DATE DUE

ALL ITEMS ARE SUBJECT TO RECALL
AFTER 2 WEEKS

D1223806

Extradition, Politics, and Human Rights

Extradition, Politics, and Human Rights

Christopher H. Pyle

TEMPLE UNIVERSITY PRESS

PHILADELPHIA

To my wife, Cindy, whose love makes all things possible,

and to my sons, Jeffrey and Jonathan, whose commitments

to justice and decency make this father proud

Temple University Press, Philadelphia 19122
Copyright © 2001 by Temple University
All rights reserved
Published 2001
Printed in the United States of America

⊗ The paper used in this publication meets the requirements of the American
National Standard for Information Sciences—Permanence of Paper for Printed
Library Materials, ANSI Z39.48-1984.

Library of Congress Cataloging-in-Publication Data

Pyle, Christopher H.
    Extradition, politics, and human rights / Christopher H. Pyle.
        p.   cm.
    Includes bibliographical references and index.
    ISBN 1-56639-822-3 (cloth : alk. paper) — ISBN 1-56639-823-1 (pbk. : alk. paper)
        1. Extradition—United States—History.   2. Deportation—United States—History.
    3. Human rights—United States.   I. Title.
    KF9635 .P95 2001
    345.73'052--dc21
                                                                        00-039283

Contents

Preface and Acknowledgments

This book began, quite oddly, in the Bow Street Magistrate's Court in London in 1978. I had been asked by Earl Dudley, former chief counsel of the House Judiciary Committee, to testify about the U.S. government's surveillance of civilian politics. His clients were British officials of the Church of Scientology, whom the U.S. government wanted to extradite for ordering the burglary of a prosecutor's office in the District of Columbia courthouse.

Earl did not want me to endorse his clients, just authenticate the final report of the Senate Select Committee on Intelligence. The report, to which I had contributed, documented the U.S. government's surveillance of a number of religious groups. The Bow Street Magistrate's Court would not accept a copy of the report unless someone could swear to its authenticity.

At the time, I knew nothing about extradition. What I knew about the Church of Scientology led me to believe that it probably had committed the burglary. Somewhat reluctantly, I agreed to testify. The Scientologists were entitled to have the document authenticated, after which they probably deserved to be extradited.

In London, the Scientologists could not have been more gracious. Among other things, they allowed me to read fifteen volumes of government surveillance reports about the church. I came to understand why they might want to steal documents from a U.S. prosecutor. The initial intelligence reports about their activities were rife with unverified gossip and rumor that, as they passed from agency to agency in Europe and the United States, lost their original source notations and were recast as the gospel truth. Dubious allegations were sent out to multiple agencies, including the Federal Bureau of Investigation (FBI) and Interpol, and then returned, unsourced and repackaged, to confirm themselves. Some of the unverified charges were leaked to the press, whose accounts were then used to confirm the original gossip.

None of this persuaded me that the defendants were innocent, but it did put the charges against them in a new perspective. Like many political fugitives, the church was locked in a propaganda war with a dozen or more law enforcement and intelligence agencies. Some wanted to ban the church from doing business in their country, others wanted to deny it tax-exempt status. Theirs was not an ordinary prosecution.

But should the British court shield the church's leaders from extradition on that account? The extradition treaty contained something called a "political offense" exception, but I quickly learned that the defendants would have to claim involvement in a political uprising to enjoy its protection.

From what I knew of my own government, I thought the Scientologists would receive a reasonably fair trial, but then be hit with unfair sentences. Unlike FBI executives who were convicted of ordering hundreds of "black-bag jobs" by armed agents against law-abiding groups for more than thirty years, the Scientologists were not likely to receive a pardon and champagne from the president of the United States. The Justice Department would seek the maximum penalty and the judge would probably grant it because the Scientologists were unpopular, in part because of the FBI's propaganda campaign. So, if the magistrate were to authorize extradition, I thought surrender should be conditioned on a promise that the defendants would be treated like other first-time, one-time, unarmed third-rate burglars.

But that was not to be. The magistrate was forbidden to question the administration of justice in the United States. The Scientologists were extradited[1] and, in due course, received maximum sentences.

I returned to the United States intrigued by the idea of a political offense exception to extradition. As a teacher of both law and politics, I was fascinated that Anglo-American jurisprudence would recognize a "political offense" for any purpose.

The more I read, the more I came to appreciate how fraught with politics extradition is—international politics, ethnic politics, and interbranch rivalries. Extradition, I discovered, was often demanded, granted, or denied for the rankest of political reasons. Worse, British and American judges were required by law to serve as the long arms of foreign injustice, much like the jurists who enforced fugitive slave laws in the nineteenth century.

Eventually my research and writing led to testimony before Congress in opposition to the Reagan administration's attempts to strip judges of what few powers they have to protect political fugitives from foreign injustice. The more I learned, the more concerned I became at how easy it was for any person under the protection of the U.S. Constitution to be surrendered to an unjust regime on the basis of false charges.

In the course of this research I have accumulated more debts than I can possibly acknowledge. Earl Dudley got me started. Professor Barbara Ann Banoff, a former Senate committee colleague, shared my concerns and co-authored a law review article in which we defended the political offense exception, proposed an exception to it for heinous crimes, and urged courts to suspend their "rule of noninquiry."[2]

As a witness before Congress in the mid-1980s, I received invaluable assistance from many people, most notably David Beier and Eric Sterling of the House Judiciary Committee and Morton H. Halperin and Wade Henderson of the American Civil Liberties Union. I was also aided by numerous attorneys for Irish Republican Army (IRA) fugitives, most notably Mary Boresz Pike, whose defense of Joseph Doherty deserves the highest possible praise.

During the late 1980s and early 1990s, I turned my attention to the extradition of alleged war criminals and received reams of documents from Radoslav Artukovic and Edward Nishnic. It took Ed Nishnic more than eight years, but he and his family eventually proved that his father-in-law John Demjanjuk was not "Ivan the Terrible" of Treblinka, as the U.S. government wrongly alleged. Rad Artukovic was not so fortunate. His father's official responsibility for the atrocities of Croatia's wartime regime was indisputable, but this loyal son clearly proved that his father was extradited by the United States and sentenced to death by a Communist court on false evidence of alleged crimes that in fact never occurred.

One cannot research such cases without being expected to take sides, for the extradition of political fugitives often has more to do with politics than with justice. Such cases are the object of intense propaganda wars, so that whatever one writes about them is likely to be viewed with suspicion. The more I have delved into these cases, the more I have come to believe that there is no sure way to tell the good guys from the bad guys. Both rebels and governments commit similar acts in the course of uprising, and the longer the armed conflict continues, the more the two sides come to resemble each other. What should be important for the United States, when judging whether a particular fugitive ought to be extradited, is the nature and quality of his acts, not the atrocities of his group or government. So, when I express some understanding of why men like Joseph Doherty join the IRA, I should not be thought to condone any of the IRA's atrocities. My interest is in how U.S. courts can best serve the cause of justice.

If I have bias, it is against those U.S. attorneys who have failed to question the foreign governments they have represented, who have committed fraud upon the court, or who have tried to abolish the time-tested political offense exception. It is not that I think these attorneys are worse than the people they would extradite. Often they are better, but I expect more of them. As a quotation outside the office of the attorney general declares: "The government wins when justice is done." I do not accept the assumption of some Justice Department lawyers that noble ends can excuse illegal means, that the liberty of individuals should be entrusted to the executive, that no one should question the willingness or capacity of any requesting regime to do justice, or that justice is served by kidnapping.

In short, I carry no brief for either the political fugitives or political prosecutors who are the subjects of this book. My objective has been to assess each according to the nature and quality of his acts, viewed in context and comparatively.

In 1987, I had the pleasure of attending an excellent conference on extradition sponsored by the Institute of Higher Studies in Criminal Sciences, in Siracusa, Italy, led by Professor M. Sherif Bassiouni of Marquette Law School. During the 1990s, I participated in the work of the International Law Association's Committee on Extradition and Human Rights, led by Professor Alfred P. Rubin of the Fletcher School of Law and Diplomacy and its learned rapporteurs, Professor John Dugard of the University of Witwatersrand, South Africa, and Professor Christine Van den Wijngaert of University of Antwerp, Belgium. To the international lawyers from many nations on this committee, I owe a special debt of gratitude. I only hope they will forgive me for concluding that human rights are more likely to be protected by domestic than by international law.

My research on this book and my participation in the important work of the International Law Association committee would not have been possible without generous assistance from the Institute for the Study of World Politics, the American Council of Learned Societies, the National Endowment for the Humanities, and Mount Holyoke College, where I have happily taught both politics and law for a quarter century.

Over the years, numerous Mount Holyoke students have helped research this book. I cannot possibly thank them all here, but Catherine Allgor (now a distinguished historian in her own right) and Bonnie Wadsworth deserve special thanks for their extensive labors.

It is difficult enough to find time to write one's own books without critiquing the manuscripts of others, so I am especially grateful to Abraham D. Sofaer of the Hoover Institution, Kenneth S. Gallant of the University of Idaho Law School, and Alfred P. Rubin for their close and critical readings of the text. Judge Sofaer was particularly considerate, given that I have criticized policies he advocated as legal adviser to the Department of State. Of course, no one has been more generous than the indefatigable Professor Rubin, whom the Fletcher School quite properly calls its distinguished professor of international law. Generosity could be his middle name.

Needless to say, I absolve these colleagues of any errors or follies committed in these pages and thank them all for their kind assistance and counsel.

Introduction

Extradition is an obscure topic about which reams have been written. It is the subject of frequent controversies between nations but rarely stays in the news long enough for the public to learn much about it. Extradition demands can draw protesters into the streets, but extradition law inspires about as much interest as the law of habeas corpus.

That is a shame, because the law of extradition is not just a bit of legal plumbing which, once laid down, can safely be taken for granted. Like the writ of habeas corpus, which protects us from arbitrary imprisonment, the law of extradition is one of those judicially protected guarantees of liberty and fairness that the executive is forever trying to erode.

Many people assume that the law of extradition is not very important because it only deals with aliens, and that aliens have no rights other than those granted to them by Congress. Those who share these assumptions are wrong, however, on both counts. American citizens are as vulnerable to surrender to unjust foreign regimes as foreign nationals are, and under our Constitution, foreign nationals are entitled to as much freedom from unreasonable detention and arbitrary surrender to regimes they may have defied as are native-born Americans. The Constitution's guarantees against unreasonable deprivations of liberty belong to all persons present in this country and not just those entitled to vote.

In the early days of the republic, the law of extradition showed special solicitude toward fugitives from foreign civil wars and from the victors' justice that often followed. It protected liberal revolutionaries and deposed royalists alike. But it did not stop there. The cast of characters in this book includes many people whom governments would like to surrender arbitrarily: runaway sailors and slaves, anarchists, fugitives from friendly police states, IRA and PLO gunmen, alleged war criminals, and drug lords. Some of the more notable are Jonathan Robbins, a sailor whose surrender to the British Navy may have cost John Adams the election of 1800; the blacks who seized the slave ship *Amistad* in 1839; IRA soldier Joseph Doherty, deported for shooting a British soldier who was trying to kill him; Andrija Artuković, a Croatian extradited to Communist Yugoslavia for war crimes that could not be proven; John Demjanjuk, a Ukrainian accused of operating the gas chamber at Treblinka; and General Manuel Noriega, removed from Panama by a U.S. military invasion so that he could stand trial in Florida for aiding drug cartels.

This book traces the evolution of American extradition law and practice from colonial times to the present. It begins with the refusal of New England Puritans to surrender the "regicides" who had ordered the execution of a British king and ends with the Reagan–Bush effort to restore the medieval practice of surrendering political fugitives for reasons of state. The book also describes what can happen to the fairness of our legal system when foreign fugitives become the targets of media-hyped "wars" against crime, or when the Supreme Court allows government lawyers to disregard the law of extradition and authorize kidnapping instead.

Among the legal luminaries who have influenced the American law of extradition are James Madison, Thomas Jefferson, John Adams, John Marshall, Daniel Webster, John Quincy Adams, and John Stuart Mill. Their contributions stand in stark contrast to more recent efforts by such lesser lights as Ronald Reagan, Margaret Thatcher, Edwin Meese, William Rehnquist, and Oliver North.

Unfortunately, much of the drama—and the sense of justice—that once animated writing about extradition has been lost to the desiccated prose of legal technicians. Most law professors treat extradition as a minor issue in courses on international law, which few students take and even fewer respect once they realize how casually their own government disregards it. Most of what has been written on extradition law has been "relentlessly academic," full of repetitious expositions, and largely oblivious to the political forces that have driven the cases and the law.[1] This book attempts to recover the stories behind the cases, including what happened to the defendants upon their surrender to the regime seeking to prosecute them.

Those who take international law seriously usually think about extradition as an aspect of international relations in which states, not individuals, are the only rights holders. This nation-centered, and therefore executive-centered, approach has the unfortunate effect of denigrating the extent to which the surrender of persons to foreign governments also raises issues of judicial independence, executive authority, individual liberty, and due process of law. Even among human rights advocates, more is made of vague treaty provisions than the "municipal" law of individual nations, where the greatest hope for judicially enforceable rights still remains.

It is often said that a nation's level of civilization can best be discerned from how fairly it treats people whose crimes generate the most public fear and loathing. In the nineteenth century, our institutional commitment to even-handed justice was most severely tested in cases involving alleged mutineers, pirates, and fugitive slaves. Today it is strained most by cases of alleged terrorists, war criminals, and drug lords— the legal pariahs of our times.

In the early days of the American republic, there was little curiosity about the criminal pasts of new arrivals. Many Americans were refugees from tyrannies of one sort or another. For them, America was the "first new nation,"[2] a place in which everyone could start anew. What a person had done in the old country was thought to bear little relationship to what he or she might do in America. To become an American in those days was to be "born again," free from the oppressions and injustices of foreign regimes. This indifference was not necessarily a virtue, but it was a necessity; there was very little organized law enforcement in the young republic. Until modern police departments were organized in the 1830s, there was little demand for the return of fugitives to stand trial. Today the United States has extradition treaties with more than one hundred foreign countries. It began signing these treaties in the 1840s, gave them out rather indiscriminately after the 1860s, and has found it inconvenient to abrogate agreements with even the most venal regimes.

Extradition remained a small-scale business until the 1970s, when advances in bureaucracy, telecommunications, and air travel radically improved the capacity of pursuing regimes to get wanted fugitives back. Then the demand for extradition burgeoned, driven in no small part by political pressures to combat hijacking, terrorism, and drug dealing, and to rid the United States of former war criminals. These developments gave rise to powerful efforts to shift responsibility over extradition from the courts to the executive. Just as the fate of most criminal suspects is now decided through executive plea bargains, so the decision of who may be surrendered for trial and punishment abroad is shifting to the executive. To any American who still believes in checks and balances, guaranteed rights, and limited executives, these developments should be profoundly disturbing.

* * *

As should now be obvious, this book is not just history; it uses history, as lawyers do, to advance an argument. My purpose is not just to recall forgotten legal roots but to reassert the centrality of individual liberty, due process of law, and humanitarian concerns in future debates over extradition law. Extradition involves the surrender of human beings—people under the protection of our Constitution—to foreign regimes, many of which are unjust. This reality was well understood in the eighteenth and nineteenth centuries, when the United States was a refuge for the victims of European oppression, but it has been disregarded frequently in the twentieth and twenty-first centuries as we have sought to stem the tide of immigration and develop advantageous economic and political relations with autocratic regimes of every stripe.

Extradition also involves the effort by our government to obtain from foreign governments people charged with violating American criminal law. The law of extradition was designed to make systems of reciprocal surrender orderly and principled, and to make abduction, military incursions, and fraudulent deportations unnecessary and illegal. Unfortunately, our own government has recently used all three methods with impunity, and with judicial blessings.[3]

A person suspected of violating U.S. criminal law cannot be imprisoned without indictment by a grand jury (or comparable judicial hearing), compulsory process to obtain witnesses in his or her defense, and trial by petit jury. These basic safeguards (or their equivalents) do not exist in many foreign legal systems, making it all the more important that our courts review extradition requests very carefully, particularly when between 10 and 20 percent of all persons extradited to foreign legal systems happen to be American citizens.[4] Unfortunately, defendants at extradition hearings in U.S. courts are usually held without bail and thus are limited in their capacity to challenge the charges against them. They are denied the right to confront the witnesses against them[5] and cannot call upon the court to refuse to admit the fruits of what, had they occurred in the United States, would be unconstitutional searches.[6] The evidence against them can be presented in the form of unsworn statements from alleged witnesses whom they cannot cross-examine or effectively contradict.[7] Neither the Federal Rules of Criminal Procedure[8] nor the Federal Rules of Evidence[9] apply. As a result, defendants (who may be Americans) are not entitled to any of the pretrial discovery rights they would enjoy if they were being prosecuted (or even sued) under American law. In seeking their extradition, both the foreign regime and the United States Justice Department attorneys who represented it can make lavish use of hearsay evidence against them.[10] Thus, in many respects Justice Oliver Wendell Holmes was right when he remarked, impatiently, that attempting to mount a defense to extradition is "a waste of time."[11]

* * *

The immediate occasion for this book was the effort by officials of recent administrations to "reform" the law of extradition by stripping the courts of jurisdiction to protect people charged with political offenses or to question the capacity of requesting regimes to do justice. But the book goes beyond recent politics to address the age-old conflict between individual liberty and *raison d'état*.

My thesis is that we should talk less about *international* law and more about *American* law when discussing extradition. I take this position for two reasons. First, international law has historically given the individual, and due process, short shrift. Second, respect for individual rights, especially constitutional rights, demands it. I do not suggest that the United States should impose its standards of justice on foreign legal systems, but I do argue that our government should not surrender individuals under the protection of our laws if by so doing it would become the long arm of foreign injustice. Nor should the United States violate international law, or principles of limited government, to recapture fugitives who have sought refuge elsewhere.

I am making this argument by book in part because I was not able to make it satisfactorily as a witness before congressional committees. There appear to be few matters of less interest to most members of Congress than extradition. In part this is because there are few votes in it, at least until nationality groups begin to complain about administration proposals. The few members who are concerned about civil liberties or their ethnic constituencies find the subject too complicated, too technical, and too arcane to justify the energy required to master extradition law.

It has not always been thus. In the early months of 1800, the entire House of Representatives extensively debated one extradition case—the case of Jonathan Robbins.[12] But that was a time when many Americans espoused a jurisprudence of natural rights.

Today lawyers, and particularly international lawyers, dominate the debate over extradition. As a group, they tend to be more interested in power than legitimacy and more impressed by the needs of states (and other large organizations) than the rights of individuals.

This diminished concern for the human rights dimension of extradition is also to be found in the scholarly literature, most of which is written by international lawyers in the bloodless prose of digests, treatises, and law reviews. The implicit assumption of modern digest writers seems to be that the incoherence of the law, or its lack of morally defensible principles, is not their problem; their task is simply to restate the precedents. Others have been content to inventory various approaches to the law of extradition without seriously questioning the underlying values, premises, or purposes. Some academic writers have attempted syntheses, but most have been more analytic than philosophic. That is to say, they have attempted to achieve coherence and principle by sewing precedent to precedent like a patchwork quilt, as if history can be made into law—and good law—solely by verbal legerdemain and the promotion of habit.

A few writers have emphasized some value, principle, or purpose, such as combating terrorism, but in so doing have underemphasized other values, including justice, liberty, or democracy. Still others have simply abandoned the jurisprudence of fundamental rights, embraced rank positivism (or the most short-sighted instrumentalism), and let judges do what they can, case by case, to repair the ever rending quilt. If politicians, diplomats, and judges today seem disoriented by the law of extradition, it may be that the relationship of law to values has been so obscured that they cannot tell where they are—or ought to be—going. This work is an attempt to restore to the debate over extradition what the framers of our Constitution would recognize as the "first principles" of good governance.

Some may see this as legal ethnocentrism. Perhaps so, but if the law of extradition is to be based on such fundamental principles as the rule of law, due process, political liberty, human rights, and judicial independence, then I know of no better place to start than American constitutional law and the political thought that informs it.

Moreover, I submit that there is no other place from which Americans can start constitutionally. One of the chief defects of the American law of extradition is that our judges and scholars, at least since the late nineteenth century, have been content largely to emulate foreign practice as if extradition is merely a matter of international law and politics and as if the only parties to an extradition proceeding are states. Of course, extradition is the product of treaties, and much is to be learned from foreign laws, court decisions, and administrative practices. But where the liberty of those under the protection of our Constitution is at stake, our politicians, diplomats, and judges can never be free agents. The Fourth Amendment's guarantee against unreasonable seizures of persons is expressly a "right of the people"—all the people—and not just those who happen to have citizenship.

It is often argued that we ought to "respect" foreign cultures, and that we must not "impose" our legal values upon them. But a refusal to extradite does not impose our values on them; it merely enforces our values against ourselves, which is precisely what the rule of law is supposed to do. Because due process is supposed to be one of the key values we enforce against ourselves, we dishonor ourselves and our law each time we pretend not to notice that a requesting regime is systematically unjust or driven by law-bending prejudice against the accused.

It is also assumed, particularly within the Departments of State and Justice, that extradition is primarily a matter of executive discretion. The chief justification offered in support of this view has been that a refusal to extradite can seriously harm our foreign relations. This claim of executive discretion is made not because the founders intended it that way, or because the courts or Congress have ceded that power to the executive, but because diplomats and prosecutors are bureaucrats and, like most bureaucrats, put efficiency ahead of principle. What happens to people surrendered by the United States to foreign regimes matters less to these bureaucrats than the government's success in negotiating the return of fugitives from American law enforcement. To this end our officials are even willing to trade in fugitives, as if the subjects of extradition are not real people with claims to justice and humanity but, rather, mere commodities to be bartered on the international law enforcement exchange.

Executive branch officials have also insisted that judges adhere to a "rule of noninquiry" and not question the motives of foreign prosecutors or the capacity of the requesting regimes to do justice. To refuse to extradite on these grounds, they argue, would be insulting to other nations and do serious harm to our foreign relations. Little in the history of American extradition, apart from our refusal to surrender the late Shah of Iran, supports this claim of harm to foreign relations, but even if a particular refusal does cause harm, the harm has to be endured because, under our system of government, liberty and justice are supposed to come first. For some, the betrayal of one dying shah for fifty Americans held hostage in Tehran seemed like a good deal in 1980, but it is worth reflecting on what ceding that much power to our politicians would do, in the long run, to make our nation even more vulnerable to foreign blackmail. That practical point is really moot, however, because under our Constitution, there are some things our politicians cannot do.

This book also argues against another rule of noninquiry—the rule that allows courts to pretend it is no concern of theirs that the prisoner before them was not extradited in the normal course of law but was abducted in violation of international law, the domestic law of the host country, and the American law of kidnapping.

Some say that the United States should cease pretending it is better than other nations and get on with the business of fighting crime and terrorism. I submit that we are—or ought to be—better. What is pretentious is the executive's claim that there is, for crime-fighting purposes, something akin to a "family of nations." Most of the one hundred or so countries with which we have extradition agreements are not constitutional democracies with independent judiciaries. In recent years, they have included police states like South Korea and Taiwan, military oligarchies like Chile and Panama, tribal oligarchies like Ghana and Nigeria, and Communist regimes like Yugoslavia, Romania, Bulgaria, and Albania. The prosecutorial motives and capacity to do justice of such governments ought to be questioned. So, too, should the motives and capacities of leading Western democracies, because democratic party politics does not guarantee either the rule of law or independent courts. If foreign officials are insulted by the answers, so be it. Conversely, the courts of other nations ought to question the motives and capacities of our government to do justice, for no regime on earth can be trusted in all circumstances to provide wholly apolitical and wholly fair investigation, prosecution, trial, or punishment.

That just legal systems are rare ought to be as stark a reality as international drug smuggling, terrorism, embezzlement, or murder. Unfortunately, U.S. administrations are selective about the realities they emphasize. Under recent administrations, efforts to undermine Marxist revolutions, stem the tides of immigration (particularly of poor blacks and Hispanics from the Caribbean), and combat terrorism and drug smuggling replaced human rights as priorities of our government. The result was a shameful gap between our nation's principles and our government's treatment of political fugitives wanted by foreign regimes. Closing that gap is what this book is about.

Readers who feel rusty about the basics of extradition law are invited to scan the Appendix.

CHAPTER 1

A Nation of Asylum

The evil of protecting malefactors of every dye is sensibly felt here as in other nations, but until a reformation of the criminal codes of most nations, to deliver fugitives to them would be to become their accomplice.

Thomas Jefferson, Secretary of State, September 6, 1793

On September 1, 1675, armed Indians swept down on the little settlement of Hadley, in western Massachusetts. "The people were in grave confusion," Governor Hutchison later wrote.[1]

> Suddenly, a grave, elderly person appeared in the midst of them. In his mien and dress he differed from the rest of the people. He not only encouraged them to defend themselves, but put himself at their head, rallied, instructed, and led them on to encounter the enemy, who by this means were repulsed. As suddenly the deliverer of Hadley disappeared. The people were left in consternation, utterly unable to account for this strange phenomenon. It is not probable that they were ever able to explain it.

The "Ghost of Hadley," as he later became known, was Colonel William Goffe, one of the "regicides" who had signed the death warrant of King Charles I. With the restoration of Charles II, Goffe had fled to New England with Colonel Edward Whalley, another regicide. Massachusetts and Connecticut received royal directives demanding their return, and royal messengers were sent out from Boston to track them down. Wherever the messengers went, however, they were frustrated by dilatory displays of cooperation. As the deputy governor of New Haven explained: "We honor his Majesty, but we have tender consciences."[2]

Regicides who had fled to the Netherlands were delivered up to the king's vengeance;[3] those who fled to the colonies were not. The most wanted men in the British empire were hidden from capture and supported for the rest of their lives. The New England Puritans had been divided on the wisdom of executing Charles I; some would have surrendered the regicides, but those in positions of power did not. Why they did not is central to understanding the American approach to extradition.

* * *

The political explanation is obvious. The New Englanders were Puritans and cared more for their coreligionists in England, whatever their excesses, than for Charles II and his bishops. A legal basis for their noncooperation could be found in a 1641 statute of the Bay Colony. It provided that "if any straingers, or People of other Nations, professing the true Christian religion, shall fly to us from the Tyranny or Oppression of their Persecutors . . . they shall be entertained and succourd amongst us according to that power and prudence God shall give us."[4] Colonists could not invoke this law against the king without causing his privy council to invalidate it, but they could obey it quietly.

The colonists' unwillingness to surrender the regicides not only reflected the law and politics of the moment; it was emblematic of a tidal shift then taking place in English political thought on both sides of the Atlantic. During the Middle Ages, the dominant political thought viewed insurrectionists with alarm. Most people were deemed subjects, not citizens, and therefore not entitled to take law into their own hands. Insurrection was both a crime against the person of the king, to whom his most likely rivals owed personal loyalty, and an offense against the society that the king personified. Insurrection was also an offense against God's holy ordinances, because kings traced some of their authority to the divinity and received frequent blessings from his priests. Thus, political offenders—especially religiously motivated regicides—were looked upon with special horror.

In England and her American colonies, this horror was diminished by the Puritan and Whig revolutions of the seventeenth century. The Puritan movement separated loyalty to God from loyalty to king and thus diminished the horror of crimes against the state. The Puritan Revolution hastened the transformation of subjects into citizens, after which Parliament won political supremacy and the sovereignty of the king became the sovereignty of the Crown—an abstract conception in which less emotional loyalty could be vested.[5]

In America, the doctrine of popular sovereignty arose early and naturally from the experience and necessity of self-government. The colonial officials who resisted the king's demand for return of the regicides asserted the de facto sovereignty of their own political systems. They did not think of themselves as agents of the English sovereign in the sense that the king's sheriffs did in England. They thought of themselves more as elected officials of their towns and colonies, in which congregations of freemen were the de facto sovereign. Accordingly, an attack on a public official could not be the same as an attack on a divinely ordained king. Public officials were more in the nature of public servants, which meant that an attack on them was not treason but an ordinary crime. In colonial America, power was not hereditary; it had to be earned through service to the community. Officials who earned the respect of other freemen could expect cooperation; those who did not, like Charles II, could expect little.

As long as the crowned heads of Europe created political alliances through inter-marriage, they could not be indifferent to the presence of foreign political fugitives on their soil. But as the "family of princes" was gradually replaced by the "family of nations," and as commerce became the primary source of new wealth, the greater interest of maritime peoples like the English, the Dutch, and the American colonists was in maintaining neutrality during foreign civil wars. The Scottish philosopher Francis Hutcheson spoke for them all when he wrote in the 1750s:[6]

> As to state criminals; as frequently good men are on both sides of civil wars and state-fac-tions, as well as in solemn wars, the general custom is very humane, that they should uni-versally find protection in foreign states; and refusal to deliver them up . . . is never deemed a just cause of war, if while they reside abroad, they are forming no conspiracies or hos-tile attempts against the present governors of their country.

The unwillingness of nations to surrender political fugitives grew as feudalism and its structure of personal obligations disintegrated and as the criminal law became less politicized. This occurred in Great Britain during the seventeenth and eighteenth cen-turies with the abolition of torture, elimination of the Star Chamber and the Court of High Commission, reduction in the severity of punishment for treason and sedition (in fact if not in law), and the extension to accused traitors of procedural rights rou-tinely accorded criminal suspects.[7] It also grew with freedom of the press, the decline of revealed wisdom, the rise of scientific (and relativistic) thinking, the proliferation of Protestant sects, and the religious toleration that gradually arose out of the priva-tization and diversification of Christian faith.

Simultaneously with these developments, Great Britain ceased to negotiate extra-dition treaties with European states, even as they intensified their efforts to extra-dite ordinary criminals.[8] In part this may have been due to Britain's loss of fron-tiers on the Continent,[9] but it may also be attributed to a growing commitment to the principles of limited executive authority, guaranteed liberties, and due process of law.

Resistance to exclusive executive control over many powers, including the extra-dition of British *subjects,* began early in the seventeenth century. Parliament led the way in 1606 when it exempted Englishmen from extradition to Scotland, even though the two kingdoms had been united. The reason given was concern over the treatment British subjects might receive at the hands of Scottish law,[10] but behind that concern was a growing conviction, as Holdsworth reports, "that a subject could not be com-pelled to leave the realm except by virtue of an Act of Parliament."[11]

In support of this view, Sir Edward Coke invoked chapter 29 of Magna Carta. Chap-ter 29 provided that "No freeman shall be taken or imprisoned or disseised [dispos-sessed] of his freehold or otherwise destroyed, nor will we pass upon him nor con-demn him, but by lawful judgment of peers or the law of the land." In his comments on that chapter, Coke wrote: "by the law of the land no man can be exiled, or ban-ished out of his native country, but either by authority of Parliament, or in case of abjuration for felony by the common law."[12] At this point in British history, executive control over extradition might have been established had not common law judges like Coke and the proponents of Parliamentary supremacy fought to bring the Stuart kings within the rule of law.

More generally, Coke opposed the surrender of fugitives from foreign lands: "It is holden, and so it hath been resolved, that divided kingdoms under several kings, in league with one another, are sanctuaries for servants or subjects flying for safety from one kingdom to another; and upon demand made by them, are not, by the laws and liberties of kingdoms, to be delivered; and this, some say, is grounded upon the law in Deuteronomy, 'Thou shalt not deliver unto his master the servant which is escaped from his master unto thee.'"[13]

Parliamentary supremacy over the making of laws affecting individual liberties triumphed with the passage of the Habeas Corpus Act of 1679. In addition to abolishing executive detention of persons without trial, that act provided that no "*inhabitant*" or "*resident*" could legally be sent prisoner "beyond the seas." Any who were so treated were granted the right to sue those who transported them.[14] Whether Parliament intended to protect *aliens* as well as subjects from executive surrender is not clear,[15] but this broad language can be seen as the beginning of both a solicitude for the human rights of aliens and the modern Anglo-American practice of treating aliens and citizens alike for extradition purposes.

The Habeas Corpus Act had two other effects. One was to destroy the assertion that Great Britain had a duty under natural law to extradite accused felons in the absence of treaties—an assertion that tended to enhance claims of inherent executive power over extradition.[16] The second was to make the crucial decision regarding extraditability a *legal* decision to be made by the *courts*.

This was the legal legacy that Britain bestowed upon her American colonies well before their revolution. It was a legacy that the Americans would take to heart as they struggled to allocate authority between their executive and their courts, to establish due process, and to develop fundamental rights.

But British law and Deuteronomy were not the only sources of colonial thought. The emerging American people were also children of the Enlightenment who recognized a moral right of revolution against despotic regimes. During the seventeenth and eighteenth centuries, the right was supported by the most influential philosophers, including Locke, Montesquieu, Hutcheson, Voltaire, Diderot, Helvetius, Condorcet, and Beccaria.[17] Even conservatives who had doubts about the legitimacy of that right (or when it should be exercised) came to recognize a need to shelter refugees from liberal revolutions. For conservatives, the most convincing event was the Reign of Terror during the French Revolution.

Enlightenment thinkers also placed high value on the rights of man, arguing, among other things, that it was morally wrong for a nation to send an accused back to a foreign legal system that was manifestly arbitrary, inequitable, unnecessarily severe, or highly politicized. The leading spokesman for this view was the Marquis de Beccaria, an eighteenth-century *philosophe* and one of the founders of modern penology. Asked whether he favored extradition, Beccaria replied:[18]

Although the certainty of there being no part of the earth where crimes are not punished may be a means of preventing them, I shall not pretend to determine this question, until laws more conformable to the necessities and rights of humanity, and until milder punishments, and the abolition of the arbitrary power of opinion, shall afford security to virtue and innocence when oppressed; and until tyranny shall be confined to the plains of Asia, and Europe acknowledges the universal empire of reason, by which the interests of sovereigns, and subjects, are best united.

Becarria's views were widely shared by liberal statesmen and penal reformers during the eighteenth and nineteenth centuries.[19]

* * *

The American colonists did not derive all their ideas from European sources. Some they developed for themselves through the daily business of governing their own affairs, which they did for a century and a half before they broke from England. During the colonial period, there was no extradition with foreign nations at all. Some extradition agreements existed with Indian tribes, but these were not reciprocal.[20] Like Englishmen everywhere, the colonists preferred to be tried at home, by their own kind. This became a major issue at the time of independence, when Jefferson's Declaration complained that the Crown had wrongly transported colonists "beyond the seas to be tried for pretended offenses." In that instance, the foreign courts were British admiralty courts sitting in Nova Scotia without juries; the "pretended offenses" were violations of the Navigation and Stamp Acts by colonial shipowners. Technically speaking, no extradition was involved. The shipowners were still British subjects, and they did not have to go to Halifax if they were willing to lose their ships and cargoes by default, but the principle was similar. To colonists accustomed to being tried in their own common law courts before sympathetic juries drawn from their local communities, trial in Nova Scotia before a prerogative court by a judge paid from the forfeitures he levied was to "subject us to a jurisdiction foreign to our constitution and unacknowledged by our laws."[21] The practice heightened colonial feelings that Great Britain was becoming a foreign country from which independence would have to be won by force.[22]

The first call for a national policy on extradition occurred in 1784 when the Virginia legislature sought to prod the national government to improve relations with Spain, which had repeatedly threatened to close trade down the Mississippi River.[23] One impediment to improved relations along the western border involved American frontiersmen who murdered Indians and committed other crimes in Spanish territory while using American states as places of refuge. To combat this filibustering, the Virginia legislature enacted what was probably the first extradition statute in modern history.[24] It was a modest effort that had no tangible consequences, but it revealed the early outlines of American thinking about extradition.

The bill, sponsored by James Madison, had two main parts. The first authorized Virginia's governor to cooperate with the federal government, should the federal government seek (by treaty or statute) to surrender "any citizen or inhabitant of this commonwealth" who "within the acknowledged jurisdiction of any civilized nation in amity with the United States, shall . . . commit any crime." The second part authorized the Virginia courts to prosecute "any citizen of this commonwealth" who "shall [go] into the territory of any christian nation or Indian tribe, in amity with the United States, and shall there commit murder, house-burning, robbery, theft, trespass, or other crime, which, if committed within this commonwealth, would be punishable by the laws thereof."[25]

Madison's bill was nothing more than a prod to the federal government—a promise of assistance should extradition be arranged with Spain. It was highly controversial and passed by only one vote. Among those voting for it was John Marshall, the future Chief Justice of the United States.[26]

To Virginia's more radical whigs, the extradition bill was an assault on section 8 of the Virginia Bill of Rights. Section 8 guaranteed a right to trial "by an impartial jury of [the] vicinage" and provided, in the tradition of Magna Carta, that no man shall be deprived of his liberty "except by the law of the land or the judgment of his peers."[27]

To the bill's opponents, the rights to a trial by jury and to due process of law were not just rights derived from a specific governmental system, but natural rights of all men to fundamental fairness. Accordingly, they recoiled at the thought that their governor might collaborate with the national government to surrender Americans to any foreign regime. To surrender Americans to a Spanish regime in Florida or Louisiana was even worse because it revived their Protestant contempt for his Catholic Majesty's infamous Inquisition.

The more conservative whigs who supported the bill refused to accept such a broad theory of rights. In their view, the constitutional rights of criminal suspects were not rights of personhood derived from a respect for all members of the human race. They were not even rights of citizenship derived from a theory of social compact. They were positive rights—rights bestowed by the governing authorities to assure fair trials in American courts. From that perspective, the surrender of a Virginian or American to Spanish justice did not violate the Virginia Bill of Rights because it only specified the kind of justice people could expect from Virginia courts. The conservatives were also reassured by a provision in the bill that conditioned Virginia's cooperation on the expectation that the national government would only engage in extradition with "civilized nations in amity with the United States."

Madison had tried to assuage the critics' fears with a provision that, he later informed Jefferson, "provides . . . for a domestic trial in cases where a surrender may not be justified."[28] This vague "extradite or punish" provision may well constitute the earliest legislative effort to avoid American complicity with foreign injustice. It did not single out political offenders for protection; it applied to all cases in which the capacity or willingness of the foreign regime to do justice might be in doubt.

In a letter to Jefferson, Madison concluded from his reading of Grotius, Pufendorf, and Vattel that extradition was an inherent power of all nations.[29] This may suggest that Madison was willing to entrust specific extradition decisions to the executive. However, he did not say that; he said that if the power was ever to be exercised,

Congress would have to act. This made sense. In 1784, under the Articles of Confederation, there was no national executive to assert any inherent national powers.

Madison could have claimed extradition authority for each state, to be allocated by its legislature to either the courts or the executive. But Madison was too much of a nationalist to do that. Extradition was, for him, a national power, and he wanted to strengthen, not weaken, the confederation of American states.

So Madison's bill provided that Virginia would cooperate with "the judgment of the United States, *in congress assembled*, the law of nations, or any treaty between the United States and a foreign nation."[30] This provision might be taken to suggest that Madison viewed extradition as a political rather than legal matter, but that, too, would be a mistake because he went on expressly to define it as a matter of law. His bill expressly provided that "the sovereign of the offended nation shall exhibit to the United States, in congress assembled, due and satisfactory evidence of the crime, with a demand of the offender to be tried and punished where the same was committed."[31] Since there was no federal court system, and Madison did not want to entrust extradition to the states, he had no choice but to vest it in Congress, sitting as a court, under the Articles of Confederation.

In short, Madison's early bill treated extradition as a legal, not executive, decision to be undertaken according to traditional legal proofs, with the safeguard of a trial in Virginia if surrender would lead to injustice. It also envisioned extradition as a national, not state, matter to be arranged by legislation or treaty and not by executive officials alone.[32] Following Vattel's treatise, Madison even anticipated the surrender of citizens as well as aliens, thus deriving liberty from personhood, not citizenship.[33] However, the statute he wrote was nothing more than an offer of state cooperation, which the national government chose not to accept.

* * *

The first significant effort to articulate a truly national policy regarding extradition occurred during Washington's first term and again involved Spain. Governor Charles Pinckney of South Carolina asked President Washington which level of government, the nation or the state, had the authority to ask the Spanish governor of East Florida to surrender two fugitives charged with forging securities. Washington referred the inquiry to Secretary of State Thomas Jefferson, who looked first to the question of authority.

In the absence of a treaty or statute, Jefferson advised Washington, the executive lacked the authority to deliver criminals to—and therefore request criminals from—foreign countries.[34]

> England has no [extradition] convention with any nation, and their laws have given no power to their executive to surrender fugitives of any description; they are, accordingly, constantly refused, and hence England has been the asylum of the Paolis, the LaMottes, the Calonnes, in short, of the most atrocious offenders as well as the most innocent victims, who have been able to get there. The laws of the United States, like those of England, receive every fugitive, and no authority has been given to our executive to deliver them up.

In fact, the laws of the United States were only silent. Jefferson could have read the constitutional powers of the executive narrowly in the tradition of the British Habeas Corpus Act or broadly in the tradition of Grotius and other advocates of an inherent national power to extradite in the absence of a treaty. He chose the narrow reading, not only because he was a strict constructionist, but because he recognized the difficulty of drawing lines between "crimes, acknowledged to be such by all mankind . . . and acts rendered criminal by tyrannical laws only."[35]

Jefferson also knew that Congress was opposed to casual extradition arrangements. He reminded Washington that the Senate had rejected a consular convention negotiated with France by Benjamin Franklin because it would have allowed French consuls in the United States to forcibly repatriate not only French seamen who jumped ship in American ports, but passengers as well.[36] To avoid American complicity in the tyrannies of foreign regimes, Jefferson told Washington, "the first step always, is a Convention defining the cases where a surrender shall take place."[37] Washington agreed, Pinckney reluctantly acceded to the Secretary's judgment,[38] and the Spanish authorities in East Florida were not asked to surrender the fugitives.

In 1792, Jefferson further developed his views on extradition in the course of an unsuccessful attempt to negotiate a more general treaty with Spain.[39] In addition to requiring a prior treaty, Jefferson proposed limiting extradition to serious crimes and vesting the decision of who may be surrendered squarely in the judiciary. His preference for a short list of very serious crimes was based on the assumption that for most fugitives, exile from their own countries was punishment enough for whatever minor offenses they might have committed.[40] It was also grounded in a preference for the minimal policing of society. Accordingly, Jefferson proposed limiting extradition with Spain to "murder, of malice prepense, not in the nature of treason."[41]

Treason should be exempted, Jefferson wrote,[42] because the legal codes of most nations

> do not distinguish between acts against the *Government* and acts against the *oppressions of the Government*. The latter are virtues, yet have furnished more victims to the executioner than the former. . . . The unsuccessful strugglers against tyranny have been the chief martyrs of treason laws in all countries. Reformation of government with our neighbors is as much wanting now, as reformation of religion is or ever was any where. We should not wish, then, to give up to the executioner the patriot who fails and flees to us.

Whether Jefferson meant to suggest that an exception for political offenses be written into the treaty is not clear,[43] but it is more than possible. The need to draw a line between political and other offenses in any extradition treaty with Spain had been suggested during the previous summer by Governor Charles Pinckney of South Carolina in a letter to President Washington.[44] The most obviously political of all offenses in the eighteenth century, of course, was treason.

By excluding treason from the list of extraditable crimes permitted by treaties, Jefferson sought to shield revolutionaries against oppressive regimes. However, he did not imply that only conservative regimes could be oppressive, and he did not bestow his humanitarian sympathies on liberal revolutionaries only. He was willing to protect counter-revolutionary conservatives too. In so doing, he seems to have believed, as the British then did, that political fugitives of the right or left pose no threat to the nation that gives them asylum, because the cause for their violence effectively ends when they flee their homeland.

In addition, Jefferson saw beyond the problem of political fugitives to the more general question of whether (and if so, how) free countries with fair legal systems should deal with extradition demands from unfree countries with unfair legal systems. As he wrote to Pinckney in April 1792:[45]

> Two neighboring and free governments, with laws equally mild and just, would find no difficulty in forming a convention for the interchange of fugitive criminals. Nor would two neighboring despotic governments, with laws of equal severity. The latter wish that no door should be opened to their subject flying from the oppression of their laws. The fact is, that most of the governments on the continent of Europe have such conventions; but England, the only free one till lately, has never yet consented either to enter into a convention for this purpose, or to give up a fugitive. The difficulty between a free government and a despotic one, is indeed great.

To the extent that extradition was to be allowed, Jefferson reasoned, it should be a legal process, administered by judges, because the liberty of persons was at stake. If the Spanish government wanted an alleged murderer returned, he wrote, it should have to "apply to any justice of the supreme court of the United States, or to the district judge of the place where the fugitive is, exhibiting proof on oath that the murder has been committed by the said fugitive" in order to have the accused arrested.[46] Alternatively, the Spanish government could ask a U.S. marshal (or his deputy) to arrest the fugitive in order to bring him before a district judge. Either way, the procedure Jefferson outlined was a legal one, with no direct role for U.S. diplomats or politicians, including the president.

Once the accused was before the court, Jefferson continued, it should convene a "special inquiry" before a grand jury. The standard of proof should be the same as a grand jury would normally apply in deciding whether to bind an ordinary American over for trial for the same crime. If the grand jury chose to return a "true bill" against the accused, then the judge was to order the officer holding him to arrange for his delivery to the Spanish government.[47] Again, Jefferson did not envision any role for the president or the State Department in deciding whether to surrender an accused to Spain.

Not surprisingly, the Spanish government rejected Jefferson's proposals. It wanted the treaty to cover all "malhechores" (malefactors), and not just murderers and forgers as Jefferson had proposed. It also wanted to arrange for the exchange of fugitive slaves, a matter of importance to Spain, South Carolina, and Georgia, but which Jefferson ignored.[48] Spain also wanted surrender on demand, whereas the American negotiator, Thomas Pinckney (one of Charles Pinckney's Federalist cousins), insisted that the request for surrender be "supported by testimony of the commission of the crime which would be sufficient in the country to which the fugitive has flown to cause him to be arrested and brought before the tribunals of justice if the crime had there been committed."[49] By insisting on this last condition, which was similar to Jefferson's grand jury proposal, Pinckney in effect sought to make extradition from Spain to the United States a judicial process too.

Pinckney's treaty (also known as the Treaty of San Lorenzo) ultimately did not provide for extradition.[50] However, it did allow for the return of ships and cargo driven into U.S. (or Spanish) ports by storms or similar exigencies, and the Spanish would later try to use these return-of-property provisions to recover fugitives from slave revolts.[51]

* * *

If border-jumping by criminals drove Americans to consider extradition with Spain, ship-jumping by sailors caused them to contemplate limited extradition with France. The first effort to control French sailors who fled their ships while in American ports had been negotiated by Benjamin Franklin in 1782 and 1783. Franklin's convention was rejected by Congress on the recommendation of John Jay, its secretary for foreign affairs, in part because it would have allowed French consuls to repatriate both French seamen and French passengers from French ships without applying to American courts.[52] To grant French consuls this power would also have interfered with the right of Frenchmen to emigrate to the United States and would have violated the growing belief that where individual liberty is at stake, independent judges should make the decision.

Franklin's successor, Thomas Jefferson, was directed to renegotiate the convention to avoid these defects. Article 9 of the revised agreement, signed in 1788, provided that:[53]

> The Consuls and Vice-Consuls may cause to be arrested the captains, officers, mariners, sailors and all other persons being part of the crews of the vessels of their respective nations, who shall have deserted from the said vessels, in order to send them back and transport them out of the country; for which purpose the said Consuls and Vice-Consuls shall address themselves to the courts, judges, and officers competent, and shall demand the said deserters in writing, proving by an exhibition of the registers of the vessel or ship's roll that those men were part of the said crews.

The new agreement provided only for the return of seamen, and then only through the judicial processes of the United States. Contrary to what the French had wanted, their consuls were not allowed to hold their own courts or issue arrest warrants under their own authority within the United States; they had to apply to the relevant American "courts, judges, and officers." This treaty, the first adopted under the new Constitution and the first to deal with the return of fugitives, clearly established that decisions involving the liberty of alleged foreign fugitives were for courts, not diplomats, to decide.

In negotiating the convention, Jefferson thought he was helping merchant ships recover their crews. He did not anticipate that France would be torn apart by revolution and that some ship-jumpers would be fugitives from political conflict and state terrorism. Thus, the consular agreement took on new significance on August 1, 1793, when a large convoy of French ships packed with refugees from Santo Domingo sailed into New York harbor. The refugees were Creoles (French people born on the islands) who had attempted to seize control of the colony in 1791 for their planter class. They met with resistance from the French Assembly in Paris, which in April 1792 decreed that the more numerous men of color on the island were entitled to the same political rights as their white masters. This infuriated the whites, and when commissioners sent from France to enforce the decree allied themselves with armed mulattos, the whites resisted, choosing as their champion General Thomas Francis Galbaud, the newly appointed governor-general (and husband to a wealthy Creole heiress). The tumultuous reception Galbaud received when he landed at Cap François (now Cap Haitien) in May 1793 provoked the commissioners to invalidate his credentials and order him returned to France. Before that could be accomplished, French sailors who had been harassed by mulatto soldiers decided to seize the city on behalf of the whites. The general agreed to lead them, but when they stormed ashore, the commissioners called upon insurgent slaves for aid. Thousands responded, and Galbaud's undisciplined force, together with most of the white colonists, was driven into the sea.[54]

Americans received the refugees enthusiastically, but the French minister to the United States, Edmond C. Genêt, recognized their hatred for the French republic and their determination to retake the island—in alliance with the British, if necessary. He was determined to disperse the refugees throughout the United States and use their ships to attack Louisiana and the Floridas (then under Spanish control), to raid British shipping from U.S. ports, and to recapture two French islands off the coast of Canada.

To do this, the French minister had to buy off the sailors and soldiers, which would require blaming Galbaud and his aides for their disastrous plot to seize the island. Genêt was encouraged in this scheme by naval officers who, in order to protect themselves from reprisals, had made the general their prisoner on board the seventy-four-gun flagship *Jupiter*. Galbaud, in short, was to be the scapegoat. Knowing this, he, his wife, and three aides escaped from the warship and fled toward Canada. The French minister then asked state and federal authorities to help recapture the "traitors," claiming that they were conspiring to use the United States as a base from which to capture Santo Domingo in concert with Britain and Spain. Genêt wanted to ship them to France for trial, where they most certainly would have been executed for treason,[55] but Secretary of State Jefferson refused. Jefferson sympathized with the French Revolution, but he was even more partial to individual liberty. On September 12, 1793, he informed Genêt that because Galbaud and his aides had been passengers, and not sailors, on the *Jupiter*, they could not be arrested under the 1788 convention. If Genêt could furnish proof that the fugitives were violating the U.S. neutrality acts, he added, the United States could have them arrested; otherwise they were entitled to go free.[56]

This should have been a sufficient response to Genêt's demand, but the secretary of state went further. He explained why the United States was not willing to surrender fugitives to countries like France:[57]

The laws of this country take no notice of crimes committed out of their jurisdiction. The most atrocious offender, coming within their pale, is received by them as an innocent man, and they have authorized no one to seize and deliver him. The evil of protecting malefactors of every dye is sensibly felt here as in other countries; but until a reformation of the criminal codes of most nations, to deliver fugitives to them, would be to become their accomplices: the former, therefore, is viewed as the lesser evil.

Jefferson could have confined his concern to political offenders; Galbaud and his aides were accused only of treason. But, as Jefferson had already intimated to Governor Pinckney with regard to extradition with Spain, the question was one of justice for all persons, not just for political fugitives.[58]

Jefferson's explanation was not calculated to please the French envoy, but a year later Genêt had ample reason to appreciate the policy when his own surrender for alleged "criminal conduct" was demanded by his Jacobin successor, Jean Fauchet. Despite everything Genêt had done to outrage the Washington administration, the request for his extradition was denied "upon reasons of law and magnanimity."[59]

Fauchet then asked if the U.S. "government would wink at an attempt to seize and send Genêt to France," but this, too, was rejected. Unlike late-twentieth-century presidents and justices, Washington would not countenance abduction, and Genêt lived out the remainder of his days as a country gentleman in New York.[60]

The Washington administration's hostility toward the extradition of Galbaud and Genêt was not just an expression of diplomatic neutrality toward the internal political conflicts of a European power. It also reflected the humanitarian views of Enlightenment reformers and the confidence of American lawyers that the judicial-centered common law was manifestly more just than the executive-centered civil law. This conviction was to persist, despite many liberal reforms on the Continent, until the late nineteenth century.[61]

* * *

Galbaud and his staff were not the only ship-jumpers sought by the revolutionary French government. French consuls frequently went into U.S. courts to obtain the arrest of fugitives from the undisciplined French navy, which was riven with class conflict between an older officer corps drawn from the aristocracy and a newer, more politically correct corps, which had been promoted from the lower ranks.

One of the aristocrats was Captain Henry Barré of the corvette La Perdrix, who had the misfortune of getting into an altercation with Captain Mahé of the frigate La Concorde in July 1794 after a convoy for which Mahé was responsible had been scattered by a larger British fleet off New Jersey.[62] Mahé was furious at Barré for not sailing down to the mouth of the Delaware to give him some protection. He called Barré a "Muscadin"—a war slacker opposed to the revolution—and declared that the corvette captain would be guillotined if he ever returned to France.[63] Barré, although respected by the French consul as an officer who had done well by his crew, needed no further warning.[64] He jumped ship at Cape Henlopen, Delaware, and took refuge with friends in New York.[65]

Fauchet, the French envoy, obtained a warrant for Barré's arrest from a federal judge in Philadelphia, but it was only valid in Pennsylvania. The French vice-consul in New York then sought another from federal district court judge John Laurance, but the judge refused on the grounds that the vice-consul could not prove that Barré had been a member of the ship's company. The vice-consul submitted a number of accounts and dispatches to prove Barré's captaincy, but Laurance insisted on enforcing the letter of article 9 of the 1788 convention, which expressly required presentation of the ship's register. Not even a copy would suffice; the original *rôle d'équipage* had to be presented. By insisting upon this technicality, Laurance effectively shielded Barré, and others like him, from repatriation and death for desertion at a moment when, so far as anyone in New York knew, the Reign of Terror was still at its height. Like Jefferson, the judge also shielded the U.S. government from the ignominy of supporting French terror.

Fauchet was highly displeased but managed to persuade Attorney General William Bradford to appeal the denial on France's behalf. Since the case involved an ex parte application for a warrant, Barré was not a party to the original application or the appeal. The respondent was Judge Laurance, and the demand was for a writ of mandamus directing him to issue a warrant for the captain's arrest. Thus, the first extradition case under the new Constitution, misspelled *United States v. Lawrence*, involved a federal judge defending his decision not to order the arrest of an alleged fugitive.

When the case was argued before the U.S. Supreme Court on February 18, 1795, the judge's attorneys reiterated Jefferson's view that "absent a positive compact, no Government will surrender deserters, or fugitives, who make asylum of its territory."[66] They also argued that since the treaty derogated from the freedom that individual French citizens would otherwise enjoy under customary international law, it should be precisely construed, particularly "when we consider the existing circumstances of the [French] nation."[67]

Unlike modern attorneys general, Bradford made it clear that he was not placing the prestige of the United States behind France's reading of the treaty or of the applicable U.S. law. Rather, he was presenting France's views neutrally, as a courtesy to France, for an impartial disposition by the court. This was particularly important, he said, "in the present case," which, "from the nature of its subject, as well as the spirit of our political Constitution, the Judiciary Department is called upon to decide."[68] In other words, the attorney general recognized that cases involving the personal liberty of alleged fugitives were, under the Constitution as well as the consular convention, for courts and not the executive to decide. Nor, he added, would the executive even think of overruling a court in such cases. "It is essential," he stressed, "that judicial mistakes should only be corrected by judicial authority."[69]

At the same time, the attorney general argued—speaking for France—the Supreme Court should not inquire into what was going on in France. It should treat the case formalistically, as if the Terror did not exist. The Court's decision, he said, "ought not to be affected by any circumstances respecting the hardship of Captain Barré's fate, or the crisis of French affairs. No change or fluctuation in the interior policy of France, can release the obligation of our government to perform its public engagements."[70] Bradford thus became the first executive official in American history to propose that a court blind itself to the unwillingness and incapacity of a foreign regime to do justice in an extradition case. Although he did not so label the idea, he was advocating what would later become a judicial "rule of noninquiry."

However, Bradford also distinguished between an arrest pursuant to the consular treaty and the delivery of the prisoner. Surrender, he said, "is obviously a subsequent act, to be performed after the party has been brought before the Judge; when, not only the allegations against him, but his answers and defence, are heard, and the Judge has decided that he is an object of the article. Natural justice, and the safety of our citizens, require that such a hearing should take place."[71] Here, Bradford argued, the fugitive could attempt to prove that he had never signed the ship's roll, or had been lawfully discharged. If "he suffers any injury" (presumably as a consequence of this hearing), "he might, on Habeas Corpus, be relieved."[72] Thus, the first administration under the new Constitution accepted the primacy of the judiciary in deciding who should be arrested on charges of violating the laws of a foreign country, and whether the evidence against the person justified surrendering the person to that power.

At one level, the issue simply concerned the kind of proof necessary to justify an arrest under the convention. That agreement clearly said that the original ship's register had to be presented; France, through the attorney general, demonstrated how utterly impractical this requirement was once a ship had left port, since maritime law required that the register go with the ship. When the agreement was written, the drafters probably focused only on the need to round up crews on the eve of a ship's departure. Here, however, the French vice-consul demanded the extradition of a captain who had fled the French navy because he feared injustice at the hands of the Jacobins. In effect, the French government was attempting to transform a nonpolitical, ship-jumping convention into an extradition treaty that would deliver political fugitives into the hands of their enemies, who were almost certain to treat them unjustly.

Procedurally, the question before the Court was whether issuing an arrest warrant was a *ministerial* duty, regarding which the trial judge enjoyed no discretion, or a *judicial* duty, in which case he would be free to exercise his best judgment as to the sufficiency of the evidence. As Chief Justice John Marshall would explain a few years later in the famous case of *Marbury v. Madison*, writs of mandamus may be issued only to direct the doing of a nondiscretionary act.[73] On this question, the Supreme Court had no difficulty. In a brief *per curiam* opinion issued on March 3, 1795, the justices unanimously agreed that issuing warrants was a judicial duty "and (whatever might be the difference of sentiment entertained by this Court) we have no power to compel a Judge to decide according to the dictates of any judgment, but his own."[74] As a matter of law, this meant that a judge hearing an application for the arrest of a foreign fugitive is entitled to examine all the circumstances to determine whether there is probable cause to seize the accused. His decision was not to be controlled by the mere presentation of a piece of paper by a foreign consul.

Interestingly, the same issue had been addressed by Chief Justice John Jay in 1786 when, as secretary for foreign affairs, he had objected to a provision in Franklin's draft of the consular convention that would have made "the certificate of a consul conclusive proof of a man's being a Frenchman, and declares that he who makes *such proof* shall not lose, for any cause whatever." This, Jay had advised Congress, "does not comport with the genius and spirit, either of our constitutions or our laws; both of which secure to every inhabitant and citizen the inestimable privilege of offering, in our tribunals, every species of legal evidence that may tend to elucidate the merits of the cause before them."[75] Jay was particularly concerned with the issue of identity, but he was making a much larger point about the duty of courts to protect persons from unjust extradition by allowing them wide latitude in the evidence they could present in their defense at the probable cause hearing. Whether Jay's previous opinion was considered by the Court in its review of Judge Laurance's decision to deny Barré's surrender is not known. The chief justice did not participate in the *Lawrence* decision; he was in England negotiating yet another treaty that would provide for the surrender of foreign fugitives.

As a practical matter, the *Lawrence* case made it extremely difficult for French authorities to recapture seamen who, for any reason, took refuge in the United States. Fauchet, in a dispatch home, warned of the obstacle the Court's decision would pose to the recovery of mutineers from French warships, of which there were many at the time. He recommended that his superiors authorize him, or his successor, to negotiate a new treaty that would reverse the Court's decision, but nothing came of this proposal. A secretary of state, an attorney general, and now the Supreme Court had all recognized that the liberty of persons, even French sailors, was for courts, not the executive, to decide.[76]

* * *

Permeating these policy decisions was a generous sense of the United States as an open society. Neither the national nor state governments set standards for immigration. Had they done so, there would have been no one to enforce them. The ports of America were wide open to immigration. Short on labor, eighteenth-century America generally welcomed new settlers. From the perspective of their scattered settlements divided by huge swaths of undeveloped land, the Americans foresaw no difficulty absorbing fugitives of all kinds, from ship-jumping captains like Barré to whole fleets of French Creoles from strife-torn Santo Domingo. Many Americans were refugees themselves, and their America was a diverse, fluid, loosely structured, minimally policed society that had no interest in enforcing the oppressions of a Europe they had fled. Having left their personal as well as political histories behind by crossing over, they tended to be rather generous with the freedom they had found. Thus, it was easy for them to adopt their own "rule of noninquiry," take a humanitarian approach to foreign requests for extradition, or even deny them altogether.

When diplomacy required it, Americans could "honor his majesty," but they also had "tender consciences." Given the regimes they had left behind, they felt something of a civil responsibility to protect political fugitives of all stripes, from the brave "Ghost of Hadley" to the obnoxious Citizen Genêt. They were not eager to engage in extradition, but when it seemed necessary to preserve relations with Spain, suppress border raiders, recover fugitives, or return foreign seamen to their ships, they insisted on treaties or legislation to establish the relationship and denied the executive discretion to decide who should be surrendered. Because requests for extradition threatened the liberty of individuals, courts would have to rule upon them, using evidentiary standards similar to, and perhaps more rigorous than, those employed in domestic criminal cases. Whether an accused should be surrendered for trial abroad would have to be decided on the totality of the circumstances; a mere certificate from the foreign government would not do. Americans were not yet willing to blind themselves to the potential for injustice inherent in most foreign legal systems, whether those systems were politically conservative like Spain's, or politically radical like France's. Nor was this protection limited to political fugitives; it was accorded to all fugitives from all unjust legal systems.

Such was the American approach to extradition on the eve of Jay's Treaty with Great Britain—the first general extradition agreement to be concluded by the new republic.

CHAPTER 2

The Extradition of Thomas Nash

If you had been as Robbins was
What would you have done?
What ought you not to do?
And look at Robbins,
Hanging at a British Yard-Arm!

Like him you one day may be
Trussed up to satiate British vengeance.
Your heinous crime
Daring to prefer danger or death
To a base bondage.

Robert Slender, epitaph for an extradited seaman

When John Jay arrived in London in 1794, he discovered that the British approach to extradition was very similar to the American. Great Britain had also become a nation of asylum. Her government refused to engage in extradition in the absence of a treaty or legislation and looked upon the decision to extradite a particular individual as a matter of law, which meant that it could not become a mere matter for executive discretion. It did not take Lord Grenville long to accept Jay's proposals for extradition between their two countries.

Article 27 of Jay's treaty provided:[1]

It is further agreed that His Majesty and the United States on mutual requisitions, by them respectively, or by their respective Ministers or officers authorized to make the same, will deliver up to justice all persons who, being charged with murder or forgery, committed within the jurisdiction of either, shall seek asylum within any of the countries of the other, provided that this shall only be done on such evidence of criminality as, according to the laws of the place where the fugitive or person so charged shall be found, would justify his apprehension and commitment for trial, if the offence had there been committed. The expense of such apprehension and delivery shall be borne and defrayed by those who make the requisition and receive the fugitive.

Although modest and short-lived,[2] the provision established a number of important principles that have continued to structure the Anglo-American approach to extradition and the protection of political offenders. First, the treaty acknowledged that extradition would have to be authorized by law. In the United States, this would be the Jay Treaty itself; in Great Britain it would be the treaty and implementing legislation.[3]

Second, while the language of Article 27 seemed to say that executives of the two countries were responsible for delivering up fugitives in response to proper requisitions, the standard of proof prescribed virtually guaranteed that the question of extraditability would have to be examined by a court, either at the initial fact-finding stage, or on review by habeas corpus. Like the final version of the French consular convention, Jay's treaty with Great Britain made extradition a matter of *law*, not just foreign policy, by specifying legal proofs.

Third, this standard of proof not only echoed the common law's test for the issuance of arrest warrants; it was also consistent with the probable cause standard of the Fourth Amendment to the U.S. Constitution. The British government was no less committed than the American to this standard, which its courts had come to call a *prima facie* case requirement. Indeed, the one change that the British negotiator, Lord Grenville, appears to have made in Jay's draft of Article 27 was to insert the more emphatic word "only" in front of "on such evidence of criminality."[4]

Fourth, the treaty established the principle that no crimes are extraditable unless they are expressly listed in the treaty. Only two offenses were listed, murder and forgery. Both were nonpolitical on their face and of substantial gravity. The formalism of this approach suggests that Jay and Grenville thought of political crimes largely in the "pure" sense of treason (i.e., *lèse majesté*) and sedition or believed that the likelihood of political prosecutions in Britain and the United States was not great. If any danger of political abuse existed, they may have reasoned, the evidentiary requirement would prevent extradition by requiring that the offense be a crime in both countries—the so-called "double criminality" test. In this respect, the Federalist John Jay seems to have parted company with the Republicans Jefferson and Pinckney, both of whom had earlier recognized the need for a political crimes exemption in a treaty with Spain that they were considering.

Fifth, Jay's Treaty provided that the crime must have been committed within the "territorial jurisdiction" of the requesting state. In the 1790s, this meant that the requesting state could demand extradition only for crimes committed on its soil.[5] Extradition under the Jay Treaty would thus be limited to fugitives and would not cover shootings across borders.

Sixth, the principle of territoriality implied its corollary: trial within the vicinity of the crime. Indeed, trial within the vicinage, so important to the Americans who signed the Declaration of Independence, had become an independent principle of the American constitutions.

Finally, the treaty, like Madison's Virginia statute, drew no distinction between citizens and aliens, thus implying both a solicitude for aliens and a willingness to surrender nationals. Under the newly ratified Bill of Rights, rights against government derived from personhood, not citizenship.

Jay's Treaty did not contain an express exception for political crimes or for politically motivated prosecutions. Nor did it expressly anticipate the rule of specialty (limiting trial to the offenses for which extradition was authorized) or the rule against double jeopardy. It made the decision regarding extraditability a legal one but did not say who should make that determination, initially or on review. Nor did Congress enact legislation specifying who should decide, even though the treaty was not, by its terms, explicit enough about the allocation of decision-making authority to be unquestionably self-executing.[6] As a result, the allocation of decisional responsibilities had to be worked out politically as well as judicially.

* * *

Article 27 was largely ignored in the otherwise vehement debate over Jay's Treaty. Its meaning and significance would have to be tested in a series of cases arising out of the bloodiest mutiny in British naval history.

That uprising occurred on board the thirty-two-gun frigate *Hermione,* on patrol in the British West Indies during the Napoleonic wars. Discipline on the ship was brutal, and Captain Hugh Pigot was despised by his crew. On September 20, 1797, in the midst of a tropical storm, the captain impatiently ordered sailors down from the mizzen topsail, declaring he would flog the slowest. Three seamen leaped from the yardarm to the ratlines, lost their hold, and fell more than forty feet to the deck. Told that the men were dead, the captain is said to have replied, "Throw the lubbers overboard."[7]

The next day the crew mutinied. They killed or threw overboard ten people, including the captain and most of the ship's officers. Then they sailed the ship into La Guaira (today the seaport to Caracas, Venezuela), sold her to Napoleon's Spanish allies, and scattered.

The mutiny sent a shudder through the British naval establishment. Most of its crews had been shanghaied by press gangs and were not much different from the inmates of a prison. They were paid about half the wages offered by the American merchant marine and were ruled with iron discipline. The *Hermione* revolt, following close behind the Spithead and Nore mutinies, threatened by its example to subvert discipline throughout the fleet, then Britain's main line of defense in her life-and-death struggle with France and her allies. A reward of $1,000 was posted on both sides of the Atlantic for information leading to the capture of the mutineers, and no effort was spared to track them down.[8]

Landsmen had no more reason to care for the mutineers than did the British navy. Sailors were generally thought to be a degraded lot, uneducated, uncouth, and unrestrained by the normal ties of affection or responsibility to the ports they visited. Military deserters were positively feared; they made up a large percentage of the robbers and brigands for which European states had developed extradition treaties in the eighteenth century. Society was considered safer if sailors, particularly from warships, were closely controlled.[9]

The first of the mutineers to be traced to the United States was Simon Marcus, a common seaman. He was taken off the schooner *Hannah* at Wilmington, Delaware, in response to a request from Robert Liston, the British minister. Attached to Liston's request to Secretary of State Timothy Pickering was the affidavit of Frances Martin, who had been on board the *Hermione* during the mutiny, when her husband William, a boatswain's mate, was killed. Her account of the uprising listed Simon Marcus, Thomas Nash, and several others as the mutineers.[10]

The request and affidavit were promptly "laid before the President [Adams]," Pickering wrote Liston three days later, but the evidence presented against the sailor was insufficient to "justify his apprehension & commitment for trial, if the offense had been *here* committed." Mrs. Martin had only identified Marcus as a member of the crew; she had not offered any evidence that he participated in the killings or the sale (i.e., piracy) of the vessel.[11] Liston protested that Marcus should be presumed guilty because he had falsely denied being a member of the crew, but President Adams was not persuaded.

Marcus went free, but the legal problems his case posed did not go away. Three weeks later, authorities in Perth Amboy, New Jersey, arrested three more fugitives from the *Hermione* at the British government's behest. This time the secretary of state went to Attorney General Charles Lee, rather than the president, and asked whether the evidence against William Brigstock, John Evans, and Joannes Williams was sufficient to justify their extradition for murder and piracy.[12]

Lee found other problems with those requests. First, he noted, Brigstock claimed to be an American, and thus deserved the right to be tried by an American jury. The other prisoners might turn out to be Americans too, but even if they were not, Lee thought it was more "becoming the justice, honor, and dignity of the United States, that the trial should be in our courts."[13]

Second, Lee did not believe that the three men were extraditable under the Jay Treaty. The killings, he believed, did not come within the "territorial jurisdiction" envisioned by the treaty because they did not occur on British soil. To a twenty-first-century lawyer, this may seem peculiar, but the idea of a ship's decks being "territory" for purposes of establishing criminal jurisdiction had not then been established.[14] However, while Lee's narrow theory of territoriality barred extradition for murder on a British ship, it did not bar prosecution under the 1790 Crimes Act for murder or piracy on the high seas, especially where the alleged pirates were or might be Americans.[15]

Third, while Lee agreed with Grotius, Pufendorf, and Vattel that countries are "duty bound" morally to comply with extradition requests for "heinous offenders," he did not know how that could be done without enabling legislation. In this, he was more like a liberal Jeffersonian than a conservative Federalist. Uniform legislation was needed, he said, to prevent the delivery of anyone, and especially American citizens, to unjust regimes. "Suppose," he asked Pickering, that "it was not the British nation (whose system of jurisprudence is humane, fair, and just), but the French, Spanish, or Prussian, that had made the requisition: would it be right to comply with it? I think not."[16]

For these reasons, the attorney general opposed extradition to Great Britain and urged prosecution of the sailors in federal court for piracy and murder. The secretary of state, however, decided not to share this inconvenient view with the British minister. Instead, he asked Judge Robert Morris of the U.S. District Court of New Jersey "to detain the said William Brigstock until the President shall give directions to deliver him to the orders of the British minister."[17]

The implication of the secretary's letter seems clear; he thought that, under the Jay Treaty, the president had the power to direct a federal judge to hold and surrender to Great Britain a person who might be an American. His position was inconsistent with that taken by Madison and the Washington administration, but times had changed. Fear of domestic rebellion and foreign subversion ran high, and Colonel Pickering had become the administration's chief enforcer of the Alien and Sedition Acts. His high-handedness, therefore, was consistent with the High Federalist view that gave primacy to executive power, a view that in time would cost President Adams and his party dearly.

What happened next is not clear, but the executive power to direct surrender that Pickering asserted was not exercised in the Brigstock cases. Instead, all three sailors were rushed to trial in Trenton, New Jersey. On Friday, April 6, 1798, all were indicted for piracy. Their trial began the following Monday, with Judge Morris and Justice Samuel Chase on the circuit court bench. Thirteen hours later, the jury acquitted all three.

Given the paucity of evidence against the three men, it is curious that they were tried at all. The only witness for the prosecution was Mrs. Martin, and she could not prove that either Evans or Williams had participated in the mutiny.[18] The allegations against Brigstock were stronger, but the jury may have had doubts about the evidence against him because the British government's case against the others was so weak. Or he could have benefited from a sympathy vote. As Secretary of State Pickering started to explain to the British minister (in a too candid letter he never sent), Brigstock "is a citizen of the United States whose friends live in New York; and probably he was impressed on board the *Hermione*."[19]

Brigstock would not be extradited, the secretary decided, but he would be tried separately for murder. Lee's opinion thus prevailed, but if the British minister was upset when he learned of it (probably orally), Pickering mollified him on April 8 by asking a district judge in New York to continue the detention of "seven or eight" other fugitives from the *Hermione*.[20]

Then on June 8, 1798, Pickering called an end to the prosecution of Brigstock for murder. The reason, he said, was a letter from Admiral Sir Hyde Parker clearing the accused of that charge.[21] That may have been the reason, but it is also possible that the exculpation was arranged by Liston and Pickering so that the United States would not be on record as having refused extradition for any of the reasons set forth in Lee's opinion.[22]

Then, too, the president may have seen some merit to the self-defense claim. As a lawyer in 1769, he had successfully advanced the same argument to win the acquittal of a colonial seaman charged with killing an officer of HMS *Rose* who had tried to fill out his crew by impressing sailors from a colonial merchant vessel.[23] Or Lee might have persuaded Adams that the *Hermione* fugitives should not be sent overseas for trials without the benefit of juries: Adams had supported similar arguments that eventually found their way into the Declaration of Independence. But both explanations seem unlikely, given the administration's subsequent handling of the case of Jonathan Robbins. A more plausible speculation may be that Adams, counseled by Lee, did not want to make a martyr of Brigstock, who had supporters in New York—a state important to Adams's reelection.

Brigstock's plight was beginning to receive the attention of Republican newspapers nationwide. As early as July 4, 1795, Philip Freneau's *Jersey Chronicle* had carried an account of impressments by Captain Hugh Pigot when he was in command of the frigate *Success*. In one attack, Pigot was alleged to have carried off two-thirds of all the American sailors then in the port of Jeremie, Santo Domingo. (The *Hermione*, under a different British captain, seized still more Americans from Jeremie at the same time.) These depredations were described by Republican editor James Callender in his *History of the United States for 1796* and republished at the time of the Brigstock arrests.[24] The Adams administration protested the impressments diplomatically but did nothing else to stop them.[25]

Among Jeffersonian Republicans, there was considerable support for mutinies within the British navy in 1797, both because they strengthened France's power and because they seemed to demonstrate that impressed seamen would not endure British tyranny. When Mrs. Martin's account of the cruelty of Captain Pigot was published, the Philadelphia *Aurora*, an outspokenly Republican newspaper, applauded the sailors who had killed him.[26]

By contrast, Federalist newspapers disapproved of the mutinies. On July 3, 1798, the Charleston *State Gazette and Timothy's Daily Advertiser* published an approving account of the court-martial of several of the *Hermione*'s crew on board HMS *York* during the previous March.[27] During the late spring and early summer of 1798, Federalists in Congress were fearful of espionage, subversion, domestic rebellion, and even mutiny within the fledgling U.S. Navy, which would be the main line of defense (behind the British navy) if the nation went to war with France. French demands for bribes from U.S. diplomats in the infamous XYZ Affair had made war more likely than ever, and the Federalists moved, as the British had several years earlier, to silence seditious publications and expel aliens hostile to their party and Great Britain. Among this legislation was an alien removal act that, had it been passed in its original House form, would have substituted arbitrary deportation for extradition.

The original House bill "for restraining aliens and other disaffected or seditious persons" would have allowed deportation of any alien "convicted of a felony or other infamous crime in his native country . . . if he was a notorious fugitive from justice in any foreign country upon any charge of treasonable or seditious practices."[28] Vice President Jefferson wrote James Madison that the House bill and its Senate counterpart were "so palpably in the teeth of the Constitution as to show that they [the High Federalists] mean to pay no respect to it."[29] A few days later, however, the House chose to reject its own bill for the Senate's, and this provision was dropped. The final version of the alien removal law did not challenge the Washington administration's policy, reinforced by the Convention with France and the Treaty with Great Britain, that there could be no extradition without a treaty.[30]

Such was the political climate in February 1799 when Thomas Nash, another fugitive from the *Hermione*, was arrested in Charleston, South Carolina. Nash had come into Charleston on the schooner *Tanner's Delight*, where he was betrayed by William Portlock, one of the schooner's crew, probably for a reward. Portlock swore before a local justice of the peace that he had heard Nash tell some French privateersmen that he had been a boatswain's mate on the *Hermione* when she was seized. Portlock also alleged that when Nash was drunk, he "would mention the name of the *Hermione*, and say, bad luck to her, and clench his fist."[31] Nash was locked up in the Charleston jail, and the British navy was notified of his capture. Lieutenant John Forbes, who had served on the *Hermione* with Nash, was sent to Charleston, where he viewed the prisoner and then swore out an affidavit identifying him as Nash.[32]

Since there were no ancillary charges against Nash, who at the beginning of his proceedings was not thought to be an American, the extradition demand had to be confronted squarely. Federal District Judge Thomas Bee (supported by the local U.S. attorney) began by advising the British consul in Charleston to route his request through diplomatic channels, thus giving Pickering a chance to assert his executive-centered approach. This was done, and on May 15, 1799, Secretary of State Pickering wrote to the president in Quincy, Massachusetts, recommending extradition.

This time Pickering did not seek the attorney general's advice. He did not want to hear that the deck of a British warship was not soil enough to give the British territorial jurisdiction to make the extradition request. Nor did he put the matter before the cabinet, where the absence of implementing legislation, jury trial claims, or the self-defense argument might be raised. Instead, he sought to persuade the president privately to direct surrender.

Like any secretary of state, Pickering had a vested interest in making the new treaty work. But his determination went well beyond that. Pickering was a pro-executive High Federalist who believed that, in the absence of a treaty, governments retained discretion to surrender alleged offenders "in cases affecting the great interests of society."[33] He was also an archetypal American conservative who defined most matters as a conflict between good and evil and was thus susceptible to seeing only that part of a story that would affirm his righteousness.[34] He had no sympathy for mutineers, whom he dismissed as "pests" of the sea. Ignoring Captain Pigot's cruelty (documented in Mrs. Martin's affidavit) and his impressment of American sailors in Jeremie, the secretary of state condemned "the offence committed on board the Hermione" as "a most atrocious act of *piracy* accompanied with *murder*," and declared "that the Judge of the District Court of South Carolina should be directed to deliver up the offender in question, on the demand of the British Government, by its Minister."[35]

Unlike the Washington administration, but like many law-and-order conservatives today, Pickering believed that extradition was preeminently an executive matter and that judges in such cases were but convenient agents of foreign policy. The personal liberty of accused persons did not concern him; nor did he value the democratic scrutiny of popular juries as a check on foreign tyranny. These were Republican ideas, and the former colonel would have none of them.

President Adams replied almost immediately, agreeing with Pickering that "an offence, committed on board a public ship of war, on the high seas, is committed within the jurisdiction of the nation, to whom the ship belongs." On the other hand, he added, "how far the president of the US would be justifiable in directing the judge, to deliver up the offender, is not clear. I have no objection to advize and request him to do it."[36]

In retrospect, Adams probably wished that he had been more emphatic about the independence of the judiciary, for that was a principle in which he believed strongly. His tentativeness cost him and his party grievously in the elections of 1799 and 1800.

Today it seems preposterous that the executive would presume to *direct* a federal judge to surrender a person within the jurisdiction of his court. In the 1790s, it was not yet clear whether a judge hearing an extradition case is fully wreathed in the independence accorded to the judiciary by Article III of the Constitution, or whether he is some sort of administrator under Article II.

Unresolved too was whether the jurisdiction of federal judges was "inherent" in their offices, implicit in the judicial power given them by Article III, or a power that could be exercised only pursuant to an express grant from Congress. Neither the Judiciary Act of 1789 nor its amendments expressly authorized judges to hold hearings in extradition cases—nor did the Jay Treaty, unlike the Consular Convention with France. The Judiciary Act did not give lower federal courts sweeping jurisdiction over all "federal questions" or all issues "arising under" a treaty of the United States. So unless Article III is itself a fountain of judicial authority (rather than a restriction on what Congress can do legislatively), federal courts could be said to lack authority to hear any cases arising under Article 27 of the Jay Treaty.

On the other hand, it was possible (albeit controversial) for a federal judge to sit as a non–Article III administrative judge or treaty commissioner. That had been done before.[37] Indeed, Chief Justice John Jay had assumed non–Article III duties when he negotiated the treaty.

Yet it was one thing to negotiate a treaty and something else to make a judicial decision that could cost a person his liberty, or in Nash's case, his life. In addition, federal district judges had the authority to review detentions ordered by non–Article III officers. Would a federal judge who detained an extradition suspect as an Article II administrator have the authority then to put on his Article III robes and review his own decision pursuant to a request for a writ of habeas corpus?

The law, as Adams had observed, was not clear. He could have drawn an analogy to interstate rendition of fugitives and treated international extradition as a purely executive function, subject only to habeas corpus review, but he did not. Adams was no Republican, but he had once been what we would today call a civil liberties lawyer. He could not imagine that the decision to deliver a person to trial and possible death at the hands of a foreign tribunal could occur outside the judicial process. Therefore, he directed the secretary of state to put the issue before Judge Bee and let him decide what basis there was for American courts to take jurisdiction.

Pickering complied, but in a poorly worded letter that opened Adams to Republican charges that he had tried to direct Judge Bee's decision. Expressing his own opinions rather than the president's, the Pickering informed the judge that "Nash ought to be delivered up, as requested by the British Minister: Provided such evidence of his criminality be produced as by the laws of the United States, or of South Carolina, would justify his apprehension and commitment for trial, if the offence had been committed within the jurisdiction of the United States." Read literally, these sentences do not constitute an intrusion upon the independence of the judiciary. However, Pickering concluded: "The President has in consequence hereof authorized me to communicate to you 'his advice and request,' that Thomas Nash may be delivered up to the Consul or other agent of Great Britain, who shall appear to receive him."[38] This conclusion sounds like a directive, although literally it is not.

Meanwhile, from February to July, the accused lay in chains in the squalid Charleston jail, friendless, unrepresented by counsel, and, so far as anyone in authority knew, a British subject. Given the anti-alien fervor among the Federalists and the contempt for seamen generally, Nash had no reason to be optimistic.

Judge Bee, for his part, seems to have had no interest in either the law or the facts of the case. On July 1, 1799, without interviewing the prisoner or holding an evidentiary hearing, Bee wrote to the secretary of state that he had, that day and in court, told the British consul he intended to order Thomas Nash "brought before me on habeas corpus in order to his being delivered over agreeable to the 27th article of the treaty of amity with Great Britain."[39]

The consul requested that the prisoner be kept in jail until a ship could come for him. There Nash was discovered in mid-May by Abraham Sasportas, a commercial agent for the French Republic, while inspecting the jail as part of a state grand jury. On this visit, Sasportas later claimed in a letter to Republican editors, Nash said that he was Jonathan Robbins, a Connecticut Yankee who had been coerced into the British navy, and he showed Sasportas a certificate of American citizenship signed by a New York notary. Sasportas was so impressed, he said, that he "spoke to . . . counsel the very day."[40]

Whoever Sasportas engaged in May did nothing to prepare Robbins's (or Nash's) defense. On July 23, 1799, William Johnson—probably the former speaker of the South Carolina House who would later be appointed to the U.S. Supreme Court by President Jefferson—went before Judge Bee, identified himself as "only a few minutes engaged as Council with the Prisoner," and asked for a day's delay to study the case. He got two but never appeared again. When the court reconvened on July 25, the prisoner had two other attorneys, Colonel Alexander Moultrie and his assistant, Samuel Ker. Moultrie was well known, having been attorney general of South Carolina for sixteen years before being impeached and removed from office for embezzling state funds in order to invest in the ill-fated Yazoo land company.

The attorneys promptly introduced an affidavit by their client that claimed for the first time Robbins was actually a native of Danbury, Connecticut, who two years earlier had been taken off the American brig *Betsy* by a press gang from the *Hermione* and held on board until the ship was captured by her crew and sold to the Spanish. To support this last-minute assertion, they presented the "sailor's protection," or certificate of citizenship, that Sasportas would later claim he had seen in May.[41] The protection—a common document designed to shield American sailors from impressment—did not establish that its bearer was who he said he was. Although signed by a notary in New York, it lacked a physical description or documentation. It could have been issued to anyone, or resold to anyone willing to change his name.

At the hearing on July 25, Judge Bee heard both the British request for extradition and the prisoner's petition for release through a writ of habeas corpus. The British government insisted that the "protection" was false, that the prisoner was Thomas Nash, that he was born in Wexford, Ireland, and that he had served as a petty officer aboard the *Hermione*. They could not present the ship's last roster, which had been taken by the mutineers, but they were able to submit a copy of an earlier one indicating that the frigate's crew contained one Thomas Nash but no Jonathan Robbins.

To support his extradition request, the British consul submitted the affidavits of Portlock and Forbes. Nothing in Portlock's statement indicated that the prisoner was actually Thomas Nash or that he had participated in the mutiny or murders. Forbes's statement clearly identified the prisoner as Nash but provided no firsthand information about Nash's role, if any, in the mutiny. Forbes had left the ship before the uprising. All he could say was that he had been told by others that Nash had been "one of the principals."[42] In short, both affidavits linked the twenty-three-year-old sailor with the *Hermione,* but neither offered any proof that he was guilty of murder—the one offense for which he could lawfully be extradited under the Jay Treaty.

With better counsel, doubt might also have been cast on the lieutenant's identification. The circular calling for Nash's apprehension said that he was only five feet, six inches tall, whereas the prisoner was five feet ten, a tall man for his day. Similarly, the circular said that Nash had been a common seaman, which could have been used to cast doubt on the lieutenant's claim that he was a petty officer. But nothing was done in advance of the hearing to prepare the seaman's defense. The prisoner's attorneys did not meet with each other to plan their arguments until the day before the hearing, and Moultrie did not meet the accused until just before the hearing began. He did not prepare, he later explained, because he did not think he had a case. Not until the evening before the hearing did he learn that his client claimed to be an American citizen forced into the British navy against his will.[43] By then, of course, it was too late for the attorneys to seek confirmation of their client's story from New York or Connecticut. Indeed, the seaman seemed to hold little interest for them except as an instrument for launching another Republican attack upon the Jay Treaty.

Accordingly, where their arguments should have stressed facts, they stressed law. Ker began by suggesting that the judge take the unprecedented step of declaring the Jay Treaty unconstitutional on the ground that it purported to strip an American citizen of his right to a trial by jury. Rather than emphasize the paucity of evidence against his client, Ker stressed Robbins's right, as an impressed seaman, to "have recourse to violence in the recovery of [his] liberty."[44] He also contended that since the charges involved murder on the high seas and since the accused was an American, he should be tried in a U.S. court, presumably for piracy.

Moultrie expanded on the constitutional argument, presenting as lucid a case for declaring the treaty unconstitutional as Chief Justice John Marshall would deliver four years later in the landmark case of *Marbury v. Madison*.[45] The argument was so good, in fact, that John Marshall might have made note of it when he read the record of the case several months later. But given the similarities of British and American criminal procedure at the time, and the partisan controversies still swirling about the Jay Treaty, it was not likely that a Federalist trial judge (who had delayed the proceedings out of deference to the administration that had concluded the treaty) would take such an unprecedented and radical step.[46]

Moultrie also noted that the authenticity of Robbins's "protection" could be checked, but he did not turn that observation into a formal motion. He concluded with an equally casual reference to the vagueness of the charges, without spelling out for the judge what the standards of probable cause should be for ascertaining identity and culpability in cases like Robbins's.[47]

Whether better advocacy would have made any difference is difficult to say; Judge Bee was clearly more interested in promoting the diplomatic priorities of the Adams administration than in questioning the sufficiency of the evidence. Neither his summary of the arguments advanced in Robbins's defense nor his own decision took notice of the absence of any evidence that the accused actually committed an extraditable offense. Bee was convinced that the prisoner's claim to being an impressed American seaman was a last-minute fabrication; the first he apparently heard of it was at the hearing. Since the "sailor's protection" that Robbins exhibited was dated May 20, 1795, the judge reasoned:[48]

> It is somewhat remarkable, that a man of the name Jonathan Robbins, with the paper produced in his possession, should continue on board a British frigate for a length of time, under another name, and acting as a warrant officer, which impressed men are not likely to be entrusted with, and that he should afterwards take the name of Nathan Robbins, and lay in jail here five or six months, without the circumstance being made known until now.

The claim may well have been a fabrication; foreign seaman frequently obtained false American "protections" in an effort to avoid impressment. But in relying on this speculation, the judge in effect shifted the burden of proof from the requesting government to the prisoner, because he did not require the British government to prove the protection false.[49]

At no time did Bee expressly consider whether the mutiny was an act of justifiable self-defense. Just how much the sailor told his counsel about the actual events is not known, but no facts were included in their arguments before the court. Under the rules of evidence then in force, criminal defendants were not permitted to testify under oath in their own defense. But the sailor's attorneys could have used Mrs. Martin's affidavit in the Brigstock cases to establish this defense, had they done some home-work. A modern extradition court would normally dismiss a self-defense claim as a legal defense to be raised at the prisoner's trial. However, Bee was not bound by such a mechanical view. Like Judge Laurance in the case of Captain Barré, Bee could have viewed the case with an eye toward the realities that lay behind the formal charges. Taking notice of the hideous conditions under which sailors struggled within the British fleet, he could have demanded proof that the killings on board the *Hermione* were really "murder" within the meaning of the treaty. He could also have insisted on proof that the accused had personally committed one of those murders. On that point there was none. Neither Lieutenant Forbes's affidavit (or Mrs. Martin's statement, had it been supplied) implicated Nash in any killings. But Bee was not interested in what had actually happened on board the *Hermione,* or why British sailors had recently rebelled at Nore and Spithead.[50] That was for a British court-martial to decide.

Nor did the judge see any problem sending sailors back to naval courts-martial; juries did not sit on the decks of American warships either, and the American navy would want to make use of the threat of extradition under the treaty to enforce dis-cipline, which had recently been intensified because of the naval war against France.[51] Bee might also have appreciated Robert Liston's gift of cannon from Nova Scotia to protect the Charleston harbor from French and Spanish raids.[52] He certainly did not worry that a court-martial convened by British officers who shanghaied American sea-men into brutal service might not, in time of war, be trusted to give a fair hearing to the self-defense claims of alleged mutineers.

The judge admitted that when the case began he thought that extradition was a mat-ter for the executive alone; that was the procedure established by the federal statute governing rendition of fugitives between the U.S. states.[53] Accordingly, he had instructed the British government to route its request through the president. Later, when he realized that the treaty was silent upon the subject, he concluded that the general powers of the judiciary would have to be invoked, because Article III of the Constitution expressly extended the power of the judiciary to treaties. Thus, without recalling the Supreme Court's decision in the case of Captain Barré (*United States v. Lawrence*), the judge reaffirmed the primacy of the judiciary in extradition cases.

But this did not help the prisoner. Declaring that there was "sufficient evidence of criminality" to justify Robbins's commitment for trial, Bee ordered the U.S. marshal "to deliver the body of . . . Nathan Robbins, alias Thomas Nash, to the British Con-sul," and promptly adjourned the court. There was no opportunity for defense coun-sel to move for a stay, to file an appeal, or to petition for further review by habeas corpus. Nor was there a chance for them to advance humanitarian appeals to the sec-retary of state or the president—a procedure not formally adopted until the 1870s. The prisoner was immediately clapped into irons and delivered to a detachment of federal troops that had been guarding the proceedings from across the street. They promptly marched the hapless sailor to British war cutter *Sprightly*, which carried him off to Port Royal, Jamaica. There on August 15, 1799, the prisoner was tried without the benefit of legal counsel and convicted not only of murder, but of mutiny, desertion, and piracy.[54] Four days later he was hanged from the foreyard of HMS *Acasta*. His corpse was rehung in chains from a gibbet near the mouth of the harbor as a warning to other British sailors.

Only after the sailor had been sent to his death and the issue had became a major partisan controversy were certificates obtained by the secretary of state from the selectmen and town clerk of Danbury declaring that no person or family named Robbins had ever lived in their town.[55] However, on June 20, 1800, the *Aurora* reported that the Danbury selectmen had "found a family of that name, and a brother of Jonathan Robbins, living within a few miles of that town," across the border in New York.[56]

At the court-martial on board HMS *Hannibal*, three witnesses identified the prisoner as Nash, and one of them testified that he saw Nash shove Lieutenant Foreshaw through the larboard gangway into the sea. Nash, for his part, no longer insisted that he was Jonathan Robbins, that he had been pressed into service, or that he had acted in self-defense. Rather, in questioning a witness against him, he made a clumsy attempt to imply that he had pretended to help the mutineers so that he could later help retake the ship.[57] As part of their effort to mollify American public opinion, the British later reported that the prisoner had confessed, prior to his execution, that he was an Irishman.[58]

The extradition of the alleged mutineer was a personal victory for the High Federalist secretary of state over the more moderate attorney general. It also pleased pro-British Federalists, supporters of the Jay Treaty, and law-and-order conservatives generally. However, it was a relatively minor matter to them compared to the undeclared naval war against France, the Fries Rebellion, the sedition of Republican editors, and the threat that pro-French, pro-Republican aliens posed to national security.

The Republicans also paid little attention to the case. Colonel Moultrie was more interested in using Nash's case to attack the constitutionality of the Jay Treaty than he was in exploiting the obvious weaknesses in the British government's request. Alive, Thomas Nash was just a sorry sailor, part of the wretched refuse that washed up in American ports almost daily. Dead, however, he would become Jonathan Robbins, a legendary symbol of liberty lost to autocratic government at home and British oppression abroad.

CHAPTER 3

The Martyrdom of
Jonathan Robbins

Alas poor Robbins!
Alas poor liberty!
Alas poor humbled and degenerate country!

Robert Slender, epitaph for an extradited seaman

The surrender of "Jonathan Robbins" gave Republicans fresh reason to attack the Jay
Treaty and to portray the Federalists as anti-libertarian and pro-British. Their denun-
ciations would influence the state elections of 1799, congressional debates (including
an effort to censure Adams) in the spring of 1800, and the presidential campaign in
the fall of 1800, in which Adams would finish third to challengers Jefferson and Burr.
Before the controversy dissipated with the House's election of Jefferson in the spring
of 1801, Robbins had become a martyr and Article 27 of the Jay Treaty was doomed
never to be invoked again. No one would be extradited from the United States for
another forty years.

   In the course of the partisan debates, the two sides would often talk past each other.
The Republicans would stress the right of all Americans to trial by a jury of their peers;
the Federalists would defend Adams and executive screening of extradition requests.
The Republicans would stress liberty; the Federalists, order. But for all their wrangling,
the two parties shared many values in common, which was not to be fully appreciated
until the 1840s, when the muddy tale of "Jonathan Robbins" achieved mythic clarity.

* * *

The first major assault on Robbins's surrender was launched from Charleston on
August 3, 1799, by South Carolina's Senator Charles Pinckney. Writing as "A Southern Planter," the Republican legislator denounced Judge Bee for not caring whether

Robbins was an American or an impressed seaman.[1] "If this case becomes a precedent," Pinckney warned, "not even the most respectable citizen whose business obliges him to go abroad will be safe. Should he be pressed into the British navy and then fight his way to freedom, he will—if this case holds—be returned for trial."[2]

It was clear to Pinckney, as it had not been to Robbins's attorneys, that the British case for extradition was factually defective. But whereas the judge acknowledged constitutional authority to decide the case, Pinckney argued that Congress must first establish the judge's jurisdiction by legislation. The treaty, because it envisioned judicial proceedings and American evidentiary standards, could not be deemed self-executing. It had to be implemented by subsequent legislation.

In any case, the senator argued, Judge Bee should have recognized the significance of the case and put it off for the circuit court to decide. Under federal legislation, district judges like Bee lacked jurisdiction to try capital cases and therefore should not authorize the surrender of persons to foreign regimes on capital charges. It was particularly important to have the ablest judges decide such cases "in times of war, and particularly in revolutions, when different nations hold such opposite views upon what are piracy or murder, and what [constitutes] justifiable resistance to tyranny and oppression."[3] Moreover, as there was a claim of American citizenship and inadequate proof of criminality, the better course would have been to bind the prisoner over for trial in the United States. In any case, the judge should have given the prisoner the opportunity to send to New York and Connecticut for additional proof of his birthright.

Unlike Robbins's counsel, Pinckney addressed the question of what degree of proof of criminality should have been required. Judge Bee had not required any proof beyond the British government's allegations; the senator would have required the same degree of proof as would be required by an American or British grand jury, which he believed would have excluded "trivial suspicion and hearsay evidence."[4]

Finally, Pinckney took notice of the controversy beginning to brew over the president's alleged directive to the judge. Having not yet seen Bee's reply, however, the senator did not realize how much Judge Bee had been influenced by Pickering's misrepresentation of the president's views.[5]

Pinckney's *Letters of a South Carolina Planter* were published in numerous Republican papers and in pamphlet form.[6] He also shared them with Madison and Jefferson.[7] By then, however, Madison already may have weighed into the debate with a brief, anonymous essay in the Richmond *Examiner*. The essay itself has been lost, and Madison's authorship is not certain,[8] but the piece brought John Marshall, the future chief justice, into the fray with an essay in the *Virginia Federalist* on September 7.[9]

Marshall, then a Federalist candidate for Congress, ignored everything of interest to the Republicans, including the claims of American citizenship, the escape from impressment, and the right of Americans to trial by jury. Instead, he stressed the need for executive screening of extradition requests, both to preserve the sovereignty and unity of the national government and to protect the liberty of the persons sought. From this premise, he reasoned that it was the president's duty to "give some directions in the business," not to influence the judge but to bring the case to his attention.[10]

But the Republicans kept returning to the fact that Robbins was, or claimed to be, an *American* sailor impressed into the British navy. Like the anti-federalist opponents of Madison's bill in the Virginia House of Delegates, the Republicans believed that the right to trial by a jury of one's peers was absolute and could not be violated by remote national officials pursuant to a questionable agreement with a foreign tyrant. They did not limit jury trials to offenses against American law but saw them, like the writ of habeas corpus, as safeguards against arbitrary officialdom anywhere in the world. The jury, to eighteenth-century Republicans, was not just a device for assuring justice and checking tyranny; it was an expression of local democratic control against misguided national and foreign executives. This was the legacy of "jury nullification" that colonial juries had handed down when they defied the instructions of royalist judges; this was the local power that Jefferson had asserted when he wrote in the Declaration of Independence that the king was guilty of wrongfully "transporting us beyond seas to be tried for pretended offenses."

It also appeared to many Republicans that Adams was trying to extend the arbitrary power he had received a year earlier to exclude aliens to include Americans whose delivery might improve relations with Great Britain. Republicans distrusted the pro-British sentiments of High Federalists like Pickering and saw the surrender of Jonathan Robbins as part of a conspiracy to appease the British navy, which the president did not wish to alienate while the American navy was fighting an undeclared naval war against France.

So the Republicans would not allow the Federalists to escape blame for what they had done. Accounts of the sailor's death soon appeared in Federalist as well as Republican newspapers, because the case seemed to symbolize the most fundamental differences between the two parties. Pasteboard figures of Robbins were exhibited at election grounds throughout the fall campaigns.[11] "I think," Jefferson wrote to Pinckney on October 29, that "no circumstance since the establishment of our government has affected the popular mind more."[12]

The controversy continued beyond the fall elections, to consume much of the House of Representatives' time in the early months of 1800. Ultimately, the case became a *cause célèbre* less because there was great sympathy for impressed seamen[13] than because it symbolized party differences on a variety of issues, including foreign relations, executive power, judicial independence, and human rights.

* * *

Starting in February 1800, the Robbins case became the object of protracted debate in Congress. At issue was not just the fate of a common seaman but the larger issue of executive powers, both in relationship to the courts and regarding foreign relations. The debate also had much to do with who would be the next president of the United States.

Opening the assault on John Adams was Rep. Edward Livingston, a Republican from New York who had previously opposed Jay's Treaty. Now he focused on Article 27, which he called "unjust, impolitic, and cruel." Judge Bee's interpretation of the article, Livington said, would allow a citizen of the United States to "be dragged from his country, his connexions, and his friends, and subjected to the judgment of an unrelenting military tribunal."[14]

Unlike Pinckney, Livingston considered the president's request to the judge to be "a dangerous interference of the Executive with Judicial decisions" and an assault on "the Constitutional independence of the judicial power."[15] In his view, Robbins should have been prosecuted, not extradited in obedience to Adams's request, because all of the issues—jurisdiction, applicability of the treaty, citizenship, and impressment—were "matters of exclusive judicial inquiry."[16] Livingston therefore asked Congress to censure the president.[17]

The Republicans demanded the administration's correspondence regarding the Robbins case and the court papers.[18] When the documents were produced, they reinforced the Republicans' suspicion that undue executive influence had been used. They revealed not only Pickering's presidential "directive," but Judge Bee's reply of July 1, 1799, acknowledging that he had, without holding a hearing, and *"In compliance with the request of the President of the United States, . . .* [given] notice to the British Consul that . . . I should order Thomas Nash . . . to be brought before me on habeas corpus, in order to his being delivered over."[19] This seemed proof positive that the court had knuckled under to executive demands.

Albert Gallatin (R.-Pa.) took up the attack where Livingston left off. The future secretary of the treasury challenged the administration's theory that the president could put the extradition provisions of the Jay Treaty in force without first going to Congress for implementing legislation. The treaty, he said, was defective in that it did not specify which branch of government would decide extradition matters. Only Congress could repair such a defect. The British Parliament had enacted legislation to implement the treaty; so should the American Congress, as it had done in 1792 to give effect to the Consular Convention with France.

Similarly, whether the offense was committed within the "territorial jurisdiction" of Great Britain or whether the alleged offense was murder or self-defense were questions which Article III of the Constitution had placed "within the exclusive cognizance of the judiciary." For legal precedents, Gallatin referred to the Brigstock case, where the Adams administration entrusted these questions to the court, and to the case of Captain Barré, where the Washington administration had done the same. Both decisions, Gallatin suggested, established the primacy of the judiciary in such matters.[20]

In response to this attack, Representative John Marshall rose to Adams's defense with a conception of presidential power as generous as anything Alexander Hamilton could have penned. Today the speech is remembered for its claim that the president is the "sole organ" of the nation in foreign affairs—a rhetorical excess that would be quoted over and over again during the Cold War as justification for unlimited (and illimitable) executive power. At the time, however, Marshall was advancing a much more subtle and complex argument about extradition, one that was rhetorically sweeping but practically respectful of the system of checks and balances.

Marshall began with a tactful concession: "Had Thomas Nash been an impressed American, the homicide on board the Hermione would, most certainly, have not been a murder." Thus, in the future chief justice's view, the United States government "could never surrender an impressed seaman to the nation which, in making the impressment, had committed a national injury."[21] But Marshall would not concede this same defense to an Irishman or Englishman impressed into the Royal Navy. Like the defenders of conscription today, Marshall conceded to every nation the legal right to coerce her own subjects to fight in her defense.[22]

Livingston had suggested that Adams be censured because he had intruded into what was a purely judicial decision. Marshall disagreed. This time, however, he did not stress the advisory nature of the president's request. Rather, he counterattacked with a bold and sweeping theory of presidential power that seemed, at least rhetorically, to limit judicial authority to a degree inconsistent with his later court opinions.

The courts, he said, seeming to agree with Livingston, have no authority "to seize any individual and determine that he shall be adjudged by a foreign tribunal" absent legislation from Congress, which did not exist. However, he added, the president does possess that authority, because he is charged by the Constitution with seeing that the laws, including treaties, be faithfully executed.[23] On its face, Marshall's argument sounded like a sweeping assertion of an inherent executive power over all aspects of extradition. The president was, he said, "sole organ of the nation in its external relations," which implied that the surrender of fugitives was his sole responsibility. This impression was heightened by two breathtaking assertions: that surrender was not for courts to decide because it was a matter of "political law,"[24] and that the president had the sole power to decide "whether the nation has or has not bound itself to deliver up any individual."[25]

This was, in effect, an assertion of what would eventually be known as the "political question" doctrine—that certain issues are too "political" to come within the jurisdiction of the courts. Like some modern judges who have used the "political question" doctrine to deflect legal challenges to the conscription of troops, Marshall applied the doctrine in a way that showed little sympathy for individual freedom. The future chief justice was not a civil libertarian.

But Marshall refused to drive his assertions of presidential power to their logical extreme. He did not claim that the president possessed an authority over extradition that he could delegate to the judge. Ten months earlier Marshall had written privately to the secretary of state that "How far the President . . . would be justified in directing the judge to deliver up the offender is not clear."[26] Nor did Marshall claim that the president had the authority to order the judge to do anything. "Had the President directed the Judge at Charleston to decide for or against his own jurisdiction, to condemn or acquit the prisoner," he admitted, "this would have been a dangerous interference with judicial decisions, and ought to have been resisted. But no such direction has been given, nor any such decision been required."[27]

Thus behind the sweeping rhetoric about "sole" presidential power lay a rather modest conception of the extradition power. What Marshall really said—contrary to the practice specified by Jefferson's ship-jumping convention with France—was that the request from Britain should go to the president first. The president (or his delegate) should decide whether the request is lawful within the meaning of the treaty and, if so, order the arrest of the fugitive. This was an argument for executive screening, not executive extradition. Nor did Marshall deny the jurisdiction of the courts to decide whether the evidence was sufficient to justify extradition.[28] The question was how. Marshall again denied that the British should go into court directly, ignoring the president and the State Department, but he admitted that Congress could "prescribe the mode" for implementing the treaty.[29] That presumably meant that Congress could write a statute authorizing the president automatically to refer extradition requests from Great Britain to the judiciary, for its exclusive interpretation of the treaty's meaning.[30] Consistent with other members of his party who had not shown much enthusiasm for a Bill of Rights, Marshall reminded the Republicans (who were then outnumbered in both houses of Congress) that they could enhance the liberty of fugitives, if they wished, by legislation.

Most important, Marshall admitted that "if the President should cause to be arrested under the treaty an individual who was so circumstanced as not to be properly the object of such an arrest, he may perhaps bring the question of the legality of his arrest before a judge, by a writ of habeas corpus."[31] Thus, contrary to his rhetoric, Marshall did not deny the jurisdiction of the courts. He expressly conceded it.[32] Like Secretary Pickering, whom he had been counseling, this was precisely what had been done in South Carolina. It was the procedure that President Adams, through Pickering's letter to Judge Bee, had approved in advance.

In sum, Marshall was trying to suggest that extradition was an executive process *unless* the prisoner chose to make it a judicial one. Marshall's approach to the problem was simple and efficient, and he declared it analogous to the manner in which wrongfully seized prizes of war could be repatriated to their rightful owners and deserting seamen could be returned to their ships.

By analogizing persons to prizes, however, Marshall demonstrated his party's extreme insensitivity to the question of liberty, the very issue its Republican adversaries had been raising. Under his scheme, prisoners who lacked legal counsel or who were ignorant of their right to have the legality of their seizure tested in a habeas corpus proceeding could be surrendered by the executive with dispatch. It did not seem to bother Marshall that this would mean one law for the rich and the educated and another for the poor and the untutored. Nor did it concern him that a person could be spirited out of the country as a matter of political appeasement before he could learn of his rights or before potential defenders could learn of his plight. Marshall, whose speech on this issue may have won him appointment first as secretary of state and later as chief justice, was more interested at that moment in enhancing the Constitution of Powers than in strengthening the Constitution of Limitations or the Constitution of Rights.

But even as he conceded the power of Congress to limit the authority of the president, Marshall did not squarely answer Senator Charles Pinckney, who a year earlier had argued that neither the president nor the courts could order the surrender of anyone until Congress gave effect to the treaty by enacting legislation.[33]

To Marshall, however, the treaty was a "contract" among nations and was as much a law of the land as any statute, once it had been accepted by the Senate and signed by the president.[34] It did not worry him that important questions of individual liberty would be decided not by both houses of the legislature, but by the president and two-thirds of the Senate. Unlike Jefferson, Marshall did not proceed from the belief that the chief function of government was to secure liberty; like conservatives of every age, he put greater stress on the need for authority and order. Thus he did not acknowledge that individual liberties might suffer more if they were decided by the Senate and president in the context of an international agreement than if they were decided by the House, the Senate, and the president in the context of domestic legislation.

For all its flaws, Marshall's speech in Congress was a *tour de force*. He spoke to nearly every issue raised during the preceding weeks, and he defended Adams with knowledge and authority. Moreover, he set forth the first clear concept of how the power to surrender fugitives should be exercised under the new Constitution. The speech was also an eloquent argument for the Federalist conception of strong presidential leadership in foreign affairs—a view that would become part of the conservatives' charter for a national security state in the mid-twentieth century.

Even Jefferson was impressed by Marshall's performance, although he was not swayed by the argument. On the back of a reprint of Marshall's speech, the vice president made a note to himself:[35]

> 1. It was Pyracy by the law of nations, & therefore cognisable by our courts. 2 if alleged to be murder also, then whether he was an impressed American was an essential inquiry. 3 tho' the President as a party subordinate to the court might enter a Nolle pros, a requisition in the style of a Superior was a violation of the Constitutional independancy of the Judiciary.

Looking back upon these times, John Adams viewed the Republican effort to blame him for "the murder of Jonathan Robbins" as just another manifestation of the "terrorism" that had begun with "Chaise Rebellion" in 1786 and had continued through the seditious attacks on his administration by scurrilous Republican newspapers. To Adams, like President Reagan almost two centuries later, "terrorism" was not just random violence intended to extort concessions from officials; it encompassed any effort to discredit established authorities.[36]

Marshall's admirers would later claim that his speech destroyed the case for censuring Adams,[37] but the votes against that motion had already been disclosed in a preliminary vote of the Committee of the Whole. When the final vote came the next day, Livingston's motion was soundly defeated, 61–34.

In the days immediately following the debate, John Marshall was convinced that the Republicans' effort to "affect the next election of President . . . has completely faild of its object."[38] But the voters went on to deny Adams reelection and to replace Federalist with Republican majorities in both houses of Congress. The key states to throw their electoral votes to Jefferson were New York and South Carolina, states that had been acutely aware of the *Hermione* fugitives. The role of the extradition of Jonathan Robbins in this defeat cannot be ascertained, but many knowledgeable observers thought it was a factor.[39] In all probability, anger at the surrender of Robbins merged with hostility toward the Alien and Sedition Acts. The Alien Removal Act, in particular, granted the president summary power to deport any aliens he considered undesirable, and thus gave him far more arbitrary power than Adams had allegedly claimed in his "directive" to Judge Bee.[40] However, the "directive," along with the prosecution of Republican newspaper editors, dramatized the kind of arbitrary executive power that the Republicans found so threatening about the Adams administration.

The intensity of opposition to the surrender of Jonathan Robbins can be seen in a bill passed by the Virginia legislature in 1801. It made it a felony for anyone, on his own authority or on behalf of the Commonwealth of Virginia, to surrender a free person against his will for prosecution by a foreign power. If the accused was subsequently executed, the law continued, the person surrendering him should be put to death.[41]

The extent to which the surrender of Jonathan Robbins affected the election of 1800 is less important than the political lessons that subsequent generations gleaned from the case. The most immediate lesson was that the new nation would be truer to its republican principles if it ceased extradition altogether, which is what the Jeffersonians did when they permitted Article 27 of the Jay Treaty to lapse in 1807. As Supreme Court Justice Samuel Nelson observed in 1853, "the intense public indignation" that followed the surrender of Jonathan Robbins "prevented a renewal" of extradition between the United States and Great Britain until 1842.[42]

Even more important, presidents learned to be careful not to intrude, or even appear to intrude, on judicial primacy in extradition decisions.[43] As a result of the Robbins case, Supreme Court Justice John Catron wrote, "a great majority of the people of this country were opposed to the doctrine that the President could arrest, imprison, and surrender, a fugitive, and thereby execute a treaty himself; . . . and from that day to this, the judicial power has acted in cases of extradition, and all others, independent of executive control."[44] Not until Ronald Reagan took office in 1981 would the executive branch claim that it, rather than the courts, should decide whom to surrender and whom to shield.

* * *

The focus of the Robbins debate, then, was on the abuse of executive power, the need for judicial independence, and the need for jury nullification of high-handed, remote executive action. Less well-focused, perhaps because the requesting regime was Britain's, was whether the accused could expect a just interrogation, trial, and punishment when he was returned.

Neither the Republicans nor the Federalists thought to ask whether Nash (or Robbins) was any more likely to get a fair hearing from the British navy than Captain Barré was likely to get from the revolutionary French navy he had deserted. Modern policy makers have generally answered this question in the negative by exempting all military offenses, except war crimes, from extradition. However, neither the Jay Treaty nor its critics considered the special problem of military "justice," especially in time of war. Had they actually examined the previous twenty-four military trials arising out of the *Hermione* mutiny, they might have opposed the surrender on the same humanitarian grounds that Jefferson invoked in his famous letter to Genêt.

Dudley Pope, author of the only full-length book about the mutiny to closely examine the naval court records, has concluded that several of the mutineers tried before Nash had been sentenced to death unjustly.[45] Pope also found that the commander of the Caribbean squadron who convened the courts-martial had attempted to have Rear-Admiral Richard Bligh, the legendary martinet who survived a mutiny on the *Bounty*, barred from sitting on future *Hermione* trials for fear that he would be too lenient.[46] The proper approach, wrote the squadron commander to the admiralty, was that of "imposing discipline by the terror of exemplary punishment."[47]

Examination of the larger issues of military justice would have to wait 125 years, until the posthumous publication of Herman Melville's *Billy Budd, Sailor*.[48] Melville's hero, like Jonathan Robbins, is an inarticulate seaman, impressed from the merchant ship *Rights of Man*, who is tried and hanged on board HMS *Bellipotent* for striking a cruel officer and unintentionally killing him. The central conflict in the novel, as in the Robbins case, is between the short-term, law-and-order realism of the British navy and the long-term, human rights claims of an abused person who strikes out against oppression. The emphasis is on the sailor's humanity, not his citizenship, and his universal human "rights of man" are juxtaposed to a situation-specific, executive-centered theory of justice. The moment Captain Vere sees the stuttering boy strike his false accuser dead, he knows that the boy is innocent but must hang.[49] The politics of maintaining order within the fleet demand it; the captain, not being part of an independent judiciary, is not free to be just. Like Judge Bee, the captain sees only the realities of executive need; he reacts mechanically, without analyzing the case or exploring how he might square morality with law enforcement. Like Bee, Vere does not pause to consider whether the offense was a capital one; Budd must be punished, as Robbins was, to deter future mutinies and otherwise serve *raisons d'état*.[50] Vere, like Bee, is a legal positivist; indeed, he is a caricature of one, emphasizing that morality is a feminine virtue and has very little to do with law, which is about power in a Hobbesian world.[51] Vere, like Bee, avoids moral responsibility by taking refuge in a mechanistic theory of the law.[52]

Like the Robbins case, Melville's novel captured the ambiguities and paradoxes of trying to do justice in a political world. Budd, like the Robbins of Republican mythology, began as an apolitical figure, a child-man kidnapped into a floating prison, but he became politically significant when, by unintentionally killing a superior officer, he endangered the very system of tyranny on which the British navy depended. Unlike Colonel Goffe, General Galbaud, Citizen Genêt, or Captain Barré, Budd could not command sympathy for his political plight. He was not part of an organized uprising. He was just a Bristol lad who might be an angel but, for the sake of preserving a military regime based on kidnappings, floggings, and exemplary executions, must be hanged.

In Budd's case, a modern reader might find it difficult to appreciate Captain Vere's fear of shipboard uprisings. In Nash's case, however, Secretary Pickering, Judge Bee, and even Colonel Moultrie had no such difficulty. They—and most people of their time—knew that British (and American) warships were not the good ship *Rights of Man*, but Hobbesian tyrannies like the *Bellipotent* or the *Hermione*. They knew that the efficiency, even the survival, of these warships depended on the subordination of the interests of individuals to the ship's mission. Like supporters of conscription today, they knew that the larger society depended on these floating tyrannies, so they ignored the injustices that made discipline within them possible. Mutinies were feared then as much as jail breaks or ghetto riots are feared now, because the larger society knew, without admitting it, that members of this abused class had a genuine cause to resent the society that was indifferent to their plight. Thus Nash's own humanity could not be conceded. He had to be seen as a "mutineer"—a deadly threat to social order.

Once the label stuck, Thomas Nash became an "unperson." Curiosity shrank. Although no specific criminal acts were ever alleged against the prisoner, Judge Bee had no difficulty sending him off to his death. Even Nash's own attorneys did not think to ask what had truly happened on board HMS *Hermione* or what kind of "justice" had been meted out to other "mutineers." They knew, as well as Americans today know what really goes on in most prisons, but they refrained from asking, and there is special horror in this fact.

Captain Vere believes he is fighting for the ordered liberty of Great Britain against the anarchistic authoritarianism of revolutionary France, and at one level he is. But he is also defending a ruling class that exaggerated the extent to which the measured forms of the common law really guaranteed liberty under law. Moreover, the very navy he defends from mutiny by hanging Budd also ordered him to impress Budd in the first place. Vere claims he is defending a rational body of law, and in a larger sense he is. But the statutes he invokes against Budd derive from a series of arbitrary, brutal, and irrational assumptions about the wisdom of near perpetual warfare between Protestant Britain and Catholic France and Spain. Vere claims that Budd breached his duty of loyalty to the king, but the king himself is reputed to be mad. More to the point, the very legal system that Vere claims to enforce is mad—if madness means a pathological loss of perspective, judgment, and proportion.

Similarly, the system of law that Judge Bee enforced by extraditing Nash was pathologically unjust, in the sense that it enforced obedience to a brutal system of incarceration built on kidnapping and maintained through the terroristic use of floggings and hangings. That the terrorism of the British navy was not illogical—it could produce obedience in times of storm or battle—does not make it any less unjust. Some of the most pathological people and organizations have a certain logic about them. Morally, however, the British navy in Nash's time was a floating gulag, a collection of police statelets from which escape was not only rational, but should have been applauded by anyone who respected the right to live free. Indeed, most nations would eventually come around to the view that extradition should not be used against anyone escaping conscription or involuntary military service. But in the late eighteenth and early nineteenth centuries, not even Americans had come to demand universal freedom. For their sailors, as for their slaves, they permitted localized tyrannies in a society they otherwise declared to be free.

* * *

The Robbins debate foreshadowed conflicts to come—over executive power, judicial independence, standards of proof, and the availability of defenses. Guilty or not, a grave injustice was done, but certain salutary principles were established. Extradition in the absence of a law or treaty was not proper. The question of who was extraditable was a matter of law, not foreign policy, and thus for the courts to decide. The executive could arrest the individual, it could even argue the foreign government's case for it, but it could not direct the outcome.

These principles, thanks to the martyrdom of Jonathan Robbins, would inform the next national debate over extradition. Before then, however, the nation would have to deal with an even more frightening class of unpersons—rebellious black slaves.

CHAPTER 4

Extradition and Slavery

[For the executive] to seize any man, black or white, slave or free, who may be claimed to be a slave, and send him beyond seas for any purposes . . . would [assume] control over the judiciary by the President, which would overthrow the whole fabric of the constitution.

John Quincy Adams

The U.S. government, badly burned by the Robbins affair, pulled back from extradition for more than forty years. But it could not escape demands for the return of fugitive slaves—demands from Spanish authorities in Cuba or from Southerners who wanted government help in reclaiming slaves who had fled to Mexico, Canada, or the Bahamas.[1] The most controversial of these demands involved blacks who had seized ships, because they had engaged in collective action. If they escaped surrender and punishment, other slaves might be inspired to revolt too. Fear of slave uprisings was palpable, even among those who were opposed to slavery, so it was crucial for pre–Civil War presidents to prevent the Northern United States or British possessions in Canada or the Caribbean from becoming havens for rebel slaves.

* * *

On the eve of negotiations to reestablish extradition between the United States and the United Kingdom two revolts at sea captured popular attention. The first involved the Spanish schooner *Amistad,* which rebellious blacks brought to the United States; the second involved the American brig *Creole,* which American slaves forced into British Bermuda. In both cases, fear of what today would be called black terrorism caused successive U.S. administrations to advocate surrender of the alleged criminals to certain convictions and death, even though their "crimes" had been committed—like those of Jonathan Robbins—to achieve freedom.

The blacks who seized the *Amistad* in June 1839 were recent captives from Sierra Leone who had been brought to Cuba by Spaniards in violation of an anti–slave trade convention between the United Kingdom and Spain. In Havana, they were given slave names and sold as if they were "legal slaves" raised in Cuba.[2] While being transported by sea from Havana to Guanaja (near Puerto Príncipe), the blacks were tormented by the ship's cook, who led them to believe that the Spaniards intended to cut their throats, saw their bodies into sections, salt them down, and eat them as dried meat. Desperate, the blacks revolted, killed the captain and the cook, and seized control of the ship. They spared the two slave owners, Jose Ruiz and Pedro Montes (also spelled Ruez and Montez), on condition that they navigate the ship back to Africa. Ruiz and Montes pretended to cooperate, sailing slowly east during the day and more rapidly west during the night. For sixty-three days they tacked about in the Atlantic, eventually bringing the ship to the eastern tip of Long Island. There the *Amistad* and her half-starved company were seized by the crew of the American revenue cutter *Washington*, not to help the blacks, but to obtain salvage payments from the Spanish owners for "rescuing" their sea-worn ship and cargo from certain loss.

* * *

Knowing that slavery was illegal in New York, the captain of the *Washington* took his captives and their ship into New London, Connecticut, where slavery was still allowed and where the blacks were more likely to be treated as property for which salvage rewards could be ordered. Once ashore, the blacks were subjected to the usual double standard. On the one hand, they were held as property returnable to their "owners." On the other, they were charged as persons with the crime of piracy. This contradiction was to become central to their case, which was soon taken up by Connecticut abolitionists. Their challenge was to prevent the men, women, and children of the *Amistad* from becoming "unpersons" like Thomas Nash.

While a grand jury was deciding whether to indict the adult Africans for murder or piracy, their abolitionist attorneys made a seemingly modest request: that the U.S. circuit court for Connecticut order the release of three African children, ages 7, 8, and 9, for lack of jurisdiction. William S. Holabird, the U.S. district attorney for Connecticut, immediately objected, asking that the court place the fate of all the Africans in the hands of the federal executive. The administration of Martin Van Buren did not want them treated as real individuals; it wanted to batch-process the entire group as quickly as possible, before the abolitionists could turn them into heroes and inspire American slaves to follow their example.

Justice Smith Thompson of the U.S. Supreme Court, sitting as the circuit judge, refused to free the children. To avoid turning any of the prisoners into "persons," he dismissed the charges of murder and piracy and left the question of whether they were free men or slaves to be decided by District Judge Andrew T. Judson in the civil suit for salvage. If any crime was committed in the course of seizing the ship, Thompson ruled, it was against the criminal laws of Spain and Cuba and would have to be tried in Spanish courts.[3] Habeas petitions pleading for the release of the children and the adults were denied.[4] The possibility of a jury trial in the United States was not even considered.[5]

Politically, it would have been difficult for Justice Thompson to have ruled otherwise. Freeing the captives immediately would have presumed them to be persons, not property—an incendiary idea in pre–Civil War America. It would not only have freed these prisoners; it would have acknowledged the right of slaves everywhere to fight their way to freedom and seek asylum in Connecticut. To free the *Amistad* blacks, Thompson would have had to hold that the Cuban authorities had issued false papers in violation of Spain's treaty with the United Kingdom. Whether he did so or not, he would be accused of reaching a question that most Americans were trying to avoid: Whether the positive law of any state, foreign or domestic, could lawfully authorize slavery. This was too much for any judge to do by a summary procedure, even if he abhorred slavery, as Thompson did.

The Spanish government was furious at the court's interference in what in Spain would have been an exclusively executive matter. It had no difficulty viewing the blacks as both property and persons and demanded their surrender as cargo and as "assassins." Its ambassador's notes characterized the prisoners more as assassins than property, because his government feared slave uprisings in Cuba if the *Amistad* blacks went unpunished.[6]

Secretary of State John Forsyth, himself a slave owner, deliberately ignored this characterization, choosing to view the prisoners as mere property—part of the cargo of a Spanish ship driven ashore and subject to return under Pinckney's Treaty of 1795.[7] Nothing in that treaty (known to the Spanish as the Treaty of San Lorenzo) said anything about extradition. Efforts to include an extradition provision, including one that would require the return of fugitive slaves, had failed during the negotiations.[8] If the blacks were to be delivered for prosecution, they would have to be surrendered under provisions governing the return of property, not as alleged criminals. The consequence of their surrender, however, was unmistakable; the leaders would be convicted of murder and subjected to grisly deaths.

To preserve Southern support for the presidency of New York's Martin Van Buren, Attorney General Felix Grundy prepared a legal opinion at Forsyth's request that supported the surrender of the *Amistad*'s blacks. Grundy insisted that Spanish documents characterizing the *Amistad* blacks as Cuban slaves rather than African captives had to be accepted at face value; thus, the blacks were cargo that the president had to surrender under Pinckney's Treaty. In effect, Grundy asserted what later became known as a rule of noninquiry.

The attorney general admitted that the *Amistad*'s blacks were not pirates.[9] If they were pirates, then they would have been subject to prosecution in a U.S. court, and that would have inflamed anti-slavery opinion against Van Buren's administration in the North. But even as Grundy agreed with the court that the blacks could not be *prosecuted* for piracy in the United States, he took the seemingly inconsistent position that they could be *surrendered* for piracy, or its equivalent, under Spanish law.[10] "These negroes are charged with an infraction of the Spanish laws," the attorney general wrote. "Therefore it is proper that they should be surrendered to the public functionaries of that government, that, if the laws of Spain have been violated, they may not escape punishment."[11] Contrary to both law and logic, Grundy argued that, in the absence of an express treaty of extradition, alleged slaves could be surrendered as criminals under a treaty providing for the return of cargo, by the president acting alone, even while litigation to determine the accused persons' surrenderability was pending in a U.S. court.

The attorney general also opposed any examination of the ship's papers, which the abolitionists were prepared to prove were fraudulent. "Were the Government of the United States to permit itself to go behind the papers of the schooner *Amistad*," Grundy wrote, "it would place itself in the embarassing condition of judging upon the Spanish laws, their force, their effect, and their application to the case under consideration."[12]

In effect, Grundy argued for the same rule of noninquiry that the Supreme Court had rejected in the case of Captain Barré.[13] Ignoring also the Fifth Amendment's guarantee of due process of law, the attorney general said, "I cannot see any legal principle upon which the Government of the United States would be authorized to [investigate] whether the facts stated in those papers . . . are true or not."[14] He even went so far as to claim that to deliver the blacks into the hands of abolitionists would deny the blacks the opportunity to prove their right to freedom in a Cuban court.[15]

Van Buren's cabinet approved Grundy's opinion but did not dare implement it, because the U.S. attorney for Connecticut and the salvage claimants had already placed the matter in judicial hands. When asked by the Spanish minister to assert executive control,[16] Secretary of State Forsyth replied that the Constitution "secured the judicial power against all interference on the part of the executive authority."[17]

Forsyth's position on judicial primacy seemed principled, but it was based on the most transparent of expediencies. Van Buren was running for reelection, and could not risk alienating his Northern supporters by defying the courts on an issue of slavery. So Forsyth contented himself with providing legal representation to the Spanish government and the two slave owners, whose claims were "merged" for this purpose. The secretary of state was under no legal obligation to provide counsel to either the Spanish government or the slavers. He could have insisted that this was a dispute over salvage, not extradition, and let the slavers go it alone in court. But the political risks of letting a Northern court grant the equivalent of asylum to rebel blacks were too high.

Prudence limited the administration's intervention to providing legal counsel. Neither Forsyth nor Van Buren was prepared to defy the courts. William S. Holabird, the U.S. attorney for Connecticut, was not so cautious. "I should regret extremely that the rascally blacks should fall into the hands of the abolitionists," he wrote to his superiors, and he asked if he should enforce the president's order whatever the court decided.[18] No such authority was granted.

The case was heard before Judge Judson, a Van Buren appointee who, before his appointment, had obtained passage of a law forbidding a school for Negro girls in his home town of Canterbury from bringing in out-of-state students without the selectmen's permission. He also prosecuted the headmistress of that school when she defied the law (before a mob destroyed her school),[19] and so he seemed like a safe judge to hear the administration's case.

The key question was clear: had the blacks been free persons or slaves at the time of their revolt? The answer depended on how much credence Judson chose to give to the ship's documents, which listed the blacks as legal, Cuban-born slaves. The U.S. attorney argued, as Attorney General Grundy had, that the Cuban documents presented by the slavers had to be accepted at face value; the abolitionists argued that justice required that the court lift the veil of governmental legitimacy and look at all the evidence bearing on the captives' origins. The Van Buren administration made no inquiries into the realities of the Cuban slave trade;[20] it did not wish to be burdened with inconvenient facts that might be demanded by critics in Congress, if not the captives' attorneys. The executive branch may also have insisted on the validity of the Spanish documents in order to avoid a precedent that could undermine unquestioning judicial acceptance of documents issued by American slave states certifying the ownership of blacks who had fled north, or to British possessions in Canada or the Caribbean.

But Judson, despite his hostility to abolitionists, found himself compelled to accept their claim that the black rebels, who knew only African languages and answered only to African names, were not Cuban-bred (and therefore legal) slaves. On January 13, 1840, he ruled that as free Africans they had the right to overpower those who would carry them into bondage.[21] At the same time, the judge was careful to rule that Antonio, the black cabin boy, was legally a slave and would have to be returned to the Spaniards for delivery to his master's widow.[22] Judson thus accepted the legal principle the Van Buren administration most wanted to win—that fugitive *slaves* from Spain's colonies must be returned, under the Spanish treaty, to their owners.[23]

Technically speaking, the administration won, but politically the case was a disaster. The administration had been so confident that Judson would rule in their favor that it had secretly ordered the USS *Grampus* to stand by at New London to spirit the blacks off to Cuba before the abolitionists could file an appeal.[24] As a consolation prize, the judge ordered the administration to deliver the blacks to Africa as if they had been illegally imported slaves. Justice Thompson, again sitting as the circuit court, affirmed Judson's decision without an opinion on April 29, 1840, and the administration turned to the Supreme Court.

* * *

By the time the case arrived at the high court, Van Buren had been defeated for reelection. The president's pro-slavery strategy had alienated Northern voters, and the alienation had contributed to his defeat in six states that he had won in 1836, including his home state of New York. One example often cited against Van Buren in the Whig press was his secret plan to rush the *Amistad* captives off to Cuba before an appeal could be filed on their behalf.[25]

The pro-slavery forces had good reason to believe that the Court would rule in their favor. The new administration of John Tyler, who quickly succeeded William Henry Harrison, had fewer slave owners in high places but was no less compromised by slavery than Van Buren's. A majority of the Supreme Court's justices came from slave states; two owned slaves and a third justice had sent his off to Liberia, without changing his belief that slavery was necessary so long as large numbers of Africans lived in the United States.[26] The new attorney general, Henry D. Gilpin, was also willing to take up where Grundy had left off.

Gilpin opened his argument before the Court by noting that the *Amistad*'s papers were in order and should be accepted at face value. Like attorneys general Bradford and Grundy before him, he advocated noninquiry; whatever mistreatment there might be of slaves under Spanish law, he said, the United States was treaty-bound to accept it.[27]

Roger S. Baldwin opened for the defense, arguing that it was inherently beyond the authority of a government founded on liberty to become the instrument for the enslavement of people who were free at the moment they landed on Long Island in the free state of New York. He insisted that the Court look beyond the formal sufficiency of the *Amistad*'s papers to the fraud behind them, and he argued that Pinckney's Treaty with Spain committed the United States only to the return of property, not free Africans.[28]

Also appearing for the defense was former president John Quincy Adams. Now a seventy-three-year-old member of the House of Representatives, Adams saw the case for what it was—a major political and moral battle for the soul of the divided nation. While the case awaited Supreme Court consideration, he kept the issue alive by persuading the House to demand the government's documents on the case, and then chairing the House committee assigned to review them. Once in the well of the Supreme Court, Adams indignantly refused to let the executive branch treat the case as one for the return of fugitive slaves.[29] He briefed the justices on the politics of the case: of the administration's covert assistance to the slave owners, its refusal to deliver certain documents, and its intent to deny the blacks their right to appeal by rushing them off to Cuba in the midst of winter, through icy seas, as deck cargo on a small navy schooner. Quoting several letters from Spanish ministers to Secretary of State Forsyth, Adams made it clear that the chief purpose of the American executive's role in the case was not to restore property, but to satisfy "the public vengeance . . . of African slave traders."[30]

Adams willfully ignored that the executive branch had acceded to the jurisdiction of the court. Instead, he condemned the assertion of exclusive executive power to "seize any man, black or white, slave or free, who may be claimed as a slave, and send him beyond seas for any purposes."[31] His choice of language recalled a similar grievance in the Declaration of Independence, copies of which, he pointed out, hung in the Court's chamber. Such a power, the former president and secretary of state declared, "would overthrow the whole fabric of the constitution."[32]

Adams reserved special scorn for Grundy's argument that the authenticity of the documents enslaving the prisoners could not be questioned. "The Executive may send the men to Cuba," Adams said, "to be sold as slaves, to be put to death, to be burnt at the stake, but they [the executive] must not go behind the document, to inquire into any facts in the case. . . . I am ashamed that such an opinion should have ever been delivered by any public official of this country."[33]

Above all, Adams emphasized the principles underlying the writ of habeas corpus. Suppose the president had followed the attorney general's advice and delivered the Africans to Spain, he argued. Then "what ... would have been the tenure by which *every* human being in this Union, man, woman, and child, would have held the blessing of freedom? Would it not have been the tenure of Executive discretion, caprice, or tyranny ... at the dictate of a foreign minister ...? Would it not have disabled forever the effective power of Habeas Corpus?"[34]

Justice Joseph Story, an old Adams disciple from Massachusetts and a great scholar of the law, was amazed by the argument. It was "extraordinary," he wrote to his wife, "for its power, for its bitter sarcasm, and its dealing with topics far beyond the record and points of discussion."[35] On March 9, 1841, when Story delivered his opinion for the Court, he ignored most of what Adams had argued but granted the relief sought.[36] The district court's decision that the blacks were not legal slaves under Spanish law was upheld; they could not be surrendered. To reach this decision, the justices lifted the veil of governmental legitimacy and found that the ownership documents were fraudulent. The provision of Pinckney's Treaty allowing for the return of cargo was not applicable, Story wrote for a 6–1 majority, because the ship had not been driven into American waters by storms, pirates, or war, and the blacks had not been rescued from pirates or robbers. In the absence of any positive law authorizing the prisoners' enslavement, Story said, the Court had no alternative but to revert to natural law's "eternal principles of justice" and declare them free.[37]

The only portion of the district court's opinion not upheld was the ruling that the president had the authority, under a law barring the importation of slaves, to return the blacks to Africa. The blacks, Story ruled, were completely free to remain in the United States, or to go wherever they pleased.[38]

Abolitionists celebrated, but Southerners were furious. Five presidents refused to accept the Court's decision. Tyler, Polk, Fillmore, Pierce, and Buchanan all recommended that the United States government pay reparations for freeing the blacks, but Congress refused. In all probability, the presidents were no more concerned with doing justice for the Spanish slavers than for their captives. Rather, they did not want to alienate Cuban opinion against possible annexation by the United States.[39]

Thus, a major effort at covert extradition was blocked: blocked by a judicial system that refused to view the prisoners as nonpersons. The jurisdiction of courts to refuse to surrender alleged terrorists to foreign governments was upheld and the authority of the courts to decide such matters were accepted by two more administrations. Contrary to the lower court's decision in *Robbins*, but consistent with the Supreme Court's decision in Captain Barré's case (*United States v. Lawrence*), the trial court was permitted to question the validity of the documents on which the foreign government's demand was based, and that inquiry was upheld by the nation's highest court.

However, Story's opinion also treated natural law as secondary to the law of the American states, so that the positive law of slavery could strip a person (like the cabin boy) of the right to rebel. This decision constituted a substantial jurisprudential concession, because if the positive law of slavery could destroy such a natural right, it would not take much for future courts to accept other oppressive laws (like the law of mutiny in *Robbins* or the law of a police state in the case of hijackers to freedom) as legitimate grounds for authorizing extradition. If positive law were to be accepted without question, then the practice of noninquiry would be transformed from a mere lack of curiosity into a legal prohibition against moral understanding.

As a legal precedent, the *Amistad* decision was only a partial victory for the abolitionists and for the freedom-from-surrender they championed. They sought freedom for all slaves, not just protection for people illegally enslaved. Moreover, while Justice Story and his colleagues upheld the right of revolution in the absence of valid law enslaving the fugitives, the Court also assumed that the positive law of a foreign state or a treaty could effectively deny this right to otherwise free people. The *Amistad* captives went free because the absence of positive law permitted recognition of the natural right of revolution; in the presence of immoral positive law, the Supreme Court would have upheld their enslavement. The *Amistad* case, while not expressly about extradition, thus embraced the dubious proposition that American extradition courts might have a duty to effectuate foreign injustice, provided that requirements like probable cause and double criminality were satisfied.

* * *

The *Amistad* captives were not returned because they had never been lawfully enslaved. The question of what to do about lawful slaves who rebelled and fled abroad arose in October 1841, when nineteen of 138 black American slaves being shipped from Hampton Roads, Virginia, to New Orleans, Louisiana, on board the American brig *Creole* rose up in revolt. Led by a slave named Madison Washington, the rebels killed one of the slave owners, wounded the captain and first mate, and forced the second mate to take them to Nassau in the Bahamas. There the British authorities refused to help the U.S. consul return the ship and the slaves to their intended voyage. Instead, the authorities stood by as black islanders helped the slaves escape.[40]

The *Creole* incident provoked a major crisis for the new Whig administrations of Harrison and Tyler. Spokesmen for slavery were willing to risk war with Great Britain, while abolitionists hailed the revolt as a triumph for freedom. The new secretary of state, Daniel Webster, found himself in a position comparable to that of the Spanish ministers in the *Amistad* case. Webster could not make a convincing legal argument for the surrender of the *Creole*'s rebels as criminals, because there was no extradition agreement between Britain and the United States.[41] So he argued, not unlike the Spanish ministers who besieged his predecessor, that Britain had an obligation under the international law of hospitality to help the owners of ships and cargoes in distress, which meant suppressing slave mutinies and returning the seized ships and their human cargo.

The case was distinguishable from that of the *Amistad*, he argued (after privately consulting with Justice Story), because the *Creole*'s blacks were lawful slaves. However, unlike his slave-owning predecessor, Webster did not call for the return of the blacks as assassins, pirates, robbers, murderers, or slaves. He confined himself to demanding reparations.[42]

This equivocation did not spare Webster the wrath of William Jay, a prominent abolitionist who retained the natural law principles of his father John's generation. In an anonymous pamphlet on the *Creole* case, the younger Jay (himself a former judge) declared that "resistance of ... force ... even unto death, cannot be called mutiny or murder—because they are violating no law by such resistance, but on the contrary, vindicating their natural freedom—the gift of God alike to all."[43] Jay also linked the return of fugitive slaves to the surrender of impressed seamen who had fought their way to freedom.[44] "The right of resistance unto death," he said, "admitted both by Gallatin and Marshall in the case of Robbins, cannot depend upon the color of the skin."[45]

Further, Jay argued that the British government was under no obligation to enforce the domestic law of the United States, which because of its immorality could not be given effect in the British Isles. In the absence of an extradition treaty, or the recognition of slaves as persons protected by the absence of such a treaty, Jay was asserting a principle analogous to the rule of double criminality.[46]

Webster could appreciate Jay's argument. Like Jay, he had opposed slavery and the impressment of seamen. In his treaty with Lord Ashburton, Webster would embrace the rule of double criminality. As a politician trying to prevent civil war, however, there was little he could do. Like most national figures, he was trapped by the amoral legal positivism of Southern slave interests. To avoid civil war at home, he could not speak out forcefully for human rights in the case of fugitive slaves who had fled abroad. The best he could do was temporize.

The *Creole* case came at a particularly awkward time. Webster and his British counterpart, Lord Ashburton, were preparing to negotiate a series of grievances, including border disputes, that had recently brought their two countries close to war. In addition, Webster's new president, John Tyler, was personally angered by Britain's refusal to surrender the *Creole* blacks. A slave owner from Virginia, Tyler had special reason to fear anything that encouraged slave revolts.

If the *Creole* case haunted the U.S. government, the recent surrender of a fugitive slave haunted the British. In January 1842, the new British governor-general of Canada had taken it upon himself to order the return of Nelson Hacket, who had fled to Canada from Arkansas the previous summer.[47] Hacket's pursuers had obtained his surrender by charging that he had stolen not only his master's fastest horse, but a neighbor's beaver coat.

Hacket's surrender terrified Canada's population of 12,000 blacks, most of whom were fugitive slaves or their offspring. Abolitionists were upset, too, and turned Hacket into their own Jonathan Robbins. A delegation from the American Anti-Slavery Society visited Ashburton shortly before his return home in September 1842, and he assured them that if extradition proved injurious to fugitive slaves, the British government would put an end to it.[48]

Hacket was not tried upon his return. A trial would have acknowledged his humanity, so he was simply remanded to the justice of his master.[49] The Canadian government did not protest this perversion of the extradition process and, perhaps because Hacket had been surrendered by executive fiat, did not use the occasion to insist on the adoption of a judicially administered rule of inquiry into the capacity of the requesting regime to do justice.

If Webster was unable to win a treaty provision for the surrender of fugitive slaves, and there is no evidence that he pushed hard on this issue, Lord Ashburton was equally unable to win the surrender of mutineers and deserters from the British armed forces. As Ashburton explained to the anti-slavery group, "The governor of Canada was anxious that deserters should be included [in the treaty]," but because Ashburton had learned "that a claim would be put in [by the United States] for the delivering up of fugitive slaves, he abandoned the question of deserters from H. B. M.'s possessions. He was also very desirous to secure the delivery of mutineers, but did not press it, lest it should involve, on the part of his government, the delivery of slaves situated as were those on board the *Creole*."[50] Both diplomats appear to have understood that neither impressed seamen nor slaves who had fought their way to freedom would be open to extradition under the new treaty. Technically, the murder provision left some fugitive slaves exposed, but politically their surrender would be resisted, in no small part because of the pressure placed upon the British government by abolitionists on both sides of the Atlantic.

Nonetheless, the *Creole* affair hung like a "great plague" over the negotiations. To appease President Tyler, whom Ashburton found "sore and testy" about the *Creole* case, and Southern Senators who might seek revenge by defeating the entire treaty, the British envoy agreed to settle the matter by having his government promise to instruct its officials in the Bahamas and elsewhere to avoid "officious interference" with American ships driven by necessity, accident, or violence into British ports. As late as two days before the signing of the treaty, President Tyler still questioned the willingness of British authorities to surrender an escaped slave who had killed his master.[51] He was right; extradition under the treaty was never enforced against runaway slaves,[52] and the promised instructions not to interfere with American ships were never sent.[53]

* * *

Extradition, however, was enforced against runaway slaves within the United States. In the early nineteenth century, the United States was two nations, one free, the other slave, and it was in the extradition of fugitive slaves that the modern rule of noninquiry—of not inquiring into the willingness or capacity of the requesting regime to do justice—was born.

Noninquiry had been practiced in the Robbins case, too—noninquiry into the capacity of the British navy to do justice. In *Robbins* the potential injustices awaiting the accused were not considered; nor were they considered in most fugitive slave cases.

The injustice awaiting impressed seamen like Jonathan Robbins was captured most effectively by Herman Melville in *Billy Budd*, but Robbins may not have been his only inspiration. Melville's father-in-law was Lemuel Shaw, chief justice of the Massachusetts Supreme Judicial Court, who dominated his state's judicial system as completely as Captain Vere ruled the *Bellipotent*.[54] Shaw opposed slavery, publicly, privately, and in judicial opinions. But where enforcement of the fugitive slave law was concerned, he did his duty and was no less draconian at it than Vere.[55] There is no evidence that Shaw was the model for Vere, but the similarities between the two men—both trapped between their duty to power and the obligations of conscience—are striking. The fugitive slave was very much like Jonathan Robbins or Billy Budd. The legal system he faced was harsh and summary. Under the Fugitive Slave Act of 1850, the accused was not allowed to testify to anything.[56] He could not explain that he was, in fact, a free person. His accusers would decide that question according to their own law and customs when they had him securely back under the law of slavery. Like Robbins, the fugitive slave had no way to appeal to the court for the empathy accorded free men who use force to escape from an unjust, lifelong, life-threatening imprisonment.

The tenth section of the Fugitive Slave Act of 1850 enacted the first rule of noninquiry in American extradition law. It expressly provided what the Spanish slavers and the Van Buren administration had failed to achieve: a rule requiring the court to accept, without question, formal legal papers from the slave state attesting to fugitive's alleged enslavement.[57] The blindness to injustice that American judges would later impose upon themselves in international extradition cases was imposed by the U.S. Congress in fugitive slave cases.

To Herman Melville, the fictitious Billy Budd, like the pseudonymous Jonathan Robbins, was essentially a slave of the British navy, captured by force, held in bondage, and driven by whips to work under hideous conditions for a bare subsistence. Like slaves, both Budd and Robbins could not speak effectively in their own defense. Nor did they enjoy the assistance of competent counsel. When Robbins and his mates rose up in rebellion, struck down their oppressors, and fled, they were hunted down like fugitives from a slave rebellion. Mutineers, like rebellious slaves, were portrayed as more than mere criminals—they were the natural enemies of an artificial, and therefore fragile, social order. Justice had nothing to do with their extradition or punishment; preservation of an oppressive order was what really counted.

Melville understood this, and he understood that their persecution could operate only under a suspension of empathy, an unwillingness to look behind the formal charges, and a self-imposed rule of noninquiry whenever an unjust social order was threatened. Nothing fascinated him more than the capacity of captains like Vere, or judges like Lemuel Shaw, to extol liberty and justice in the abstract and then deny them in the course of enforcing an overriding, socially imposed commitment to a profoundly unjust system of law and order.

Melville was not so naive as to believe that the Veres and Shaws had much choice in the matter; what interested him was the presence of so much systematic evil that neither the Veres nor Shaws could resist. They were, despite their private Christian faiths, the official tools of unjust power, and the unjust power was not only an imposing military or legal hierarchy; it was the culturally pervasive force of their society's own rules of noninquiry, rules that prevented most people from actively empathizing with mutinous sailors or rebellious slaves. These enemies of the social order could not be seen and judged as individuals, on the nature and quality of their acts, in light of a realistic assessment of the context in which those acts took place. They were condemned as nonpersons, natural forces of evil to be hunted down and destroyed, much as the Spanish authorities (and Southern slave owners) had insisted on the extradition of *Amistad*'s Africans. They were, to use a modern term, terrorists.

* * *

Melville's understanding of how cultures of noninquiry operate to depersonalize and then destroy people struggling to be free was expressed not only in *Billy Budd*, but in the even more satiric, wickedly devious tale of *Benito Cereno*.[58] *Cereno*, a novella first published in 1855, is about a slave revolt on board a Spanish ship much like the *Amistad*. Melville undoubtedly knew about the *Amistad*, but he chose to appropriate the lesser known story of Captain Amasa Delano of Duxbury, Massachusetts, who had encountered a mystery ship full of slaves off the coast of Chile in 1807.[59]

The facts of the *Amistad* case did not interest Melville; there Christian gentlemen had looked behind the ship's papers and seen the slave trade beyond. Melville was more interested in those who, consciously or subconsciously, refuse to look behind the facade of law and order. So when his Captain Delano boards the mysterious *San Dominick* to offer assistance, he refuses to suspect that the Spanish captain with whom he exchanges courtly conversation is really the terrified and pliant hostage of his inseparable black servant, Babo.[60]

To Delano, the good-hearted Christian, black Africans are like Newfoundland dogs, and he looks upon them as kindly as he would Newfoundlands. Gradually, however, it becomes clear to the reader that the good Captain is as dumb as a Newfoundland and that the shrewdest men on the ship are black. Even when the desperate Spanish captain, Benito Cereno, leaps into Delano's longboat in a desperate bid to escape, Delano misinterprets his motives and has to be restrained from shoving him overboard. When the slow-witted Delano finally comprehends the truth, the truth he comprehends is the horror that a slave revolt would visit on the morally stupefied society of Melville's time—the terrorism of dogs who turn upon their masters.

Like most Americans in the "know nothing" 1850s, Melville's Yankee sea captain refuses to acknowledge the continuing atrocities of slavery, for that would have required him to concede the rightness of the slaves' revolt and, indeed, morally obliged him to aid it. All the good-hearted captain allows himself to recognize is the plight of a fellow white, Christian captain, and the salvage award that will come to him and his crew if they recapture the ship for the Spaniard.

The ship is recaptured and the slave leaders are brought to trial in Lima, Peru, where, like Thomas Nash, they are sentenced to a ghastly death. Babo's head, like Nash's corpse, is put on display as a grim warning to all other nonpersons not to challenge the tyrannies to which the society and law have become accustomed.

Meanwhile, Captain Delano remains as dumb as a dog. He admits his gullibility in a parting conversation with Captain Cereno:[61]

"Only at the end did my suspicions get the better of me, and you know how wide of the mark they then proved."

"Wide, indeed," said Don Benito, sadly; "you were with me all day; stood with me, sat with me, talked with me, looked at me, ate with me, drank with me; and yet, your last act was to clutch me for a villain.... To such a degree may malign machinations and deceptions impose. So far may even the best men err, in judging the conduct of one with the recesses of whose condition he is not acquainted. But you were forced to it; and you were in time undeceived. Would that, in both respects, it was so ever, and with all men."

"I think I understand you; you generalize Don Benito; and mournfully enough. But the past is past; why moralize upon it? Forget it. See, yon bright sun has forgotten it all and the blue sea and the blue sky; these have turned over new leaves."

"Because they have no memory," he dejectedly replied; "because they are not human."

"But these mild trades that now fan your check, Don Benito, do they not come with a human-like healing to you? Warm friends, steadfast friends are the trades."

"With their steadfastness they but waft me to their tomb, Senor," was the foreboding response.

"You are saved, Don Benito," cried Captain Delano, more and more astonished and pained, "you are saved; what has cast such a shadow over you?"

"The negro."

Three months later, Benito Cereno dies while Captain Delano is sailing home, serenely confident that he has done his Christian duty. Unlike Cereno, the New Englander still does not comprehend the enormity of the wrongs done to the blacks. He does not recognize that each of them had a right to freedom and that the only Christian thing he could have done was to aid their return to Africa, or at least stood neutral toward their attempt, as impossible as the attempt might be.

Benito Cereno is as sly a satire of the return of fugitive slaves as *Billy Budd* is a deadly mock of the return of Jonathan Robbins. Melville's captains seem trapped: Vere by his position as captain in wartime, Delano by his position as a pillar of Christian society—a society that accepts racial slavery, both because it cannot imagine any alternative and because it is too terrified to admit that slave revolts might be morally justified. What traps the captains, however, is their inability to question the very tyrannies they serve. Captain Delano cannot really see slavery from a slave's perspective; Captain Vere does not recoil at the impressment of seamen. Like Captain Pigot, whose tyranny triggered the mutiny on the *Hermione*, Vere kidnapped sailors and ordered floggings. But for a captain to admit his own tyranny would have meant conceding that seamen (or slaves) are the moral equals of their commanders, and like Justice Lemuel Shaw, Vere could not do that. His standing in society, the power he wielded, and his capacity to do good depended on his unwillingness as a judge to question the assumptions on which that social and legal system was founded.

But more than that, the "captains" of Melville's America—ship captains and judges alike—instinctively felt that blacks and sailors, and Indians and immigrant workers, were a profound threat to dominant order and had to be suppressed, at least in the short term. Repressed fury on the part of these voiceless peoples had to be presumed by anyone realistic enough to be a "captain." To ignore the danger posed by these peoples, to fail to recognize the savage potential of the genuinely oppressed, was hopelessly romantic and would lead to death, not gratitude, when the repressed revolted. This was the moral of Cereno's friend Aranda, who triggered the uprising on board the *San Dominick* by releasing the shackles of his slaves. Rather than thank their master for the respite, the slave rose up, captured and killed him, flayed the flesh from his bones, and mounted his skeleton on the ship's prow under the sardonic warning to similarly naive whites: "Follow your leader."

In the 1840s and 1850s, when the political offense exception was being developed and when Melville was gaining the insights that would shape both *Billy Budd* and *Benito Cereno*, "ship of state" metaphors permeated American literature. American society was far from egalitarian, despite its freedom from hereditary government. Many Americans assumed that humankind could be divided into natural captains and natural seamen, natural masters and natural slaves, and natural civilizers and natural savages. Lockean assumptions about liberty and equality might characterize relationships within the dominant white, male, propertied "captains" like Delano and Shaw, but for those who fell outside that blessed circle—like the felons or paupers who went to sea, slaves, and frontier "savages"—power relations were strictly Hobbesian. Captains, masters, and governors might be benevolent on occasion, but for safety's sake, they had to be autocratic. The survival of the ship, the plantation, or the settlement depended on it.

Thus Americans could demand a political offense exception for fugitives from autocratic European states and yet advocate a rule of noninquiry into the capacity of Spanish (or Southern) slave owners to do justice. They could extradite mutinous slaves and sailors by a similar suspension of curiosity regarding the circumstances that impelled their uprisings and escape. Political liberty for white male Europeans inspired empathy; equal liberty for voiceless minorities of poor seamen, black slaves, or native populations undergoing colonization or settlement escaped their imaginations.

This lack of imagination was particularly powerful when the administration of "justice" was largely executive in nature, because executives are tasked, first and foremost, with the maintenance of order and good foreign relations. It was less powerful in the courts, which also had an obligation to preserve individual liberty. In the case of Thomas Nash, Judge Bee forgot this higher duty; in the case of the *Amistad* captives, both the district court and the Supreme Court remembered it, looked behind the ship's papers, and declared the captives free.[62]

* * *

For those who could appreciate what would lead people (if only like themselves) to revolt, and who could imagine what could happen to them if they were returned, the best solution was to ban extradition entirely. It was better, they said, to grant asylum to all comers and not inquire too deeply into their backgrounds. America should be the land of the second chance, even at the risk of accepting people who did not deserve a second chance.

But that was not to be. Domestically, pressure for the return of fugitive slaves continued to mount. Internationally, the rise of professional police departments was creating bureaucratic pressure for a new round of extradition treaties. For the United States, conflict on the Canadian border also called for a new effort at extradition, if only to avert war. Extradition was to become part of America's future, with a major exception for political offenders.

CHAPTER 5

First Principles

Public opinion had settled down to a firm resolve, long before the treaty of 1842 was made, that so dangerous an engine of oppression as secret proceedings before the executive, and the issuing of secret warrants of arrest, founded on them, and long imprisonments inflicted under such warrants, and then an extradition without an unbiased hearing before an independent judiciary, were highly dangerous to liberty, and ought never to be allowed in this country.

Supreme Court Justice John Catron, In re Kaine, *1852*

Thomas Nash was the only person surrendered under the Jay Treaty, and when its extradition provision expired in 1807, no effort was made to renew it. The British navy was still impressing American seamen into its service, and the surrender of Nash had discredited the extradition process and helped to destroy the Federalist Party.

Under the Jeffersonian Republicans, the United States showed no interest in negotiating extradition agreements with any foreign powers. Like the British, the Americans felt reasonably secure behind their Atlantic moat. They were proud of their long tradition of sheltering political refugees, and they were content with the progress they had made in depoliticizing the criminal law. But the two countries could not escape the fact that they shared an unguarded, 3,000-mile common border, one crossed by ordinary criminals, revolutionaries, and counter-revolutionaries virtually at will. Eventually extradition would have to be resumed, and when it was—with the Webster–Ashburton Treaty of 1842—-a number of basic principles, first voiced in the late eighteenth century, were reaffirmed.

* * *

In the absence of an extradition treaty, demands for the extradition of common fugitives had to be addressed by the border states themselves. This quickly led to questions regarding the relative authority of the states versus the nation on matters affecting foreign relations and whether extradition could ever occur in the absence of a treaty or statute.

The colonial practice was to make treaties. As early as 1621, the Colony at New Plimoth concluded a treaty with Massasoit, sachem of the Pokanokets (Wampanoags), which provided, without reciprocity, that if "any of his did hurt any of theirs, he should send the offender, that they might punish him."[1]

Treaties—or agreements—also governed extradition among colonies. A 1643 agreement among the English colonies of New England provided for the return of fugitive servants and escaped prisoners.[2] This agreement was extended internationally, and by intercolonial compact, to the Dutch colony of the New Netherlands in 1650.[3] In 1670, the United Colonies of New England reaffirmed their mutual obligation to return fugitive servants and escaped prisoners in their new articles of confederation.[4] From earliest times, then, Americans believed that extradition should be governed by express agreements.

The first state to address international extradition after the Revolution was New York, which had an active border with Canada. In 1821, just six years after the War of 1812 ended, Governor DeWitt Clinton of New York asked the governor of Canada to surrender one Jacob Smith, alias Redington, who was wanted for forgery. In return for this assistance, Clinton wanted to promise the Canadians that New York would reciprocate in the future, but he quickly discovered that states were barred by the U.S. Constitution from making reciprocal agreements with foreign governments without the consent of Congress. Knowing that the national government in Washington was not yet disposed to reopen extradition with the British, Clinton proposed,[5] and in 1822 the state legislature passed, a statute that authorized the governor unilaterally to surrender fugitives to Canada if the crimes alleged were punishable, if committed in New York, by imprisonment or death.[6]

In prescribing the burden of proof that the requesting government would have to meet, the law seemed to track the Jay Treaty of 1794. However, it assigned that determination to the chief executive rather than to the courts. In so doing, New York ignored the federal government's unbroken practice since 1784 of having the evidentiary determinations in international extradition cases made by judges, not politicians. Five years later, in the course of a massive revision and codification of state law, the legislature decided that it may have given the governor too much power over political fugitives, and it excluded treason from the extradition law.[7] What prompted this amendment is not known, but it appears to be the first political offense exception expressly written into law anywhere, preceding similar developments in Belgium and France by six years.

Meanwhile, the national government remained powerless to extradite anyone in the absence of an authorizing treaty or statute. This was the considered opinion of four U.S. attorneys general,[8] as well as Secretary of State Henry Clay and Chief Justice Joseph Story.[9] In the early years of the republic, only Secretary of State Pickering thought that the executive might have an inherent power to surrender fugitives, and he never acted on that belief.[10]

The courts agreed with the executive. In the *Dos Santos* case, when Portugal asked for the surrender of one of its citizens wanted for murder associated with piracy, Judge (later U.S. Supreme Court Justice) Philip P. Barbour refused. Barbour rejected the argument that comity among nations required the extradition of ordinary offenders as a matter of customary international law.[11] His rejection was based not only on a review of foreign treatises and Anglo-American case law, but on the belief that such a sweeping power could require the surrender to the United Kingdom of an Englishman who had fought for the United States in the War of 1812, or to Mexico of an American who had fought for Texas independence in 1835. In other words, Barbour saw the requirement of a treaty as essential to the protection of persons who would later come to be called "political offenders."[12]

A treaty was required, Judge Barbour added, to assure that the spirit of the Constitution would be upheld, and that persons would not be surrendered to regimes that would not grant defendants such basic privileges as "trial by jury, the right to be confronted by his witnesses, [and] the privilege of not being obliged to be a witness against himself."[13] In short, the future Supreme Court justice believed that the requirement of a treaty existed not just to protect American sovereignty or to assure reciprocity, but to guarantee that the U.S. government would not deliver alleged criminals to unjust foreign regimes.

Chancellor James Kent, the conservative New York jurist, took a different view. Following Grotius, he argued that nations have a "duty" to engage in extradition—a duty arguably inferable to their executives in the absence of a treaty or statute.[14]

Opinion was not clear as to whether a U.S. state, in the absence of any federal laws or treaties, could engage in international extradition on its own. In 1796, Secretary of State Pickering had encouraged Governor Thomas Chittenden of Vermont to extradite Ephriam Barnes and James Clarkson Freeman to Canada to face charges of highway robbery and horse-stealing, even though those offenses were not covered by the Jay Treaty. According to Pickering, President Washington had agreed that delivery could be made by Vermont in the absence of a treaty.[15]

The question gained in salience in the 1830s, when Americans in New York and Vermont supported Canadian rebels against British colonial rule and pressured state officials not to accept Kent's theory of international—and potentially executive—duty. Americans did not just support the Canadian cause; they joined the fighting on both sides of the border.[16] If Kent's theory prevailed, then American governors or presidents could order the surrender of Americans as well as Canadians, for paramilitary activities carried out on American as well as Canadian soil.

Kent's theory of inherent power was tested in 1839 when Governor William H. Seward of New York was asked to surrender Benjamin Lett, who was wanted by Canadian authorities for murder. Seward, who would later serve as Lincoln's secretary of state, refused on the theory that the state's 1822 extradition statute violated the federal Constitution, which allocated the conduct of foreign relations to the nation, not the states.[17] Eager to mollify the British and avoid war, both President Van Buren and Secretary of State Forsyth urged the New York governor to exercise his authority under his state's statute until it was declared unconstitutional,[18] but the governor refused to act unless the president himself authorized the surrender.[19] Van Buren then decided that he could not surrender Lett in the absence of a treaty.[20]

Border relations were particularly tense in January and February 1839, when the governor of Lower Canada, Sir John Colborne, sent three extradition requests to Governor Silas Jenison of Vermont. One asked for a person charged with torching the Canadian village of Caldwell's Manor. Another demanded raiders who had assaulted a Canadian family, and a third called for the delivery of Dr. George Holmes, a New Hampshire man, wanted for the murder of his lover's husband.

Jenison, like Seward, turned to the federal government, but Secretary of State Forsyth still would not get involved in the absence of a treaty. The governor then decided that he, too, lacked authority to surrender fugitives to Canada because the Vermont legislature had not granted him explicit authority to do so. By April he also decided he could not surrender anyone for crimes allegedly committed in the course of the Canadian uprisings,[21] thus acknowledging a political offense exception to extradition for participants in uprisings.

Dr. Holmes, however, had nothing to do with political uprisings; he was wanted for killing his lover's husband. Thus when Vermont imprisoned Holmes in response to a British request for extradition, and he petitioned the U.S. Supreme Court for release, Seward's question was raised again: May an American state constitutionally engage in international extradition without express authorization from the national government?

The justices could not agree on an answer. In *Holmes v. Jennison*[22] Chief Justice Roger Taney took the Madisonian view that international extradition affected international relations and thus was exclusively for the national government to decide. He was joined by justices Story, McLean, and Wayne. Justices Thompson, Barbour, and Catron claimed that the power to surrender fugitives to foreign countries was concurrent, until such time as a national treaty or congressional statute preempted the matter for exclusive federal decision. Justice Baldwin voted to sustain the power of the state on the ground that it was a legitimate exercise of its police power to get rid of an undesirable inhabitant.[23] However, a majority of the justices agreed that the national government could not engage in extradition without a treaty.

The Supreme Court's indecision regarding the state's authority threw the case back to the supreme court of Vermont, which had earlier ruled that Dr. Holmes was extraditable. Augmented by its chief justice, Charles K. Williams, who had not participated in the earlier decision, the Vermont high court reversed itself.[24] According to the chief justice's opinion for the majority, the power to extradite fugitives to foreign countries could be exercised by the state, but the power to specify when and under what conditions belonged to its legislature, not its executive.[25]

The Vermont court rejected Chancellor Kent's view that extradition was required by international law even in the absence of a treaty. The weight of authorities, the court decided, was against this view. So, too, was the Jay Treaty, for if the customary law of nations clearly established a duty to extradite, Article 27 of that treaty would not have been necessary.

Moreover, to allow the executive to surrender persons in the absence of a treaty (or, presumably, a statute),[26]

> would be utterly repugnant to many of those principles, and destructive of those rights, which have been considered of the greatest importance, and which are deemed essential to the preservation of personal security. Not only those who seek the protection of our laws and an asylum under our liberal institutions, but our own citizens are liable to be sent abroad out of their country and deprived of trial by jury, at the pleasure of a single individual, and on the demand of a foreign sovereign.

The Vermont chief justice continued, as if anticipating arguments that the Reagan administration would make in the 1990s:[27]

> If the practice of surrendering exists by comity only, and the sovereign of one state delivers up to another in expectation of a similar favor, and there were no constitutional objections to the exercise of this power by the state government, there would yet remain this formidable objection to the exercise of the power by the governor, that it is no where inscribed among the executive duties, by our constitution, to determine what cases, for what offences, and with what nations this comity shall be observed. He is not the sovereign power. . . . It would still be requisite for the legislature to pass a statute on the subject, to determine the cases in which it might be exercised, the proof on which, and the tribunal by whom, it should be exercised.

Thus, in the Vermont court's view, extradition was an inherently judicial function, to be prescribed by legislation and subject to the same constitutional standards as any similar kind of adjudication. Because it was a judicial function, due process must apply in every case; it was not sufficient, constitutionally, to protect political offenders only.

The Vermont decision was consistent with the reasoning of Madison, Jefferson, and Jay. It was also consistent with Judge Barbour's decision in *Dos Santos*. It rejected New York's executive-centered extradition but embraced New York's insistence on an authorizing law and a political offense exception.[28] Taken together, these early attempts to deal with extradition confirm that the founders of American extradition law and policy were not just interested in assuring political asylum for liberal revolutionaries. They also wished to establish the rule of law in place of executive fiat and assure that rights to liberty and due process of law guaranteed by the federal and state constitutions would protect all subjects of extradition equally. In the United States, extradition was to be a matter of law, not political discretion.[29]

* * *

Article 10 of the Webster–Ashburton Treaty of 1842 authorized the resumption of extradition between the United States and Great Britain, now the United Kingdom. Much had happened over the past four decades to make extradition between the two nations conceivable again. Britain had become more liberal and more proud of its role as a nation of asylum to the political refugees of liberal revolutions on the Continent. The United States had lost much of its enmity for its ancient despot and in fact had supported liberal Britain against the conservative regimes of Prussia, Austria, and Naples. Bonaparte's ascension to emperor and the later restoration of the French monarchy also made the British look liberal by comparison. But most of all, the United States and the United Kingdom were determined to end tensions over the U.S.-Canadian border. That meant defining not only when extradition would be granted, but when it would be denied and whether it should be a matter of law or politics.

Two major border incidents in the late 1830s helped clarify when extradition would be denied, if it were to be allowed at all. The first involved a covert military raid by Loyalist Canadians against a rebel base in New York; the second involved a half-mad Canadian revolutionary whom the Canadians wanted returned.

Perhaps the greatest threat to border peace occurred in 1837, when Canadian rebels, assisted by hundreds of New York sympathizers, hired the American steamship *Caroline* to run men, guns, and supplies to a British island in the river just above Niagara Falls. Their mission was spoiled on the night of December 29 when sixty-three Canadian volunteers crossed the river to the United States, towed the ship out into the stream, put her to the torch, and set her adrift, to be destroyed on the rocks above the Falls. During the raid two Americans, Amos Durfee and a cabin boy known only as "Little Billy," were shot dead.[30]

Three years later Alexander McLeod, a deputy sheriff from Niagara, Upper Canada, was arrested in the upstate village of Lewiston, New York, and charged with personally killing Durfee. The British government protested and invoked the "act of state" doctrine, claiming that the raiders had acted on its orders.[31] It assumed full responsibility for the raid and the killings and insisted on McLeod's release.[32]

The issue was not one of extradition. The offense had been committed on American soil and Britain did not seek McLeod's release so that it could prosecute him. But the controversy highlighted the question of what to do about Canadians and Americans who were crossing the border and committing crimes for political purposes. The conflict over McLeod was also an explosive one; mob action had prevented his release on bail. Lord Palmerston advised the U.S. minister to London that McLeod's conviction and execution would be the signal for a war to settle a host of issues between the two countries.[33] Meanwhile, border strife had broken out in northern Maine, and Congress had authorized the president to call out the militia and recruit 50,000 volunteers for the army if a peaceful settlement could not be found.[34] Fortunately for relations between the two countries, a New York jury acquitted McLeod in October 1841 and he was released.[35]

In the midst of the tension caused by the McLeod case, the Canadian government asked Governor William L. Marcy of New York to extradite William Lyon Mackenzie, a half-mad former mayor of Toronto who deeply admired American democracy and sought to impose it on Canada by force.[36] Mackenzie was wanted by the Canadian Tories for his involvement in a shooting by his sentries of a man who tried to pass through their lines, the burning of a house which took place in the course of the uprising, and the seizure of mail bags and money from a mail coach.

Governor Marcy, who would later become secretary of state to President Pierce, referred the requisition to the state's attorney general, Samuel Beardsley, for an opinion. Beardsley advised the governor that he lacked authority to order the surrender because the acts charged were manifestly of a political character. The term "offense of a political character" had never been used before in American law; it had only recently been expressed in Belgian and French law, where it had yet to be given definition. But here, in upstate New York in 1837, thirty years before John Stuart Mill associated nonextraditable political offenses with uprisings, a state attorney general was advancing an uprising test. Participation in an uprising, Beardsley argued, was the equivalent of the offense of treason, which the 1827 amendment to the New York extradition statute had declared to be nonextraditable. According to British law, the attorney general reasoned, Mackenzie and his fellow revolutionaries may be "murderers and felons, as well as traitors," but in the United States they should be considered traitors only and entitled to asylum, because theirs was "a civil war . . . open, public and notorious . . . to overthrow . . . the royal government."[37]

The fact that the statute made no exception for political offenses was not dispositive, the attorney general said. The nonextradition of political offenders was "a principle in itself just and wise; in conformity with the enlightened spirit of the age, and which the [state] legislature, in enacting the statute . . . intended should in all cases be sacredly reverenced and observed."[38]

Governor Marcy agreed. He concluded that the offenses charged against Mackenzie, "being incidents of the revolt, were merged in the higher crime imputed to him of treason—a political offence, excepted by our laws from those for which fugitives can be surrendered by the Executive."[39] Thus even though Mackenzie was not formally charged with treason, he was protected by the state law barring extradition for that crime.[40] The request for his surrender was denied.[41]

In *Holmes*, the Vermont high court produced the first U.S. judicial opinion expressly acknowledging that political offenders should not be extradited. Who was a political offender, it said, was not a matter of formal charges. The European distinction between the so-called "pure" political offense,[42] like treason, sedition, and espionage, and the "relative" offenses, like killing in a rebellion, was meaningless to the majority. It fully intended to look behind the formal charges to the truth of the matter, understanding that "in all insurrections and rebellions, which are not so far successful as to be termed revolutions, persons are killed, and, in the eye of the law, if those who killed are acting against the government, they are deemed guilty of murder and must be surrendered up for trial if found among us [if extradition is allowed without restriction]." The consequences of such a view "are so disastrous," Chief Justice Williams wrote for the majority, and "so much at variance with the rights, privileges and immunities of American citizens, that [even] if the weight of authority was more forcible, I could not yield my assent to it."[43]

For this reason, the state court ruled that extradition in the absence of a statute or treaty could not be allowed. In that respect it reaffirmed the federal court's opinion in *Dos Santos*. In recognizing a political offense exception, it broke new ground, becoming arguably the first court anywhere to recognize the exception in the absence of a treaty or statute declaring it. By brushing aside any effort to restrict that exception to allegedly "pure" political offenses, the Vermont court said, in effect: We will inquire. We will not impose upon ourselves a judicial rule of noninquiry into the political reality behind the accusations.

Such was the state of judicial authority on the eve of the famous Webster–Ashburton Treaty of 1842, which would revive extradition between Britain and the United States. Before leaving London for Washington, Lord Ashburton made a point of asking the U.S. minister, Edward Everett, for his political assessment. Everett envisioned no difficulty resuming extradition, so long as it did not "extend to treason or any other political crime."[44]

* * *

Article 10 of the new treaty was drafted, at Webster's request, by Justice Joseph Story, who began with Article 27 of Chief Justice Jay's treaty.[45] Aware that extradition between the two countries had not been renewed because of what Webster called the "notoriety" of the Robbins case,[46] Story and the negotiators left no doubt that the issue of extraditability was for the courts to decide. After repeating that evidence of criminality would be determined "according to the laws of the place where the fugitive or person so charged shall be found," the new treaty declared that[47]

> the respective judges and other magistrates . . . shall have power, jurisdiction, and authority, upon complaint made under oath, to issue a warrant for the apprehension of the fugitive or person so charged, that he may be brought before such judges or other magistrates, respectively, to the end that the evidence of criminality may be heard and considered; and if, on such hearing, the evidence be deemed sufficient to sustain the charge, it shall be the duty of the examining judge or magistrate to certify the same to the proper Executive authority, that a warrant may issue for the surrender of such fugitive.

Thus Marshall's conception of extradition was rejected. Instead of an executive process subject to judicial review (via habeas corpus), the treaty mandated that the request for arrest be sent directly to a court. A judge, not a politician, would decide whether the accused should be arrested, and a judge would decide according to law, not politics, whether the accused could be surrendered. In specifying judicial rather than administrative arrest warrants, the treaty removed extradition from the summary arrest procedures that would later be used to combat illegal immigration.

Webster's rejection of Marshall's theory of extradition may be traced to the *Caroline* affair and to Britain's demand for McLeod's release. That demand was refused, Webster later wrote, because "in regular constitutional governments, persons arrested on charges of high crimes can only be discharged by some judicial proceeding."[48] Thus, if the U.S. executive lacked the authority to "forgive" killings by a foreign raider acting under British government authority, he lacked the authority to arrest and deliver a revolutionary or criminal at the behest of the Crown.

Implicit in Webster's refusal appears to have been the belief that courts have an inherent authority over all persons in custody, that no one may be discharged into the custody of another jurisdiction without court approval, and that no one can be sent out of the country without still another review, if he requests it, by filing for release under a writ of habeas corpus. "It is so," he reminded the British, "in the colonies and provinces of England."[49] It must also be so in the United States, he might have added, because the Constitution forbids the unreasonable seizure of persons and because the surrender of Jonathan Robbins (and the passage of the Alien and Sedition Acts) still rankled.

Politically, Webster could not have been any more eager to engage in executive extradition of cross-border rebels than governors Seward and Jenison, President Van Buren, or Secretary of State Forsyth. Nothing would have been more politically unpopular than for any executive to act unilaterally to deliver a fugitive rebel—or an American sympathizer—to the colonial regime they were trying to oust in conscious imitation of the American Revolution. The best they could hope for was a court that would do it.

The distrust of unbridled executive authority which so clearly affected both the Vermont court and Secretary Webster was also driven by popular recollections of the surrender of Jonathan Robbins. Because of that case, Justice John Catron of the Supreme Court later wrote, [50]

> a great majority of the people of this country were opposed to the doctrine that the President could arrest, imprison, and surrender a fugitive, and thereby execute the treaty himself; and they were still more opposed to an assumption that he could order the courts of justice to execute his mandate, as this would destroy the independence of the judiciary, in cases of extradition, and which example might be made a precedent for similar invasions in other cases; and from that day to this, the judicial power has acted in cases of extradition, and all others, independent of executive control.
>
> That the eventful history of Robbins's case had a controlling influence on our distinguished negotiator [Webster], when the treaty of 1842 was made ... is, as I suppose, free from doubt. The assumption of power to arrest, imprison, and extrude, on executive warrants, and the employment of a judicial magistrate to act in obedience to the President's commands, where no independence existed, had most materially aided to overthrow the administration of a distinguished revolutionary patriot [Adams], whose honesty of purpose no fair-minded man at this day doubts. Public opinion had settled down to a firm resolve, long before the treaty of 1842 was made, that so dangerous an engine of oppression as secret proceedings before the executive, and the issuing of secret warrants of arrest, founded on them, and long imprisonments inflicted under such warrants, and then, an extradition without an unbiased hearing before an independent judiciary, were highly dangerous to liberty, and ought never to be allowed in this country.

Justice Story had proposed a rather long list of extraditable crimes, including desertion, burglary, and theft.[51] Desertion was quickly dropped by the Americans because of the summary method of trial and punishment used by military forces,[52] and because extraditing for that offense would raise bitter memories of the surrender of Jonathan Robbins.

Burglary and theft were excluded by the British because they could be used to reclaim fugitive slaves, who could be charged with stealing the clothes on their backs.[53] Mutiny was dropped by the British in memory of the *Creole* slaves and by the Americans out of respect for impressed seamen like Robbins, while revolt was eliminated both as a political offense and as another way of shielding runaway slaves. The list of extraditable crimes was thus reduced to murder, assault with murderous intent, piracy, arson, forgery, and the utterance of forged paper.[54]

The negotiators could hardly avoid listing murder as an extraditable offense if there was to be any extradition at all, but its inclusion, without a humanitarian exemption for fugitive slaves charged with killing in order to escape, upset British abolitionists, who successfully pressured their government to stretch the rule of double criminality, if necessary, to claim that it was not murder under British or Canadian law to kill in order to escape from the illegal condition of slavery.[55]

The new treaty allowed for the extradition not only of fugitives but of any "person so charged." Citizens and aliens alike were subject to extradition and, in cases involving forgery or the firing of weapons across borders, did not have to leave their own soil to violate the laws of the other nation.

Article 10 looked like a straight law-enforcement measure and could be so regarded—once the border was settled. However, the primary purpose of its murder, arson, and assault provisions was to end a species of politically motivated crime: cross-border raids arising out of disputes over territorial sovereignty. Justice Story explained that "I have purposely excluded political offences, as involving [many] debatable matters . . . that . . . might hazard the ratification by our Senate [due to] popular clamour."[56]

Story did not wish to trigger a debate over what constituted a political offense because he knew that Webster wanted to put all cross-border raiders on notice that if they persisted in fomenting revolution in Canada, they would be returned for trial as criminals. In modern parlance, Article 10 was intended to end "terrorism." Extolling his treaty years later, Webster claimed that the "happiest consequences" had flowed from its extradition provision. "No more was heard of border forays, 'Hunters' Lodges,' 'Associations for the Liberty of Canada,' or violences offered or retaliated across the line. The mild, but certain influence of law imposed a restraint, which even costly and formidable military means had not been found entirely adequate to produce."[57]

* * *

Webster's treaty was not appreciated by many of his Democratic opponents in Congress. In particular, it was denounced by representatives of the slave states, who were angered by the treaty's failure to require the United Kingdom to return fugitive slaves. Senator Thomas Hart Benton (D.-Mo.) was particularly outspoken in the ratification debate. As the representative of a slave state, Benton attacked the treaty for authorizing judges to ascertain criminality. This, he said, would make it impossible for the South to recover fugitive slaves, because[58]

> in the eye of the British law, they have no master, and can commit no offence against such a person in asserting their liberty against him, even unto death. A slave may kill his master, if necessary to his escape. This is legal under British law; and in the present state of abolition feeling throughout the British dominions, such killing would not only be considered fair, but in the highest degree meritorious and laudable.

In effect, Benton understood what the British government intended—that the rule of double criminality, carried over from the Jay Treaty, would bar British courts from certifying the extraditability of a slave who had fought (or stole) his way to freedom. Like the British sea lords who did not want American courts to grant a similar defense to impressed seamen who had fought their way out of the British navy, the senator wanted to curb the impulse of judges to do substantial justice.

Jay's Treaty was better, Benton argued, relying on Marshall's interpretation, because "the delivery was a ministerial act; ... under this treaty, it becomes a judicial act, referring itself to the discretion of the judge." Better by far to leave things as they are, he continued, and let executive officials decide which fugitives shall be surrendered. Executives, he argued disingenuously, would act "from a sense of propriety, and the dictates of decency and justice. Not so with the judge. He must go by the law; and when there is no law against the offense, he has nothing to justify him in delivering the offender."[59]

To this extent, Benton misread the most obvious lesson of the Robbins case. But he did not oppose judicial protection for Irishmen like Robbins, or Irish rebels against British rule. He opposed applying the judicial law of extradition to slaves, because that would acknowledge that they were people, and recognizing them as persons would be the first step to ending slavery altogether. However, if the executive were to remain in charge of returning slaves, political considerations could reign supreme, and the fugitives could be returned like chattels.

The senator from Missouri did find four serious weaknesses in the new agreement. One was the lack of a provision limiting extradition to serious crimes only. The new treaty authorized extradition for five additional offenses—assault with the intent to commit murder, piracy, robbery, arson, and the utterance of forged paper—which,[60]

> though high in name, might be very small in degree. Assault, with intent to murder, might be without touching or hurting the person; for, to lift a weapon at a person without strik-ing is an assault: ... and the offense being in the intent, is difficult to prove. Mr. Jefferson excluded it, and so did Jay's Treaty; because the offence was too small and too equivocal to be made a matter of international arrangement. . . . The robbery might be of a shilling's worth of bread; the arson, of burning a straw shed; the utterance of a forged paper, might be the emission or passing of a counterfeit sixpence. All these were excluded from Jay's treaty, because of their possible insignificance, and the door they opened to abuse in harassing the innocent, and in multiplying the chances for getting hold of a political offender for some other offence, and then punishing him for his politics.

A second flaw in the treaty was the lack of what in modern times would be called the "rule of specialty." As Benton put it,[61]

> under the head of murder, the insurgent, the rebel, and the traitor who has shed blood, may be given up; and so of other offences. When once surrendered, he may be tried for any thing. The fate of Jonathan Robbins, alias Nash, is a good illustration of all this. He was a British sailor—was guilty of mutiny, murder, and piracy on the frigate *Hermione*— deserted to the United States—was demanded by the British minister as a murderer under

Jay's treaty—given up as a murderer—then tried by a court-martial on board a man-of-war for mutiny, murder, desertion, and piracy—found guilty—executed—and his body hung in chains from the yard-arm of a man-of-war. And so it would be again.

Third, Benton feared that the American legal process could be used as an instrument of foreign persecution: [62]

> In the number and insignificance of the offences for which he might be surrendered, there would be no difficulty in reaching any victim that a foreign government chose to pursue. If this article had been in force in the time of the Irish rebellion, and Lord Edward Fitzgerald had escaped to the United States after wounding, as he did, several of the myrmidons who arrested him, he might have been demanded as a fugitive from justice, for the assault with intent to kill; and then tried for treason, and hanged and quartered; and such will be the operation of this article if it continues.

Fourth, Benton noticed the lack of any express protection for political offenders. He did not claim any need to protect political offenders on the northern border. Rather, he invoked the more neutral example of Irishmen who had fled to America after supporting Wolfe Tone in the unsuccessful French-backed rebellion of 1798.[63] Benton presumably did not imagine that the fugitives from slave uprisings could also claim political offender status, because he did not think of them as contestants for governmental power.

The absence of special protection for political offenders provoked the greatest criticism in Congress. This criticism was not assuaged by a special message from President Tyler, who tried to explain that "in the careful and specific enumeration of crimes, the object has been to exclude all political offences, or criminal charges arising from wars or intestine commotions. Treason, misprison of treason, libels, desertion from military service, and other offences of a similar character are excluded."[64]

The Democrats could not block ratification of Webster's treaty, or even condition senatorial consent on changes in the extradition provisions. Benton's demand for the return of fugitive slaves fell on deaf Northern ears, while his civil liberties concerns were swamped by the desire to avert yet another war with the British by settling the Canadian boundary. After extensive secret debate in the Senate, Benton's resolution calling for rejection of the entire treaty was defeated.

However, in 1843, when the United States agreed to engage in extradition with the then-liberal government of France, the treaty expressly barred surrender for "any crime or offense of a purely political character."[65] The Tyler administration thus made express what it had considered implied by the treaty with the United Kingdom.[66] Whether this satisfied the administration's critics is not known. The term "purely" could be interpreted to limit the scope of the exception to such formal political offenses as treason, lèse majesté, and sedition, and to avoid judicial decisions questioning the integrity of foreign officials seeking the return of politically controversial figures for seemingly ordinary crimes. But that does not seem to have been the Tyler administration's intent. Even before Benton's attack on the Webster–Ashburton Treaty, the president had assured Congress that the object has been to exclude all political offenses, and not just formal (or "pure") ones like treason and sedition.[67]

* * *

In failing to exempt impressed seamen, political offenders, or fugitive slaves from extradition for the crimes they committed in the course of their escapes, neither Webster nor Ashburton left their respective governments—or courts—wholly unable to protect them. The Vermont court in *Jennison* had recognized a political offense exception even before there was a treaty; other courts might do likewise. Judges could embrace an expansive view of what constitutes a crime under the rule of double criminality, taking self-defense (and therefore the immorality of the requesting nation's law) into account. Or they could rummage through the legal papers and find a technical excuse for not honoring a morally distasteful extradition request.

This challenge was first faced in 1843 by a British court sitting in Nassau when asked by Americans to surrender seven slaves charged with killing their master in Key Biscayne while escaping from Florida. The court refused, claiming insufficient evidence but implicitly invoking both the rule of double criminality and the exculpatory principle of self-defense:[68]

> An indictment *per se* can never be received as evidence. It is not enough for us to know that the American jury thought the parties guilty: we ought to know the *grounds* upon which they thought them guilty. What may constitute the crime of murder in Florida may be very far from doing so according to the British laws, or even to the laws of the northern States of America. By issuing a warrant, then, to apprehend the parties in virtue of these indictments, we might be doing so on evidence which would not justify the apprehension by true British law, and should thereby be proceeding in direct violation of the act.

In 1860, however, self-defense was disallowed by a Canadian court in the case of a fugitive slave from Howard County, Missouri. John Anderson had, as Jack Burton, been butler to Moses Burton, a prominent businessman whose wife had raised the slave in her home as a playmate and nurse to her two daughters. As a result, Jack developed a profound unwillingness to submit to punishment, and Moses eventually sold him to a more brutal owner, thereby dividing him forever from his wife and four children. Jack stole a mule from his new master and fled, only to be challenged north of Fayette by Seneca Digges, a white farmer, who rightly surmised that Jack was a fugitive. Jack fled, pursued by Digges's slaves, but suddenly found Digges blocking his way again. In desperation, Jack stabbed the man who would have reenslaved him and fled north to Canada. Digges subsequently died of his wounds, making Jack, by the laws of Missouri, the most heinous and feared of murderers.[69]

Changing his name to Anderson, Jack reestablished himself as a plasterer, but another fugitive eventually informed on him. A justice of the peace had him arrested and notified Missouri authorities, who demanded his extradition. His case made its way in due course to the Queens Bench in Toronto, which upheld his extradition as a murderer.[70]

By the law of Canada, Anderson was no murderer. But the court decided, despite the rule of double criminality, that the definition of "murder" should be decided by the law of the requesting state. Had the stabbing taken place in Canada, it would have been recognized legally for what it was morally—a justifiable act of self-defense. Indeed, Digges would have been the criminal for having tried to reenslave Anderson. But self-defense was considered then, as it is today, to be a legal defense that the accused may raise only at his trial. To claim self-defense in an extradition proceeding was considered as premature as raising it before a grand jury.

Then, as now, this rule made sense if it could be assumed, as it often can, that self-defense means the same thing in both jurisdictions. But Anderson's was no ordinary case, any more than the operative law of Missouri was ordinary so far as fugitive slaves were concerned. The courts of Missouri were not about to allow an escaped slave to plead self-defense against a white person, any more than the British navy would have granted the same right to impressed seamen like Jonathan Robbins or Billy Budd.

But the Canadian court would take no notice of, or brook any inquiry into, these obvious facts. There was simply nothing in the text of the treaty, Chief Justice John B. Robinson decided, that would exempt fugitives slaves from extradition for killing a slaver in order to escape. The Queen's Bench knew that the British government, in negotiating the treaty, did not intend to return fugitive slaves to the United States any more than the United States intended to surrender impressed seamen to the British navy, but those understandings were not written into the treaty, so the judges refused to honor them or, more precisely, left their implementation to the executive.

"We may be told," the Chief Justice added, "that there is no assurance that the prisoner, being a slave, will be tried fairly and without prejudice in a foreign country; but no court . . . can refuse to give effect to an act of parliament by acting on such an assumption; nor can we be influenced by the consideration, a very painful one in all such cases, that the prisoner, even if he shall be wholly acquitted . . . , must still remain a slave in a foreign country."[71]

Thus the rule of noninquiry came to Canada. Its logical force derived, in no small part, from the fact that courts in Canada (and the United Kingdom) lacked the authority to refuse to enforce legislative acts on the grounds they violate constitutional guarantees of due process. Unfortunately, American courts and writers would later ignore this special circumstance when citing opinions like this one as persuasive authority for similar acts of moral blindness.

The majority's decision was immediately and widely denounced, making the Anderson case to Canada what the Robbins case had been to the United States. Abolitionists even persuaded a court in Great Britain to ignore Canadian autonomy and order the matter of Anderson's liberty to be reheard in London.[72] But as moral outrage increased, Canada's Court of Common Pleas accepted another habeas petition and, in a triumph of the technical over the moral, ordered Anderson released. The Missouri warrant, the justices discovered, had reported the killing of Seneca Digges but had neglected specifically to charge Anderson with murdering him.[73]

Within the Canadian parliament, liberals denounced conservatives for attempting to surrender Anderson to slavery. The government responded by amending the Fugitive Offenders Act to increase the amount of evidence necessary to justify extradition but refused to accept a broader rule of noninquiry.[74] Thus the Anderson case came to an end, framing without resolving the clash between law and morality, and order and liberty, in cases where the requesting regime cannot be expected to do justice.

* * *

Louis Hartz has written that the political thought of nations is established at their moment of founding, and that all subsequent thought enters into dialogue with the founders' concepts, values, and concerns.[75] The same may be said, with even greater force, for new doctrines and practices in a stable legal system built upon precedent. For the U.S. law of extradition, the founding moment was probably the 1840s, when extradition began in earnest, but was built upon principles that had been developing since the 1780s.

The first principle, articulated by Madison, Jefferson, Jay, and Webster, followed by officials in New York and Vermont, by the federal courts, and numerous U.S. attorneys general, was that extradition could not occur in the absence of law, set forth either by a treaty or by legislation. Second, whether the executive had the authority to surrender a person under the protection of the Constitution, laws, and treaties of the United States to a foreign power was clearly for the courts to decide. It was not to be confused with deportation, which was essentially an administrative process; it was part of a legal process following the basic rules of evidence and due process of law appropriate to preliminary hearings in criminal prosecutions. The treaty might not specify that judges should decide who is extraditable and who is not, but there was never any doubt among American officials that they would, as was repeatedly demonstrated by the cases of Captain Barré, Thomas Nash, the *Amistad* captives, Dos Santos, Mayor Mackenzie, and Dr. Holmes. Third, the appropriate focus was on legal criteria, not foreign policy considerations. The refusal to surrender Nash, or the *Amistad* captives, or Mackenzie might cause international repercussions, but that was unavoidable. Extradition constituted a deprivation of liberty, which made it too important to be left to the discretion of politicians (or government lawyers), even if judges were not always immune to political pressures.

The fourth founding principle of American extradition law was that the United States would not surrender political offenders. This principle might be poorly worded or, in the case of the Webster–Ashburton Treaty, not made express, but eventually it had to be acknowledged. Americans would argue for another century and a half over what an exception for political offenders would encompass, but the basic principle was established by Charles Pinckney and Thomas Jefferson, the New York State legislature, the Vermont high court, the Tyler administration's assurances regarding the Webster–Ashburton Treaty, and that administration's more explicit 1843 treaty with France. The United States was capable of surrendering fugitive slaves to certain injustice, but it would not long ignore the plight of political fugitives from European conflicts. The United States was still a nation of asylum.

Other principles were not established. Before extradition treaties were entered into, Jefferson insisted, the negotiators should take into consideration the requesting regime's capacity to do justice. This consideration, among others, deterred the United States from negotiating extradition treaties for its first fifty years and limited the list of extraditable offenses for years thereafter. However, a formal principle of inquiry was never explicitly embraced. Jefferson knew why he should not give General Galbaud to Genêt; Washington knew why he should not surrender Genêt to the Jacobins. Judge Laurance knew why he should not surrender Captain Barré to the guillotine. But there is no evidence that anyone would have shielded the *Amistad* blacks from the Spanish stake had a more credible case for their enslavement been made. Similarly, neither Daniel Webster nor Lord Ashburton worried that the legal systems of each other's country might not always be just.

Evidentiary standards were also in flux. On the one hand, Jay, Marshall, Story, and Webster insisted on a level of proof roughly comparable to the Constitution's requirement of probable cause. Some, like the Supreme Court in the *Amistad* case, would lift the veil of national legitimacy and question the authenticity of documents. Others, like the Vermont high court, would look behind charges of murder for evidence of involvement in a political uprising by way of explanation and excuse. During the American Civil War, Canadian courts would accept evidence that the alleged crime had been carried out under orders of the Confederate States of America. Killing civilians under military orders could be a defense to extradition in Canada even when killing to avoid reenslavement was not.

In nonpolitical cases, however, Anglo-American extradition courts soon refused to consider alibis or claims that the accused acted in self-defense. These assertions were left for the trial court in the requesting state to consider. Participants in political revolts could expect some systematic protection from extradition, but nonpolitical defendants, including fugitive slaves, could not. Judge-made rules of noninquiry would see to that.

CHAPTER 6

Offenses of a Political Character

To surrender political offenders ... is not a duty; but, on the contrary, compliance with such a demand would be considered a dishonorable subserviency to a foreign power, and an act meriting the reprobation of mankind.

William L. Marcy, Secretary of State, September 6, 1853

The American origins of an exception to extradition for political offenders lie, as we have seen, in the young nation's tradition of political asylum.

In the seventeenth and eighteenth centuries, liberty was a condition that white Americans were willing to share with European immigrants of all political persuasions. Confident of liberty's curative qualities, they were willing to extend that condition to both the radical executioners of Charles I and the aristocratic fugitives of the French Revolution. A nation of immigrants influenced by Puritan notions of spiritual rebirth, they viewed the experience of "crossing over" as morally transformative. Those who crossed the Atlantic were deemed to have left the politics and decadence of old-world tyrannies behind, and to have joined a new order that had no obligation to return European political offenders to the courts of their oppressors.

* * *

These views stood in sharp contrast to old-world practices during the same period. From the seventeenth century to the nineteenth, the asylum principle in Europe tended to run in one direction only. The principle was recognized when the state sympathized with the politics of a fugitive to its shores and was ignored when the state sought to recover a rebel. During the French Revolution, the Jacobins adopted a Constitution that proclaimed their new republic a haven to all foreigners banned from their countries for the cause of liberty, but denied the same protection to "tyrants."[1] In 1798, the Directory forced Switzerland to sign a treaty promising to extradite political offenders against France.[2] In 1799, the British demanded and obtained the surrender of Napper Tandy and other participants in the Irish Rebellion of 1798 who had fled to the German state of Hamburg. Napoleon denounced that surrender,[3] but later demanded that the British turn over some fugitives who had opposed his regime.[4]

After Napoleon was defeated in 1815, the conservative regimes of Europe fought against the emerging doctrine of political asylum and tried to coerce smaller states into extraditing political offenders.[5] In 1817, for example, the Netherlands were forced to sign a treaty with Hanover stipulating the surrender of political offenders.[6] When Switzerland defied Austria, Prussia, and Russia by refusing to return some Piedmontese revolutionaries, Count Metternich of Austria arranged for the French monarchy of Louis XVII to mass troops on the Swiss border. Shortly thereafter, Switzerland closed her borders to political refugees and in 1828 agreed with France to extradite political fugitives.[7]

However, attitudes were changing. In 1815, the British governor of Gibraltar provoked a storm of indignation by surrendering some political fugitives to Spain. Sir James Mackintosh announced to Parliament, somewhat prematurely, that the nonextradition of political offenders had become a "venerable principle" and "part of the consuetudinary law of nations."[8] A year later, Lord Castlereagh declared that to make British law an instrument for punishing foreigners for their political offenses was an abuse of law.[9]

Scholarly opinion was also coming to favor the nonextradition of political offenders. In 1812, Vicomte Louis de Bonald, perhaps the most conservative philosopher in France, declared that "Extradition should not be accorded for . . . political offenses and, as the right of asylum is no longer attached to temples, the whole universe is a temple for the unfortunate."[10] In 1829, Hollandais Kluit, a respected Dutch jurist, published the first full-fledged argument against extraditing political offenders.[11] Like Sir James Mackintosh, Kluit claimed that states "universally refuse to surrender fugitives accused of political crimes."[12]

France was not one of them, but it too ran into a firestorm of liberal protest when it surrendered Antonio Galotti to the reactionary regime of Naples. Although he was charged with robbery and crimes against property, Galotti was no ordinary criminal; he was a member of the Italian *carbonari* movement and had participated in an unsuccessful revolution in 1820. Popular protests forced the Bourbon monarchy to revoke the order for Galotti's extradition (claiming that it had been obtained by deception), and to dispatch a naval squadron to the Bay of Naples to seek his release. The show of force did not obtain Galotti's immediate freedom, but it did shield him from execution until his exile could be negotiated.[13]

Following the Galotti affair, France abrogated the extradition treaty that she had imposed upon Switzerland, but concessions of this sort were not enough to save the monarchy, which was swept away in the Revolution of 1830. The men who rose to power with Louis Philippe, the "bourgeois king," were liberals intent on barring future governments, including their own, from using the legal process to destroy political rivals. Thus began a series of laws providing special protections, such as jury trial and more lenient incarceration, for politically motivated offenders.[14] The purpose of these laws was not to express respect for the practitioners of political violence, but to defuse sympathy for them in a romantic age. In particular, the liberals did not want to make martyrs out of radicals by being seen to suppress them with autocratic techniques. The French liberals who enacted these laws presumed, in defiance of both logic and experience, that it was possible to draw legally respectable distinctions between political and nonpolitical crimes, and the special protections became the basis for legislation and treaties exempting political offenders from extradition.

To the British and Americans, such assumptions were hopelessly naive. To them, the rule of law—as opposed to the commands of politics—meant the absence of political crimes, not leniency and respect for political killers. Thus the political offense exception, which entered Anglo-American law primarily through treaties, has always set uneasily within the Anglo-American legal traditions. Its humanitarian basis appealed to American sensibilities and fit well with American traditions, but its implication that one revolutionary might be as morally good as any other became increasingly less persuasive as the experience of "crossing over" came to be seen as less transformative. Eventually, the rule of noninquiry into the capacity of the requesting regime to do justice would undermine the humanitarian impetus behind the American exception for political offenders, making the exception more difficult to justify.

As we have seen, the first legislature to exempt political offenders from extradition was New York's, in 1827. However, its exception was for "treason," which could mean anything from political dissent to armed rebellion.

The first judicial acknowledgement that an exception to extradition for "political offences" was appropriate appears to have occurred in Canada two years later. In the case of *Rex v. Ball*, counsel for an alleged thief from Vermont named Joseph Fisher observed that extradition could never be allowed for political offenses. The King's Bench, sitting in Montreal, agreed. "Offences of a political nature, arising out of revolutionary principles, excited in any government" were different, it ruled. "The authority of the state to which the accused has fled may well be extended to protect rather than deliver [the political fugitive] up to his accusers, and this upon a wise and humane policy, because the voice of justice cannot always be heard amidst the rage of revolution, or when the sovereign and subject are at open variance respecting their political rights, and therefore no state will ever be induced to deliver men up to destruction, not even to malicious prosecution."[15]

The Canadian court understood, better than most courts since, that the risks of injustice and malicious prosecution are particularly high in cases were political fugitives are sought for extradition. It did not clearly state that it would refuse to grant extradition in such cases, but it did implicitly reserve the right to do so if the executive did not refuse surrender first.

The political offense exception germinated differently, but more or less contemporaneously, on both sides of the Atlantic. The first national statute expressly to exempt "political offenses" from extradition was enacted on October 1, 1833, by French-speaking Belgium, which had just recently won her independence from the Netherlands.[16] A month later, Belgium and France also became the first countries to incorporate that exemption into an extradition treaty.[17] In 1834, legislatures in France and Switzerland incorporated the exception into their municipal law.[18] Thus, to most international lawyers, the political offense exception is of European origin.

Although the verbal formula may have come from Belgium and France, it would be a mistake to assume that Americans, Canadians, or the British interpreted the purposes of the exception in exactly the same way. The British, for example, refused to include a political offense exception in their 1843 treaty with France, preferring instead to rely on a short list of presumably nonpolitical offenses like murder and forgery, and excluding such obvious political offenses as treason, lèse majesté, and sedition. This approach, which the Webster-Ashburton Treaty had embraced, would prove inadequate, but it reflected an Anglo-American skepticism about revolutionary politics—particularly class-based revolutionary politics.

Today most politically motivated killers are denounced as terrorists, but to many mid-nineteenth-century European liberals, rebels against reactionary regimes were genuine heroes. Leaders of the unsuccessful revolutions of 1830 and 1848 like Mazzini, Kossuth, and Garibaldi were lionized by the liberal societies to which they fled.[19] "With rare and notable exceptions," Barton Ingraham has written, the political offender "was seen as motivated by moral considerations: fighting for liberal democracy against autocratic and repressive regimes, fighting for the cause of nationalism or self-determination, fighting on behalf of the poor and enslaved classes for a fair share of the national wealth, but never acting from personal considerations of greed or lust for power."[20]

This romanticism dominated the writings of European criminologists. For example, Cesare Lombroso, the leading Italian scholar of crime, characterized political criminals as men of "powerful intellect, exaggerated sensibility, great altruism, patriotic, religious, or even scientific ideals."[21] Lombroso also exempted political criminals from common criminals who he believed were impelled to crime by their biological natures.[22] Romanticism, couched in the language of social science, led countries like France to treat domestic political criminals with leniency.[23]

European romanticism never really caught hold in America, where revolution had meant independence from colonial rule, not class conflict. Americans, who had always been rather measured and legalistic about their revolutionary goals, were even more cautious after witnessing the excesses of the Jacobins in France and the slave uprising in Haiti. This skepticism was reawakened in 1852 when Louis Kossuth, on tour in the United States, made clear the extent of his socialist, rather than liberal, aspirations. Americans would accept the Kossuths of Europe, as they had Galbaud, Genêt, and Barré, as individuals "crossing over," but as a maritime nation they were less passionate about taking sides in European conflicts.

On the other side of Western Europe, the conservative states of the Holy Alliance turned a hard face to the political crimes defense and sustained that hostility throughout most of the century. There was a brief lapse in 1830 when Austria and Prussia refused to surrender some Polish revolutionaries to Russia,[24] but in the 1830s Austria, Prussia, and Russia agreed with the Germanic Confederation to provide for the return of all persons charged with high treason and *lèse majesté*, conspiracy against the safety of a throne or legitimate government, or participation in a revolt.[25] Spain, under a conservative monarchy, followed suit.[26]

In 1849, following unsuccessful revolutions throughout Europe, Austria and Russia mounted a major diplomatic effort to recover by extradition about 5,000 Hungarian and Polish revolutionaries (including Kossuth) who had fled to Turkey. Although three treaties committed Turkey to either extradite or punish the refugees, the Sublime Porte, backed by the British fleet, refused.[27]

Shortly thereafter, the unity of the Holy Alliance's policy demanding the extradition of political offenders began to fall apart. In 1856, Austria-Hungary became the first autocratic state to sign an extradition treaty containing a political crimes exception.[28] The North German Federation and Russia followed in the 1860s.[29] The political crimes exception became the diplomatic price autocracies had to pay for the regular extradition of ordinary criminals from liberal states.[30]

By the 1860s, the political offense exception had become "boilerplate" language in most extradition agreements among Western nations, and it would continue to spread as former colonies joined the "family" of nations. What the words meant, however, was left wholly undefined.

* * *

Meanwhile, yet another sea change in attitudes toward revolution was occurring, away from the romantic view of political crime and toward a more positivistic, power-centered attitude regarding the legitimacy of foreign requests. The shift began with a series of assassinations and bombings directed at high government officials in Europe and the United States. Between 1854 and 1911, nineteen heads of state died at the hands of assassins, including presidents Lincoln, Garfield, and McKinley of the United States, the moderate Tsar Alexander II of Russia, the apolitical Empress Elizabeth of Austria, King Humbert of Italy, and President Carnot of France. These murders, the atrocities of the Paris Commune in 1870, and frequent bombings by anarchists, nihilists, and socialists convinced even the most liberal regimes that not all politically motivated criminals were men of honor and sanity. On the contrary, some were shockingly indifferent to the carnage they inflicted on innocent bystanders by bombings that had no immediate, practical objective. Moreover, some made it clear that they did not intend to confine their attacks to reactionary regimes.

One result of this collective experience was a series of interpretations that narrowed and broadened—and muddled—the rule against surrendering political offenders. Another result was a series of exceptions to the undefined rule. The exceptions and the revised definitions developed gradually and in tandem, although for analytical clarity it is useful to focus on them separately.

For the modern definition of what constitutes a political offense in American extradition law, it is necessary to begin with the United Kingdom, because for over a century the American thinking on this subject has been influenced by the British. This was not always so. Attorney General Beardsley of New York, writing for Governor Marcy in 1837, made support of an uprising the crucial test for nonextradition under a statute that sought to protect political offenders by barring surrender for "treason." In 1840, the Supreme Court of Vermont recognized a moral difference between killing as part of an insurrection or rebellion and ordinary murder and, in dicta, refused to extradite rebels.[31] However, when U.S. courts finally got around to defining what constituted a "political offense" within the meaning of American extradition treaties, they did not look to these early American opinions; they looked to British sources.

Unlike the United States and France, the United Kingdom was slow to join the extradition movement during the mid-nineteenth century. By 1870, she had ratified only three extradition treaties.[32] One reason the British government was reluctant to negotiate more, Attorney General John T. Coleridge told Parliament in 1870, was that "they might be required to surrender political offenders, and violate the right of political asylum always afforded here to political refugees."[33] Another reason was the close scrutiny given to proposed treaties by Liberal members of the House of Commons like John Stuart Mill.

The pride that the British took in their policy of asylum was also expressed in one of their earliest treatises on extradition. Writing in 1868, Frederick Waymouth Gibbs contrasted British and French practice:[34]

> In England, a foreigner immediately on landing is, as regards his liberty, on the same footing as an Englishman. The same judicial forms are necessary to restrain his freedom as to restrain the freedom of any of us. He is not subject to any exceptional power of removal on the part of the police.
>
> In France, on the other hand, a foreigner comes within the jurisdiction of the administrative Government. If considered obnoxious, he may be passed on from gendarme to gendarme till he arrives at the frontier, and be forbidden to return under pain of punishment.

When the United Kingdom finally entered the modern age of extradition, she did so by enacting a comprehensive statute that brought some coherence to her subsequent treaties and court decisions. The statute itself was the outgrowth of a substantial debate in Parliament in 1866, and the report of a select committee of Parliament that took extensive evidence in 1868.[35] Its origins went back to 1852, when the Earl of Derby's Conservative government tried to make extradition to France of a properly identified person automatic on the presentation of a sentence of conviction or a warrant of apprehension from a French court, and had tried to make this rule of non-inquiry more palatable by adding to the treaty a political offense exception cognizable in the courts.[36]

The Liberals who blocked implementation of this treaty were not content to have a political offense exception to extradition; they wanted to preserve judicial scrutiny of the evidence on which the extradition request was based. Like the Americans, they were not just committed to protecting liberal revolutionaries from foreign persecution; they wanted to protect people of all political persuasions and rightly saw the blind acceptance of mere documents as a threat to liberty and justice. Thus, what began as a debate over the seeming technicalities of proof grew into demands for judicial control, due process, and special care in the protection of political offenders.

Although this book is about the American law of extradition, the 1866 debate in Great Britain is worth reviewing at some length, both because it influenced American thinking about extradition and because it foreshadowed many of the issues raised in modern times. The initial focus of the debate was a seemingly technical amendment to the law implementing the 1843 treaty with France. The amendment would have allowed British courts to accept certifications by French judges that copies of depositions against the accused were accurate without requiring that a witness (usually a French policeman) swear to the British court that the copies were accurate because he had personally compared them to the originals.[37]

The amendment might have passed without debate except for the fact that the liberal monarchy of Louis Philippe had been replaced by the more repressively militaristic regime of Napoleon III. Louis Blanc, a former member of the provisional government that had ruled France briefly during the socialist revolution of 1848, warned Liberal members of the British Parliament:[38]

> I could give you many illustrations of the way in which the meaning of the depositions made before our *Juges d'Instruction* is sometimes distorted by them under the influence of party spirit. To form a correct idea of the dangerous and mischievous character of the present Bill it is necessary to bear in mind that in France justice has always been much more or less subservient to the purposes of the ruling power; that the liberty of the press has been entirely suppressed, and that there is not a shadow of what is called public control. To pass the present bill would be, to a certain extent, to forge a weapon not unlikely to be used against innocent persons, and to incur the accusation of having surrendered to a foreign despotic power the dignity of a free nation.

Blanc's concern with the political manipulation of lax evidentiary requirements was expanded upon by John Stuart Mill, the noted philosopher of liberalism and member of Parliament for Westminster. Like Jefferson, Mill began his analysis by raising the larger question of due process of law:[39]

> I do not mean to say anything against the French Government, but I think it is neither in any way improper nor at all impertinent . . . to say something about the French law, and particularly those parts of it which are thought most defective by the best Judges in France itself. There are many things in that law which are worthy of great praise, . . . but I never met with any enlightened Frenchman who did not think that the mode in which the preliminary evidence is taken is the worst part even of that. The depositions which are taken preparatory to a criminal trial in France by the *juge d'instruction* are taken in secret. . . . It is, therefore, the easiest thing in the world to get up a false charge against a person, if . . . there is the slightest disposition to do so.

For Mill, the problem was how much weight British judges should give to French depositions, given that requests for the punishment or extradition of seemingly ordinary criminals could mask the persecution of a political rival.[40]

If the laws of any country afford facilities for getting up a false case, that false case is very much more likely to be got up where political offences are concerned. Political offences *eo nomine* are not, it is true, included in the Extradition Treaty, but acts really political often come within the definition of offences which are so included. Apply this observation to the case of the French Emperor at Boulogne [where Louis Napoleon wounded a soldier during a scuffle that broke out while he was trying to exhort members of a French regiment to support his second "invasion" in 1840] and you will perceive—as doubtless the Emperor himself would perceive—the force of what I am saying.

Mill's reference to Louis Napoleon's crime was pregnant with significance, because the proposed treaty was with *le petit Napoleon*'s government. The French emperor, who finally seized power in 1851, had been pressuring the British government for nearly a decade to enact a new alien control law (or a broader conspiracy statute) in order to punish political fugitives who, from their safe haven in England, had been plotting his assassination. Mill's reference to Louis's ludicrous "invasion" at Boulogne was a reminder to the Frenchman's Tory sympathizers that violence happens even when conservatives attempt bloodless uprisings, and it warned Liberals that a foreign government's extradition request against alleged plotters in England could easily be a false one, based, as it probably would be, on reports from French spies who had infiltrated the fugitives in England.

Mill's use of Louis Napoleon's crime also reinforced the Liberal view that Britain was, and ought to be, a haven for political fugitives of all stripes, from Louis Philippe, the Bourbon king whom Louis Napoleon tried twice to depose, to Louis Blanc, whose interim socialist government in 1848 was supplanted by Napoleon's, to Louis Napoleon himself, who staged his landing at Boulogne from England and then fled back to England after escaping from prison in 1846. But the French emperor did not believe in neutral principles of asylum, or neutral application of a political offense exception to extradition. Like most continental autocrats, he considered asylum a partisan, and not a neutral, policy. Despite the protection he had received in England, he wanted British authorities to punish liberal and socialist exiles who sought to blow him off his throne.

The extradition provision to which Mill objected was part of a series of attempts by Tory governments to appease the emperor, if not with a new alien control bill, then with a law watering down the evidentiary requirements for proving conspiracy to commit murder.[41] Mill did not object to extraditing those charged with trying to assassinate foreign heads of state—he agreed with the objectives of the *attentat* clause, but he was concerned with political prosecutions, and what lax evidentiary requirements in cases alleging conspiracy would do to facilitate them:[42]

> When there has been an actual attempt at political assassination, it is not difficult, in most cases, to distinguish between a false charge and a true one. But it is often uncommonly so in the case of complicity in such an attempt; and these are precisely the cases in which there is most danger of a false charge.... If I may offer, merely by way of illustration, a case fresh in the memory of every member of this House, I will say that Governor Eyre [who brutally suppressed a revolt in Jamaica by killing and torturing hundreds of per-

sons] felt convinced that Mr. Gordon [a black Jamaican] was an instigator of the insurrection . . . , and on that ground Mr. Gordon was put to death, although the evidence has
been pronounced by those who have examined it judicially . . . utterly insufficient to establish this charge. Well, we have heard no end of testimony from both sides of the House
as to what a good man, a clever man, and a blameless man Mr. Eyre was. Well, then, let
Mr. Eyre be all this: it follows, that let a man be as good, and wise, and blameless as it is
possible for a man to be, he may yet make this mistake. . . . The great majority of people
are ready to believe almost anything against their political enemies, especially those who
have said or published things tending to excite disapprobation of their conduct; as witness the case of Mr. Gordon.

Mill's concern here was for what would eventually become the "second limb" of
the Anglo-American political offense exception—the limb that mandates inquiry into
the political motives of the requesting regime.

The Conservative government of 1866, again led by the Earl of Derby, opposed the
idea of any political offense exception at all, even though they had acceded to the
inclusion of one in the 1843 treaty with France. When the debate began in 1852, the
focus had been on fugitives from the socialist revolutions of 1848. By 1866, the British
government was preoccupied with Irish rebels, whom it regarded as mere criminals,
and whose extradition from foreign lands it did not want blocked by applications of
the political offense exception. An express exception was not really needed, Foreign
Secretary Lord Stanley argued (like President Tyler after the Webster-Ashburton
Treaty), because it was already understood (presumably as an executive power). However, Attorney General Hugh Cairns had to admit that the understanding was not
expressed in diplomatic correspondence; it was only inferred by his government from
an apparent lack of requests for political refugees.[43]

Government spokesmen argued that an exception for political offenders should not
be made express because it could not be defined with precision. This was not acceptable to Mill or his Liberal colleagues, who wanted the exception to be administered
by the courts, not politicians. As Mill put it:[44]

There was at the present moment the utmost uncertainty as to the nature of the inquiry
which an English magistrate was bound to make, previous to delivering up any persons
charged with a political offence. . . . By the treaty . . . , the prisoner might be delivered up
on the production of written depositions. But . . . conformable with our practice, it would
be open to the prisoner to produce counter evidence in contradiction of them, which
might show them to be untrustworthy. But now look at the memorandum of the Conference at the Foreign Office. . . . [It says] that when the prisoner was brought before the
magistrate he would be entitled to have the depositions read in his presence; but that he
would not be allowed to controvert the truth of those depositions, or to produce counter
evidence, except as to his identity. Could there be a more flagrant case of contradiction
between theory and practice?

The government's spokesmen admitted no contradiction. In their view, executive
screening would intercept and reject all improper requests for the extradition of political refugees. The government thereby advanced the standard executive position in

most debates over the allocation of power: to demand maximum discretion for themselves, to give personal assurances of benign intentions, and to ignore the possibility that their successors might not be as wise or just as they deemed themselves to be. If French officials were to abuse the extradition agreement, Attorney General Cairns argued, the British government would simply terminate the treaty. If a political refugee were sought, the secretary of state could refuse to pass the request on to a magistrate, or inform the French (or allow a judge to decide) that the offense was not one for which extradition would be granted.[45]

Mill's response was the equally standard Liberal position. He commended "the noble Lord's assurance that he would not deliver up such persons," but added that "they ought to have some more complete security" since "the country was not likely to be always so far favoured" with such leadership.[46] Mill expressed the classic Madisonian argument for checks and balances.

Charles N. Newdegate, a Conservative from Warwickshire, saw quite clearly that the Liberal argument would undermine executive power, and, unlike his party's spokesmen, he addressed that issue candidly. Newdegate was willing to accept a statutory rule against the surrender of political offenders, but he wanted its administration left to the councils of the government. If any violation took place, he argued, that should be a matter for Parliament to consider. Newdegate strongly opposed any measure that would authorize the courts to scrutinize the documents for evidence that the offense was really political. This, he saw, would "require the courts to define political offences" and that, he believed, "was to require them to undertake a duty beyond their competency."[47]

The debate then turned to the question of whether it was possible to write a rule against the surrender of political offenders that was sufficiently specific to be made law. Mill thought it was and favored denying extradition for "any offence committed in the course or in furtherance of any civil war, insurrection, or political movement."[48] Unlike many later supporters of this "incidence test," Mill believed that the political offense exception should encompass not only violent acts committed in the course of an uprising, but criminal solicitations to violence voiced during the earliest stages of an uprising, if the ultimate purpose of those exhortations was to effect changes in the government. The image of Louis Napoleon exhorting the regiment at Boulogne to take up arms on his behalf was still uppermost in his mind.[49] Mill's version of the incidence test encompassed sedition, treason, and criminal solicitation to achieve political change, and it would have exempted persons for statements made, and acts committed, in the earliest, nonviolent, organizing, stockpiling stages of an uprising.

The liberal philosopher did not advocate complete neutrality toward the means employed to achieve revolution abroad. In response to a letter asking him to support amnesty for certain Irish prisoners, Mill expressed the belief that "in rebellion, as in war, . . . a distinction should be made between fair weapons or modes of warfare and foul ones," thus suggesting that he would be amenable to exceptions for war crimes, or for wanton, indiscriminate acts of violence. In refusing to support amnesty for the Irish Fenians who blew a hole in the wall of the Clerkenwell Prison on December 13,

1867, in order to rescue two of their members, Mill may also have rejected indiscriminate violence, because the overcharged explosion had devastated the neighborhood, killing fourteen people and maiming or wounding forty others.[50] Mill did not agree with the French government, which in 1867 refused to extradite two suspects in the Clerkenwell bombing.[51] In addition, he did not support release of those who had participated in Fenian attempts to invade Canada from the United States, perhaps because that military action was not related to "a legitimate insurrection on Irish soil." On the other hand, Mill was willing to support full pardons to "those political prisoners who have shed no blood, or have shed it in the way of what may be called fair or legitimate insurrection on Irish soil."[52]

Sir Francis H. Goldsmid, England's first Jewish barrister and a Liberal member from Reading, proposed a political motives test instead.[53] The first part of his proposed amendment would have barred extradition for any offense that "had for its motive or purpose the promotion or prevention of any political object."[54] The second part would have required all requesting regimes to promise not to prosecute the accused for any offense "other than the offence specified in the requisition." As Goldsmid explained, his rule of specialty was designed to protect political offenders from surrender for ordinary crimes where subsequent political prosecutions were likely.

In contrast to Goldsmid's more radical (and, with its focus on motives, very French) proposal, the Conservative government's ministers preferred the more narrow and formalistic definition of "pure" political crimes. This would give the executive the most discretion to decide who would be accorded protection. But since Goldsmid had proposed the more radical political motives test, the government was driven onto the middle ground already proposed by Mill. Attorney General Cairns therefore sought to define political offenses in terms of attempts to overthrow governments or to alter systems of law, which, he claimed, "had nothing to do with murder." Political offenses, he suggested rather vaguely, were the sort of offenses that "had led to wholesome changes in our Constitution."[55]

At the same time, Cairns spoke out against the political motives test. It was not acceptable, he said, because it would forbid the surrender of criminals who, like those who had plotted the assassination of President Lincoln of the United States, had shocked "humanity and the whole civilized world." In particular, he wished to deny protection to those who sought to assassinate heads of state or to murder police sergeants and informers in Ireland "in cold blood from motives of revenge or a desire to promote the Fenian movement."[56]

The attorney general's arguments were supported by Acton S. Ayrton, a leading Liberal M.P., who pointed out that the political motives test might "appear to give some moral right to murder people for political differences." He "should regret exceedingly if any person who shot him in the lobby were to find a safe haven in France, on the ground that he did not like his speeches in the House."[57]

However, time for the debate ran out before any agreement could be reached. The French treaty was renewed for a year, and the larger questions of extradition policy were delegated to a select committee containing representatives of both parties. As a member of the select committee, Mill questioned whether the rule of double criminality could protect a person charged with the killing of a sentry in the course of an uprising. Since the act would constitute the crime of murder if committed in Great Britain, he reasoned, the rule would not bar surrender of the accused to a foreign regime.

The government responded by proposing that a formal rule against the surrender of political offenders be included in legislation, but that the definition of a political offense be confined to acts in the nature of treason. This definition was much narrower than the one recommended by Mill in 1866. It would cover acts connected with attempts to overthrow governments and insurrections, but it would not cover crimes committed in support of a political movement but prior to a formal uprising, like Louis Napoleon's or those then being committed by the Fenian Movement in Ireland, England, and Canada. More specifically, the government argued, persons should be extradited for the murder of police agents (even where the police had taken political prisoners), or for forging documents to get money to fund an uprising.[58]

In answer to a question from Mill, the chief metropolitan police magistrate was willing to concede that it might be proper to exempt from extradition acts committed with a view toward inciting insurrection.[59] He probably made this concession because incitement itself would be in the nature of treason or sedition. However, neither he nor other government witnesses would shield from extradition those whose alleged crimes were not connected to an organized, planned effort to seize political power.

The Conservative government's definition of a political offense was as romantic in its own way as the Liberals' concept of a political offender. Just as European liberals tended to idealize political refugees as freedom fighters, British Conservatives tried to hold revolutionaries to a gentlemanly style of civil war. Formal forces were favored, with identifiable political and military leaders and politically accountable chains of command. Thus, conservative judges in Upper Canada had no difficulty authorizing the surrender of Bennet G. Burley, a captain in the Confederate Army, who with others, and dressed as civilians, seized the U.S. mail packet *Philo Parsons* off the Ohio shore of Lake Erie and relieved a passenger of his money. Although Burley was able to prove that he was acting as a soldier under orders, with a manifesto from Confederate President Jefferson Davis, the justices held that he could be extradited to Ohio to be tried for robbery. Robbery, they ruled, was contrary to legitimate warfare and not, therefore, a political offense.[60]

By contrast, a more liberal judge in Montreal, Lower Canada, refused to authorize the surrender of Confederate soldiers who, also in civilian clothes, had raided St. Albans, Vermont, shot up the town, tried to burn it, and made off with bank deposits estimated at $208,000.[61] The Webster-Ashburton Treaty did not contain a political offense exception for soldiers in a civil war or rebellion, but Justice Smith had no difficulty reading one into it as an essential background norm:[62]

> The United States themselves, and all civilized countries, make a wide distinction between offences committed during a normal state of things, and those which are incident to political convulsions. . . . Under this distinction, political offenders have always been held to be excluded from any obligation of the country in which they take refuge to deliver them

up, whether such delivery is claimed to be due under friendly relationship, or under treaty, unless in the latter case, the treaty expressly includes them. The case of fugitive slaves appears to me to rest to some extent on the same ground; and on principle, the extradition of a fugitive slave for taking life in defence of his right of personal freedom, would seem to me to be unsustainable, except by a nation recognizing by its laws and within itself the institution of slavery. And deserters have been usually treated as belonging to the same category. Political offenders, however, form the most conspicuous instances of exclusion from the operation of the extradition law. No nation of any recognized position has been found base enough to surrender, under any circumstances, political offenders, who have taken refuge within her territories—or if there be instances, they are few in number, and are recorded as precedents to be reprobated rather than followed.

The St. Albans raid, like the seizure of the steamboat *Philo Parsons*, was a hit-and-run operation—guerrilla warfare behind enemy lines and targeted against civilians, not soldiers. Its primary purpose, beyond terrorizing Northern citizens, was to rob banks to finance the rebel cause. In Lower Canada, however, that made no difference, as the court and counsel recognized that the American Civil War was being fought, on both sides, with a variety of regular and irregular tactics. In any case, the court assumed that neutral countries should not try to second guess the war-fighting tactics of belligerents.[63]

In England, however, hit-and-run attacks on the police, like those practiced by the Fenians in Ireland and England, were viewed as unworthy of protection. This attitude may be attributed to the natural reluctance of any regime to concede legitimacy to the violent opponents of their own rule, but the Conservatives justified their position on the principle that attacks on policemen, rather than armed forces, are subversive of social order. When a member of the select committee drafted a report suggesting that acts preparatory to an insurrection should be protected so long as they did not violate the rules of legitimate warfare, the committee balked.[64]

The draft report of the select committee also considered several exceptions to political offender protection for heinous crimes, drawn by analogy to the laws of war. "As it is not lawful in war to kill peaceful citizens," the committee observed, so "the killing by rebels of those not engaged in the work of repression, or not challenged to defend themselves by open attack, whether they be ministers of state or officers of justice, or ordinary citizens, should be subject in all countries, and as between one country and another, to the consequences of murder."[65]

Ultimately, the select committee could not agree on a statutory definition of what should constitute a nonextraditable political offense, so that task was left to future generations. The committee merely proposed that the political offense exception be denied to persons charged with assassinating a reigning sovereign or members of his family.[66] This provision, known as the *attentat* clause, was taken from the treaty between France and Belgium and was the first of many exceptions to the political offense exception. But the clause was not adopted in the United Kingdom's 1870 Act because attacks on a reigning sovereign were regarded by British law as treason, the quintessential political offense.

Like the select committee, the Liberals who drafted the 1870 statute made no effort at defining what would constitute a political offense. However, their bill did assign the task of definition to the courts as well as to the executive.[67] Section 3(l) provided:

> A fugitive criminal shall not be surrendered if the offence in respect of which his surrender is demanded is one of a political character, or if he prove to the satisfaction of the police magistrate or the Court before whom he is brought on habeas corpus, or to the Secretary of State, that the requisition for his surrender has in fact been made with a view to try or punish him for an offence of a political character.

Section 9 made it clear that the magistrate would receive any evidence tended to show that the offense was of a political character, while sections 7 and 2 authorized the British secretary of state to refuse to refer requests for arrest to a magistrate if he believed that the offense charged was of a political character. Thus, both judicial definition and executive screening were expected.

Most importantly, the law had two limbs. The first limb referred to offenses of a political character and eventually evolved into a prohibition against surrender for offenses relating to or furthering a political uprising. The second limb sought to bar extradition where the request was contaminated by partisan political motives. By a plain reading of the statute, which (with minor variations) was incorporated into numerous British and American extradition treaties, the courts and the executive were to enforce both provisions.

When the law was finally passed by Gladstone's government, John Stuart Mill was no longer a member of Parliament, but he took great pleasure in its passage. Or more precisely, he took pleasure in the defeat of the Conservative government's 1866 proposal because it saved political offenders from being "dealt with by the criminal courts of the government against which they had rebelled, thus making the British government an accomplice in the vengeance of foreign despotisms. . . . The cause of European freedom [was] thus . . . saved a serious misfortune, and our country from a great iniquity."[68] Following enactment of this statute, the United Kingdom proposed renegotiation of the 1842 treaty with the United States. However, the conservative U.S. secretary of state, Hamilton Fish, objected strenuously to the idea that judges—and inferior judges at that—should define what constitutes a nonextraditable political offense. In Fish's view, that task of definition should be transferred to the executive branch because of its superior wisdom in such matters, and because entrusting the task to the courts could produce contradictory definitions.[69]

Fish's pro-executive opinion was clearly a regression from the whig libertarianism of earlier decades, when memories of the unhappy case of Jonathan Robbins were still fresh. Extensive negotiations were conducted, but British Liberals stood firm, and the U.S. government was held to the traditional American policy of judicial primacy. When the extradition agreement with the United Kingdom was finally renegotiated in 1889, the historic role of the judiciary in defining what constitutes a political offense was left undisturbed.[70]

The 1870 Act also provided that all British extradition agreements contain a rule of specialty obliging requesting regimes to limit prosecution of the surrendered person to the "extradition crime proved by the facts on which the surrender is grounded."[71] But when the British tried to invoke this principle with the United States, Secretary of State Fish again objected. Since the Webster-Ashburton Treaty had contained no such principle, he argued, it could not be made binding on the United States except by a new treaty. Until that time, he insisted, the United States could prosecute surrendered persons for other crimes in addition to the one for which surrender had been made.

The British solicitor general insisted that the principle of specialty was implicit in the 1842 treaty because it was meant to prescribe a limited number of exceptions to a general principle of asylum, but the American secretary would not agree. He wanted the principle to be explicit and political—as a justification for diplomatic protest and not as an individual right that courts could make into a binding condition on extradition. His view was consistent with the theory that only nations, not individuals, have rights under international law, and it would gain powerful support in succeeding years.

In 1886, the U.S. Supreme Court agreed with Fish that only nations have rights under customary international law, but ruled that U.S. treaties could confer judicially enforceable rights on individuals.[72] In *United States v. Rauscher,* the Court agreed with the British government that the principle of specialty was implicit in the Webster-Ashburton Treaty's short list of extraditable offenses, and held that courts could enforce (via habeas corpus) that principle against the State of New York, which was attempting to try Rauscher for a different offense than the one for which the British government had extradited him.[73]

Even so, the diplomats got their way. In renegotiating the Webster-Ashburton Treaty in 1889, they included a provision expressly barring trial on charges for which the accused had not been extradited. However, the prohibition could only be invoked by governments, and not by the individual on whom the injustice would be visited.[74] Despite this end-run on *Rauscher,* the broader principle of that case still stands: Defendants who have been extradited to the United States may invoke the principle of specialty, provided that the applicable treaty does not expressly strip the courts of jurisdiction to hear them.[75] Of course, nothing would prevent future courts from holding that the Constitution's guarantee of due process requires, as a matter of *in personam* jurisdiction, that trial of an extradited person in the United States be limited to the charges for which he was surrendered.

* * *

The first and most important decision interpreting the British Extradition Act arose in 1890 when Switzerland asked the United Kingdom to return Angelo Castioni for the murder of Luigi Rossi. Castioni had led an armed uprising in the canton of Ticino; it was alleged that Rossi, a member of the canton's government, had been shot to death by Castioni during an attack on the municipal palace. Some saw the revolt as a mere "commotion," but the attack was more than a riot. The attackers succeeded in establishing a provisional government. Thus, Castioni could be seen as one of a long line of revolutionaries for whom the defense had been written. The demand was rejected by the Queen's Bench.[76]

Had the court left the matter there, the *Castioni* decision would have been unexceptional, but the judges used the occasion to narrow the uprising test. Counsel for the defense had urged the court to define as nonextraditable "any offence committed in the course of a furthering of civil war, insurrection or political commotion."[77] This formulation was broader than anything Mill had supported. His version would have applied the uprising test to violence involving "political movements," but offered no protection to fugitives from less organized, less focused, more spontaneous "political commotions." Read literally, the term "commotions" would have permitted rioters of almost every stripe to escape extradition.

The court seized on this point to justify a much narrower uprising test. The judges were not about to protect people who happened to commit ordinary crimes for personal reasons in the course of, but not in the furtherance of, a struggle for control of the government. Their rejection of a "commotions" test made it appear, quite erroneously, as if Mill had advocated a patently overbroad test.[78] Rather, Mill had argued for a need to protect revolutionaries before they are able to organize themselves into military or paramilitary units or win international recognition as belligerents in a civil war. The time to begin protecting foreign political activists from extradition, he believed, was when they had become part of a discernable political movement with distinctive ideas and programs. Mill used the term "movements," rather than "parties" or "organizations," indicating that he understood that most repressive regimes do not wait for their opponents to create well-developed organizations. Politically motivated prosecutions begin when critical ideas are first expressed by individuals who attract a following, and continue in a manner calculated to deter new dissidents from joining established opposition groups.

But the Queen's Bench was no more interested in Mill's "movement" test than it was in Castioni's "commotion" standard. It preferred a test that placed even greater stress on organization and popularity, and therefore looked for acts that furthered an insurrection or rebellion. As Judge George Denman stated:[79]

> In order to bring the case within the words of the Act ... it must at least be shewn that the act is done in furtherance of, done with the intention of assistance, as a sort of overt act in the course of acting in a political matter, a political rising, or a dispute between two parties in the State as to which is to have the government in its hands.

It has been suggested that the source of this formulation was Justice James F. Stephen,[80] a legal scholar who, before joining the court, had been a member of the Royal Commission of 1878 that reviewed the 1870 statute. In a treatise published in 1883, Stephen had interpreted the law to mean that "fugitive criminals are not to be surrendered for extradition crimes if those crimes were incidental to and formed a part of political disturbances."[81]

In fact, the court chose a formula even narrower than Stephen's "political disturbances" test—an "uprising test" made easy by the facts in *Castioni*. The court's formulation was not as narrow as the treason test advocated by the Conservative government in 1866; nor was it necessarily confined to civil wars and full-fledged insurrections, or to the final acts inciting insurrections. But in choosing to stress political uprisings, the court denied protection to rioters and to hit-and-run killers in the Fenian tradition. They were classified as mere criminals. To reap the benefits of political offender status, the court effectively said, incipient revolutionaries must organize themselves into disciplined military or paramilitary organizations in the tradition of the American Confederacy or Louis Napoleon's invasion force. Mere participation in a political movement whose informal supporters use selective violence to force limited changes will not entitle them to protection. Nor will they be safe from extradition if the movement they support is not ready to risk everything in an all-out effort to overthrow the established regime.

In choosing this narrow definition of the uprising test over Mill's broader "movement" version, the court ignored the "second limb" of the definition set forth in the Act of 1870—the part that forbids surrender when the requisition "has in fact been made with a view to try or punish him for an offence of a political character."[82] That clause, if read with a skeptical eye toward the capacity of foreign partisans to apply the law fairly to their political challengers, could have become a second, more liberal shield for participants in violent political movements that had not yet gained the status of uprisings. But since no such reading was necessary to protect Castioni, that clause remained unexplicated by the court.

However, the clause had not gone unexamined by the executive. As early as 1878, a Royal Commission on Extradition had foreseen the possibility that "cases ... may occur in which it would be undesirable to surrender a person accused of a crime instigated by a political motive, even though a magistrate or judge could not pronounce that there existed either civil war or open insurrection, and consequently could not discharge the accused as of right. To meet this possibility, a discretionary power in favor of the prisoner should be reserved to the government, to refuse to deliver up a prisoner so accused."[83] The 1870 Act made it clear that both the courts and the executive could deny surrender in situations not involving uprisings, where the request has been made "with a view to try or punish him for an offence of a political character," but the commission recommended that this power be exercised by the executive only. In both the United Kingdom and the United States, that recommendation would, in due course, become law. Thus, while the 1870 statute was a triumph for judicial primacy in extradition, that primacy ultimately came to be limited to applications of the *Castioni* uprising test. In nonuprising situations, where partisan motives infected the request, the executive came to dominate, with predictably adverse results for both liberty and justice.

CHAPTER 7

Judicial Primacy

There is no liberty, if the power of judging is not separated from the legislative and the executive powers.

Alexander Hamilton

Most of the extradition treaties negotiated by the United States in the nineteenth century followed Daniel Webster's lead in acknowledging that extraditability was a matter for the judiciary to decide. Where the judicial role was not expressly provided for in the treaty, as it was not with the first extradition treaties with the United Kingdom and France, it was assumed by both the executive and the courts.[1] Extradition by executive directive was not to be allowed; Jonathan Robbins was not forgotten.

In 1847, however, the legality of entrusting such decisions to the courts without an express grant of jurisdiction was challenged by Nicholas Lucien Metzger, whose extradition was sought by France on a charge of forgery.[2] The French government began the case by making an application on its own behalf in a New York court. It was assisted, at Secretary of State James Buchanan's request, by Benjamin F. Butler, the U.S. attorney for the Southern District of New York (and himself a former U.S. attorney general). The state court ordered Metzger's arrest.

Metzger challenged his arrest on jurisdictional grounds. Because the treaty with France did not expressly grant jurisdiction over extradition to any court, he argued, the court had no alternative but to release him. The French minister reported this argument to the U.S. secretary of state, who instructed Butler to inform the state court judge that judicial determinations of extraditability had been intended by the treaty's American negotiators. But the judge accepted Metzger's argument, so the French government asked President James K. Polk to order Metzger's arrest and treat extradition as a matter of executive discretion.

Secretary of State James Buchanan refused the request. Extraditability, the future president insisted, was a matter for a court to decide, and he suggested that an application be made to one of the federal judges in New York.[3] Metzger was subsequently arrested on a federal warrant and brought before Judge Samuel R. Betts, where he again contended that the court could not act in the absence of express authorization by treaty or legislation. Judge Betts disagreed. He held that treaties were self-executing and that courts had inherent jurisdiction to enforce treaties without implementing legislation.[4]

There was precedent for this view, but Betts might just as well have rejected the idea that treaties are self-executing on the ground that law affecting liberty should be made by the entire Congress, acting through its two judiciary committees, and not by the president and the Senate alone, acting perhaps with the aid of the Senate Committee on Foreign Relations. But this was an idea whose time still has not come.

Metzger then petitioned the Supreme Court of the United States for a writ of habeas corpus directing his release. Speaking through Justice John McLean, the Court decided that it could not issue the writ to review the decision of a judge given in chambers.[5] The Supreme Court did not consider whether extradition treaties should be self-executing. It was more interested in whether the courts had jurisdiction in the absence of express authorization by treaty or statute. The first article of the treaty with France provided that requisitions for extradition be made through diplomatic channels; the third declared that "on the part of the government of the United States, the surrender shall be made only by the authority of the executive thereof."[6] Together these provisions could have been read as providing that extradition of fugitives to France was a strictly executive matter. That, indeed, was the policy in France.

However, there was no political support for such an interpretation in the United States. The shadow of Jonathan Robbins eclipsed that possibility completely. The State Department had made it clear that extradition was a matter for the judiciary, and the Supreme Court endorsed this policy as "proper" and "the most appropriate, if not the only, mode of giving effect to the treaty."[7]

Why it was appropriate for the courts to exercise this authority, without express permission from Congress or a treaty, was not explained, but Webster's whig principles seem to have prevailed. Simply put, the deprivation of liberty is not a power to be entrusted to the executive.[8] To accept the idea that the executive could arrest a person without judicial authority and then surrender him without a judicial determination, rendered according to law, would negate a basic function of an independent judiciary and a basic check on arbitrary power.

To acknowledge such a power would also mean, in effect, that the president and two-thirds of the Senate could, merely by concluding a treaty, suspend the privilege of the writ of habeas corpus. The power to suspend the privilege of that writ is granted by Article 1, Section 9, of the Constitution to the entire Congress, but it is confined to moments of rebellion or invasion, and then only when the public safety requires it. As the Supreme Court ruled in 1865 in the famous Civil War case of *Ex parte McCardle*, the power to suspend that privilege is an emergency wartime power. It does not extend to prosecuting emergency detainees in executive tribunals and, one may reason by extension, to extraditing them for reasons of state.[9] In short, suspension of the privilege is not something that the executive may do, even with the approval of two-thirds of the Senate (or a unanimous Congress), to satisfy the demands of foreign governments.

Even John Marshall would not have supported Metzger's argument that extradition was, under the treaty with France, an exclusively executive process. Marshall would have allowed the request to go through the State Department, with the arrest being made on the authority of the executive. But were the executive to decide that the accused was extraditable, Marshall argued, it would have to allow the accused to seek judicial review by requesting a writ of habeas corpus.[10] Unless the accused consents to extradition, uniform legal standards, administered by courts, must prevail.

* * *

The effect of Metzger's claim was to force not only the executive but Congress to entrust questions of extraditability to the courts. In 1848, Congress, with the support of President Polk, passed the first and only extradition law in American history.[11] It attempted to do what both John Marshall and Philip Nicholas had tried in 1800: to set forth the procedures that would govern all extradition cases. But unlike Marshall's proposal, the 1848 statute rejected an executive-dominated process for a judicially centered one, very much in the spirit of Webster's treaty with Ashburton. In particular, nothing in the statute required that requests for extradition be routed first through the president or secretary of state. Foreign governments could take their requests directly to whatever federal or state court had authority to order the arrest of the person sought. Philip Nicholas's proposal was also rejected. The new statute did not bar extradition in cases that might also be tried in American courts.

If the court were to decide that the accused was extraditable, the new law provided, it was to "certify the same, together with a copy of the testimony taken before him, to the Secretary of State, that a warrant may issue upon the requisition of the proper authorities of such foreign government, for the surrender of such person, according to the stipulations of the treaty or convention." While arguably ambiguous, this language did not say that the executive would have the power to decide, either before or after court action, that the accused ought not to be surrendered.[12]

When the bill was presented to the House of Representatives, it was characterized as nothing more than a measure to implement the treaties with England and France.[13] In the Senate, the bill was challenged on due process grounds but saved from amendment by assurances that it would not allow for the surrender of political offenders.[14] It became law on August 12, 1848, and has survived virtually unchanged as the basic extradition statute of the United States.[15]

It has been argued that the 1848 statute was meant to give courts authority to decide whether there is probable cause to believe that the accused committed an extraditable offense, but not to shield him as a political offender, because that power is nowhere mentioned in the statute.[16] However, nothing in the legislative debates suggests that this was the intent of Congress, any more than it was the intent of American negotiators to impose executive extradition on the United States.

To say that the framers of the 1848 statute intended to limit judges to probable cause determinations is to misread the whig spirit of the age. Tory faith in executive discretion and tory blindness to executive and foreign abuses would come later, but in 1848 they had nothing to do with the making of American extradition law and policy. Metzger's attempt to escape extradition through a tory reading of the French treaty was rejected by all three branches of the federal government and by both sides of the debate over the Webster–Ashburton Treaty. His sterile literalism—seeking to enhance executive power without reference to the whiggish values of those who made the treaty—was overwhelmingly rejected by politicians and judges.

* * *

Metzger was not the only defendant to challenge the jurisdiction of the courts. In 1852, Thomas Kaine claimed that extradition was a national act involving foreign relations; therefore, court proceedings had to be initiated by the chief executive of the United States or not at all.

Kaine, like Metzger, was not a political fugitive. He was an Irish farmer wanted by the British for attempting to murder another farmer in Westmeath, Ireland. The incident arose out of a dispute over who had the right to till a particular plot of land, a life-and-death issue in potato-famine Ireland. When the U.S. commissioner granted the British consul's request for Kaine's arrest, Kaine immediately asked federal Judge Samuel R. Betts to release him under a writ of habeas corpus, claiming, in effect, that all foreign requests had to be routed through the president and approved by him or his delegate. According to Kaine, the request for a fugitive's arrest had to be made by the U.S. executive, not by a foreign executive.[17]

This was not what Congress had specified when it passed the 1848 statute. That statute said that the foreign government did not have to seek prior permission from the federal executive but, on the contrary, could go directly into court and initiate extradition proceedings.[18] Congress did not even require that the federal executive be informed of the request as a matter of courtesy.

Kaine's argument did not persuade Judge Betts, who ruled that the executive could still refuse to surrender a fugitive whom a court found extraditable. That was a legitimate exercise of "a political power"—the power to grant asylum. But nothing in the law required that the president approve, in advance, the initiation of a judicial hearing to determine whether the accused was extraditable.[19] That might be practical, because the executive could have the fugitive arrested, but arrests are not always necessary to establish a court's jurisdiction.

Failing with Judge Betts, Kaine's attorneys tracked Supreme Court Justice Samuel Nelson to his vacation home in Cooperstown, New York, and presented him with a second request for release pursuant to a writ of habeas corpus. Nelson thought that the issue was important enough to refer to the entire Supreme Court, which then consisted of eight justices because of the death of John McKinley.[20] At the same time, Kaine's attorneys also asked the Supreme Court to review the case on appeal (certiorari) and in response to yet another habeas petition for release.

For procedural reasons unnecessary to recount here, the justices chose not to accept the case for decision under any of the three procedures. Even so, most had a great deal to say about the question of executive screening of extradition requests, even though all of it was dicta.

Four justices, led by John Catron, were disposed to uphold the constitutionality of the statute.[21] They agreed that extradition was a national power, but they did not make the common mistake of equating the nation with the executive. Rather, the justices confirmed Congress's authority to specify by legislation how that power was to be exercised.[22]

Kaine probably hoped that executive screening would help people like himself, by bringing ethnic-group pressures to bear on the State Department screeners early in the process, but the four justices read his argument—as Judge Betts had—as an effort to subordinate the courts to executive power. This was intolerable, they said, and precisely what John Adams had done when he "ordered" Judge Bee to surrender Jonathan Robbins.[23]

A fifth justice, Benjamin R. Curtis, also agreed that the lower courts had jurisdiction to hear extradition requests initiated by foreign regimes without prior executive screening, but he did not believe that the Supreme Court had authority to review this case by any of the three procedures.[24] Thus, while a majority of the justices voted to uphold the constitutionality of the Act of 1848, which gave the courts this power, they established no legal precedent in Kaine's case.

Justices Samuel Nelson, Roger Taney, and Peter V. Daniel dissented. They agreed that the case was properly before the Court on Kaine's petition for a writ of habeas corpus, and that the U.S. commissioner could not hear the extradition request "except as authorized by treaty stipulations, and Acts of Congress passed in pursuance thereof." Nothing in the language of the U.K. treaty, Nelson argued, specifically allowed the British consul to make his demands upon the United States by going directly into one of its courts. Under "our system of government," he reasoned, "a demand upon the nation must be made upon the President, who has charge of all foreign relations, and with whom only foreign governments are authorized, or even permitted, to hold any communication of a national concern."[25] The president, he argued, quoting from Marshall's argument in the Robbins debate, is "the sole organ of the nation, in its external relations, and its sole representative with foreign nations. Of consequence, the demand of a foreign nation can only be made on him."[26]

Although this argument sounded like an effort to revive Marshall's executive-centered approach to extradition, it was not. Both the plurality of four and the minority of three were concerned about undue political pressure on extradition magistrates. The plurality, recalling the case of Jonathan Robbins, was concerned about undue presidential influence at the beginning of a case and spoke out forcefully on behalf of an independent judiciary as essential to civil liberty. The minority worried that without centralized screening of applications, weak cases might be put before obscure judges and commissioners, who might then succumb to pressures from either the foreign nation or an ethnic mob. In Kaine's case, mob pressure had been so fierce that at one point the U.S. marshal did not dare bring Kaine into court for fear he would be freed by a mob.[27] Another mob later tried to prevent Kaine's delivery to British authorities.[28]

Thus, seven of the eight justices agreed on the need to protect the existing, judicially centered process from outside pressure. Their dispute was over how best to achieve that end. The plurality trusted the independence of the courts and feared executive interference with them. The minority feared the malleability of "humble magistrates" and sought to prevent extradition from becoming a routine, low-level, bureaucratic practice by providing for high-level screening.[29] In short, the argument within the Court was essentially a policy dispute, which may be why the justices chose to deliver their views in so much dicta.

When Justice Nelson recovered the case as a circuit judge, he stuck to his minority opinion and ordered Kaine's release for lack of a proper requisition to the president and authorization from him to the court, a concomitant lack of jurisdiction in the magistrate, and lack of competent evidence as to the authority of the British magistrate who authorized Kaine's arrest.[30] "The case immediately before me may be one of comparative unimportance," Nelson wrote, "as the fugitive demanded is an obscure and humble individual. . . . But I cannot forget that the principles and rule of construction to be applied to him will be equally applicable to the case of a demand for the surrender of a political offender, and to all other cases falling within [the statute's] provisions." Then he said,[31]

> a political question . . . must be decided by the political, and not by the judicial, powers of the government. It is a general principle, as it respects political questions concerning foreign governments, that the judiciary follows the determination of the political power which has charge of its foreign relations, and is, therefore, presumed to best understand what is fit and proper for the interest and honor of the country.

Overstating his point still further, Nelson declared that the political dimensions of extradition requests are "questions unfit for the arbitrariment of the judiciary."[32] This statement would later be cited by the Reagan administration to support its unsuccessful effort to persuade the federal courts to foreswear jurisdiction to grant the political exception.[33] But the citation was not appropriate. In the very next paragraph, Justice Nelson made it clear that he was not advocating court-stripping. All he really wanted was for extradition requests to be referred to the executive "in the first instance," so that improper demands, corrupted by politics, could be recognized and denied.[34]

Political persecution was only one of Nelson's concerns. He was also concerned with potential denials of due process. Concern for due process, he wrote, recalling Jefferson's letter to Genêt, was central to the kind of extradition treaties the United States had negotiated:[35] "An enlightened nation, with a criminal code ameliorated by the advance of civilization, would not enter into a treaty with a barbarous one, whose code is bloody and cruel. And, even among enlightened nations, the stipulations for surrender are cautiously limited to a few specified crimes, of atrocious character, against persons and property."

Nelson was particularly concerned with the threat to liberty posed by lax procedures, insufficient evidence, and insufficient proof of the authority of foreign magistrates to certify the evidence. In his opinion, the proof, in all cases under a treaty of extradition, should be, not only competent, but full and satisfactory, that the offence has been committed by the fugitive in the foreign jurisdiction—sufficiently so to warrant a conviction, in the judgment of the magistrate, of the offense with which he is charged, if sitting upon the final trial and hearing the case. No magistrate should order a surrender short of such proof.

In short, Justice Nelson wanted to enhance civil liberties, not limit them, by keeping extradition an extraordinary procedure, limited to the most serious crimes where strict adherence to legal standards and a very high standard of proof would be more likely because of the unusual, rather than routine, nature of the requests. The routinization of extradition, he foresaw, posed a serious threat to the liberty of political fugitives. His confidence in executive screening was probably enhanced by knowledge that both the U.S. secretary of state, William L. Marcy, and the British prime minister, Lord Palmerston, had been especially vigilant against the political use of extradition by Austria.[36]

Nelson's concerns encouraged Attorney General Caleb Cushing to give foreign regimes the option of initiating their requests through the president, so that some screening would occur. The change, Cushing informed Secretary of State Marcy, would not allow the president to control the magistrate's decision; it would simply meet the concerns of a minority of the Supreme Court.[37]

As the politics of extradition changed, executive screening would do more than that, but what is most interesting about this particular legal opinion—particularly because it is evidence of "founders' intent"—is the attorney general's insistence that "in the execution of this treaty, as of other treaties of the same class, the arrest, examination, and decision of fact, are judicial functions and acts. They are not, and they cannot be, performed by the President."[38] According to Cushing, this was not just a requirement of treaty law; it is a constitutional requirement.[39]

> The two governments have by treaty agreed to make the question [of extradition] a judicial one; and they could not do otherwise; for the Government of the United Kingdom is a constitutional one, as well as that of the United States; and in both countries the writ of *habeas corpus* presents itself as a safeguard, in the hands of the judges, of individual freedom against all possible encroachments on the part of the executive.

Thus, all talk of extradition as a nonjusticiable political question was repudiated by the Pierce administration, as it had been by the Supreme Court in 1795 in the case of Captain Barré.

* * *

From 1848 until the 1970s, government lawyers and diplomats accepted the principle of judicial primacy in extradition decisions. The only exception took place in 1864, when Secretary of State Seward, who was then asserting war powers to incarcerate thousands of people without trial, took it upon himself to surrender a Spanish slave trader named Don Jose Augustin Arguelles to Cuba. Arguelles was the lieutenant-governor of a district in Cuba where a cargo of African slaves was supposed to have been freed on the order of higher authorities. Arguelles falsely reported that 141 of the slaves had died of smallpox; in fact, he had sold them and fled to New York. Spanish authorities in Cuba asked the Lincoln administration to surrender Arguelles, even though no extradition treaty existed between the two countries at the time. Secretary of State Seward, with President Lincoln's approval, ordered Arguelles surrendered as a purely executive act.[40] A storm of protest followed Arguelles's surrender, with Seward justifying his act on the grounds that "a nation is never bound to furnish asylum to dangerous criminals who are offenders against the human race."[41] A congressional resolution condemning the surrender as unconstitutional was defeated. Instead, the matter was referred to a committee, where it died unresolved.[42]

Seward's action would seem to establish an historical precedent in favor of Chancellor Kent's (see Chapter 5) view that international law permits (but does not require) extradition in the absence of a treaty.[43] But Seward went beyond Kent (and Marshall) by refusing to concede that the alleged slave trader had a right to judicial review of the legality of his detention through a petition for a writ of habeas corpus.[44]

Given the Lincoln administration's contempt for civil liberties, Seward's arbitrary approach to extradition is hardly surprising. Perhaps the best that can be said in the secretary's defense is that the surrender of Arguelles was somehow necessary to the successful prosecution of the war, but even that argument would have been rejected by the Court that decided *Ex parte McCardle*.[45]

In any case, the power that Seward asserted was repudiated in 1873 by Acting Secretary of State Bancroft Davis.[46] No administration since has adopted the theory of inherent executive power advanced by Seward.

* * *

The mid-nineteenth century can be called the whig era in the American law of extradition. The period was characterized by congressional limitations on executive discretion, belief in the primacy of the judiciary over matters of individual liberty, and concern for protecting foreign revolutionaries against the autocrats they attacked. Extradition was accepted in principle but was to be used sparingly, without any presumption that requests from regimes with which the United States had treaties were, for that reason alone, entitled to the benefit of any doubts.

Similarly, it was recognized that courts (and the executive) should not presume that requests for extradition would never be corrupted by wrongful motives. As the leading U.S. treatise on international law put it in 1866:[47]

> Nations bound by treaties of extradition must still have the right to protect themselves against being defrauded of their right to give asylum. If, for instance, a political refugee, an escaped slave, or a deserter from military service, has asylum by the practice of nations, it will look behind the mere formal proofs of a crime committed by such a person, to see that the real object is not to get possession of him for a purpose to which the treaty does not apply.

But it would be a mistake to assume full consistency in the government's practices. The most striking failure to specify a political offense exception occurred in 1856, when the Pierce administration concluded a treaty of commerce and navigation with the Kingdom of the Two Sicilies. Although the kingdom had a notoriously reactionary government and a corrupt legal system, extradition was authorized. The surrender of political offenders was forbidden, "unless the political offender shall also have been guilty of some one of the crimes enumerated in article 22."[48] Because one of these enumerated crimes was murder, the exemption largely destroyed the political offense exception. More treaties with reactionary regimes were to follow, but no one was to attack the political offense exception again in this manner until 1981.[49]

The concern for due process and fundamental fairness that had characterized Thomas Jefferson's approach to extradition reached its high point during the 1840s and 1850s, when the modern law of extradition was just getting started. A British court allowed slaves who had killed their masters while escaping to plead self-defense. An American court admitted alibi evidence. Justice Nelson of the Supreme Court even applied a "beyond reasonable doubt" standard of proof in Kaine's case, instead of the much lower probable cause standard required in domestic indictments.

But this liberalism began to decline after the Civil War. Broad evidentiary hearings gave way to narrower examinations by magistrates and narrower reviews under habeas corpus. As American jurisprudence left its faith in natural law behind and embraced the positivism of John Austin and the formalism of Christopher Langdell, certain "rules of noninquiry" would develop to blind U.S. judges to foreign injustice. Before that happened, however, there was the difficult task of defining an "offense of a political character."

CHAPTER 8

The Uprising Test and Illiberal Revolts

> *During [the] progress [of the revolutions] crimes may have been com-*
> *mitted by the contending forces of the most atrocious and inhuman*
> *kind, and still the perpetrators of such crimes escape punishment as*
> *fugitives beyond the reach of extradition. I have no authority, in this*
> *examination, to determine what acts are within the rules of civilized*
> *warfare, and what are not.*
>
> Judge William W. Morrow, In re Ezeta, 1894

In exempting political offenders from extradition by application of the uprising test, nineteenth-century liberals looked back with admiration to Washington, Bolivar, Mazzini, and Kossuth. They could extend respect for the ambitions of Louis Napoleon and the soldiers of the Confederate States of America. They thought in terms of popular revolutions, political movements, or spontaneous "commotions" challenging autocratic government, and on occasion they could stretch these concepts to protect people whose offenses had little to do with uprisings.

But liberals were hardly ready for a new age of rebellion from the left and the right—uprisings of isolated cabals of nihilists, anarchists, and socialists, and coup attempts by corrupt caudillos (military dictators) or roaming bands of brigands. It had been politically easy for the United States and the United Kingdom, the Low Countries, and France not to surrender failed liberals or failed monarchists; it was much more difficult to shelter failed assassins, dictators, or robbers. The former made respectable citizens; the latter were not so easily trusted. As political violence moved away from disciplined military and paramilitary revolts and toward random acts of indiscriminate killing, the political offense exception became harder to justify, except as an expression of the political neutrality of a country that still was not ready to accept sustained international responsibilities.

* * *

The anarchist movement of the late nineteenth and early twentieth centuries administered the *coup de grâce* to most romantic notions about the supposedly innate nobility of revolutionaries. Liberal faith in revolutionaries had been undermined by the socialist revolutionaries of 1848, who had advocated class warfare and violent redistributions of wealth. Liberal support for revolutionaries was further eroded by the indiscriminate violence of the Irish Fenians, whose bombings showed an appalling indifference to the lives of innocent bystanders and callous disregard for the presumed rules of "civilized" warfare. The old revolutions had occurred in largely agrarian societies; the new revolts occurred more often in cities, where the risk to bystanders was higher and the disruption of society greater. Liberal romanticism suffered a severe blow when the socialists of the Paris Commune of 1870 brutally assaulted bourgeois liberals. But the crimes of anarchists were the most disturbing of all to the rising middle class, precisely because they seemed so pointless, terroristic, and cowardly.

In societies dominated by the practical ethos of industry and commerce, the killing of politicians or bystanders merely to express an opinion was pointless. The new middle class could respect revolutionaries who organized others to fight for political change in some foreign land.[1] They could understand nationalistic aspirations, too, and accept violence organized to shake off foreign domination. Liberal businessmen of the *la belle époque* often sympathized with middle-class revolts against corrupt aristocracies in the Germanies, Russia, Austria, Italy, and Spain, but they were horrified when working-class anarchists and communists defined the entire middle class, including women and children, as the source of all oppression. To nineteenth-century, laissez-faire liberals, the Industrial Revolution and the middle class that led it promised economic opportunity for all and a degree of political stability unprecedented in history.

The anarchists threatened all this by attacking the very idea of structure, order, and authority. Liberals—and especially American whigs—knew that all concentrations of power were prone to corruption and oppression, but they were equally convinced that some government, indeed, almost any government, was preferable to none. Thus, liberals saw anarchists as potentially more dangerous than reactionary kings and dictators, precisely because anarchists would destroy all government and leave nothing but chaos in their wake.

To liberals of the late eighteenth and early nineteenth centuries, revolutionaries were men of principle and restraint who organized armies of national liberation that were no more savage than their adversaries. In victory, they were expected to be magnanimous; in defeat, honorable. Their killing was supposed to focus on enemy soldiers in military or paramilitary engagements. Liberal revolutionaries sought practical military advantage but did not assassinate kings or politicians in futile gestures. Nor did they terrorize civilian populations with hit-and-run bombings and murders. They were soldiers with republican virtue who fought for democratic reform and were thus worthy of respect.

Anarchists, by contrast, were generally viewed as cowards. They stabbed elected politicians in the street, bombed cafés and barracks, and ran off into the night. Unlike liberal revolutionaries, they specialized in killing defenseless people. Nor did they evince manly concern for the women and children who might be harmed by their dynamite. Indeed, killing strangers without pity was what anarchists did best. Anarchists also killed innocent people out of revenge for the arrest of comrades, thus proving, in an age of sportsmanship, that they were persons without honor.[2]

Indeed, at the very moment when nineteenth-century opinions about morality and character were being challenged by early notions about psychology and genetics, anarchists were denounced as moral degenerates, psychological freaks, and genetically predisposed to be criminals.[3] Most acted alone or had only the most tenuous ties to other anarchists, therefore reinforcing "scientific" claims that they were too "abnormal" to be "political" in any respectable sense.

Like communists (and some Fenians), the anarchists alienated liberal nations of asylum by carrying their violence across borders. Liberal revolutionaries had fought for national self-determination largely within their own borders, which made them relatively easy for foreign liberals (or conservatives) to accept. Anarchists, on the other hand, exported their violence from one country to another in tiny cabals without popular support. Their politics drew no distinctions between monarchies, dictatorships, republics, or democracies. In their pitiless way, the anarchists opposed all systems of power and proclaimed their contempt for all governments.

Theodule Meunier was one of them, wanted by the French government for bombing a barracks at Lobau on March 15, 1892, and the Café Véry in Paris on April 25. Two people were killed at the restaurant and many others injured in what appears to have been an act of revenge for a waiter's role in bringing about the arrest at the café of the infamous French anarchist Ravachol. The waiter escaped, but the café's owner was blown to bits, giving new meaning, some anarchists said, to the word "verification."[4]

The police immediately suspected Meunier, but he gave them the slip and took refuge in London. Two years later he was arrested at France's request and, in July 1894, extradited to Paris. In authorizing Meunier's surrender, the Queen's Bench revised John Stuart Mill's uprising test:[5]

> In order to constitute an offence of a political character, there must be two or more parties in the State, each seeking to impose the Government of their own choice on the other, and that, if the offence is committed by one side or the other in pursuance of that object, it is a political offence, otherwise not. In the present case there are not two parties in the State, each seeking to impose Government of their own choice on the other; for the party with whom the accused is identified . . . namely, the party of anarchy, is the enemy of all Governments.

The ruling denied benefit of the political offense exception to a terrorist—one who deliberately killed and injured innocent people for symbolic reasons. In result, the outcome in *Meunier* could be read as establishing the first exception to the political offense doctrine for "wanton crimes." However, the wantonness of the bombing was not what the court focused on. Rather, the justices defined opposition to all government as "nonpolitical" and, under that theory, rendered an opinion broad enough to permit the extradition of all anarchists as ordinary criminals—even those essentially charged with sedition. Anarchists, by definition, could never be political offenders, because to be "political" in the liberal view meant believing in government enough to want to supplant one with another. At the very least, they had to be contenders for power (uprisers), and thus potentially subject to victors' justice (and the moderating effects of having to win a measure of popular support).[6]

In re Meunier could be read to deny political offense protection to people charged with nonterroristic crimes of protest against the very existence of government. Taken literally, the decision may also imply that people who are not anarchists can be surrendered for nonterroristic crimes committed in the course of rivalry between two regional factions, neither of which is currently vying for national power. This could occur if the party in office perverts the criminal law and extradition in order to persecute members of the regional faction it dislikes most.

By further emphasizing the wanton nature of the anarchists' crimes, the court in *Meunier* could have preserved the political offense exception for fugitives who, in the tradition of Louis Napoleon or Louis Kossuth, had committed crimes in the hope of sparking an uprising but had misjudged the extent of their support (or the strength of their opposition). But the focus of most governments' attention during this law-and-order period was on the "anarchy" of the anarchists, not the indiscriminate nature of their crimes. This focus, which essentially opened the anarchists to extradition for their beliefs, expressed the rising conservatism of traditionally liberal governments at the turn of the twentieth century.

The sweeping nature of the court's holding in *Meunier* also fit well with the *attentat* clause that the Belgians, French, and other more conservative nations had been adding to their laws and treaties since 1856, after the political offense exception prevented two Frenchmen from being extradited from Belgium to France for trying to blow up a train carrying the new French Emperor, Napoleon III. The *attentat* ("outrageous attempt") clause simply declared that all attempts to assassinate heads of state, members of ruling families, or sometimes diplomats were outside the protection of the political offense exception. Assassinations, whatever their motive and by whomever ordered, were categorically declared to be nonpolitical.[7]

Like the *Meunier* decision, the *attentat* clause was too broad, protecting all heads of state, no matter how richly they deserved to be shot. It was also too narrow, protecting only high government officials and their families from assassination. Those who would attempt to end the murderous reign of a dictator would be subject to return, to be tried by his courts, but dictators who became refugees might still be able, under some circumstances, to avoid extradition for atrocities committed in trying to suppress a revolt.[8] In practice, however, the *attentat* clause has rarely been used.[9] The British were particularly opposed to it, because most assassinations of heads of state constitute treason, the quintessential political offense.

As for Theodule Meunier, he was rushed to trial almost immediately upon his return to France. To "verify" the heinousness of the bombing and overshadow all protestations of innocence, the prosecution displayed a dismembered leg of the restaurant owner, Véry, preserved in alcohol in a large glass jar. A broken bone protruded through charred flesh and fabric. Meunier was quickly convicted and sentenced to hard labor for life. He died in prison, unrepentant to the end.[10]

Americans, who had lost two presidents to assassins, became even more concerned about anarchists than the British, especially after anarchists were blamed for the Chicago Haymarket bombing in 1886. In 1900, American officials helped Italian authorities investigate a number of Italian anarchists in Paterson, New Jersey, who were suspected of participating in the Bresci plot to assassinate King Humbert I.[11] In 1901, President William McKinley was assassinated in Buffalo, New York, by an anarchist sympathizer, Leon Czolgosz, and Congress moved to bar from immigration (and therefore asylum) anyone "who disbelieves in or is opposed to all organized governments."[12] The *attentat* clause was added to several U.S. extradition treaties during this period, but the *Meunier* doctrine categorically excluding attacks on heads of state or diplomats from the political offense exception was never expressly adopted by an American court.

* * *

A variant of the United Kingdom's uprising test came to the United States in the same year that *Meunier* was decided. This time the defendants were not nihilists or socialists but a corrupt caudillo and his aides.[13] Antonio Ezeta had helped his brother Carlos overthrow the government of Salvador (now El Salvador) in 1890 and, as vice president, army commander-in-chief, and later president, had dealt brutally with his opposition. In 1894 another revolution deposed the Ezetas, and Antonio and his aides were driven to the sea, where they found refuge on board the USS *Bennington*. The pursuing forces demanded their surrender, but the warship's captain refused. However, to protect American citizens still in Salvador, he agreed to hold the fugitives in custody and transport them to San Francisco, from which their extradition could be requested. The new government sought their return for a number of serious crimes, including murder, attempted murder, and robbery. All but one of these offenses (charged against an aide) were alleged to have been committed during the two revolutions. They included the execution of four persons for refusing to defend the government, the execution of one person suspected of spying for the opposition, and the taking of a "forced loan" from a bank.

Judge William W. Morrow denied extradition for all offenses associated with the actual conflict of arms, reasoning by analogy from the British court's opinions in *Castioni*.[14] The "uprising test" thus gained a foothold in American law. Morrow's decision also established the legitimacy of judges deciding what the political offense exception meant and when it would be applied.

But the uprising test adopted in *Ezeta* was less liberal than what Mill had in mind, because the judge recognized no exceptions for acts of exceptional cruelty. He made this very clear:[15]

> My duty will have been performed when I shall have determined the character of the crimes or offenses charged against the defendants, with respect to that conflict. During its progress crimes may have been committed by the contending forces of the most

atrocious and inhuman kind, and still the perpetrators of such crimes escape punishment as fugitives beyond the reach of extradition. I have no authority, in this examination, to determine what acts are within the rules of civilized warfare, and what are not.

John Stuart Mill would not have approved of Judge Morrow's ruling. Enforceable distinctions, he believed, could be drawn between "fair means and foul."[16] Morrow might have agreed, but he did not consider the drawing of those distinctions to be his duty. So far as he was concerned, the political offense exception no longer existed just to shield liberal revolutionaries (like Simon Bolivar) against autocratic colonial powers. The exception had to change to accommodate the ignoble realities of Latin American politics, which led the court to preserve American neutrality toward all sides in those highly personal struggles for power, money, and status.

* * *

Those ignoble realities emerged during the 1880s and 1890s as the United States struggled with how to characterize opponents of the Mexican dictator Porfirio Diaz, who launched a series of supposedly "revolutionary" border raids from the United States. The U.S. government had no respect for the Mexican dictator, but considered his opponents no better.

The first group to challenge the Diaz regime from the United States rode out of the Arizona territory into the Mexican town of Magdalena, Sonora, in 1880. The raiders extracted money from the local populace, allegedly for revolutionary purposes, and then returned to Arizona, where they were promptly arrested for violating U.S. neutrality laws. The Mexican government demanded that the United States extradite eight of the raiders, but the U.S. State Department refused, noting: "the fact that they are charged with being revolutionaries shows that, whatever may have been their other crimes, they may also have been guilty of a political offense."[17]

In 1887, Secretary of State Bayard refused Mexico's demand for the surrender of Francisco Cazo, whose band had crossed into Mexico to occupy the town of Agualeguas, Nuevo Leone, for three days—July 11–13, 1886. Before the raiders departed, Cazo left a political proclamation behind, with orders that it be published. Residents in the town were also reported to have shouted "Hurrah to Don Francisco J. Cazo" and "Death to the Garra party." On the basis of this slim record, Bayard concluded that "the affair was an avowedly partisan political conflict" and refused to surrender Cazo.[18]

On December 10, 1892, another group of about 130 Mexican "bandits" led by Francisco Benavides rode out of Texas, across the Rio Grande, and attacked a Mexican army garrison in the village of San Ygnacio in the state of Tamaulipas.[19] The commander, two of his lieutenants, and four enlisted men were killed. Some were burned alive in their thatched-roof jacal. The raiders seized some forty horses (both military and civilian) and a number of saddles, rifles, and revolvers. They also extorted small sums of money from women and took sixteen Mexican soldiers back to Texas as captives. Two of these later died of their wounds.[20]

When three of the raiders, Inez Ruiz, Juan Duque, and Jesus Guerra, were finally captured in Texas, they sought to avoid extradition by claiming that the attack was part of a revolutionary movement against Diaz, begun by Catariono Garza in 1891 and led, in this instance, by an American named Benavides.[21] Garza's followers denied that their leader would have ordered the attack; at that moment he was on trial in U.S. federal court in San Antonio for other violations of U.S. neutrality. Instead, they said, the raid had been carried out by remnants of his defeated band.[22] About ten days before the attack, a revolutionary manifesto, supposedly signed by about 150 men including Benavides, declared that a second invasion of Mexico would be undertaken.[23] However, most ranchers, marshals, and sheriffs in the area did not take the political ambitions of Garza's men seriously and characterized them as mere cattle rustlers, smugglers, and robbers.[24] Secretary of State Walter Q. Gresham agreed: "The idea that these acts were perpetrated with bona fide political or revolutionary designs was negatived by the fact that immediately after this occurrence, though no superior armed force of the Mexican Government was in the vicinity to hinder their advance into the country, the bandits withdrew their booty across the river to Texas."[25]

Gresham's analysis picked up on a peculiarity of the U.S.-Mexico Extradition Treaty of 1862, which barred extradition only for "an offence of a *purely* political character."[26] These were not traditional revolutionary soldiers, he reasoned, but bandits, and even if they had some vague political aspirations, the criminal nature of their conduct outweighed their political motives. Gresham pioneered the Anglo-American approach to political offenses, which was to focus judgment on the more objective facts of the uprising and the organization behind it, rather than the subjective motives of participants, as the French did.

The local U.S. commissioner accepted Gresham's reasoning but was overturned on a habeas review by U.S. District Judge Thomas S. Maxey.[27] The three raiders were exempt from extradition, he held, because their attack was part of an uprising against the Mexican government begun by Garza in 1891. The Mexican consul at San Antonio, Plutarch Ornelas, then appealed to the U.S. Supreme Court, which threw out the district judge's decision for lack of jurisdiction.[28]

Ornelas v. Ruiz thus became the first case involving alleged political offenders to come before the U.S. Supreme Court. Unfortunately, the Court's opinion had nothing to do with the uprising test. It focused instead on the scope of the district judge's power to review the commissioner's findings of fact.[29] The uprising test was imported from the United Kingdom to become part of U.S. case law solely through Judge Morrow's amoral disregard of General Ezeta's brutality.[30]

In 1897, Guerra's surrender was again requested by the Mexican government. This time Secretary of State John Sherman refused. Ignoring the narrow language of the treaty, which granted the political offense exception only to persons charged with "pure" political offenses like treason, sedition, and espionage, Sherman stressed the *Ezeta* test with its emphasis on "relative" political offenses, which could be political or nonpolitical, depending on the circumstances or motives. Like Secretary Gresham, Sherman rejected the French motives test and looked instead for more objective evidence of a movement and uprising against Mexican authority.[31] The attack, he said, had to have been predominately military in nature, because the petition filed with the magistrate stressed the shooting of Mexican officers and soldiers, the burning of military barracks, the seizure of cavalry horses, and the taking of soldiers as prisoners. This, and not the extortion of small sums of money from women or horses from civilians, was "the gravamen of the charge." Moreover, Sherman speculated, the extortion of money might well have occurred without Guerra's knowledge or approval. Accordingly, it would be wrong to hold a principal responsible for every nonpolitical crime carried out by his subordinates in the course of an uprising. In any case, he reasoned, if the primary purpose had been to pillage the countryside, the attackers would have continued to do so, and their nonpolitical objectives would have become clear.[32]

In rejecting Mexico's plea that the State Department take a purists' view toward how uprisings should be fought, Sherman quoted with approval from the opinion of Sir Henry Hawkins in *Castioni*:[33]

> I can not help thinking that everybody knows that there are many acts of a political character done without reason, done against all reason; but at the same time one can not look too hardly and weigh in golden scales the acts of men hot in their political excitement. We know that in heat, and in heated blood, men often do things which are against and contrary to reason; but none the less an act of this description may be done for the purpose of furthering and in furtherance of a political rising, even though it is an act which may be deplored and lamented, as even cruel and against all reason, by those who can calmly reflect upon it after the battle is over.

Judge Hawkins's opinion was consistent with the less romantic, more realistic spirit of the late nineteenth century, especially regarding rebellions in Latin America. By then the colonial wars for independence were over, and what now passed for "revolutions" were more often coups among cabals of oligarchs, or gang wars among roving bands of armed men, led by a self-styled "general," who supported themselves by taking what they needed from civilians at gunpoint. As a Colombian diplomat explained to an International American Conference in Washington:[34]

> In the revolutions, as we conduct them in our country, the common offenses are necessarily mixed up with the political in many cases. A revolutionist has no resources. My distinguished colleague, General Caamano [of Ecuador] knows how we carry on wars. A revolutionist needs horses for moving beef to feed his troops, etc.; and since he does not go into the public markets to purchase those horses and that beef, nor the arms and saddles to mount and equip his forces, he takes them from the first pasture or shop he finds at hand. This is called robbery everywhere, and is a common offense in time of peace, but in time of war it is a circumstance closely allied to the manner of waging it.

In rejecting the distinction between "pure" and "relative" political offenses, Secretary Sherman denied that the term "pure" had ever been meant by Americans to limit the scope of the exception to cases in which the accused had been formally charged with treason, sedition, or espionage.[35] In this he was on sound historical ground, going back to Attorney General Beardsley's opinion for Governor Marcy and the Vermont Supreme Court's dictum in the case of Dr. Holmes.[36]

Sherman was on sound philosophical ground too. In the United States, liberty came first; police power came later, and then only tentatively, and in ways that were supposed to be consistent with the primacy of liberty. That was the assumption, at least, although administrators (like Secretary Seward) were sometimes tempted to violate it in practice. Sherman was not one of them. His theory of treaty interpretation, and presumably all legal interpretation, favored personal liberty, which he said may not be taken away by "mere judicial construction" of ambiguous adjectives like "pure." This was especially true in cases of extradition, where the preference for liberty requires that, "in cases of doubt, the obligation of extradition is interpreted in a limitative manner and in favor of the right of asylum."[37] Jesus Guerra thus became the first fugitive to be shielded from extradition as a political offender by the secretary of state after being ruled extraditable by a court.

The decision to shield Guerra came under sharp criticism when the newly formed American Society of International Law debated how the United States should deal with the new, nonliberal rebellions of the late nineteenth and early twentieth centuries. James B. Scott, the State Department's solicitor, wondered "whether the progress of constitutional and representative government will not cause political offenses to be looked upon with less favor than formerly, and that uprisings against a well regulated and orderly government will deprive the fugitive of the sympathy lavished upon him not many years ago when constitutional government was being forced from unwilling hands."[38]

Frederic R. Coudert, a distinguished New York attorney, noted the irony that the United States should regard armed bands of brigands fighting U.S. rule in the Philippines as common criminals, while treating the same kinds of people who rebel against other countries as political offenders.[39] To justify the extradition of a political fugitive, he suggested, the United States should adopt the Swiss preponderance test and find that the ordinary criminal elements of a mixed criminal-political attack outweighed the political elements. Coudert endorsed the *Meunier* decision and the *attentat* clause and thought that the United States should also look to the laws of war, as the Swiss and Spanish did (and as the Institute of International Law had recommended in 1890) for guidance as to what constituted acceptable modes of warfare in foreign uprisings.[40] In a sense, Secretary of State Sherman had applied the preponderance test in shielding Guerra, just as Judge Morrow had implicitly used it to shield General Ezeta, despite the "forced loan" he had ordered his men to take from the vaults of the International Bank of Salvador and Nicaragua. Neither Sherman nor Morrow expressly invoked the Swiss test in justifying their decisions, but Sherman came close when he characterized the robberies that took place during the San Ygnacio raid as "incidental" to the larger political purpose.[41]

The chaos on the Mexican border not only strengthened the U.S. commitment to the political offense exception; it also led the State Department to suspend its own rule of noninquiry into the capacity of a requesting regime to do justice. This rare act took place in the midst of the Mexican Revolution, a multisided civil war rife with banditry and cold-blooded slaughter. The revolution had begun in 1911 with the overthrow of the Diaz dictatorship and the restoration of constitutional liberties under President Francisco I. Madero. In 1913, Madero was deposed and killed by General Victoriano Huerta, who sought to restore a reactionary dictatorship. A year later, however, Huerta was just one of several caudillos contending for power at the head of ragtag armies. In 1915, he was arrested in El Paso, Texas, while attempting to lead a foray back into Mexico. The de facto regime of General Venustiano Carranza promptly demanded Huerta's surrender, along with a number of subordinates, for the murder of Madero and his vice president.[42] The U.S. State Department refused, noting that Carranza's "so-called Constitutionalist Government" had not been recognized by the United States. That should have been sufficient, but the department went on to suggest that a fair trial would be impossible, given "the well-known conditions existing throughout the Republic."[43]

* * *

Robberies created an even more difficult problem when the rise of secret police in Russia made large-scale acts of rebellion impossible, and small, clandestine revolutionary groups ordered robberies to obtain much needed funding. One particularly controversial case arose when Russia demanded the extradition of Kristian Rudewitz, a fugitive from Russia. On the night of January 3, 1906, he and fifteen other masked men went into the village of Benen and killed Kristian Leshinsky and his wife Trina, robbed their daughter Wilhelmina Kinze and her husband, killed her, and then burned the house in which they had found her mother. At the extradition hearing, Rudewitz sought the protection of the political offense exception, claiming that the killings had been carried out pursuant to a resolution of the Zhagarn group of the Russian Social Democratic Party. He claimed that the daughter, Wilhelmina, had been executed for spying against the Party on behalf of the Tsarist police. The U.S. commissioner was not persuaded and authorized extradition for that murder. However, Russian émigrés staged a mass protest rally in Chicago, and the State Department decided not to surrender him. The killing of the woman and her parents and the burning of their home was "clearly political in their nature," Secretary of State Elihu Root informed the Russian minister, and "the robbery committed on the same occasion was a natural incident to executing the resolutions of the revolutionary group."[44]

While the Swiss courts were trying to develop a preponderance test to permit the surrender of revolutionaries whose terrorist means were morally disproportionate to their political ends, American authorities suspended moral judgment. As Secretary Root explained to the Russian ambassador who had urged adoption of the Swiss test:[45] "However much the Government of the United States may deplore or condemn acts of violence done in the commission of acts bearing a political purpose, however unnecessary or unjustified they may be considered, if those acts were in fact done in the execution of such a purpose, there is no right to issue a warrant of extradition therefor."[46]

The amorality of the State Department's position on these early "death squad" cases bothered attorneys like Frederic Coudert, because the line between vengeance on behalf of the "party" and personal vengeance was often blurry, particularly where clandestine parties were dominated by authoritarian leaders. To traditional liberals, there were standards of warfare that revolutionary soldiers did not cross. These standards, they believed, were shared by all men of honor, like Generals Washington and Howe, Grant, and Lee. They did not understand the savagery of the new terrorists of Russia, or why their parties had to operate so clandestinely, and so they tended to support the extradition of men like Rudewitz. Only the political influence of these new ethnic groups, particularly within the American Democratic Party, gave the liberals pause.

For those open-minded enough to notice, reasonable distinctions could be drawn between the Social Democrats on the one hand and nihilists and anarchists on the other. The Russian Social Democratic Party in 1906 was not a nihilist group; its Menshevik and Bolshevik factions were vying for power. It was not an armed revolutionary band, like Francis Marion's "Swamp Foxes" or Ethan Allen's "Green Mountain Boys;" nor was it a group of brigands with vaguely political goals, like those on the Mexican border. Like the anarchists, some Party members carried out assassinations, but as part of an arguably purposeful group strategy, and the attacks were against people associated with the Tsarist autocracy, not innocent bystanders.[47] In short, the Party fit within Mill's definition of a "political movement," even if it had not yet arrived at the "uprising" stage. Given the power of the Tsarist secret police, the Party seemed doomed to failure, but potential for success had never been part of the uprising test. The laws-of-war approach advocated by Coudert could not be applied; the Party was not strong enough to conduct paramilitary operations and would have been destroyed if it did. It had to fight clandestinely against more vulnerable, often civilian targets, which posed serious moral problems for those who had idealized the heroes of liberal revolutions in the age of massed musketry. So liberalism collided with ethnic politics, and neutrality, not liberty, became the dominant value behind the political offense exception for much of the twentieth century.

* * *

In marked contrast to British and Canadian law, which demanded a direct relationship between the alleged crime and a political uprising, American law during the early twentieth century took a rather relaxed view as to what offenses might be "incidental" to an uprising, and thus shielded from extradition. Like Mill, the Americans seemed willing to apply the exception to protect participants in political movements as well as armed uprisings, and did not necessarily require that the movement be well organized or that it actually order the attacks.

The political offense exception received its broadest and morally most outrageous application in 1903, in the case of James Lynchehaun, a Catholic Irishman wanted by the British to complete a life sentence for a particularly brutal attack on his Protestant landlady, Agnes MacDonnell. The 1894 attack had taken place on Achill Island, in County Mayo, on Ireland's west coast. The police alleged that Lynchehaun, who had recently been fired as MacDonnell's rent collector, scaled the wall of her farm, set fire to the sheds and stable, and then attacked her when she came out to investigate. In the course of the attack, her nose was bitten off, her right eye crushed to a pulp, her stomach stomped, and spines of whin bush (gorse) kicked deep into her vagina. Her house was set on fire, and the police believed that Lynchehaun tried to throw his victim into the flames.[48]

For the next year, the accused was hidden from the police by the peasants, especially women, of Achill Island. The defiance involved in hiding him was so emblematic of Irish resentment of the British that John Millington Synge used Lynchehaun as one of the models for *The Playboy of the Western World*.[49] The constables finally dug the fugitive out from under the floorboards of a remote cottage, convicted him of attempted murder at Castlebar, County Mayo, and imprisoned him, first in Mountjoy and later in Maryborough, from which he escaped and fled to Chicago.

There, at the Grand Pacific Hotel in November 1902, Lynchehaun introduced himself to Michael Davitt, head of the Irish Land League. Davitt was a hero to the fugitive because Davitt and his League had successfully persuaded the British to return most of the English-owned land to Irish farmers. However, the fugitive was not a hero to Davitt, who promptly reported the encounter to the mayor of Chicago. The Chicago police informed the British government, which demanded extradition, and Lynchehaun was arrested in Indianapolis.

On the face of it, there seemed to be nothing political about Lynchehaun's crime. As he explained in a letter to the *Chicago American* before he fled, Mrs. MacDonnell's "misfortunes" were the result of "crossing the wrong man" by trying "to have me evicted from my home and land."[50] In Indianapolis, however, Irish Americans quickly formed a defense committee, and Lynchehaun's story changed. He now claimed that he had attacked the woman not out of spite, but as part of a movement of oppressed tenants belonging to the Irish Republican Brotherhood, who sought to drive her out of Ireland and regain her lands for the Irish people. The defense claimed that Lynchehaun was the Brotherhood's district organizer and that the attack was an organizational decision, which he carried out after the drawing of lots. Lynchehaun admitted to hitting Mrs. MacDonnell with his fist but insisted that the bulk of her injuries were inflicted by members of the crowd that pretended to help fight the fires. The uprising in her barnyard was like the Boston Tea Party or the French Revolution, he claimed, and entitled him to protection from extradition.

There is evidence that even the defense committee did not believe all of Lynchehaun's claims,[51] but Commissioner Charles W. Moores did. Following several mass demonstrations on the fugitive's behalf, Moores ruled against extradition because the assault and arson, while "futile," were "incidental to and formed a part of political disturbances." They were also connected to "riots for political purposes" designed to "overthrow landlordism," and thereby promote land reform legislation, a change in the governing class, and possibly independence from British rule.[52]

Little in Lynchehaun's life story inspired trust in anything he said, and his defense seems to have relied heavily on perjured testimony. But the accused symbolized a larger truth, which was oppression of the Irish by the British, and so he received the benefit of many doubts. Senator Mark Hanna (R.-Ohio) intervened with President Theodore Roosevelt to prevent a parallel effort to deport Lynchehaun, and when the fellow lay seriously ill in January 1906, Vice President Charles W. Fairbanks paid a well-publicized sympathy call upon him.[53] As usual, extradition was a matter of politics as well as law, and Republicans like Democrats courted the ethnic vote.

* * *

In retrospect, it is curious that more was not done earlier, in both the United Kingdom and the United States, to exclude wanton crimes from the scope of the political offense exception. But in *Meunier, Ezeta,* the Mexican border-raid cases, the Russian death-squad cases, and *Lynchehaun,* the terroristic nature of the crimes was downplayed, as was the requirement of a full-scale, popular revolution. So long as the "movement" did not export its killing to Western Europe or the United States, its atrocities and futility could be tolerated by an America that was still sufficiently uninvolved in international relations to be able to see the rebels (or their adversaries) for what they were.

The cases of Lynchehaun and Rudewitz, like those of Ezeta and the Mexican-border bandits, illustrate more than the demands of ethnic politics. They also reflect a decline in popular support for universal rules of right conduct, an increase in ethical relativism, and a greater unwillingness on the part of American jurists to take a moral position on the legitimacy of revolutionaries or, as we will see in the next chapter, on the capacity (or willingness) of the requesting regime to do justice.

CHAPTER 9

Noninquiry

We are bound by the existence of an extradition treaty to assume that the trial will be fair.

Justice Oliver Wendell Holmes, Glucksman v. Henkel, *1910*

Contemporaneous with the Civil War, a new era in American jurisprudence was born—an era of statist theories of government, positive law, and individual rights derived from positive law, formalistically applied, without reference to the larger structure of liberty envisioned by the founders of the American republic. Whig theories of checks and balances would come to be regarded as quaint relics of Newtonian physics; American universities would teach John Austin's positivism, Herbert Spencer's Social Darwinism, Christopher Langdell's legal syllogisms, and John Burgess's organic state. Oliver Wendell Holmes's "bad man's theory of the law" would come to dominate the "realistic" teaching of law, even as the realists criticized the Langdellian formalists. Aggressive new law firms would teach that law is a disparate collection of positive rights and duties to be asserted on behalf of corporate clients without reference to larger conceptions of morality or the old Madisonian science of structuring and limiting power in order to assure a general condition of liberty. The U.S. government would assert leadership within the "family of nations" and seek the benefits of reciprocal extradition with as many foreign regimes as possible, while the compilers of international law digests would record the effects of these developments on the law of extradition as if they had no moral consequences at all.

Out of this new jurisprudence would evolve a number of "rules of noninquiry"— rules that blinded judges to how they had obtained jurisdiction or what could happen if they authorized extradition. This deliberate unrealism would contrast sharply with the traditional skepticism regarding the capacity of foreign regimes to match American standards of justice.

Of course, all was not blindness. The corruption of justice achieved by the French Jacobins had much to do with Washington's decision to shield both General Galbaud and Citizen Genêt from the Jacobins, and it was probably behind Judge Laurance's decision not to surrender Captain Barré. Assessments regarding the likelihood of prejudice informed the political offense exception, which presumes that political fugitives are not likely to receive justice from the regimes they have fought to overthrow. The desire to minimize the potential for foreign injustice also inspired the practice of allowing extradition for only a few serious, nonpolitical crimes (short lists), the rule confining subsequent prosecution to those crimes for which the accused is found extraditable (the rule of specialty), and the treaty requirement that the offense be criminal within the requested as well as requesting state (the rule of double criminality). The same, too, can be said for the probable cause rule. Much of early Anglo-American extradition law was based on principles of due process of law and a realistic assessment of foreign capabilities and intentions. In tandem with these rules, however, was an often willful blindness to the requesting state's potential for injustice, particularly where the surrender of disfavored people—like deserting seamen and fugitive slaves—was demanded.

* * *

One of the earliest and most infamous applications of the rule of noninquiry can be found in a 1829 decision of the North Carolina Supreme Court. At issue was whether courts could inquire into the capacity or willingness of slave owners to treat their slaves with justice or humanity. Chief Justice Thomas Ruffin had no doubt as to where the courts' duty lay:[1]

> There may be particular instances of cruelty and deliberate barbarity where, in conscience, the law might properly interfere.... But we cannot look at the matter in that light. The truth is that we are forbidden to enter upon a train of general reasoning on the subject. We cannot allow the right of the [slave's] master to be brought into discussion in the courts of justice.

In 1842, as we saw in Chapter 4, the U.S. Supreme Court followed suit, striking down a Pennsylvania "liberty law" that sought to shield alleged fugitive slaves from abduction by slave catchers.[2] In 1850, Congress made the rule of noninquiry mandatory in all fugitive slave cases.[3] As we saw in Chapter 5, a Canadian court in 1860 refused to question the willingness or capacity of the U.S. state of Missouri to do justice in the case of John Anderson, the slave who found it necessary to kill a white man in order to escape.

This kind of moral blindness would gradually infect other principles of extradition as well. In 1871, the rule of specialty came under attack when Richard B. Caldwell failed to persuade a U.S. circuit court that he could not be tried in New York for bribery when Canada had extradited him only on charges of forgery.[4]

In effect, Caldwell asserted the rule of specialty as a personal right, but Circuit Judge Charles L. Benedict did not agree.[5] The rule limiting trial to the offenses for which the accused was extradited, he said, was "a good cause of complaint between the two Governments," but no business of the courts. Benedict would no more have excluded Caldwell from trial than he would have excluded illegally obtained evidence from consideration; that would "permit a person accused of crime to put the Government on trial for its dealings with a foreign power."[6] Benedict did not pause to consider whether the rule of specialty might not be a requirement of due process, as inherent to the extradition process as the political offense exception or judicial primacy. To this nineteenth-century positivist, the right did not exist because it had not been expressly included in the Webster-Ashburton Treaty. Benedict turned a blind eye to how the prisoner had been brought before his court. Whether the prisoner had been extradited in bad faith, the judge said, was a question for the executives concerned, as if the treaty were a mere agreement among executives and not also the law of the land, for courts to enforce as they would any other law.[7]

Judge Benedict's blindness to the illegality that had brought Caldwell before him on charges of bribery did not go unchallenged. State and federal courts divided on the issue,[8] and the judge's views were finally tested in 1886, when he and his colleague, William J. Wallace, could not agree on whether William Rauscher, second mate of the American ship *J. F. Chapman*, could be tried in the United States for inflicting cruel and unusual punishment on a seaman under his command when Rauscher had been extradited from the United Kingdom only on charges of murder. Certifying their disagreement, the judges passed the case up to the U.S. Supreme Court which, in *United States v. Rauscher*, rejected Benedict's view.

A majority of that Court ruled that the rule of specialty was not only a diplomatic right of the extraditing nation, but the personal right of any person extradited from a foreign country to stand trial in a U.S. court.[9] According to Justice Samuel F. Miller, U.S. trial courts were responsible for seeing to it that no "implication of fraud" or "bad faith" could be imputed to the United States in making the original extradition request.[10] Protecting the integrity of the United States was not just an executive function.

To protect that integrity, Justice Miller wrote for the Court, the prisoner must have the right to ask that the additional charges be dismissed, on the grounds that they violate the treaty and the foreign government's extradition order.[11] Or, Miller implied, the U.S. trial court could dismiss the additional charges on its own motion or on a motion from the offended foreign government. Whoever points out the violation, American courts have the authority to see to it that they do not become unwitting parties to treaty violations, because a treaty is not just an arrangement between our executive and a foreign power; it is the supreme law of the land.[12]

So defined, *United States v. Rauscher* has never been overruled. The rule of specialty may be enforced by U.S. courts at an extradited person's request against U.S. prosecutors who overreach the terms of the individual's extradition.

However, the Supreme Court has refused to bar extradition where it appears likely that the requesting foreign government will try the accused for crimes other than those for which he was surrendered by the United States. Even where the requesting state has a record of abuse, the rule cannot be asserted by the accused in an American extradition court for the rather simple-minded theory that only states have rights under treaties. Nor can the rule be judicially enforced by a conditional finding of extra-ditability. When an American court "certifies" a defendant's extraditability, it must assume that the rule of specialty will be followed.[13] Any conditions on the subsequent trial must be imposed diplomatically by the U.S. executive.[14]

* * *

Miller's opinion in *Rauscher* offered hope that the courts would insist on a measure of integrity in the extradition process, but that hope was dashed on the very same day by the Court's opinion in *Ker v. Illinois*. In *Rauscher*, the moral issue had been the obtaining of an accused for trial under false pretenses; in *Ker* it was abduction. Fred-erick M. Ker had embezzled $56,000 from a Chicago bank and fled to Lima, Peru, where he was tracked down and kidnapped by Pinkerton detective Henry G. Julian, operating without a judicial warrant for Ker's arrest. Arriving in Peru in the midst of a Chilean invasion and unable to find any local officials to help him, the detective made the seizure himself and arranged to have his captive brought back to the United States on board the USS *Essex*.[15] Both the Illinois court and the U.S. Supreme Court ignored the fact that Ker had been kidnapped with the assistance of the U.S. Navy.[16] Justice Miller, again writing for the U.S. Supreme Court, saw nothing wrong with Illi-nois taking jurisdiction in Ker's case. Treaty rights, the Court ruled, belong to states, not individuals, and Peru had not objected. Moreover, Miller added, "we do not see that the Constitution, or laws, or treaties of the United States guarantee him any pro-tection."[17]

In refusing to question how the accused had been brought before them, the Illinois court and U.S. Supreme Court in effect condoned the detective's law-breaking. They implied that extradition treaties are not meant to bar more primitive forms of self-help and that courts do not have to dissociate themselves from private (or executive) wrongdoing. Implicit in *Ker's* rule of noninquiry into abductions was what Oliver Wendell Holmes would soon call "the bad man's theory of the law"—law is no more than what one cannot get away with.[18]

* * *

No decision was more significant to the evolving rules of noninquiry than *In re Ezeta*. Judge Morrow's opinion shielding the Salvadoran dictator is best known for making participation in a violent contest for power integral to the definition of a nonextra-ditable political offender under the uprising test.[19] *Ezeta* is less well known for Judge Morrow's refusal—consistent with *Ker*—to inquire into the fact that the former dic-tator and his aides were brought to San Francisco against their will by the U.S. Navy.[20]

The case is even less well known for the judge's decision allowing Ezeta's body-guard, Lt. Col. Juan Cienfuegos, to be sent back to Salvador to stand trial for an attempted murder committed between the two uprisings. The prosecution, Cienfue-gos charged, was "nothing more or less than an effort on the part of the present gov-ernment of Salvador to secure the person of the accused for the purpose of wreaking their vengeance on him for the part he took against them in the late war."[21] Granting that "This argument is not, perhaps, destitute of force," Judge Morrow nevertheless ruled: "it is not a matter of which I can properly take cognizance. . . . If, as is claimed, [Cienfuegos] is being extradited for a political purpose, that is a matter which can very properly be called to the attention of the executive when he comes to review my action."[22]

This blind formalism was not confined to the judiciary. As early as 1864, law officers for the British Crown, including the attorney general and the solicitor general, advised that "Her Majesty's Government cannot of strict right refuse to deliver a criminal [to China] on the ground that there is reason for suspecting that torture will be applied."[23] In 1878, their view was endorsed by the Royal Commission on Extradition, and became law in the United Kingdom in 1896.

* * *

Six years after the *Ezeta* decision, a British court refused to question whether justice would be done in the case of Émile Arton, wanted by French authorities for fraud, larceny, and embezzlement in connection with the disastrous efforts of two companies, the Société de Dynamite and the Compagnie de Panama, to dig a canal through the Isthmus of Panama.[24] The venture, begun in 1880, had lost its investors over 1 billion francs by 1888. The Compagnie de Panama desperately needed to issue more stock, but the government refused. So Arton, its "advertising agent," was given 1 million francs with which to bribe members of the French Assembly. The necessary legislation was passed, but only half of the new stock could be sold. In December 1888, the Compagnie de Panama suspended payments to its subcontractors, and in 1892 the Société de Dynamite sued Arton for embezzlement. A newly founded muckraking newspaper, *La Libre Parole*, exposed the bribery and Arton fled the country.

For three years the French police went through the motions of pursuing him; there was great fear in parliamentary circles of whom he could implicate. But the Assembly's critics would not let the scandal go away, and in November 1895 Arton was finally arrested in London, where he had reestablished himself as a tea merchant and changed his name, wryly, to Newman.

Like Cienfuegos, Arton invoked the "second limb" of the political offense exception, claiming that the French government really wanted to question him about certain political secrets and would punish him for his refusal to reveal those secrets, whatever offense they chose to allege for the purpose of obtaining his return.[25] However ordinary his crime appeared, he said, he was wanted by political enemies whose motives had nothing to do with justice. In addition, Arton argued, independently of the treaty, that the demand for his extradition should not be complied with because it "was not made in good faith and in the interests of justice."[26]

Both claims were plausible. Arton was the bag man in a pervasive system of legislative bribery. The political culture that demanded his return had raised hypocrisy to the highest of social art forms; bribery and corruption pervaded not only the French legislature and executive, but the courts as well.[27] More significant still, the driving force behind the demand for Émile Arton's extradition was not the criminal justice system, but the virulently anti-Semitic *La Libre Parole,* which alleged that Arton and his associates had been born Alsatian Jews and were part of a pervasive Jewish conspiracy to steal the wealth and betray the morals and security of Catholic France.[28] By 1895, anti-Semitism was being exploited politically by the Left and the Right, and especially by royalists and Boulangists in their efforts to discredit parliamentary government.[29] Whatever the French courts decided to do with "le juive Arton," justice was not likely to have anything to do with it.

But the British court was unmoved. "The Court cannot permit you to argue," Lord Russell told Arton's counsel from the bench, "that a friendly State is not acting in good faith in making this application; that is not a question which the judicial authorities of this country have any power to entertain."[30] "Such considerations, if they exist at all," he added in his opinion, "must be addressed to the executive of this country."[31]

In taking this view, Lord Russell followed the recommendation of the 1878 Royal Commission on Extradition.[32] Like the Commission, he went beyond the plain meaning of the statute, which said nothing about leaving the bad motives provision of the political offense exception to the executive, and only the executive, to apply.[33] On the contrary, the statute explicitly gave the courts and the executive concurrent authority to administer this "second limb," but Russell ruled that such assessments were political questions, for the sole consideration of politicians, and his colleagues agreed.[34]

Judge Wills went further, denying that courts had any power to question the capacity of the requesting legal system to do justice. "We must assume," he wrote, "that the French Courts will administer justice in accordance with their own law; and so long as they do that, or whether they do it or not, we cannot interfere beforehand."[35] Unanimously rejecting both of Arton's bad faith claims, the justices made the rule of noninquiry part of British extradition law.

* * *

In 1901, the U.S. Supreme Court followed the rationale of *Arton* in refusing to question the systemic *capacity,* rather than the political *willingness,* of the requesting legal system to do justice in the case of Charles F. W. Neely, an American wanted for embezzlement by the government of Cuba, then being managed by the U.S. Army.[36]

Neely tried to escape surrender with the Jeffersonian argument that, if surrendered, he would be tried in Cuba under procedures that would not satisfy the guarantees of the U.S. Constitution. Cuba, he noted, had no equivalent of the writ of habeas corpus, no provision against bills of attainder or ex post facto laws, and no trial by jury.[37]

The Justices were not persuaded. Nothing in the U.S. Constitution, they said, bore any relation to crimes committed abroad.[38] The rule of double criminality governed the substance of the crime but did not require equivalent procedures. Nor did anything else, including the Fifth Amendment's due process clause, authorize them to question the capacity of a requesting regime to do justice.[39] In addition, the Court ruled, U.S. citizenship did not give Neely the right to a trial "in any other mode than that allowed to its own people by the country whose laws he violated and from whose justice he has fled."[40]

Ironically, Neely's extradition was not sought pursuant to a treaty between the United States and Cuba (or Spain). It was sought pursuant to a special extradition statute hurried through Congress during the postwar occupation of Cuba by the United States Army.[41] Neely was not sought by an independent Cuba; the papers demanding his extradition were signed by General Leonard Woods, who was then in command of the U.S. army of occupation and the Cuban government it was in the process of creating.[42] Implicit in the Court's decision, then, may have been the assumption that Neely would be surrendered to a fair and impartial court system supervised by Americans. If so, the *Neely* decision may be of very limited precedential value.

On the other hand, the Supreme Court may have implicitly embraced the trial court's view that since Neely "himself had selected the forum for the commission of his crime, he will not be heard to object [to] the procedure of its courts."[43] If so, then the case should be accorded no precedential value at all, because it would be based on the constitutionally impermissible assumption that a finding of probable cause is equivalent to a finding of guilt. Whatever motivated the Court in *Neely*, the result was the same—a rule of noninquiry into the capacity of the requesting regime to do justice.[44]

In 1910 the Supreme Court repeated this abdication in *Glucksman v. Henkel*, the case of a Russian wanted for forgery.[45] Speaking for a unanimous bench, Justice Oliver Wendell Holmes declared: "We are bound by the existence of an extradition treaty to assume that the trial will be fair."[46] The statement was not necessary to the decision of the case, but it put the Supreme Court squarely in the ranks of those who assumed that the State Department would make and keep extradition agreements only with fair legal systems.

Why foreign regimes (especially Tsarist Russia) should be given the benefit of such an assumption Holmes did not say. He refused to extend the same presumption to the state of Georgia in 1915, when it was accused of allowing a courtroom mob to intimidate a jury into convicting Leo Frank, a Jewish businessman, of murdering a young Christian woman in his employ.[47] The issue before the Court had to do with the scope of federal court review pursuant to Frank's petition for a writ of habeas corpus. The majority took the narrow, technical American view of habeas corpus; Holmes, the more expansive British view. For himself and Justice Hughes, Holmes dissented:[48]

> Habeas corpus cuts through all forms and goes to the very tissue of structure. . . . Whatever disagreements there may be as to the scope of the phrase "due process of law," there can be no doubt that it embraces the fundamental concept of a fair trial, with opportunity to be heard. . . . This is not a matter for polite presumptions; we must look facts in the face. Any judge who has sat with juries knows that they are extremely likely to be impregnated by the environing atmosphere. When we find [that] the judge [believed that] neither prisoner nor counsel would be safe from the rage of the crowd, we think the presumption overwhelming that the jury responded to the passions of the mob.

In *Frank*, palpable injustice was clear from the record; in an extradition case, probably injustice would have to be anticipated from facts outside the record, and this step the Court and Holmes were not willing to take.[49] But every probable cause hearing is an exercise in speculation. In no extradition case are the facts ever fully known, much less tested for credibility. Educated guesses have to be made about what can, ultimately, be proven at trial. Even appellate judges must speculate, as Holmes and Hughes did when they concluded that the jury in Frank's case was probably intimidated by the mob.[50]

But Holmes saw no connection between his concern for what he saw as the jury's "lynching" of Leo Frank and his indifference to the risk of future "legal lynchings" by foreign regimes in cases like Glucksman's. Holmes's job was to review state court abuses, not anticipate foreign ones. Justice had little to do with his work; law was his business, and national wrongdoing he accepted with a shrug.[51] As Morton Horowitz has observed, "For Holmes, . . . law is the product of social struggle. Nothing stands between the state and the individual."[52] Holmes understood the systemic rationalizations that led to the extradition of Thomas Nash, the return of fugitive slaves, the hanging of Billy Budd, or the decapitation of the desperate men who commandeered Benito Cereno's ship. The "Yankee from Olympus" was a witting participant in the lawful processes that made such injustice possible, and he was as fatalistic about that role as Melville's Captain Vere was about his. But where Melville took great pains to camouflage his cynicism beneath layers of satiric ambiguity, Holmes candidly admitted it. For his own epitaph he proposed: "Here lies the supple tool of power."[53]

Allied with this impassivity toward systemic injustice was the new legal positivism, which rejected anything approaching a universal theory of human rights not squarely grounded in municipal legislation. "The sacredness of human life," Holmes wrote to Sir Frederick Pollock, "is a purely municipal ideal of no validity outside the jurisdiction [of a national legal system]. I believe that force, mitigated so far as may be by good manners, is the *ultimo ratio*, and between two groups that want to make inconsistent kinds of worlds I see no remedy except force."[54] Accordingly, there was no room in Holmes's jurisprudence, or that of most of his colleagues, for a rule of inquiry, unless it was mandated by Congress or a treaty. Neither the due process clause of the Fifth Amendment nor the natural rights jurisprudence seemingly authorized by the Ninth Amendment's reference to rights preexisting the establishment of government were sufficient to justify judges' questioning the intentions of foreign politicians or the systemic injustice of foreign legal systems.

Holmes and his colleagues could have made their presumption about the fairness of the requesting regime's legal system rebuttable, but they did not. They made it irrebuttable, so that extradition judges would hear no evil, see no evil, and speak no evil of foreign regimes.

Watching the emergence of this positive law was none other than Herman Melville, who wrote *Billy Budd* between 1886 and 1891. In *White Jacket*, written in 1850, Melville had allowed military discipline to be tempered by a higher moral law. In *Budd*, however, he abandoned all romanticism and sardonically allowed one of nature's innocents to be killed by the jurisprudence of Oliver Wendell Holmes Jr., his Berkshire neighbor's son. The "vows of allegiance" which Captain Vere had sworn were to "martial duty," not to natural law, eternal principles of justice, or compassion. Like

Holmes, the captain was committed to deciding cases "objectively," according to the facts and law, leaving abstract considerations of justice and subjective considerations of mercy to "psychological theologians"[55] (or to the Parliament that enacted Britain's articles of war). Like Tennyson's calvarymen, Vere's job was not to reason why; it was to judge sailors mechanically, according to the dictates of an imperial law. In this, Melville's captain was a prescient parody of the judges in *Arton* and *Neely*, who blindly insisted that they had no authority to question the capacity of any foreign regime to do justice.

* * *

The Neely decision was applied to the British treaty in 1915 in *In re Lincoln*, where the accused argued that the real purpose behind the request was not to punish him for forgery but to silence him for statements made while in the United States.[56] Judge Thomas Chattfield was not persuaded. "It is not part of the court proceedings," he ruled, "nor of the hearing upon the charge of crime to exercise discretion as to whether the criminal charge is a cloak for political action, nor whether the request is made in good faith. Such matters should be left to the Department of State."[57] Nothing in the treaty's two-limbed political offense exception divided enforcement duties in this fashion.[58] Chattfield, following Judge Morrow's lead in *Ezeta*, simply decreed that the judiciary would enforce the first limb and the executive the second. In so doing, he abdicated a major function of an independent judiciary in the American system of checks and balances.

Moreover, in placing this evaluation exclusively with the executive, Chattfield ignored two potential conflicts of interest. First, the U.S. executive was unlikely to question the requesting regime's commitment to justice because, in most instances, it had undertaken to represent that regime in court, and had done so, as most lawyers do, before knowing all the facts. Second, U.S. attorneys would naturally seek to maintain good relations with the requesting (and presumably friendly) regime, both to encourage the reciprocal surrender of American fugitives and to avoid damaging other national interests and relationships.

At the State Department, attitudes had not changed much since the days of Hamilton Fish. American diplomats did not limit their extradition agreements to constitutional democracies[59] but bestowed them, along with treaties of navigation, as gestures of friendship upon most newly recognized regimes.[60] Nor did successive secretaries of state ask their presidents to abrogate (or formally suspend) extradition treaties when dictators overthrew parliamentary regimes and politicized their legal systems, as frequently occurred in Latin America. Like most diplomats and administrators, they valued order more than liberty. This priority can be seen quite clearly in an article by John Bassett Moore defending the treaty with Russia against an attack by Sergei Stepniak, the Russian writer and nihilist who had fled to the West after assassinating the St. Petersburg police chief with a stiletto.[61] To Stepniak's argument that "no civilized country extradites criminals to China or Turkey where the judicial proceedings are entirely barbarous," Moore replied: "No government is perfect, and some governments are simply terrible, but the worst of all is immeasurably better than none at all."[62]

Moore may have been right, but his rejoinder was beside the point. The issue was not whether order is preferable to chaos, but whether an American court has any business extraditing people to unjust legal systems. To that question Moore made no reply, except to say that the Russian legal system looked reasonably regular to him.[63] Like most formalists, Moore attributed no significance to the secret policemen whom Stepniak had attacked with both blade and pen.

* * *

One partial exception to the rule of noninquiry would emerge in cases where the accused was being returned not for trial, but for incarceration pursuant to a conviction *in absentia*. It began in 1911, in *Ex parte Fudera*, when a circuit court refused to permit the surrender of an alleged murderer to Italy because the court that had convicted him *in absentia* had relied on hearsay so thin that it would not establish probable cause in the United States.[64] Technically speaking, the rule of noninquiry was not suspended; the court simply looked at the submissions before it and found them wanting. But the implication was clear. By examining the inadequate record of the previous trial, the court looked through the screen of national legitimacy and saw the injustice that the extradition of Fudera would implement.

There is much to be said for refusing to enforce *in absentia* convictions by extradition, or for conditioning extradition on retrial, so that both sides can be heard and the prosecution's evidence and witnesses challenged. But American courts have not yet gone that far. The most they have done, beginning in 1913, is to subject the records from *in absentia* convictions to what can best be called heightened scrutiny.[65]

* * *

How low considerations of humanity and justice had sunk by the eve of World War I can be seen most dramatically in the Canadian case of Savaa Fedorenko, a former Social Democrat from Tsarist Russia, who was sought for killing a village watchman.[66] Fedorenko had been arrested as a "suspicious stranger" in a district that had been placed under martial law because of the revolutionary violence of other Social Democrats and had shot the watchman, he claimed, only to escape what was certain to be a brutal interrogation. The brutality of the Tsarist police was well known; so too was the Russian practice of trying alleged police killers before a special tribunal, but the Canadian court still authorized his surrender.

Fedorenko was extraditable, the judge ruled, because he had been "in no way identified with any [revolutionary] political movement."[67] Like Jonathan Robbins, he had fought to escape brutal custody, and like Robbins, he was sent back to drumhead justice. Such was the reasoning of judges in a positivist age. Self-defense and likely injustice were ignored because the legitimacy of the oppressive regimes was now beyond question. The humanitarian spirit of the political offense exception had been lost to a jurisprudence of blind rules.

By adopting the rule of noninquiry and trusting diplomats to deal only with just legal systems, the British and American courts undermined the moral underpinnings of two major principles of extradition law: the rule of specialty and the second limb of the political offense exception. American judges kept responsibility for enforcing the rule of specialty in cases tried in the United States, but they delegated its enforcement against foreign regimes wholly to the Department of State. They remained willing to deny extradition where previous *in absentia* trials had produced a record of accomplished injustice, but they refused to speculate on either the willingness or capacity of the requesting regime to do justice, no matter how much extrinsic evidence there might be of political motives or systemic injustice. As to these, the courts would not speculate but would presume, against all reality, that the foreign regime must be fair because the United States had an extradition treaty with it. Worse still, the courts turned a blind eye to the substitution of abduction for extradition.

The Supreme Court did not surrender all power to define the political offense exception; the courts still retained control of the uprising test. But the justices conceded power to the executive where it probably mattered most—in cases where appearances of regularity masked political motives behind the request or a corrupt legal system.

Concern for what might happen to extradited persons on their return to their country of origin thus went into judicial eclipse. The humanism of Becarria and Jefferson succumbed to nationalism, pragmatism, and statism. Political expediency was the dominant value, and for a nation that remained relatively isolated from international relations, expediency consisted of an indifferent, Holmesian shrug.

Thus, on March 4, 1933, a U.S. commissioner in Boston authorized the extradition of Harvard Professor Joao F. Normano (also known as Isaak Lewin) to Hitler's Germany on charges of fraud, despite defense claims that, as a Jew, Normano could not possibly receive a fair trial from the Nazis.[68] Today we know just how right the defense was, but in March 1933, Hitler was busy persecuting communists and had not yet mobilized the legal system against Jews. Moreover, because the request for Normano had been filed before Hitler came to power, the case had an aura of legitimacy to it.

Even so, Hitler's suspension of all constitutional guarantees of liberty on February 28 should have caused the executive and judicial departments of the United States to stop all extradition to Germany. That did not happen, because there was no procedure for suspending the operation of treaties. The State Department allowed Normano to file an administrative appeal but refused to concede that he would not receive a fair trial.[69] The most it was willing to do was ask if the German government would be willing to withdraw its request. When the German government refused, Normano's surrender was ordered.[70]

Normano's attorneys filed a habeas petition, but on May 31, 1934, Judge Elisha H. Brewster refused to take notice of Hitler's increased persecution of Jews. "Such considerations," he ruled, "ought not to influence the decision. Whatever may be the situation in Germany, the Extradition Treaty between that government and the United States is still in full force, and it is the duty of the court to uphold and respect it just as it is bound to uphold the laws and the Constitution of the United States."[71]

Despite this denial, Brewster had taken judicial notice of Nazi injustice and, like the Canadian justices who finally shielded John Anderson from American injustice,[72] found refuge in a technicality. By law, the warrant directing Normano's surrender should have been delivered to the U.S. marshal within sixty days of the commissioner's decision. It had not been and, without asking the State Department to explain why, Brewster ordered the prisoner released.[73] The decision was something that only a lawyer could take pride in.

CHAPTER 10

Cold War Justice

*Altho[ugh] it appears that deportation proceedings should be insti-
tuted, [the accused] should not be sent to apparently certain death at
the hands of the Yugoslav communists. Unless it can be established
that he was responsible for the deaths of any Americans, I think that
deportation should be to some non-communist country which will give
asylum. In fact, if his only crime was against communists, I think he
should be given asylum in the U.S.*

Internal Justice Department note, circa April 1951

In the late eighteenth century, fugitives, but not governments, were released from
moral judgment. Most foreign governments were known to be despotic, and most
political fugitives were presumed to be victims. By mid twentieth century, most noncommunist governments had been exempted from moral condemnation, while the
morality of fugitives was being drawn into doubt.

In the nineteenth century, exempting revolutionaries from extradition could be justified on the grounds that despotic rulers had broken their social contract with the
people. By the twentieth century, even the most despotic governments were allowed
to escape such judgments by calling themselves "democratic" and by committing
their injustices in the name of the people, the state, the nation, or the tribe.

In the late eighteenth and early nineteenth centuries, respect for human rights was
regarded by enlightened thinkers as the acid test of governmental legitimacy. In the
twentieth century, positivists assumed that the mere control of the instrumentalities
of state coercion was enough to establish a requesting government's legitimacy.[1] They
denigrated the idea that law should be based on moral principles that respected social
needs. Having concluded that there could be no "natural law" based on reason, the
positivists believed that there was no rational basis for arguing for or against the
legitimacy of any particular government. Governments did not exist by consent fully
granted but by imposition or acquiescence. Morality, respect for liberty, or obedience

to an implicit social contract had nothing to do with legitimacy. Power was the chief basis for authoritative rules.

As power displaced morality in the interpretation of law, the morality of the accused became irrelevant to the definition of a nonextraditable political offense. Political neutrality, not moral purposes, came to dominate judicial assumptions regarding the implicit purposes of the political offense exception. Carried to its logical conclusion, this position meant that despotic former officials charged with genocide could become beneficiaries of the political offense exception.

* * *

The power-centric approach to governmental legitimacy was embraced most fervently by conservative Catholics who supported the anti-communist crusades of Senator Joseph McCarthy (R.-Wisc.) Many of these ethnic Catholics agreed with the radio priest, Father Charles E. Coughlin, who was an apologist for the Nazis and an outspoken anti-Semite.[2] They considered Jews to be agents of "Godless Communism," and were furious at the Yugoslavian Communists' arrest of Archbishop Stepinac, who had collaborated with the pro-Nazi Ustaše.[3] Like many fundamentalist Protestants, these ethnic Catholics felt no urgent need to conduct war crimes trials, "deNazify" Germany, or take special care to exclude Nazi collaborators from postwar resettlement in the United States. Such trials would disclose the extent to which the Catholic Church had failed to resist Hitler or, in Croatia, supported his collaborators. The emphasis that conservative Catholics placed on fighting communism, rather than punishing fascists, was thus self-protective as well as an expression of their anti-Semitism. They lobbied to expand immigration quotas for Balts and Ukrainians, restrict immigration quotas for Jews who had survived the Holocaust, and persuade Congress not to ratify the United Nations treaty defining genocide as a universal crime.[4]

Nowhere was this Catholic prejudice against Jews stronger than in Brooklyn, New York, where the *Tablet*, the unofficial voice of the Brooklyn diocese, was openly anti-Semitic and led a McCarthyite purge of alleged communist teachers, mostly Jews, from New York City's public schools.[5] In 1949, Catholic opposition defeated a measure, sponsored by Congressman Emmanuel Celler (D.-N.Y.), that would have admitted 25,000 Jewish victims of the Holocaust.[6]

Power-centric, anti-communist, anti-Semitic conservatism was particularly strong among European Catholic and Eastern Orthodox émigré groups who lived in urban and suburban ethnic enclaves and who lobbied on behalf of the "captive peoples" of Eastern Europe. They were particularly effective working through their congressional representatives to ensure that the Immigration and Naturalization Service (INS) would not place anti-Nazi barriers in the way of relatives, friends, and associates wishing to emigrate from war-torn Europe to the United States.

One successful Croatian American road builder in Long Beach, California, asked his conservative Republican congressman to introduce a private bill in Congress making the builder's brother and his brother's family legal residents of the United States, despite the fact that they had entered the country illegally from Ireland in 1948 using false names and documents. The brother for whom this request was made was Andrija Artuković, former minister of the interior in the Nazi puppet regime of Croatia during the war.[7]

The request put the Truman administration on the spot. Artuković was not a minor figure; he was second in command in one of the most murderous regimes spawned by Hitler and Mussolini. Since the Artukovićs had entered the United States by fraudulent means, the Justice Department could have moved immediately to deport them back to Ireland, if not Yugoslavia. But Deputy Attorney General Peyton Ford, possibly mindful of the congressional interest in the Artukovićs' fate and the political clout and energy of the Croatian American community in Southern California, did nothing until the Yugoslavian Communist government of Marshal Tito obtained Artuković's address and demanded his surrender as a major war criminal. This time the State Department, which was not eager to appear supportive of a communist regime, sat on the case. It did not move until April 29, 1951, when syndicated columnist Drew Pearson went on the air with the Artuković story.[8]

The charges were credible on their face. When Hitler dismembered Yugoslavia in 1941, he allowed Mussolini to authorize a band of anti-Serbian, anti-Semitic Croatian separatists called the Ustašhe (from the verb "ustati," which means "to rise up") to establish the "Independent State of Croatia." The Ustašhe immediately began slaughtering Serbians, who had dominated the Yugoslavian state since its creation following World War I, and who were old enemies in the religious and ethnic rivalries of Balkan politics. The Ustašhe also assisted the Germans in eliminating Jews and Gypsies. The chief of Britain's military mission to Tito's partisans—who were often the victims of Ustašhe terror—described the situation in 1941:[9]

> Bands of Ustase roamed the countryside with knives, bludgeons and machine guns, slaughtering Serbian men, women and little children, desecrating Serbian churches, murdering Serbian priests, laying waste to Serbian villages, torturing, raping, burning, drowning. Killing became a cult, an obsession. The Ustase vied to outdo each other, boasting of the numbers of their victims and of their own particular methods of dispatching them. . . . Some Ustase collected the eyes of Serbs they had killed, sending them, when they had enough, to the *Poglavnik* ["head man"] for his inspection or proudly displaying them and other human organs in the cafes of Zagreb.

Even their German and Italian patrons were revolted by the Croatian savagery. As the head of the German Secret Service in Zagreb put it: "Efforts to educate the Ustase bands to civilized warfare were quite useless."[10]

While Mussolini installed the Ustašhe in power, the Germans contributed its secret police chief, an intensely pro-German, former Austrian officer named Slavko (Eugene "Dido") Kvaternik. He arrived with the invading German troops on April 10, 1941, and immediately declared Croatia independent of Yugoslavia. On April 15, Kvaternik assumed command of the new government's security apparatus and, by all accounts, undertook his work with grim and savage zeal.

On the following day, a former Zagreb lawyer named Andrija Artuković was made commissioner of the public security apparatus, which gave him overall responsibility for Kvaternik's operations and for implementing the regime's "racial policy." On the 17th, Artuković was also made minister of interior affairs[11] which meant, organizationally and legally, that he was second in authority only to Ante Pavelić, the new regime's head man.

In reality—if the reality of that regime can ever be reconstructed—Kvaternik appears to have maintained his independent power base with the Germans and reported directly to Pavelić. Artuković, if his defenders are to be believed, was more of a figurehead, chosen for his legal credentials and reputation as a defender of the Roman Catholic faith. Their version of history is plausible; Western accounts of Croatia's wartime carnage emphasize Kvaternik and Pavelić and ignore Artuković, who was demoted into obscurity in 1943.[12]

In recent years, Justice Department attorneys have insisted that Andrija Artuković was widely known within wartime Yugoslavia as "The Butcher of the Balkans," but no historical sources have been found to support that claim. While the records of wartime chaos and carnage are often incomplete, the historical record on Artuković's wartime activities is virtually blank.

Before the war, Artuković had been a sufficiently active opponent of the dictatorship of the pro-Serbian King Alexander to be tried for complicity in the assassination of the monarch in 1934. He was acquitted of those charges by a Yugoslavian court, and it is now generally believed that the killing was carried out by a Macedonian on orders from Pavelić.[13] However, while Artuković may not have been as central to the Ustaše regime as the Justice Department would later claim, he could not have been an innocent dupe, or wholly ignorant of what his actual or nominal subordinates were doing.

In his formal capacity as minister of the interior, Artuković cosigned the order that formally created the Directorate of Public Order and Security. The order made its director directly subordinate to the minister, and reserved to the minister the power to appoint all of the directorate's personnel.[14] Artuković's defenders would later claim that Kvaternik, as director, reported directly to Pavelić, bypassing Artuković almost completely. However, in 1986, Artuković admitted that he might have signed documents paying for the operating costs of, and appointing guards to, a concentration camp at Danica, because, he said, he often signed documents without reading them.[15]

The aim of the Ustaše regime was not to turn the Croats into a racially pure people, but rather to eliminate from Croatia all peoples who did not share its ethnic identity, including its fervent Roman Catholic faith.[16] Today we would call this activity "ethnic cleansing." In pursuit of this goal, Artuković signed a variety of Nazi-style laws that led to the persecution of Serbs (who were mainly Eastern Orthodox in their faith), communists (who were against all religions), and Jews as enemies of the new, pro-Catholic state. Orthodox Christians were required by law to convert to Catholicism. Jews were ordered to wear yellow badges, stay off sidewalks, and observe a 6:00 P.M. curfew. Artuković's son, Radoslav, would later characterize the signing of these laws as "lip service" to Nazi demands and necessary to protect Croatian independence.[17] However, they are more indicative of a state and party that had a "purification" mission of its own, which it carried out with unspeakable savagery. Unlike the Italian army, which occupied Croatia but resisted orders to deport Jews, the Ustaŝhe slaughtered thousands of Jews in their own camps.[18]

Artuković's defenders claim that he was not an active supporter of these policies. However, prosecutors could point to a 1941 Zagreb newspaper that quoted Artuković as saying he planned to copy Nazi racial laws relating to Jews,[19] and a 1942 speech in which he told the parliament that the Croatian people had to "rid their national and state body of poisonous scourge and greedy imposters; Jews, communists, and Freemasons." Indeed, in that speech Artuković reported that his government had "solved this so-called Jewish question with a resolute and radical measure to protect not only itself and its nation, but also that which is most beautiful and the most noble in the Croatian people."[20] The April 30, 1941, decree that began the elimination of Croatia's Jews was virtually identical in its criteria to that adopted by the Nazis in Germany.[21]

The scale of the wartime slaughter among Yugoslavians was so great that very few witnesses survived to identify those most directly responsible. Those Ustaŝhe who might have implicated Artuković directly were slaughtered on Pavelić's orders before he fled,[22] killed by the Communists when they came to power,[23] or fled abroad and now had every reason not to volunteer information. The strongest evidence against Artuković lay in the position he held and in the orders he had cosigned establishing the directorate and its death camps. As damning as these were, however, they would not establish probable cause that he had personally committed *an extraditable offense*. To establish that, complicity in specific murders would be required.[24]

The flood of publicity generated by Drew Pearson's accusations intensified the Truman administration's discomfort. On the one hand, it did not want to cooperate with communists. On the other, it did not want to be seen as harboring a Nazi collaborator and war criminal. A handwritten note from Deputy Attorney General Peyton Ford's assistant to the Immigration and Naturalization Service (INS) reveals the Justice Department's thinking at the time.[25]

> Altho[ugh] it appears that deportation proceedings should be instituted, [Artuković] and/or his family should not be sent to apparently certain death at the hands of the Yugoslavia communists. Unless it can be established that he was responsible for the deaths of any Americans, I think that deportation should be to some non-communist country which will give him asylum. In fact, if his only crime was against communists, I think he should be given asylum in the U.S.

Two days later the deputy attorney general telephoned the INS commissioner to make it clear that he did not believe that Artuković should be delivered into the hands of his enemies.[26]

Considered together, the note and the telephone call suggest both a laudable unwillingness to cooperate with unjust regimes and a shocking ignorance of, or callousness toward, the war crimes of Croatia's Nazi collaborators. Indeed, if the war crimes were against communists, the aide's note seems to say, then they were hardly crimes at all and should be rewarded with asylum.

The note may sound aberrational, but in the anti-communist, anti-Semitic politics of the 1950s, it was not. The driving force of American immigration politics at the time was to characterize every fugitive from communism as a "freedom fighter," not to avenge the slaughter of millions of Jews and Gypsies who had died at the hands of the Nazis and their collaborators. With the Rosenberg spy case dominating the news, Jews were still widely associated with communism. The Justice Department, together with the Department of State, decided that the best solution was to deport the Artukovićs to a noncommunist nation, but Yugoslavia complicated matters by demanding Artuković's extradition. The Yugoslavian government had to go to court on its own; the Departments of State and Justice did not wish to lend their prestige to a communist request in any way. Artuković was arrested pursuant to a court order on August 29, 1951, brought before a U.S. commissioner, and locked up in the Los Angeles County jail.

Before an extradition hearing could be held, however, Artuković's attorney, on a petition for habeas corpus, had the case shifted to the federal district court, where he won Artuković's release on bail by portraying him, not inaccurately, as a family man.[27] In this proceeding, the primary issue involved the applicability of the 1902 extradition treaty with Serbia, on which the Yugoslavians had based their request.[28] This treaty, Artuković's attorney argued, could not be still in force because the subsequent Yugoslavian governments after World Wars I and II were federations of several states and not an expanded Serbia. After carefully surveying Yugoslavian history, Judge Peyton Hall agreed,[29] but his decision was overturned on appeal.[30] The Court of Appeals for the Ninth Circuit was apparently persuaded by an amicus brief from the Department of State to grant almost complete deference to presidential decisions regarding the continuity of foreign governments and treaties. No thought was given to the idea that extradition treaties should be deemed abrogated whenever a radical change in political regimes undermines the willingness or capacity of the requesting nation's courts to do justice.

The case was then sent back to Judge Hall to hear Artuković's other argument: that his extradition was barred by the political offense exception. Again, Judge Hall agreed. On April 3, 1956, he found "that all of the asserted offenses for which extradition is sought were the result of 'orders' issued by [Artuković] acting as [an] official of the [Croatian] government during the time of war." Accordingly, a "plain reading of the Indictment ... makes it immediately apparent that the offenses for which the surrender ... is sought, were offenses of a political character."[31]

Yugoslavia appealed, and on June 24, 1957, the Court of Appeals for the Ninth Circuit upheld Judge Hall's decision. The common crimes with which Artuković was charged, it reasoned, "show a marked degree of connection [with] a political element," because the crimes were alleged to have been committed on his orders, and not by him personally. "Various factions representing different theories of government were struggling for power during this period in Croatia." Therefore, if issuing those orders was a crime, it was an offense of a political character.

The judges did not seem to notice that the victims of these mass murders were not parties to the factional struggles for power. The court's focus was on the struggle for power, not the quality of the defendant's alleged acts. Accordingly, they observed, if a new exception was to be made for war crimes, "Perhaps changes should be made [in the treaties]."[32]

Other nations had tried to do just that, only to encounter stiff resistance from the State Department, motivated by conservatives in Congress. Of course, there was nothing to prevent the Court of Appeals from exercising its interpretive powers to exempt war crimes or crimes against humanity from the political offense exception. The scope of that exception had never been articulated in treaties or legislation but had been left to judges to define, case by case. But the court was not disposed to innovate and chose to rule—consistently with the Justice Department's view—that foreign officials who order genocide are entitled to protection from extradition, provided that they do not personally carry out their own orders.

This appalling decision was short-lived. On January 20, 1958, the Supreme Court vacated the ruling without comment and ordered the extradition hearing to go forward.[33] Its cryptic decision would later be interpreted by the hearing commissioner as simply recognizing that applicability of the political offense exception was best left to the fact-finding extradition hearing, and not to a judge reviewing the case on habeas corpus.[34] But it is more reasonable to conclude that the Justices were revolted by the idea that foreign officials who had committed war crimes should be given blanket immunity from extradition.[35]

On June 16, 1958, an evidentiary hearing was finally held before U.S. Commissioner Theodore Hocke. The atmosphere was tense as Croatian and Serbian refugees, some survivors of the atrocities on both sides of the conflict, crowded into the courtroom along with scores of reporters. Speaking for Yugoslavia, Los Angeles attorney (and later Republican Congressman) George E. Danielson declared that Artuković was responsible, among other things, for the murder of innocent peasants, whose mutilated bodies had been concealed in mines or caves, or thrown off cliffs; for the beating to death of three-year-old children as they cried out for their mothers; for the families burned alive in their homes or stables; for the slow and tortured deaths of pregnant women; and for the murder of forty-seven Serbian priests and forty-eight Jewish rabbis and cantors, all named.

But when the time came to present evidence, the Yugoslavian government did not present a single eyewitness to back up its charges. Its entire case rested on a pile of affidavits, all of which had been taken down by Communist officials not as verbatim transcripts, but as summaries of what the officials believed the affiants had said or meant. Of the 119 statements, only twelve mentioned Artuković by name, and not one contained firsthand knowledge of Artuković's words or deeds.

Because the affidavits appeared contrived, Commissioner Hocke allowed Artuković's counsel to rebut them with witnesses. Witness after witness blamed the Ustašhe's killings on "Dido" Kvaternik, the director of public order and security. Defense counsel also portrayed their client as a staunch anti-communist who was now being victimized by his old communist adversaries. The Yugoslavian government presented no live witnesses of its own and did not ask for time to obtain any.

On January 15, 1959, Commissioner Hocke ruled that Artuković could not be extradited, both because the Yugoslavian government had not established probable cause to believe that he was responsible for the war crimes and because, if he was responsible, he was shielded from extradition by the political character of his actions.[36] Hocke began his opinion by chastising the Yugoslavian government for waiting until almost the eve of the extradition hearing to present a batch of additional documents. The delay, he said, hampered the defendant's capacity "to obtain evidence to refute them."[37] In recognizing a right to rebut, the commissioner was clearly following the precedents at that time, which allowed evidence to disprove probable cause but barred evidence (e.g., of insanity) that would be a defense at trial.[38] As Hocke summarized Justice Brandeis's opinion in *Collins v. Loisel*, "It is not the function of the committing magistrate in foreign extradition proceedings to determine whether or not the accused is guilty, but merely to decide whether or not there is *competent* evidence which according to the law of the surrendering state would justify his apprehension and commitment for trial if the crime had been committed in that state."[39]

Hocke did not believe the Communist government's affidavits; he did believe the testimony of Croatian refugees who blamed Kvaternik for the regime's atrocities.[40] "The live witnesses [for the defense] were in the United States and under no fear, inducement, or compulsion to testify falsely," Hocke noted. "History indicates that this might not have been true in Yugoslavia at the time the evidence was taken."[41]

Although Artuković had signed the orders creating the security apparatus and the death camps, that alone was not enough to make him responsible for what happened in those camps. To hold superiors responsible for the crimes of their subordinates, the commissioner reasoned, "would probably result in failure to find any candidate who would accept the responsibilities of such a position if he was going to be held to answer for crimes committed by his underlings without more definite proof that they were acting under his orders."[42]

The commissioner's reasoning on this point defied common sense. To say that a superior should not be held responsible for the sporadic crimes of his subordinates is reasonable; no one can be expected to know everything his underlings do. In this case, however, the Ustašhe killings were so pervasive and savage that it strains credulity to say that a man in Artuković's position did not know of them, approve of them, and even applaud them. The atrocities in Yugoslavia cannot be characterized as isolated massacres brought on by the regrettable but understandable hysteria of battle. They were part of a sustained policy of mass killings that began in 1941 and did not end until Pavelić's regime fell in 1945. It also strains credulity that the Ustašhe would put a nonbeliever at such a crucial point in their chain of command if they thought he was not one of them. Nor is it likely that Artuković could have remained in such a position for two years if he had not been, morally and at least semi-actively, one of them.

However, extradition law, like criminal law (but unlike the law of impeachment), requires probable cause that a specific crime has been committed. The one extraditable crime for which the statute of limitations had not run out was murder, and to prove probable cause that Artuković was personally responsible for specific murders the court needed more than the accused's signature on a nonspecific order. It needed "a smoking gun" or an eyewitness, and the crucial fact for Hocke was that the Yugoslavian Communists—who were not above using torture to produce the sort of testimony they needed to convict an adversary—failed to produce the affidavit of a single witness personally linking Artuković to any of the mass killings. The commissioner was so appalled by the Yugoslavian government's performance that he was moved to declare: "I hope I do not live to see the day when a person will be held to answer for a crime in either the California or United States courts upon such evidence as was presented in this case on behalf of the complainant."[43]

A cynic might conclude that Yugoslavians did not really want Artuković back. To try him in Zagreb would have reopened old wounds that the Tito regime presumably wanted to heal. That regime's leaders may have felt they had to demand Artuković's return, but chose to submit inadequate evidence in order to preserve the tenuous unity of their divided state. However, it would be just as plausible to assume that no witnesses who could implicate Artuković in any particular killings survived the war. Or it could be that Artuković was a shrewd enough politician not to become personally implicated in specific killings.

Similarly, it is likely that Commissioner Hocke did not wish to be the first U.S. magistrate to send a staunch anti-communist, supported by a politically influential émigré group, back to certain death at the hands of a communist regime that had committed many atrocities of its own. Eisenhower's administration undoubtedly felt more obligation than Truman's to help Yugoslavia after its break with the Soviet bloc in 1954, but there is no reason to believe that the Republicans wanted to surrender fugitives of any stripe to communists at the height of the Cold War. So they, too, may have collaborated in the presentation of a weak case.

Given the politics of southern California at the time, the most popular way for the commissioner to have decided the case would have been to suspend the rule of noninquiry and deny extradition on the Jeffersonian ground that a Nazi collaborator could not possibly get a fair trial from the communists his regime had fought. Such a ruling would have made Hocke out to be both a defender of American justice and a staunch anti-communist.

If the commissioner were even more prudent, he could have decided the case solely on probable cause grounds. This would have tossed the hot potato straight back to the Yugoslavs. All they had to do, he could have said, was come up with direct evidence of Artuković's involvement in the war crimes. Then they could file a new request for his extradition.

But the commissioner did not chose either alternative. Instead, he granted Artuković the benefit of the political offense exception.[44] In so doing, he did not analyze the competing values. He simply endorsed the prior opinions of Judge Hall and the Ninth Circuit. As a result, he gave himself—and indirectly the courts—a deserved reputation for being monumentally insensitive to what he called "so-called war crimes."[45]

The decision to grant Artuković benefit of the political offense exception has been called "one of the most roundly criticized cases in the history of American extradition jurisprudence."[46] More than any other decision, it caused the political offense exception to lose its reputation as a shield for liberal revolutionaries and come to be seen as a "legal loophole," benefiting every sort of tyrant its inventors most despised. Read together, the *Ezeta* and *Artuković* decisions suggest that the humanitarian basis for the political offense exception had been supplanted by blind neutrality toward the conduct of foreign strife. But the neutrality was really not blind, except in the most formalistic sense, because the court and the Justice Department knew how politically unpopular it would be to extradite anyone back to a communist regime.

Knowing this, the court took judicial notice of communist injustice without saying so. Communist injustice, in those times, was considered too obvious to require proof. Knowing this, the United States, like most Western nations, had long refused to engage in extradition with either the Soviet Union or most of its satellites.[47] On the other hand, the court was forced to invoke the uprising test in a morally repellant way precisely because the rule of noninquiry forbade a candid inquiry into the capacity or willingness of the requesting regime to do justice.

The court was forced into this position in large part because the Department of State refused to review the wisdom of maintaining extradition with dubious regimes. The treaty with Yugoslavia (actually Serbia) should have been abrogated (or suspended) in 1928 when King Alexander became dictator, or in 1941 when the Germans and Italians invaded, or in 1945 when Tito's Communists consolidated their control. But the State Department never did. While the executive branch had diplomatic and administrative reasons for keeping the 1902 treaty with Serbia on the books, the courts were not so bound. They could have declared the old treaty inoperable because of intervening dictatorships. Or they could have refused to do business with communist regimes on straight due-process grounds. Instead, they put more weight on the first limb of the political offense exception than over time it could bear, morally or politically.

* * *

The first limb of the political offense exception was strained again in two other cases arising out of the Cold War, and in both instances it was made to perform a service that judicial enforcement of the second limb could have done better. In the first case, *In re Kolczynski*, a British court decided to stretch the uprising test to protect seven Polish seamen who had overpowered the skipper of their Communist fishing trawler out of fear that they would be returned to Poland to stand trial for anti-Communist remarks.[48] The seamen had not been part of any political movement or uprising; they had simply fled to avoid prosecution for their political beliefs. Not willing to trust the executive to deny extradition by invoking the second limb of the 1870 statute (thereby accusing the Polish government of engaging in political persecution), the British court simply ignored the uprising requirement and, "if only for considerations of humanity," declared the sailors to be protected political offenders.[49]

In the second case, an American court stretched the facts just as far to protect a Greek anti-Communist from surrender to a Communist town council on charges of embezzlement of municipal funds. Federal district judge Harlan H. Grooms of the

Northern District of Alabama had one perfectly good excuse not to surrender George B. Mylonas: The record of his *in absentia* trial was what one should expect of a politically charged communist trial.[50] The entire case could have been disposed of on the basis of the earlier *in absentia* case of *Ex parte Fudera*.[51] But Grooms went further to invoke the second limb of the political offense exception as if it was for the judiciary to enforce, noting that the Supreme Court had warned that "[c]are should ... be taken that the treaty not be made a pretext for collecting private debts, wreaking individual malice, or forcing the surrender of political offenders."[52] Then, apparently fearful that judicial reclamation of the second limb might not hold up against a claim of executive monopoly, Judge Grooms went on to also grant Mylonas benefit of the first limb—or uprising test—on the ground that the offense "was incidental to, formed a part, and was the aftermath of political disturbances, and accordingly [was] 'of a political character.'"[53]

This was stretching the point; nearly a decade had transpired between the end of the Greek civil war and Mylonas's alleged embezzlements. In the context of Balkan politics, however, the claim was plausible. The region is legendary for sustaining bitter political, ethnic, and family feuds for generations, if not centuries. However, what impressed the American judge was not the long memories of Balkan rivals, but the fact that Mylonas had fought in the Greek civil war against communists who were now the very officials charging him with a seemingly nonpolitical crime. So the judge stretched the political offense exception to give Mylonas shelter.

* * *

Technically speaking, Grooms did not remove his judicial blinders in order to predict future injustice; he found past injustice on the record and refused to perpetuate it. To this extent, his decision was not a full-fledged suspension of the rule of noninquiry but more of a modification where the foreign regime's injustice had already been established. So it could be argued that the executive's exclusive power to enforce the second limb of the political offense exception established in *Normano* survived. But the rule of noninquiry was undermined. Taken together, the Artuković, *Kolczynski*, and *Mylonas* cases present mute testimony that the rule of noninquiry has its limits and that there are certain requesting regimes that even formalists cannot stomach.

Unfortunately, to reach these results required intense anti-communism and strong ethnic opposition. Had the requesting regime been merely fascist, as in Normano's case, extradition might have occurred. The Germans, after all, were Christian capitalists committed to law and order, reciprocal extradition, and international trade. Similarly, had Yugoslavia's communism not been so salient, or had Artuković's ethnic support been countered by Holocaust remembrance groups demanding his expulsion, the result in his case might well have been different. In an era of positivist jurisprudence, ethnic politics and executive priorities continued to vie for dominance, while considerations of liberty, due process, and neutral principles of law remained on the shelf, to be applied only when necessary to clothe an essentially partisan purpose with moral respectability.

CHAPTER 11

Police Wars

We have before us the opportunity to forge for ourselves and for future generations a new world order, a world where the rule of law, not the law of the jungle, governs the conduct of nations.

President George Bush, January 16, 1991

The law of extradition, like most bodies of law, has grown spasmodically. Its history, like that of science, has consisted of long periods of administration marked by short bursts of innovation.[1] As with developments in science, each spasm of law-making has been dominated by paradigms that have liberated lawmakers from habitual modes of thought and blinded them to some of the implications of their reforms.

For the whigs who championed the political offense exception during the mid nineteenth century, the image that inspired their law-making was of liberal revolutionaries who fought militarily (like Bolivar, Mazzini, and Kossuth) to overthrow autocracies that the whigs despised. For the tories who subsequently sought to limit the exception, the image that provoked their law-making was of radical socialists, anarchists, war criminals, and terrorists whose political hatreds were not admired and whose attacks recklessly or deliberately killed bystanders.

Behind these competing images, and the ethnic empathies and antipathies they embodied, lay differing views regarding law, liberty, and order. Liberals (i.e., civil libertarians) were more prone than conservatives to respect the right of oppressed peoples to revolt, whereas conservatives tended to stress order over liberty, and sympathize with friendly foreign governments against those who would overthrow them. Civil libertarians were more likely to tolerate (moderate) socialists but reject authoritarians of the left and right. Conservatives, on the other hand, were more sympathetic to authoritarian capitalist regimes and quick to condemn even the most benign socialist regimes or revolutions.

Cutting across these political dispositions were a variety of ethnic sympathies, which could turn conservatives into libertarians and vice versa. When ethnic (or nativist) sympathies ran deep, invocations of principle often rang hollow.

During the nineteenth century, the young United States did not automatically ally itself with established foreign regimes. Rebellious by birth, it had a natural sympathy with colonial peoples fighting for their independence. Proudly republican, Americans had little sympathy for the autocratic regimes of Central and Eastern Europe and their efforts to put down popular revolts. U.S. officials often agreed with politically influential ethnic groups on the need to grant asylum to foreign revolutionaries and to deny demands for their extradition because, in the spirit of Washington's Farewell Address, the United States was oceans away from the conflicts and had no immediate political or economic stake in the outcomes.

In the twentieth century, the United States became an old nation, with an old nation's preference for order and regularity in its foreign relations. It became a great power and acquired a great power's obligations to allies. Intensely opposed to "communism," American officials saw little need to explore differences between degrees of "socialism" or "capitalism," either in governments or in rebel groups. They did not consider that these terms might have been rendered obsolete by the complexities of modern economics. As American business interests spread to the Middle East and Latin America, successive administrations found themselves defending authoritarian capitalist regimes against no less authoritarian socialist revolutionaries. As U.S. presidents acquired the capability to intervene covertly in foreign conflicts, they found the temptation to use that capability irresistible. The result was a loss of political distance between American interests and foreign conflicts, and an attendant loss of neutrality.

At the beginning of the twentieth century, American extradition policy could be used to shield fugitives from all sides of a foreign conflict and to declare, if necessary, a plague on both houses. Such was the spirit of isolationism. After World War II, the U.S. government became more interventionist, eager to defend capitalism against socialism, even when the capitalists were dictators and the socialists maintained modified market economies. The justification was something called "national self-interest," but the rhetoric was often moralistic. Rebels against "communist" regimes were assumed to be "democratic" fighters for "freedom," and most rebels against regimes the United States supported were assumed to be "terrorists." Linguistic integrity disappeared.

Moreover, from the U.S. government's point of view, the integrity of the foreign regime's legal system was irrelevant to the debate. Like most Americans, Justice Department lawyers rarely had the language skills and overseas experience to comprehend other legal systems well. Understanding those systems and the cultures in which they were imbedded was deemed unnecessary.

Confusing American military force with more subtle forms of political influence, successive administrations assumed they could "solve" internal conflicts in foreign lands with well-timed applications of military power or covert manipulation. Driven to refinance part of the American military machine with the sale of outmoded weapons to "Third World" countries, the United States also developed stronger ties with foreign armed forces than with civilian opposition groups. As a result, the United States became increasingly vulnerable to demands for the extradition of political fugitives from some of the world's less reputable regimes. This was the new world order that emerged from Cold War rivalry and the rise of international commerce.

* * *

In the eighteenth and nineteenth centuries, liberty and popular government had preceded the development of law enforcement agencies, the Justice Department, a full-fledged foreign service, and clandestine agencies. Consequently, the U.S. government, like the people it represented, was generally hostile to the return of fugitives to authoritarian regimes. By the late twentieth century, however, the United States had become as bureaucratic as France had been two centuries before. The result was a very different approach to extradition—one powerfully sympathetic to foreign law enforcement agencies and indifferent, when not downright hostile, to political fugitives.

Prior to the 1970s, the United States received fewer than a dozen extradition requests a year. By 1978, it was receiving about one hundred; by 1987, the number had grown to 239 as international police cooperation, aided by computers and telecommunications, grew apace.[2] About a third involved white-collar crimes like embezzlement and banking fraud. Another third involved narcotics trafficking, while the remainder included crimes of violence, including terrorist killings and war crimes.[3] The desire of American law enforcement agencies to recover fugitives from American law grew, too, as the technology for tracking fugitives improved.

Within the Departments of Justice and State, legal bureaucracies were established to deal with these requests and to handle requests for the return of fugitives from American law. Joining the State Department's Office of Legal Advisor (OLA) was a new Justice Department Office of International Affairs (OIA), which not only coordinated extradition policy but also helped redraft treaties and plan litigation and legislative strategies. In addition, the Justice Department created the Office of Special Investigations (OSI) to rid the United States of war criminals. Within U.S. attorneys offices in major cities like New York, Los Angeles, and Miami, legal aid to foreign regimes burgeoned.

The institutional ethic of the attorneys who handled the new international trade in fugitives was, not surprisingly, to increase the recovery of fugitives from American law, not to protect the right of foreigners to revolt or to preserve the neutrality of American courts toward foreign disputes. Nothing in the attorneys' work made them sensitive to, or disposed them to become informed about, the politics that might lie behind a foreign government's request. Considerations of foreign policy and career advancement encouraged them to presume that the requests were legitimate. Justice Nelson's hope in *Kaine* that the executive branch would screen extradition requests for corrupt motives did not materialize, precisely because the routinization that Nelson had feared numbed executive and judicial sensibilities.

The triumph of administrative routine over independent judgment, national neutrality, or considerations of justice was completed in the mid-1970s, when the Justice Department decided, in order to enhance the reciprocal surrender of American fugitives, to represent all requesting regimes in American courts. The decision was most commonly portrayed as a mere administrative arrangement. In fact, it had serious policy implications, because it put U.S. attorneys automatically on the side of requesting regimes and against the persons whose extradition was sought.

* * *

On top of these developments were intense demands for effective legal action against drug trafficking, war criminals from the Holocaust, and terrorism. Extradition as a procedure involving isolated crimes was replaced by extradition as a weapon in "wars" against crime. Sub-bureaucracies were set up to wage these police wars, subject to congressional oversight and pressure. Politicians demanded "results," and results demanded "body counts," so the defendants were no longer individuals entitled to justice, but symbolic pawns in partisan political games. The facts of individual cases became less important than their potential for demonstrating that politicians were getting "tough on crime." Common to each of these "wars" on crime was an effort to limit or destroy many of the inconvenient constraints on extradition, including the political offense exception and due process of law.

During the late 1970s, a well-publicized "war on drugs" was declared. This war would become distinguished both by an effort to abolish the political offense exception, because it might protect politically connected drug lords, and an effort to circumvent the law of extradition by abducting suspects from abroad.

The first two U.S. treaties of modern times to drop the political offense exception were negotiated by the Carter administration with Colombia[4] and Mexico.[5] Both countries were major sources of marijuana and cocaine, and their drug lords had used their vast wealth to corrupt law enforcement. These treaties were presented as mere technical changes in the law, given a perfunctory review by the Senate Committee on Foreign Relations, and approved without notice to civil libertarians or ethnic groups that might have recognized the larger implications of the changes. A similar treaty with the Netherlands slipped through the Senate at the same time.[6]

A second war on crime was launched in the late 1970s to expel from the United States Nazi war criminals wrongly admitted after the World War II. Like other wars on crime, this was a no-holds-barred operation driven by intense congressional oversight and energized by Holocaust remembrance groups in the United States and abroad.

Finally, there was the "war on terrorism," which began in the late 1960s with a major international effort to combat aircraft hijacking. One strategy of this war was to conclude multilateral treaties to facilitate the surrender (or prosecution) of aircraft hijackers and saboteurs.[7] Proponents of these treaties proceeded on the assumption that hijacking, like the bombing of aircraft, was such a heinous offense that it could never be justified on political or libertarian grounds, or excused as a form of political resistance.

But hijackings were only part of the problem. Western nations were plagued with all manner of terroristic conflict. West Germany was victimized by the neoanarchism of the socialistic Baader-Meinhoff Gang; France and Spain, by the Basque independence movement. The United Kingdom and its citizens were attacked by the provisional wing of the Irish Republican Army, the Irish National Liberation Army, and a variety of Protestant paramilitaries in Northern Ireland. Starting in the late 1960s, Palestinian groups began exporting their violence far beyond the borders of Israel and its occupied territories, while in Italy the Red Brigades kidnapped and killed a former prime minister.

But not all terroristic violence was directed against the state or the symbols of economic and political power. Police and military terrorism against terrorists became commonplace in Latin America, Northern Ireland, and Israel. In Argentina, the kidnapping and killing of the left-wing Tupamaros was answered by a massive program of government-run killings and "disappearances" conducted by covert military "death squads." These practices soon spread throughout Central and South America, and when the practitioners ultimately sought refugee in the United States, they presented special problems for the evolving law of extradition.

The United States was relatively exempt from terrorist attacks at home. There were occasional aircraft hijackings by black American dissidents from U.S. airports to Cuba, France, and Libya during the 1960s, and some domestic bombings by the Weatherman Faction of the Students for a Democratic Society, Puerto Rican nationalists, the Ku Klux Klan, and other groups on the extreme left and right of the political spectrum. But fear of terrorist attacks was rampant, particularly at the height of anti-war protests against the Nixon administration. When a Weatherman unit blew up a restroom in the U.S. Capitol, most public buildings in Washington were brought under tight security, and American politicians lost whatever residual tolerance they might have had for revolutionaries.

During the 1960s, 1970s, and 1980s, diplomats and officials of many nations became the object of assassinations and kidnappings. In 1963, President John F. Kennedy was assassinated; in 1968, his brother Robert was murdered. In Iran, Lebanon, and Kuwait, U.S. embassies were attacked, and in Iran in 1980, fifty-three U.S. embassy staffers were taken hostage. During the early 1970s, the United States, in violation of its long-standing commitment to the political offense exception, signed a multilateral convention which labeled all attacks on diplomats inexcusable under all circumstances.[8] Later in the decade a similar effort was undertaken to condemn the taking of hostages under all circumstances.[9]

Common to these actions was a sense that aiding foreign prosecutions of international "outlaws" was more important for its symbolic than tangible effects. These wars were often characterized as a form of moral and cultural self-defense. In some respects, they provided a new outlet for moral and cultural fervor as the Cold War wound down. Unfortunately, when terms like "war" and "self-defense" are used, and when conflicts are seen as a clash of cultures rather than the prosecution of routine criminals, the end is assumed to justify almost any means. Instead of promoting a respect for law, this new world order reduced extradition to a tool of partisan politics.[10]

* * *

Starting in 1981, the Reagan administration launched a three-fold attack on the political offense exception. The first strategy was to remove the exception from all U.S.

extradition treaties by legislation. The second was to eliminate it treaty by treaty. The third was to persuade the courts to interpret it out of existence, or to transfer its administration to the State Department as a "political question."

According to the Reagan administration, the courts were soft on terrorists and could no longer be trusted properly to administer the political offense exception. As proof, administrative spokesmen cited judicial delays in authorizing the extradition to Israel of an alleged bomber for the Palestine Liberation Organization (Abu Eain), judicial refusal to extradite to the United Kingdom several members of the Provisional Irish Republican Army (McMullen, Mackin, Doherty, and Quinn), and the judicial decision in 1959 to grant the political crimes defense to Andrija Artuković, the alleged Nazi war criminal.

However, extradition requests for these alleged terrorists and war criminals did not just arise in the normal course of business. They were solicited, shaped, timed, and engineered by government lawyers as part of a larger administration plan. The campaign was conducted in secret. At no time did the Justice Department disclose its litigation strategy to the press or make public its representations to foreign governments. Had those governments been required to appear in court with their own attorneys to press their extradition requests as they had in the first *Artuković* case, a coordinated campaign could not have been conducted in secret. The department would have had to disclose its litigation strategy openly and independently, as an intervening "friend of the court." As counsel for the requesting regimes, however, U.S. attorneys and Justice Department officials could camouflage their strategy behind a seemingly neutral facade of legal representation, and behind this facade, manipulate, coordinate, and control the cases to serve their policy ends.

Because the lawyers were fighting "wars" rather than just enforcing law, the extradition cases of the 1970s and 1980s would be marred by government abuses of the legal process. Justice Department attorneys would wrongly accuse several men of being heinous war criminals and achieve the incarceration of one for more than eight years. They would persuade the U.S. Supreme Court to turn deportation into a form of executive extradition and accept kidnapping as a lawful alternative to extradition. They would even defend military invasion as an alternative to extradition, giving new meaning to the old maxim "When arms speak, the laws are silent."[11]

As in all wars, urgent ends came to justify normally illegal means. Applying wartime metaphors to police work permitted politicians and government attorneys to relabel individual defendants as nonpersons, stripping them of the fair treatment that should proceed from a formal presumption of innocence. As with fugitive slaves, American judges looked the other way, and American law again became an instrument of oppression.

CHAPTER 12

Exempting Terrorists

*The [political offense] exception does not make a random bombing
intended to result in the cold-blooded murder of civilians incidental to
a purpose of toppling a government, absent a direct link between the
perpetrator, a political organization's goals, and the specific act.*

Eain v. Wilkes, *1981*

The political offense exception was developed for an age of muskets and swords, when rebel troops usually met government forces in open fields in close military formations that massed their inaccurate firepower against other close formations. At that time, it seemed possible for armies to minimize the loss of civilian lives. In 1863, for example, 75,000 Confederate troops fought 95,000 Union troops for three days in and around the town of Gettysburg, Pennsylvania. Twice the battle swept through the town itself, then inhabited by about 1,800 civilians huddled in their cellars. When the smoke cleared, 51,000 soldiers lay dead, but only one civilian had been killed— by a stray bullet that pierced two doors.

   As long as civilians were left alone, and as long as civilians left the fighting to soldiers, it was possible to think of war as limited and limitable. Nineteenth-century military doctrine fostered this belief by portraying commanding officers as noble, disciplined, honorable men who would naturally respect and protect the lives of women and children. Some civilian casualties could not be avoided, of course, especially during the siege of cities, but these were the regrettable by-products of war and not its object. To those Anglo-Americans whose knowledge of war came mainly from heroic paintings, civilian populations were deliberately savaged mainly in "barbaric," non-Christian societies (which the honorable soldiers of the colonial powers were then attempting to "civilize.")

   Of course, Europe had known bitter ethnic and religious strife in which large portions of the civilian population were tormented and killed, often for the greater glory of God. It had, for example, suffered the religious massacres of the Thirty Years War and the class warfare of the French Revolution. But memories of these bitter conflicts had receded during the century of peace that followed the defeat of Napoleon and the Congress of Vienna. The destruction of civilians was now confined to the barbaric margins of Europe's empires, so that truly civilized nations, which did not expect to meet on the battlefield again, could safely promise to obey self-imposed "laws of war."

Louis Napoleon's shooting of a grenadier during a scuffle in Boulogne did not disturb such beliefs. The unfortunate violence harmed only a soldier and seemed "incidental" to a political speech that was meant to inspire two companies of soldiers to join an uprising meant to restore Napoleonic "honor" to bourgeois France. So John Stuart Mill could argue that Louis Napoleon deserved protection from extradition as a political offender—even though his "uprising" had not yet matured into a full-fledged armed rebellion.

More disturbing by far was the attempt by two Frenchmen in 1852 to blow up the train on which the new Emperor Napoleon was traveling. This was terrorism. The attack was not narrowly focused on military personnel who could be said to have assumed the risk. It showed utter disregard for the lives of civilians on the train, and it was intended, in a hare-brained way, to advance the vague purposes of a clandestine group that enjoyed little popular support and was unequipped to contend for state power by putting uniformed forces into the field.

Similarly, there was great reluctance to extend the political offense exception to small bands of Irish rebels. They, too, did not fight military style but set off bombs in public places where they were likely to wreak carnage on people uninvolved in the struggle for state power.

By the same reasoning, it was possible to shield some rioters like Castioni from extradition. The uprising in which he participated was spontaneous, and thus lacked the sustained organization and discipline of more inspired efforts, but it did involve a bid for municipal power, however fleeting. The killing, so characterized, was not pointless.

Unlike Castioni, the anarchist Theodule Meunier had no interest in seizing the reins of government. He only wanted to destroy the state, by the militarily futile, socially terrifying act of killing or maiming anyone who happened to be in the café at the time. Other anarchist attacks were more focused but still operated at a highly abstract, symbolic level where wins and losses could not be counted. So the anarchists threatened the stability of civil society and were deemed, like mutineers and rebellious slaves, to constitute an intolerable threat to all society.

To the Jacobins, asylum was to be granted only to fighters for liberty; to the autocrats of Austria, Prussia, and Russia, it was to be denied to the enemies of the established order. By contrast, the more moderate Americans in the late eighteenth and early nineteenth centuries understood that liberty depends on a system of habitual order, and that lasting order depends, perhaps paradoxically, on liberty. Accordingly, they saw the need for a complex, law-driven system of "ordered liberty" so that revolution against tyranny would not be necessary. Unlike most societies, their new nation was not so riven by religious, ethnic, or class rivalries that both order and liberty were impossible to achieve.

But the United States was an aberration, not the norm. The norm in most nations, then as now, was not law but politics—and not a politics of "E Pluribus Unum" but of exclusion, where one group's gain was likely to be another's loss. The Americans who developed their nation's extradition law believed that their political culture (and England's) was exceptional, and expected that many countries—especially in Latin America—were probably doomed to exchange orderly tyranny for disorderly rebellion for decades, if not centuries, to come.

In this whiggish perspective, reflected in Melville's *Benito Cereno* and *Billy Budd* (and the writings of Nathaniel Hawthorne), the history of most peoples, most of the time, was one of victimization and tyranny. Without the sort of legal constraints the British and American people had imposed on their governments, foreign officials could be trusted to victimize those over whom they held power. The United States would have to deal with some of these regimes and their comparably oppressive successors. If it chose to engage in extradition, it would have to find ways to maintain neutrality during inevitable periods of upheaval. From this "liberal" understanding of the moral ambiguity and complexity of foreign civil strife, then, came a second reason for shielding political fugitives from extradition—the need for neutrality.

For the United States, neutrality toward foreign power struggles was relatively easy so long as transportation across oceans was difficult, overseas trade was limited, and the capacity to project American military power to other lands was minimal. Neutrality was also a relatively easy stance for U.S. presidents (or British prime ministers) to take when ethnic groups demanded partisanship on one side or the other of a foreign conflict. Liberal toleration could be pleaded as a basis for giving asylum to fugitives from both sides, and so there was broad support for a political offense exception to extradition.

The most reprehensible of fugitives were those who tried to destabilize government without organizing an alternative. Accordingly, in response to the attack on Louis Napoleon's train, the *attentat* clause was born. Because they bombed French cafés (and barracks) without organizing any alternatives, the anarchists were denied protection too. Such were the early attempts to develop humanitarian exceptions to the exception for political offenders.

* * *

Since World War II, efforts to mitigate the immoral potential of the political offense exception have accelerated. In 1949, the victorious Allies adopted the Geneva Conventions on land warfare to prohibit some of the worst conduct of their adversaries. The common Article 3 to these conventions denies benefit of the political offense exception to soldiers in international wars who commit atrocities against "persons taking no active part in the hostilities."[1]

Starting in 1948, the United Nations tried less successfully to win equally wide support for a convention against genocide. Article 6 of this convention proposed to strip persons charged with genocide of the protection of the political offense exception, and defined genocide, among other things, as causing "mental harm to members of . . . a national, ethnical, racial or religious group."[2]

This sweeping definition provoked stiff opposition, particularly from conservatives in the U.S. Senate who feared that Americans could be extradited to stand trial elsewhere for interracial harms.[3] The United States did not finally ratify the U.N.'s Genocide Convention until 1986,[4] and its implementation statute does not provide for extradition.

In 1977, an effort was made to bring fighters in noninternational conflicts under the same war-fighting limitations as soldiers in international conflicts. Protocols 1 and 2 to the Geneva Conventions of 1949, as these proposals were called, advocated a "war crimes exception" to the political offense exception.[5] Most proponents of a war crimes exception would deny rioters like Castioni benefit of the political offense exception.

The Geneva Conventions governing the behavior of individual soldiers toward prisoners of war, women, children, and the sick won the immediate and widespread endorsement of politicians, even though their extradition provisions have never been enforced. The Genocide Convention and the 1977 Protocols, by contrast, ran into immediate resistance, particularly in the United States. One reason for resistance to the Genocide Convention was the indiscriminate nature of much modern warfare. So long as wars could—at least in theory—be fought according to rules of engagement that kept military operations away from civilian populations, then military men were reasonably safe from charges that they indiscriminately annihilated noncombatants. But with technological advances in the ability to create carnage from the air, of the kind visited on Antwerp and London by Hitler's *blitzkrieg*, on Tokyo and Dresden by Allied firebombing, and on Hiroshima and Nagasaki by U.S. nuclear bombs, it was more difficult for governments to claim that the massive destruction of civilian populations was not a war aim.

The moral proposition advanced by the 1977 Protocols to the Geneva Conventions seemed as unassailable as the prohibition against genocide. Fighters on both sides of noninternational wars ought to have as much respect for the lives and well-being of noncombatants as soldiers in international wars. But they do not. No insurgent group has ever agreed to abide by the Protocols' standards, which, among other things, deny prisoner-of-war (POW) status to people caught with concealed weapons.[6] Most insurgent groups also lack the capacity to take and hold prisoners of war.

However, opposition has not been confined to insurgent groups. President Reagan flatly refused to submit Protocol 1 to the Senate for its advice and consent. To do so, he declared, would legitimize "terrorists" and other participants in Soviet-sponsored, anti-colonial "wars of national liberation" by giving them legal standing, including prisoner-of-war status, under international law.[7] Reagan wanted people he defined as terrorists to be treated as ordinary criminals, politically and legally, which meant, among other things, denying them shelter under the political offense exception.

The U.S. Joint Chiefs of Staff objected vociferously to both Protocols.[8] Like the president, they did not want client regimes in countries like El Salvador to have to grant POW status to captured guerrillas, since they were struggling to characterize their conflicts as something closer to police actions than belligerencies.[9]

The Joint Chiefs also understood that it was virtually impossible for any military or paramilitary force of the sort the United States had been sponsoring in the "Third

World" to pacify armed civilian populations (or to minimize casualties among American "advisors") without attacking civilian targets, because many of the guerrillas were civilians, or obtained shelter and intelligence assistance from civilians, including members of their own families. Since the war in Vietnam had persuaded many Americans that it was virtually impossible to fight popularly based insurgencies by traditional military means, the United States chose not to ratify Protocols 1 or 2. Thus this effort to add a "war crimes exception" for alleged terrorists to the law of extradition was defeated.[10]

Like the Joint Chiefs, many rebel commands around the world recognized that victory in the traditional military sense was not possible, either for them or for the governments they opposed. It was manifestly impossible for most insurgents to organize large-scale military units. They had to operate in small, self-contained, plainclothes units and live as individual civilians. Anything more organized or visible would soon be detected and destroyed by the technologically superior state forces.

Successful guerrilla wars, like those that drove the British out of Palestine, the French out of Algeria, the Americans out of Vietnam, and the Soviets out of Afghanistan, were wars of attrition, calculated more to win psychological victories over civilian populations than to defeat armies in the field. Psychological control over the local population had to be achieved by a combination of tactics that simultaneously terrorized potential informants into silence and brought state terrorism down upon the local community. Each time the rebels goaded the regime to punish the civilian population for the rebels' actions, the rebels gained civilian support.

That support, however, was based on bitterness, not hope, and led to a civil war of brutal reprisals. As a result, most uprisings are today seen by outsiders as more criminal than military, more dirty than clean, and more repugnant than noble. Because most regimes today have extensive surveillance capacities, most rebels cannot wear uniforms, mass in large numbers, and thus demonstrate their own capacity to achieve order and discipline. Indeed, to achieve their objective, which is to destabilize the regime in power, most rebels must create civilian fear and disorder, because they have to prove, as part of their psychological warfare, that the regime is incapable of achieving order or protecting its civilian supporters. But the more rebels pursue this strategy, the more outsiders come to view them as enemies of public order and think of them as more like anarchists than like Washington or Lee. Such rebels become known as "terrorists."

In military wars, evidence of success is fairly objective. It can be measured in men killed, territory controlled, and resources captured or destroyed. In psychological wars for the hearts, minds, fears, and exhaustion of civilian populations, wins and losses are much more subjective. As in Vietnam, guerrillas may score a major victory simply by mounting an impressive offensive, even though they are beaten in the process. The local population may give up on the regime that fails to protect them, or outsiders may give up on sending troops to fight in a seemingly endless war that cannot be won.

Further undermining the sympathy on which support for a political offense exception depends is that many rebellions today involve ethnic, religious, or class hatreds that go back centuries. In such contexts, where a short-term military victory is not expected, the tactics of the insurgents and counterinsurgents often become wantonly vicious. Reprisal killings, rapes, indiscriminate bombings, assassinations, and massacres become so commonplace that insiders and outsiders become inured to them. The fighting becomes so bitter that all sense of tactics is lost, and vengeful actions actually strengthen, rather than weaken, the opposition's resolve. In the blind bitterness of religious conflicts, defeats can be transformed into victories by declaring that the dead are martyrs to one God or another. The typical uprising of the late twentieth century is one in which all sides commit atrocities, as in French North Africa, Northern Ireland, Israel/Palestine, Angola, Afghanistan, Nicaragua, El Salvador, Rwanda, Liberia, Somalia, or the Sudan.

Eventually the violence from such dirty wars spills over into the international arena. Extremists shoot up international airports, hijack airliners, and otherwise try foreign patience for their cause. Bystander nations eventually conclude that it is in their interest to aid the regime in power. The regime in power may be bad, but the rebels are no better, and someone has to win, if only to end the "pointless suffering," particularly of innocent foreigners. As President Franklin Roosevelt is supposed to have said of the Nicaraguan dictator Anastazio Somoza, he might be a son-of-a-bitch, but he was our son-of-a-bitch.[11] Thus governments come to characterize the paramilitary operations of repressive regimes as "law enforcement" and hit-and-run attacks by insurgents as "terrorism," even though both sides are employing terrifying violence for political ends, and neither has shown the least capacity or intention of promoting the liberal politics of inclusiveness that are essential to the creation of ordered liberty. To bystander nations who care more about safe trade, tourism, or great-power rivalry than the seemingly impossible dream of ordered liberty, this failing seems less important than that somebody win and the violence and instability end.

During most of the Cold War, it was virtually impossible for many nations to dissociate most insurgencies (and counter-insurgencies) from great-power rivalries. Indeed, most of the civil wars of the Cold War era were influenced at one point or another by covert assistance from the United States, the Soviet Union, or their surrogates. The United States was particularly prone to underestimate the power of local ethnic, religious, or class hatred and to see most insurgents as proxies for the Soviet Union or China. This led American officials to treat socialist rebels as terrorists, and to disbelieve or dismiss the atrocities of the capitalists and generals who fought them as the mere excesses of justified law enforcement.

As hot wars gave way to the Cold War, and as the Cold War blended with local police wars, the political offense exception came to depend for its justification ever more heavily on the slender reed of neutrality. At the same time, a shrinking globe, protracted conflict, and spillover violence made neutrality harder to sell, and so the political offense exception fell deeper into disfavor.

* * *

The case that most undermined the exception—during the Carter administration—involved Peter Gabriel John McMullen, an Irishman who had fled to the United States to escape both the British army and the IRA. McMullen was a Northern Irish Catholic who had, for lack of other employment, joined the British army. He was stationed near Belfast when, on "Bloody Sunday," January 30, 1972, soldiers from his unit fired into a crowd of unarmed protesters in his home county of Derry. Thirteen were killed, twenty-eight wounded. Outraged by these killings and by the unwillingness of Unionists and the British to respond constructively to more than five years of nonviolent protests by Catholics, McMullen deserted the army, leaving behind a bomb in the barracks. For the next two years, according to his own testimony, he was active in the IRA, training members in military tactics and, from within the United States, "coordinating a considerable number of arms shipments back to Northern Ireland."[12]

By mid-1974, however, McMullen was disenchanted with the IRA and attempted to resign. His objections, he later said, were to its "indiscriminate bombing . . . and the fact that they had grown away from the grass-roots people in the streets." Moving his family to Dublin, he took a job as a butcher. However, as he later testified, "once in [the IRA], you never get out."[13] In November 1974 he was arrested by the Irish authorities, convicted of membership in the IRA, incitement to riot, and possession of a gun, and incarcerated as a "non-aligned" (i.e., non-IRA) prisoner.

Following his release from prison in 1977, McMullen testified, he was pressured back into IRA service. He sheltered members in his home, trained them, and coordinated more arms shipments from the United States. However, he refused to help kidnap an American bar owner, Daniel Flannigan, for ransom. For this, he claimed, an IRA court of inquiry sentenced him to death. Thus, when he left his family and fled to the United States early in 1978, McMullen saw himself only as a fugitive from the IRA.[14]

That, of course, was quite enough. Desperate not to be sent back to Northern Ireland and to probable death at the hands of the IRA, McMullen contacted the Oakland office of the U.S. Bureau of Alcohol, Tobacco, and Firearms, offering to exchange information about the IRA in return for political asylum. Much to his surprise, the U.S. government used the information he volunteered to arrest him for illegal entry and to invite a British request for his extradition. The bomb he had left behind in the barracks in Ripon, Yorkshire, had gone off, slightly injuring a cleaning woman, whose presence he had not anticipated.

Even so, McMullen cooperated with both U.S. and Scotland Yard investigators. He could not believe that the United States—and particularly the pro–human rights Carter administration—would condemn him as a terrorist and seek, by extradition and deportation, to deliver him to the very regime he had fought to overthrow.[15] Nor could he imagine that the United States, an historic nation of asylum, would ship him off to a British prison where the IRA would be able to kill him.

Because McMullen had broken with the IRA and described it unfavorably in court, most Irish American groups despised him. Among other things, he testified that the IRA "engages in beatings, kneecappings (crippling by shooting into or crushing the victim's knees), and murder to maintain discipline within its membership."[16] But Paul O'Dwyer, the New York civil rights activist and lawyer, recognized that the fate of all IRA members who sought refuge in the United States was at stake and, in conjunction with San Francisco lawyer William Goodman, undertook McMullen's defense. O'Dwyer and his associates would subsequently become involved, in one way or another, in all the IRA extradition cases. If the Justice Department could conduct a coordinated campaign, so too could Irish American republicans.

The defense was successful. Relying on the "essence" of the *Castioni* case, Magistrate Frederick J. Woelflen ruled in May 1979 that McMullen was entitled to the protection of the political crimes defense because the bombing of which he was accused "occurred during an uprising," was "incidental" to that uprising, and was committed in furtherance of that uprising. McMullen was also "a member of a group participating in the uprising" and was "engaged in acts of political violence with a political end." Relying on the *Artukovic* decision, which was binding on his court as part of the Ninth Circuit, the magistrate went on to declare that "even though the offense be deplorable and heinous the criminal actor will be excluded from deportation [actually extradition] if the crime is committed under these pre-requisites."[17]

The decision attracted little attention in the press, but it outraged Carter administration officials involved in the new and highly publicized war against terrorism. To protect members of a terrorist group from extradition simply because they were "political" was totally unacceptable to them. So too was the judge's reiteration of the Ninth Circuit's willingness to protect even "the most deplorable and heinous" offenders. If the decision stood, they declared, the United States would become a haven for terrorists. In their opinion, the magistrate had actually extended the political crimes defense by applying it to a barracks bombing in England, remote from the focus of the alleged uprising. Ignoring that the term "United Kingdom" included Northern Ireland, U.S. officials claimed that the *McMullen* decision would protect Irish or Palestinian terrorists operating in Europe or the United States.

The British government was not pleased either. While the magistrate agreed that the IRA was a terroristic organization,[18] he also found, by the British government's own admissions, that the IRA was engaged in an uprising.[19] The decision was a clear setback for British efforts to portray Northern Ireland as beset by crime rather than revolution.[20]

Even so, the magistrate narrowed the political offense exception in one respect: He asserted that *membership* in a rebel organization was a necessary criterion for applying the uprising test. That was not what the British court had required in *Castioni;* there was no rebel organization behind the mob Castioni joined. The magistrate also refused to deny extradition on the ground that McMullen might be subject to "physical or mental mistreatment . . . should he be incarcerated in a British prison in either England or Northern Ireland."[21] The second limb of the political offense exception was still for the executive to enforce.

The opinion in *McMullen* was brief, casual, and imprecise. Administration officials would later refer to it as proof that U.S. magistrates lacked the ability to understand the legal, moral, or political implications of extradition in an age of terrorism, and it inspired them to intensify their efforts to change the law, in the courts, by treaties, and by legislation.

* * *

The core issue in McMullen's case was the bombing of an army barracks by a member of a disciplined, paramilitary organization who was acting on its behalf. The target was military and the degree of violence used was appropriate to the IRA's political and psychological warfare objective. The act itself could not be condemned as heinous, even though it was meant to intimidate soldiers and civilians outside the conflict's locale (although not outside the nation under attack) and one civilian employee of the British army was injured.

The next case to come before the courts raised, in starker terms, the question of when, if ever, fugitives who attack presumptively innocent persons should be accorded protection under the political crimes defense. The defendant, Ziad Abu Eain, a twenty-year-old Palestinian living in Chicago, was charged by the Israeli government with planting a bomb in a trash bin in a crowded marketplace in Tiberias—a resort town on the Sea of Galilee, within the State of Israel, north of the Israeli-occupied West Bank of the River Jordan. The bomb, which exploded on May 14, 1979, killed two Jewish boys and wounded thirty-six others. Some lost limbs.

Like Peter McMullen, Abu Eain put his trust in the American legal system. Instead of going underground after an initial visit from the FBI, he turned himself in, only to be arrested on August 21, 1979. His case came to the attention of Arab American groups, and his attorneys included Abdeen M. Jabara, a noted Arab American lawyer from Detroit, and Ramsey Clark, the former attorney general of the United States. The Israeli government was represented by U.S. Attorney Thomas P. Sullivan, assisted by Louis G. Fields, head of the Office on Terrorism and Narcotics, U.S. Department of State,[22] and Israeli officials. The U.S. government's strategy in the case was supervised by Warren Christopher, then deputy secretary of state. In short, this was no ordinary criminal case.

Indeed, passions were intense. The U.S. Attorney's conduct of the case so offended an expert witness that he later wrote to a member of Congress: "In my opinion, Mr. Sullivan's purpose in appearing personally was to convert the hearing on the issue of probable cause into a criminal trial of 'a terrorist,' but without either the procedural or substantive due process of law which would be applicable in a criminal trial."[23] Sullivan had reason to be passionate. He believed that Abu Eain's friends and relatives were plotting to kill him and free the prisoner when he appeared before the magistrate.[24]

On the other side, the American-Arab Anti-Discrimination Committee sponsored a Ziad Abu Eain Defense Committee. Seventeen ambassadors from Arab countries (mostly friendly to the United States) wrote to Secretary of State Cyrus Vance to inform him that the extradition of the accused would contribute to "a profound sense of injustice" among nations in the Middle East. Petitions on Abu Eain's behalf were signed by 30,000 Arab Americans.[25]

A secondary issue in Abu Eain's case concerned the extent to which a defendant may challenge the veracity of the charges against him. The Israeli government alleged that Abu Eain drove ninety miles from his home in Ramallah on the West Bank to plant the bomb, but the only evidence supporting this contention was the confession of an alleged coconspirator, a young Palestinian named Jamal Hassan Yasin. At the extradition hearing, Abu Eain's attorneys pointed out that the confession was in Hebrew, a language Yasin did not understand. The Israeli government countered with a document bearing the young man's signature that declared he had been brought before an Arabic-speaking judge, understood his statement, and stood by its truthfulness. However, within a few weeks of this court appearance, Yasin twice repudiated his confession in sworn statements to his attorneys—one Israeli and one Palestinian—claiming that he accused Abu Eain only because he knew he was out of the country and presumably beyond the reach of Israeli law.

Abu Eain's attorneys argued that self-serving accusations by alleged coconspirators should be received with caution and warned that the statement might have been extracted from Yasin under duress; Israeli interrogators were known to beat suspected terrorists. Abu Eain insisted that the accusation was false, that he had been in Ramallah on the day of the bombing, celebrating the birth of a nephew. He offered fourteen affidavits in support of this contention.[26] However, the affidavits and Yasin's recantations were not accepted into evidence. Magistrate Olga Jurco adhered to the longstanding doctrine that "the accused does not have the right to contradict the demanding country's proof or pose questions of credibility."[27] In other words, she would not suspend the rule of noninquiry to consider allegations that the charges against the accused were obtained by torture.

Abu Eain's attorneys had to rely on the political offense exception. However, the magistrate refused to find the existence of the sort of "uprising" contemplated by the exception. The most she would acknowledge was the existence of a "conflict," which the U.S. Court of Appeals for the Seventh Circuit later observed might not rise to the level of strife envisioned by the political offense exception. In fact, the Court of Appeals suggested that the threshold of conflict required to invoke the defense might be something approaching "on-going, organized battles between contending armies."[28] However, it avoided such a ruling by associating Abu Eain's alleged crime with the polar opposite of war: isolated acts of anarchistic violence. The bombing, the Court of Appeals ruled, "was not shown to be incidental to the conflict in Israel"; thus, the magistrate was correct in ruling that it was not covered by the political offense exception.[29]

The bombing was not incidental to the conflict, the court reasoned, because it was not aimed at disrupting "the political structure of the state." Rather, it was an attack upon the social structure. In the court's view, the political offense exception "does not make a random bombing intended to result in the cold-blooded murder of civilians incidental to the purpose of toppling a government," at least not "absent a direct link between the perpetrator, a political organization's political goals, and the specific act."[30]

The Court of Appeals then advanced a new exception to political offender status. "The indiscriminate bombing of a civilian populace is not recognized as a protected political act even when the larger 'political' objective of the person who sets off the bomb may be to eliminate the civilian population of a country." [31]

This "wanton crimes exception" to the protection of political offenders was a major innovation. It responded more effectively to the same concerns that had led to the adoption of the Belgian *attentat* clause in the 1850s, the *Meunier* exception for anarchistic crimes in 1894, and the exception for aircraft hijackers adopted in multilateral conventions in the early 1970s. It refused to embrace the moral neutrality of *Ezeta*, *Artukovic*, and *McMullen* and set a precedent that might, in time, bring the law of extradition for at least some noninternational conflicts into line with the law governing international wars.

On its face, the new wanton crimes exception offered a justification for not granting benefit of the political offense exception to people charged with war crimes or crimes against humanity. But the Court of Appeals refused to go that far. It characterized the killings alleged in *Artukovic* as political because the victims were from racial and ethnic groups officially designated as enemies of the Croatian state. This, it ruled rather dubiously, was not the same as selecting victims at random or killing people indiscriminately.[32] (By the same reasoning, ironically, the PLO and IRA could argue that many of their bombings were not indiscriminate. They were planted in places where they were likely to kill British soldiers and their collaborators.)

In recognizing a "wanton crimes" exception, the Court of Appeals went a long way toward restoring the humanitarian concerns that underlay the political offense exception. It also protected—or promised to protect—the political offense exception from Justice Department efforts to abolish it, or transfer its administration to the executive branch.

However, implicit in the court's opinion were some unexamined assumptions—Western and perhaps white assumptions—about what constitutes a political movement and a nation state. In the Palestinian view, the civilian population of Israel—an armed civilian population—was the functional equivalent of an invading force engaged in a moderate version of what might be called "ethnic cleansing." The judges did not consider that Abu Eain was an Arab victim of Israeli's seizure of the West Bank in 1967, or that he was forced to grow up in the privations of a displaced persons' camp because his family had been dispossessed by the Israelis in 1948.[33] The court simply assumed that the presence of Israelis in Tiberias (or Ramallah) was legitimate. Abu Eain's motives, experiences, and political goals were deemed irrelevant to the court's analysis.

The Departments of Justice and State should have been pleased with their victory, but the opinion took away much of what it granted by allowing application of the exception in instances where the seemingly anarchistic violence was conducted at the direction of a revolutionary organization. Had there been solid evidence that the PLO had ordered Abu Eain to plant the bomb, and had the PLO announced such bombings as part of a deliberate campaign to destabilize the Israeli government (or occupation), the young man might not have been extradited.[34] According to government attorneys, this part of the court's opinion negated whatever force its recognition of a "wanton crimes exception" might have had.

In fact, government attorneys did not want the political crimes defense modified to permit extradition of persons charged with wanton crimes. That was a liberal half-solution; they wanted a radical change that would abolish the exception altogether or transfer its administration to the executive. They wanted to decide who would be surrendered and who would not, subject only to the most *pro forma* judicial hearings to determine probable cause.

While the Justice Department attorneys sought to politicize extradition, they continued to insist that Israel's pursuit of Abu Eain was an ordinary criminal prosecution. To maintain this illusion, they first had to persuade the Israelis to try the accused in a civilian court. As a Palestinian charged with terrorism, Abu Eain ordinarily would have been tried by a military court.

At the extradition hearing in Chicago, Abu Eain's attorneys tried to persuade the magistrate to suspend the rule of noninquiry and question the capacity of Israeli's legal system to do justice in the case of a Palestinian charged with terrorism.[35] The magistrate refused, possibly relying on assurances that the accused would be tried by a regular rather than special counter-terrorist court.[36]

Abu Eain was returned to Israel on December 13, 1981. The following morning his Israeli attorney charged that he had been abused by Israeli authorities. She said that his hair had been pulled, that he had been slapped, hit, and verbally abused, and that he had been forced to stand for long periods at night with a bag over his head. The manacles used on him had cut sores in his wrists. As punishment for his alleged crimes, his family's house was ordered torn down.[37] On June 17, 1982, Abu Eain was convicted and sentenced to life imprisonment solely on the basis of the recanted, Hebrew-language confession of his alleged Arab accomplice.

Throughout the extradition case, U.S. government attorneys insisted that Abu Eain was an ordinary criminal, not an enemy soldier. But after he was convicted (at U.S. insistence) as a common criminal in a civilian court, the Israelis reclassified him a prisoner of war so that he could be included in a POW exchange.[38] The State Department should have been embarrassed by this tacit acknowledgement that Abu Eain's imprisonment could not be disassociated from war and politics, but there is no evidence that it protested this abuse of the criminal justice process.

Following a judicial ruling that he is extraditable, the accused is entitled to appeal to the Secretary of State, who may decide, notwithstanding the court's finding, that reasons of justice, humanity, or international politics warrant a refusal to surrender.[39] In Abu Eain's case, however, the outcome of his appeal was foreordained. Louis G. Fields had already testified that the State Department considered the bombing in Tiberias to be an ordinary crime to which the political crimes defense should not apply.

Thus, the Department of State, then proclaiming the primacy of human rights in American foreign policy under the leadership of Secretary of State Cyrus Vance and Deputy Secretary of State Warren Christopher, did not maintain even the appearance of neutrality. It threw its prestige against Abu Eain just as it had intervened against Peter McMullen. Not since the case of Jonathan Robbins had the State Department behaved in so partisan a manner.

* * *

The wanton crimes exception was invented in Chicago and would spread to New York (see the next chapter), but when the chance came to extend it to the west coast, in a case involving one of the IRA's most murderous gangs, the Ninth Circuit Court of

Appeals balked. All three judges agreed that IRA member William Joseph Quinn should be extradited to the United Kingdom, but no two could agree on why.

Judge Ben C. Duniway embraced the wanton crimes exception, but Judges Stephen R. Reinhardt and Betty C. Fletcher, consistent with Ninth Circuit neutrality, refused to second-guess the uprising group's tactics. Reinhardt voted to permit Quinn's surrender on the theory that the exception was never meant to apply to terrorists who export their revolutionary violence abroad, while Fletcher disqualified Quinn from protection on the theory that the exception does not apply to an outsider who volunteers his services to an indigenous uprising.[40]

The Quinn decision is so incoherent that it is tempting to dismiss it for the non-precedent it is. But even a failed decision can be instructive of how judges may be tempted to rule in future cases, particularly when understandable rage gets the better of cool reason.

Unlike McMullen, Liam (or Bill) Quinn was not a native Irishman outraged by British army wrongs in his own hometown. He was an American, raised by Irish American parents in a Catholic, working-class neighborhood of San Francisco, who volunteered his services to the IRA in 1971 and was eventually assigned to an active service unit in London.

According to the British government, Quinn first came to their attention on February 26, 1975, when a London constable, Adrian Blackledge, saw a man leave a house on Fairholme Street, West Kensington, acting as if he feared observation. Thinking the man might be a burglar, Blackledge stopped him for questioning and, when his answers seemed suspicious, informed him that he would have to be searched, either then or at the station.[41] The man fled, with Blackledge and other constables in hot pursuit. An off-duty constable, Stephen Tibble, who happened to be riding by on his motorcycle, joined the chase. Tibble drove ahead of the suspect, jumped off his cycle, and crouched in a blocking position. The suspect then pulled out a pistol, shot Tibble dead, and escaped. Shortly thereafter, the police discovered a bomb-making cache in a nearby house. Quinn's fingerprints were found on a map and on other items in the house. Also found at the house were the fingerprints of four other members of the active service unit the police later linked to fifty-eight bombings, shootings, and kidnappings. According to subsequent testimony, Quinn's fingerprints were found in two IRA "safe houses" used for bomb-making and on the packaging of several bombs, including a booby-trapped Bible sent to the Catholic bishop of the British armed forces. Quinn's prints also were found on a letter bomb that exploded in the hands of Crown Court Judge John H. Buzzard, injuring his face and destroying parts of two fingers, and on an unexploded parcel bomb left in a black bag on the front step of the Charco-Burger Grill, Heath Street, London.[42]

On April 4, 1975, Quinn was arrested in Dublin, Ireland, in connection with the kidnapping of and assaults upon two soldiers in Donegal. Finding Quinn's appearance similar to that of the suspect wanted for killing Constable Tibble, the Irish Gardai contacted Scotland Yard. On May 14, Constable Blackledge flew to Dublin, surreptitiously viewed Quinn as he sat in the prisoner's dock, and made an immediate, positive identification.[43]

Quinn was acquitted of kidnapping the soldiers but convicted of membership in the IRA and sentenced to a year in prison. No request for his extradition to London awaited his release on January 2, 1976, and in 1978 he returned to California, from which the British government did not seek his extradition until August 1979.[44]

Why the decision to recover Quinn took three years is not clear. Perhaps the British government was still investigating other members of his unit, or possibly it knew his surrender was barred by *Ezeta* and its progeny. The request may also have been initiated by the U.S. Justice Department, which began its campaign to abolish the political offense exception in 1979, starting with the McMullen case. Whatever the reasoning, the British government waited until after a wanton crimes exception was recognized in *Abu Eain* and *Mackin* (next chapter) before requesting his surrender. The FBI arrested Quinn on September 30, 1981, in Daly City, California. By this time, the statute of limitations had run out for all but the killing of Constable Tibble and conspiracy to bomb.

In September 1982, federal magistrate F. Steele Langford ruled that Quinn was not entitled to the protection of the political offense exception on the theory that neither the bombings nor the killing were necessary to achievement of the IRA's goals, and thus were not incidental to an uprising.[45] Not since the *Ezeta* decision had a Ninth Circuit magistrate expressly claimed the power to second-guess the efficacy of an uprising group's tactics. As to the conspiracy-to-bomb charge, the second-guessing made sense, especially to anyone who believes that there must be some moral limits to revolutionary violence.

The opinion was also unprecedented in its backhanded invocation of a motives test. Langford ruled that killing the constable was not incidental to an uprising because Quinn could not have known that the civilian blocking his escape was actually a constable. The magistrate ignored that capture would have removed Quinn from IRA operations and might have forced him to reveal IRA activities. Nor did the magistrate acknowledge that the first duty of every covert operative is to avoid capture.

By narrowing the Ninth Circuit's uprising test in this manner, Langford essentially accepted the wanton crimes exception pioneered by the Seventh Circuit in *Eain*. He sought proof of a "direct link" between each of the alleged offenses and what he considered to be reasonable actions in furtherance of the uprising.

Like Magistrate Buchwald in *Mackin* (next chapter), Langford insisted that the accused prove membership in a revolutionary organization. In Quinn's case that posed no problem: He had already been convicted for IRA membership in Ireland. But Langford went farther, demanding that the accused also prove membership in the active service unit that did the bombings. When Quinn refused to incriminate himself in this manner, the magistrate denied him protection under the political offense exception.

In Langford's view, Quinn should not only establish his membership in the unit that carried out the attacks, but he should also prove that the attacks were carried out under specific orders (presumably by disclosing the identity of his superiors in the clandestine unit), not just from his unit in the field but from higher authorities. This, too, was unprecedented, although it had been suggested by the Court of Appeals in *Eain*.[46]

Quinn's counsel promptly petitioned for a writ of habeas corpus, and in October 1983, U.S. District Judge Robert P. Aguilar overturned Langford's decision.[47] Aguilar ruled that the magistrate had been wrong to rule that the bombings or shootings were not incidental to an uprising and rejected Langford's belief that courts should second-guess what is necessary to the success of an uprising, or what the motive of Tibble's killer might have been.

Aguilar based his decision squarely on Ninth Circuit precedents, which did not recognize humanitarian exceptions for wanton attacks on noncombatants. Quoting from the *Ezeta* decision, he declared: "I have no authority, in this examination, to determine what acts are within the rules of civilized warfare, and what are not."[48] Courts should remain neutral regarding a revolutionary group's tactics.[49]

The judge also ruled that an accused could not be required to prove membership in an uprising group in order to invoke the political offense exception.[50] Requiring such an admission, he said, would violate the U.S. constitutional privilege against self-incrimination.[51]

Moreover, requiring proof of membership could lead to awkward evidentiary problems. For example, what kinds of organizations would qualify as uprising groups? Would protection be granted only to persons whose organizations issued membership cards? It was enough to invoke the political offense exception, he ruled, that the accused could show that an uprising was occurring and that the offenses of which he was charged would, if proved, support that cause.[52]

The Justice Department promptly appealed. The U.S. Court of Appeals for the Ninth Circuit held oral argument in July 1984 but did not render a decision for eighteen months. While Quinn languished in maximum security, the court dragged its feet, either hoping that Congress would abolish the exception, or because the judges themselves were badly divided. Their fragmented and garbled decision, issued in February 1986, dismayed nearly everyone associated with the case.[53]

Before reaching its decision, the entire panel properly rejected the U.S. government's claim that the "political question doctrine" barred judges from applying the political offense exception. In so doing, the judges recalled Justice Catron's opinion that "extradition without an unbiased hearing before an independent judiciary [is] highly dangerous to liberty, and ought never to be allowed."[54]

The court also rejected the government's plea that it abstain from a decision so as not to "embarrass" the executive branch in the conduct of foreign affairs. "Far from embarrassing the executive branch," Judge Reinhardt wrote, "[judicial] responsibility for determining when the exception applies actually affords a degree of protection for the executive branch [from] undue pressure when public and international opposition ... creates conflicts with the treaty obligation created by the political offense exception."[55]

Next, the court reaffirmed the "incident to an uprising" test of Anglo-American law but ruled that allowing courts to second-guess the appropriateness of the means chosen by the uprising group would invite judges to entertain some "highly subjective and partisan political considerations."[56] Similarly, the majority rejected the Seventh

Circuit's suggestion that the uprising test be limited to conflicts with formal armies in the field, a view implicit in Magistrate Langford's opinion. Instead, the majority sided with the district court's opinion in *Doherty* (next chapter), which rejected the notion that the political offense exception protects only "actual armed insurrections or more traditional and overt military hostilities."[57] "It is understandable," Judge Reinhardt wrote, "that Americans are offended by the tactics used by many of those seeking to change their governments. . . . Nevertheless, it is not our place to impose our notions of civilized strife on people who are seeking to overthrow the regimes in control of their countries in contexts and circumstances that we have not experienced, and with which we can identify only with the greatest difficulty."[58]

As a caution to moralists who tend to judge the tactics of modern revolutionaries by those of their own nation's founders, the statement made sense. But, as an abdication of all moral judgment, the opinion seemed to many to go too far.

No reasons were given for these rejections, although they were consistent with the Ninth Circuit's tradition of staunch neutrality. No rebuttal was offered to Judge Duniway's concurring opinion, who would have applied the wanton crimes rationale of *Eain v. Wilkes* to both the killing of Tibble and the bombing conspiracy.[59] Instead, Reinhardt went on—without the support of any other judge—to distinguish between "international" and "domestic" terrorism and to claim that Quinn was extraditable as an international terrorist.

The political offense exception, he asserted, was meant to apply only in cases of "domestic" terrorism and need not apply when domestic savagery is taken abroad. The exception, he continued, presumes that each government has an obligation to remain neutral toward internal struggles among foreign peoples, but need not tolerate foreign strife when it is exported to lands beyond dispute.

Reinhardt's opinion was extraordinary not only for its lack of historical understanding but for its conclusion that exporting revolutionary violence from Belfast to London was "international." Reinhardt had to know that Northern Ireland was ruled from London and that Northern Ireland was part of the United Kingdom. Both the magistrate and Judge Fletcher, in her dissent, reminded him of that fact.[60] Even so, he decided that Quinn was extraditable because there was no uprising in England.[61]

To Judge Reinhardt, Northern Ireland must have appeared more of a colony than a province, but if a revolutionary can become an extraditable terrorist simply by carrying the colony's revolt to the imperial state, then, as Judge Duniway pointed out, John Paul Jones was a terrorist for bringing the American Revolution to the shores of England in 1777.[62] Implicit in this portion of Reinhardt's opinion (which neither of the other judges endorsed) is the assumption that rebels against foreign occupation must treat the oppressing nation as neutral territory, and its people and officials as innocent bystanders.

Moreover, Reinhardt reasoned, if the occupying power drives a people from their land, and they subsequently launch paramilitary forays from a neighboring state, their fighters are not entitled to protection from extradition, because there is no uprising within the land that the irredentists are trying to retake. "When PLO members enter Israel," he wrote, "and commit unlawful acts, there is simply no uprising for the acts to be incidental to."[63] If that were true, however, then irredentist groups like the *contras* were not entitled to the political offense exception until they could set up base camps within Nicaragua—a theory neither the Carter nor Reagan administration were likely to support.

Returning to the case at hand, Reinhardt suggested yet another reason men like Quinn should be extradited. "It is not clear," he observed, "whether . . . a foreign citizen who voluntarily joins [an indigenous uprising] is protected by the exception."[64] Although he did not expressly rest his decision to extradite Quinn on this point, Judge Fletcher did, thereby asserting yet another reason for not enforcing the political offense exception.[65]

In advancing her "interloper exception," Fletcher assumed, in effect, that the Marquis de Lafayette had no business volunteering his services to the American Revolution. But she and Reinhardt were still focusing on Abu Eain, assuming that the Jordanian had no business revolting against the Israeli occupation of Jordan's former West Bank because he "was not a national of that country."[66] Both judges ignored the fact that Eain lived in Ramallah, a city on the West Bank that had been seized by Israel from Jordan in the 1967 war. Ignored too was the fact that Israel itself was created in 1948 by the seizure of Palestinian lands, including the property of Abu Eain's own family. By their reasoning, Americans who fought for Texas against Mexico would not have been protectable, and American Jews like Golda Meir, who fought to wrest a new Israel from both Palestinian Arabs and the British, would have been extraditable terrorists, because they were not full-fledged members of a revolt "by an indigenous people against their own government or an occupying power."[67]

In fact, the political offense exception had been developed precisely to help irredentists like Bolivar, Mazzini, Garibaldi, and Kossuth. Equally to the point, there is nothing in its history or in the uprising requirement of Anglo-American law to confine the exception's application to "indigenous peoples." Indeed, if this reasoning had been applied at the time of the American Revolution, the only people entitled to rebel would have been the native tribes.[68]

Judge Fletcher joined Judge Reinhardt in rejecting the wanton crimes exception and the membership requirement. She agreed that the killing of the constable by a fleeing member of the IRA would normally be incidental to its uprising, but disagreed with Reinhardt's claim that no uprising existed in England. Like Duniway, she rejected the "export exception" and based her vote on the interloper theory. She did not believe "that mercenaries or volunteers in a foreign conflict can claim protection under the political offense exception."[69]

Accordingly, the only elements of this complicated case that have precedential value are the initial rejection of the "political question" claim, the affirmation of the amoral uprising test of *Ezeta,* and the rejection of the membership requirements. As to why Quinn should not be protected by the political offense exception, no two judges agreed.

Despite this incoherence, William Quinn became the first person—and the first American—to be extradited to the United Kingdom for crimes committed in the cause of Irish independence. His surrender is best explained not by any legal theory but by waning sympathy for the Irish cause on the part of an increasingly conservative U.S. government and judiciary. Fifteen months later, Quinn was convicted at the Old Bailey in London solely for the arguably nonwanton crime of killing Constable Tibble in order to escape; he was sentenced to life in prison.

Ironically, had Quinn been tried on the same evidence and jury instructions in the United States, his conviction would have been overturned for violating due process of law and the privilege against self-incrimination. The burden of proof that Quinn was the man Constable Blackledge saw kill Tibble was set extremely low. The lack of any line-up was excused, and the jury was instructed that it was enough if the killer "must have looked something like the defendant." In addition, the judge pointed out, as no American judge could, that by not taking the stand in his own defense, the accused had failed to rebut the prosecution's case.[70] As Quinn's solicitor remarked to an American observer before the trial, "Your U.S. Constitution is a kind of bottom line beneath which the government cannot go. Here, there is no bottom line."[71]

* * *

The search for ways to deny alleged terrorists benefit of the political offense exception continued in New York, where a U.S. district court briefly embraced a "war crimes" exception before being overturned by the Court of Appeals for the Second Circuit. The case involved Mahmoud El-Abed Ahmad (aka Mahmoud Abed Atta), a PLO member wanted by Israel for murdering the driver of a regularly scheduled civilian bus outside of Tel Aviv in the occupied West Bank on April 12, 1986. Two of the three men who attacked the bus with an Uzi submachine gun and Molotov cocktails were captured and confessed, naming their cousin Ahmad, a naturalized American citizen, as their leader.

Acting in cooperation with the Israeli government, U.S. agents tracked Ahmad through Mexico to Venezuela, where U.S., Israeli, and Venezuelan agents interrogated Ahmad, not about his entry into Venezuela, but his alleged crimes against Israel. Lacking an extradition treaty with Israel, the Venezuelan government agreed to turn him over to U.S. agents at the Caracas Airport. On May 5, 1987, they brought Ahmad to New York against his will, arresting him on the plane.[72] This arrest, but not Ahmad's previous seizure, was authorized by a warrant issued in New York by U.S. Magistrate John L. Caden.

At the extradition hearing, Caden ruled that Ahmad could not be extradited because he had been brought to the United States illegally and because he was entitled to benefit of the political offense exception.[73] Ahmad's intended victims, Caden held, were armed settlers of occupied territory, not innocent civilians shopping in a marketplace.[74] The attack was carried out pursuant to orders from the Abu Nidal faction of the PLO, which had conducted other attacks along the road as part of an effort to prevent consolidation of Israeli control over lands it had seized from Jordan in 1967. Responsibility for the attack was assumed by the Nidal faction, making Ahmad's alleged crime more clearly incidental to an uprising than Abu Eain's.[75] Without condoning the attack, Caden reaffirmed the importance of judicial neutrality toward foreign strife, observing presciently that "today's rebels in the West Bank may be tomorrow's rulers there, and it is not this court's objective or purpose to impair future foreign relations by prejudging the legitimacy of the Palestinian objectives."[76]

Unhappy with this result, the Department of Justice filed a new request for Ahmad's extradition with U.S. District Judge Edward R. Korman. He decided that Ahmad had lawfully been "found" in the United States at the time of his arrest and was not entitled to protection under the political offense exception because his alleged actions were in the nature of "war crimes."[77] Reasoning on analogy to the "rules of engagement" set by national armies for fighting international wars pursuant to the Geneva Conventions of 1949, Korman held that "an act which would be properly punishable even in the context of a declared war or in the heat of open military conflict" could not be protected by the exception.[78]

Korman also rejected the magistrate's view that Israeli settlers of the occupied West Bank were fair targets of PLO attacks. Only a majority of the male settlers carried weapons, he found, and only "some engaged in the kind of vigilante activity cited by the defendant." Therefore, attempting to "murder every passenger, . . . simply because one or more . . . could be described as arguably non-civilian [was] an indiscriminate act of violence . . . not within the political offense exception."[79]

Ahmad's counsel, former U.S. Attorney Ramsey Clark, then petitioned for a writ of habeas corpus overturning Korman's decision. Chief Judge Jack Weinstein, a distinguished jurist and former Columbia Law School professor, was assigned the case. Weinstein began his opinion by restating the incidence test to require a level of political violence comparable to a civil war, thus raising the bar far higher than John Stuart Mill, the *Castioni* decision, and the IRA cases had set it.[80] He disagreed with Magistrate Caden that there was "a substantial revolt . . . in the occupied territory" at the time of the attack and to which it might be considered incidental.[81] The picture he painted was of a suburban community serviced by civilian buses on civilian routes and schedules, implying that periods of quiet imposed by an occupying force could properly strip long-standing rebellions of their legitimacy. In this, his view was similar to that of Judge Reinhardt, who reasoned that Quinn was not entitled to protection of the political offense exception because the people of London were not then in revolt.

Weinstein was on stronger ground when he embraced the "wanton crimes" standard without relying on *Eain v. Wilkes.* "Sporadic acts of violence," he observed in passing, "cannot justify deliberately waylaying a civilian bus operating on a regularly scheduled run and deliberately attempting to kill the civilian driver and passengers. [The] alleged attack . . . must be characterized as a random act of murderous terrorism, rather than a protected political offense."[82]

The judge recognized "the anomaly of . . . blowing up whole cities by air raids while condemning by law the deliberate killing of even one civilian" but insisted that "the civilities of war" require punishment of "face-to-face inhumanities" in order to reaffirm "the sanctity of life."[83] The only justification he could offer for this admittedly double standard was the improbable one that punishing individuals keeps hope alive that the inhumanity of war might someday be controlled.[84]

Weinstein also denied Ahmad protection of the political offense exception because his alleged acts violated the "Law of Armed Conflict."[85] In effect, he endorsed Korman's war crimes approach, but he took his lead not from the "rules of engagement" adopted for a particular conflict by a particular warring state, but from allegedly "universally accepted principles of human rights," as evidenced by the 1977 Protocol 1, which also sought to regulate international wars.[86]

This ruling was extraordinary, given that Protocol 1 had not been ratified by the United States, Israel, the PLO, or most nations. Even if it had, Weinstein's version of the war crimes exception offered little help to most rebels, because Protocol 1 provided that the only legitimate targets of attack could be uniformed soldiers, or combatants with fixed insignia recognizable at a distance. The judge's exception would not have protected Ahmad if the bus had been full of soldiers out of uniform or militia in mufti. Nor would it have protected IRA member Joseph Doherty from extradition for shooting the leader of a British army hit squad who, dressed in civilian clothes, tried to wipe out Doherty's paramilitary unit in a premeditated, direct assault upon their position (see next chapter). Weinstein's war crimes exception clearly loaded the scales of justice against foreign revolutionaries and would, if adopted nationwide, deny most rebels benefit of the political offense exception.

The former professor also asserted a due process exception to the rule of noninquiry, but this turned out to be more apparent than real. While presuming that a trial in the requesting state would be fair, Weinstein was willing to suspend the rule of noninquiry if the accused could demonstrate a "substantial probability" that he would face procedures and treatment "antipathetic to a court's sense of decency."[87] Ahmad established that probability and won a full evidentiary hearing on Israel's capacity to do justice, but in the end Weinstein found that the defendant's trial was likely to be fair. Ignoring extensive evidence that Israeli interrogators used torture and other forms of inhumane treatment on alleged terrorists (because they had occurred prior to this particular round of violence),[88] Weinstein concluded that Ahmad could be safely extradited because "no person tried in Israel after extradition by the United States had been denied due process."[89] The judge also relied on assertions by the U.S. State Department that the trial would be fair.[90]

The very act of inquiry had the salutary effect of inspiring the Israeli government to offer the sort of promises that normally could be achieved only by conditional surrender.[91] However, by narrowing the inquiry to proof of what had happened to previous extraditees from the United States, rather than focusing on what happened to PLO defendants generally, the judge demonstrated minimal curiosity.

Weinstein's rulings reflected a level of intelligence and thoughtfulness rare in extradition opinions, but they did not survive appeal. On August 10, 1990, a three-judge panel of the Court of Appeals for the Second Circuit unanimously rejected each of his innovations.[92] "It is not the business of our courts," they ruled, "to assume responsibility for supervising the integrity of the judicial system in another sovereign nation."[93] Of course, Weinstein had denied any wish to supervise Israeli courts; he simply refused "to blind ourselves to the foreseeable and probable results of the exercise of our jurisdiction."[94]

To this Second Circuit panel, such blindness was mandatory. What may happen to the accused upon his return, including risks to his life, Judges Ellsworth A. Van Graffeiland, Jon Newman, and Amalya Kearse ruled, are "within the exclusive purview of the executive branch."[95] The fact that the executive branch was representing the Israeli government did not bother them, because they could not imagine a case in which the Secretary of State had or would direct extradition in face of proof that the accused would be treated in a matter that would offend "a federal court's sense of decency."[96] The three judges either had low standards of decency (which has been typical of courts in abduction and torture cases) or they had not heard of the *Robbins* and *Normano* cases, where the State Department clearly ignored common knowledge that the accused would not be treated fairly, either as an alleged mutineer from the British navy, or as a Jew wanted by Nazis. The judges were certain, however, that "the interests of international comity" would be "ill-served" if courts asked such embarrassing questions.[97] Thus, reasons of state were to deny an accused—and an American at that—both liberty and justice.

* * *

The 1980s were marked by repeated judicial attempts to exempt alleged terrorists against civilians from protection of the political offense exception. As executive and public pressure mounted, the judiciary became more inventive, devising not only one exception for "wanton crimes" and two for "war crimes," but additional exceptions for exported violence, violence in pacified areas, and violence by nonindigenous interlopers. In addition, one district court was willing to shield an otherwise extraditable defendant if he could show that he would be tortured or treated unjustly upon his return. Of these efforts, only the exception for wanton crimes would gather additional judicial support.

CHAPTER 13

Urban Guerrillas Versus Army Death Squads

We are not faced here with a situation in which a bomb was detonated in a department store, public tavern, or a resort hotel, causing indiscriminate personal injury, death, and property damage. . . . The facts of this case present the . . . political offense exception in its most classic form.

Judge John E. Sprizzo, In Matter of Doherty, 1984

The effort to strip alleged terrorists of political offender status was as much a propaganda war as it was a legal one. In this effort, success would depend on preserving noninquiry. The requesting state, and its representatives in the U.S. Department of Justice, could not afford to allow the courts or the public to see how much the tactics of the foreign government and its rebels resembled each other.

For the British government, sustaining an American practice of noninquiry was not difficult. Most Americans assume that British law enforcement is at least as fair as their own. It is not always fair, of course, any more than the American government has always been fair toward its minorities. Structurally, however, the American government has more ways to correct abuses than the British. The United Kingdom lacks a body of constitutional law that can trump mere acts of Parliament, or a Bill of Rights enforceable by an independent judiciary. It does not separate the judicial and legislative functions; the twelve Law Lords who constitute the court of last resort are also members of the upper house of Parliament. The Lord Chancellor, who is both a member of the ruling party's cabinet and speaker of the House of Lords, is also head of the judiciary and can sit as a Law Lord whenever he wishes. He also gets to choose the judges.

The United Kingdom is not a democracy as Americans understand the term. In the United States, "constitutional" modifies "democracy." The United Kingdom labors under no such legally enforceable restraints, or the implicit assumption that the rights of the people preexist the prerogatives of government. In the British tradition, liberty and due process are not rights guaranteed against the government by a higher law; they are "privileges and immunities" dispensed by the Crown to its subjects. The United Kingdom has elections, but parliamentary democracy without a legally enforceable constitution does not guarantee liberty, especially where minorities are concerned. As the people of Ireland have known for centuries, there are no checks on what Parliament, controlled by one or another alternating party oligarchy, can do to deprive them of liberty or govern them arbitrarily. Politics occurs largely within, rather than between, the major parties, neither of which has traditionally campaigned in Northern Ireland. Moreover, the party in power almost always has the votes it needs, without the help of opposition members, to pass emergency legislation or criminal justice bills expanding the power of the police to detain and interrogate suspected "terrorists." During the 1970s and 1980s, draconian measures for Northern Ireland were often passed as "orders in Council," which obviated the need for public debate in advance of the enactment.

Americans do not understand these important details. They assume that because their government is derived from the British that the United Kingdom must be like the United States, only better, because its officials seem more proper and polite. Thus Americans have difficulty imagining that British politicians might allow their army to use lawless tactics to "pacify" the Catholics of Northern Ireland, including plainclothes hit squads with "shoot to kill" orders.

The British government has shrewdly managed public opinion both at home and abroad. The Northern Irish civil rights movement of the late 1960s and allegations of the torture of prisoners in the early 1970s (when many IRA members were interned without trial) received little coverage in Britain, in part because of press laws that denied alleged terrorists the right to speak for themselves on television.[1] British government spokesmen insisted that Northern Ireland had a democratic system of politics when it was actually being run by a largely Protestant police force and army regiment under emergency legislation.[2] Reports of a "shoot to kill" policy against IRA members, documented by a team of international lawyers,[3] were successfully denigrated, and an independent constable's investigation into six very suspicious deaths was sandbagged.[4] The conventional wisdom advanced by the British government was that the "troubles" in Northern Ireland were caused by a few terrorists with limited popular support who were seeking to disrupt ordinary law enforcement. If only the terrorists were defeated, the theory went, Northern Ireland would be like the rest of the United Kingdom. This was also the view of lawyers for the Carter and Reagan administrations, who relied uncritically on what the Thatcher government told them. Why should they be critical when the British government was their client? From the litigators' point of view, the United Kingdom was as much their client as the CIA, the army, or the Federal Reserve. If there were any doubts, however, they were silenced by the counter-terrorism professionals, for whom, simply put, "the enemy of our friend is our enemy." Forgotten in all this was President Washington's Farewell Address, in which he counseled against the naive belief that nations can really have "friends."[5]

This uncritical view was obvious in the cases of Peter McMullen and Ziad Abu Eain, and it became even more pronounced in the effort to extradite Desmond Mackin and Joseph Doherty, IRA members.7 wanted for shooting British soldiers. Their cases are worth examining at some length for many reasons, not the least of which is that they were not—morally speaking—anything like what the anti-terrorism lawyers at Justice said they were.

Neither was an innocent, of course. Both Mackin and Doherty were disciplined members of paramilitary, urban guerrilla units fighting a war of independence against what they considered a foreign army of occupation. The "army" to which the two men belonged did not operate by the laws of war. It did not wear uniforms, mass in large numbers, or set up a government in exile. In addition to semiconventional guerrilla operations, it terrorized civilians into silence, ran protection rackets, and bombed populated streets with reckless disregard for passing noncombatants.

However, the army that Mackin and Doherty opposed did not fight by the conventional rules of warfare, either. Nor did it conduct itself according to the conventions of law enforcement. Faced daily with the threat of ambush by men like Mackin and Doherty, the British counter-insurgency forces responded in kind, pouncing on suspected IRA members, more often with a view to kill than to capture and prosecute.

* * *

Desmond Mackin's story was typical of young men who joined the IRA in the 1970s. Mackin was only eight years old when he and his family (which had IRA connections going back to the 1920s)6 were first driven from their home in East Belfast by gun-wielding Protestants in 1963. The family moved to a mixed Protestant–Catholic neighborhood in West Belfast between the Protestant Shankhill and the Catholic Falls Road. There in 1967, Mackin followed his family's tradition and joined the Republican youth group, Na Fianna Eireann ("Soldiers of Ireland"). He participated in civil rights marches, did neighborhood scouting for the IRA, and attended some indoctrination sessions. The mixed neighborhood was relatively peaceful, but in July 1969, Protestants went beyond their annual parade of nationalistic symbols. Supported by uniformed Protestant police and B Special constables, they attacked Catholic enclaves, evicting approximately 500 Catholics and firebombing their homes. Desmond Mackin, then thirteen years old, fled with his mother and three younger sisters down the Falls Road in a hail of stones. The family was reduced to living in a barricaded community on public welfare until emergency housing became available in the Andersonstown section of East Belfast.7

These acts of Protestant terrorism, which the British authorities lacked the ability or will to stop, drove Mackin to become an active member of the IRA. Starting in 1971, he saw many of his friends interned without trial. He was too young to be interned, but he was tried for attempting to murder a policeman. Unable to convict him on that charge for lack of evidence (despite efforts to beat a confession out of him), the authorities prosecuted him for membership in a proscribed organization. In 1972, Mackin was sentenced to five years in Long Kesh, a prison then known for its brutal conditions. Released in

1976, he continued to work for the IRA and was, according to the magistrate, kept under close and harassing surveillance by undercover British troops.[8] At this time, he later testified, he was a member of the Belfast Brigade of the IRA's First Battalion.[9]

On March 16, 1978, while out searching for a "lost" taxicab,[10] Mackin and an IRA colleague found themselves surrounded by clusters of plainclothes soldiers on the ground, two surveillance helicopters overhead, and a minivan with someone inside taking photographs. Fearing harm (to put it mildly), they tried to overpower one of the plainclothes soldiers and break away.[11] According to Mackin, the soldiers pursued him down a back ally and continued to shoot at him although he was unarmed and had raised his hands in surrender. Neighborhood residents, sympathetic to the IRA, came out into the ally and forced the soldiers to cease shooting by shielding Mackin with their bodies. They also insisted that he be taken to a civilian hospital because they feared what might happen to him at a military facility. This community support, Mackin believes, saved his life.[12]

During the chase, Mackin, his colleague, and a soldier were shot. The soldier, Stephen Wooten, received one gunshot wound. Mackin received three and his companion seven, all in the back. Released on bail, Mackin fled to the Republic of Ireland and from there to the United States, where he lived openly and where his activities on behalf of civil rights in Northern Ireland won him a commendation from the Pennsylvania state legislature. On October 6, 1980, he was arrested in New York on charges that he had shot the plainclothes soldier.[13]

There was no reason for the British government to expect Mackin to be extradited; his was precisely the sort of case for which the political offense exception had been developed in both British and American law. However, the U.S. Departments of Justice and State were out to change the existing law.[14] In addition, Prime Minister Margaret Thatcher felt a strong political need, given the IRA's indiscriminate bombings in London, to do something about terrorism. (This need became intensely personal after the IRA tried to kill her with a bomb in 1984.) Otherwise, the British civil service, which had defended the political offense exception for more than a century, would have made a *pro forma* request for Mackin and then forgotten him.[15]

The U.S. Department of Justice demanded Mackin's extradition, even though the United Kingdom's evidence against him was dubious at best.[16] Among other things, the British could not produce the gun that Mackin was alleged to have fired, although they had captured him at the scene. They admitted that their forensic laboratory could find no traces of gunpowder on his hands or clothing, and their medical expert agreed that the soldier was probably wounded from a distance of more than one hundred feet, which means that he was probably shot by another British soldier firing at Mackin.[17]

Even so, the U.S. Justice Department repeatedly and publicly called Desmond Mackin a "terrorist." Within pro-IRA circles in the United States, Desmond Mackin was not a terrorist but a hero. His defense, like that of the IRA defector Peter McMullen, was organized by Frank Durkan, a partner in Paul O'Dwyer's law firm in New York. It was handled in large part by Keara O'Dempsey, a young attorney who came so to admire her client that she named a son after him.

Special U.S. Attorney Thomas H. Belote opened the case by arguing, first, that the role of the magistrate was limited to determining whether there was probable cause to extradite the accused. The magistrate, he claimed, lacked the competence and authority to decide whether the alleged crime was political. Whether the offense was political, the U.S. attorney asserted, was a nonjusticiable "political question" that only the executive branch could decide. Judicial determinations of what constitutes a political offense, he argued, could not be allowed because such decisions could be politically embarrassing to U.S. foreign policy. The same argument would be repeated, sometimes vehemently, in subsequent extradition cases and before Congress.

Second, Belote tried to persuade the magistrate that there was no uprising in Northern Ireland, only organized crime. Third, he argued that the alleged crime was not incidental to or in pursuance of the uprising—if one existed.

The magistrate, Naomi Rice Buchwald, disagreed on all points. Her one-hundred-one–page opinion was as comprehensive and scholarly as the opinion in McMullen's case had been short and casual. Issued on August 31, 1981, it covered all the issues of the case with the erudition of a law-review article.

Buchwald began by ruling that there was probable cause, based solely on the "eyewitness testimony" of the soldiers, to believe that Mackin was guilty of possessing and firing a gun, but that there was no probable cause to believe that he was guilty of attempted murder. The fact that British authorities could not produce the gun and that the United Kingdom's forensic experts could not find residues of gunpowder on Mackin's hands or clothing were not sufficient to overcome the soldiers' depositions. Nor did the magistrate reject depositions claiming that Mackin had shot the man he struggled with at close range, despite the likelihood that a bullet fired at that range would have gone through, and not remained in, the soldier's body. Under these circumstances, she could not find sufficient proof that the shooting amounted to attempted murder. In effect Buchwald found probable cause to believe that Mackin did fire a gun, but in self-defense.

Probable cause, she declared, was "evidence sufficient to cause a person of ordinary prudence and caution to conscientiously entertain a reasonable belief of the accused's guilt."[18] "In dealing with probable cause," she added, "we deal with probabilities. These are not technical; they are factual and practical considerations of everyday life on which reasonable and prudent men, not legal technicians, act."[19]

After reciting these well-established standards, however, the magistrate chose not to apply them. Consistent with the rule of noninquiry, she simply accepted the soldiers' depositions at face value, even though they were inconsistent with each other, were contradicted by the forensic evidence, and had been found insufficient by a British appeals court in the collateral case of Mackin's companion.[20]

If the case had ended here, the most Mackin could have been extradited for was possessing and firing a gun.[21] But that was not the end of the matter, for Buchwald was prepared to rule that the prisoner was shielded from extradition by the political offense exception. She dismissed the Reagan administration's claim that the political offense exception was a political question beyond her competence or authority to decide. "All precedent is to the contrary," she wrote. "Throughout more than eighty years of jurisprudential history in every case in which the political offense exception has been squarely presented . . . the courts have never declined to receive evidence on and consider the applicability of the political offense exception."[22]

The magistrate had no difficulty finding that there was an uprising at the time and site of the alleged offense, that Mackin was a member of the uprising group, and that his alleged offense was incidental to, and in furtherance of, the uprising.[23] In finding an uprising in Northern Ireland, Buchwald rejected testimony by Frank Perez, the State Department's "terrorism expert," that the IRA was indistinguishable from the Red Brigades. It was obvious from a secret intelligence analysis prepared by the British army and introduced by the defense that the IRA was a disciplined and highly organized guerrilla army.

In ruling that Mackin was a member of the uprising group, Buchwald decided that membership in an organization was a necessary element to invoking the political offense exception. This ruling contradicted both John Stuart Mill's advice and the British decision in *Castioni,* but it was consistent with the American decisions in *McMullen* and *Abu Eain.* With those more recent decisions, Buchwald's ruling constituted a further narrowing of the historic exception.

The narrowing had the benefit of expecting a measure of organization and perhaps discipline from those who would use force in the contest for political change. The magistrate seemed to say that *Castioni,* like John Stuart Mill, went too far in shielding those whose violence was too spontaneous to enjoy support from persons of considered judgment. The organizational requirement also made some practical sense. The political offense exception was not meant to shield politically motivated lunatics.

On the other hand, the requirement of an organizational base meant that the exception could not be used to shield fugitives from police states, like the sailors in *Kolczynski* or like the Chinese students who protested in Tiananmen Square. Forcing fugitives to admit membership in an uprising organization might not seem bad in the United States, where mere membership in any political organization cannot be a crime. But in the United Kingdom and many other countries, it can be a crime simply to belong to a proscribed group. Accordingly, to require an accused to admit that association in order to claim benefit of the political offense exception could have the effect of forcing him to incriminate himself.

Finally, in deciding whether the alleged offense was "incidental" to and "in furtherance" of an uprising, Buchwald found that Mackin was not an anarchist out to destroy the social fabric, that his alleged crime was focused on a soldier, that it was part of the traditional goals and strategies of the IRA, and that the accused was motivated by political, not personal, motives.[24] Accordingly, she ruled that he was not extraditable.

One issue the magistrate did not examine was whether Mackin was likely to get a fair trial if he was extradited to Northern Ireland. Unacknowledged was the fact that he would not be tried by an ordinary English court but by a special court created solely to try political offenders. Nor would he be entitled to a jury of his peers; the special

"Diplock Courts" (after the chairman of the commission that recommended them) are staffed by judges only. The Diplock Courts also operate under emergency legislation that strips IRA suspects of due process guarantees enjoyed by ordinary criminals in ordinary British courts. Buchwald, however, ignored each of these defects in British justice and limited Macken's protection to his status as a political offender.

* * *

The United States promptly challenged Buchwald's decision in the U.S. Court of Appeals for the Second Circuit. The Justice Department advanced three arguments, each clearly contrary to established legal precedents. First, its attorneys repeated their claim that the U.S.–U.K. treaty of 1972 vested the decision as to who was a political offender exclusively with the executive branch.[25] Second, the Justice Department asserted that the United States, on behalf of the United Kingdom, had a right to appeal a magistrate's refusal to allow extradition, and third, it insisted that the Court of Appeals could issue a writ of mandamus directing the magistrate to authorize extradition.

The claim to exclusive executive control over the political offense exception was based on the argument that the "requested party" referred to in the treaty was not the entire United States government but the executive branch alone. A decision to regard an offense as "one of a political character," the Justice Department now insisted, could only be made by the executive.[26]

The argument was straight out of Justice Sutherland's opinion in *United States v. Curtiss-Wright Export Corp.*,[27] a statist (or royalist) argument that equated the sovereignty of the United States solely with the powers of the chief executive. The roots of this argument lay in Representative John Marshall's defense of President Adams's conduct in the Robbins Case, where Marshall incorrectly referred to the president as the "sole organ" rather than the authoritative negotiator and spokesman for the United States in foreign relations. The argument relied on a rigid theory of separation of powers that, contrary to precedent, denied both Congress and the courts the authority to make any decisions affecting international affairs.[28]

The Court of Appeals rejected the Justice Department's argument. "Whatever we might decide if we were writing on a clean slate," Judge Henry Friendly wrote, the courts have always decided on the applicability of the political offense exception.[29] This was true whether the treaties explicitly assigned the task to the courts or not. "The government has suggested no reason, and we are unable to envision any, why courts should determine political offenses under some treaties, but not under others."[30]

The reason for assigning such decisions to the court was also obvious from rereading the 1852 Supreme Court case of *In re Kaine*.[31]

> This principle [of judicial control of the political offense exception] was in existence at least as long ago as when . . . Justice Catron, speaking for four members of the Supreme Court, wrote that "extradition without an unbiased hearing before an independent judiciary . . . [is] highly dangerous to liberty and ought never to be allowed in this country. . . ." Although this statement is directed at extradition proceedings in general and not specifically to the political offense issue, Justice Catron's opinion gives no indication that the

political offense issue ought to be treated differently from other issues at the extradition hearing. More importantly, an example cited by Justice Catron, relating to the alleged mistreatment of one Jonathan Robbins, suggests that the members of the Court joining in his opinion were of the view that "an unbiased hearing before an independent judiciary" was particularly necessary in cases where the political offense exception was at issue.

According to Judge Friendly, *In re Kaine* demonstrated that "it was precisely the political offense exception that was of the greatest concern to Congress in passing the Act of August 12, 1848," granting courts jurisdiction over extradition cases.

The precedent against the appealability of court decisions denying extradition was equally obvious. There was the Supreme Court's decision in *In re Metzger*, denying an appeal in the absence of jurisdictional legislation;[32] the jurisdictional statute of 1848, which did not provide for appeals;[33] and an 1853 opinion of Attorney General Cushing acknowledging that no right to appeal existed.[34]

Finally, the Court of Appeals denied the Justice Department's claim that a court order (here a writ of mandamus) could be issued to the magistrate directing her to issue a certificate of extraditability. In so doing, the Court of Appeals did not stress the trial court's discretion, as the Supreme Court had in the ship-jumping case of Captain Barré,[35] but relied on the more general principle that the writs are reserved for "exceptional cases" in which there is a "usurpation of power, [a] clear abuse of discretion and the presence of an issue of first impression."[36] In no way, the Court of Appeals ruled, had the magistrate abused her authority.

Whether the administration abused its discretion in making such patently weak arguments is a separate question. The court apparently thought so, for it ordered the government to pay the costs Mackin had incurred in contesting this appeal. Mackin, who had entered the country illegally, was then promptly deported to the Republic of Ireland, the country from which he had come and to which he had chosen to go. There Mackin found work as an editor in the Dublin office of Sinn Fein, the political arm of the IRA. The British government, confirming the weakness of its case against him, did not seek his extradition from Dublin to Northern Ireland, even after a new treaty with the Irish Republic made that easier.

* * *

If the evidence against Desmond Mackin was shaky, the case against Joseph Patrick Thomas Doherty was airtight. He and his "M-60 Gang" had been captured during a shoot-out with British soldiers. Like Mackin, Doherty was a product of Belfast's Catholic ghettos and a family with IRA and republican ties.[37] Like Mackin, Doherty was a victim of Protestant pogroms, and his commitment to revolution had been hardened by abuse from British soldiers.

In 1969, as Desmond Mackin and his family were fleeing a Protestant pogram in the Falls Road section of Belfast, violence was also breaking out in the tough New Lodge District, in the north end of the city above the docks. At first, the British troops were welcomed by Catholics as protectors against Protestant attacks. When fourteen-year-old Joe Doherty saw Protestant boys with a sawed-off shotgun stalking a British soldier, he ran to the top of the street to inform the officer in charge. The soldier was shot and wounded, but as a result of Doherty's information, the stalkers were arrested. A newspaper reported his role, and the next day on his way to school, Joe was set upon by Protestant boys, who kicked his face in. His family was told that their home would be firebombed if he testified in court.[38]

Doherty did testify, but he also concluded, as did most Catholics in their embattled enclave, that the British army would not protect them. Indeed, as members of the old IRA predicted, the largely Protestant army (which drew many of its troops from Calvinist Scotland) grew increasingly partial to the Protestants, who had controlled the Northern Irish government for over fifty years. Thus, when the Provisional Wing of the IRA set up barricades to protect the neighborhood, young Joe Doherty, like Desmond Mackin, joined its youth arm, Na Fianna Eireann.

At sixteen, Joe Doherty was clearly identified by the army as an IRA scout who lived on a street that uniformly supported the "Provos." In keeping with the counter-insurgency policy employed at the time, the soldiers regularly "lifted" the boy off the street and subjected him to abusive interrogations, not so much to gain information as to frighten him.[39]

By this time, the IRA was conducting bombings without warning and goading soldiers to overreact, knowing their brutality would build support for independence. In August 1971, the army conducted house-to-house searches for IRA supporters throughout Northern Ireland, and the Dohertys' home was on their list. At four o'clock one morning, armored personnel carriers roared into their narrow street. A squad of soldiers kicked the front door in and occupied the tiny row house, which was less than fourteen feet wide. Holding Joe and his father at gunpoint, a dozen soldiers in battle dress and blackface forced his mother and three sisters to get out of bed and stand clad only in their nightclothes while their bedrooms were searched. When Mrs. Doherty asked for privacy in which to put on her robe, she was called an "Irish bitch" and forced out of bed at gunpoint.[40]

By the time Doherty was seventeen, he was a veteran of "deep interrogation" (physical abuse) by the army and the police. Knowing that he had become an officer in Na Fianna Eireann, they kept him under continual surveillance and searched his home repeatedly. On the day after his seventeenth birthday, the army included him in a round-up of IRA suspects. For three days he was beaten, deprived of sleep, and subjected to disorienting electronic noise. "I wasn't one of the serious ones," he recalled. "Down the hall I could hear guys screaming getting electric shocks. I was just given run-of-the-mill beatings; stripped naked, beaten with sticks and slapped around."[41] As his mother would later recall, the treatment left some marks. "My son did not have a stutter before he was interned." Among the words that now gave him difficulty were "British" and "prisoner."[42] The European Court of Human Rights would later rule that the interrogations of this period constituted "inhuman and degrading treatment" in violation of the European Convention on Human Rights.[43]

Following this interrogation, Doherty was interned for five months, first in the hold of the *Maidstone,* a prison ship anchored in Belfast Lough, and then at Long Kesh. No

charges were lodged against him; he was held on a nonjudicial order that characterized his detention without trial as "expedient" to "the preservation of peace and the
maintenance of order."[44]

Shortly after arriving on the *Maidstone*, Doherty and his fellow internees received
reports of "Bloody Sunday," the same event that had driven Peter McMullen into the
IRA. Doherty recalls: "Nearly everybody in the room, IRA and non-IRA, started cry-
ing. People said this has got to end; we can't let them get away with it."[45] Upon his
release, Doherty joined the IRA, determined to drive the British government from its
last major colony. In 1973, he was sentenced to a year in prison for possessing a starting pistol. In 1974, he received a ten-year sentence for transporting eighty pounds of
gelignite explosives for the IRA. Released five years later, he joined an "active service unit."[46]

During the time Doherty was imprisoned, the nature of the armed conflict changed.
On a "Bloody Friday" in July 1972, twenty-two bombs went off without warning at
numerous businesses all across Belfast. Nine people died. Over a hundred were hos-
pitalized, including some who were maimed for life. The IRA would later claim that
they had given warnings but that the authorities had ignored them. In reality, there
were too many bombs for warnings to do much good.[47]

At the same time, the British army and Royal Ulster Constabulary (RUC) were
developing a massive surveillance system, using sophisticated electronic eaves-
dropping devices, networks of informants, and secret squads of highly trained
plainclothes soldiers, like those who had surrounded Desmond Mackin. Unable to
function in loose brigades, the IRA reorganized its soldiers into isolated, cell-sized
"Active Service Units." It was to one of these units that Doherty was reassigned late
in 1979.

On May 2, 1980, Doherty's unit seized a Victorian house at 371 Antrim Road in
North Belfast. They locked two women and a three-month-old baby in a back room
and took up positions at upper windows, from which they planned to ambush a
British army convoy as it slowed for the intersection below. The street corner below
was crowded with traffic and pedestrians, many of them children from neighboring
schools who bought sweets at Cassidy's, a newsagent's store next door, but as the IRA
men positioned their high-powered rifles and American M-60 machine gun on the
windowsills, they were not worrying about ancillary casualties.

Unknown to Doherty and his unit, however, an informant had revealed their plans
to the Army Special Air Services Regiment (SAS), an elite, covert unit comparable in
some ways to the U.S. Delta Force. According to Martin Dillon, a journalist with considerable access to British intelligence and no fan of Joe Doherty, the hallmark of the
SAS was "speed, firepower and aggression." As Dillon reports, "The SAS frequently
ambushed IRA active service units and rarely took prisoners. The shooting of
unarmed IRA bombers in Gibraltar was such an exercise, and a complete IRA active
service unit was wiped out at Loughgall.... Use of the SAS habitually signals an
order to 'terminate with extreme prejudice,' and is rarely an arrest operation."[48]
Among IRA supporters, "SAS" means "special assassination squad."[49]

Informed of the IRA unit's plan, the British army's Task Coordinating Committee requested that all army and police activity in the area cease early in the morning of May 2, so that Doherty and his associates would not be deterred from going ahead. The IRA unit was allowed to seize the house, even though that entailed great risk to the occupants, and to set up their ambush, even though a firefight would seriously endanger civilians.[50] The army, Dillon believes, wanted to kill the ambushers, not capture them, because killing them would give the authorities an advantage in the propaganda war.

The task of assaulting the ambushers was assigned to SAS Captain Herbert R. Westmacott and two teams of plainclothes soldiers under his command. One team was to come up on the house from the rear; the other, led by Westmacott, would attack from the front. But withdrawing all surveillance from the neighborhood turned out to be a mistake, because when the attack came, Westmacott and his team pulled up to the wrong front door.

At No. 371, Doherty and his associates were getting suspicious. No Army units had passed by, and traffic had gotten unusually light. They were thinking about pulling out when, shortly after 2:00 P.M., a carload of men dressed in blue jeans and anoraks, and carrying submachine guns and a sledgehammer, drove to the house next door and jumped out. At this moment, Dillon writes, Doherty and his mates must have known from the red armbands on the anoraks that they were "suddenly facing the most efficient killing machine in the British army."[51] Doherty himself recalled: "They were coming in on a kill mission. . . . They don't exactly take prisoners."[52]

The IRA team immediately opened fire and Captain Westmacott was killed almost instantly by bullets to his head and shoulder. The house was quickly surrounded. When the SAS unit realized that it could not engage the IRA team without risking additional casualties, it called for regular troops and, consistent with its covert status, melted away.

The commander of the new unit called upon Doherty and his associates to surrender. The men could have tried to negotiate their escape by using the occupants of the house as hostages and shields, but, consistent with IRA policy, they did not. Instead they called for a priest and negotiated their surrender.

The IRA men were charged with murdering the captain, attempting to murder the other soldiers, possessing illegal firearms, and belonging to the IRA. Their trial, before a one-judge Diplock Court, was a foregone conclusion and Doherty offered no defense. Indeed, he denied the authority of the court to try him. In the year between his capture and trial, he spent his time plotting an escape. On June 10, 1981, after the trial but before the judge's ruling, Doherty and seven other IRA men broke out of Crumlin Road prison across the street from the courthouse. Using two pistols smuggled into the prison, they captured several warders (guards) and solicitors. Doherty and another IRA man put on warders' uniforms and "escorted" their fellow gunmen out through the front gate.[53] There they came under fire from a plainclothes unit of detectives who just happened to witness the breakout as they were passing by. Doherty made good his escape by standing up, claiming to be a warder, and insisting that he be allowed to escort his "prisoner" back to the prison. Once out of the line of fire, both men bolted, commandeered a car, and disappeared.[54]

That night, there were bonfires and dancing in the streets of Catholic Belfast to celebrate the breakout. Doherty and his fellow escapees became known as the "A-Team," after an American television program about a paramilitary unit that performed improbable feats. The IRA and its supporters had needed this victory badly; its morale had hit rock bottom when their hunger strikers were allowed to die by prison authorities. Two days after the escape, however, Doherty and his codefendants were convicted, *in absentia,* on all charges, and Doherty was sentenced to prison for life.

Of the eight who escaped, six were soon recaptured in the Republic of Ireland. Fearing that Doherty would also be caught, if not killed by the SAS in retaliation for Westmacott's death, the IRA gave him a false passport and sent him off to New York. There, on the morning of June 18, 1983, Doherty was arrested on an INS warrant while tending bar at Clancy's Bar in Manhattan. At first, he thought that the he had been caught in a routine sweep for illegal aliens. Later it bacame clear that the FBI had sought him out at the request of the British government.[55] Doherty was a prestige asset; as much as the IRA wanted Doherty free as a symbol of its unquenchable spirit, the British government wanted him behind bars, because the propaganda war was always more important than the paramilitary conflict. A second provisional warrant for his arrest was issued on June 27, to hold him for extradition, and a formal extradition request was received two months later. Bail was denied and deportation proceedings suspended until the extradition request could be heard.

* * *

Before the extradition hearing was held, the British government made an all out effort to persuade the Reagan administration that Joseph Doherty was a terrorist. At a secret meeting in London on February 15, 1984, U.S. government representatives were informed that Prime Minister Thatcher took a "personal interest" in the case and had asked to be briefed on all developments.[56]

Once the extradition process was underway, the British and American governments launched a fierce propaganda effort to portray Doherty as the archetypal terrorist, a man not fit for the company of decent human beings. The crux of this message, which the British ambassador personally carried to the editorial boards of major American newspapers, was that the British role in Northern Ireland was no longer a paramilitary one but simple law enforcement, making Doherty nothing more than a criminal in paramilitary disguise. At no time did the British government disclose that it could have arrested Doherty and his mates before the planned ambush. The full story of their attempt to neutralize Doherty militarily, just as he would have killed them militarily, was withheld from the courts, the Congress, and the press.

At the extradition hearing, which took place in March and April 1984, the only issue was the applicability of the political offense exception. A representative of the U.S. State Department urged Judge John E. Sprizzo not to apply it, on the ground that its application "could cause damage in relations between Great Britain and the United

States" and that the damage "would not necessarily be limited to Great Britain, but could extend to other countries with strong national policies against terrorism."[57] In short, whether to grant the exception was a nonjusticiable "political question" for the executive and not the judiciary to decide. But Judge Sprizzo, a conservative Reagan appointee, was not persuaded. In December 1984, he ruled against the Reagan administration and barred Doherty's extradition.[58]

The judge had no difficulty finding that there was an uprising in Northern Ireland, that the shooting was in furtherance of that uprising, and that it was ordered by a revolutionary group with historical roots and popular support. It was unnecessary, he ruled, for the IRA to command majoritarian support; even the American revolutionaries could not claim that a majority stood behind them.[59] Nor was it necessary that they prove probable success; history, he recognized, was replete with examples of revolutionary groups that succeeded against the odds.[60] Sprizzo did require proof that the uprising group was not just an isolated group of fanatics, and his review of the long history of rebellion in Northern Ireland convinced him that the IRA was not, as the British claimed, just another group of criminals.[61] The keys to distinguishing the IRA from ordinary fanatics, he ruled, lay in the nature of its organization, structure, and discipline. Captain Westmacott's widow expressed a similar view. "I don't feel revenge," she told a London newspaper in 1981. "Richard's killing wasn't a personal murder. It was part of the war in Ireland."[62]

But Judge Sprizzo did not rely on these criteria alone. He also invoked the "wanton crimes" test of *Abu Eain* on the basis of two comparisons, one of which was to the laws of war. "Surely," he wrote, "an act which would be properly punishable even in the context of a declared war or in the heat of open military conflict cannot and should not receive recognition under the political exception to the treaty."[63] Sprizzo's second comparison was to attacks on innocent bystanders: "We are not faced here with a situation in which a bomb was detonated in a department store, public tavern or a resort hotel, causing indiscriminate personal injury, death, and property damage. Such conduct would clearly be well beyond the parameters of what [is] and should be regarded as encompassed by the political offense exception to the treaty."[64] Accordingly, he ruled, "the facts of this case present the assertion of the political offense exception in its most classic form."[65]

Crucial to Judge Sprizzo's decisions were the existence of an uprising and the nature of what the accused did to further that uprising. The politics of counter-terrorism were irrelevant for his purposes, as were allegations of terrorist activity by IRA members in other circumstances. Joseph Doherty was to be judged on the facts of his case and not on a generalized indictment of his organization. Guilt by association had no place in the law. This was the significance of the judge's decision to invoke the wanton crimes exception. As the U.S. government pushed to abolish the political offense exception for all IRA members, the judge pushed back by distinguishing ever more clearly between Doherty's participation in paramilitary operations and the wanton crimes of other IRA men.

The most innovative portion of the judge's opinion had nothing to do with the political offense exception *per se*, but with the larger question of whether the accused could receive justice as a rebel against Britain and as a defendant in the Diplock courts of Northern Ireland. Sprizzo observed that "both Unionists and Republicans who commit offenses of a political character can and do receive fair and impartial justice and that the courts of Northern Ireland will continue to scrupulously and courageously discharge their responsibilities in that regard."[66]

In fact, the record of the Diplock Courts was mixed, at first accepting and later doubting the testimony from informants with improbably powerful memories.[67] The emergency legislation under which those courts operated would not have met due process standards in the United States.[68] The British army's counter-insurgency techniques at times resembled the *modus operandi* of hit squads,[69] and lawful inquiries into a "shoot to kill" policy were covered up by the highest authorities.[70] Eventually even the British government and its judges would have to admit what was widely known in Ireland and the United States—that the police had fabricated forensic evidence or coerced confessions to put seventeen alleged IRA terrorists behind bars.[71]

Thus, while Judge Sprizzo's decision does not reflect how unjust British law enforcement was toward IRA suspects,[72] his opinion stands as the first instance in which a federal judge actually employed the political offense exception's "second limb" due process test as well as its "first limb" uprising test. By so doing, Sprizzo set a precedent for the proposition that where evidence of injustice in the courts of the requesting regime is clear, extradition cannot be allowed.

Whether the courts of the requesting regime are fair, the judge decided, was *a question of fact* for the extradition magistrate to determine. In this connection, he noted with obvious understatement, "it is certainly at least arguable that the United Kingdom may not be entirely neutral with respect to the issue of Irish independence because it is the end of British rule in Ireland that has been and continues to be the principal objective of the Irish Republican movement."[73]

* * *

Sprizzo's application of the uprising test was entirely consistent with precedent. Given the law, the facts, and the precedents before him, he could not have decided otherwise. Nevertheless, the head of the Justice Department's Criminal Division denounced the decision and vowed to overturn it. "I think it is outrageous," Assistant Attorney General Stephen S. Trott told the *New York Times*,[74] "that terrorists can run across a border and repeal the whole penal law of a country, and we're part of the problem. We've got to get rid of this 'political offense' nonsense among free, friendly nations. We're going to have to attack this treaty by treaty and redo the extradition language."

Trott's statement was, in effect, a declaration of war against the political offense exception. The intemperance of his remarks offended many, including the *National Law Journal*, which declared that his "sarcastic comments . . . demean[ed] the judicial process and the Justice Department itself."[75] But Trott brushed aside all criticism, and his opinion accurately reflected the views of the highest officials in the Reagan and Thatcher administrations. Margaret Thatcher was particularly angered by Sprizzo's decision. The IRA had tried to kill her and her cabinet at the Tory Party's annual conference in Brighton,

England, in 1984. Eight people had died in that attack, including one of her close associates, and Thatcher was determined to break the organization that ordered it. According to Dillon, a senior Foreign Office official told him that Sprizzo's opinion had taught the prime minister that U.S. courts "were not to be trusted," and that, in Dillon's paraphrase, "power politics were required to seal Doherty's fate."[76]

Denied the right to appeal Judge Sprizzo's decision,[77] lacking any new evidence that might justify reopening the extradition request before Sprizzo or another judge, yet determined to keep Doherty behind bars, the Department of Justice tried a new gambit. It asked another district court judge to issue a declaratory judgment accepting the department's interpretation of the treaty in place of Sprizzo's. Technically, this was not an appeal. It was a request for "an authoritative construction of the treaty," which then could be used as the basis for a new extradition request and for the inevitable review that would follow via a habeas corpus petition initiated by Doherty's counsel. In effect, however, it was a request for review, because Sprizzo had already given the government an authoritative construction of the treaty in the same case.

The Declaratory Judgment Act had been adopted in 1934 to allow a person who was legitimately uncertain of his legal rights to avoid damages by asking a court to clarify an ambiguous point of law.[78] Its purpose was to permit a declaration of rights not already determined, not decide whether a previous adjudication had been done properly.[79] Nothing in its legislative history indicates any intent to change the well-established doctrine of extradition law, by which only the accused has a right to higher court (or collateral) review via the "great writ" of habeas corpus. Also, it was patently obvious that if the government were to change the law in this regard, then there would be no sound legal reason it could not seek to overturn every legal interpretation by an arraigning magistrate, and thus keep any accused person behind bars for months or years while the lawyers wrangled.

All these points and more were apparent to any lawyer.[80] Nonetheless, the Justice Department asked federal district court judge Charles S. Haight Jr. to declare that the law of extradition required Joseph Doherty's surrender and to issue the necessary certificate allowing the secretary of state to surrender him. Six months later, Haight denied the request.[81]

The government's willingness to abuse the legal process did not escape the judge's attention. Noting that the government's brief had warned that failure to grant its request "would literally compel the Government to continue refiling the request [for extradition] until a favorable decision is obtained, however long that might take," Haight replied: "If this statement was intended to intimidate this Court, it does not; and *quaere* whether unlimited repetitions of judicially rejected contentions comport with the dignity of the United States Attorney's office. But I will leave that determination for, say, judge number 14 on the list."[82]

Haight's sardonic warning did not intimidate the Justice Department. It was playing for time until Congress could be persuaded to accept changes in the treaty. Filing a frivolous request for a declaratory judgment had the predictable effect of keeping Doherty behind bars until a supplementary treaty abolishing the political offense exception could be negotiated; an appeal of Haight's decision would keep Doherty there for another six months to a year, by which time a new treaty capable of being applied retroactively might be in place. If the treaty were to be delayed for any reason, deportation proceedings could also be strung out for a year or two until ratification was achieved.

The Court of Appeals for the Second Circuit heard argument in December 1985 and upheld Haight's opinion on March 13, 1986. Judge Henry Friendly, writing for a unanimous panel, found the administration's claim to appellate review by means of a declaratory judgment request "startling" but patiently went about rejecting it, much as he had rejected the government's claim of a right of appeal in *Mackin* more than four years earlier.[83] For an administration that had berated the Supreme Court for ignoring "framers' intent," he reviewed the origins of the political offense exception, why it had been entrusted to the courts rather than politicians, and why the executive branch had not been given authority to appeal. "If an analogy must be found," he wrote, "the closest . . . lies in the power of a magistrate, after a preliminary hearing, to discharge a person against whom a criminal complaint has been filed and to dismiss the complaint, after which the prosecutor's remedy is to institute a new proceeding."[84] Indeed, Judge Friendly found the government's assertions especially startling because it had been arguing for years in Congress that new legislation was needed to give it a right of appeal. "The Government now tells us that everything . . . it has told the Congress within the last few years has been wrong."[85]

* * *

Both Judge Haight and the Court of Appeals understood that the Justice Department was playing fast and loose with settled law, and they expressed their distaste for the arrogance and dishonesty involved. However, neither court was sufficiently outraged or courageous to take the political heat involved in releasing Doherty pending the completion of deportation proceedings. Indeed, their refusal to release him on bail and the leisurely pace at which they considered his case revealed the extent to which he had been turned into a symbol and, thereby, stripped of his humanity.

On the other hand, the political offense exception survived. Its defenses were strengthened by Judge Sprizzo's endorsement of *Abu Eain's* wanton crimes exception, and its humanitarian function was enhanced—precedentially, at least—when Sprizzo actually examined the capacity of the courts of Northern Ireland to do justice in IRA cases. By so doing, the judge actually breached the rule of noninquiry and claimed, if only for a moment, judicial administration of the second limb of the political offense exception.

By endorsing *Abu Eain's* wanton crimes exception, Judge Sprizzo also reaffirmed two ancient principles: First, U.S. courts exist to judge individuals, not advance foreign policy or facilitate the surrender of persons for reasons of state. Second, any person who is accused of a crime is entitled to be judged by the nature and quality of his acts and not the apparent guilt of his associates. That the U.S. Justice Department (or the British government) would sink to challenging these principles was a measure of the extent to which the police war against terrorism had come to threaten the impartiality of law.

CHAPTER 14

Hijacking to Freedom:
Extradite or Punish?

*Pray heaven! ... they may find a way to loose their bonds without a
drop of blood. But hear me, Oro! were there no other way, and should
their masters not relent, all honest hearts must cheer this tribe ... on;
though they cut their chains with blades ... gory to the haft! 'Tis right
to fight for freedom, whoever be the thrall.*

Herman Melville, Yoomy's
speech in Mardi, 1849

*They must be universally condemned, whether we consider the cause
the terrorists invoke noble or ignoble, legitimate or illegitimate.*

U.S. Secretary of State
William P. Rogers, 1972

One strategy for denying alleged terrorists protection from extradition is the categorical exclusion of certain heinous acts from the protection of political offender
status. The first of these exclusions was the famous *attentat* clause, which simply
declared—with breathtaking illogic—that the assassination of heads of state was an
ordinary, not a political, crime.

From the 1960s through the 1980s, additional attempts were made to bar from
political offense protection other actions, including the hijacking (and sabotaging)
of airliners,[1] the assassination of diplomatically protected persons,[2] the taking of
hostages,[3] or crimes unrelated to uprisings.[4] To many people, this seemed simple:
Define what is too heinous to warrant protection, label it a nonpolitical offense, and
thus achieve a long overdue humanitarian exception to the outmoded political
offense exception.

There were obvious flaws in this approach, of course, like how to protect the assassins of a latter-day Hitler, but these were brushed aside as something the executive could solve with a grant of asylum or clemency.[5] Categorical exclusions effectively strip the courts of the need to inquire into *why* the alleged terrorist did what he did, and *to whom*. All the courts would have to determine is *what* he did, *when* and *where*, and, if it was categorically excluded from protection as a political offense, authorize his extradition or trial.

* * *

Hijacking historically has posed a special moral problem because it usually involves violence and the taking of hostages. Robbins and his fellow mutineers, the *Amistad* captives, and the *Creole* slaves were all hijackers, and their challenge to the safety of transportation was highly disturbing to many. But no move was made until the 1970s to categorize all hijackings as inexcusable in all circumstances.

During the Cold War, "captive peoples" who hijacked their way to freedom were welcomed in the West as heroes. The British court stretched the uprising test completely out of shape in 1955 to shield the Polish seamen who commandeered their fishing trawler rather than suffer a Communist trial for their political opinions.[6] The Swiss Federal (Supreme) Court likewise refused in 1980 to extradite three Yugoslavians for diverting a Communist airliner to Zurich in their bid for freedom.[7] In both instances, the courts did not just ask what, when, and where; they also asked why and to whom. Once they knew the answer to these questions, extradition was more or less out of the question. Just as the British court was willing to characterize the hijacking of the Polish trawler as an "uprising," the Swiss court was willing to excuse the diversion of the Yugoslavia airliner, because the political purpose of achieving "freedom from the compulsion of a totalitarian state" outweighed the ordinary crimes of subduing the radio operator, firing a pistol into the cabin ceiling, and putting the plane through terrifying maneuvers.[8]

The U.S. executive, in its capacity as a postwar army of occupation in West Germany, refused in 1950 to surrender Czechs who commandeered three airliners and diverted them to Munich. In his note to the Communist regime in Prague, the U.S. ambassador quoted Secretary of State Marcy's famous answer to the Austrians in the Kosta affair: "To surrender political offenders . . . is not a duty; but, on the contrary [is] an act meriting the reprobation of mankind."[9]

Official morality changed, however, when disaffected Americans began seeking asylum abroad by hijacking planes to Europe and Communist Cuba during the late 1960s.[10] Particularly galling to the American government was a French court's decision to grant the political offense exception to two African American hijackers on the strength of their vague references to Black Panther leaders and Hanoi, even though they had demanded $500,000 as well.[11] In another case, hijackers demanded and received $1 million and then forced their captives to fly them from the United States to Algeria. Following their subsequent arrest in Paris, another French court concluded that theirs was a political offense because they were escaping racial segregation.[12]

These French rulings, which found the existence of a black "uprising" in the United States, outraged American officials and went a long way toward discrediting the political offense exception.

Then, on the Labor Day weekend of 1970, a Palestinian commando group (later known as Black September) simultaneously hijacked four New York–bound airliners from different European cities. Three of the planes were diverted to a desert in Jordan and blown up after their passengers had been taken off.[13] A fourth made an emergency landing in London after an in-flight battle.[14] Within a few months these hijackings galvanized the political will necessary to conclude the 1970 Hague Convention for the Suppression of Unlawful Seizure of Aircraft, which eventually 115 countries signed.[15]

The Black September hijackings also helped to trigger the movement to undermine, if not destroy, the political offense exception to extradition. The United States, together with the Soviet Union, asked the convention delegates to deny the political offense exception categorically to all aircraft hijackers, regardless of their motives. Theirs was an extraordinary alliance: a police state determined to keep its people imprisoned and the West's leading democracy, worried not only about Black September operations but about anti-war radicals who might hijack their way to Cuba or Libya.[16] Fortunately, cooler heads prevailed. The American-Soviet proposals were rejected by West European nations in favor of an obligation to extradite or prosecute.

The obligation was artfully worded. If extradition was refused, then the host country was required "without exception whatsoever ... to submit the case to its competent authorities for the purpose of prosecution."[17] The phrase "without exception whatsoever" seemed to withdraw all protection from politically motivated hijackers and thus addressed the politics of the problem. However, the concluding language effectively left host countries free to protect future Kolczynskis by sham prosecutions or hung juries.

* * *

The first test of the Hague Convention's categorical exclusion of hijackers from the political offense exception occurred in April 1972, when two miners hijacked a small Czech airliner and forced its crew to land them in Nuremberg, West Germany. During the takeover, one of the miners shot the copilot in the shoulder.

The Czech government demanded extradition, the miners pleaded for political asylum, and the West German government was caught in a political bind. It wanted to provide a refuge for anyone who could breach the Iron Curtain, but it did not want to encourage hijacking, which endangered innocent people. An occasional wall-jumper could be celebrated; hijackers—particularly those who shot copilots—were not to be encouraged, even if they were fighting their way to freedom. Politically, West Germany could not extradite anyone back to the Communists, so it decided to prosecute. The miners were convicted and sentenced to seven years each in prison.[18]

For the United States, the first major test of the Hague Convention occurred on August 30, 1978, when Hans Tiede and Ingrid Ruske, along with her twelve-year-old daughter Sabine, hijacked a Polish airliner from Gdansk, Poland, to Tempelhof Airport in the American sector of West Berlin. Theirs was a truly desperate act; their original plan had been to escape using forged documents, but it failed when Ingrid's West German lover was captured by the East German secret police while trying to bring forged papers to her. Knowing that it was only a matter of hours before the police would track them down, Tiede, Ruske, and her daughter got on a Polish flight to Schoenefeld Airport in East Berlin. Minutes before the plane was to land, Teide walked through the curtain to the forward crew area, brandished a toy pistol, and persuaded the pilots to divert the plane to Tempelhof.

After the landing, Tiede flashed "V" for victory signs, grinned broadly, and tossed his toy gun to an American colonel. "Welcome to free Berlin," said another colonel. The first colonel gave Ruske a kiss and escorted the trio from the plane. Eight other passengers, all East Germans, promptly joined them in defecting.[19]

For a brief moment, Tiede and Ruske were genuine heroes; they had dared to be free. But then East Germany demanded their extradition under the Hague Convention. West Germany happily washed its hands of the case. It is your problem, they told the American occupation force, because the plane had landed in the American sector of West Berlin. Having sought a no exceptions approach to airplane hijackers, the American government could not now say that the treaty did not apply. The West Germans had declared the treaty applicable to West Berlin, and the United States had, as part of the military command structure for West Berlin, acquiesced in that decision. Unwilling to extradite Tiede and Ruske, the Americans decided to prosecute them instead.

This posed a problem because U.S. courts normally sit within the United States and try people for crimes committed on American territory and against American law. In this instance, however, the relevant territory belonged to West Germany. So the decision was made to employ an American court, using American procedures, but applying the substantive law of West Germany, in a city under allied military occupation. A "United States Court for Berlin" was established and Herbert J. Stern of the U.S. District Court for New Jersey became its judge.[20]

The case against Tiede and Ruske was assembled by the same military command that had welcomed them to freedom. Indeed, much of the evidence against them was collected while the Polish airliner was still on the ground. When the plane took off, Tiede, Ruske, and her little girl were taken into custody. They were not arrested or charged but were kept on the base, so far as they knew, to achieve a friendly resolution of their situation. Meanwhile, military investigators opened and read all their incoming mail and secretly copied all their outgoing mail.[21] The U.S. government later admitted that it had held them incommunicado for more than two months in order to prevent them from obtaining legal assistance, even though it had decided within forty-eight hours of their arrival to appoint a prosecutor, in case U.S. (or West German) officials chose to have them tried.[22] When authority to prosecute Tiede was received, the trio still were not informed or offered counsel, even though a courtroom was being constructed at the other end of the building in which they were being held.

During the sixty-four days that Ingrid Ruske and her daughter were held in what the U.S. government falsely called "protective custody," the investigators had no evidence whatever that they had helped Tiede carry out the hijacking. Finally, on the sixty-fifth day of their confinement, Ruske and her daughter were released for lack of evidence. In return, Ruske was asked to sign a document promising not to sue the United States or any of its employees. She did so willingly, for, so far as she then knew, the U.S. officials were her friends.

Ruske's release posed no diplomatic problem so long as Tiede could be prosecuted. If all the U.S. government needed was a show trial, it could forget her. But that was not to be. When military investigators learned that Ruske had been in on the plan to defect from the beginning but had kept silent to protect her imprisoned lover, U.S. Attorney Andre Surena and Special Prosecutor Roger Adelman ordered the military to construct a case against her too. The investigators did so by pretending friendship and leading her to believe she would not be prosecuted if she told the full story about her role and that of her lover.

The decision to prosecute Ruske along with Tiede was made with full knowledge that convicting her might well doom her daughter—whom the investigators also pretended to befriend—to spend the rest of her youth in a state institution. Government lawyers also knew that by disclosing the escape plot behind the hijacking, which they would have to in order to convict Ruske, they would help the East German secret police clinch their case against her imprisoned lover. Thus the prosecutors would not only betray her trust; they would deceive her into betraying the persons she most loved, with and for whom she had risked her life.

The decision to prosecute Ruske was clearly imprudent, for once the government sought to introduce her confession and her lawyers moved to suppress it on a variety of constitutional grounds, there was grave danger that the case against her would have to be dismissed. But that was not the most imprudent choice the State Department made. The department also created a civilian court with a civilian judge, rather than a military tribunal, which an occupying power would normally do. So when it chose to argue that the defendants were not entitled to a jury trial because the U.S. Court for Berlin was a "conqueror's court"—free from all constitutional constraints, including the Sixth Amendment's guarantee of a right to trial by jury,[23] Judge Stern was profoundly shocked.

The State Department did not want a jury trial for two reasons. First, letting jurors decide would be seen by communist regimes as a way of preventing convictions and would motivate those regimes not to return the hijackers of Western planes. Second, a jury would have to be drawn from the population of West Berlin. As a matter of law, this was no problem; nothing in the U.S. Constitution said that the members of an American jury must be Americans. But the West German government, which was paying for the trial, would be upset if the moral onus for acquitting the defendants was placed on Germany through the instrument of a German jury. So the State Department continued to argue that the U.S. Constitution did not apply in this court.

Of course, were Judge Stern to accept that argument, then the American "conquerors" would be free to treat everyone in their sector as arbitrarily as they would like. The U.S. Court for Berlin would have no legal authority to restrain them.[24]

The implications of this argument were extraordinary. Not only would the judge of that court lack all independence; he could not apply any principle of law that the prosecutors did not approve. If they disagreed with his rulings, they could—as their brief threatened—ignore them.[25] This was more power than even an American military command would dare claim.

Moreover, if the due process clause of the U.S. Constitution did not apply, then the State Department could extradite the defendants at any time—during their trial, after their acquittal, or after their conviction and incarceration. Anything could be done with Tiede, Ruske, and her daughter because "foreign policy," not law, would govern.

Indeed, anything could be done to anyone in the American sector, because the U.S. military would, under "conqueror's law," acquire near dictatorial powers.[26] It was a doctrine, Judge Stern noted, "worthy of Adolf Hitler himself. Not since the 'People's Courts' of the Nazi Era had Berlin heard of such a thing in a 'court of law.'"[27] It was also an embarrassing argument for the United States to make in Germany, where the American policy was supposed to foster liberty, democracy, and the rule of law among former Nazis.

Worse still, it was more than an argument; it was, as the judge later noted, the basis on which the suspects had been held incommunicado for more than two months.[28] It was also a threat against the court. If Stern did not accept the argument, then the State Department was reserving the right to dismiss him.

The decision to frame the argument as a threat to the judge's independence was not made by the two junior attorneys in Berlin. They received their orders from Washington. Who issued the orders is not known, but State Department Attorney Roger Adelman informed the court that "these are the rules that the Secretary of State has dictated for this court."[29] The secretary of state was Cyrus Vance; his deputy was Warren Christopher.[30]

Judge Stern saw the threat but was not intimidated. On the contrary, he pressed the State Department's prosecutors to admit that they were not directing him to deny Tiede and Ruske their right to a jury trial, but only arguing for it as a matter of law.[31] Once they did that, he rejected their arguments and ordered a jury empanelled.[32]

Stern knew this decision would put the State Department in a triple bind. If the department accepted his order, then the German government, which was paying for the trial, would object to shifting the onus of decision onto German jurors, while the Russians would object to allowing conquered Germans to judge the facts in an occupation court. On the other hand, if the State Department revoked the judge's mandate, then the U.S. would be bound to extradite the defendants to Poland, which would embarrass the Carter administration's campaign for human rights and cause objections among the people of West Germany. Or the State Department could fire the judge for not collaborating and try to appoint another—an act that might well spark criticism within the United States and damage Secretary Vance's reputation as a lawyer-statesman.[33]

Under the circumstances, the State Department chose to retreat, if only temporarily, and allow the trial to proceed. The domestic political costs of flouting the Constitution outweighed the foreign relations benefits of insisting on a conqueror's court. However, the very fact that its lawyers could make such an argument revealed that justice under law was a low priority for the State Department, even as it was commanded by two of the most distinguished attorneys in American public life.

Before the trial began, Judge Stern ruled—over the State Department's vociferous objections—that incriminating statements obtained by the military from Ruske could not be used against her, because the manner in which they were obtained had violated her Fifth Amendment privilege against self-incrimination.[34] Without this evidence, the prosecution's case against her collapsed, and her lawyers successfully moved to have the charges dismissed with prejudice. She and her daughter went free.

However, the prosecution was concerned with more than a lack of evidence. It did not want a federal court in Berlin that could challenge its authority in any way. So the State Department decided to prevent Stern from giving effect to his opinion that U.S. constitutional rights limited its officials in Berlin. To do this, government attorneys made Tiede an unusual offer. If he would plead guilty, they would guarantee that he would be released from jail by Christmas, regardless of what sentence the judge imposed.[35]

In most American courts, where plea-bargaining is essential to clear crowded dockets, such an agreement, *if approved by the judge,* would be proper. But the judge must approve each plea bargain, because due process requires that the judge ascertain that the accused was not pressured or tricked into waiving a fundamental constitutional right. In this instance, however, the offer was made in secret, after the U.S. ambassador had been ordered by the State Department to change the law under which parole would be granted. The law was changed, by the ambassador's decree, to give the government's lawyers what they wanted, not as a general rule but in this case only. Equal justice under law had nothing to do with it; neutral principles were irrelevant. The State Department sought to fix the case much as a politician might fix a traffic ticket. It was, as Stern later noted, a "fraud upon the court"—an attempt to turn a judicial proceeding into a "charade."[36]

But Tiede did not cooperate. He elected to exercise his constitutional right and was tried by a jury of West Berliners. His principal defense, which would not have gotten him far under American law, was "justification and excuse." Articles 33, 34, and 35 of the West German Penal Code allowed the jury, in its efforts to determine criminality, to weigh all the circumstances to decide whether the defendant's law-breaking and the risks it posed to others was justified or could be excused because of the desperate circumstances he was in, the value of the goals he sought on behalf of himself and his two companions, and the nature of the means he used.[37] This defense is very similar to the Swiss "preponderance of the motive" test for nonextraditable political crimes.

In a sense, the concepts of justification and excuse had already been applied, *sub silentio,* in *Kolczynski.* There the British court essentially concluded that assaulting a fishing boat captain and locking him up was justified and excusable, because the purpose was to avoid certain return to a political trial for mere dissent. If the Polish sea-men could be justified in beating their captain, then Tiede might be justified in point-ing a toy gun at a flight attendant and threatening to shoot her if the plane did not land in free Germany, and this justification could just as easily be claimed in an extra-dition proceeding as in a trial.

In Tiede's case, there was persuasive evidence that the flight attendant and cock-pit crew were not very frightened by their hijacker. They smoked cigarettes with him, looked at pictures of his children, and tried to get the plane back in the air before any-one could question them. The State Department claimed that Tiede endangered the passengers and crew, and West Berliners living near the airport, by forcing a seventy-two-passenger plane to land on a too-short runway, but this claim was rebutted by evidence that President Carter's jumbo jet had recently used the same runway with-out difficulty. Nor did the passengers know that a hijacking was in process. Finally, the Polish customs agent who examined the hijackers' "gun" before they boarded con-sidered it a "toy" and returned it to Ruske's daughter.[38]

How the jury went about processing this information in the course of considering the questions of justification and excuse is not known, but they acquitted Tiede of hijacking, depriving persons of their liberty, and doing bodily injury to the flight attendant, although they convicted him of taking a hostage.[39] This put the judge in a difficult position, for now he had to pass sentence and, with that decision, consider the significance of the State Department's effort to nullify his sentencing authority. Faced with the State Department's persistent contempt for limited government and the rule of law, Judge Stern made an unusual decision. "Gentlemen," he told a pha-lanx of government lawyers,[40]

> I will not give you this defendant. You have persuaded me that you recognize no limita-tions of due process. I don't have to be a great prophet to understand that there is prob-ably not a great future for the United States Court for Berlin here. Under those circum-stances, who will be here to protect Tiede if I give him to you for four years [the sentence they had requested]? Viewing the Constitution as non-existent, considering yourselves not restrained in any way, who will stand between you and him?

Stern recognized that, given the State Department's disregard for law, there was nothing to prevent it from surrendering Tiede to the Polish government by executive fiat, if that proved diplomatically advantageous. So he sentenced Tiede to the time he had already spent in custody and declared him a free man.[41]

Stern's decision was in the highest tradition of American jurisprudence. However, when the U.S. Court of Appeals later heard a challenge to the State Department's deci-sion to abolish the U.S. Court for Berlin in order to prevent additional cases from com-ing before it, the court upheld the State Department and criticized Stern because he had "ordered that 500 unsuspecting Berliners be rounded up to make a venire for the trial."[42] No notice was given to the popularity of Judge Stern's actions in Berlin, or the example of integrity he set for a people eager to get out from under arbitrary gov-ernment of any sort.

The Court of Appeals also refused to endorse Stern's "attractive position" that "the Bill of Rights is fully applicable to the conduct of U.S. judges and officials in Berlin." Rather, the court accepted that principle *arguendo,* as if contemplating so basic a principle of American law was too difficult, or too unimportant, for it to consider.[43]

Reviewing Stern's 1984 book about the case, Andreas Lowenfeld, a deputy legal adviser to the State Department between 1964 and 1966, defended the State Department's lawyers against the judge's criticism. Like the Court of Appeals, Lowenfeld refused to wrestle with the fundamental principles at stake. Rather, he disparaged Stern for thinking of himself as the "Valiant Defender" of "the Values of American Justice," and asked whether Cyrus Vance, Warren Christopher, or the lawyers who worked for them to convict Tiede and Ruske had really advanced "so unworthy" an argument?[44]

The answer, of course, is yes. The U.S. military investigators were as treacherous to Ruske as any secret police, while the Departments of State and Justice actively defied the most basic principles of American justice. To examine their conduct is like stepping through Alice's looking glass, where:[45]

> The cat, whose name was Fury,
> Said to a mouse
> that he met in the house,
> 'Let us both go to law:
> I will prosecute *you.–*
> Come, I'll take no denial.
> We must have a trial,
> For really this morning
> I've nothing to do.'
>
> Said the mouse to the cur,
> 'Such a trial, dear sir,
> With no jury or judge,
> would be wasting our breath.'
> 'I'll be the judge,
> I'll be the jury,'
> Said cunning old Fury:
> 'I'll try the whole cause
> And condemn you to death.'

* * *

How should we deal with aircraft hijackings, which most people regard as quintessential acts of terrorism, regardless of the hijackers' motives? Thomas Franck, a professor of international law, has written that the U.S. government was right to prosecute Tiede. "While the dissident hijackers [in that case] may have our sympathy, most Americans probably do not regard that their punishment reduces the law to an absurdity."[46] Most Americans who saw *Judgment in Berlin,* the 1988 film based on Judge Stern's book, thought that the prosecution had behaved despicably, but Franck is probably right that "Americans widely believe hijacking . . . of airplanes an unacceptable practice no matter what the 'why' or 'to whom' factors are."[47] The problem is how to square this general sentiment with individual justice, which Americans also support, and which the Constitution requires.

According to Franck, we should not try to reconcile these conflicting values. "Pity the criminal all you like," he says, quoting Porfiry Petrovich, the Russian police inspector in Dostoevsky's *Crime and Punishment*, "but don't call evil good."[48] The law against hijacking must be pitiless, because the social utility in deterring similar crimes outweighs the moral value of doing justice in each individual case. In this belief, Franck (and Dostoevsky's inspector) are very much like Melville's Captain Vere, who admonished: "let not warm hearts betray heads that should be cool. Ashore, in a criminal case, will an upright judge allow himself off the bench to be waylaid by some tender kinswoman of the accused seeking to touch him with her tearful plea? Well, the heart here, sometimes the feminine in man, is that piteous woman, and hard though it may be, she must be here ruled out."[49]

Hijacking, like mutiny in the fleet, must be deterred at all costs. In saying this, Franck admits that he is endorsing a form of "idiot's law"—an absolute prohibition that he knows will lead, on occasion, to "absurd consequences."[50] But in this situation, he believes, "idiot's law" is better than "sophist's law"—law which, in its effort to plumb the depths of the issues for their "multilayered complexity," produces a "complex, exculpatory, . . . case-by-case approach" that deters no one and, therefore, cannot merit popular support.[51]

In the 1970s, Franck's view enjoyed almost universal acceptance. Over one hundred nations ratified the Hijacking Convention, and the U.S. Congress backed up its "extradite or punish" provision by making the destruction of aircraft a separate federal crime.[52] If the only hijackings had come from communist police states, most people would probably have stayed with the Cold War practice, but beset by an epidemic of hijackings, they opted for a draconian rule.

The trouble with such unequivocal laws, of course, is that they require courts to presume that what the accused did was heinous before the court knows enough about the acts, in context, to make an accurately informed, fully considered moral judgment. The lawmakers, in effect, prejudge the accused, much as Vere (or Parliament) did in *Billy Budd*, because they fear that the deterrent effect of their law will be undermined by the "womanly" subjectivity that comes from daring to see the accused as a person. Where deterrence is the primary objective, people in power do not want to try individuals; they want to punish symbols.

Legislative enactments, like the Articles of War, are "idiot's law." Passed in haste to confront a crisis, they are intended to deter large numbers of people by the very unreasoning nature of their declarations.[53] Such positive rules are usually hostile to "sophist's law," which draws upon the traditions of the common law and natural rights to produce decisions that judge the behavior of individuals in light of potentially conflicting moral standards.[54]

Legislative prohibitions tend to be simple-minded for several reasons. They are usually the result of political compromises (or inattention) which conceal (or ignore) irreconcilable differences in values and priorities. Legislative drafters often find it impossible to specify, let alone agree upon, all potentially exculpatory factors in advance, particularly when the law is passed in haste as part of an urgent "war" on crime.[55] In the intensely pluralistic politics of the U.S. Congress, specification of all potentially exculpatory factors might also be seen, by the often righteous sponsors of laws against terrorism, as subversive of the moral sentiment and deterrent force that their bills are supposed to convey.

By stressing the *what* and *when*, to the exclusion of the *why* and *to whom*, Franck would essentially impose a rule of noninquiry where considerations of self-defense, extreme provocation, or dire necessity are morally relevant—at least to the "womanly" among us. In so doing, he would effectively transfer such womanly considerations to the executive branch, with all its political conflicts of interest.

Clemency, in the Anglo-American tradition, is an executive, and therefore political, function. But in hijacking cases, where U.S. attorneys represent foreign regimes, the chances of executive clemency are virtually nil—unless the Justice Department is willing to sacrifice reciprocal extradition services by rejecting the requesting regime's demands. If there is to be any clemency for hijackers like Tiede and Ruske, it must be something courts can grant (and thereby shield the executive from foreign policy repercussions).

An American court that seeks to learn why these "terrorists" did what they did need not fully embrace a subjective French or even Swiss-style "political motives" test. To seek to understand why somebody did something so seemingly heinous is not to decide in advance to excuse it. Rather, the inquiry into motives or purposes can be used to frame Robert Slender's haunting question: "If you had been as Robbins was/What would you have done?"[56] If we do not allow our courts to ask this question, we must conclude with the proponents of categorical prohibitions that it is simply not relevant that Nash might have been an impressed seaman or that Captain Pigot's brutality might have justified hijacking the *Hermione*. If these questions are not relevant to a court that is trying hijackers rather than extraditing them, then we should not wish to know whether the *Amistad* captives were really free men, why the *Amistad* and *Creole* were hijacked, or that Tiede and Ruske resorted to hijacking only because they feared imminent capture by the secret police.

Of course, while self-defense may be raised where the accused is being tried rather than extradited, it cannot be raised if the government choses to seek extradition. This may make sense where the alleged oppressor was a private person; the court of the requesting state presumably can decide that question fairly. But where the act of self-defense was directed at the requesting state, allowing it to decide the legitimacy of that resistance makes little sense, unless its courts are unusually independent and principled. In hijacking cases, claims of self-defense, extreme provocation, or dire necessity need to be heard by the host country's courts, if injustice is to be avoided.[57]

If such claims are heard by the courts, then it may be possible, over time, for courts and legislatures to make reasoned moral distinctions between different kinds of hijackers. Absolute prohibitions can be applied to the likes of D. B. Cooper, the legendary hijacker who extorted $200,000 in return for the passengers' lives and then parachuted into oblivion over Oregon on November 24, 1971.[58] Something like the "wanton crimes" exception can facilitate the extradition or punishment of hijackers who execute innocent passengers like Robert Stetham or Leon Klinghoffer in order to extort concessions or commit reprisals.[59] A suspension of the rule of noninquiry can be used to shield hijackers like Tiede and Ruske (and the Polish seamen) from return to police states. In cases like those of Billy Budd, Jonathan Robbins, the *Amistad*, and the *Creole*, we may decide that the requesting state can have no jurisdiction over seamen it has impressed or human beings it has enslaved. Similarly, we might decide, perhaps by legislation, to refuse to engage in extradition with any regime that does not allow its citizens the right of emigration.

To adopt such rules is not to romanticize people like Tiede and Ruske. Hijacking a plane from East to West during the Cold War was a dangerous act, even if it was done with a toy gun and a child. So too was Billy Budd's crime—striking a superior officer at a time when many ships in the British navy were rife with mutinous resentments. But it is also wrong to declare Budd a "mutineer" or Tiede and Ruske "terrorists." In both instances, the worst offense to justice was the exaggeration of their offenses that the law imposed upon the courts, and which in Budd's case was compounded by making him into a symbol of something he wasn't. In both instances, the effort to make the defendants seem truly heinous obscured grave injustices by their governments, who kept them imprisoned under miserable circumstances against their will. Laws can draw sharp lines, but provision needs to be made for judicial mitigation where good cause can be shown. Judges must be granted enough "wiggle room" to "do the right thing." We need order and we need liberty, and to achieve both we need to moderate the "idiot's law" of legislatures with the "sophisticated" interpretations of judges in the common law, natural rights tradition.

To achieve ordered liberty, it helps to think of the criminal law as something more than a service that politicians render to their constituents. If law is merely a response to political demands, then we will have a surfeit of "idiot's law" well expressing the simple-minded consternation or vengeance of an alarmed public or righteous politicians. If law is something we produce merely to please our superiors, then we will get decisions like Captain Vere's. If law is mere adherence to social convention, then we will get decisions like Captain Delano's, who could not imagine that he had any obligation, as a Christian gentlemen, to help Benito Cereno's captors get to Sierra Leone. The criminal law should conform to a higher morality than everyday politics, which may be why the Supreme Court freed the hijackers of the *Amistad*, even as they lamented the "dreadful acts" by which the captives seized the ship and forced their enslavers to serve them.[60]

The problem with the Hijacking Convention, like the Fugitive Slave Acts, the Articles of War, and the rule of noninquiry, is that they force judges to operate "railroads." Any system of extradition that bars judicial examination of the charges in their full moral context delegitimates the judicial system by forcing courts to bum's rush fugitives to injustice.

Finally, we need full judicial inquiry in order to preserve our humility and avoid becoming complacent collaborators in systemic injustice, like Captain Delano. Before we too harshly judge fugitives from foreign uprisings, police states, slavery, or impressment, we should reflect on whether our own nation is not complicit in similar wrongs. As a nation of settlers whose ancestors displaced and destroyed a native population, we should reflect humbly on our instinct to so harshly judge members of the PLO. As the sponsor of numerous Cold War conflicts, we should be careful not to insist on humanitarian standards for "terrorists" that the armed forces of our client states could not meet. We should not loudly condemn all persons who use guns and bombs in the course of uprisings and then turn around, as the Reagan administration did, and claim that the killing of over one hundred innocent civilians in a nighttime bombing raid on Libya was not an act of terrorism or an attempt to assassinate a head of state.

Tiede's case should have caused excruciating embarrassment at the Departments of Justice and State, even before it became a major motion picture. But lawyers are not easily embarrassed and governments have short memories.[61] The attack on the political offense exception was carried still further into precincts where "idiot's law" is most popular—the Congress of the United States.

CHAPTER 15

Gutting the Political Offense Exception

The Prime Minister believes you owe us this one. She allowed your Government to use our territory for your F-111s when they were on their way to Libya.

> British diplomat Sherard Cowper Coles
> to U.S. Attorney Otto Obermaier, 1986

Simultaneously with its efforts in court, the executive branch sought to destroy the political offense exception in Congress, both by the revision of treaties and by the introduction of "reform" legislation. Its first strategy was to transfer administration of the exception from the courts to the executive; the second was to eviscerate the exception itself.

The driving force behind these changes was the extradition bureaucracy of the Departments of State and Justice. The attorneys there preceded and outlasted the elected officials who superintended them, and they set the agenda for politicians to exploit with anti-crime slogans. Democratic and Republican appointees to State and Justice quickly discovered that their primary function was not to initiate policy but to adopt as their own the policies favored by their nominal subordinates.

It was in this posture that the Carter administration came to attack the political offense exception to extradition even as it sought, within other compartments, to promote human rights abroad. While liberal Democrats fought conservative efforts to strip the federal courts of jurisdiction to decide cases involving racial segregation, internal security, and abortion, the Departments of State and Justice quietly persuaded the Senate to strip U.S. courts of jurisdiction to apply the political offense exception in extradition cases involving three foreign countries: Colombia, Mexico, and the Netherlands. Actually, "persuaded" is too strong a word. "Tricked" would be more accurate. According to one of its attorneys, the Senate Committee on Foreign Relations had no one on its staff at the time who knew enough about extradition to recognize that bestowing exclusive authority on the executive to decide who was entitled to the political offense exception was no mere technical change.[1]

When the Reagan administration assumed office in January 1981, it was determined to abandon Carter's solicitude for international human rights and to intensify the government's wars on terrorism and illegal drugs. Blithely claiming that the political offense exception was a "legal loophole" for terrorists, the new administration sought to close it.

* * *

The first extradition treaty negotiated by the Reagan administration was with the Marcos regime in the Philippines. The proposed agreement did not abolish the political offense exception outright, but it sought essentially the same result by transferring administration of the exception exclusively to the executive branch.[2] In summarizing the treaty for Congress, the new administration, like the one before it, did not disclose the revolutionary nature of the change it was proposing. When challenged, it disingenuously claimed, in an unsigned document, that the political offense exception would still exist.[3]

The purpose of the treaty was to combat communist terrorism, the administration said, neglecting to mention that the Marcos regime had destroyed that country's democratic institutions and murdered and terrorized its political opponents for years.[4] Any regime that opposed communism was, according to the Reagan administration, "democratic." At a luncheon in Manila on June 30, 1981, Vice President Bush warmly toasted the dictator: "We stand with the Philippines. . . . We stand with you, sir. We love your adherance to democratic principles and to democratic processes, and we will not leave you in isolation."[5]

A few months later, administration officials told Congress that the proposed treaty was possible because Marcos had ended martial law and largely phased out the military tribunals he had used to harry and suppress his opponents. They did not acknowledge that the Marcos Constitution authorized him to rule by decree and continue to suspend the privilege of the writ of habeas corpus.[6] The State Department reported that "the Philippine government agreed in the treaty that extradited persons shall not be tried by extraordinary or ad hoc tribunals," but did not disclose that Marcos had replaced almost the entire judiciary with judges beholden to his patronage.[7] Nor did the State Department note that in September 1980 Marcos had secretly signed the Public Safety Act, giving himself extraordinary powers.[8]

The administration added that "We have no reason to believe that the Philippine government would jeopardize the treaty by making improper extradition requests."[9] But, even as the treaty was being negotiated, FBI agents were helping the Marcos regime link opposition leaders in exile to bombers in the Philippines. Among those investigated by the FBI was former Philippine senator Benigno S. Aquino Jr., then in exile and a fellow in international affairs at Harvard. In putting Aquino under close surveillance, and even raiding his home, the Bureau did not act on its own but responded to allegations by Imelda Marcos, the dictator's wife, that Aquino had sent assassination teams to Manila.[10] While Marcos supporters were assassinating Filipino American labor leaders in Seattle,[11] the U.S. Justice Department launched a grand jury probe into "terrorist" activities by Philippine exiles in Los Angeles.[12]

When the text of the treaty was finally released in November 1981, numerous human rights and nationality groups denounced its court-stripping provision. Their protests intensified as word spread that Marcos had obtained warrants for the arrest of forty people charged with various "subversive" and "seditious" acts and a series of bombings. Among those charged with conspiracy to plant bombs in Manila was former senator Aquino, Marco's most distinguished rival. The charges against him and others were based primarily upon allegations by Victor Burns Lovely, who, once he was released from police custody, recanted, claiming that the accusations had been extracted from him under torture.[13]

These disclosures took their toll, and by March 1982 the Philippine treaty was in trouble. Fearing that its defeat could scuttle the larger campaign to do away with the political offense exception, the State Department decided to withhold the treaty from the Senate. Instead, it tried to achieve the same end by pushing legislation it had introduced the previous September—comprehensive legislation to strip all courts of jurisdiction to grant the exception in any case arising under any extradition treaty. Reagan emissaries continued to praise the Marcos regime for its commitment to "democracy,"[14] until senator Aquino broke his exile in August 1983 and returned home, where he was immediately dragged from his plane by security guards and executed with a single shot to the back of his head.[15]

*　*　*

Senator Strom Thurmond (R.-S.C.) introduced the administration's bill to a Republican-controlled Senate on September 18, 1981, two months before the proposed treaty with the Philippines was revealed. At about the same time, Representative William J. Hughes (D.-N.J.) proposed an alternative in the Democrat-controlled House. Both versions were characterized as necessary to modernize the law of extradition, combat terrorism and drug-smuggling, and reverse judicial decisions that had barred the extradition of IRA members and delayed the surrender of Abu Eain.

Support for an executive-centered approach to extradition was strongest in the Republican-controlled Senate, where the Committee on Foreign Relations was chaired by Richard G. Lugar (R.-Ind.). Opposition to the legislation was greatest in the House, where Representative Hughes, who was chair of the Subcommittee on Crime, was willing to accept the court-stripping provision.[16] The House committee's staff, however, gave opponents every opportunity to be heard. Opposing the House and Senate bills were most scholars of extradition, the American Civil Liberties Union, and a coalition of ethnic groups, including Arab Americans, Irish Americans, Salvadoran refugees, and Filipinos.[17]

The battle in Congress was, as almost always, a tournament of slogans: how best to protect "freedom fighters" while assuring the surrender of "terrorists." The administration insisted that such distinctions could best be drawn by the executive, with its

superior political "expertise," but Senator Charles Percy (R.-Ill.) and the Senate Judiciary Committee were not persuaded. When they insisted on keeping the administration of the political offense exception in the courts,[18] the Reagan administration was
forced to switch tactics. It proposed to keep the political offense in name but sought
to exclude from its protection a wide variety of alleged offenses.

The categorical exclusion approach was not new. It had begun with the Belgian
attentat clause in the mid nineteenth century and was employed, most recently, by the
1977 European Convention on the Suppression of Terrorism.[19] The European treaty,
however, contained a much more limited list of excluded offenses[20] than the bill, and
even these were often nullified by little-noticed reservations that effectively preserved
the political offense exception.[21]

The administration's list began innocuously with rape and drug smuggling but
moved on to more problematic offenses, including the hijacking of aircraft and attacks
on internationally protected persons. The revised bill also claimed that homicide,
assault, kidnapping, the taking of hostages, unlawful detentions, and the use of
firearms in a dangerous way could not be considered political offenses except under
"extraordinary circumstances."[22] Attempts and conspiracies to commit these offenses
were brought under the same umbrella,[23] effectively denying the political offense
exception to most persons involved in foreign uprisings.

Opponents of the bill insisted that administration of the political offense exception should remain with the courts. They offered three ways of dealing with the
problem of protecting freedom fighters but not terrorists. One was to suspend the
rule of noninquiry, which would allow the courts to protect foreign fugitives from
"victors' justice" and other forms of oppression.[24] Another was to follow the courts'
lead and add a "wanton crimes" exception to the political offense exception,[25] and
a third was to impose some or all of the laws of war on participants in noninternational armed conflicts.[26]

The first of these alternatives was the broadest, because requiring inquiry into the
capacity of the requesting regime to do justice could protect fugitives who had not
necessarily been a part of an uprising and had not otherwise contended for power.
The "wanton crimes" exception was more narrow, and it focused more squarely on
the immediate political problem, which was how to preserve the political offense
exception and yet permit prosecution (in either country) of war criminals and terrorists who targeted presumptively innocent civilians. The "wanton crimes" approach
drew upon a developing body of law and left the door open to further developments
on a case-by-case basis. The "war crimes" and "grave breaches" approach was narrower still. It would have limited protection of the political offense exception to persons who were engaged in rather well-organized, paramilitary or military uprisings
of a subnational character.

The three approaches were not mutually exclusive. Preference for one over the
other often had more to do with the direction from which the advocates approached
the problem than with the measure's merits. Suspending the rule of noninquiry
appealed to lawyers with a strong commitment to due process of law and a desire to

keep American courts from functioning as the long arms of foreign injustice. They were less concerned with protecting former participants in foreign uprisings than with maintaining the integrity and neutrality of American courts in the face of strong executive pressures to politicize the law of extradition.

Advocates of the "wanton crimes" approach shared these concerns but doubted whether it was possible, under the existing political conditions, to win suspension of the rule of noninquiry. They viewed the "wanton crimes" approach as a way of defending the political offense exception by appealing to Congress's normal disposition to maintain the status quo while appearing to be innovative.

Advocates of an exception for "war crimes" or "grave breaches" came to the extradition controversy from the perspective of international law. They were searching for ways to develop rules of warfare that could be extended to subnational conflicts. Their approach, however, could lead courts to think of the political offense exception as shielding participants in civil wars but not protecting rioters like Castioni, fugitives from police states like Kolczynski, Tiede, and Aquino, or revolutionaries like Kossuth, Mazzini, and Bolivar before they led armies. Courts would not have to leave these fugitives unprotected, of course. They could use the moral standards behind the "war crimes" approach to inform judgments about unacceptable wantonness in conflicts not rising to the level of civil war.

The inquiry advocates went further and sought to protect the American legal system from being an instrument of foreign injustice. To this end, they were willing to shield from extradition (although not necessarily from trial) some rather despicable people, including former war criminals, dictators, and torturers.

George W. Crockett (D.-Mich.), an African American congressman with a strong Arab American constituency in Detroit, came to see the problem as primarily one of foreign injustice driven by racial, religious, and ethnic prejudice. Drawing upon the "nonrefoulement principle" of international refugee law, he proposed a partial suspension of the rule of noninquiry for fugitives who could show that they would be persecuted on their return because of their "race, religion, nationality, membership in a particular group, or political opinion."[27] Crockett's language was lifted almost verbatim from a U.N. treaty to which the United States was a party, and thus seemed almost unexceptional.[28] The persecution clause also invoked a human rights mantra, which made it more politically acceptable in some circles than a "wanton crimes" or "grave breaches" exception.

Crockett's amendment became known as the Ninoy Aquino test, and it gained sufficient support from the senator's martyrdom to doom the bill's prospects in the House.[29] Undeterred, the Reaganauts, led now by State Department legal adviser (and former judge) Abraham D. Sofaer, returned to the treaty-by-treaty approach.

* * *

In 1985, the Reagan administration proposed a supplementary extradition treaty with the United Kingdom.[30] Its purpose was to help Britain suppress IRA terrorism,[31] not just in the future, but retroactively in the cases of McMullen and Doherty. This treaty, like earlier versions of the bill, used the categorical exclusion approach to gut the political offense exception.

Two justifications were offered. Stephen Trott, head of the Criminal Division of the Justice Department, envisioned the U.S.-U.K. treaty as a prototype for swapping alleged criminals with all U.S. "friends and allies." [32] Sofaer was more subtle. He claimed that "the political offense has no place in extradition treaties between stable democracies, in which the political system is available to redress legitimate grievances and the judicial process provides fair treatment."[33]

Sofaer's argument called for a large measure of uncritical thinking, if not outright gullibility, for while Great Britain (England, Scotland, and Wales) might be considered reasonably democratic and just under normal circumstances, the so-called United Kingdom operated a police statelet in Northern Ireland.[34] Sofaer knew this but counted on most Senators to assume that the United Kingdom possessed the sort of legal system worthy of being mother to their own. Of course, whether the United Kingdom was or would remain stable and democratic was irrelevant. The crucial issue was, or should have been, Protestant Britain's capacity to do justice, especially toward Catholic Irishmen alleged to have taken up arms against it. That, ultimately, was a factual question that had little to do with openness of the political system for Englishmen living east of the Irish Sea.

Sofaer misrepresented the state of the law when he claimed that "terrorists who commit . . . wanton acts of violence" could not be extradited under existing law. To support this claim, he cited two cases in which the French, with their motives test, had refused to return aircraft hijackers to the United States.[35] But these French cases revealed nothing about the political offense exception in U.S. courts, where the "wanton crimes" exception was gaining support.[36]

Diplomatic pressure from the British government to help "get" the IRA was intense, particularly in the wake of the IRA bombing on October 12, 1984, that nearly killed Prime Minister Thatcher in Brighton.[37] The Iron Lady raised the matter with President Reagan during state visits to Washington in December 1984 and February 1985, while the British ambassador actively lobbied American newspaper editors.

But this alone proved insufficient as opposition mounted in the Senate Committee on Foreign Relations. A broad coalition of liberals and conservatives, from Senator Edward M. Kennedy (D.-Mass.) to Senator Jesse Helms (R.-N.C.), blocked the treaty for nearly a year. The votes did not shift until April 1986, when Prime Minister Thatcher allowed U.S. warplanes to attack Libya from bases in Great Britain. Then a payback was demanded and the balance of power shifted.[38] The president turned up the heat on May 31 when, in his weekly radio address, he declared that rejection of the treaty would be an affront to the British prime minister who, "at great political risk, stood shoulder-to-shoulder with us during our operations against Qadhaffi's terrorism."[39] "Suddenly," as one senate staffer observed, the issue was "bigger than ethnic politics."[40]

The administration's allies in Congress also helped to shift the balance of power by conditioning approval of a $250 million aid package to Northern Ireland on approval of the extradition treaty.[41] Thus Senators who had opposed the treaty chiefly as a gesture to their Irish American constituents were effectively whipsawed.[42] The final vote in favor of the treaty was 87 to 10, far more than the two-thirds majority needed to consent to a treaty.[43] Then the Senate, by voice vote, quickly approved the aid package.[44] Most Senators ultimately came to look upon the vote as getting tough on terrorism, for they even opposed, by a vote of 65 to 33, an amendment by Senator Alfonse D'Amato (D.-N.Y.) that would have denied the treaty retroactive application to IRA fugitives like Doherty and McMullen.[45]

The vote also indicated a shift away from the IRA and toward "law and order" among Irish Americans. Opposition to the treaty had been led by liberal Democrats John Kerry of Massachusetts and Christopher Dodd of Connecticut, supported by liberal Republican Lowell Weicker of Connecticut. Voting for ratification were three liberal to moderate Democrats from Irish American constituencies: Daniel Patrick Moynihan of New York and Bill Bradley and Frank R. Lautenberg of New Jersey.

Voting against ratification were conservative Republicans Alfonse D'Amato of New York, Orrin Hatch of Utah, and Jesse Helms of North Carolina. Helms even sponsored an amendment that would have permitted extradition in cases of criminal violence but would have barred it in cases of insurrectional violence, so as to distinguish between "criminal terrorists" and "genuine freedom-fighters."[46] The idea of preserving asylum for foreign revolutionaries burned more strongly among conservative nativists, who cared less about funding foreign aid or paying back Thatcher than internationalists like Senators Richard Lugar (R.-Ind.) and Thomas Eagleton (D.-Mo.). But the fix was in, and Helms's amendment was tabled by a vote of 87 to 9.[47]

In confidential negotiations preceding the floor debate, the administration won acceptance of its categorical exclusion of most crimes of violence from the political offense exception by accepting Crockett's Ninoy Aquino clause, which permitted courts to suspend the rule of noninquiry and deny extradition when the accused is able to "establish, by a preponderance of the evidence," that he would be persecuted on his return.[48]

In a colloquy carefully scripted in advance,[49] Senator Joseph Biden (D.-Del.) claimed that Article 3(a) was meant to "create a right of inquiry into the fairness of the foreign judicial system."[50] Senator John Kerry (D.-Mass.) added that the "Ninoy Aquino test involves not only the issue of trumped-up charges, but also the issue of due process and the fairness of the system of justice to which a fugitive would be extradited,"[51] adding that "the Committee on Foreign Relations is sending a strong signal to the court system of our Nation that the standard of justice in Northern Ireland is unacceptable to us, until changed to reflect basic safeguards for the individual."[52]

But the often erratic Senator Thomas Eagleton broke ranks. Defying the agreement, he falsely claimed to a nearly empty chamber that he was the principal author of Article 3(a) and that it was "not intended to give courts authority generally to critique the abstract fairness of the foreign judicial systems." Its purpose, the former vice-presidential candidate said, was simply to protect the accused from trumped-up charges or from political or religious persecution that he could prove were personally directed against him.[53] Senators Carl Levin (D.-Mich.)[54] and Joseph Biden[55] tried to reassert the understanding, pointing to the committee's report and declaring that the members had intended that American courts question the administration of justice in Northern Ireland. But Eagleton's interpretation, rather than that of the treaty's deal-making opponents, would subsequently be adopted by two courts.[56]

As a result of Eagleton's spin on the Aquino amendment, proof of systemic prejudice in similar cases may not be enough to protect the accused, even though there may be substantial recent evidence that the requesting state has generated dubious accusations through threats, torture, and inducements (Abu Eain, Aquino, and Artuković), has conducted show trials (Artuković and Demjanjuk *infra*), or has subjected similar persons to cruel and unusual punishments. To take advantage of the Aquino test, the accused may have to meet an impossible burden of proof—that his accusers have already made specific plans to visit the same injustices on him and have been foolish enough to put their plans on paper. This is not what the proponents of the Aquino test intended.

* * *

Another provision of the supplementary treaty allowed for retroactive application.[57] New requests could now be made for the extradition of McMullen and Doherty under a treaty specifically intended to strip them of protection as political offenders. Sponsors of the treaty made no secret of the fact that the treaty was meant to "get" these two men.[58]

The retroactivity provision forced Doherty to negotiate for deportation to the republic of Ireland, where he had dual citizenship, and ultimately exposed him to deportation to the United Kingdom. (See the next chapter.) The new treaty also was used against McMullen, who briefly succeeded in having it declared unconstitutional as a "bill of attainder."[59] But in a triumph of formalism over substance, the Court of Appeals for the Second Circuit reversed, claiming that the clause was not a true bill of attainder because it did not explicitly impose punishment; it only exposed McMullen to it.[60]

In consenting to the U.K. treaty, the Senate declared that "it will not give its advice and consent to any treaty that would narrow the political offense exception with a totalitarian or other non-democratic regime and that nothing in the Supplementary Treaty with the United Kingdom shall be considered a precedent by the executive branch or the Senate for other treaties."[61] The Departments of Justice and State, under both the Reagan and Bush administrations, then proceeded with this strategy, negotiating protocols or supplementary treaties with friendly governments they considered "democratic." West Germany[62] and Canada[63] agreed, but Australia refused,[64] and the agreement with Belgium never went into force.[65]

By these agreements, the U.S. government decided, in effect, that it could not imagine a circumstance under which it would ever be legitimate to assert a right of revolution against these favored governments. George Washington would never have been so naive.

* * *

When the debate over the supplementary treaty was over, New York University law professor Thomas M. Franck criticized both sides. As we saw in Chapter 14, he considered the categorical exclusion approach of the Reagan administration to be "idiot's law" in its "single-minded passion for arrow-like truths" and "simple principles."[66] However, he believed that the opposition view, which proposed "a complex, exculpatory, judicially determined case-by-case approach,"[67] was far too "sophisticated" to achieve legitimacy in the primitive precincts of international law.

Between "idiot's law" and "sophist's law," Franck argued, there is no certain choice except functionality. In his view, the U.S.-U.K. treaty is functional because the United States "has not repealed the legal concept of sanctuary for all political offenders, but only for those from Britain, which we believe to have a relatively open legal-political system capable of accommodating legitimate dissent and change supervised by a legitimate judiciary."[68] Like Sofaer, Franck came close to arguing that, for law enforcement purposes, Americans should think of the United Kingdom as a fifty-first state, despite the fact that its courts cannot hold their executive to constitutional standards and their decisions are not reviewable by a common high court, which might be relied upon to enforce uniform constitutional standards.

The trouble with both sides of the debate, Franck seemed to say, is that they endorse a version of the "just war" theory. The Reagan administration presumed that all Soviet-backed "wars of national liberation" were unjust, and that all rebels against friendly democracies were "terrorists." Conversely, he suggested, the opposition—and particularly this author—wanted U.S. courts to conduct sufficiently deep inquiries into the story of the accused and his uprising group to find justification for what he did.

Neither criticism is particularly apt. While it is true that most partisans in hot and cold wars think their cause is just, and would like judges to declare their larger cause to be just, that was not the position of most opponents of the treaty. They saw the political offense exception as an instrument of individual justice, not foreign policy. Like Jefferson and Washington, they did not believe it should only protect liberal revolutionaries. They thought it should protect people like Captain Barré, General Galbaud, and Citizen Genêt, whom they viewed as political fugitives, not pawns in some geopolitical game. They understood that courts exist not as instruments of foreign policy but to pass judgment on the behavior of individuals, according to the nature and quality of their acts, properly understood in context.

For an American court to ask why a Mackin or Doherty might have done what he is charged with doing is not to embrace a subjective, French-style "political motives" test in the process. The inquiry into motives or purposes can be used to ask, yet again, "What would you have done?" This was the moral inquiry that Robert Slender raised in his epitaph for Jonathan Robbins, and which New England answered when they refused to surrender the regicides. It was the inquiry that judges had to face in fugitive slave cases, and what the U.S. State Department flubbed, both when it supported delivering a Jew to the Nazis and when its lawyers betrayed the two hijackers in Berlin. It is the question Herman Melville posed to Captain Vere: Would you enforce the "law" of an unjust regime against a person who acts reasonably under the circumstances?

Judicial neutrality, then, is something very different from executive neutrality. Executive neutrality (or assistance) is based on political calculations that have little to do with what any one individual may or may not have done. Judicial neutrality is based on an obligation to render justice in each individual case, quite independently of what the judges may think about the politics, practicalities, wisdom, or desirability of the defendant's cause. For a century and a half, it has been the court's duty to ascertain whether the conduct of the accused was incidental to, and in furtherance of, the interests of one side or the other in a foreign uprising and, more recently, to evaluate whether, under the circumstances, the individual's actions were too heinous to merit protection under the political offense exception.

Far from pushing a theory of "just war," opponents of the U.S.-U.K. treaty sought to keep the focus of American courts on whether the accused should be surrendered to the regime seeking to prosecute him, which meant understanding what he did and why, and what the requesting regime would be likely to do to him upon delivery. They thought that Judge Bee should have investigated who Nash (or Robbins) was, and why the crew of the *Hermione* mutinied. They supported the Supreme Court's approach in the *Amistad* case, in which the justices sought to know who the prisoners were and why they rose up. They thought that extradition judges ought to assess whether a Nash (or Robbins) could receive justice from the British navy, or the *Amistad* captives could receive justice from the slave courts of Spanish Cuba. They took these views out of a concern for justice and the integrity of American courts, not out of partisanship for the IRA or the PLO.

In their view, to deny extradition in such cases would not constitute approval of what the accused (or uprising group) had done. It would be nothing more nor less than what William Leete of New Haven told the king's men in 1661 when he refused to help them capture the regicides: "We honor his Majesty, but we have tender consciences."[69]

CHAPTER 16

Deportation to Achieve Extradition

The [deportation] laws of this country were not enacted to facilitate the punishment of one convicted of an offense against another country's laws.

Fong Yue Ting v. United States, *1892*

It's quite clear that in the extradition proceeding, the objective was to get Doherty to the United Kingdom. And in the deportation proceeding, our objective is to get him to the United Kingdom. This is just an alternative means to accomplish that.

Jay Scott Blackmun, Assistant Director,
U.S. Immigration and Naturalization Service, 1987

Ratification of the supplementary extradition treaty, with its provision for retroactive application, put IRA member Joseph Doherty in a bind. He could wait for a new extradition attempt and challenge the treaty's constitutionality, or he could request voluntary deportation to the Republic of Ireland, where he was also a citizen. Chances were not good that a court would find the retroactive application of the treaty an unconstitutional bill of attainder, even though proponents of the treaty had proclaimed in legislative debate that the chief purpose of the treaty was to strip Joseph Doherty and Peter McMullen of rights previously recognized, in their cases, by courts.[1] The Reagan administration had packed the courts with pro-executive judges who could be "trusted," as Margaret Thatcher might say, to overlook such admissions.

Deportation was not an ideal choice for Doherty, but it was better than being extradited to Northern Ireland. The Irish government would probably sentence him to ten years (for his prison escape, under a reciprocal agreement with the United Kingdom) but did not seem disposed to extradite him to the United Kingdom, where he might be prosecuted for other offenses. So on September 3, 1986, three months after the Senate approved the supplementary treaty, Joseph Doherty formally requested voluntary deportation to the Republic of Ireland.[2]

*   *   *

Under U.S. law, aliens who have entered the country illegally have traditionally been able to choose the country of their deportation.[3] The right to choose follows from the very definition of deportation, which is "the removal of an alien out of this country, simply because his presence is deemed inconsistent with the public welfare, and without any punishment being imposed or contemplated . . . under the laws of the country . . . he is sent to."[4] Unlike the law of extradition, "the immigration laws of this country were not enacted to facilitate the punishment of one convicted of an offense against another country's laws."[5]

The Departments of State and Justice had long respected this distinction. As Charles Cheney Hyde, one of the State Department's most distinguished legal advisers, acknowledged:[6]

> The immigration laws of the United States provide for the exclusion or deportation of aliens who have been convicted or who admit the commission of certain classes of crimes in foreign countries. These laws are separate and distinct from the laws and treaties relating to extradition. They are not enacted for the benefit of foreign governments or for the purpose of bringing fugitives to justice; rather they are for the protection of the United States.

Few legal distinctions could be clearer. Deportation has for centuries been a largely executive process for getting rid of illegal aliens. Extradition, by contrast, had been developed to bring the rule of law, rather than the corruptions of politics, into the surrender of people wanted for crimes against other nations.

Even so, the Justice Department adamantly opposed Doherty's request. The Immigration and Naturalization Service (INS) invoked an obscure provision of the immigration law that authorized the attorney general to disallow "deportation to such country [if it] would be prejudicial to the interests of the United States."[7] According to the INS, this discretionary provision not only gave the attorney general a veto over the deportee's first choice of destinations, but it allowed the government to select the second choice, thereby using deportation politically, as a form of disguised extradition. The claim was both novel and unprecedented[8] and, taken literally, threatened to destroy the very difference between deportation and extradition. It was another effort to strip courts of their authority to protect political offenders from their enemies.

The obscure provision did not state clearly that the attorney general could deport a political fugitive to the regime he had fought to overthrow. Nor did it purport to overturn the established distinction between deportation and extradition. It simply said that "No alien shall be permitted to make more than one such designation."[9] Nothing in the provision or its legislative history suggested that Congress intended to allow the executive to substitute political considerations for the judicial processes of extradition.

On September 19, 1986, Immigration Judge Howard Cohen rejected the administration's claim. Without pausing to consider Congress's intent, Cohen found no reason to believe that deporting Doherty to the Republic of Ireland would adversely affect U.S. interests, and Cohen ordered him deported there.[10] The INS promptly sought review by the Board of Immigration Appeals, while Doherty sought judicial release under a writ of habeas corpus so that he could do as the immigration judge directed and leave for Ireland. But the district court, concerned that the provision had never been litigated, refused Doherty's request,[11] forcing him into the Court of Appeals, where he alleged that the INS and the attorney general were dragging out the administrative appeals process in order to keep him in jail, thereby assuring his availability for extradition once the new treaty was ratified.[12]

That, of course, was precisely what the government was doing. As the INS's assistant director for deportation in New York openly admitted: "It would be prejudicial to the interests of the U.S. to permit a member of a terrorist organization to leave the U.S. and travel to a country where he might escape punishment for his crimes."[13]

For its part, the U.S. Court of Appeals for the Second Circuit rejected Doherty's bid for freedom and deportation and allowed the Board of Immigration Appeals review to go forward.[14] Writing for a unanimous panel, Judge Ralph Winter refused to lift the veil of executive legitimacy. Nor did he doubt Attorney General Meese's motives or question his bid to circumvent the judicial process of extradition with executive deportation.

The only issue, Winter wrote, was "whether there is any reasonable foundation at all for the Attorney General's actions" in the deportation case.[15] Where the liberty of a human being is a stake, courts are supposed to apply "strict scrutiny," not mere reasonableness, but Joseph Doherty was, like mutinous seamen and fugitive slaves, no longer considered a real person. He was a "terrorist," because the government said he was. Accordingly, Winter gave the Justice Department benefit of every doubt, ignoring its efforts to intimidate extradition magistrates and its use of dilatory tactics to keep Doherty locked up until the political offense exception to extradition could be abolished. Far from applying "strict scrutiny," Winter treated these deprivations of liberty as the moral equivalent of decisions to store grain.

The court identified only two significant questions: whether there was cause to believe that Doherty was an IRA terrorist, and if so, whether the attorney general might reasonably conclude that deportation to the Republic of Ireland would be prejudicial to U.S. interests.[16] The court did not acknowledge that the highly prejudicial label "terrorist" was as vague and subject to political abuse as the label "subversive" had been in the McCarthy era. Winter did not even notice that, by the government's own definition, Doherty was not a terrorist.[17] Nor did he consider that the Justice Department, by litigating the extradition case against Doherty on behalf of the United Kingdom, had a conflict of interest.

Instead, the judge reached out to decide a question that was not before the court. "There are no statutory guidelines," he declared, "regarding what quality or quantity of prejudice to United States interests is necessary, or even what constitutes 'interests.'" Accordingly, these matters were "essentially political," not legal.[18]

Judge Winter's performance was remarkable. By focusing narrowly on deportation (and the allegedly plenary power of Congress and the executive to deal with aliens), Winter endorsed a "Catch 22"[19]: A revolutionary could not be extradited to the regime he fought to overthrow unless an independent judiciary found that he had committed a heinous act, but he could be deported to that same regime if the politically pressured executive chose to label him a "terrorist" and decide that refusing to deliver him would prejudice diplomatic relations with the requesting regime.

No recognition was given to the fact that Joseph Doherty had far greater cause to revolt against the United Kingdom in 1980 than the Minutemen of Lexington and Concord had against Great Britain in 1775. The lands of the American revolutionaries had not been expropriated by hostile settlers. The Americans had not for centuries been discriminated against in voting, housing, and employment by a hostile religious majority backed by the British government. Nor had they been interned without trial on prison ships or tortured in interrogations. The American revolt was largely anticipatory; the colonists realized that Britain was trying to establish control over the colonies after more than a century of benign neglect. Not wishing to lose the self-government they enjoyed, they rose up against what was then arguably the world's most "democratic" government.

Judges with any historical sense should have seen this parallel and understood that Irish revolutionaries were entitled, no less than their American forebears, to be judged according to the nature and quality of their acts, in the context in which those acts were committed, and not as they were demonized by British and American politicians. This right to be judged fairly should exist whenever the U.S. government is judging a political fugitive for purposes of extradition, deportation, or political asylum.

Doherty's counsel raised this point clearly on appeal, but the court rejected it, ruling that the executive's power under the deportation law can be exercised regardless of the laws and principles governing extradition.[20] A clearer rejection of legislative intent in favor of "mechanical jurisprudence" would be difficult to imagine.

The contrast between Judge Winter's tunnel vision and Judge Friendly's political realism is so stark that some have argued it can only be explained in terms of contrasting ambitions. Friendly was known as "a judge's judge," whereas Winter was repeatedly mentioned as a potential Reagan nominee to the Supreme Court. However, both decisions regarding Doherty were unanimous, suggesting that other explanations are needed. The most charitable explanation is that the judges had their blinders on.

Their only frame of reference in this case was the law of deportation, which had been developed by the executive branch in order to rid the United States of illegal immigrants, foreign criminals, anarchists, communists, and terrorists. The Immigration Service, which administers the law of deportation, has always been driven more by considerations of domestic and foreign politics than are attorneys and judges involved in extradition who are required by law to at least address issues of liberty, equality, and justice. Nor had Congress attempted to reconcile the two bodies of law to form a comprehensive and impartial policy toward political fugitives.

It is almost certainly no coincidence that the Court of Appeals chose to release its decision upholding Meese's action on December 23, 1986, the very day that the new extradition treaty went into effect. The Reagan administration now had two ways by which it could deliver Doherty to his enemies: extradition and deportation. But the Board of Immigration Appeals would not cooperate. On March 11, 1987, it rejected the Justice Department's claim that deporting Doherty to Ireland would be prejudicial to the nation's interest.[21] The board found that the Immigration Service had failed, despite ample opportunity, to come up with any evidence that deportation to Ireland would adversely harm foreign relations.[22] The board also agreed with Doherty that the INS and Justice Department were employing a conscious strategy of delay.[23]

Anticipating this decision, but playing for time until the new extradition treaty went into effect, the INS claimed that it had "new evidence" justifying a motion to return the case to the trial judge. However, when forced to show its hand, all it had to offer was a short, conclusory statement by Associate Attorney General Trott dated February 19, which had been cribbed from old testimony given to a Senate committee in 1985. Attached to the statement was a still older affidavit by a State Department official that had been rejected by Judge Sprizzo in 1984.

On May 22, 1987, an irritated Board of Immigration Appeals dismissed the Justice Department's case and ordered Doherty deported to Ireland, as he had requested.[24] The board observed that "the glacial pace at which any tangible proof of this [national] interest was produced seems to belie any sense of urgency or responsibility on the part of the government to proceed promptly in this case."[25] The majority was particularly annoyed that the Justice Department could not explain why this "new evidence" had not been submitted earlier, especially since government counsel had assured the immigration judge that the matter was "enjoying the attention of certain high officials ... including the Attorney General."[26]

The Board of Immigration Appeals' decision was a public-relations debacle for Attorney General Meese, but the law allowed him to review and reverse the board's rejection of his claims.[27] On May 29, 1987, the INS quietly took advantage of this rarely used power,[28] appealing to Meese without bothering to inform Doherty's counsel.

For months nothing happened, except that Doherty became the longest-held prisoner in the history of the Metropolitan Correctional Center in Manhattan, locked in his cell for over twenty hours a day. Although the new extradition treaty, which went into effect on December 23, 1986, had been sold to Congress as the only way to "get" Joe Doherty, the Justice Department chose not to use it. Instead, it moved to circumvent extradition entirely. On June 9, 1988, as one of his last acts in office, Attorney General Meese reversed the board's decision, ruling that Doherty was deportable only to the United Kingdom.[29] In so doing, Meese made the extraordinary and unprecedented claim that he was not bound by the INS's failures to produce evidence, the board's rules regarding the timely submission of evidence, or the legal principle that facts are for the board, as initial factfinder, to determine. Indeed, he claimed the authority to "receive additional evidence and to make de novo factual determinations,"[30] without being bound by the ordinary rules of administrative due process.

The only "evidence" that Meese purported to consider was Trott's affidavit and a letter (not part of the hearing record) from Michael H. Armacost, the under secretary of state for political affairs, reporting that the United Kingdom had been greatly disappointed by Judge Sprizzo's opinion and claiming that failure to deliver Doherty would significantly harm relations with the British government.[31] By treating these assertions as conclusive (and beyond challenge by the defense), Meese reiterated his contempt for Judge Sprizzo's decision and for his own Board of Immigration Appeals.

Beyond that, Meese claimed the power to use the law of deportation to subvert the law of extradition and to evade the import of Sprizzo's holding that Doherty was a "political offender," not a wanton terrorist. More shocking still, Meese's decision was upheld on appeal.[32] Without reflecting on what its decision would mean for the distinction between extradition and deportation, the principle of nonrefoulement, or due process within the system for immigration appeals, the Court of Appeals declared that Attorney General Meese's action was "within the scope ... of his broad discretion to determine what constitutes prejudice to national interests."[33] Again, the power of pejorative labels ruled supreme over the judicial imagination, as it had during the World War II internment of Japanese and Japanese Americans[34] and in the McCarthy era.[35] From hot war to cold war to police war, the result was the same—judicial unwillingness to question the basis of executive-branch claims.

* * *

While the INS's appeal to Meese was pending, Irish law changed, making Doherty vulnerable to extradition from the republic to Northern Ireland.[36] On December 3, 1987, his counsel asked the Board of Immigration Appeals to send the case back to the immigration judge so that Doherty's deportation could be stayed and his earlier request for political asylum heard. Failing that, she asked that he be allowed to designate a new country of deportation where, as a political fugitive, he might live in freedom.[37]

Eleven months later, the board decided that his petition for asylum should be considered, not because Irish extradition law had changed, but because Doherty had established a prima facie case that he would be persecuted if returned to Northern Ireland.[38] The board thus acknowledged a basic principle of refugee law called "non-refoulement," which forbids states to return fugitives to countries where they are likely to be persecuted or where their lives or freedom would be endangered.[39]

The board also ruled that Doherty's failure to pursue political asylum was excusable because, at the time he opted for deportation, he had a reasonable expectation of being deported to the country of his choice.[40] The board dismissed as premature the Immigration Service's claim that Doherty had engaged in conduct that would render him unworthy of asylum.[41] However, the board also refused to allow Doherty to redesignate the country to which he wished to be deported. So he was now stuck with requesting political asylum from the very Justice Department that had so long harried him on behalf of the British government.

Not surprisingly, Meese's successor, Richard Thornburgh, accepted the Board of Immigration Appeals' decision that Doherty could not pick another country, but he refused to allow Doherty's petition for political asylum to go forward, despite the principle of nonrefoulement. The former governor of Pennsylvania was willing to assume, for the purposes of argument, that British security forces had pursued a shoot-to-kill policy against suspected IRA members, but he would not concede that such lawlessness might extend to the treatment of IRA prisoners, as Amnesty International had alleged.[42] Thornburgh acknowledged that the British security forces had taunted Doherty's sister with talk about "what would be done to him on his return," but the attorney general chose to treat these threats as "ambiguous" and therefore not proof of the sort of persecution envisioned by the nonrefoulement principle.[43] Accordingly, he did not intend to grant Doherty political asylum.[44] Moreover, the attorney general added, it was "inconceivable," given the politics of the situation, for Doherty to expect that the United States would not deliver him to the British government.[45]

The nation's highest legal officer thus decided that the humanitarian principles of asylum and nonrefoulement could, at his discretion, be subordinated to political conceptions of the "national interest." Similarly, the same principles that underlay the political offense exception (and had caused its administration to be entrusted to an independent judiciary) could properly be removed from a treaty when necessary to repay a foreign power for letting the United States bomb another country from its bases.[46]

Here, however, the Court of Appeals agreed that the attorney general had abused his discretion in ordering Doherty deported to the United Kingdom.[47] Thornburgh was wrong, the appeals court ruled, to prejudge the merits of Doherty's asylum claim and to assume that foreign policy considerations alone justified its rejection.[48] Congress had amended the immigration laws in 1980 precisely to make fugitives from all countries eligible for asylum if they could demonstrate a well-founded fear of persecution.[49] The same law that denied the attorney general power to refuse asylum for reasons of political or administrative convenience[50] imposed upon Thornburgh a positive obligation to withhold deportation if the alien's life or liberty would be threatened by persecution, even though the withholding might impair foreign relations.[51] The Court of Appeals therefore remanded the case to the immigration judge with orders to reconsider the asylum claim.

* * *

Before the immigration hearing could take place, however, the Supreme Court reversed the decision of the appeals court, holding that the attorney general had unlimited discretion to decide whether to reopen a deportation or asylum proceeding.[52] Chief Justice William H. Rehnquist found "no statutory provision for reopening a deportation proceeding"; rather, "authority for such motions derives solely from regulations promulgated by the Attorney General."[53]

The chief justice ruled that the attorney general did not have to give himself express authority to reopen a proceeding; like any court, his power to reopen one was inherent. In reaching this conclusion, the Court ignored the fact that the attorney general had issued regulations formally authorizing the Board of Immigration Appeals to decide such cases on his behalf, and that, after applying standards and procedures approved by him, his board had ruled in Doherty's favor. In Rehnquist's opinion, the attorney general's discretion over aliens is so broad that he may violate his own commitment to administer justly the laws of deportation and asylum.

The five-member majority went on to claim that "motions for reopening of immigration proceedings are disfavored for the same reasons as are petitions for rehearing and motions for a new trial on the basis of newly discovered evidence. This is especially true," Rehnquist continued, "in a deportation proceeding where, as a general matter, every delay works to the advantage of the deportable alien who wishes merely to remain in the United States."[54] No basis was cited for this claim. Unmentioned was the long record of dilatory practices by which the U.S. government had kept Doherty behind bars until it could circumvent Judge Sprizzo's opinion.[55]

The Court of Appeals had based its decision squarely on Congress's intent in *requiring*—and not just allowing—the attorney general to withhold deportation where the individual has a well-founded fear of persecution.[56] But the Supreme Court chose to ignore this law, its legislative history, and the Court's own prior interpretations of that law.[57] It also disregarded the Court of Appeals' reasoning, the U.N. treaty and protocol banning the return of political refugees,[58] and the U.N. high commissioner's manual for interpreting that obligation.[59] Instead, it chose to subsume the attorney general's mandatory duty to withhold deportation on humanitarian grounds under his separate, and arguably discretionary, power to grant or deny asylum on political grounds.[60] That was not what Congress intended, but the majority was not interested in "framers' intent." The justices claimed that "abuse of discretion" is the appropriate standard of judicial review,[61] but then ruled, inconsistently, that the attorney general's discretion in withholding deportation is not limited.[62] Nor, they held, was the nation's chief law enforcement officer bound to follow the regulations of his Board of Immigration Appeals until such time as he chose formally (and prospectively) to change them. Therefore, no abuse of discretion could have taken place.

In February 1992, a month after the Supreme Court's decision (and after the New Hampshire presidential primary was over), Joseph Doherty was taken at dawn from the federal prison at Lewisburg, Pennsylvania, flown to a U.S. airbase in England, and from which the British government returned him to Belfast. (Ironically, he was no longer an IRA member in good standing, having criticized the organization for bombing a military hospital in Northern Ireland the previous year.) The National Committee to Free Joe Doherty held its last march to the Metropolitan Correctional Center in Manhattan, where the city has renamed a street corner for him. Charles J. Hynes, the Brooklyn district attorney, declared that "it is a very, very low day in the history of American justice."[63] Five months later, Patrick Mayhew, minister of state for Northern Ireland, announced that Doherty would not receive credit for the nearly nine years he spent in American prisons and would have to serve another ten years before his life sentence would be reviewed.[64]

* * *

The Supreme Court's decision doomed Joseph Doherty to a life behind bars for committing a quintessentially political offense, but its ruling had implications far beyond him. The justices effectively granted to the attorney general the unprecedented power to extradite by executive deportation any foreign revolutionaries who enter the United States illegally in order to escape regimes (fellow revolutionaires or rival groups) seeking to kill them. The power of kings and dictators to surrender foreign revolutionaries for reasons of state, which Western democracies sought to abolish by adding the political offense exception to their extradition treaties, now resides with the politicians who command the U.S. Department of Justice.

In the end, Doherty's case had little to do with law and much to do with politics. Had the British army not sided with the Protestants against the Catholics in Northern Ireland, Doherty might never have joined the IRA. Had the propaganda mills of the British and U.S. governments not labeled him a terrorist, the law of extradition might not have been circumvented, first by abolishing the political offense exception in several treaties, and next by permitting executive deportation as an alternative to judicial extradition in all cases involving illegal aliens wanted for political crimes.

To recognize this shoddy record is to carry no brief for the IRA, which on countless occasions has acted dishonorably. Had other Irish revolutionaries not committed unspeakable atrocities, like the bombing of the elderly Lord Mountbatten and his family on their yacht, and a campaign of terror against British civilians, including the bombing of a band concert, the Queen's horse guards, and Harrod's Department Store in London, Doherty might have been judged fairly in the United States—on the nature and quality of his acts. But that was not to be. In the war for American (as well as for Irish and British) public opinion, the IRA defeated itself. Overcoming the sympathy their aspirations had evoked during the civil rights movement, "Bloody Sunday," the internments, and the hunger strikes, the "hard men" of the IRA managed to so discredit their cause that the American legal system, normally disposed to protect political fugitives, chose to treat Joseph Doherty not as a revolutionary soldier, but as a terrorist by association. The IRA was helped in this venture by the PLO's atrocities and the propaganda efforts of the Thatcher and Reagan administrations, but much of the discredit they brought upon themselves and, therefore, Doherty. By acting viciously rather than politically, they not only undermined the political offense exception but also exposed all political fugitives seeking refuge in the United States to politically driven extradition by deportation.

The IRA changed American law by altering the stereotypic images that dominate most people's thinking, most of the time. They made it difficult, if not impossible, for government lawyers and judges to recognize that Doherty was not a terrorist. Their atrocities made it difficult for U.S. officials to see that Northern Ireland was a police statelet, that the British government was not "democratic" toward the people of Northern Ireland, and that the British legal system, lacking a constitution, failed to provide many of the legal safeguards that Americans have come to believe are part of a common legal heritage.

Irish American groups with strong Irish republican sympathies demonstrated remarkable unity and considerable organizational skill in fighting for Joe Doherty's freedom, but they were defeated in the propaganda wars by a larger fear of terrorism, which even some prominent Irish American politicians (like Senators Kennedy and Moynihan) dared not challenge too aggressively. The intensity with which Irish (and other) Americans identified with the politics of their nations of origin was also diminishing, as the political influence of recent immigrants declined and the old ethnic neighborhoods, with their revolutionary support groups, broke up. At the same time, ethnic Americans came to rely on television as their chief source of news, and to view shootings and bombings by foreign revolutionary groups almost entirely apart from the oppression that provoked them. Thus, the political context in which American judges came to view extradition cases changed, and the weight of empathy—the most critical ingredient in any political offender case—shifted from the revolutionaries to their victims, and then to the regime the offender challenged.

* * *

It would be a mistake to assume from Doherty's deportation that the Departments of State and Justice are genuinely committed to "getting" all terrorists. On the contrary, the U.S. government has refused to surrender a number of "hard men" for "humanitarian" reasons. One was Orlando Bosch, whose anti-Castro group, Accion Cubana, sought to punish countries doing business with Communist Cuba by bombing eight tourist or diplomatic offices in New York and Los Angeles, damaging a British ship off Key West, and blowing up a Japanese freighter in Tampa, Florida.

In 1968, Bosch was convicted of firing a bazooka at a Polish freighter in Miami harbor and sentenced to ten years in federal prison. Four years later, he was paroled and in 1974 fled the country rather than answer a subpoena in a murder case. The governments of Venezuela and Costa Rica both offered to return the parole jumper to the United States, but the Justice Department expressed no interest in recovering him.

In 1976, Venezuelan authorities arrested Bosch and three colleagues for blowing up a Cubana airliner en route from Venezuela to Cuba. Seventy-three civilians plunged to a fiery death, including Cuba's Olympic fencing team. Bosch and two others were convicted, had their convictions overturned on appeal, but were nonetheless imprisoned until 1987. In 1988, Bosch returned to the United States, where he was sent back to prison for his attack on the Polish freighter, and from which Cuba requested his deportation to face charges arising out of his many terroristic activities. The Justice Department agreed that Bosch planned the bombing of the jetliner and denied him political asylum. But it also refused to deport him to Cuba, claiming that Cuba could not be trusted to give him a fair trial.[65]

How Yugoslavia could be trusted (see the next chapter) and Cuba not, the Justice Department did not say, for in truth, its decision to shield Bosch was politically driven. Anti-Castro Cubans, whose votes the Republican Party was actively courting, conducted rallies, hunger strikes, and shop closings, ultimately winning the support of President Bush's son Jeb. Moreover, Bosch was widely believed to have worked with the CIA.[66]

More recently, the State Department refused to accept Haiti's request for the extradition of Emmanuel Constant, wanted for his role as a founder of Fraph, a paramilitary group that tortured, murdered, raped, and mutilated thousands of Haitian supporters of former president Jean-Bertrand Aristide. Extradition was denied by the State Department, the Haitian government was told, because its petition was insufficiently specific. However, the U.S. government refused to share with the Haitians thousands of pages of documents seized when U.S. troops raided Fraph headquarters in Port-au-Prince in 1994.[67] During that raid of Constant's headquarters, the troops found photographs of mutilated bodies taped to the walls and bits of human flesh and bone in the cells. A score of Fraph members and supporters were arrested, but no effort was made to seize Constant so that he might be tried in a Haitian court set up under U.S. supervision. Instead, he was allowed to enter the United States on a tourist visa. When that expired in 1995, he was temporarily arrested (in what was later said to be a "bureaucratic lapse"). Unlike Joseph Doherty, Constant was released pending his application for asylum.[68] Deportation for trial, which had been arranged in January 1996, was also withheld, according to the State Department, because it might "place an undue burden on Haiti's judicial and penal system."[69]

According to attorneys for the Haitian government, the former Fraph leader and paid CIA informant was shielded because the U.S. government feared what he might disclose at trial about CIA support for efforts to block the Clinton administration's goal of restoring President Aristide to power.[70] Further, the Haitian government alleged that denying deportation without prosecuting Constant in the United States was a violation of U.S. obligations under the international convention against torture.[71]

Clearly, the U.S. government does acknowledge both fair trial and humanitarian grounds for withholding deportation and barring extradition. Unfortunately, it only grants these protections to anti-communist mass murderers who have worked for the CIA.

CHAPTER 17

Retributive Justice and the Second Artuković Case

I hope that I will never live to see the day when a person will be held to answer for a crime ... upon such evidence as was presented in this case.

Commissioner Theodore Hocke, in
United States ex. rel. Karadzole v. Artukovic, *1959*

Throughout the twentieth century, the relative political influence of organized ethnic groups was a major factor in the ability of most defendants to assert the political offense exception. The willingness of Irish Americans to stage mass demonstrations may well have saved James Lynchehaun from extradition for stomping his Anglo-Irish landlady. It certainly brought Vice President Fairbanks to his bedside.[1] Conversely, the relative political weakness of Jewish Americans nearly cost Joao Normano his life at the hands of the Nazis.[2]

In the 1970s and 1980s, these positions changed. The suburban migration of second- and third-generation Irish Americans had weakened organized Irish influence within the Democratic Party, and Irish American supporters of the IRA found themselves unable to protect Liam Quinn and Joseph Doherty from surrender to their British enemies.[3] At the same time, Jewish American groups were becoming more adept at using the political process not only to advance the interests of Israel, but to force the extradition or deportation of persons implicated in the Holocaust. The latter effort brought Jews into open political conflict with predominately East European Catholic and Eastern Orthodox ethnic groups that had, in the anti-communist 1940s and 1950s, persuaded the federal government not to inquire too deeply into the pro-Nazi pasts of some of their fellow émigrés.

This ethnic group conflict arose repeatedly as Congress and successive administrations confronted liberal and Jewish demands that the United States ratify the United Nation's 1948 convention against genocide. That multilateral treaty, first opened for signature in 1948, flatly prohibited signatory states from invoking the political offense exception in order to shield alleged war criminals from extradition.[4] Liberal Democrats, responding to their Jewish constituency, favored ratification. Conservative Republicans, eager to use their opposition to the U.N. and "world government" to draw East European Christians away from the Democrats, opposed the treaty and associated legislation that would have made war crimes and crimes against humanity part of federal criminal law.[5]

So long as the treaty and implementing legislation were not part of American law, extradition on charges of genocide could not be allowed without violating the rule of double criminality. The genocidal offenses would have to be recharacterized as common murder.[6] This requirement was important. It had saved Andrija Artuković from extradition in the 1950s, because evidence that he was responsible for specific murders, rather than for signing laws that would authorize others to commit genocidal crimes, was lacking.

With the beginning of détente in the early 1970s, the political situation changed. As hope for international cooperation rose and the Cold War waned, distrust of secret-police evidence declined. Fear that the Holocaust would be forgotten drove Jewish American organizations and Holocaust remembrance groups to accuse the executive branch of sheltering former Nazis after the war.

There was some truth to the charges; the U.S. Army Counter-Intelligence Corps had employed former Nazis as intelligence resources against the communists during the early years of the Cold War.[7] The most infamous of these was Klaus Barbie, "the Butcher of Lyon," whose surrender to France the Army denied, before helping him find refuge in Bolivia.[8] Postwar immigration laws permitted numerous former Nazis to enter the United States as displaced persons, and efforts to deport those who had entered fraudulently were not vigorously pursued. No basis would be found for charges that there had been a "conspiracy" by government lawyers to prevent deportation of former Nazis,[9] but lack of evidence did not prevent Jewish members of Congress, including Reps. Joshua Eilberg (D.-Pa.) and Elizabeth Holtzman (D.-N.Y.), from publicizing those accusations. The hearings these liberals organized before the Immigration, Citizenship, and International Law Subcommittee were tainted by the berating of government witnesses and the demand for detailed information about cases that had not yet been brought to trial. Members of the subcommittee also traveled abroad, meeting with foreign prosecutors and soliciting promises of cooperation.[10]

The refusal of the intelligence agencies to disclose which former Nazis they had used and helped only intensified the subcommittee's demands, which eventually settled on the Immigration Service, its politically weakest target. In 1977 the service conceded that it had not done enough to rid the country of former Nazis (most of them now in their seventies and eighties), and it agreed to create a Special Litigation Unit (SLU) with a nationwide mandate. In 1978 the subcommittee forced the transfer of the SLU to the Department of Justice, where it was renamed the Office of Special Investigations (OSI).[11]

* * *

With powerful congressional sponsorship, OSI soon employed about fifty people, including lawyers, historians, paralegals, secretaries, and clerks, and it received an annual budget during the early 1980s of about $3 million.[12] Like the State Department's office of counter-terrorism, the OSI quickly concluded that the traditional political offense exception, administered by the courts, was an obstacle to the achievement of its mission. One focus of OSI lawyers was the 1959 decision that had granted Andrija Artuković benefit of the political offense exception.[13] At first they tried to reopen Artuković's deportation to Yugoslavia; then they sought to have him extradited.

Artuković had been found deportable, but his deportation to Yugoslavia had been stayed in 1960 because a law at that time barred the deportation of a person to a country where he was likely to be persecuted.[14] In 1979 the Justice Department asked the Board of Immigration Appeals to lift this stay on the ground that the law had been changed. The new law, added to the Holtzman Amendment of 1978, provided that persons could be deported to a country where they might be persecuted if they themselves had engaged in persecution.[15]

This provision was known to Washington insiders as the "Artukovic clause," and it had been added to the law (with State Department and Justice Department support) precisely to facilitate deportation of the former Croatian official.[16] Indeed, the members of the subcommittee had gone to Yugoslavia before passage of the provision to encourage that government to try yet again to obtain Artuković's return.[17]

In passing the Holtzman Amendment, Congress intended to retain the traditional standard that a person cannot be deported unless the evidence against him is "clear, convincing, and unequivocable [sic]."[18] However, the Justice Department's petition to the Board of Immigration Appeals in the new case against Artuković did not ask for a hearing at which the sufficiency of the old evidence could be tested against this evidentiary standard. It simply asked that the old stay be lifted, as if the old evidence was sufficient or that the "clear and convincing" evidentiary standard was irrelevant. The Board of Immigration Appeals accepted the claim. Ignoring the fact that the evidence on which the old deportation order was based had been found insufficient to meet even the lesser requirements for extradition, the board lifted the stay and reinstated its original order.[19]

Success, however, was not immediate. In December 1982 the Court of Appeals for the Ninth Circuit reversed the board's decision and granted Artuković a new evidentiary hearing. The board's previous findings, it said, were the product of a "hearing convened thirty years ago for a different purpose raising different issues under a different statute" and could not be used "as a substitute for the evidence required by the 1978 [Holtzman] law." OSI would have to prove its case for deportation by "clear, convincing, and unequivocal evidence."[20]

Faced with this seemingly impossible task, the Justice Department chose to seek extradition instead. In so doing, it ignored the obvious fact that an old anti-communist like Artuković could hardly be expected to get a fair trial from his former enemies. Yugoslavia was still a communist dictatorship, and the first premise of its legal system—like all communist systems—was that the administration of justice must serve the "Revolution," that is, the Party's ends.

The fundamental injustice of communist legal systems was well understood by Americans in the mid-1950s, when Artuković's extradition was first requested. Memories of postwar show trials still rankled.[21] But after Yugoslavia broke with the "international Communist conspiracy" in 1956, such memories began to fade. As the Cold War wound down, anti-communism within the United States also diminished, so much so that when Jewish Americans demanded Artuković's expulsion in the mid-1970s, a new generation of Justice Department lawyers could pretend not to notice that Tito's Yugoslavia was still a communist dictatorship with a politically managed legal system.

According to Neal M. Sher, OSI's director, Yugoslavian diplomats proposed the new extradition effort,[22] but in July 1983, OSI sent a delegation of lawyers to Belgrade that included Director Sher, Mark M. Richard, deputy assistant attorney general for the Criminal Division, and Murray Stein, associate director of the Office of International Affairs. Sher would later testify that this delegation only sought to gather evidence for the deportation hearing, and not to press for extradition.[23] However, a contemporaneous State Department cable reported that "the principal purpose of the visit [was] to raise the possibility of a Yugoslav extradition request to the U.S. for Andrija Artukovic."[24] In addition, Gojko Prodanić, a former official of the Yugoslav Ministry of Justice, reported that an assistant attorney general from the United States (presumably Mark Richard) had visited him in July 1983 and had emphasized "that the U.S. Justice Department wishes to actualize anew the extradition proceeding of Andrija Artukovic. Representatives of the American ministry," Prodanić recalled, "proposed that the Yugoslav side submit a new request for the extradition of Artukovic."[25]

Sher would later call assertions that OSI had initiated the extradition case "outrageous,"[26] but the evidence from both sides of the Atlantic proves otherwise. The Yugoslav government, having been burned before, needed persuasion. It also had to decide whether to use Artuković's case as a means of discrediting Croatian nationalists determined to rehabilitate the Ustashe. OSI, on the other hand, had every reason to push forward. Ousting former Nazis was its only mission, and expelling Artuković was its "Number 1 priority."[27]

In pushing forward, the OSI took a narrow view of the meaning of justice. The fact that the Yugoslavian Communists had massacred thousands of Ustashe soldiers delivered to them by the British after the war did not cause the U.S. attorneys to doubt whether Artuković could receive justice upon his return.[28] They had already satisfied themselves that he was guilty; all else was mere formality. Nor were they bothered by memories of "show trials" or the ideology that had repeatedly led communist regimes throughout Central and Eastern Europe to subordinate considerations of justice to the mission of their party. Indeed, the OSI lawyers were not even deterred by the fact that most of the affidavits which the Yugoslavians would have to resubmit had already been rejected by a U.S. commissioner as unreliable.[29] The delegation simply urged the Yugoslavians to come up with "new" eyewitness testimony to add to the old, inadequate allegations.

This lack of concern that they might be inspiring fraud upon the court should not surprise any student of institutional behavior. The job of the OSI was not to do justice, but to avenge atrocities and thereby educate the public. The theory of justice implicit in this mission was eye-for-an-eye justice, not the due process morality of the U.S. Constitution. Like the Communists, the Justice Department attorneys did not believe that law has to be impartial and protect even the most despised persons from persecution. As partisans of a particular cause against a specific enemy, they did not worry about the integrity of the law itself. If they had to ally themselves with one set of murderers in order to punish another, they could do so; the rightness of their ends could justify less than perfect means.

OSI's acceptance of dubious evidence from Communist sources was criticized by several federal judges in the 1980s. For example, Judge Norman Roettlinger, sitting in South Florida, condemned one joint OSI-KGB venture for using "despotic tricks, paid informers, hearsay as evidence, lack of documentation, blatantly perjured testimony, coaching of witnesses, trick photos and totalitarian-type police methods totally unacceptable by American standards."[30] In another case, OSI lawyers did not inform defense counsel that some of the Soviet witnesses had been coached before giving depositions in OSI investigations.[31] Reversing an order for the deportation of Edgar Laipenieks, the Court of Appeals for the Ninth Circuit ruled that OSI had relied on depositions that the immigration judge had found were "tainted" by the "prejudicial and highly suggestive language used by [a] Soviet official."[32] In shielding Juozas Kungys, whom the OSI sought to deport for participating in Nazi killings of Lithuanians, another U.S. district court criticized "an unusual cooperative effort of the Office of Special Investigations and Soviet authorities."[33]

Government attorneys also knew that the "evidence" presented against Artuković by Yugoslavia, or uncovered by OSI researchers, would be insufficient to support a conviction under American evidentiary standards. David Nimmer, the assistant U.S. attorney who handled the case for OSI in Los Angeles, admitted in 1985 that "we would not take this case into a [U.S.] criminal court."[34] Nimmer's superiors in the Justice Department thought no differently. Under Nixon's Attorney General William French Smith, as under Carter's Griffin Bell and Reagan's Edwin Meese, the "Department of Justice" was not an agency dedicated to doing justice but a law firm that represented clients. In the case of the OSI, the client was a powerful lobby of Jewish Americans who had very good reasons to demand that the government find a way to punish or expel former Nazis and Nazi collaborators. Resisting OSI's assignment in the interests of a larger, more constitutional concept of justice would have been difficult for even the most sensitive attorney general. After all, the U.S. government had failed to take a number of measures that could have mitigated the effects of the Holocaust. The Roosevelt administration knew of the persecutions of 1938 but did not move to rescue the German Jews while time remained.[35] During the war, administration officials refused to divert bombers to destroy gas chambers.[36] After the war, U.S. Army intelligence officers helped smuggle former Nazis into Latin America or the United States in return for helping to spy on communists.[37]

At first the Yugoslavians balked at renewing the extradition request. In September and October 1983, an OSI historian went to Zagreb to help research the case against Artuković, and in December the Yugoslavians finally agreed. In March 1984, an OSI attorney accompanied an OSI historian to help select the legal documents that would be offered in court.[38] On April 5, a Yugoslavian attorney appointed to defend Artuković against the new charges asked OSI to notify Artuković that he was the subject of new legal proceedings. They promised to do so but never did.[39] In August 1984, the new extradition request was formally transmitted to the United States.

* * *

Shortly after dawn on November 14, 1984, twenty armed men from the U.S. Marshal's Service surrounded Artuković's home near Seal Beach, California. Three police units stood by on shore while a Coast Guard vessel blocked escape by sea. Marshals with guns drawn seized the elderly invalid as he was being spoon-fed breakfast by his nurse. They lifted him onto a stretcher and took him by ambulance to a waiting helicopter. The nurse was not allowed to accompany his patient or told where he was being taken; nor were any relatives notified. Not surprisingly, the old man was terrified and, while airborne in the throbbing helicopter, suffered a heart attack. The marshals then delivered him to the University of Southern California Medical Center, where his condition was diagnosed as critical.[40]

That same morning, the Office of Special Investigations held a press conference at the federal courthouse in Los Angeles to announce their arrest of the "most dangerous high-ranking Nazi ever to enter America."[41] The OSI briefers did not mention that the "dangerous Nazi" they had just captured so dramatically was eighty-six years old, legally blind, had experienced a series of strokes, and suffered from chronic brain syndrome, Parkinson's disease, and Alzheimer's.

In their effort to garner publicity, the OSI lawyers nearly killed the man. Even so, when Artuković was arraigned that evening in the prison ward of the hospital, OSI attorneys successfully argued that the prisoner was too dangerous, and too likely to flee (though confined to a wheelchair), to be granted bail. The magistrate agreed, even though the prisoner had not absconded when he was free on bail in the 1950s.[42]

The extradition proceedings were held before U.S. Magistrate Volney V. Brown Jr. in February 1985. One of the first issues was whether the prisoner was sufficiently competent to stand trial. The Justice Department argued that Artuković's mental state was irrelevant to the extradition proceeding and could only be raised at trial in Yugoslavia, but the magistrate ruled[43] that to allow an extradition proceeding to go forward against an incompetent person would violate the Sixth Amendment's assurance of effective assistance of counsel.[44]

Expert witnesses were then called. The government's expert, a cardiologist, claimed that Artuković was mentally competent; the defense's expert, a psychiatrist, said he was not. To break this deadlock, the magistrate appointed his own expert, a forensic psychiatrist, who concluded that Artuković was not competent but could be made so by the administration of anti-depressant drugs. The doctors agreed that Artuković had moments, even hours, when he was lucid, so Brown decided to schedule a series of half-day hearings and to hold them on those days that the government's cardiologist, who was also treating Artuković for his heart problem, believed that his patient was competent.[45] Bail continued to be denied, possibly on the belief that if Artuković were released, no family doctor would ever find him sufficiently competent to attend legal hearings.

The new case against the former Croatian minister of interior affairs was based on two affidavits.[46] In the first (originally prepared in 1952), Franjo Truhar claimed to have heard Artuković order the killing of Jesa Vidić in order to give his land to a supporter of the Communist Party. The extradition request, which OSI helped to prepare, declared that Truhar had made only one prior statement. In fact, he had made four, and they contradicted the one that OSI chose to submit to the court. OSI possessed copies of these contradictory statements but did not inform the court or the defense of their existence.[47] It also let the Yugoslavian government know, rather emphatically, that it was not necessary for any witnesses to appear before the extradition court.[48]

The second affidavit, by Bajro Avdić, dated July 6, 1984, charged that Artuković, in November 1941 near the Kerestinec collection camp, had ordered the machine-gunning of between 400 and 500 captured Partisans—helpless men, women, and children—and that he, Avdić, had personally heard the order and witnessed the killings. Avdić also alleged that Artuković, again in Avdić's presence, had ordered the machine-gunning of women and children from villages near Vrgin Most and the Moscenica monastery as reprisals for the destruction of one of his government's military units. Finally, Avdić claimed that in early 1942 Artuković had ordered the machine-gunning and crushing by tanks of hundreds of Partisans captured at Zumberak, and that Avdić had seen this order carried out, too. The first affidavit added nothing to what had been rejected in 1959, but the second was new.[49] OSI knew from its own research that the new affidavit contradicted earlier ones Avdić had signed, and that past Yugoslavian investigators had not considered him a credible witness, but it chose not to disclose any of this knowledge to the court or to the defense.[50]

The extradition hearing was attended by Croatian nationalists and members of a variety of Jewish organizations, including the militant Jewish Defense League (JDL). Passions ran high, and one of Artuković's attorneys, Gary Fleischman, received threats by mail and telephone. He was also spat on by members of the JDL for being willing, though a Jew, to defend an alleged Nazi war criminal.[51]

In March 1985, Magistrate Brown ruled that Artuković could be extradited on one count: the alleged murder of Jesa Vidić. However, the prisoner could not be extradited on other counts derived from the Avdić affidavit because Yugoslavia had neglected to indict him on those counts. This oversight was remedied in April, and on May 2, the magistrate amended his opinion to permit extradition for the killings near Vrgin Most, outside the Kerenstinac camp, at Samobor Castle, and near the Moscenica monastery.[52] Ironically, none of the crimes for which Artuković was declared extraditable had anything to do with the Nazi Holocaust. The alleged crimes were just as bad, however, and if committed today would be subject to prosecution before a special international tribunal. On June 3, 1985, while Artuković's application for a writ of habeas corpus was still pending, Assistant Secretary of State Kenneth Dam signed a warrant authorizing Artuković's surrender.[53]

Magistrate Brown's amended opinion, filed on August 8, 1985, began by acknowledging that much of the evidence presented in this new case had been rejected by Commissioner Theodore Hocke in 1959.[54] However, Brown ruled, that made no difference because the doctrine of *res adjudicata* is not applicable to subsequent extradition requests. The magistrate also rejected Artuković's argument that reopening an extradition case after twenty-five years denied due process of law. In so doing, Brown ignored how difficult it would be for Artuković to find other Ustashe who had survived the Communist slaughter and would be willing to risk testifying on his behalf more than forty years after the alleged events.[55] Nor did Brown recognize, as Commissioner Hocke had, that by extraditing Artuković the United States would be delivering him to certain injustice. If the accused had due process claims to raise, the magistrate concluded, he should save them for the Communist court.[56]

Brown refused to accept evidence that the extradition case had been reopened at the Justice Department's behest, in response to political pressures within the United States, and not as a result of the normal process of Yugoslavian justice. But after refusing to hear that evidence, he ruled that "there is no evidence, nor indeed suspicion, that the United States government, or any of its agents, has been guilty of wrongful conduct in connection with the instigation of this proceeding."[57]

Magistrate Brown agreed that there had been an "uprising" within Yugoslavia at the time of the alleged killings, but he ruled that the killings for which extradition was granted had nothing to do with the suppression of that uprising. They were murders "for personal gain, racial or religious hatred, and/or impermissible vengeance upon disarmed enemy soldiers."[58] Thus, Artuković could not avail himself of the political offense exception because the magistrate, in effect, had adopted the wanton crimes proviso that the Ninth Circuit had traditionally rejected.

Brown saw no difficulty extraditing Artuković for "murder," even though the extradition request specifically charged him with "genocide." Genocide was not then recognized as a crime under American law and thus could not be grounds for extradition under the rule of dual criminality expressly recognized in the treaty.[59] This, Brown seemed to reason, was a mere technicality, ignoring the possibility that a person charged with war crimes, and thus labeled a pariah, might need more judicial protection from prejudicial "background evidence" than one charged with ordinary murder.[60] Continuing his studied blindness to the political and ethnic hatreds still raging in Yugoslavia, Brown assumed that by labeling the case one of ordinary murder he could make it ordinary in Yugoslavia.

Finally, in authorizing Artukovic's extradition, Brown accepted both affidavits, even though Truhar's had been rejected as not credible in the 1959 proceeding. Offers to prove that Avdic's had been fabricated were rejected. Following the rule of noninquiry, the magistrate refused to accept evidence that cast grave doubts on the credibility of its claims.[61] In so doing, Brown refused to consider that the secret police of Communist Yugoslavia might well have manufactured the second set of charges in order to get a pro-Nazi enemy.

Brown may have felt that blindness on his part was required by the rule of noninquiry. However, it is more likely that he was responding to the political pressures of the moment, since there was nothing to prevent him from admitting much of the evidence discrediting the new affidavit for the purpose of "clarifying" the facts, rather than "rebutting them." In other words, allowing the defense to prove from independent, public-record evidence that Avdic could not possibly be telling the truth would not have transformed the probable cause hearing into a trial on the merits. It would have simply allowed the U.S. court to establish whether there was enough merit in the charges to justify binding the accused over for trial.

The Justice Department, however, objected to all efforts to discredit Avdic's affidavit. First, the department claimed, it would be unfair to Yugoslavia to question the veracity of its key witness when he was not available to defend himself; second, it claimed that the rule of noninquiry absolutely forbade "the fugitive" to "attack any affiant's credibility."[62] This second argument appeared to contradict an earlier assurance by OSI Director Sher that no injustice would come of OSI's reliance on evidence from the Soviet Union. "In the final analysis," Sher had told a B'nai B'rith meeting, "*American* law and *American* procedures provide ample opportunity for a defendant to uncover falsehoods and fabrications. . . . Our system is designed to expose the truth."[63]

The American practice of accepting accusations by affidavits was not designed to expose the truth, however, as OSI attorney Mark Richard had informed the reluctant Yugoslavian government nine months earlier. Knowing that the Yugoslavians were hesitant to rely on the dubious affidavits of Avdic and Truhar, Richard assured their minister of justice that, under American law, "no witness for the fugitive can attack your system of justice, the integrity of your courts or the truthfulness of the statements made by your witnesses."[64]

Offering such an assurance to a communist police state was tantamount to encouraging fraud, but that does not seem to have bothered OSI's attorneys, either. They also withheld evidence that Truhar had given contradictory testimony in three prior affidavits, at least one of which was in OSI's possession.[65] In two of the statements, Truhar backed away from claiming direct personal knowledge that Artukovic had ordered Vidic's death. In the third, he did not even mention Artukovic but said he learned of Vidic's death from a pharmacist.[66] OSI, however, recognized no legal or moral obligation to share these prior inconsistent statements with either the extradition magistrate or the defense.

Magistrate Brown accepted OSI's argument that he could not legally accept any evidence challenging the affidavits. "I'm sympathetic with your plight," he told defense counsel, but refused to allow any "rebuttal" evidence.[67] He could have allowed the defense to "clarify" the affidavits, but even this, OSI claimed, would be too much of a stretch. Brown agreed, thus dooming a man against whom there was no reliable evidence to a Communist trial and death sentence.

In refusing to allow Artuković's attorneys to discredit the affidavits with public-record information, Brown may have confused extradition hearings with *ex parte* hearings for arrest warrants, at which the suspect is not present to challenge the "facts." In reviewing an application for an arrest warrant, judges do not usually question the veracity of alleged informants or whether they even exist. In an extradition case, however, the magistrate has no opportunity (or motivation) to impose sanctions for misrepresentations made by foreign police in foreign courts. Just as American judges will accept jurisdiction over abducted persons,[68] so foreign judges are not likely to care how extradition was obtained from the United States. Thus the accused has no protection against false or misleading affidavits submitted by less than scrupulous U.S. attorneys.

The evidence challenging Avdić's credibility was substantial when first offered, and it became even more so by February 1986, when Artuković's counsel tried to reopen the issue with a scholarly report by Henry L. De Zeng.[69] Drawing primarily from German, Italian, and Yugoslavian war records, De Zeng showed that Avdić could not have graduated from the military driving school as he claimed and thus come to witness the alleged killings near Kerestinec in November 1941. The school did not exist until 1942. Second, the "Leader's Bodyguard Brigade" to which he claimed to have belonged, and from which he claimed to have observed the 1941 killings, did not come into existence until 1942. Third, Avdić could not remember the name of the man who had been his commanding officer at the time, although war records indicated that Avdić had worked for the same man for most of the war. Fourth, the evidence suggests that the Kerestinec camp outside of Zagreb was closed "soon after" July 1941, making it unlikely that Artuković would have encountered Partisans being transported to that camp during the following November.

The portion of Avdić's affidavit describing atrocities Artuković allegedly ordered at the beginning of 1942 was similarly suspect. It charged, among other things, that the accused ordered army tanks mounted with turrets and cannon to crush the homes of Partisan sympathizers at Zumberak while their occupants were locked inside. However, De Zeng found public record evidence that the Croatian army did not then possess tanks of that size or armament. Similarly, the kind of machine guns Avdić said were used to execute civilians near Vrgin Most in 1941 were not delivered to the Croatian army until 1943. In addition, De Zeng reported, neither German nor Italian war records mentioned a Croatian operation at Zumberak in early 1942, when the town was under Italian, not Croatian, control.

Avdić also alleged that he witnessed mass killings ordered by Artuković as part of a large Ustashe operation in the vicinity of the Moscenica monastery. However, according to the defense study, there was no mention in German war records or Yugoslavian histories that Artuković visited the area (where the German army then operated), that a battle there involved the Ustashe and that they suffered heavy casualties, or that reprisals were taken for these deaths against local civilians. Similarly, the defense could find nothing in the records of the Yugoslavian Partisans indicating that the Ustashe had captured, interned, and killed several hundred of their number in a castle near Samobor.[70]

Under the rule of noninquiry, this defense study could not be accepted as proof that Artuković did not commit the atrocities for which he was charged. The ultimate truth or falsity of the charges is not for the extradition court to decide, and the magistrate so ruled. But the defense study raised a different question, which was whether the Avdić affidavit was sufficiently believable to establish probable cause. At this point, it is also worth recalling that the Yugoslavians and their OSI attorneys were only charging Artuković with these specific murders. His extradition had not been sought, and could not be sought, simply for his official responsibility for the genocide carried out by his subordinates. Genocide, at the time, was not an extraditable offense.

* * *

"Rough justice" simply demands that the accused meet the fate he deserves. It was rough justice that led to the hurried conviction and execution of Japanese General Tomoyuki Yamashita, after World War II, for crimes committed by his subordinates in the Philippines. General Yamashita was not charged with personally ordering or participating in any killings. There was no evidence that he knew of the atrocities at the time they were committed, or that he could have stopped them had he known. He was convicted because troops under his command slaughtered thousands of Filipino civilians, and his conviction was, unfortunately, upheld by the U.S. Supreme Court.[71] To believers in rough justice, it is sufficient to know that Artukovic was the titular head of the Ustashe Ministry of the Interior; that alone is sufficient to make him morally responsible for all the crimes committed by his subordinates.

In ordinary criminal cases, it is not usually sufficient to say that an official is morally responsible for the wrongful behavior of subordinates. To hold the official legally responsible, evidence should link him to those crimes. It should not be enough to claim, as the prosecution successfully did in the Yamashita case, that "he must have known." Without evidence of direct, personal culpability, the criminal justice system can have no integrity, and without integrity, those who run it come to resemble the very persons they would judge.

If there is to be any integrity to the extradition process, the believability question must be asked by the Justice Department even before it is considered by the court. This analysis, in court or in the department, should be essentially the same as a probable cause analysis in a domestic arrest case—a commonsense analysis based on the totality of the circumstances and keyed to the precise charges against the accused. Where the requesting regime is known for corrupting law with politics, or where the accused is an old political enemy of the accusers, commonsense demands stricter scrutiny than in ordinary criminal cases. To treat the inquiry formalistically, to ignore the totality of the circumstances, and to ignore clear evidence that the case is not an ordinary one is to open the legal process to serious abuse.

In the Artuković case, the Office of Special Investigations did send its historian to Yugoslavia. However, his mission was to help the Yugoslavians build OSI's case against Artuković, not check the veracity of the Yugoslavian allegations and witnesses with a view to assuring that impartial justice could be done. One particularly disconcerting item that should have piqued OSI's curiosity was that the accused was not mentioned once, according to his son Radoslav, in the massive research on atrocities done for the Nuremberg war crimes trials.[72] OSI also ignored the son's private and public demands that the defects in Avdić's claims be investigated, so that the appropriateness of Justice Department reliance on them could be reconsidered.

Of course, it would be naive to expect more than intense partisanship from such a specialized legal unit. Lawyers employed to wage war against the Mafia, drug cartels, or war criminals are evaluated almost solely in terms of how many convictions they obtain and whom they put behind bars. Thus, their political mandate to do retributive justice is likely to overwhelm what should be their moral and legal obligation to prevent injustice in each particular case. Judges, however, are supposed to assure that justice is done in each case. That is why they are granted so much independence from ordinary politics and so much discretion in determining what constitutes probable cause. Unfortunately, judges tend to be least skeptical of prosecutors at the initial stages of a criminal proceeding, where the sheer volume of cases is overwhelming, when the evidence is most amorphous, and when the opportunity to repair mistakes later seems greatest.

Whatever his reasons, Magistrate Brown did not ask the Justice Department to produce corroborating evidence that the alleged events had occurred, or had happened in roughly the way Avdić claimed they did. He did not ask for proof from the standard histories of the war and Holocaust (or the Nuremberg investigations) that the alleged massacres had actually occurred or that Artuković was the kind of official he was accused of being.[73] Nor did Brown ask the Justice Department to respond to the defense's offers to show that Avdić's crucial affidavit was not to be trusted. On the contrary, he rejected all defense attempts to prove that Avdić was a liar whose allegations were offered by a regime that had been notorious for corrupting legal processes in order to achieve political advantages, a regime whose previous attempt to obtain Artuković's extradition had been condemned by Commissioner Hocke as unworthy of trust.

* * *

In the second Artuković case, as in the first, hard facts specific to the charges were less important than political perceptions of who Artuković was and who his alleged victims were. In both instances, the label placed on the accused by contemporary politics determined his fate. In the first case, Artuković was labeled an anti-communist war criminal—a characterization that probably required, under the politics of the Cold War, closer than normal scrutiny of the "facts" against him. In the second case, Artuković was labeled a Nazi and therefore a leader in the European slaughter of Jews. Ironically, not one of the alleged offenses for which he was ultimately extradited involved the killing of Jews. Andrija Artuković was morally responsible for the crimes of his subordinates, but he could only be extradited to stand trial for something else—something probably false, but symbolically true.

In the first Artuković case, facts mattered, but only because politics mattered first. In the second case, politics guaranteed that what mattered was the public's perception. In the first Artuković case, the magistrate was free to examine the inadequacy of Yugoslavia's evidence because public support for anti-communists was great and because public awareness of communist purge trials remained strong. In the second case, however, most Americans no longer thought of Yugoslavia as a communist nation. For them, it was something indeterminate, a quasi-capitalist state that exported inexpensive automobiles and allowed its citizens to emigrate. Americans no longer remembered—if they even knew about—the savagery of Yugoslavia's internal warfare or the historic roots of its ethnic and religious conflicts. But they did know of Hitler's atrocities against the Jews. They also knew of their own country's failure to help the Jews, and of the assistance that the U.S. military and intelligence services gave to former Nazis after the war. In the public mind, these wrongs had to be corrected. Thus Magistrate Brown had much less freedom than Commissioner Hocke to follow the facts. If Brown were to decide the case solely on the facts, he would not be praised for preserving the integrity of the American legal system. He would be remembered for shielding a Nazi war criminal and preventing the U.S. government from atoning for its wrongs against the Nazis' victims.

By labeling Artuković a pariah, the OSI was able to inflict some punishment on him prior to trial. Its first move was to transfer the old man from the U.S. Naval Hospital in Long Beach, California, to a U.S. prison hospital in Missouri, 2,000 miles away from his family and attorneys. When asked to justify this unusual move, the OSI claimed that it was too expensive to keep Artuković in a California hospital.[74] But if expense was truly a consideration, the government could have transferred him to the nearby federal prison hospital on Terminal Island in Long Beach. More to the point, the expense and anguish inflicted on his family was of no concern to the OSI. When Artuković's wife was finally able to visit him, she found him in solitary confinement. She could not determine if a doctor had seen him, or even if any doctor at the prison knew about her husband's medical history.[75]

When U.S. Magistrate John R. Kronenberg saw no reason for this treatment and indicated that he was disposed to free the elderly man on bail,[76] Chief District Judge Manuel L. Real swiftly removed him from the case. The removal order was issued by telephone from a bar association convention in Washington, D.C., in violation of the standard federal practice that forbids judges to issue orders while outside of the district.[77] Bail continued to be denied. Stung by the bad publicity, however, OSI agreed to return Artuković to the federal prison hospital in Long Beach.[78]

The only means by which an accused can obtain review of a magistrate's decision authorizing extradition is to ask for a writ of habeas corpus ordering his release. This petition was also taken up by Chief Judge Real, who on February 6, 1986, adopted Magistrate Brown's opinion as his own.[79] Artuković's counsel immediately asked the

Court of Appeals for the Ninth Circuit to stay the extradition order pending an appeal, but the request was rejected on February 11 before the attorney could even submit a brief. Without taking time to review the record, the three-judge panel declared that Artuković would probably not prevail on appeal. In any case, the judges added, extradition to Yugoslavia would not, on a "balance of hardships," cause the accused "irreparable injury."[80]

The scales of justice were thus prejudicially misloaded. On one side were the interests of a single individual whom the government had, by its press campaign, stripped of his right to be judged as a real person and not a symbol. On the other were the foreign policy interests of the United States and the justice interests of the foreign nation. In loading their scales in this manner, the judges' refusing to recognize, as Commissioner Hocke had, that the delivery of a pro-Nazi Ustasha to a Communist government was tantamount to a sentence of death—an injury as irreparable as the delivery of Thomas Nash to the British Navy or the *Amistad* captives to the Cuban slavers. Nor did the court add to Artuković's side the collective interest of all Americans in protecting their courts from complicity in foreign injustice. The judges did not even admit that the right to life and liberty of even the most despised individuals is, under the U.S. Constitution, fundamental.

In rendering their judgment, the judges should have acknowledged that the evidence against the accused was doubtful at best, but they did not. They accepted the Justice Department's claim "that the public interest will be served by the United States complying with a valid application from Yugoslavia under the treaty."[81] "Such proper compliance," the judges continued, "promotes relations between the two countries, and enhances efforts to establish an international rule of law and order." Although they concluded that "the probability of irreparable injury to Artuković if we deny his motion is evident," the judges nevertheless found that the balance of hardship was tempered by Artuković's "ability to defend himself at trial in Yugoslavia."[82] Andrija Artuković was to be surrendered, like Jonathan Robbins before him, for reasons of state.

Technically speaking, the judges did not dismiss Artuković's appeal, but their decision left OSI free to surrender him. Without notifying his attorneys or family, its agents put Artuković on a flight east. While he was in the air, his attorneys asked for a stay, but that request too was denied.[83] Artuković was transferred to a waiting Yugoslavian plane and flown out of the country. "I find it disgraceful," attorney Gary Fleischman said of his client's nighttime departure. "He was whisked out of the country without the opportunity to say goodbye to his wife, children and grandchildren he will probably never see again. Why? For what reason?" Countering Fleischman's statement, Assistant U.S. Attorney David Nimmer replied, "He had fifteen months to say goodbye to his family."[84] Justice Department official Murray Stein added: "That's basically our policy all the time, to get rid of people as fast as we can. We try to treat foreign governments as we want to be treated."[85] Judge Bee or Martin Van Buren could not have said it better.

* * *

When Andrija Artuković arrived in Zagreb on February 12, 1986, strapped to a stretcher, he was immediately charged with 230,000 additional killings.[86] These charges were later presented as a preamble to the formal indictment, and thus technically satisfied the rule of specialty (or speciality), but their purpose clearly was to prejudice the court and observers before the case got underway. They were accepted by the court under a Yugoslavian law that permits the prosecutor "to complete the picture of the accused."[87]

Artuković's Yugoslavian attorneys were allowed only thirty-two minutes alone with their client, but the president of the court ruled this sufficient because they had been permitted to confer with him in other meetings monitored by security officials.[88] Artuković's son Radoslav, the defense's chief investigator and press spokesman, was denied a visa to enter Yugoslavia until the eve of the trial, and then only on condition that he not help the defense or criticize Yugoslavia's legal system.[89]

Artuković's trial was the first of a former Croatian government official since 1948;[90] it would become the last of the Yugoslavian Communist Party's show trials against its wartime adversaries. The term "show trial" seems appropriate, given that many of the accusations and much of the testimony offered by the prosecution had nothing to do with the specific charges and had the effect of violating the rule of specialty. Seventy-five journalists from sixty foreign countries covered the proceedings, which were conducted under heavy security. Like Adolf Eichmann, the defendant was caged in a bullet-proof glass booth.[91]

The trial began with the interrogation of the accused by the judges; no privilege against self-incrimination was allowed. Nor was the defense allowed a verbatim transcript of the proceedings; the presiding judge created a "summary," which under Yugoslavian law is supposed to capture the essence of the defendant's answers and omit remarks which the judge believes are not relevant or admissible. The summary made it appear that Artuković had replied to questions in coherent, complex, complete sentences and had volunteered information when, in fact, he has answered in monosyllables.[92]

Only two government witnesses directly accused Artuković of a crime. The first, Franjo Truhar, had earlier signed an affidavit claiming that the defendant had told him he would have Jesa Vidić killed in order to get his land. On the stand, however, the eighty-five-year-old former police chief proved as senile and forgetful as the defendant. Throughout much of his testimony he gaped blankly, not seeming to comprehend the questions. Only through leading questions, which would not be allowed under American law, was the court able, finally, to coax the bewildered witness into saying that Artuković had told him that he would kill Vidić. Unable to draw a coherent statement from this crucial witness, the presiding judge finally read Truhar's 1952 affidavit into the record and got him to say that he would stand behind its accuracy.[93]

The most damning testimony came from Bajro Avdić, who repeated his claims that as one of Artuković's motorcycle escorts he had witnessed him order the machine-gunning of Partisans near Kerestinec, women and children from villages near Vrgin Most and the Moscenica monastery, and the machine-gunning and crushing by tanks of Partisans captured at Zumberak.[94] The defense was prepared to prove that the events alleged had not happened, but the presiding judge—this time in violation of Yugoslavian law—barred the defense from presenting any witnesses. In particular, Artuković's attorneys were not allowed to challenge Avdić's credibility, which was highly suspect. In the U.S. extradition proceeding, Justice Department lawyers had argued that it would be unfair to challenge the credibility of a man who was not present in court to defend himself. In Yugoslavia the man was present, but defense counsel could not challenge his credibility, and the United States did not protest.

According to the court's president, there was no need for further evidence. The facts had been established well enough by the prosecution's witnesses and documents.[95] The Communist government was satisfied that it had proven its case against the pro-Nazi Croatians; it did not wish to give them a forum to respond.

The defense was allowed to present closing arguments, but the decision was a foregone conclusion. On May 14, 1986, Andrija Artuković was found guilty on each of the four counts. In violation of the rule of specialty (which the U.S. government did not protest), the court also found him guilty of ordering "the persecution, torture, and murders of . . . hundreds of thousands of Jews, Serbs, Croats and Gypsies, many of them women and children," not one of whom was identified by name in any indictment.[96] For all these offenses, the court sentenced him to die by firing squad.

With the additional, enlarged verdict, Zagreb newspapers proclaimed, the court had not only convicted Artuković; it had convicted the Independent State of Croatia and had helped to discredit the current Croatian independence movement.[97] A U.S. diplomat confirmed that the trial had given the Communists an opportunity to lash out once again at Catholics.[98]

Back in the United States, attorneys in the Office of Special Investigations celebrated the verdict. Director Sher assured the press that the evidence against the former interior minister was "staggering, absolutely staggering. . . . To claim that he was not accorded due process or proper rights is absurd."[99] Murray Stein, associate director of international affairs at the Justice Department, defended Yugoslavian justice: "You can't expect the European judicial system to be like our own. Over there, before you go to trial, they have investigated and examined you so thoroughly, they've already determined there's between zero and no percent chance you'll be exonerated."[100]

In April 1987, a Yugoslavian court decided that Artuković was too ill to be executed, and in January 1988 he died in prison of natural causes. A few months later, Milan Bulajić, a former legal adviser to the Yugoslav Foreign Ministry who had assisted in efforts to obtain Artuković's extradition in both the 1950s and 1980s, published a four-volume work concluding that the massacres for which Artuković was extradited never happened.[101] "There was no legal reason for the extradition," he told a Belgrade newspaper. "Andrija Artuković was sentenced for crimes which never took place."[102]

In September 1990, Dennis Reinhartz of the University of Texas at Arlington, who had served as an OSI historian in the Artuković case, admitted that he had serious doubts about the Avdić affidavit at the time it was submitted: "[Avdić] was quite clearly cutting himself a deal with the government that had him imprisoned. On those events, there is no corroboration."[103] Historian Charles McAdams of the University of San Francisco, who was barred from testifying on Artuković's behalf at his extradition hearing, was even more emphatic. The charges, he said, "were absurd. A joke. I'm part Jewish myself. The Holocaust was a tremendous tragedy. But there was not credible evidence against Artukovic on these crimes. The OSI wanted him badly and they got him. None of the standards of justice used in the U.S. were applied."[104] In 1990, the Justice Department's Office of Professional Responsibility began a review of OSI's conduct in the Artuković case. Its findings were submitted to Deputy Attorney General Jamie Gorlick in 1996 but have yet to be made public.[105]

In the second Artuković case, rough justice was done. A former official whose ministry was responsible for unmerciful torment and slaughter of hundreds of thousands of innocent people received neither justice nor mercy from the United States government. In their zeal, attorneys for the U.S. Department of Justice came to resemble the very fascists they sought to condemn, while enabling communists guilty of comparable atrocities to commit still further injustices, all in the name of justice.

CHAPTER 18

Extradition as a Substitute for Deportation: Getting Ivan

It is crucial that the moral force of the criminal law not be diluted by a standard of proof that leaves people in doubt whether innocent men are being condemned.

Justice William J. Brennan Jr., In re Winship, 1970

Each age, and each zealous group, has its monster labels, like "heretic," "Papist," or "Communist," which are meant to deny moral worth to the accused and enable the government to punish him or her with the severity due the embodiment of evil.

Such was the case with Thomas Nash. So long as government lawyers successfully labeled him a "mutineer," no one—not even his own counsel—cared if justice was done. Once Joseph Doherty was labeled an IRA "terrorist," the similarity between his actions and those of the Minutemen at Lexington and Concord could no longer be seen. Once the Croatian Andrija Artuković was labeled a "Nazi war criminal," suspicion that the "evidence" against him might have been falsified by Communist and Serbian enemies could be casually dismissed.

The framers of the U.S. Constitution well understood the condemnatory power of politically freighted labels. The most politically charged offense of their age was "treason," and they were so concerned with the corruption of justice common to allegations of treason that they took the power to define that offense away from politicians and wrote it into the Constitution. For the same reason, Jefferson refused to list treason as an extraditable offense in his proposed treaty with Spain. Real treason, he believed, was a most heinous offense and deserved severe punishment, but pretended treasons were too common to entertain extradition requests based on them. It would be better, he thought, to grant asylum to all persons charged with treason, even though some were unworthy, than to risk helping a foreign regime corrupt justice.

Of course, political sympathies can also work to shield the most heinous offenders from extradition. Thomas Nash was probably not an impressed American seaman, although he did fight his way to freedom from a brutally unjust British navy. Acceptance of his claim to American citizenship by the Jeffersonian Republicans was as blind, in its own way, as the Adams administration's acceptance of the allegations against him. Similarly, sympathy for the Irish victims of absentee British landlords was sufficiently powerful in the early 1900s to blind the supporters of James Lynchehaun to the hideous offense for which he was charged. Hostility to communist regimes was sufficiently strong in the 1950s for a myopic U.S. magistrate to grant Artuković the protection accorded political offenders.

As blind as these judgments were, however, the system was weighted, as Jefferson thought it should be, on the side of freedom, due process, and asylum. Doubts were to be resolved on behalf of the accused and against the requesting regimes, whether those regimes governed autocratically or through populist terror.

The founders of the American republic could ground their legal system on republican and liberal values because they had no great stake in Europe's conflicts, and because they had no great need for reciprocity. Nor did they feel much need to use extradition as another form of deportation. In the United States, liberty had preceded bureaucracy, and so long as the law enforcement and diplomatic bureaucracies were weak, the system could favor liberty, not just for the failed leaders of liberal revolutions, but for more politically problematic people like Citizen Genêt, General Galbaud, Captain Barré, the Mexican border raiders, and General Ezeta.

The preference for liberty in American extradition law began to decline with the rise of anarchism and the spread of legal positivism. However, it did not reach significant proportions until the 1970s, when the anti-drug, anti-terrorism, and anti-Nazi bureaucracies were formed. With these highly politicized legal bureaucracies in place, the traditional presumptions in favor of liberty, due process, asylum—or individual justice—were replaced by a presumption in favor of administrative need. The careers of anti-Nazi lawyers depended on highly visible "body counts." Just as the first victim of every military conflict is truth, so the first victim of this "war" on ex-Nazis was truth. The Office of Special Investigations was not expected to engage in the dispassionate, systematic enforcement of the law. It was expected to "get" ex-Nazis, so it was organized, like an anti-organized crime task force, into a hard-driving, legal combat unit.

* * *

No case brought out the combat mentality of OSI more dramatically than that of John Demjanjuk, a retired Ford Motor Company mechanic from Cleveland, who was charged in 1976 with being "Ivan the Terrible," the man who slashed and bludgeoned Jewish prisoners as he herded them into the gas chambers at Treblinka. Treblinka was the most efficient of three killing stations built by the German Schutzstaffel (SS) in Eastern Poland between February and July 1942. Established primarily to kill the survivors of Warsaw's ghetto, its abattoir would destroy, in just one year, approximately 875,000 men, women, and children.[1]

Treblinka was divided into two camps. The victims were brought into Camp One by train, separated by sex, forced to disrobe, and then driven naked to Camp Two along a narrow path that the SS called the Himmelstrasse, or Road to Heaven. At the end were the gas chambers, run by a motor mechanic known as "Ivan the Terrible" or, in Polish, "Ivan Grozny." He operated the engines that pumped lethal carbon monoxide fumes into the chamber. When his victims did not move fast enough, he beat them with a pipe or whip. He also hacked at the prisoners with a sword and severed the breasts of women.[2]

The man accused of being this ogre was one of hundreds of thousands of displaced persons who had emigrated to the United States from Europe following World War II. According to his account, he was born Ivan Demjanjuk in the Ukrainian village of Dub Marcharenzi on April 3, 1920. His parents were partially disabled by war and poverty. His father had lost several fingers in World War I; his mother never recovered the use of her right leg after a difficult childbirth. Their son was enrolled in the village school for nine years but only completed the first four grades because of excessive absences. The boy would have gone more often, but whenever his father found work, he had to take the only pair of shoes. During the famine of 1932–1933, which left 7–10 million Ukrainians dead of starvation and disease, Demjanjuk recalled, "People were lying dead in their homes, in the yards, on the roads, exposed to sunlight. Nobody collected them; nobody brought them to burial."[3] The family had to sell their house for the equivalent of eight loaves of bread and move to a collective farm outside of Moscow, but lack of work on the farm soon drove them back to their village.[4]

In 1940, after Hitler invaded Poland, Demjanjuk received his first draft notice from the Soviet army. It said, among other things, that he must have "two pairs of underpants, a spoon, and a plate." He was too poor to have underpants, and when he reported to the induction center without them, he was sent home. A year later, after Hitler had invaded Russia, the Soviet army was less particular, and the boy was inducted without underpants.[5]

After basic training, he was assigned to a front-line artillery unit that soon found itself retreating before the German onslaught. Near the Dnieper River, Demjanjuk was struck in the back by a piece of shrapnel, which left a permanent scar. By early 1942, he was back in combat on the Crimean peninsula, where he and his unit were captured by the Germans.[6]

These facts have never been in dispute. Nor is there doubt that the end of the war found him in a displaced persons camp in Landshut, Germany, where he met Vera Kowlowa, his future wife. Over the next four years the couple lived in several camps, and Vera gave birth to their first child in one of them. In 1950 the Demjanjuks applied to emigrate to the United States, and two years later they sailed into New York harbor on a troopship. At the height of American anti-communism, Ivan changed his name to John and hid the fact that he had grown up in the Soviet Union and had once joined the *Komsomol*, a communist youth organization.[7] Some time after the war, he also removed an SS-type blood-group tattoo from the inside of his left arm.

In August 1952, after briefly working on a farm in Indiana, John took a job with the Ford Motor Company as an engine mechanic. Vera went to work in the coiling department at General Electric, and both remained with their companies until retirement. John spent most of his off hours gardening or playing with his children. The family regularly worshipped at St. Vladimir's Orthodox Church in Seven Hills, Ohio. "We were," John Jr. would later say, "the perfect family."[8]

These facts also were not questioned. What was disputed was what John Sr. did during most of the war. The first allegation against him came in the mid-1970s, when Michael Hanusiak, a member of the American Communist Party and a pro-Soviet editor of the New York–based *Ukrainian Daily News*, returned from the Soviet Union with a list of Ukrainian nationalists who the Soviets believed had committed crimes against Jews.[9] Hanusiak privately published some of his charges in a 1976 broadside entitled *Lest We Forget*.[10] He also shared additional information with the Immigration and Naturalization Service (INS). Among his later claims, which presumably came from Soviet interrogations of former Ukrainian prison guards, was one that Ivan Demjanjuk had been a *wachmann* (guard) at the death camp at Sobibor.

The INS collected photographs of all the alleged collaborators and sent them to the Israeli police, who pasted them on sheets of cardboard and advertised for survivors of Sobibor and Treblinka who might be able to identify "the Ukrainians Ivan Demjanjuk and Fedor Fedorenko."[11] None of the Israeli survivors recalled an Ivan Demjanjuk at either camp, although several Treblinka survivors remembered Fedorenko's name and face well. No one in Israel who had survived Sobibor remembered an Ivan Demjanjuk by name or recognized his unnamed photograph, but nine survivors of Treblinka did associate Demjanjuk's round face, protruding ears, and high forehead with an Ivan they did know: Ivan the Terrible.[12]

The positive identifications were reported to the American authorities. The more numerous failures were not, even though some of the survivors who did not recall Demjanjuk's face had known Ivan the Terrible well.[13] Nor was the actual number of failed identifications, especially by people who knew Ivan well, presented to the courts in Cleveland (or later in Jerusalem). If the purpose of the American and Israeli investigations had been simply to establish the truth, then both the positive identifications and the failures to identify would have been equally desired, since exoneration would have been as important as incrimination. But the American investigators who created the case were not impartial historians; they were attorneys who would be judged, personally and as a budgetary unit, by the number and apparent notoriety of the people they "got." The truth that mattered most to them was any truth that would tend to incriminate, not exonerate, John Demjanjuk. They did not act as members of a justice department, but as advocates of a cause.

* * *

Problematic eyewitness identifications had plagued INS and OSI efforts from the start. In 1978, six survivors of Treblinka testified in Miami at the denaturalization trial of Feodor Fedorenko. Fedorenko admitted that he had been a *wachmann,* but he denied he was a volunteer. The Nazis "didn't ask" for volunteers, he said; "if you didn't go they'd shoot you down like a dog."[14] Fedorenko also claimed, less persuasively, that his role had been limited to perimeter duty. The survivors contradicted him, recounting criminal acts they had seen him commit.

The key issue before Federal District Judge Norman Roettger was whether the eyewitness identifications could be relied on. He was skeptical from the start; the memories were now thirty-five years old. The photo spread presented to camp survivors by the Israeli police, he decided, was "impermissibly suggestive."[15] The police actually told one of the witnesses that the person in photograph 17 was Fedorenko and asked if the witness recognized him; after a while, the witness did.[16] OSI wanted the camp survivors to identify Fedorenko through depositions only; the judge insisted that they be brought into court and made to identify the accused in person. The first walked about the courtroom and initially picked the wrong person; the second correctly picked the one elderly person at the defense table, convincing the judge that the witnesses were, at the very least, "discussing the trial among themselves," or, "at worst, someone was coaching them."[17] Witness Joseph Czarny misidentified a photograph as that of the defendant, after declaring that he could never make such a mistake. Other witnesses attributed physical characteristics to the accused that he did not have.[18] Judge Roettger rejected their testimony and refused to strip Fedorenko of his citizenship.

Assessing this defeat for the Justice Department, Allan A. Ryan Jr. (who would later head OSI) recommended against an appeal. The department's factual and legal position, he concluded, was insupportable.[19] That conclusion was disputed by Nathan Dershowitz of the American Jewish Congress, who protested to the solicitor general, Wade McCree Jr. About the same time Rep. Joshua Eilberg, chairman of the House Judiciary's Subcommittee on Immigration, Citizenship, and International Law, wrote to Attorney General Griffin Bell to denounce the government's handling of the entire case.[20] Shortly thereafter, Ryan reversed himself and personally persuaded the Court of Appeals that whether the eyewitness identifications were correct was not relevant to denaturalization, because undisclosed service as a death-camp guard was, in itself, sufficient to strip Fedorenko of his citizenship.[21] In affirming the Fifth Circuit's decision, the Supreme Court ignored both the issue of duress and the unreliability of the eyewitness identifications, contenting itself with interpreting the language of the denaturalization statute.[22]

In another case challenging the reliability of eyewitness identifications, Judge Julius Hoffman (the irascible curmudgeon who had presided over the Chicago Seven trial) stripped Frank Wallace (born Franz Walus) of his citizenship for concealing membership in both the SS and the Gestapo. Twelve witnesses swore that Wallace, as Walus, was a brutal Gestapo agent in Kielce and Czestochowa. They described, in graphic detail, atrocities they had seen him commit between 1939 and 1943.[23]

However, SS records in Germany contained no reference to a Storm Trooper named Frank Walus, Franz Walus, or, in Poland, Franciszek Walus. OSI claimed a Nazi cover-up,[24] but the more plausible explanation was that the German SS did not admit Poles or young men as short as the accused.[25] OSI's investigators could not find Walus's name in the records of any other German military organization, and they refused to search the files of the Polish war crimes commission for evidence that he was either a member of the German military or a collaborator.[26] On the other hand, German health records and records of the International Red Cross substantiated Wallace's claim that he spent the war as a forced laborer on Bavarian farms.[27] The defense was able to produce photographs showing him with German farmers,[28] and Bavarian farm wives testified that he had worked for them during the period in question.[29]

Given this countervailing evidence, the Court of Appeals decided that Judge Hoffman and the witnesses had been mistaken and ordered a retrial. It would be "an intolerable injustice" not to retry the accused, the appeals court ruled, predicting that a new trial would "almost certainly compel a different result."[30] In addition, the court found that Judge Hoffman's attempts to impeach Walus's witnesses had evinced an "unrestrained and almost irreconcilable reliance on bias" and barred him from retrying the case.[31] Nine months later, OSI dropped the case, leaving Walus's name uncleared and his family deeply in debt.[32]

* * *

According to Allan Ryan, OSI's second director, "the most enduring lesson to come out of the Walus case is that an office like OSI was needed not only to prosecute the guilty but to protect the innocent."[33] But the lesson was not learned. When OSI began denaturalization proceedings against John Demjanjuk in Cleveland in February 1981, it relied primarily on the thirty-five-year-old memories of six survivors of Treblinka. Indeed, in an earlier denaturalization case against Feodor Fedrenko, Judge Roettger had found testimony of those survivors incredible.[34] But Federal District Judge Frank J. Battisti had more confidence than Judge Roettger in eyewitness identifications.

The OSI offered an identity card from KGB files that purported to place Demjanjuk at Trawniki, the camp at which, in 1942, the SS trained captured Ukrainians to work as guards in the extermination camps of Sobibor and Treblinka.[35] The card was a problematic piece of evidence. It correctly gave Demjanjuk's full name, date of birth, father's name, hair color, and location of scar. It incorrectly reported that he was five feet, nine inches tall; in fact, he was closer to six feet. The photograph glued to the front of the card certainly looked like Demjanjuk. It contained staple marks, as if it had been taken from some other document, but that alone did not make it any less authentic. The signatures also appeared genuine.[36]

But the card did not mention Treblinka. It said that Demjanjuk had been sent to L. G. Okzow, a work farm near Chelm, on September 14, 1942, and had been transferred to the death camp at Sobibor on March 27, 1943. If true, the card proved that Demjanjuk had lied about being at the prisoner-of-war camp at Chelm until the spring of

1944. It also indicated that he had been a death-camp guard at Sobibor during the spring and summer of 1943, at which time several of the eyewitnesses placed him at Treblinka. Thus, it discredited eyewitness testimony that he was Treblinka's Ivan while supporting the conclusion that he was a death-camp guard—a conclusion that would justify both denaturalization and deportation.

Of course, the postings on the card might not have been complete. Demjanjuk could have been at both death camps and the farm too at different times, but there was no documentary evidence to support this supposition.[37] No roster, no identification card, no payroll record, and no survivor placed an Ivan *Demjanjuk* at Treblinka. Several survivors recalled Ivan Grozny—Ivan the Terrible—and insisted, solely from photographs, that Demjanjuk was Treblinka's Ivan.

Unlike Frank Walus, Demjanjuk could not present documentary evidence or eyewitness testimony that would prove he had remained a POW at Chelm. Nor would he have wished to admit that he had been trained at Trawniki and become a guard at Sobibor. That would have opened him to deportation to the Soviet Union and probable execution there for collaborating with the Nazis. On the other hand, no survivors of Sobibor could confirm the card's notation that he had been with them. If OSI chose to rely on the Trawniki card, all it could claim was that Demjanjuk had been a guard, which was not enough to prove, beyond a reasonable doubt, that he had committed any specific murders at Sobibor, let alone Treblinka, for which he could lawfully be extradited.

By placing Demjanjuk at Sobibor when several Treblinka survivors swore he was at their camp, the card seemed to cast more than a reasonable doubt on the eyewitnesses' claims. But as Ryan had demonstrated in the Fedorenko case, the government did not have to make out a criminal case against Demjanjuk; it had only to meet the lower standards of denaturalization, deportation, or extradition. In the denaturalization and deportation cases, OSI could prevail with the card alone; in the extradition case, it could rely on the eyewitnesses from Treblinka and thereby establish probable cause. OSI's job was not to proceed as if this were just another criminal case, assuring itself that it truly had the right man before denouncing him to the world as Ivan the Terrible. Its job was to get rid of former Nazis, with as little solicitude as possible. Accordingly, its attorneys had no difficulty advancing contradictory statements of fact in different legal proceedings.

In the wake of the Walus, Fedorenko, and other debacles, OSI was under intense pressure from Congress to justify its existence.[38] For that it needed dramatic victories, which could only come if the persons it accused were especially atrocious. Although the first published accounts of Treblinka recorded that a Ukrainian named Ivan had helped run its gas chambers, not one of them reported that he was known as Ivan the Terrible.[39] OSI's witnesses were the first to give him that apocalyptic name—a label that would recall one of the great tyrants of Russian history, create powerful presumptions of guilt against the accused, and, not insignificantly, bring added glory to OSI.

To prove that Demjanjuk was Treblinka's Ivan, OSI offered the videotaped testimony of Otto Horn, a former member of the Gestapo who had supervised the burning of corpses.[40] His time at Treblinka overlapped Ivan's by about a year and he claimed to have known the gas chamber operator well. Horn was first questioned by a team of OSI investigators, including attorney Norman Moskowitz, on November 14, 1979, at his home in West Berlin. Three months later, Moskowitz asked him, on videotape, to recount how he had come to identify Demjanjuk as Ivan from two different sets of photographs that the investigators had shown him separately. Horn's answers persuaded Judge Battisti that Demjanjuk had been at Treblinka and, consequently, was not entitled to citizenship.[41]

Stripped of his citizenship, Demjanjuk was now subject to deportation, and OSI moved quickly to send him to the Soviet Union, where he would almost certainly be tried and executed, both for being a guard at Sobibor and for joining a Nazi-sponsored, anti-Soviet army of Ukrainian nationalists at the end of the war.[42] The USSR could not request his surrender through normal channels; no extradition treaty existed between the two nations. There were good reasons, founded on disrespect for the fairness of the Communist legal system in politically charged cases, that no extradition treaty had ever been concluded with the Soviet Union. Where alleged war criminals were concerned, however, the absence of an extradition treaty was, for Justice Department lawyers, a mere technicality. Having convicted the accused in their own minds, they were happy to deport him to the Soviet Union, even if deportation was likely to result in a sham trial and certain execution. The INS began deportation proceedings in December 1982 and received authorization in February 1985.[43]

* * *

The war crimes cases, like those involving terrorism, engaged the passions and resources of conflicting ethnic groups. Of these, none had more clout than American Jews newly conscious of their country's failures to shelter refugees from the Holocaust, bomb the camps, punish the killers, or bar them from immigration. In the 1970s and 1980s, American Jews possessed the organization, political influence, and money to make their concerns known. More important still, they held the moral high ground.

Organized against the prosecutions were a number of East European émigré groups, who would eventually raise over $2 million for Demjanjuk's defense.[44] Unlike the Jews, these groups were not united in a moral cause; they supported particular defendants against what they saw as communist conspiracies. The more extreme among them were deeply prejudiced against Jews and argued that the Holocaust never happened. The less extreme were politically conservative, staunchly anti-communist, and tended to view European Jews as socialists. Political support came from right-wing publications like *Human Events* and conservatives like Patrick Buchanan, who sought to forge an electoral alliance between conservative Catholics and evangelical Protestants. As a result, most liberal Democrats and pragmatic Republicans were deaf to the pleas of the East European émigré groups supporting Demjanjuk.

The émigré groups had great difficulty persuading Congress and the public that men like Demjanjuk, Walus, and Fedorenko had been prisoners of the Nazis too. The issue of "duress" was more difficult to raise in the cases of death-camp guards than it had been in the cases of hijackers to freedom. The guards had driven thousands of innocent people to their deaths; the hijackers threatened harm but had not wantonly killed anyone. Yet the guards claimed that they were not free moral agents but had been victims of a separate "holocaust" against Soviet prisoners of war.

To young men like Fedorenko and Demjanjuk, incarceration at the Nazi-run POW camp for Soviet prisoners at Chelm was tantamount to a sentence of death. On this point there is no better authority than Alfred Rosenberg, the Reich minister for the Eastern Occupied Territories. In 1942 he reported that "Of the 3,600,000 [Soviet] prisoners of war, only several hundred thousand are still able to work fully. A large part of them had starved, or died, because of the hazards of the weather. Thousands died from spotted fever. . . . In various camps, all the 'Asiatics' were shot."[45] However, when East European émigré groups attempted to point out this "other Holocaust," Jewish groups denounced the comparison. The sufferings of the two groups are not comparable, they argued, both because the Holocaust against Jews was genocidal and because many Slavs, Balts, and Poles had collaborated in that effort.

As an historical judgment this is undoubtedly true; Soviet prisoners did die by the millions, but not in human abattoirs. The mass murder of most European Jews was unprecedented in a way that the death of prisoners of war was not, and anti-Semitism was rife among Balts, Slavs, and Poles. But as a matter of individual justice, the émigré groups also had a point, which John Demjanjuk Jr. made most starkly:[46]

> If my father were to stand up today and say, 'I lied. I was a guard someplace,' I would have to put that into the context of what happened in World War II. Knowing what POW camps were like—at Chelm, where he testified he was, where people were dying from typhus, dysentery, and starvation. Does a boy put in a situation like that, given the opportunity to have a real meal and put meat on his bones, and faced with a choice of living or dying—is he morally wrong for choosing the option of living? Is he any more culpable than the Jew that made the decision to live and spent twelve months pulling gold out of the mouths of corpses? I don't think so.

The answer under Anglo-American law (and Israeli law is based on British law) is that duress is not a defense to murder, whether the accused is a kapo or a guard. The common law historically excused a variety of lesser crimes if they were committed under threat of "imminent death or serious bodily injury,"[47] and two-thirds of the American states have statutes that follow the common law rule.[48] However, the American Law Institute's Model Penal Code, which some American states have adopted, takes the opposite view, more in line with the German Law invoked in the *Tiede* case.[49] The code recognizes that duress can be a defense to any crime, including murder, if the accused was subjected to coercion that "a person of reasonable firmness in his situation would have been unable to resist."[50]

In *Fedorenko*, Judge Roettger considered the duress question, much as the Model Penal Code would, when he asked whether the Treblinka guard's service was truly "voluntary." He concluded it was not: "With the benefit of hindsight seated in a comfortable chair in an air-conditioned office," the judge stated, "it would be relatively easy to conclude that the defendant should have turned his rifle on the SS . . . or that he should have attempted to escape once he got to the nearby village." The judge reasoned, however, that if Fedorenko had refused to carry out orders at Treblinka, "his execution would have been swift and sure. It no doubt would have occurred before a formation of other prisoner-guards to serve as an example to them. . . . As a court of equity, this court cannot impose such a duty on the defendant."[51]

On the other hand, the Ukrainian guards were not totally without moral choices. It is not clear just how much the Nazis told them about the death camps they were being recruited to guard, but probably not much while the Ukrainians were still in the POW camp. Once on duty, however, the guards had rifles, access to confiscated possessions, and the opportunity to take two- to four-hour leaves in neighboring communities, which gave them some opportunity to escape. Of course, they could not travel far before their absence would be noticed and the Nazis would start tracking them down. Nor did they have maps, or any place they might go that was less dangerous to their survival than the camps. War-starved Poles were not likely to shelter them, and if they fled to the Soviet Union, they would face execution as enemy collaborators. Fedorenko testified that four Treblinka guards had tried to escape but were captured and shot. Accordingly, Judge Roettger concluded that chances for a successful escape were slim and refused to second-guess the guard's failure to flee.[52] The restricted world of the Nazi death camp was utterly Hobbesian.[53]

Judge Roettger's decision infuriated death-camp survivors. They believed that the defense of duress should be granted to kapos and lesser collaborators like themselves, but they insisted that the guards were "volunteers."[54] Comparatively speaking, they were. The survivors had no choice at all; the guards presumably could have found a way to stay at the POW camps and gamble, against very high odds, that they would not die of starvation or disease. Many of the guards were vehemently anti-Semitic, and some, like Ivan the Terrible, took sadistic pleasure in their work.

But however valid these generalizations may be for most of the guards, they cannot be applied to any individual without imputing guilt by association. Each individual must be judged in terms of actions and choices specific to him or her, and not in terms of generalizations about others, if due process is to be done.

Roettger acknowledged duress in a civil case involving denaturalization. Had he been deciding an extradition case, he would not have been able to claim the same degree of equitable discretion. He would have been duty-bound to follow the rule barring duress as an exception to extradition (or as a defense to murder). In fact, his decision in *Fedorenko* did not last very long. In 1981 the Supreme Court rejected his reliance on duress, holding that the immigration and naturalization laws did not give courts that discretion.[55]

In short, the American law that judges are bound to enforce in extradition and denaturalization cases is draconian by nature. It is the law of deterrence and retribution, better suited to making examples out of individuals with free will than judging desperate Nazi prisoners with compassion, perspective, or proportion. In a social sense, this legal rule is highly utilitarian; as a matter of morality, it virtually guarantees that political offenders will be subjected to victors' justice in order to satisfy a predetermined greater good. It is the kind of law that led Judge Bee to surrender Thomas Nash and that impelled the Spanish authorities (and American slaveholders) to seek the return of the *Amistad* captives. It is the law of power, designed to deter prohibited behaviors or, where that is not possible, to satisfy the very human demand for vengeance. Where the demand for vengeance runs high, as it certainly did in the case of alleged camp guards like Fedorenko and Demjanjuk, attention to facts that might exonerate the accused runs low. What the accused actually did mattered less than what his choices could be made to symbolize.

* * *

While the deportation proceeding wound its way through the courts, OSI tried to persuade the Israeli government to ask for Demjanjuk's extradition. This effort began in January 1982 when an OSI delegation led by Neal Sher visited the Ministry of Justice in Jerusalem, but they encountered stiff resistance.[56] In many ways, Israeli officials understood the larger questions posed by renewed war crimes trials better than their American counterparts. They had wrestled with the moral ambiguities of prosecuting Nazi collaborators during the 1950s when they tried several Jewish kapos for brutal acts committed against fellow prisoners.[57] Following that experience, the Israelis had resolved to focus their energies on major organizers of the Holocaust whose responsibility was clear, whose depravity was beyond doubt, and who were more than mere cogs in the Nazis' killing machine. Indeed, after Eichmann was hanged in 1962, the Israeli government ceased to prosecute any Holocaust cases.

There were many reasons for this policy, not the least of which was that Israel did not have many extradition treaties and had been roundly criticized for going outside the law in kidnapping Eichmann. During the 1960s, Israel established diplomatic relations with West Germany, received substantial reparations from that country, and sought to persuade its government to assume responsibility for trying Nazis, including those who had run Treblinka. At that time Israel also had no need to educate its people about the Holocaust; a majority of them were refugees from it. Many did not want to be reminded of the old pains but preferred to focus their energies on raising new families and creating a secure home for them. By 1973, Israel had proven that Jews could defend themselves, and Israeli leaders may have wished to spare the founding generation from having to answer the painful question: Why did members of the older generation not fight back more than they did?

Punishing Eichmann had posed no moral difficulties for Israel's new legal system; he had had some alternatives and was not, as he claimed, just following orders. Punishing mere cogs in the Nazi killing machine raised more difficult questions, because the moral line between a Ukrainian guard and a Jewish prisoner who led others to their deaths was not always clear. Each was a Nazi captive; each was subject to instant execution, and each had to "collaborate" in order to survive.[58] Renewed war crimes trials would also ask a new generation whose moral stamina had not been tested under comparable conditions to second-guess the awful choices made by people trapped in insane circumstances, where the only "law" was survival, and the only unquestionably "moral" choice was suicide.[59]

The Israeli government also knew that prosecuting any war criminals would trigger demands for more such prosecutions, drawing Israelis back toward moral questions they had tried to put behind them. Thus, when Neal Sher of the American OSI appeared in Jerusalem in April 1983 to propose the extradition of Valerian Trifa, a former leader of Romania's Iron Guard who had incited pogroms in Bucharest, the Israeli government refused. It even stood by its refusal after a former U.S. Justice Department investigator working for the Simon Wiesenthal Center leaked news of the refusal to the press and Gideon Hausner, Eichmann's prosecutor, attacked the decision publicly.[60]

However, the pressure from Holocaust remembrance groups did not let up. On the contrary, their numbers and influence grew dramatically in the 1970s and 1980s. New histories documented not only the extent of the atrocities, but the failures of the allied governments to pursue war criminals. Shocked by how little both German and Jewish youth actually knew of the Holocaust, Jewish leaders in the United States and Europe decided that the Holocaust had to be remembered. Remembrance groups were created, monuments constructed, and museums planned. Much of the demand was driven by extreme right-wing claims that the Holocaust never happened. However, some of the demand also came from extreme Jewish groups, like the American Jewish Defense League, which demanded vengeance at any price.[61]

In the face of this pressure, the Israeli government finally agreed to prosecute some lesser Nazis and their collaborators. However, to reduce the number of cases, minimize the moral difficulties, and assure legitimacy of the new prosecutions, it set three conditions. First, the accused must have committed murder with his own hands. Second, he must be relatively young and in good health. Third, there must be Jewish eyewitnesses who could testify about the crimes in Israel.[62]

The Demjanjuk case met all three criteria. If he was Ivan the Terrible, he also met an earlier test, which was that he would be a figure of some symbolic significance. So after a six-month delay, the Israeli government finally asked for his extradition, in late October 1983.[63] The request was heard in Cleveland by Judge Frank Battisti, who had already decided some of the issues in the course of stripping Demjanjuk of his citizenship.

* * *

In most criminal trials, proof of identity and criminality merge. The crime is relatively recent; memories are presumed to be fresh, and the risk of mistaken identity is less because alibis are easier to prove when the trial takes place close to the locus of the crime. As time elapses, however, the risk of mistaken identifications increases, and the standards of probable cause should be adjusted accordingly, especially where the accused is to be sent across seas to stand trial in a foreign legal system, with all of the expense and evidentiary problems that entails. Fairness to the accused should impel the extradition judge to be certain that the government has the right man.

In Demjanjuk's case, Judge Battisti had no doubts. Having heard the testimony of Ivan's victims at the denaturalization proceeding, he was convinced that Demjanjuk was Ivan. Moreover, Demjanjuk, unlike Walus, had done nothing to prove otherwise. On the contrary, he had clearly lied on his immigration and naturalization papers, and he seemed unwilling and unable to invent a plausible alibi. On April 15, 1985, Battisti certified that the former auto worker could be extradited.

Analytically, Battisti recognized the need to distinguish between probable cause of identity and probable cause of criminality, but his prior experience led him to set the same low threshold of proof.[64] The crucial issue before Battisti was whether the evidence against the accused was "competent and adequate,"[65] and the law of evidence in extradition proceedings continued to load this determination in favor of the state and against the accused. The requesting state could present witnesses and rely on properly authenticated depositions and documents for its proof,[66] but the respondent could not present any documents disproving the government's claims.[67] Demjanjuk's lawyers could present "explanatory" evidence, but the judge refused to allow them to present experts who might demonstrate that the photographs had led witnesses to confuse Demjanjuk with the Ivan they remembered. Nor would Battisti allow the defendant to argue that he could not have committed crimes at Treblinka because he had been elsewhere at the time. Under U.S. extradition law, that was considered an alibi and could only be presented at trial.[68]

Finally, Battisti noted that the government only had to make out a prima facie case that Demjanjuk was Ivan.[69] For this purpose, he said, even affidavits by persons not present to testify would suffice.[70] The survivors could not be cross-examined about how they had come to identify Demjanjuk as Ivan. OSI did not have to present the Trawniki card, and the defense could not question its authenticity.[71]

Lost to history was John Jay's decisive rejection of Benjamin Franklin's ill-advised 1784 convention with France, which had attempted to make a consul's certificate of a man's identity irrebuttable. Such reliance on formal documents, Jay had persuaded Congress, "does not comport with the genius and spirit of our constitutions or our laws; both of which secure to every inhabitant and citizen the inestimable privilege of offering, in our tribunals, every species of legal evidence that may tend to elucidate the merits of the cause before them."[72]

Given the low burden of proof, OSI had no difficulty persuading the court that the accused was extraditable. As proof that Demjanjuk was Ivan, they offered the unrebutted affidavits of four Israeli survivors of Treblinka. Unlike Judge Roettger in *Fedorenko*, Judge Battisti was willing to accept these statements without testing the witnesses' memories in court. He even accepted the statements of two survivors whose recollections Roettger had found not credible in *Fedorenko*.[73] For extradition purposes, OSI argued, the Trawniki card that placed Demjanjuk at a different camp was irrelevant,[74] and Battisti evidently agreed. However, he used the photo on the card as evidence of what Demjanjuk looked like in 1942–1943 and concluded that the "obvious and striking resemblance" between that photo and the sixty-four-year-old Demjanjuk confirmed the eyewitnesses' identifications.[75]

Beyond the question of identity, there was the issue of whether Israel had jurisdiction to try Demjanjuk for offenses committed outside its territory and before Israel itself had been born. Battisti ruled that it did, on the theory that war crimes and crimes against humanity were, like piracy, "universal" and therefore within the jurisdiction of any nation's courts.[76]

Battisti's analogy to the law of piracy was not exact, because Ivan's crimes, unlike those of stereotypic pirates, were committed inside the territorial jurisdiction of a nation. In truth, the analogy was very poor, because most pirates and hijackers commit their crimes on the ships or planes of some state and are tried in courts of that state under a quasi-territorial concept of jurisdiction. In the case of both pirates and war criminals, "universal jurisdiction" is asserted when territorial jurisdiction (or its equivalent) exists but cannot (or will not) be exercised.

In the normal course of events, OSI and Battisti should have expected Poland, not Israel, to have requested Demjanjuk's surrender. OSI, however, did not ask Poland to request his extradition because the United States did not have an extradition treaty with that country. If OSI and Battisti thought that jurisdiction over Ivan's crimes was really "universal," they could have tried him themselves. But the Justice Department was not willing to accept that responsibility. Nor was OSI's mandate to do justice. Its job was to drive ex-Nazis from American soil. So no trial by the United States was proposed. Instead, trial by Israel was arranged.[77]

Battisti refused to extradite Demjanjuk for "manslaughter and malicious wounding," since trial for these offenses were barred by both the U.S. and Ohio statutes of limitations.[78] However, he did permit surrender for "murder," even though the specific (and retroactive) Israeli statute under which he would be tried punished "crimes against humanity" and "against the Jewish people."[79] The labeling problem that had so concerned Jefferson did not concern Battisti. If a person could be extradited for murder, the judge reasoned, he certainly could be surrendered for mass murder, which was covered by the Israeli statute.[80]

The judge easily dismissed claims that the alleged offenses were "political," and therefore exempt from extradition. "The murder of Jews, gypsies and others at Treblinka was not part of a political disturbance or a struggle for political power within the Third Reich," he ruled. "The murders were committed against an innocent civilian population in Poland after the invasion of Poland was completed."[81]

But just in case, Battisti also embraced the wanton crimes exception and applied it to genocide. "The . . . United States does not regard the indiscriminate use of violence against civilians as a political offense," he wrote,[82] adding, on analogy to the laws of war, that " 'Surely an act which would be properly punishable even in the context of a declared war or in the heat of open military conflict cannot and should not receive recognition under the political exception to the Treaty.' "[83] By embracing this view, Battisti extended to genocide an exception developed by the Second,[84] Seventh,[85] and Ninth Circuits[86] to deal with terrorists.[87]

Demjanjuk's attorneys promptly challenged the extradition decision by filing for a writ of habeas corpus. The petition was assigned to Judge Thomas D. Lambrose, but he handed it to Judge Battisti on the theory that it was "related" to the extradition decision.[88] Demjanjuk's attorneys then asked Battisti to recuse himself, on the ground that a judge should not review one of his own decisions. Battisti refused and eventually denied their petition.[89] He ruled, consistent with precedent, that he was bound to affirm his previous finding of probable cause if *"any* evidence as to probable cause exists."[90] Moreover, he said, the issue of misidentification could not be considered by a habeas court.[91]

Five months later, the Court of Appeals for the Sixth Circuit upheld these rulings, again confirming that the modern law of extradition was heavily loaded against the accused.[92] It was a decision the judges would come to regret, because they had authorized the surrender of the wrong man.

CHAPTER 19

Ivan Who? Getting the Wrong Man

We hold that the OSI attorneys acted with reckless disregard for the truth. . . . This was fraud upon the Court.

U.S. Court of Appeals for the Sixth Circuit, 1993

On February 27, 1986, John Demjanjuk became the first person ever extradited to Israel from the United States or any other country to stand trial for Holocaust-related crimes. Because his extradition was engineered by the United States, Israeli prosecutors found themselves unprepared to file an indictment. When he descended the airplane's steps in manacles, they had not even begun preparations for his trial.[1] The prisoner was held in solitary confinement for six months while the case against him was assembled, and another six months while the defense prepared for trial.[2]

Under Israeli law, trial by jury was not an option. Demjanjuk would be judged by a panel of three judges, in a theater converted into a courtroom to accommodate hundreds of reporters and busloads of Israeli students and soldiers. The proceedings would be broadcast to millions by radio and television. The court and prosecutors had a nation to educate. Most Israelis living in 1988 had been born after the Holocaust.

In Cleveland, Ohio, Demjanjuk had been extradited to face charges of murder; in Jerusalem, he would be tried for crimes against humanity and crimes against the Jewish people. The language of Israel's Nazis and Nazi Collaborators Law, as well as the label "Ivan the Terrible," guaranteed that Demjanjuk could not be tried as an ordinary criminal. He had become a symbol of Hitler's "Final Solution," and was destined to be tried as such.[3] For better or worse, Demjanjuk's prosecution would be a show trial.[4]

The trial did not begin, as Battisti's extradition hearing had, with a narrowly focused inquiry into whether the government had the right man. Nor did it open with testimony about specific murders, or the accused's alleged role in the torture and gassing of hundreds of thousands of nameless victims. Instead, the court allowed Ytzhak Arad, a distinguished historian of the Holocaust, to paint a broad picture of the rise of the Nazi Party, the construction of the concentration camps, and the roles played at them by the SS officers, Ukrainian guards, and work prisoners. None of these facts was in dispute. The defense had not denied that Treblinka' abattoir or Ivan the Terrible existed. It simply asked that these highly prejudicial facts not contaminate the threshold question, which was whether John Demjanjuk was really Ivan the Terrible. But this was not to be. With all the risks of prejudice, the story of the Holocaust had to be told first. Then the prosecution was allowed to tell the court what the sadistic Ivan had done, again without first proving that the man in the dock was Ivan.

Five camp survivors who had identified Demjanjuk as Ivan from photographs they had been shown in 1978 were put on the stand. The first to testify was Pinhas Epstein, whose testimony against Feodor Fedorenko had been rejected by a U.S. judge in Florida eight years earlier as not credible.[5] For eleven months, Epstein had dragged corpses from the gas chamber where Ivan worked to the burial pit where they were burned. Among other things, he described how Ivan had tortured inmates suspected of plotting an escape by breaking their arms, hands, and legs with an iron pipe before they were hanged. He also told how Ivan had ordered a Jewish worker to rape a girl of twelve or fourteen, and lashed him with a whip until he took off his pants and mounted her. But the act was not performed, he said; the girl was shot instead.[6] Only after this presentation was Epstein asked to identify John Demjanjuk as Ivan. He did so easily, even though he admitted that he had never heard Ivan called Demjanjuk at the camp.[7] Asked how he could be sure he had the right man, Epstein replied: "I see Ivan every night. My poor wife. I dream of Ivan every night. I envision him every night, he is imprinted in my memory." Then, moments later, he glared at Demjanjuk and pounded the witness stand with his fist: "There he is! There he is! There he is!"[8]

Four other survivors also identified Demjanjuk as Ivan. Two of them, Gustav Boraks and Josef Czarny, worked in Camp One, and thus had relatively little contact with Ivan, but a third, Yehiel Reichman, had seen Ivan often in the course of extracting teeth from the corpses.[9]

The most important witness was Eliyahu Rosenberg, whose job was to pack sand under the doors of the chamber before the gas was pumped in, and then to haul the corpses out afterwards. He also washed blood from the chambers. Rosenberg had been positioned to know Ivan well. On one occasion, Rosenberg said, Ivan had ordered him to copulate with a corpse—an order that was countermanded by an SS officer—and on another occasion Ivan whipped him for stealing some bread. "I would see him holding a sort of sword in his hand, . . . and sometimes he would cut off a piece of nose, a piece of ear, stab, you just cannot comprehend why, why."[10]

The most chilling moment at the trial came after Rosenberg's testimony, when he was asked to identify Ivan. He asked the defendant to remove his glasses, and Demjanjuk did so. Then Demjanjuk asked Rosenberg if he would come closer and take a really close look. Rosenberg agreed, but as he approached the defendant's box, Demjanjuk suddenly grinned, offered his hand, and said "Shalom." Horrified, Rosenberg screamed "Murderer! Bandit! How dare you put out your hand to me." In the third row of the theater, Rosenberg's wife fainted and had to be carried out by the police.[11]

Returning to the witness stand, Rosenberg positively identified Demjanjuk as Ivan. "This is Ivan. I say so unhesitatingly and without the slightest doubt. Ivan from Treblinka. The man I am looking at now. I saw those eyes, those murderous eyes."[12]

Rosenberg's memory of what went on in the camp may have been substantially accurate, but there was a problem with his identification of Demjanjuk that should have caused the judges pause. In separate statements given in 1945 and 1947, Rosenberg had described how, during the August 2, 1943, uprising he had broken into the engine room with several other prisoners and had seen another prisoner kill Ivan by hitting him on the head with a spade.[13] Now, more than forty years later, he was certain that the man before him was Ivan. His earlier statements were wrong, he said. He had not actually seen Ivan die; he had been throwing blankets over a barbed wire fence at the time.[14]

Ytzhak Arad, the historian who testified for the prosecution, accepted this explanation, explaining away the inconsistency as mere wishful thinking. However, when Yoram Sheftel, Demjanjuk's Israeli lawyer, asked whether the survivors' identifications of the accused might also be "wishful thinking," Judge Dov Levin barred Arad from answering. "That is a question," he said, "for a psychologist, not a historian."[15]

The defense did call a psychologist, but not before Mark O'Connor, their chief American attorney, attempted by an extraordinarily insensitive cross-examination to erase all moral distinctions between Ivan, who stabbed, beat, and gassed his prisoners, and Rosenberg, who had to stand by helplessly as they were herded into the chambers, and then had to pack the doors with sand. Whether the point of this inquiry was to discredit the witness or to imply that Ivan was also a victim is not clear, but it did neither. It only compounded the cruelties that Rosenberg had already suffered, detracted from evidence that Demjanjuk was not Ivan, bolstered the sense that he could have been, or pleaded for a mindless relativity.[16]

Against this background, it was perhaps too much to expect that anyone could have cast effective doubt on the identification of Demjanjuk as Ivan, but Willem A. Wagenaar, the Dutch expert on the psychology of line-ups and photographic displays, tried. His analysis, later turned into a book entitled *Identifying Ivan*,[17] was extraordinarily systematic. Wagenaar could not prove that any one of the eyewitnesses was absolutely wrong in his identification, but he did establish a substantial possibility that they were all inadvertently led to identify Demjanjuk as Ivan by the way they were recruited and shown pictures by Israeli police. In other words, while Wagenaar could not prove that Demjanjuk was not Ivan, he could show that the eyewitness identifications were not sufficiently reliable to be trusted as the sole basis for establishing his identity as Ivan beyond a reasonable doubt.

Moreover, as Wagenaar's book would document in detail, a number of other survivors who had been shown the same photographs could not recall Demjanjuk at all.[18] This information was not made available to the defense or the court at any proceeding. In other words, both Israeli and American prosecutors believed what they wanted to believe and buried potentially discrediting evidence in their files.

So, too, did the courts. They could have looked upon the issue of identity as an exercise in probabilities, weighing the positive identifications against the non-identifications. But courts do not normally do this. No less than lawyers, judges employ a theory of truth that often excludes inconvenient facts. In Demjanjuk's case, the judges and prosecution analogized the survivors' identification of Demjanjuk to what longtime classmates might do at a reunion. In such situations, the judges reasoned, none of the precautions used at ordinary criminal line-ups or photo sessions would be necessary.

But the survivors who placed Demjanjuk at Treblinka did not pick him out of a crowd on the street or at a reunion. Some responded to an advertisement seeking persons who might be able to identify Ivan of Treblinka, and were thus predisposed to find in the photographs someone who looked like Ivan if Ivan himself was not pictured. They talked with each other at their own reunions and while traveling to America to testify.[19] The photographs they were shown initially were not well selected or grouped so as to assure that viewers would not mistakenly claim someone was Ivan because he had Slavic features.

Israeli police would later say, in their defense, that they simply did what OSI asked them to do, and OSI simply asked for what police departments generally do. Unfortunately, as Wagenaar would demonstrate in his book, the art and science of photo displays is in its infancy and is thus wide open to unintentional, as well as deliberate, abuse. Given that the Ivan they knew had an oval face, a thick neck, and protruding ears, the probability was great that the survivors would be drawn to pictures of the man with these features and call him Ivan.

Moreover, because the survivors' descriptions of Ivan's atrocities were so vivid and credible, and were so consistent with vivid and credible accounts of the larger Holocaust, the judges predisposed themselves, and most observers, to want to accept the survivors' impassioned belief that Demjanjuk was Ivan, without further corroboration. Being so predisposed, it was relatively easy for the judges to accept the prosecution's supposition—and it was nothing more than a supposition—that the Trawniki ID card must have been wrong or incomplete to place Demjanjuk at Sobibor when survivors as convincing as Rosenberg swore he was at Treblinka.

But this supposition was not the only basis for the judge's belief that Demjanjuk might be Ivan. When Demjanjuk took the stand in his own defense, and tried to explain that he was a POW at Chelm when he was allegedly at Treblinka and Sobibor, he was totally unconvincing. On the contrary, by what he said and did not say, by what he could and could not remember, he left the powerful impression that he had, indeed, been a death-camp guard somewhere.[20]

At trial, the defense could not shake the authenticity of the Trawniki card or its photograph,[21] despite the prosecution's inability to offer any "chain of custody" evidence that might establish its authenticity. After the trial, a German forensic laboratory would conclude that the card was a forgery,[22] but the Israeli judges did not recognize any need for independent forensic tests.

Authentic or not, the card did not place Demjanjuk at Treblinka. Only the witnesses could do that, and on the basis of probabilities, their identifications—as opposed to their atrocity stories—could not establish beyond a reasonable doubt that the accused was Ivan. Morover, if the card was authentic and accurate, then it proved that the witnesses were mistaken to place Demjanjuk at Treblinka from July 1942 to August 2, 1943, because the card indicated that he had been transferred to Sobibor on March 27, 1943.

But courts do not require that every element in the chain of evidence be established beyond a reasonable doubt. Nearly all findings of guilt are a mishmash of probabilities, suppositions, and moral certainties, and so it was with Demjanjuk. The judges believed what they wanted to believe, and what the show-trial circumstances demanded they believe. In April 1988, despite the many reasons not to trust the eyewitnesses' memories, the court found Demjanjuk guilty as charged and sentenced him to die by hanging.[23]

* * *

Under Israeli law, all death sentences are automatically reviewed by the Supreme Court. At this point, Yoram Sheftel, an Israeli attorney, took over the defense. He recruited Dov Eitan, a former district judge, to assist him. But on November 28, 1988, a week before the appeal was to be heard, Eitan fell to his death from the fifteenth-story window of a building one block from his office. According to the police, who conducted a brief investigation but no autopsy, Eitan committed suicide. His wife does not believe he was murdered but said that he had received death threats for representing Demjanjuk and may have been driven to jump by a blackmailer who threatened to expose what she would only characterize as a "personal matter."[24]

At Eitan's funeral on December 1, acid was thrown in Yoram Sheftel's face by a seventy-year-old man who had lost a number of relatives at Treblinka. The attorney's left eye was severely burned (he was able to regain some sight in the eye through surgery).[25] These attacks on the attorneys, which had followed vitriolic criticism of them in the press, caused the Supreme Court to put off the appeal for a year and a half. During this time the Soviet Union fell apart and new evidence emerged from the files of the KGB. The new evidence came from the KGB's file on Feodor Fedorenko. In it were reports on the interrogations of twenty-one Soviet citizens who, like Ivan, had worked at Treblinka under the Nazis during World War II. Interrogated by the KGB between 1944 and 1961, all recalled a gas chamber motorman named Ivan. But the Ivan they recalled was not John Demjanjuk; he was Ivan Marchenko. Almost as significant, none of the statements placed Demjanjuk at Treblinka. Indeed, they did not mention him at all.

Demjanjuk's son, John Jr., had tried unsuccessfully to obtain these statements during a trip to the Crimea in September 1990. Their existence also came to the attention of Michael Shaked, one of the Israeli prosecutors, after Demjanjuk's conviction. Shaked went to Moscow in December 1990 to read the documents, and by March 1991 had copies of them in Jerusalem. Five months later, the prosecutors braved a firestorm of protest to turn this material over to the Israeli Supreme Court, effectively admitting that they had convicted the wrong man.

The statements by former guards confirmed the survivors' testimony about Ivan's savagery, but they consistently described Ivan Marchenko and Nikolai Shalayev as the men who had operated the gas chambers. Shalayev's confession was particularly significant, because it said that in June 1943, two months before the prisoners revolted at Treblinka, he and Marchenko were transferred to Trieste, Italy, where they guarded political prisoners.[26] He last saw Ivan in Fiume the spring of 1944, when Marchenko escaped the Nazis and joined the Yugoslav Communist partisans.[27]

During the fall of 1991, the Israeli Supreme Court received copies of more confessions of former Treblinka guards, most of whom were later shot by the Soviets as war criminals. By June 1992, the court was in possession of sixty-one statements, some dated in the 1960s and 1970s.[28] Of these, at least thirty-seven identified Ivan as Marchenko. None identified Demjanjuk as Ivan.

If true, these statements proved that John Demjanjuk was not Ivan the Terrible; nor was he a guard at Treblinka. They also established that two American courts and one Israeli court had relied on mistaken identifications by six camp survivors and one Nazi. In addition, one statement indicated that survivors like Rosenberg were wrong when they claimed, shortly after the war, that Ivan had been killed in the August 2 uprising. According to Shalayev, Ivan and he had left the camp two months earlier.[29] In December 1991, Demjanjuk's son-in-law, Edward Nishnic, and Jaroslaw Dobrowolskyj, a Ukrainian-born attorney from Detroit, went to Ukraine, to the city of Kryvy Rog, where they found Marchenko's daughter. She later supplied them with his wedding picture, which, when placed next to Demjanjuk's 1951 immigration photograph, revealed distinct similarities. Both men had oval faces, short necks, and protruding ears.[30]

Confronted with this new evidence, the survivors stuck to their identifications. The prosecutors changed their argument. Ignoring the fact that Demjanjuk had been extradited solely for alleged murders committed at Treblinka, the prosecutors insisted that his conviction should be upheld on the ground that he had been at Sobibor.[31]

Ivan the Terrible he wasn't, but Ivan the Less Terrible he might have been. The new documents did not support his claim that he had sat out the war at Chelm; they indicated that he had been at Sobibor and Flossenburg. In addition to the original Trawniki ID card (obtained for the Court by Armand Hammer), the court now had a confession from Ignat Danil'chenko, a guard at Sobibor, which named an Ivan Demjanjuk as another guard but said nothing about his actions.[32]

Nikolai Malagon, another former guard, told Soviet interrogators in 1979 that he knew both Marchenko and Demjanjuk. Marchenko, he said, drove the gas chamber van, while an Ivan Dem'yanyuk cooked for the guards.[33] In addition, the Israel prosecutors also obtained a log book from the death camp at Flossenburg, Germany, indicating that a person named Demjanjuk—no first name given—had been issued a pistol. Two other Flossenburg documents listed a Demjanjuk, again with no first name, with the same serial number—1393—that appeared on the Trawniki card.[34]

But the accused could not be convicted merely for being at Sobibor or Flossenburg, and no survivor of either camp has been found who remembers him. Approximately twenty survivors of Sobibor were still alive in the late 1980s. One of them, Dov

Freiberg, polished the Ukrainian guards' boots but did not remember Demjanjuk. "If he was at Sobibor," Freiberg speculated, "he must have been small, maybe a short-timer. If he was one of the big sadists, destroying the people, I think I would remember him."[35]

But this lack of evidence did not slow the Israeli prosecution. "What we're dealing with here is a murderer, and it makes no difference whether he committed this crime at Treblinka or Sobibor," Shaked argued before the high court.[36] Justice Aharon Barak was not convinced: "We know nothing about him at Sobibor," he said. Then, in an apparent reference to the rule of specialty, the judge added: "If you do not have proof that he was at Treblinka beyond a reasonable doubt, there is no point in proceeding."[37]

* * *

By June 1992, the new evidence tending to show that the accused was not Ivan the Terrible was beginning to bother the U.S. Court of Appeals for the Sixth Circuit. Judges Pierce Lively, Damon Keith, and Gilbert S. Merritt had become so concerned that they might have cleared the wrong man for surrender that they took the unusual and probably unprecedented step of reopening the extradition case.[38] But their concern went much deeper. From other information in the press, they suspected that OSI had known from the beginning that Demjanjuk was not Ivan.[39]

This was serious business. Government prosecutors are not supposed to be unrestrained partisans; they are officers of the court. Their job is not to get convictions at any price, but to see that justice is done. If OSI's attorneys deliberately concealed evidence that Demjanjuk was not Ivan, leading one court to strip him of citizenship, another to authorize his deportation to the Soviet Union, another to authorize his surrender to Israel, and still another in Israel to convict him of sadistic war crimes and sentence him to hang, then they deserved not only to be disbarred, but to be jailed for fraud upon the court. They, and the U.S. government, would also owe heavy damages to Demjanjuk and his family for their sixteen-year legal ordeal, for the enormous cost of his legal defense, for the three years he had spent behind U.S. bars during the extradition and deportation proceedings and the six years he had spent in solitary confinement in Israel.

The first hard evidence that OSI might not have played fair with the courts was uncovered by John H. Broadley, a partner in the Washington, D.C., office of Jenner and Block, a prestigious and influential Chicago law firm. An attorney for railroads by trade, Broadley had agreed to represent the Demjanjuk family *pro bono* in their efforts to obtain documents from OSI under the Freedom of Information Act that could be used in Demjanjuk's defense at his trial in Israel. Years of correspondence had produced little, so in January 1987, a month before Demjanjuk was to go on trial for his life, Broadley sued the Justice Department in federal district court in Washington, D.C., asking for all potentially exculpatory documents in OSI's files.

Having worked at the Justice Department for fourteen years, Broadley had seen "a lot of result-oriented legal work, but nothing like OSI." At first hearing before Judge Louis Oberdorfer, the government's attorney argued that the search for potentially exculpatory documents would take a considerable amount of time, but when Broadley tried to identify which files to search first and to set up a schedule for the work, the government's attorney could not promise swift results. OSI was a civil litigating unit, the attorney said. "They didn't know what exculpatory material is."[40]

As the suit progressed, OSI excised extensive passages from the few documents they turned over to Demjanjuk's lawyer. They even blanked out the Department of Justice file numbers, which the defense was supposed to refer to in making further document requests. One set of documents was from the Ministry of Foreign Affairs of the USSR. The English translation was heavily censored, but the Russian version was not. Using what Russian he remembered from college, Broadley discovered that the blacked-out passages referred to one hundred pages of KGB interrogation reports on former camp guards that the Soviets had given OSI back in 1979. None of these reports had ever been shared with the defense or any judge in the denaturalization, deportation, and extradition cases.[41]

One of these reports of investigation contained the recollections of Ignats Danil'chenko, another guard who had been sent to Sobibor in March 1943. In 1949 he told Soviet interrogators that a Demjanjuk was already at that camp when he arrived and was there into 1944.[42] He also said that he saw this Demjanjuk herd prisoners while armed with a rifle, but he never saw him shoot anyone.[43]

Danil'chenko's confession contradicted eyewitness claims that Demjanjuk was at Treblinka in the spring and summer of 1943. It also contradicted Rosenberg's claim that Demjanjuk had been attacked and killed during the August 2, 1943, uprising during which Rosenberg escaped. OSI had possessed a copy of Danil'chenko's confession in 1979 but had not shared it with the court or the defense in any of the three cases brought in federal court by OSI against Demjanjuk. If Justice Department officials had not failed to excise the Russian-language version of the document they surrendered so reluctantly, it might never have become available to defense lawyers fighting to save Demjanjuk's life.[44]

In June 1987 the Demjanjuk family received additional assistance from an unusual source. A janitor had been throwing OSI's trash into the dumpster of a McDonald's Restaurant at 14th and K Street, NW. Unknown to him, a group of East European émigrés had been removing it, taking it home, and searching it on behalf of one or more other defendants. Demjanjuk's son and son-in-law were invited to join the search. In a garage in Northern Virginia, the two men put on gloves and coveralls and searched through the bags, covered with cheese, ketchup, and rotting meat, for anything relevant to the defense.

In one of the bags they found reports on the original interview with Otto Horn, prepared by the two OSI staffers who had helped OSI attorney Norman Moscowitz with the questioning and photographic display. The reports, by investigator Bernard Dougherty Jr. and historian George W. Garand, were written within days of the interrogation and were consistent with each other.

Dougherty's report stated that when Horn, whose videotaped affidavit had been crucial evidence in the extradition hearing, was shown the first set of eight photographs, he "studied each [photograph] at length but was unable to positively identify any of the pictures, although he believed he recognized one of them (not Demjanjuk). . . . The first series of photographs was then gathered and placed in a stack, off to the side of the table—with that of Demjanjuk lying face up on top of the pile, facing Horn." Then Horn examined the pictures in a second stack and "upon glancing at the earlier picture of Demjanjuk, identified them as the same person. As he continued to study the picture from the second set, Horn indicated that it certainly resembled the man that he had known as 'Iwan.' . . . After a few more moments of careful study, Horn positively identified the photographs of Iwan Demjanjuk as being the 'Iwan' that he knew at the gas chamber in Treblinka."[45] Garand's report was similar, but less detailed.[46]

Experts on photo identifications argue that this method of questioning is unduly suggestive—that it is a form of "leading the witness" to come to a desired conclusion. OSI investigators Dougherty and Garand may have thought so too; they went to some effort to describe a method of photo identification which could, if made available to the defense, discredit his identification. OSI attorney Norman Moscowitz may have understood this, for in the videotaped reinterview three months later, when asking Horn to recount the identification process, he specifically asked: "When you looked at those photographs—this other set—where was this first set of photographs?" Horn replied: "They had been removed again." A little later Moscowitz asked again: "At the time that you were looking at these photographs now in front of you . . . were you looking at the other set of photographs? No. Were those photographs anywhere in your view? No. They went back into an envelope and away."[47]

From this exchange, it would appear that the OSI attorney twice led his witness to commit perjury in order to cure the defect in his identification of Demjanjuk. By discarding both the originals and all copies of the reports that could have proven the perjury, OSI destroyed evidence of this crime.[48]

When Broadley complained of this failure to the Justice Department's Office of Professional Responsibility (OPR), it immediately began an investigation, not of the concealment or perjury, but of how the Dougherty and Garand reports had been obtained by the defense. At first the Justice Department suspected that the defense had burglarized OSI's offices, because Broadley had specified the file location of a document. Then they accused the Demjanjuk family of planting a "mole" in OSI's office. Finally, OPR cleared OSI of wrongdoing, blaming Demjanjuk's counsel for not taking depositions from Dougherty and Garand, and finding that their reports had been "negligently discarded."[49]

In the garbage retrieved from the dumpster, the defense also found a memorandum written by Martin H. Sachs, an OSI attorney, to his director, Neal M. Sher, on June 3, 1986, arguing against the release of any of the documents sought by the Demjanjuk family under the Freedom of Information Act on the ground that they might be needed to support deportation of Demjanjuk from the United States to the Soviet Union if the Israeli court failed to convict him.[50] To the defense, it appeared that OSI feared that disclosure of the Soviet reports in its possession would destroy any future attempt to deport Demjanjuk, by showing that OSI had not told the whole truth in previous proceedings.

Broadley was able to obtain copies of State Department cables from the U.S. Embassy in Moscow indicating that OSI's predecessor, the Special Litigation Unit of the INS, had received, as early as August 1978, information from the KGB's interrogations of Ivan Shevchenko and Pavel V. Leleko—two other Ukrainian guards.[51] In a 1981 summary of this information, OSI informed the Polish commission on Hitlerite crimes that Shevchenko had expressly identified Ivan Marchenko as the "motorist of the gas chamber." Leleko called him the "motor mechanic of the 'dushehubka.'"[52] In June 1992, the Justice Department finally admitted that it had received one of these two reports in full and the other in excerpts in 1978.[53] The same summary prepared by OSI for the Polish commission also indicated that the Justice Department knew by or before July 1981 that another former guard, Sergey S. Vasylyenko, had identified Ivan Marchenko as the "motor mechanic of the gas chamber."[54]

Broadley also obtained a State Department cable to the Polish war-crimes commission dated June 1981 indicating that the U.S. government was in possession of Soviet interrogation reports on Leleko and Vasylyenko—two on each. Thus, before Demjanjuk was stripped of his citizenship and cleared for deportation and extradition, OSI had documentary evidence that Marchenko, not Demjanjuk, was the Ivan they had denounced to the press.[55]

With the State Department cables in his possession, Broadley now demanded full disclosure of the thirty-one Soviet "Reports of Investigation," about one-hundred pages, that it had possessed since 1979. But the Department continued to stonewall, arguing that the court could not compel their disclosure under the Freedom of Information Act because they were "lawyers' work product." The argument was silly; OSI's lawyers had not put any work into these "products," but the tactic won the government more months of delay. Only when the trial in Israel was over and Demjanjuk had been convicted did the Justice Department release them. Even then, the department blacked out the names of the former guards, making further investigation by the defense impossible. None of the thirty-one statements placed Demjanjuk at Treblinka; four clearly identified Marchenko as Treblinka's Ivan, and all had been in OSI's possession before it had gone into U.S. court to claim that Demjanjuk, not Marchenko, was the sadistic Ivan of Treblinka.[56]

On February 25, 1990, the CBS television program *Sixty Minutes* broadcast the results of its own investigation of the Demjanjuk case. Among other people, CBS was able to interview Maria Dudek, a lifelong resident of a village near Treblinka, who had known "Ivan Grozny" when he came to her village to buy sex and vodka with gold taken from the Jewish prisoners. Grozny's real name, she said, was Ivan Marchenko.[57]

* * *

As this information and more gradually came out in the press, the U.S. Court of Appeals for the Sixth Circuit began to suspect that they had extradited the wrong man. In January 1992, Chief Judge Gilbert S. Merritt asked his clerk to request a response from the Justice Department. Six months later, when none had been received,

Merritt ordered the Demjanjuk extradition case reopened.[58] The court also appointed a special master to investigate whether OSI attorneys had committed fraud upon the court.[59] The willingness of the Court of Appeals to reopen the extradition case in Cleveland put great pressure on the Israeli high court in Jerusalem to take the new evidence seriously.[60] Shaked and other Israeli prosecutors did their best to rejustify the conviction of Demjanjuk on grounds that if he wasn't Ivan the Terrible of Treblinka, then he was Ivan the Less Terrible of Sobibor or Flossenburg. But they had no evidence that he had participated in any killings anywhere, and Demjanjuk had been extradited solely to answer charges that he was the Ivan of Treblinka. OSI might be able to persuade the Justice Department to waive the rule of specialty,[61] but even that was in doubt, now that the grounds for extradition were being reexamined for possible fraud upon the court.

The special master, District Judge Thomas A. Wiseman Jr., spent a year holding hearings and gathering information. His report, issued on June 30, 1993, established clearly that exculpatory information had been deliberately and systematically withheld from the defense for years. In his judgment, "the Soviet evidence, viewed in its entirety, casts a substantial doubt [that] Demjanjuk . . . was Ivan the Terrible of Treblinka's gas chambers."[62] However, Wiseman found no intentional wrongdoing on the part of OSI's attorneys. In reaching this judgment, he granted OSI's attorneys the benefit of every doubt, even as the number of its supposed mistakes and oversights reached almost ludicrous proportions.[63] Ignored also were the political pressures that members of Congress and Jewish American organizations had put on OSI to "get" Demjanjuk, the hardball litigation that OSI had mounted to limit pretrial discovery, and OSI's repeated efforts to evade attorney Broadley's document requests.

Wiseman recommended that the case be closed without restoring Demjanjuk's citizenship, overturning the extradition order, or punishing OSI's attorneys.[64] Nevertheless, his report was clear on the facts: important, exculpatory material had been withheld from Demjanjuk's lawyers.

Politically, these findings made it much easier for the Israeli Supreme Court to overturn Demjanjuk's conviction, which it finally did on July 29, 1993, five years after his conviction.[65] The court did not just overturn the conviction on grounds of "reasonable doubt"; it set the prisoner free, ruling that to retry him on different charges would continue the proceedings "beyond proper measure."[66] Israeli prosecutors agreed.[67] Wherever Demjanjuk worked for the death-camp system, prosecutors had no evidence implicating him in the slaughter. Perhaps he was a cook, perhaps he did more, but no one knew what he did, and the forty-year-old memories of death camp survivors, the justices now knew, could not be trusted. "The matter is closed," the court concluded, but "not complete. The complete truth is not the prerogative of the human judge."[68]

Back in the United States, OSI lawyers were furious and unrepentant. Demjanjuk "got off on a technicality," Director Neal Sher declared."[69] OSI immediately launched an effort to block Demjanjuk's return to the United States.[70] There was nothing wrong with the decision to extradite him, they declared, ignoring the special master's report;

therefore, the extradition should be treated as de facto deportation. Demjanjuk was free to go anywhere he wanted, they said in a blizzard of legal papers, but without American citizenship he was not free to reenter the United States. As a war criminal, he was barred from entry by the Holtzman Amendment, which the executive branch had exclusive authority to enforce.

These were not just OSI's views. The argument had been authorized by Attorney General Janet Reno, on the recommendation of Deputy Attorney General Philip B. Heymann, who had first consulted with Representative Charles E. Schumer (D.-N.Y.), chair of the powerful House Judiciary Committee. Schumer represented the same Jewish constituency that had pressed Congresswoman Elizabeth Holtzman fifteen years earlier.[71]

The Court of Appeals was not persuaded. The extradition and denaturalization cases had been decided mainly on accusations that Demjanjuk was Ivan the Terrible; he had a right to participate in their reopening.[72] The judges did not conceal their irritation with the executive branch's claim that it alone could decide Demjanjuk's fate. The judges' order had effectively sent him to Israel in the first place.[73]

Jewish organizations denounced the court's decision and urged the Justice Department to appeal it, all the way to the Supreme Court if necessary. But when the full Court of Appeals declined to reverse its three-judge panel, the Justice Department retreated and let Demjanjuk return home.[74]

On November 17, 1993, the Court of Appeals overturned its extradition decision, finding, contrary to the special master's opinion, that OSI had committed fraud upon the court. In a unanimous decision, the judges held that OSI attorneys had "acted with reckless disregard for the truth and for the Government's obligation to take no steps that prevent an adversary from presenting his case fully and fairly."[75] Specifically, the court found that the government should have produced the statements of two former Treblinka guards, Leleko and Malagon, which the Soviet Union had supplied in 1978, and which implicated Marchenko as the gas chamber operator. Whether the law required it or not, OSI should also have produced the list of Ukrainian guards supplied by Polish authorities in 1979, which placed Marchenko at the camp but not Demjanjuk. Finally, the lawyers should have disclosed the Garand and Dougherty reports discrediting the crucial photo identification by the former Nazi, Otto Horn.[76]

The judges did not conceal their contempt for OSI's "'win at any cost' attitude," which, they said, "contrasts sharply with the attitude and actions of the Israeli prosecutors, who were under domestic political pressures themselves. But for the actions of the Israeli prosecutors," the judges observed, "the death sentence against Demjanjuk probably would have been carried out by now."[77]

* * *

The lessons to be drawn from the Demjanjuk case are too obvious to dwell on at length. First, and most obvious, is the danger of allowing the Justice Department to represent foreign regimes in extradition cases. This role almost inevitably leads to conflicts of national interest that corrupt prosecutorial and judicial integrity.

Second, so long as Justice Department lawyers continue to represent foreign regimes, they should be forbidden to solicit extradition requests in order to satisfy political demands within the United States. Extradition requests should be initiated by foreign regimes; extradition should serve the ordinary criminal-justice purposes of those foreign regimes. American courts and prosecutors should have no other objectives than to see to it that those legitimate criminal-justice purposes are served.

Third, extradition and deportation should be kept separate, as a matter of practice and a matter of law. When one is used as a substitute for the other, as in the Doherty, Artuković, and Demjanjuk cases, justice gets corrupted and the purpose of the Justice Department is no longer to do justice but to "get" people.

Fourth, the shameful performance of the Office of Special Investigations should remind us of the dangers posed whenever special task forces are set up to "get" a particular class of criminal because political pressures demand it. Units that are evaluated solely on their record of "getting" symbolic figures like Andrija Artuković and John Demjanjuk inevitably become corrupted by their own zeal to satisfy political demands.

Fifth, the injustices committed by OSI in the Artuković, Walus, Fedorenko, and Demjanjuk cases should warn us yet again that justice is not served when members of an ethnic, racial, or religious group are allowed to dominate any branch of law enforcement. The government's obligation to do justice in each individual case is never the same as a group's desire to achieve social justice in politically freighted cases.[78]

Finally, so long as the Justice Department continues to "represent" foreign demands for extradition, the politics behind the cases are not likely to be discerned clearly. In Demjanjuk's case, Israel was drawn into a prosecution it had good reasons for not pursuing. Instead of developing the case themselves, Israeli prosecutors relied on the work of U.S. prosecutors, who had their own reasons not to do it well.[79] Had the entire case been handled from beginning to end by Israeli prosecutors, the U.S. courts would have been more appropriately skeptical of the evidence, and this miscarriage of justice, profoundly embarrassing to both governments, might have been averted.

To draw these conclusions is to carry no brief for war criminals. It is to carry a brief for justice and the integrity of American and foreign judicial proceedings. We will not always be able to punish suspected war criminals or terrorists, but we should be able to say that, in trying, we did not compound their crimes. We owe this obligation to our own integrity for, as Chief Judge Gilbert Merritt reminded OSI's lawyers, "in our law, each step must itself be just."[80]

CHAPTER 20

The Law of Stolen People I

Ruin can come to a society not only from the furious resentments of a crisis. It can be brought about in imperceptible stages by gradually accepting, one after another, immoral solutions for particular problems.

Eugene Rostow, 1952

It is a crime for private persons to receive stolen goods, but it is lawful for American courts to receive stolen people. It is unconstitutional for American courts to accept evidence that the government has obtained illegally,[1] but it is not unconstitutional for judges to try alleged criminals who have been brought to them by government or private kidnappers.[2] Such is the bizarre state of American law today.

Technically, courts do not approve of kidnapping. No court would authorize an abduction in advance; to do so would be to exceed the reach of their warrants.[3] But if a police officer (or private citizen) exceeds the limits of his authority and carries out the premeditated seizure of a human being in a foreign country without first demonstrating probable cause to an independent magistrate, most judges will pretend not to notice, even though the officer may beat the captive into submission, strip his family of his love and support, and imprison him for years in advance of trial. Occasionally a court will threaten not to hear a case if American officials are responsible for torturing an abductee,[4] but most of the time, judges simply look the other way.[5]

Abductions tend to occur most frequently when the abducting government's respect for international law, human rights, and the sovereignty of other nations is low. This was true of Nazi Germany, which conducted a number of kidnappings in the 1930s,[6] and of the Soviet Union and East Germany in the late 1940s. It seems equally true of the United States in the 1980s and 1990s.

Within the United States, judicial tolerance for abductions has tended to reflect contemporary attitudes toward international law, human rights, and the rule of law. For example, in 1886 abduction was first approved by the U.S. Supreme Court in *Ker v. Illinois*,[7] a decision that upheld the jurisdiction of the Illinois court to try an American abducted from Peru by a private detective who had transportation assistance from the U.S. Navy. At the time, the United States was preoccupied with domestic affairs and largely indifferent to the opinions of other nations.[8] The 1880s were also a time when most Americans showed little respect for the rights of racial minorities, including immigrants from China.[9] Due process was defined largely in terms of fair procedures at trial, not as the source of substantive liberties or pretrial protections against police misconduct.[10] The "exclusionary rule" had not yet been applied to non-testimonial evidence.

But it would be a mistake to think of judicial tolerance of abduction solely in terms of xenophobia or the low state of civil liberties for aliens and minorities. Abductions within the United States were also tolerated, and not just in sparsely policed states of the western frontier. State courts were divided on the practice,[11] but the Supreme Court accepted it in 1952, in *Frisbie v. Collins*.[12] Shirley Collins was wanted for murder in Michigan, and when Michigan police tracked him to Chicago, beat him with blackjacks, threw him in the trunk of their car, and took him back for trial, the high court winked, just as it had in *Ker*.

The *Ker-Frisbie* doctrine, as this rule of noninquiry became known, should have been undermined by the Warren Court's "due process revolution" of the 1960s. Instead noninquiry continued, while the exclusionary evidence rule, which should have destroyed it, was itself gutted by the more conservative Burger and Rehnquist Courts.

A century after *Ker*, the United States was again hostile to alleged criminals and aliens, and its foreign policy again expressed contempt for international law,[13] the sovereignty of foreign states,[14] and the human rights of fugitives from noncommunist dictatorships in the Caribbean and Central America.[15] Successive Congresses stood by ineffectually while the Supreme Court tolerated violations of human rights and international law with the same moral myopia and parochialism that had blessed the abduction of Frederick M. Ker a century earlier.

* * *

Ker v. Illinois was not just symptomatic of a low point in public morality; it was also indicative of a formalistic approach to judging that involved mechanical adherence to outmoded legal precedents.[16] The cases on which the Supreme Court relied in *Ker* did not speak to the circumstances facing the legal system in the late nineteenth century. They had been decided a half-century earlier, at a time when the absence of extradition treaties had made abduction the only alternative to surrender by executive comity.

The chief American precedent was *State v. Brewster*, in which a county court sitting on the Vermont frontier in 1835 accepted jurisdiction over an alleged burglar who had been tracked across the border to Caldwell's Manor, Canada, captured, and brought back against his will by a group of irate Americans.[17] "[I]t is not for us to inquire," the judge said, citing no precedents, "by what means, or in what precise manner, [Brewster] may have been brought within the reach of justice." Whatever illegality violated Canadian law and sovereignty, he added, was for the political branches of the two governments to settle between themselves.[18]

The justices in *Ker* also relied on the British case of Susannah Scott, who had been brought back from Belgium by a British police officer armed with a warrant for her arrest.[19] Whether the officers showed that warrant to Belgian authorities and obtained their cooperation is not known, but Scott, unlike Ker, did not ask the trial court to decline jurisdiction. Rather, she sought release via habeas corpus, which enabled the prosecution to argue that the Habeas Corpus Act did not require the government to prove the legality of her apprehension, but only that the warrant under which she was being held was valid. The chief justice, Lord Tenterden, agreed with this narrow point, so the court never considered whether jurisdiction should have been declined because Scott had been abducted by a government officer in violation of British or Belgian law, or customary international law.[20] Ironically, had Scott been abducted for a civil offense, like failure to pay a debt, the court would have declined jurisdiction.[21] Then, as now, the courts would only tolerate the abduction of criminal suspects, perhaps because most were fugitives for whom probable cause could be assumed.

The Court in *Ker* did not need to follow either *Brewster* or *Scott*. Neither considered questions of constitutional due process. Both predated the creation of professional police forces, and neither anticipated the adoption of extradition treaties. Both ran counter to the dominant theory of extradition in America in the early nineteenth century, which was opposed to abduction except in the case of fugitive slaves. Unfortunately, a paint-by-the-numbers approach to precedent led judges to treat them as settled law.

* * *

Philosophically, the Americans who negotiated the first extradition treaties were whigs. They valued liberty, judicial procedures, and limitations on executive authority, and they accepted extradition to extend the rule of law, not undermine it with abductions.[22] The kidnapping of criminal fugitives—or the acceptance of foreign kidnappings on American soil—was not what a government of limited powers could do. Thus, when the French minister Jean Fauchet asked President Washington if he would "wink" at the abduction of Citizen Genêt, the president refused. Washington did not like Genêt, but he did not believe that his administration could—or should—allow kidnapping on American soil.[23]

The United States began its history adamantly opposed to the abduction of sailors from American ships by the British navy. Many of these sailors were deserters from the British fleet and faced military trials upon their return. Their seizure was a chronic source of conflict, and when the HMS *Leopard* attacked the USS *Chesapeake* in 1807 and abducted sailors from her crew, Jefferson ordered an embargo on trade with Great Britain and armed coastal forts. The abductions did not end, however, and the practice became one of the causes of the War of 1812.[24]

In 1837, war with Great Britain again loomed, in part because of an abduction of sorts. This time the seizure involved the steamship *Caroline*, which British raiders captured on the American side of the Niagara River and destroyed before it could run any more guns to Canadian rebels. Two Americans were killed in the process, and an outraged United States prepared for war. Fortunately, cooler heads prevailed and the Webster-Ashburton Treaty of 1842 defused the situation.[25]

From then on, the two governments agreed, with rare lapses, that extradition precluded abduction.[26] That agreement was possible because the United States and Canada respected each other's legal systems and needed routine cooperation more than occasional abductions. Thus, while the courts of both nations refused to question how the accused had been brought before them,[27] executive officials accepted the principle that abducted persons should be returned if the other country protested. Thus, in 1872, prior to the *Ker* decision, the British government protested the seizure of a Canadian by an American citizen. The United States arranged for the charges to be dropped, promising that it "would lend no sanction to any act of its officers or citizens involving a violation of the territorial independence or sovereignty of her majesty's dominions."[28] The promise was kept until 1991.[29]

The most celebrated abduction case in the nineteenth century involved Martin Koszta, a former captain in the failed Hungarian revolution of 1848, whose 1853 kidnapping in Smyrna (now Izmir), Turkey, by Austrian officials caused a major international incident.[30] Koszta had applied for American citizenship the year before in New York and had an arguable claim on the United States for protection,[31] but the Austrians were adamant and diplomatic efforts failed to win his release from the Austrian brig *Hussar*, at anchor in Smyrna Bay. The captain of the U.S. corvette *St. Louis* rolled out his guns and forced a surrender.[32]

The rescue was as much an act of war as the seizure of the *Caroline*, but it was enthusiastically backed by "Young America" nationalists in Washington. Secretary of State Marcy told the Austrian ambassador that to surrender political offenders would be "an act meriting the reprobation of mankind,"[33] and Congress voted the captain a medal.[34]

Not until the Civil War did the United States government succumb to the temptation of self-help. In 1861, a Union warship stopped the British mail packet *Trent* on the high seas and removed two Confederate commissioners. The British government protested the violation of its neutrality and ordered 8,000 troops to Canada in preparation for war. The Lincoln administration released the prisoners.[35]

Abduction by invasion was attempted in 1916, when Brig. Gen. "Black Jack" Pershing led a U.S. expeditionary force into Mexico in pursuit of Francisco (Pancho) Villa, one of several contenders in the Mexican Revolution. Villa had robbed several U.S. banks, ordered the murder of sixteen American engineers traveling in Mexico, and raided the town of Columbia, New Mexico. At the time, Mexico, like Peru in *Ker's* case, had no established government capable of administering the extradition treaty. The treaty had actually been suspended, along with diplomatic relations, when the Madero regime fell in 1913. Villa was never captured and Pershing's expedition was a fiasco.

During the Cold War, American officials were infuriated by abductions carried out by the East German secret police in the American sector of Berlin.[36] They also objected strongly when Soviet officials in New York tried to force two asylum-seeking teachers to return home.[37]

There is no record that American police have ever pushed unwanted persons over the border, or onto a ship or plane bound for a country waiting to punish them. In those rare instances in which U.S. officials have been tempted to circumvent the judicial safeguards of extradition with executive action, they have done so—as in Doherty's case—by using, or misusing, the law of deportation.[38]

Only once has the federal executive surrendered an alleged criminal to a foreign nation as a matter of executive comity. That occurred during the Civil War, when Secretary Seward made his much criticized decision to deliver the slave seller Arguelles to Spain.[39]

Until the 1970s, abductions were rare, and those that came to the attention of U.S. courts usually were carried out by private persons (or local police). The reason for this is plain. The federal executive did not believe that kidnapping was a legal or necessary law-enforcement measure. No U.S. extradition treaty or statute has ever authorized government kidnapping. On the contrary, the United States has ratified several international agreements promising not to engage in unlawful arrests and detentions.[40] However, violation of these treaties has never been held to grant an abductee standing to challenge the court's jurisdiction to try him.[41] Not until the 1980s did the United States attempt, by diplomatic correspondence or otherwise, to claim kidnapping as a legitimate law-enforcement option.

* * *

Despite the belief that kidnapping was not a necessary law-enforcement measure, there was one exception. Fugitive slaves could be abducted back to slavery by their owners before they did anyone any harm. Rebellious slaves were considered potential terrorists. Freedom for them in the North raised fears of slave revolts in the South, and few white Americans, south or north, wanted slave revolts.

Freedom for slaves just outside U.S. borders was equally intolerable to the white majority. In the late eighteenth and early nineteenth centuries, hundreds of black slaves fled into Spanish Florida, from which they staged cross-border raids, plundering white settlements and encouraging other slaves to join them.[42] The U.S. conquest of East Florida in 1817 was triggered, in part, because the Mikasuki Seminoles refused to allow U.S. troops to recover fugitive slaves from their territory.[43]

Slave owners demanded the right to recover fugitive slaves, much as they might recover runaway horses, and the Supreme Court complied. In 1842 the Justices refused to allow Northern states to protect free blacks from Southern slave catchers, by declaring unconstitutional a state "liberty law" under which a slave owner's agent had been convicted. The agent, Edward Prigg, had tried to obey Pennsylvania law in pursuing his quarry, first by obtaining a warrant and then by having a constable bring the fugitive before a Pennsylvania court. But when the judge refused to hear the case,

Prigg decided not to waste more time appealing, and he abducted Margaret Morgan and her children (including at least one who had been born free) back to Maryland and into slavery.[44]

Nothing in the Constitution or laws of the United States authorized the Morgan family's abduction. The fugitive slave provision of the Constitution contemplated the right of slave owners to make good their ownership claims in nonslave states but did not strip free states of their authority to establish procedures and standards of proof to protect free blacks, even if the measures did make the recovery of slaves more difficult and expensive.[45]

But the Supreme Court did not consider whether Margaret Morgan had been freed, or whether one or more of her children abducted with her had been born free.[46] Nor was it concerned with the plight of free blacks generally who could be mistakenly (or fraudulently) "returned" to slavery.[47] Toward their plight, as well as the plight of fugitive slaves, all of the justices but one turned a blind eye.[48] Writing for the majority, Justice Story claimed that laws governing the rendition of fugitive slaves were for Congress, not the states, to enact. As a result, free states like Pennsylvania were stripped of their authority to enact "liberty laws" to protect alleged slaves and their children from arbitrary capture and removal.

Abduction was permissible, the justices believed, because slaves (and free blacks) were, like seamen, a lower class of persons. Story, who was opposed to slavery, had no difficulty equating slaves to fugitive "idlers, vagabonds, and paupers" whom states could remove summarily.[49] To the pro-slavery Chief Justice, Roger Taney, fugitive slaves were "dangerous or evil-disposed persons."[50] Eight years later, Congress passed a new Fugitive Slave Law making the rule of noninquiry mandatory on all courts.[51]

* * *

Today, *Prigg v. Pennsylvania* is no more than a relic of a shameful past. But *Prigg's* rule of noninquiry, like the moral obtuseness of Capain Delano in Melville's *Beneto Cereno*, remains with us still. In 1993 the Supreme Court again approved the abduction of black fugitives and their forced return to poverty and oppression. In *Sale v. Haitian Centers Council*, the justices ruled that the U.S. government could seize Haitian refugees on the high seas, sink their boats, and return them, against their will, to the murderous regime they had tried to flee.[52] The *nonrefoulement* provisions of the U.N.'s Convention on Refugees[53] and the U.S. Immigration and Nationality Act[54] barred the forcible return of any refugee to conditions of persecution, but these were brushed aside, much like the "liberty laws" in *Prigg* a century and a half earlier.

In *Sale* as in *Prigg*, the political pressures were immense. The opposition to the northward migration of Haitians in the 1990s was as great, in its own way, as opposition to the movement of fugitive slaves in the 1840s, and much for the same reasons: The Haitians were poor, uneducated, and black. As a candidate for president, Bill Clinton denounced the interdiction of Haitian boat people on the high seas; as president, he continued the policy.[55] Like the abolitionists who defended the *Amistad* captives in the 1840s, students from Clinton's former law school took the Haitians' cause to court,[56] but the Supreme Court rejected their plea. The *nonrefoulement* principle, it said, only protects refugees who enter U.S. territory; the government is free to abduct them at sea.[57]

As in *Prigg*, only one justice acknowledged the plight of the fugitives. Dissenting, Justice Harry A. Blackmun admitted, as the Captain Delanos in the majority could not, that "the United States, land of refugees and guardian of freedom," was forcibly driving the Haitians "back to detention, abuse, and death."[58]

* * *

To defenders of abduction, the right to due process of law begins when the trial begins, not before. Judges have no business questioning how the accused was brought to court, any more than they should question what might happen to the accused were he or she to be extradited to a foreign land.

Critics of the *Ker-Frisbie* rule argue that judges are not mere bureaucrats who process cases blindly; they are responsible for the integrity of the legal system and can decline jurisdiction, when necessary, to avoid complicity in and deter executive misconduct. Theirs is not a theory of hermetically sealed judicial and executive branches, operating in isolation from each other. It is a theory of limited government, guaranteed liberties, and checks and balances adopted by the U.S. Constitution.[59]

The clash between these two perspectives can be seen most clearly in the contrast between two drug cases involving abductions, one from the Second Circuit, the other from the First. The Second Circuit case arose in 1974, before drug smuggling became the major crime-control issue in the nation. It involved an alleged heroin dealer, Francisco Toscanino, who claimed that he had been kidnapped in Montevideo by Uruguayan policemen in the pay of the United States, knocked unconscious, and taken to Brasilia. There he was questioned under torture for seventeen days by Brazilians who pinched his fingers with pliers, flushed alcohol in his eyes and nose, and forced other fluids up his anal passage. He was also shocked unconscious by jolts of electricity sent through wires attached to his earlobes and testicles. Toscanino alleged that his torturers worked for the U.S. Bureau of Narcotics and Dangerous Drugs and that an agent of the bureau occasionally participated in, or was present at, his interrogation.[60]

The Court of Appeals for the Second Circuit was disturbed by these allegations, which the U.S. government refused to confirm or deny.[61] The judges acknowledged that a "constitutional revolution" had occurred since *Frisbie* affirmed *Ker* in 1952. Due process now meant more than "the guarantee of 'fair' procedure at trial"; it barred "the government from realizing directly the fruits of its own deliberate and unnecessary lawlessness."[62] The *Ker-Frisbie* doctrine had been eroded by a series of decisions, starting with *Rochin v. California* in 1952, which reversed a conviction based on evidence obtained by holding the suspect down and forcibly pumping an emetic solution into his stomach.[63] "Regard for the requirements of the Due Process clause," the appellate judges in *Toscanino* said, quoting Justice Frankfurter in *Rochin*, "'inescapably imposes upon this Court an exercise of judgment upon the whole course of the proceedings [resulting in a conviction] in order to ascertain whether they offend those canons of decency and fairness which express the notions of justice of English-speaking peoples even towards those charged with the most heinous offenses.'" The court ruled that what Frankfurter had said about stomach-pumping in *Rochin* applied equally to torture in *Toscanino:* "'This is conduct that shocks the conscience.'"[64]

The underpinnings of *Frisbie,* the Second Circuit added, had been further weakened by *Mapp v. Ohio* (1961), which held that the due process clause of the Fourteenth Amendment forbade illegally obtained evidence from being introduced at trial in state courts.[65] The philosophy behind the exclusionary evidence rule, the judges pointed out, was best expressed by Justice Brandeis's famous dissent in *Olmstead v. United States:*[66]

> The court's aid ... is denied despite the defendant's wrong. It is denied in order to maintain respect for law; in order to promote confidence in the administration of justice; in order to preserve the judicial process from contamination. ...
>
> In a government of laws, existence of the government will be imperiled if it fails to observe the law scrupulously. Our Government is the potent, the omnipresent teacher. For good or for ill, it teaches the whole people by its example. Crime is contagious. If the government becomes a lawbreaker, it breeds contempt for law; it invites every man to become a law unto himself; it invites anarchy. To declare that in the administration of the criminal law the end justifies the means—to declare that the government may commit crimes in order to secure the conviction of a private criminal—would bring terrible retribution. Against that pernicious doctrine this court should resolutely set its face.

Accordingly, the Second Circuit concluded that due process requires "a court to divest itself of jurisdiction over the person of a defendant where it has been acquired as the result of the government's deliberate, unnecessary, and unreasonable invasion of the accused's constitutional rights."[67]

All of this, however, was dicta, comments unnecessary to the decision, and therefore not binding as precedent. The dicta only interpreted the due process clause of the Fourteenth Amendment and thus only applied to state courts and state cases like *Ker* and *Frisbie.* It did not apply to Toscanino, who was challenging in federal court an abduction ordered by federal agents. The analysis should have been the same, but the Second Circuit failed to extend its Fourteenth Amendment reasoning to the Fifth Amendment's identical clause, or to the Fourth Amendment's prohibition against the unreasonable seizure of persons. Instead, it decided that jurisdiction should be declined in a federal case like Toscanino's pursuant to the nonconstitutional supervisory powers that federal judges have over the federal government's administration of justice.[68] *Toscanino's* actual holding, then, was a narrow one, limited to preserving the integrity of *federal* courts from complicity in *federal* misconduct. Moreover, the holding did not focus on the claim that Toscanino had been tortured but on the allegation that he had been abducted by agents of the United States in violation of treaties meant to safeguard the sovereignty of Uruguay.[69]

For all its brave promise, *Toscanino* did little to extend the exclusionary remedy from stolen evidence to stolen people. It did not even hold, as many have assumed, that federal abductions violate the due process clause of the Fifth Amendment. It did not hold that federal abductions involving torture require federal courts to decline jurisdiction in exercise of their supervisory powers. The court's dicta was an eloquent warning to states, but its holding left federal courts within the Second Circuit free to admit abducted persons for trial so long as their kidnappings have been consented to by the foreign government whose sovereignty (or extradition treaty) had been violated.[70]

* * *

The *Toscanino* decision was widely applauded by legal scholars and human rights advocates, but it never took hold. Even Toscanino himself could not persuade the trial court that the abduction and torture he had suffered had been ordered by U.S. agents.[71] A few years later, a more conservative Second Circuit panel held that only "government conduct of the most shocking and outrageous character" would justify declining jurisdiction over an abductee.[72]

Toscanino's promise faded as more conservative jurists were appointed to the federal bench, as the Fourth and Fourteenth Amendments' exclusionary evidence rules were gutted,[73] and as the courts and public became increasingly hardened to allegations of police misconduct.[74] Most federal courts have refused to embrace either the dicta or holding in *Toscanino*. As a result, most abductees have been tried and convicted by federal courts, regardless of how badly U.S. agents or their surrogates treated them.[75] Not one has been released.

Typical of these cases was *United States v. Cordero*,[76] in which the U.S. Court of Appeals for the First Circuit held that two suspected cocaine smugglers lacked standing to challenge a violation of formal extradition procedures. "[E]xtradition treaties," Judge (and future Justice) Stephen Breyer observed, "are made for the benefit of the governments concerned," and the defendant has no right to complain when their violation results in her abduction and trial.[77]

Breyer's statement was partially true, but his conclusion did not necessarily follow. Extradition treaties are made for the benefit of governments or, more precisely, for peoples beset with crime and the need to recover fugitive criminals, but that does not mean that they do not also exist to protect individuals from arbitrary treatment. Judicial safeguards for individuals were not included in the Jay and Webster-Ashburton Treaties or in the statute of 1848 simply as the price our executive had to pay for the recovery of fugitives. They were part of the whig philosophy, which the executive proposed and supported. At no time during the formative years of American extradition law did the executive assert or reserve a power to abduct, even when extradition was not possible.[78]

Josephine Cordero and her pilot, William Sorren, were not abducted from Panama by American agents; they were seized by Panamanian officials after their expulsion had been requested by the Drug Enforcement Agency (DEA). They were not taken before a judge; after an abusive incarceration, they were hustled onto a plane that took them against their will to Venezuela, and then, with the permission of Venezuelan police, to Puerto Rico, where they were arrested. This "disguised extradition" was lawless executive action by foreign officials, carried out at the behest of the American authorities, but Judge Breyer saw no reason these irregularities should defeat the trial court's jurisdiction. American officials did not personally kidnap or abuse the defendants, or commit crimes in foreign lands. They just asked a friendly dictatorship to do that for them.

Nor did Breyer and his colleagues agree that the existence of extradition procedures precluded the use of more arbitrary modes of rendition. According to Breyer, "nothing in these treaties suggests that the countries involved *must* follow the extradition procedures set out in [them] when they return criminal defendants to the United States."[79] In other words, extradition treaties are not law; they are options. They are not meant to provide a measure of protection to presumptively innocent persons, so that the police of both nations cannot seize them in the night and spirit them off to foreign lands. They simply prescribe one of several procedures that a government may use, if it wishes. The U.S. government's obligation to obey the treaty and Constitution as U.S. municipal law ceases at the border, and a concomitant duty to obey foreign law never arises, despite what customary international law says, and despite the reservation of rights secured by the Ninth Amendment to the Constitution. If U.S. agents corrupt foreign policemen, that is not our courts' concern, because American judges have no obligation to defend the broader principle of government under law. They don't have to enforce customary international law; they just have to run the domestic criminal-justice mill. That is the essence of what Judge Breyer said in *Cordero*, in an opinion that would lay the foundation for the Supreme Court's endorsement of abduction in *Alvarez-Machain*.

The amorality of this approach is far from the ethic that led Jefferson, Washington, and Webster to refuse to engage in extradition with corrupt and unjust regimes. But American law enforcement was in its infancy then. As law-enforcement agencies grew and as international extradition became progressively easier, the institutional demand for exchanging fugitives grew stronger and more bureaucratized. With bureaucratization came resentment for the "niceties" of judicial procedures and a demand for ways to circumvent the legal processes of extradition. The United States accumulated extradition treaties with over one-hundred countries, and then circumvented those treaties in many instances with disguised extradition, as in the *Cordero* case. Indeed, by the 1970s there was probably more disguised extradition than lawful extradition.[80]

* * *

The popularity of kidnapping in modern times is largely due to the Israeli government's successful abduction of Adolf Eichmann from Argentina on May 11, 1960. There was no extradition treaty between Argentina and Israel at the time Eichmann was seized (although one was being negotiated); nor was there an Israeli warrant authorizing his arrest. The man who superintended Hitler's mass murder was abducted in a paramilitary, covert operation, probably by agents of the Mossad, although the Israeli government implied that they were private parties.[81]

Eichmann's abduction clearly violated international law and the domestic law of Argentina. Argentina expelled the Israeli ambassador and broke off diplomatic relations. The U.N. Security Council requested that Israel pay reparations,[82] which it did, virtually admitting that the abductors were government agents who had violated international and Argentine law.[83] Even so, the Israeli court, with its roots in the common law tradition, accepted jurisdiction, citing, among other cases, *Ker v. Illinois*.[84]

In time, the Eichmann decision would be cited by American advocates of abduction in less egregious cases. Together with the Entebbe raid, in which Israeli commandos rescued hostages from Uganda in 1976, Eichmann's abduction became the inspiration and justification for American self-help operations in the 1980s.

Under the Reagan and Bush administrations, the United States became the first country to adopt kidnapping as a national policy. The chief targets were alleged terrorists and drug lords, for whom there was little public sympathy. The initial plan focused primarily on Middle Eastern countries with which the United States had no extradition treaties, but which were known to harbor—and use—terrorists as national policy. Secondarily, there was a growing belief that abduction would be appropriate in countries like El Salvador and Colombia, where lawful authority was shaky or corrupt.

The abduction policy was rooted in the Reagan administration's frustration with not being able to do much about a series of terroristic attacks against Americans abroad. These included the 1983 bombings of U.S. embassies in Lebanon and Kuwait, the 1985 machine-gunning of off-duty Marines and U.S. businessmen in El Salvador, the hijacking of TWA flight 847 in June 1985, the hijacking of the *Achille Lauro* cruise ship that fall, and the machine-gunning of the Rome and Vienna airports that December.

Within the National Security Council, the dominant ethic was supplied by Colonel Oliver North and CIA Director William Casey. Having secretly sold weapons to Iran in order to fund the *contras* in Nicaragua (contrary to the Boland Amendments),[85] North and Casey had no qualms about kidnapping alleged terrorists or drug dealers. They were infuriated that some of the hijackers, including three who had seized TWA flight 847 and murdered Navy diver Robert Stethem, had been seen on the streets of Beirut. They wanted those killers taken, not just because they were murderers, but because their continued freedom was an affront to the super-power status of the United States.

* * *

The Reagan administration's first opportunity to avenge itself on Middle Eastern terrorists came not with the TWA hijackers, but with four PLO gunmen who seized the Italian cruise ship *Achille Lauro* on October 7, 1985.[86] As members of the Palestine Liberation Front (PLF), a more radical faction within the PLO, they had planned to use the ship for a raid on shore. But when a crew member saw their weapons, they were forced to seize the liner and improvise a way to freedom. They began by herding all the American, British, and Jewish passengers together and threatening to kill them if Israel did not release fifty Palestinian prisoners. Of the twelve Americans on board, one was singled out for execution. Sixty-nine-year-old Leon Klinghoffer, a Jewish American invalid, was wheeled in his chair to the ship's rail, shot twice, and thrown overboard.[87] Negotiations with the Egyptian government then commenced and, on the ship captain's assurance that no one had been harmed, Egypt agreed to grant the hijackers safe and secret passage to PLO headquarters in Tunis.

However, Israeli intelligence was listening to the Egyptian president's phone calls and informed the White House not only of the plan, but of the escape plane's number. Colonel North thereupon proposed a plan as daring and illegal as the Koszta rescue and the *Caroline* raid.[88] On the evening of October 10, four F-14 Tomcat fighters from the USS *Saratoga* intercepted the Boeing 737 near Crete and threatened to shoot it down if it did not land at the NATO base in Sigonella, Sicily. The airliner complied.

On the ground, in post-midnight darkness, the airliner was surrounded by fifty "armed and ready" American Delta Force commandos, who had arrived almost simultaneously on two C-141 troop transports. Their orders, direct from the White House, were to "arrest the terrorists" and take them to the United States. Before they could storm the airliner, however, their own planes were surrounded by Italian soldiers, whose orders were not to allow the Americans to remove the hijackers from Italian soil.[89]

A tense standoff ensued, during which American and Italian soldiers threatened each other with weapons.[90] Italy had the strongest legal claim to jurisdiction; the hijacking and killing had occurred on an Italian ship in international waters. Italy also had the most at stake diplomatically; to free the ship, passengers, and crew, Italy had agreed with Egypt to give the hijackers safe passage. Italy's resentment at the armed intervention was palpable; Rambo tactics might thrill Americans, but Italy would still have to share the Mediterranean with Palestinian gunmen after the abduction was over. In late-night negotiations, Prime Minister Bettino Craxi promised to prosecute the gunmen if the United States would back off.

Fortunately, the extradition treaty with Italy gave the American president a face-saving way out. While frustrated that the Delta Force could not complete its triumph, Reagan announced that he would seek the hijackers' extradition. He also urged the Italian government to arrest the PLO representatives traveling with them. The Egyptian government, now aware that Klinghoffer had been killed, allowed the Italians to take the four gunmen into custody but objected to the arrest of the PLO representatives, and Italy permitted them to escape. This infuriated the United States because it believed that one, Abul Abbas, also known as Mohammed Abbas Zaiden, had masterminded the hijacking. The United States rushed the Italians a warrant for his arrest, but the Italian government, on the advice of three judges, found the evidence insufficient to hold him.[91] Italy eventually tried and convicted the four hijackers,[92] but Abbas remained free.

* * *

Although furious at Abbas's escape, the Reagan administration was elated at the domestic applause it received.[93] Politically, the interception was a rare victory in a largely frustrating "war" against Middle Eastern terrorists, and during the following winter and spring, hawkish members of Congress and the administration pushed hard to make abduction more central to the counter-terrorism strategy.

In Congress, the most aggressive leadership came from freshman Senator Arlen Specter (R.-Pa.), who proposed legislation authorizing the attorney general to permit the CIA, the FBI, or the armed forces to conduct snatches on their own authority.[94] This was already legal and appropriate, the Senator argued (ignoring international and foreign law), because the Supreme Court had not rejected it in *Ker* and *Frisbie*. By his reasoning, the *Ker-Frisbie* rule was not just a rule of noninquiry; it was a grant of positive authority.

Specter's bill was opposed by two former federal judges, FBI Director William Webster and State Department Legal Adviser Abraham Sofaer. Both recognized the dangers and the illegalities. Webster was also concerned with the threat posed to cooperative relations with foreign police;[95] Sofaer worried that the bill would allocate this power to law-enforcement agencies the State Department could not restrain.[96]

The bill was also opposed by two successive deputy directors at the CIA, John McMahon and Claire George, who distrusted cowboys like Colonel North and William Casey, even as they worked with them to resupply the *contras*. In 1984 the agency had been required, against its better judgment, to assemble a counter-terrorism force of Lebanese, Palestinians, and other non-Americans, only to be embarrassed when renegade members of the group hired other Lebanese to car bomb the Beirut home of Party of God leader Mohammed Hussein Fadlallah. The cleric survived, but more than eighty other people were killed.[97]

* * *

In the public arena, the opponents of abduction appeared to win.[98] Congress did not enact Specter's bill. In the secret precincts of the Reagan White House, however, the cowboys prevailed. While Congress and the press thought that abduction was still an option to be explored, the president secretly authorized the CIA to kidnap criminal suspects.[99] This "finding," which violated the CIA's statutory mandate,[100] was signed in January 1986, about the same time that President Reagan authorized illegal arms sales to Iran. It allowed the agency not only to abduct alleged terrorists, but to sabotage their supplies, finances, travel, recruiting, and operations in foreign countries. A month later, Colonel North won approval to create a secret interagency committee called the Operations Sub-Group (OSG), to oversee kidnappings and other covert operations.[101]

In 1987 this secret authority was used by the CIA, for the first time, to lure a suspected terrorist to Cyprus and onto a yacht where FBI agents captured him. Their prey was Fawaz Younis (misspelled Yunis by the court), who with four other Lebanese militiamen had hijacked a Royal Jordanian airliner in Beirut on June 11, 1985. After severely beating several Jordanian sky marshals (in order to find their weapons), the hijackers demanded to be flown to Tunis, so that they could impose their demands on a summit meeting of the Arab League. But the Tunisian government would not permit them to land. After two days of flying around the Mediterranean, the hijackers had no choice but to return to Beirut. There Younis, speaking for the others, demanded that all Palestinians be removed from Lebanon and threatened to kill the passengers, one by one, if the demand was not met. It could not be met, and the hijackers finally released the passengers and crew. Amal militiamen then blew up the plane while Younis and his associates escaped in a waiting jeep.[102]

American jurisdiction over the crime was even less substantial than it had been in the hijacking of the *Achille Lauro*; only three of the plane's seventy passengers were Americans, and none of them was hurt. Younis did not belong to the PLO; he was an Amal militiaman opposed to the PLO, and he later claimed to have acted on orders from Nabih Berri, Justice Minister of Lebanon.[103] Unlike most hijackers, Younis lived openly in Beirut and seemed vulnerable to capture.[104] Sometime in the fall of 1986, the White House Sub-Group on Terrorism decided to make an example of him, thereby affirming President Reagan's pledge to terrorists: "You can run, but you can't hide."[105] The CIA, managing an informant supplied by the DEA, lured Younis to Cyprus and onto a yacht with promises of a lucrative drug deal. There, FBI agents posing as drug dealers patted him down, handed him a beer, and then "took him down."

Because the seizure took place in international waters, the Justice Department claimed that no nation's sovereignty had been violated. The claim was dubious; the sting was set up by the informant in the course of several days in Cyprus, and the yacht, "Skunk Kilo," was registered there. Under customary international law, the law of the ship's registry should have governed. But Cyprus—with which the U.S. had an extradition treaty—did not protest, and the court would later hold that Younis lacked standing to challenge these illegalities.[106]

Both of Younis's wrists were broken when the FBI agents slammed him to the deck of the yacht. Later he became violently seasick while being hoisted onto the USS *Butte* in heavy seas. Despite this illness, he was confined to an exceedingly hot, windowless mailroom below decks. FBI doctors did not bandage his bruised and swollen wrists or give him any motion-sickness medicine, and FBI interrogators gave him little rest until they obtained his confession. According to Judge Barrington Parker, the operation appeared to have been designed so that the suspect could be questioned, incommunicado and in great discomfort, for four days while the munitions ship steamed westward toward the carrier *Saratoga* and the plane that would fly him to America.

Parker found this treatment sufficiently improper to bar the prisoner's shipboard confession from evidence,[107] but not shocking enough to decline jurisdiction under *Toscanino's* due process or judicial integrity standards.[108] The Court of Appeals subsequently decided that the confession was not coerced but did not challenge the trial court's ruling that the defendant could assert the Fifth Amendment privilege against self-incrimination.[109] Younis was eventually sentenced to thirty years in federal prison.

Jurisdiction over Younis depended on a new "passive personality" statute that made holding American citizens hostage outside U.S. territory a federal crime.[110] According to the 1984 Hostage Taking Act, the accused had to be "found in the United States."[111] This could be read to imply a voluntary entry, but the court was not interested in how he came to have been "found" on a Navy plane at Andrews Air Force Base, strapped to a stretcher and under sedation. That inquiry, Judge Parker ruled, was foreclosed by the *Ker-Frisbie* doctrine.[112]

* * *

Buoyed by their victories over Younis and the *Achille Lauro* hijackers, the Bush administration turned to the war on drugs, which was just then being transformed into a joint law-enforcement, military operation. The armed forces were not eager to enforce civilian laws; they had hoped that the Posse Comitatus Act would protect them from such demands,[113] but as the Cold War wound down, the demand for military assistance was increasingly difficult to resist. As military involvement in this form of law enforcement became more common, so the idea of "lifting" suspects became more attractive.

The chief target for abduction in the Latin American drug trade was General Manuel Antonio Noriega, Panama's *de facto* head of state. In the early 1980s, Noriega had allowed Panama's banks to become deeply involved in the laundering of drug money. Drug processing centers and trans-shipments were also allowed by the general, who became rich from payoffs. The U.S. government had known of Noriega's role in the drug trade since the early 1970s[114] but had tolerated it because he helped the DEA capture some rival drug smugglers and supported the CIA and Colonel North in their secret war against the Nicaraguan Sandinistas. So long as anti-communism was the administration's top priority, Noriega was not only safe; he was paid a stipend by the CIA that in some years rivaled President Reagan's salary.[115]

By late 1986, however, Noriega's chief protectors, Director Casey and Colonel North, were no longer able to help him. Casey was dying of cancer and North was facing prosecution for his role in the Iran-Contra scandal. Once U.S. support for the *contras* ended, only the DEA wanted the general's services, but even it had to back off when U.S. attorneys in Miami indicted him for cocaine trafficking, racketeering, and money laundering.[116] Tremendous pressure to get rid of Noriega had arisen from Congress and the press, particularly after he nullified free elections in 1989. Noriega had become the first narco-dictator, and the Bush administration, goaded by senators as different as John Kerry (D.-Mass.) and Jesse Helms (R.-N.C.), now had powerful domestic reasons for wanting to bring him down.

Extradition was impossible. Panama's judges would have needed no prompting to decide that he was immune from extradition both as their *de facto* head of state and as a Panamanian national. Nor would Noriega's opposition have surrendered him willingly, in part because Panama's constitution frowned on the surrender of nationals.[117] In Noriega's case, abduction was preferable to extradition because a number of the charges against the general would not satisfy the rule of double criminality. The racketeering charges, in particular, had no counterpart in Panamanian law.[118]

Other alternatives were considered, including assassination or killing the general in the course of a coup or invasion. Direct assassination was out of the question; that technique had been forbidden by Executive order 12,333.[119] Extensive support for coups raised the same issue, since the executive order appeared to prohibit assassination by proxy too.[120] So abduction was the chief focus of a White House meeting on May 29, 1988. Secretary of State George Shultz, a former marine, was all for it, particularly if invasion were the only alternative. President Reagan ordered snatch plans drawn up. One proposed seizing Noriega in the Dominican Republic during a visit to a married daughter. Another was to interdict his plane over the ocean.[121] Still another was to send a Special Forces unit into Panama to snatch him, perhaps from his mistress's bed. Attempts to snatch the dictator may have been tried unsuccessfully at Easter in 1988[122] and again in early December 1989.[123]

To create a patina of legal authority for abducting Noriega, the Bush administration commissioned a series of legal opinions favorable to its plans. On June 21, 1989, Justice Department lawyers, without consulting the State Department or the president, reversed a nine-year-old Carter legal opinion opposing the use of FBI agents to conduct arrests abroad.[124] In October, after a second coup against Noriega failed, Senator Jesse Helms (R.-N.C.) proposed legislation authorizing the army to go in and kidnap him.[125] Publicly, the administration opposed this measure, but on November 3 it generated yet another legal opinion declaring that the Posse Comitatus Act did not forbid the military to make overseas arrests.[126] Fearful of what legal scholars would say about these opinions, the Justice Department kept them secret even from Congress and, when their existence became known, refused to release their text.[127]

On December 20, 1989, the United States conducted the most ambitious snatch operation in history.[128] More than 24,000 troops attacked Panama, 13,000 from inside the country.[129] Twenty-six Americans and more than 700 Panamanians, mostly civilians, died as a result,[130] and property damage exceeded $1.5 billion.

The invasion force was essentially a giant posse. Its chief mission was to seize and carry off one man before nationalist sentiment could force the successor regime to keep him there. At midnight, an hour before the invasion was to begin, a snatch squad of Delta Force commandos raided one of the general's haunts, only to find that its occupants had just left. The general evaded the invasion force for four days, finally taking refuge in the Papal Nunciature until he could be persuaded to surrender.

In Miami, Noriega was tried by Judge William Hoeveler. To no one's surprise, the judge donned his *Ker-Frisbie* blinkers and refused to examine how the general had been captured.[131] The invasion clearly violated international law,[132] including the United Nations Charter, which obligated the United States to "refrain . . . from the . . . use of force against the territorial integrity or political independence of any State,"[133] and the Charter of the Organization of American States, which declared the customary law principle that "the territory of a State is inviolable."[134] But nothing in either charter or customary international law expressly granted the general standing to challenge the jurisdiction of an American court.[135] To divest the court of jurisdiction to try Noriega, Judge Hoeveler ruled, the charters (or some other treaty) would have to say so.[136] As for declining jurisdiction as a matter of discretion, he could not do so either, because that choice had been barred by the *Ker-Frisbie* doctrine and its narrow reading of the due process clauses.[137]

Nor could the judge decline jurisdiction because the invasion constituted a shocking violation of international law. The invasion might be illegal under international law, but that was a nonjusticiable "political question."[138] In other words, while the abduction of ordinary people by American police or their paid surrogates remained a legal matter that judges could review under *Toscanino*, the abduction of a foreign head of state by invasion is a political matter that only politicians could resolve.

The indictment, abduction, and conviction of a foreign head of state was unprecedented in modern times. It was doubly unusual because the alleged crimes had not been committed on U.S. territory but wholly within Panama, and were not crimes against all mankind, like piracy and genocide. Moreover, Panama clearly had primary jurisdiction. If Panama's legal system had been working, or had any integrity, it could have tried and convicted Noriega under its own laws. Or it could have reviewed the U.S. evidence and extradited him. But the successor regime did not have a prison secure enough to hold the general.

* * *

No U.S. court has ever cited the violation of foreign sovereignty as grounds for refusing to try an abducted defendant. In large part this has been because most foreign nations, like Canada in *Brewster*, Peru in *Ker*, Uruguay in *Toscanino*, Panama in *Cordero*, Cyprus in *Yunis*, and Panama in *Noriega*, have not objected to the abduction.[139] But if courts are expected to take law seriously, should the absence of a protest be conclusive?

In the normal course of events under both the common law and the Fourth Amendment, a search warrant must be issued by an impartial magistrate before the police can carry out most premeditated seizures of evidence of a crime. Similarly, an arrest warrant must normally be issued before the police can go out and arrest a suspected criminal. This is clearly the rule in the United States, and was intended by both the makers of the common law rule and the Fourth Amendment to protect "the people" from government overreaching.[140] Should the rule be any different just because the overreaching by American officials occurs on foreign soil or affects people who are not Americans?

To allow such a double standard is to assume that the individual rights granted by the Fourth Amendment are based on nationality, not personhood. However, unlike most nations (at least until recently), the United States has not defined freedom from unreasonable searches and seizures in terms of citizenship. Nor is it practical to do so, since potential arrestees do not wear their citizenship on their sleeves. Within the United States, a rule that would deny Fourth Amendment protection to aliens would grievously endanger Americans who can be mistaken for aliens. But if the American people can be endangered by a rule that makes resident aliens Fourth Amendment outlaws, they can also be endangered by one that leaves U.S. officials unrestrained when they operate against foreigners abroad.

Before the U.S. government abducts anyone from a foreign land, should it not have to obtain an arrest warrant, as the British police officer did in *Scott*, Henry Julian did in *Ker*, the FBI did in *Younis*, and U.S. officials did in *Noriega*? But may a U.S. court go further and, as part of the warrant, authorize American law-enforcement officials to execute it in a manner that violates the sovereignty and kidnapping laws of a foreign nation? If so, where does that authority come from? Certainly not from what may loosely be called the foreign affairs or war powers. May it be implied from some allegedly inherent power of the courts,[141] or must it be expressly granted by Congress?

Let us assume that the American agents have an American warrant authorizing them to abduct a person, or bribe foreign officials to do the deed for them. Should that be sufficient? Or should similarly valid legal authority have to be issued, in advance, by the host nation so that there is no doubt as to the legitimacy of the seizure under its law? That, of course, is what an extradition order does. It certifies that the removal was legitimate under the host country's law. If the American court does not require such a certification, and assumes jurisdiction over a person who has been kidnapped in violation of a foreign law, is the judge not an accessory after the fact to the kidnapping? If he or she authorized a kidnapping in advance with some sort of overseas arrest warrant, and the host nation does not lawfully consent to the arrest on its soil in advance, would the judge not be guilty, under the host country's law, of authorizing the commission of a crime? Similarly, if U.S. courts are obliged to extradite American bounty hunters to Canada for kidnapping,[142] are they not compelled to extradite (or allow the abduction of) an American judge who orders the same offense against Canadian law?

The foregoing analysis is based on the assumption that no foreign government has objected to the abduction. The question of what to do when the host country does object is the subject of the next chapter.

CHAPTER 21

The Law of
Stolen People II

*If we are to see the emergence of a "new world order" in which the rise
of force is to be subject to the rule of law, we must begin by holding our
own Government to its fundamental legal commitments.*

Judge Stephen Reinhardt, in
United States v. Verdugo-Urquidez, 1990

On February 7, 1985, Enrique Camarena-Salazar, a U.S. drug agent operating lawfully
in Mexico, was kidnapped from in front of the U.S. consulate in Guadalajara, taken
to a ranch outside the city, tortured brutally for days, and then bludgeoned to death.
His kidnappers were members of the Guadalajara drug cartel. They wanted to know
not only who his informants were, but what he knew of their relationships to the Mexican police and military. They also kidnapped, tortured, and killed Camarena's pilot,
Alfredo Zavala-Avelar, in reprisal for a series of U.S.-sponsored raids on marijuana
plantations that had cost their cartel billions.[1]

To the U.S. Drug Enforcement Agency, these were not ordinary crimes; they were
atrocities to be avenged and a declaration of war to be answered. As in the war against
terrorism in the Mediterranean, the dignity of the United States was at stake. Over
the next decade, DEA would devote extensive resources and millions of dollars to get
those responsible for these crimes.

Obtaining the killers by extradition was not likely. Mexico had never extradited
one of its own nationals to the United States. Even if Mexican politicians made an
exception in this case, corrupt police and military officers would see to it that the
drug dealers escaped.[2] The Guadalajara cartel enjoyed the protection of officials at
all levels of the Mexican government; leading members of the Mexican police, military, and intelligence agencies were alleged to have been present at Camarena's

interrogation.[3] Resolved to get the killers at any cost, DEA spent $2.7 million just on informants and by 1990 had indicted twenty-two people.[4] Of these, three were abducted from Mexico.

Rene Martin Verdugo-Urquidez, the chief west coast distributor for the cartel, was snatched for the DEA by six Mexican police officers in January 1986 and shoved through a border fence to U.S. marshals near Calexico, California. According to the Mexican government, which protested, no request for Verdugo's extradition had been made. The police did not act pursuant to Mexican law; they had been bribed by DEA agents to violate it.[5]

Juan Ramon Matta-Ballesteros,[6] a cocaine chemist and intermediary to the Medellin cartel, was wanted, among other things, for ordering Camareno's murder. A billionaire, he lived openly in Tegucigalpa, Honduras, under the shelter of that country's constitution, which prohibited the extradition of nationals.[7] The DEA had tried several times without success to kidnap him before turning to the Honduran military for help.

Early on the morning of April 5, 1988, an elite force of sixty military police called the "Cobras" seized Matta as he returned home. Violating their country's constitution, they delivered him to waiting U.S. marshals, who handcuffed him, put a hood over his head, and pushed him to the floor of their Toyota Land Cruiser for a fast trip to the airport. A U.S. marshal drove; two Honduran soldiers with stun guns guarded the prisoner.[8] During the trip to the Honduran airport, Matta later complained, he was repeatedly shocked and burned with a "double pronged electric."[9] On the first leg of his flight to the U.S., he said, he was beaten on his head and shocked on his testicles and feet. According to the prison doctor who examined him in the United States, the abrasions and blisters on his body, including his penis, were consistent with having being shocked with a stun gun.[10]

The third abductee was Humberto Alvarez-Machain, a prominent Guadalajara obstetrician and gynecologist. He was wanted for injecting Camarena with the stimulant lidocaine to prevent his heart from failing during torture. The Mexican Federal Judicial Police (MFJP) first offered to abduct Alvarez as they had Verdugo, if the United States would deport (not extradite) one Isaac Naredo-Moreno to Mexico. Naredo was wanted for stealing $500 million from Mexican politicians. The exchange was broached by MFJP *commandante* Jorge Castillo del Rey, who claimed that he was working for Javier Orosco-Orosco, chief of the MFJP fugitive detail in Mexico City. Castillo assured the DEA agents that he was making the proposal with the full knowledge and authority of Mexico's attorney general, but that the exchange would have to occur "under the table" because its revelation would "upset" Mexican citizens.[11] In anticipation of this arrangement, the Mexican Federal Judicial Police actually apprehended Alvarez and held him in a safe house.[12]

DEA agents agreed to initiate deportation proceedings against Naredo if Alvarez-Machain was delivered to them, but balked at paying the $50,000 the *commandante* and his associates demanded in advance. The deal fell apart, and the Mexicans permitted Alvarez to bribe his way out of custody.[13]

But the U.S. government did not quit. One of DEA's informants, who had once been a member of the MFJP and an adviser to a drug lord,[14] arranged for the abduction to be carried out by former associates who were willing to accept a $50,000 reward, plus expenses, on delivery. The group, known as the "Wild Geese," included former military police officers, civilians, and at least two current policemen.[15] According to the special agent in charge, the bribe was approved by DEA officials in Washington and was at least discussed with the office of the attorney general.[16]

On April 2, 1990, five or six men wearing federal police uniforms broke into Alvarez's office, put a gun to his head, locked his secretary and maid in a closet, and hustled the doctor away to a house in Guadalajara.[17] The next day he was flown to El Paso, Texas, where the abductors turned him over to the DEA.[18] The Mexican government protested the abduction and demanded extradition of the abductors, but the Bush administration refused.[19]

* * *

None of the three snatches was formally authorized by the U.S. Department of Justice, a U.S. court, or the Mexican government.[20] None was cleared with the Department of State, although each would have substantial foreign-policy repercussions. But each was prosecuted with great passion by the Reagan and Bush administrations, and each produced some of the worst law ever handed down by the federal courts.

In *Matta*, the courts simply refused to apply the *Toscanino* test, although an American prison doctor had recorded the many stun-gun burns on Matta's body.[21] Matta was one of the more brutal of the central American drug lords, so it was no surprise that the trial judge ruled that "the allegations of torture do not meet the required level of outrageousness."[22] But instead of leaving it at that, he went on to explain that the abuse was not sufficiently shocking because Matta was already an escapee from an American prison.[23] In other words, no degree of torture by U.S. abductors could ever justify a judicial refusal to try an escaped prisoner.

Verdugo was the subject of several court decisions. The first to reach the U.S. Supreme Court involved a warrantless search of his home in Mexico by DEA agents. The trial and appellate courts found it unconstitutional,[24] but the Supreme Court reversed, 6–3, with an opinion that would lay the groundwork for accepting abductions.[25]

Writing for the majority, Justice Rehnquist upheld the search, which took place after Verdugo was abducted, but which was not authorized in advance by an American or Mexican judge. The chief justice ruled, in effect, that the Fourth Amendment was like an overcoat that U.S. investigators could remove when conducting searches abroad. Because Verdugo was only a Mexican in Mexico, he had no reasonable expectation of privacy or freedom from lawless searches by American agents. The only persons entitled to such an expectation were Americans and aliens within the United States whose "voluntary connection with the country" had placed them "among the 'people' of the United States."[26]

The immediate source of this "social contract" theory of the Fourth Amendment was Judge J. Clifford Wallace's dissent in the Ninth Circuit's decision in the *Verdugo* search case,[27] but its doctrinal roots lay in the infamous case of *Dred Scott v. Sanford*,[28] in which the U.S. Supreme Court held that blacks lacked sufficient nexus to the constitutional compact to be protected against reenslavement.[29]

This theory of limited "belonging" had once been advanced by Attorney General A. Mitchell Palmer to justify the infamous "Red Raids" of 1919–1920. The immigrants whom the FBI arrested and searched without cause, Palmer claimed, were not people whom the Fourth Amendment was meant to protect. This theory was also embraced, briefly, by Attorney General Edward Levi in 1975 in an effort to remove aliens from constitutional protections against wiretaps, bugs, and the burglaries necessary to install bugs.[30] Reawakened for the war on drugs, this theory is sweeping enough to be used in all sorts of "wars," to strip noncitizens of all rights, including free expression and legal counsel, and the right not to be subjected to cruel and unusual punishments.

The chief justice's social contract theory is not only bad law; it is bad political theory. The U.S. Constitution was not meant to be another medieval, commercial, or colonial contract between the rulers and the ruled. That concept of social structure had been left behind with the colonial charters, early state constitutions, and the Articles of Confederation. The U.S. Constitution was written by a convention, not a house of delegates or a sovereign legislature. It was ratified by conventions of the people in the states, and was thus more in the nature of a Puritan covenant among the people than a ruler's contract with the ruled. It was a covenant among a sovereign people to delegate limited authority for limited periods of time to public servants.[31] Thus Alexander Hamilton could argue with some force that where governmental authority is inherently limited to those powers that are delegated, no Bill of Rights is really necessary.[32] The anti-federalists disagreed and insisted on a Bill of Rights, but they did not reject the Federalist principle of limited government; they simply demanded "auxiliary precautions."[33] Both the Federalists and anti-federalists were, at the core, civic republicans for whom liberty was more of a collective condition, achieved by limiting authority, than it was a recognition of individual rights against the collectivity.[34]

As Justice Brennan pointed out in his dissent in *Verdugo-Urquidez*, the drafting history of the Fourth Amendment supports this view. The conventions that ratified the Constitution in the key states of Virginia and New York both recommended an amendment which would have provided "That every freeman has a right to be secure from all unreasonable searches and seizures."[35] The Massachusetts constitution, which provided most of the Fourth Amendment's provisions, spoke in the pre-independence language of "subjects." But Madison's draft rejected these narrow affirmations of individual rights for the broader limitation on government we have today, and no one in the congressional or ratifying debates objected to the change.[36] Limiting the right to be free from unreasonable searches and seizures to "freedmen" would have denied it to indentured persons, and thus to all persons who might be mistaken for indentured persons. Defining rights holders as "subjects" would have reiterated the royal theory that rights are bestowed by rulers on the ruled, rather than possessed by the people who institute government from a "state of nature." Those who associate rights with power find terms like "freedmen," "subjects," and "citizens" congenial, but the framers of the Constitution committed the United States to the logic of popular sovereignty, which means limited government.

They also thought largely in terms of the Protestant theory of natural rights based on what we would today call personhood. Rights, to them, had nothing to do with politics or membership in a political order. They accrued at birth, belonged to all people equally, and were endowed by their Creator directly to each person, without the intercession of lords temporal or spiritual. Analytically, these rights preceded government. Constitutions could express them; constitutions and statutes could restate them; but positive government could not create them. The Ninth Amendment reaffirmed this basic theory by reminding future generations that the Bill of Rights is not a closed-ended list of liberties as they were understood circa 1791.

Expressing Fourth Amendment rights as collective may have been meant to give them extra weight on those inevitable occasions when judges have to weigh governmental assertions of need against individual assertions of autonomy. The framers had lived through a period in which societal interests, as defined by Crown officials, had tended to outweigh the rights of lone individuals. By expressing the freedom from unreasonable seizures as a societal interest, the framers may have meant judges to view search and seizure issues in the light of conflicting societal interests transcending politics, rather than in terms of the large, important government against the isolated, unimportant, and perhaps despised individual.

This interpretation accords with the text of the Fourth Amendment, which speaks of the "right of the people," not the right of "persons", "citizens", or "subjects." The "reasonable expectation of privacy," then, is not Verdugo's; it belongs to the people.[37] There is no reason, under a theory of limited government, to confine this expectation to the territorial boundaries of the United States, or to citizens and resident aliens within those boundaries, leaving tourists in the U.S. and foreigners and U.S. citizens outside the United States vulnerable to that overreaching. Properly understood, the Fourth Amendment is, like the First, primarily a guarantee of limited government, which individuals necessarily must have standing to enforce.

Limited government and guaranteed liberties can also be understood as two sides of the same coin. At least, that is what the framers intended. Their separation in American jurisprudence, enforced by opinions like *Verdugo*, was a later development and owes more to Adam Smith and laissez-faire capitalism than to James Madison and civic republicanism. Chief Justice Rehnquist, who has devoted his career on the bench to releasing executive government from constitutional restraints, has always looked upon the Fourth Amendment as a statement of personal rights only. This has allowed him to decide cases in an ad hoc fashion, free from the principle that limited government means, above all, a limited executive.[38]

The principle of limited government, in a system where constitutions are ordained by "we, the people," is a system of authority from the bottom up, the very antithesis of the Chief Justice's belief in government from the top down. From his perspective, individual rights (like corporate charters) are bestowed by rulers on the ruled. If a right is not expressly granted or secured by an explicit limitation on authority, then it does not exist.

Logically speaking, the *Verdugo* decision eliminated all constitutional deterrents to torture, assassination, and abduction by U.S. agents overseas. It also rejected the major premise of *Toscanino*, which was that foreign nationals could invoke the Fourth Amendment's protection against illegal searches both within the United States and abroad. Writing for the Second Circuit in *Toscanino*, Judge Walter R. Mansfield had reasoned that the Fourth Amendment was more than a guarantee of individual rights; it was a structural provision like the exclusionary evidence rule, and was meant to protect the people from institutional lawlessness.[39] But most of this reasoning was swept aside in *Verdugo-Urquidez*, which, like *Cordero*, prepared the way for the toleration of government-sponsored kidnapping in *Alvarez-Machain*.

* * *

Alvarez, not surprisingly, challenged the court's jurisdiction to try him on the grounds that his abduction violated the due process clause of the Fifth Amendment, the integrity of the judicial system, and the extradition treaty between the United States and Mexico. Federal District Judge Edward Rafeedie brushed aside the doctor's due process claim, declaring that it had been settled by the *Ker-Frisbie* doctrine.[40] He admitted that no court should allow itself to be made "an 'accomplice in willful disobedience of law,'"[41] but he refused to find the abduction so outrageous as to require him to decline jurisdiction in the exercise of his supervisory powers.[42]

However, Rafeedie also ruled that Alvarez had been kidnapped in violation of the treaty and must be repatriated, without trial, to Mexico. The treaty, he decided, established the exclusive means governing rendition between the two countries. It did not say so expressly, but that was the import of its provisions, particularly Article 9, which declared that if Mexico (or the United States) refused to extradite a person because he was a national, it would have to prosecute him instead.[43] Theoretically, then, the treaty guaranteed that no criminal would escape justice, making abduction (or irregular deportation) unnecessary.

The doctor had standing to raise this argument, the judge said, because Mexico had formally protested his abduction.[44] He had to be given standing in order for Mexico's protest and its treaty rights to have legal effect. Rafeedie was not willing to decide—as courts had in the exclusionary evidence and First Amendment chilling effect cases—that the doctor should enjoy standing in his own right to preserve limited government, guaranteed liberties, or the integrity of the judicial system. The judge based Alvarez's right to be free from abduction solely on the existence of an extradition treaty. A right that most people would consider fundamental, and which the framers of the Constitution would certainly have considered a God-given or natural right, like the privilege of the writ of habeas corpus, was reduced to a mere artifact of transient, positive, power-based law.

But the existence of the treaty was not enough to create the right; the right had to be invoked by the other country's politicians or it was no right at all. Thus, while extradition treaties are self-executing as a matter of American law,[45] the right they create in this instance is not. The right is more of a political option, to be exercised by the foreign government when and if it wishes to do so. According to Judge Rafeedie, the right does not exist because the United States is committed to liberty, due process, or the rule of law. The right does not exist, he reasoned, because the extradition treaty is no more than an executive arrangement, rather than the supreme law of the land, as Article 6 of the Constitution clearly provides.[46] It exists only if politicians of the wronged country find it politically advantageous to assert it, and its assertion can be bought off by diplomatic concessions from the abducting country. In short, the right not to be kidnapped in violation of both country's laws is not a right at all; it is diplomatic trading stock.

The *Alvarez* decision also means that Americans have no right not to be kidnapped from the United States by a foreign government for trial—unless it is in the political interests of the State Department to protest the abduction and demand their return. This is not law; it is power politics.

Moreover, in the absence of a treaty, there is no legal deterrent to abductions by American agents. If Alvarez had been abducted from Russia and the Russian government had protested, Judge Rafeedie would not have granted him standing to challenge the court's jurisdiction, because the U.S. has no extradition treaty with that nation. The bedrock principle of customary international law, that the law-enforcement agents of one country cannot arrest persons in another country without that country's consent,[47] would count for nothing among countries that had never attempted, let alone failed at, extradition with the United States.

Politically, Rafeedie's decision was courageous—given what passes for courage among federal judges. Legally, however, its scope was severely limited; morally, its positive rights approach was a far cry from the natural rights of the founders of the American republic and their British progenitors. From Sir Edward Coke, through the Habeas Corpus Act of 1679, to the American Declaration of Independence, nothing was more basic than the right not to be uprooted from one's home and sent beyond the seas to be tried for alleged offenses (or simply banished).[48] It was a right the founders associated with the protections offered by the Great Writ, grand and petit juries, and the requirement that the accused be tried within the vicinage where the crime had been committed.

In the *Alvarez*, *Verdugo*, *Matta*, and *Noriega* cases, these fundamental rights were ignored, because the courts no longer respected the principle of limited government. If these people ought to be let off, it could not be because of general principles of justice and humanity. It had to be because of some loophole in the law, like a treaty few have ever read, which can be fixed by yet another grant of unlimited power to the executive. In a war against crime, limited government is the enemy. Limited government means fighting crime with one hand tied, and few judges want to be seen as crippling law enforcement. A judge might believe that there are some things that anti-drug warriors should not be able to do, even to avenge the murder of one of their own, but to say so at the height of the drug war would be considered fastidiously Victorian. It was much easier and more credible to find a loophole in the treaty, opened by Mexico's diplomatic protest.

Similarly, Rafeedie did not address the all important *ultra vires* question—where did the U.S. government obtain authority to steal people (or subvert foreign police with bribes)? Only a fool would ask soldiers in a war where they got their authority to seize people. In a war, soldiers can do just about anything that is not expressly forbidden, and they usually can get away with what is forbidden, too. Although the liberty of individuals was at stake, Rafeedie did not demand proof of affirmative statutory authority before allowing the executive to carry out abductions in the absence of a treaty. He limited his inquiry to proof that authority to abduct had been denied, and found that denial implicit in the extradition treaty with Mexico.

* * *

Rafeedie's decision was affirmed by the U.S. Court of Appeals for the Ninth Circuit,[49] only to be overturned, 6–3, by the U.S. Supreme Court in *United States v. Alvarez-Machain*.[50] The reversal was widely expected, not only because of lower court decisions like *Cordero*, but because the weight of public opinion had shifted against criminal suspects.

Most legal scholars have considered the *Ker-Frisbie* rule indefensible and obsolete, and have urged courts to deny the admissibility of stolen persons.[51] But most law-and-order politicians favor it, and most members of the Rehnquist Court were appointed by law-and-order presidents and approved by law-and-order Senators.

Abductions have been supported by politicians because the spirit of the times has been punitive, not judicious. Politically and philosophically, a majority of the Court has favored emasculating, not extending, the exclusionary rule.[52] Popular culture, reflected in television and films, romanticizes police who break the rules to capture or kill criminals. In Washington, members of Congress continue to demand that the armed forces be unleashed against drug smugglers, insensitive to the dangers of militarizing law enforcement.

As in most of his opinions supporting broad claims of executive power, in *United States v. Alvarez-Machain* Chief Justice Rehnquist simply ignored the strongest arguments against the position he wished to take. In upholding the *Ker-Frisbie* rule and extending it to government-sponsored kidnapping, he did not pause to address the inconsistency of allowing people, but not evidence, to be stolen. The Fourth Amendment's ban on unreasonable seizures did not apply because the Court had said so in a domestic rendition case (*Frisbie*). That was all there was to it. Rehnquist did not bother to consider whether jurisdiction should be declined in order to protect the integrity of the courts. The sole issue was whether the extradition treaty barred abduction. It did not, he concluded, because the treaty did not expressly forbid the practice.

Rehnquist's opinion was as result-oriented as Captain Vere's insistence that Billy Budd, a sailor, must be tried under the army's Mutiny Act.[53] It was as morally obtuse as the Court's decision in *Prigg v. Pennsylvania*,[54] but it was fully consistent with the Chief Justice's personal agenda, which had been to sever the judicial brakes which might restrain executive actions affecting foreign relations or infringing individual rights.[55]

The "critical flaw" in the majority's "monstrous" opinion, Justice Stevens wrote in a dissent that Justices Blackmun and O'Connor endorsed, was its failure to distinguish between private and official kidnapping.[56] But Stevens did not link this failure to the

Fifth Amendment, which forbids federal officials to deny any person liberty without due process of law. His dissent focused wholly on the treaty, thereby suggesting that all nine justices agreed that no one, citizen or alien, has a constitutional right not to be abducted from a foreign land by the U.S. government. The three dissenters disagreed with the majority only as to what the treaty with Mexico provided. In the absence of a treaty, they seemed to say, there is nothing in the values of due process, law-enforcement integrity, or international law that should lead an American court to refuse to receive stolen—and even tortured—persons.

Even so, the dissenters read the treaty as forbidding federal kidnapping. This narrow interpretation was not necessary; it would have been much more consistent with the history and purpose of American extradition law to hold that everyone, federal, state, and private, is bound to obey—or defer to—the treaty's scheme. A finding that the extradition treaty had preempted all means for obtaining alleged criminals from foreign lands would also have been consistent with the Supreme Court's holding in *Rauscher* that extradition is an exclusively federal responsibility.[57]

When the treaty specified how federal officials could recover fugitive criminals, the dissenters argued, it essentially said that they could not do it any other way. This was consistent with what American officials have historically said about extradition—in the absence of a treaty, it could not be done, even by agreement among executives.[58] The treaties created authority where none existed before; they did not create authority by their silences. In a government of limited powers, silence usually means that no authority exists, not that the government can do anything it wants. This is why Chancellor Kent's contemporaries rejected his pro-executive, inherent powers opinion that the United States could, as a matter of comity, surrender alleged fugitives.[59] Whatever powers the United States possesses by virtue of being a nation belong to the "people," to be allocated pursuant to their Constitution, and do not inhere automatically in the executive.

The dissent argued persuasively that treaties do not need to contain express prohibitions in order to limit the jurisdiction of federal courts to hear cases.[60] Justice Stevens noted that the Court had held in *Rauscher*[61] that the jurisdiction of American courts to try a person obtained by extradition was limited to the offenses for which he was extradited to the United States. The treaty did not include this rule of specialty. Nor did it have to. The rule was the logical consequence of limiting extradition to those crimes specified in the treaty and requiring the U.S. prosecutors to prove to foreign courts or officials that there was reason to believe that the accused had committed the crimes charged. In *Rauscher* the Supreme Court expressly rejected the idea that the executive can do anything not expressly forbidden by the treaty.[62]

The protection from additional prosecutions afforded by the rule of specialty did not belong just to the extraditing government; it belonged to the individual. It did not come into existence only when the other country's politicians decided to protest the additional prosecution. It existed to make sure that no "implication of fraud" or "bad faith" could be imputed to the government of the United States.[63] Nor could it be destroyed by a political waiver of objections, purchased perhaps by diplomatic favors. The right existed to assure some integrity to extradition decisions and, therefore, belonged to the individual. Similarly, the dissent reasoned, a right not to be abducted should belong to the individual, not the foreign executive.

Missing from both opinions in *Alvarez* was any sense of the larger history of extradition law and policy. Neither the majority nor the dissent seemed to know that most officials in the early years of the republic believed that the only way to recover a fugitive was pursuant to an extradition treaty. The founders of American extradition law took the whig view that officials could only do what they had *authority* to do, and authority, they believed, came from laws, not the absence of laws. Justice Story, speaking for the Supreme Court in the case of an abducted ship, was emphatic on this point: "It would be monstrous to suppose that our revenue officers were authorized to enter into foreign ports and territories, for the purpose of seizing vessels which had offended against our laws. It cannot be presumed that Congress would voluntarily justify such a clear violation of the laws of nations."[64] The majority in *Alvarez* ignored the liberal tradition of American jurisprudence to embrace a European statist view more common to Louis XIV, Napoleon, Hitler, or Stalin: The executive can do whatever the people have not expressly forbidden it to do. Oliver Wendell Holmes could not have expressed this "bad man's theory of the law" better.[65] Herman Melville would have been appalled.

This statist view was not new; it had been asserted with increasing frequency since the late nineteenth century by advocates of executive-centered government.[66] Most, like Lincoln, tried to limit the broad claims to periods of grave national emergency, but as the United States emerged as a world power, that self-restraint weakened. The first president to allege that the "bad man's theory" applied to routine as well as emergency powers was Theodore Roosevelt, who claimed that "the executive power was limited only by specific restrictions and prohibitions appearing in the Constitution or imposed by the Congress under its constitutional powers."[67] By the 1970s, Richard Nixon was convinced that the Cold War had made emergency powers so routine that the old whig theory of limited government was dead. Thus he could assure an interviewer that nothing he did during the Watergate affair was illegal, because "when the President does it, that means that it is not illegal."[68] William Rehnquist won Nixon's nomination to the Court because, as an assistant attorney general, he found constitutional-sounding ways to justify Nixon's assertions of unlimited executive authority to spy on domestic political dissent.[69]

Government by abduction, then, is not an aberrant idea. It is in the tradition of executive-centered government during the Cold War—which involved assassination plots overseas and the harassment of political dissenters at home. It is government by James Bond, Hoover's "counter-intelligence programs," Nixon's "plumbers," or General Secord's corporation—clandestine government without prior authority or subsequent checks.

To create this kind of unrestrained government, it is necessary first to dismiss the idea that treaties and statutes must be interpreted in light of a larger, ethically informed body of political thought. Law has to be reduced to little more than a series of self-contained, essentially arbitrary expressions of transient power, to be interpreted with little concern for the Constitution's larger scheme, the customary usages of other nations, the opinions of humankind, or the probable consequences of ignoring them all. Mere textual analysis will do; reference to analogous bodies of law, to other extradition treaties, or to the general patterns and purposes of extradition law is not necessary. Law is to be interpreted formally, with little reference to anything but de facto rules. Policy is for the legislature or executive, not the courts. Under this jurisprudential approach, extradition treaties are mere episodic expressions of executive interests.[70]

Thus, in *Alvarez,* the majority read the extradition treaty with Mexico as they would a single contract between two parties, but stood contract law on its head by ruling that, because the agreement did not expressly forbid abductions, the United States had no obligation to return stolen people. By this theory, a U.S. company would not breach its contract with a Mexican company if it dispatched covert agents to seize delivered goods from the purchaser's warehouse in Mexico because its agents had heard that payment might be delayed. Because the contract could not be breached by a mere act of theft, restitution of the goods would not be required. Nor would the contract have to be read in light of the common, customary, domestic law of theft, fraud, or conversion in a manner that would require restitution. The contract, in other words, would not be read to incorporate general principles of contract law. It would merely present each side with the option of following contract law, if they wished.

If the reasoning in *Alvarez* is valid, then the president should also be free to ignore the common law when interpreting contracts between the federal government and domestic corporations. For example, if one of the Pentagon's suppliers is unable to deliver promised equipment because of labor problems, the president should be able to order his agents to snatch the equipment by stealth and force, even when the nation is at peace and the law of forage does not apply. So long as the contract does not forbid self-help, the government should to be able to help itself.

The Court's reasoning in *Alvarez,* of course, is inconsistent with the Supreme Court's decision in the famous steel seizure case of 1952, which struck down President Truman's seizure of the nation's steel mills in order to settle a labor dispute that threatened to disrupt arms production during the Korean War. The Court found that Congress, by enacting the Taft-Hartley Act, had specified a solution to impending strikes that the president was bound to try—at least first.[71] The Taft-Hartley Act did not say that its procedures were mandatory, but the Court held that they were. Congress would not have prescribed such a procedure, the Court reasoned, if it had meant it to be ignored. Truman, like the DEA in Alvarez's case, did not try the prescribed procedure first. Like the DEA, he had some very practical reasons for not doing so, but they were not legally sufficient, and the Court ordered Truman's secretary of commerce to return the mills to their owners.

If the customary law of theft, fraud, or conversion must be read into the law of contracts, so the customary law of nations should be read into the meaning of treaties.[72] On remand, the Court of Appeals conceded that customary international law might provide an exception to the *Ker-Frisbie* doctrine if the government's conduct was outrageous, but the court decided that it wasn't in this case.[73]

Thus, customary international law was reduced to little more than an exhortation that any executive officer, no matter how lowly, could flout at will. This was a departure from the Supreme Court's traditional view, which had been that customary international law—at least in the realm of admiralty law—was part of the domestic law of the United States. It could not be disregarded, the Court had ruled in 1900 in the famous prize case of *The Paquete Habana,* unless and until Congress, or the president by a "controlling executive . . . act," authoritatively rejected it.[74] The Court had also held, in an 1804 admiralty case, that an intent on the part of Congress or the executive to depart from customary international law was not to be inferred lightly.[75]

In *Alvarez,* these basic principles were violated. Without saying so, the Supreme Court effectively scuttled *The Paquete Habana.* President Bush had not put the world, or even Mexico, on notice by any "authoritative act" that the United States would no longer respect the sovereignty of foreign nations but would commence kidnapping at will.[76] The president hadn't done anything;[77] he had not even been told of the three Camarena case abductions.

The idea had been growing for decades that the president's subordinates can make "authoritative" decisions on his behalf to abridge individual liberties and violate international law. Institutionally, the idea was a consequence of the increased size of the federal bureaucracy, the withering of the anti-delegation doctrine, and a shattering of Congress's ability to achieve the unity of purpose necessary to check executive abuse. Politically, this downward shift of power was also the result of a politics of "plausible denial," by which presidents (and their congressional allies) reserve the option of blaming underlings if controversial covert operations go wrong.

Courts, as much as the executive, were complicit in undermining the traditional requirement that abrogations of customary international law be decided at the highest levels of the legislative or executive branches. In the mid-1980s, for example, the U.S. Court of Appeals for the Eleventh Circuit held that Attorney General Meese had the authority, without any permission from Congress or the president, to imprison indefinitely a group of Cubans who had entered the United States illegally, even though prolonged, arbitrary detention was forbidden by customary international law.[78] In other words, abrogation of international legal obligations not longer require a formal, across-the-board decision on the part of a law-abiding president or Congress. A Cabinet officer could now decide for himself what international law he wished to obey, and when.[79] International law had been reduced to a subordinate's option.

In *Garcia-Mir,* the Court of Appeals insisted that the attorney general's assertion of power (there is no evidence the power was actually delegated to him by a formal act of the president) was legitimate because it had been asserted by a Cabinet officer, rather than a mere admiral, as in the case of *The Paquette Habana.*[80] In *Alvarez,* however, Justice Rehnquist went far beyond this limited "delegation" to uphold the selective breach of customary international law by DEA agents in the field.

International law itself was not repudiated; its protections were implicitly reserved against any foreign government with the temerity to conduct kidnappings on American soil, but the law itself was broken selectively, as when the CIA mined a Nicaraguan harbor.[81] This was President Bush's "new world order," and it was upheld by the Supreme Court.

The majority in *Alvarez* also implied that American courts, in interpreting a treaty with a foreign nation, were entitled to ignore that nation's interpretation of the agreement. Mexico and Canada had both filed *amicus* briefs, and one might presume that a "decent respect for the opinions of mankind" would have prompted some acknowledgement of them.[82] But the majority ignored these briefs completely; all that counted was how the United States read the treaty.

But which United States? The current administration insisted that the treaty permitted abduction by failing to ban it; however, all prior administrations that had addressed the issue agreed with Canada and Mexico that abduction was not a lawful option. As early as 1881, Secretary of State Blaine informed the governor of Texas that the extradition treaty with Mexico "does not authorize either party, for any cause, to deviate from [its] forms or arbitrarily abduct from the territory of one party a person charged with crime, for trial within the jurisdiction of the other."[83] In 1887, Secretary of State Thomas F. Bayard protested as kidnapping the removal from Texas of Francisco Arresures by three Texas deputy sheriffs in collusion with a Mexican policeman, and the apparent murder of Arresures while in the policeman's custody in Mexico. Although Arresures's removal had been approved by a Texas state judge, Bayard denounced the policeman's representations as "in fraud of existing treaties" and instructed the American ambassador to seek reparations.[84] In 1987 and 1989, the United States and Mexico reaffirmed their opposition to abduction in treaties providing for mutual legal assistance and drug law enforcement.[85]

Despite this historical record, the Court accepted the Bush administration's interpretation of the treaty. In so doing, the majority did not pause to explain why the views of one current administration should prevail over the opinions of several prior administrations and the governments of Mexico and Canada.

* * *

Most striking, the majority in *United States v. Alvarez-Machain* did not pause to consider the morality of allowing the executive to kidnap people. It did not consider Justice Louis Brandeis's observation that "Decency, security and liberty alike demand that government officials shall be subjected to the same rules of conduct that are commands to the citizen.... Crime is contagious. If the Government becomes a lawbreaker, it breeds contempt for the law."[86]

Hannah Arendt, the philosopher, addressed the issue of governmental rules of conduct in her widely acclaimed book about Israel's kidnapping and trial of Adolf Eichmann. She asked, "What are we to say if tomorrow it occurs to some African state to send its agents into Mississippi and kidnap one of the leaders of the segregationist movement there?"[87] Arendt suggested a criterion for judging such governmental actions: "the unprecedentedness of the crime."[88] But the Nazi Holocaust was not unprecedented; "ethnic cleansing" against Jews and countless other groups had gone on for centuries, if not millennia. Mass murder has been all too common in the twentieth century. The Nazi Holocaust seems worse because it occurred in Christian Europe and was industrialized, but murder on a large scale was not unprecedented.

If the law can make an exception in Eichmann's case and allow the Israeli government to abduct him because of the enormity of his crimes, then how are we to know when another crime is of comparable enormity?[89] Does Stalin's reign of terror, which killed more people than the Nazi Holocaust, qualify? What of the "ethnic cleansing" in Bosnia and Kosovo, or the mass murders in Rwanda? Or, for that matter, what of Iran's *fatwa* against the novelist Salman Rushdie? The answer, of course, is that we cannot draw clean, nonpolitical lines where abduction is concerned. The extent to which we will allow for kidnapping in some but not other cases will have less to do with the heinousness of the individual's conduct than with the relative balance, at the moment, between our urge for retribution and our commitment to lawful law enforcement.

According to Arendt, Eichmann's abduction could be justified not only because of the enormity of his crime, but because of the overwhelming case against him. Putting these two elements together, she attempted to limit the lawlessness to a few exceptional cases. But the eyewitness evidence against John Demjanjuk was also "overwhelming" to those disposed to believe it. Would Israel have been justified in abducting him from the United States?

Arendt's approach, then, is very much like the "gravity of the evil, discounted by its improbability" test that the Supreme Court used to justify prosecuting American Communists for their opinions.[90] Unfortunately, under that test, the gravity of the evil (or hysteria about it) frequently overshadowed the fact that specific evidence of personal, as opposed to group, culpability, often did not exist. Arendt was no wiser than the impetuous young Roper in Robert Bolt's *A Man for All Seasons*, who declared his willingness to cut down all the laws in England in order to get at the Devil.[91] But Arendt did have a point. As long as one views an abduction in terms of politics rather than law,[92] it is possible to cut down some laws some of the time and still stand erect in the winds that blow. All it takes is the right blend of intellectual inconsistency, moral hypocrisy, and raw power, of the sort Bolt expected from kings like Henry VIII, courtiers like the Duke of Norfolk, and lawyers like Richard Rich. We can get away with an occasional abduction and not do too much damage to the rule of law, if we are careful to provide due process at trial and impose an ordinary sentence afterwards. This, at least, is what former judge Abraham Sofaer advocated when he wrote of "bending" the law to get at the Reagan administration's devils.[93]

Abductions, then, are concessions that law must make to politics—like false oaths in *A Man for All Seasons*. But when we allow practical ends to justify lawless means, we do not just compromise our own souls; we set bureaucratic forces in operation and create legal precedents for even bolder immoralities. If abduction can be winked at, why not the concealment of exculpatory evidence by the OSI, torture by DEA's hirelings, or assassinations by the Mafia on contract from the CIA? To the Richard Riches at the Departments of Justice and State and their subordinate agencies, and to the Norfolks on our current Supreme Court, adherence to a mere "theory"—like limited government, human rights, or old-fashioned integrity—is naively idealistic. Law, to them, is whatever their clients want it to be. Principled restraint, essential to the achievement of liberty and due process of law, is rare (and professionally suicidal) in this environment. The law of the executive branch will be what the politics of the moment and institutional self-interest demand. It will not be what some higher body of principle recommends, because, as Robert Bolt's play reminds us, there are always more house lawyers like Richard Rich and courtiers like Norfolk than there are Sir Thomas Mores.

George Kennan shared Arendt's belief in the need for occasional abductions but understood the institutional risks. "Such operations," he warned, "should not be allowed to become a regular and routine feature of the governmental process, cast in the concrete of unquestioning habit and institutionalized bureaucracy."[94] "Government," he has observed, "is an agent, not a principal. Its primary obligation is to the *interests* of the national society it represents, not to the moral impulses that individual elements of that society may experience."[95]

Politically, Kennan was right; most government officials, most of the time, do subordinate means to ends. They are driven by politics and irritated by legal constraints. But the United States was meant to be different. It was meant to be a government under law, with a political morality to its laws, which politicians are bound to obey— so long as the courts read assertions of positive authority in light of the more fundamental principles of limited government, guaranteed rights, popular sovereignty, and checks and balances.

Arendt was not wholly insensitive to the dangers of bureaucratic zeal. There are those, she said, "who are convinced that justice, and nothing else, is the end of the law," and that they "will be inclined to condone the kidnapping act . . . as a desperate, unprecedented and not a precedent-setting act, necessitated by the unsatisfactory condition of international law."[96] If they are not allowed to kidnap people like Eichmann, she argued, they will want to assassinate them, which, she thought, would be all right "if the facts [are] beyond dispute" and if the killers were willing to give themselves up and take their punishment, like the practitioners of civil disobedience.[97] Arendt's analysis is what one would expect of a philosopher. It defines justice in the abstract, without placing it in institutional structures, as lawyers must do.[98]

Like the Reagan and Bush administrations, Arendt did not dwell on the systemic implications of lawless law enforcement. In a system of limited government, however, someone has to authorize each seizure. Unless authority is properly granted, the action cannot be legitimate. Under the American system, and particularly under the Fourth Amendment to the Constitution, a premeditated seizure of a person for a past crime has traditionally required prior judicial authorization in the form of an arrest warrant. American courts have limited authority to make exceptions to that principle; the president has even less.

If exceptions are to be made to prior judicial authorization, they must be done affirmatively, not by a wink and a nod. Abductions must be legal or illegal. They cannot be illegal for some purposes but not others. Lawless law enforcement can never be legitimate. It does not help to say, as Arendt did, that the abduction and prosecution of Eichmann was "unprecedented" and, therefore, did not set a precedent.[99] His abduction was not unprecedented and it did set precedents, both legally and politically. Moreover, to be legitimate, all decisions in a common law system must have precedent or be capable of setting precedent. That is what "neutral principles" of law means. Law cannot be legitimate if it does not transcend the case at hand. It cannot be part of a system of justice unless it is capable of standardized application.[100] If cases can be *sui generis*, as Arendt claimed Eichmann's was, then they cannot be not part of the law. They can only be lawless.[101]

Resolving to limit abduction to cases involving persons who tried to exterminate a whole people and then escaped to countries that will not give them up does not limit the precedential force of the example either, for someone eventually will argue by analogy that abduction should be used to extract other heinous criminals from other uncooperative states. In *Eichmann* the suspect was a mass murderer; in *Yunis* he was a "terrorist" who had hijacked an airliner but killed no one. In *Matta, Verdugo,* and *Alvarez*, the suspects had allegedly tortured and murdered a U.S. agent and his Mexican pilot. Before long, the chief question will not be the heinousness of the crime but simply a choice among "options." If extradition is unlikely to work, or would not assure delivery for the right charge (because of the legal limitations set by the rules of specialty and double criminality), abduction will be used.

* * *

In developing legal doctrine in the course of adjudicating individual cases, courts have an obligation not only to consider the relevant texts and legal precedents, but to imagine how the proposed doctrine might work out in practice. Unfortunately, nothing in Justice Rehnquist's opinion suggests that the majority in *Alvarez* gave the slightest thought to the political, legal, or human consequences of permitting bureaucracies to engage in abduction.

Recent history had demonstrated what some of those consequences could be. The interdiction of the Egyptian airliner played well in the American press but was responsible for the collapse of the most pro-American administration in Italy in forty years.[102] It also humiliated the president of Egypt and provoked attacks on his pro-American policies.[103] The Camarena case abductions sent a message to drug traffickers but damaged relations with Mexico and other Latin American countries.[104] The government of Mexico restricted DEA operations within the country, demanded extradition of the abductors, and insisted on renegotiation of the extradition treaty to ban abduction. It also lodged criminal charges against the DEA agents who authorized the abduction.[105] To restore DEA operations in Mexico, President Bush[106] and later President Clinton had to promise in writing that they would not authorize any abductions in Mexico during their presidencies, and the Clinton administration had to agree to a new extradition treaty that would bar abductions in perpetuity.[107]

In Honduras, the abduction of Juan Ramon Matta set off anti-American riots. On April 7, 1988, more than a thousand people, organized by left- and right-wing university students, sacked the U.S. embassy, set its annex on fire, and destroyed the consulate. Attorney General Meese blamed the violence, which killed five people and caused $4–6 million in damage, on drug traffickers, but the opposition transcended class and ideology. Even the police withheld protection from the embassy for more than two hours after the violence began.[108] As an automobile mechanic explained, "It doesn't matter whether he is a drug trafficker or a law-abiding citizen. There are certain procedures that should be followed, and they were not. He was treated like a dog picked up on the streets and taken away to the pound."[109]

In Teheran, the Majlis, or parliament, retaliated against the decision to permit the FBI to arrest persons abroad by passing a law which gave its executive authority to arrest Americans anywhere on earth for offenses against Iranian interests and deliver them to the Islamic Republic for trial by Islamic courts. The first target, an Iranian newspaper urged, should be Will Rogers III, the captain of the USS *Vincennes* when it mistakenly shot down an Iranian airbus over the Persian Gulf in 1988.[110] Other targets could include Salman Rushdie, who was wanted, dead or alive, for writing the allegedly blasphemous *Satanic Verses*.[111] The abduct-or-kill order and bounty included his foreign translators and publishers, too.[112]

Muslim extremists are not the only ones who might challenge freedom of the press with law enforcement abductions. On September 30, 1986, agents of Israel's intelligence service kidnapped author Mordechai Vanunu from Italy for publishing articles in the *Sunday Times* of London on the development of Israel's nuclear arsenal. Following *Ker* and *Eichmann*, the Israeli courts accepted jurisdiction and convicted the author of treason and espionage.[113]

The legal consequences for American agents involved in foreign abductions can be substantial, as State Department Legal Adviser Abraham Sofaer warned congressional committees in the mid-1980s. The abductors would risk not only their lives but could find themselves clapped in foreign prisons.[114] Few countries, he suggested, are likely to grant U.S. soldiers POW status for their role in a snatch operation on their soil. The U.S. Justice Department presumably would not honor an extradition request for any of its official kidnappers, but other countries might, should the kidnappers come within their jurisdiction. Refusals to extradite the kidnappers could provoke the offended government to cancel cooperative law enforcement, not just in drug investigations but in other areas, including anti-trust cases, bank fraud inquiries, and prisoner exchanges. As Sofaer summed up, "Reciprocity is at the heart of international law; all nations need to take into account the reactions of other nations to conduct which departs from accepted norms."[115]

Unmentioned in most risk analyses is the danger that abduction poses to the surrounding population. Alvarez's nurse and maid could have died before anyone found them locked in the closet. Italians could have been killed in the night, on the tarmac in Sicily, by Delta Force troopers. Bystanders in Buenos Aires could have been injured by Eichmann's kidnappers for intervening in what, to them, would have looked like a civilian crime, not a legitimate arrest. If an injured bystander were to sue U.S. kidnappers in a foreign court,[116] the kidnappers would not be entitled to assert the "Eichmann defense" of following lawful orders. The United States government itself might be sued civilly in a foreign country for the harm done to bystanders.[117] Apart from these legal questions, there is a larger one: Should bystanders in any country have to assume, when they see a kidnapping underway, that it is an act of a government?

Neither the Reagan and Bush administrations nor the Rehnquist Court have provided satisfactory answers to these questions. Nor have they adequately answered Hannah Arendt's basic question: "What are we going to say" to those foreign governments that attempt to abduct (or assassinate) persons in the United States? We cannot duck the question by insisting that it can't happen here. The United States has notoriously porous borders; abductions and assassinations have happened here. In 1956, a Columbia University professor was abducted from Morningside Heights by enemies from the Dominican dictatorship, never to be seen again.[118] In 1976, agents of the Chilean dictator August Pinochet assassinated Orlando Letelier and one of his American assistants with a car bomb in Washington, D.C.,[119] and on October 5, 1984, members of a Taiwanese criminal syndicate murdered Henry Lui, the author of a biography critical of Taiwan's president, in Daily City, California.[120] The political offense exception—the original *sine qua non* of American extradition policy—will mean little if abduction comes to be accepted as a legally and morally "viable option."

When the United States makes abduction a national policy, it must assume some responsibility for the reciprocal hostage-taking that follows. During the 1980s, for example, so many Americans and Europeans were kidnapped by anti-Israeli factions in Lebanon that the abduction of alleged terrorists by Israel and the West became increasingly risky. Israel's abduction from Lebanon of Sheik Abdul Karim Obeid on July 28, 1989, is a case in point. The Sheik was accused, among many things, of having planned the February 1988 kidnapping of U.S. Colonel William R. Higgins. Hezbollah, however, announced that the colonel had been hanged as a reprisal, and Israel postponed its criminal proceedings against the sheik in order to have him to trade for other hostages held by the Hezbollah.[121] Thus, what can begin as a law-enforcement abduction can degenerate into reciprocal hostage-taking—another power the U.S. government presumably does not possess.

Moreover, abductions abroad necessitate violations of U.S. law at home. The abduction of Humberto Alvarez did not just violate Mexican law; it violated federal and state laws against kidnapping from the moment the Mexican plane carrying him entered U.S. airspace.[122]

If we are truly honest about these matters, we should admit that all abductions are unlawful, brutal, and dangerous. No kidnapper should be trusted to tell the truth about any aspect of the case, including how the suspect came to have been injured. Kidnapping is criminal behavior, and no one who engages in it (especially bribed police officers) should be trusted to tell the truth afterwards. No court should accept the claim that the foreign government's protests really mask an approval that cannot be voiced publicly.[123]

Abduction is the political equivalent of crack cocaine. It gives elective politicians an immediate high but does long-term damage to the criminal justice system. Courts need to recognize that a real war against crime is actually a war against law, because war is the antithesis of law.

Finally, abduction is morally corrupting. As Thomas Paine warned two centuries ago: "an avidity to punish is always dangerous to liberty" because "it leads men to stretch, to misinterpret, and to misapply even the best of laws. He that would make his own liberty secure must guard even his enemy from oppression; for if he violates this duty, he establishes a precedent that will reach to himself."[124]

* * *

When Alvarez's case was finally returned to Los Angeles for trial, Judge Rafeedie discovered that the charges against the accused were based on "the wildest speculation" and ordered him released.[125] The judge also chastised federal prosecutors for failing to disclose that they had been told by Mexican authorities, well prior to trial, that the man they abducted and imprisoned for three years (and labeled "Dr. Mengele" to the press) had nothing to do with Camarena's torture or death. If the Mexican Federal Judicial Police are to be believed, the doctor who kept the U.S. drug agent alive during torture was not Humberto Alvarez but Costonoy Gonzales, the personal physician of Rafael Caro-Quintero, the drug lord at whose ranch the torture and interrogation took place.[126]

CHAPTER 22

Rethinking Extradition

It is true ... of journeys in the law that ... where one comes out ... depends on where one goes in. It makes all the difference in the world whether one recognizes [the law as] a safeguard against ... abuses, or one thinks of it as merely a requirement for a piece of paper.

Justice Felix Frankfurter, 1950

This book was meant to be long on law and reforms and short on history and politics. It has grown with increased realization that many of the articles and treatises in the field are of little use to practitioners, while many case summaries are not what they seem to be. Behind the truncated fact statements are complicated stories of real people who deserve more detailed attention than even the experts have given them. Ironically, the rule of noninquiry seems to have infected scholars as well as judges, making much of the literature excessively dependent on official versions of reality. Much of this book is an effort to reclaim that lost history.

In the early days of the republic, Americans tended to be sympathetic toward fugitives and contemptuous of most foreign legal systems. Unlike modern Americans, they felt no compulsion to police the world, favor foreign regimes over their internal challengers, or place the prestige of the United States behind a foreign regime's request. They distrusted extradition alliances because they knew how unjust governments could be. Their solution was not to engage in extradition, but to share their vision of America as a place where fugitives of all stripes could start over.

As immigration increased, the need for extradition grew. The price for extradition treaties was protection for political offenders, just as the price for a more powerful national government was adoption of a Bill of Rights. Refusing to surrender foreign rebels was not a foreign idea to which the United States acceded in order to appease foreign nations; it was the moral consequence of beginning life as a nation of asylum.

The chief threat to this tradition of asylum has always been bureaucratic. History demonstrates that U.S. government lawyers will betray the liberties of foreigners and citizens if the political (administrative, or career) advantages are great enough. They will deny such an intent, but that is what they do each time they choose not to ask what might happen to the accused upon surrender, why surrender was sought in the first place, or whether the accusations are credible. It is what they do each time they fail to share with the accused documents that would tend to discredit the charges.

In no small part, the growth of this book has been prompted by the discovery of repeated instances of judicial myopia and executive misconduct. The rule of noninquiry has repeatedly led to unjust surrenders. From Secretary Pickering's intervention against Thomas Nash to President Bush's military abduction of General Noriega, the U.S. government has been two-faced about the rule of law, particularly when foreign policy goals are at stake.

Domestic politics have also played their part, regarding not only the *Amistad* captives and fugitive slaves, but immigrants either shielded or denounced by powerful ethnic groups. The most potent threat to justice in extradition cases today, however, has come from the federal bureaucrats who, in their "police wars" against alleged terrorists, war criminals, and drug lords, have sought to remove extradition from the realm of law to the precincts of politics. In waging these ethically dirty wars, the Justice Department has too often demeaned the rule of law and rendered its own name ironic.

The record of the federal judiciary has been mixed. There have been moments of principle and courage, as in the cases of the *Amistad* captives and the East German hijackers, but more often than not, U.S. judges have functioned as judicial *apparachiks*, thoughtlessly applying the political offense exception without concern for the wantonness of the accused, or invoking the rule of noninquiry without concern for what is likely to happen to the accused after extradition. For the most part, judges have decided extradition cases mechanically, as if they were merely responsible for connecting the numbered dots on a child's drawing, or daubing colors into numbered spaces.

Like any body of law, extradition today is permeated with unwarranted assumptions, fictions, delusions, and myths. The time has come to take stock of the misguided doctrines and practices on which extradition law is now based, and to suggest some reforms.[1]

*   *   *

The mother of all delusions is that extradition does not affect "us"; it only affects "them"—fugitives from other lands, who are probably guilty anyway. In 1799, for example, no one cared about Jonathan Robbins until he claimed to be a Connecticut Yankee and an impressed seaman. Then the Jeffersonian Republicans took up his cause, insisting that he was entitled not only to a proper hearing, but to an American jury trial.

Today, few Americans know that 10 to 20 percent of all persons extradited to foreign countries in recent years have been citizens, not aliens.[2] However, because most targets of extradition are both foreigners and fugitives, all are thought to have assumed the risk that "their" own country's legal system may treat them unjustly.[3] This belief persists even when a foreigner effectively disowns his country's legal system by raising arms against it or by seeking refuge in the United States. This reasoning is applied just as thoughtlessly to third-country nationals and Americans.[4]

Many Americans believe, unlike the founders, that a person wanted for extradition must be guilty of something very serious, and will probably continue a "life of crime" if given refuge. Americans today are less likely to assume, as they once did, that the experience of "crossing over"[5] will cause foreign criminals to "reinvent themselves."[6] In the age of sail, political fugitives were not considered much of a threat to the United States or its foreign relations. Return home was unlikely, and the United States had very little government to rebel against. In the modern age of flight, however, international terrorism has given Americans good reasons to fear at least some political fugitives. Unfortunately, too much fear can lead to adverse stereotyping rather than thoughtful curiosity.

Moreover, popular fears are heightened today by the Justice Department's endorsement of a foreign regime's allegations. In the early days, foreign governments had to make their own case in court. Today, the Justice Department lends its prestige and resources to most foreign requests, not after a careful investigation of their merits, but because it wants something in return. As a result, the department has fronted for some very unsavory regimes. It has used the media to prejudice the public and the courts by attaching heinous and false labels, like "Ivan the Terrible," "Butcher of the Balkans," and "Dr. Mengele," to persons who are entitled to a presumption of innocence and dispassionate, factual assessments. Similarly, it has grossly distorted the record to make rebels like Joseph Doherty look like wanton terrorists, while extolling Nicaraguan contras as "freedom fighters."

* * *

Extradition defendants, it is assumed, do not need the protection that domestic criminal suspects enjoy, because extradition is a civil proceeding.[7] These are civil cases, according to government lawyers, "because the respondents have not been charged with an offense under U.S. law."[8] As a result, "many of the rights accorded to criminal defendants in the United States are not afforded to respondents in international extradition cases."[9]

The protection afforded by the pro forma, *ex parte* hearings that precede the issuance of domestic arrest warrants is not great, but the Fourth Amendment does require that bailable domestic defendants (who can afford it) win release within a day or two.[10] In extradition, however, many defendants are "provisionally" arrested on the basis of a mere allegation and jailed for months until the Justice Department is prepared to present the foreign regime's proof of probable cause.[11] During this time the defendants cannot support their families, which may be impoverished or torn apart because of the imprisonment.[12] Although they have committed no offense against the laws of the United States, extradition defendants must languish in jail, where they may be beaten or raped, while the Justice Department trashes their reputations in the press and while potential witnesses who might aid their defense disappear.[13]

The defendant in an extradition proceeding is more likely than a domestic suspect to be convicted unjustly at trial but is not allowed to present any elements of a legal "defense" at the extradition hearing. For example, the court will not permit the defendant to prove that he was elsewhere at the time of the crime,[14] or that the so-called new evidence against him comes from a witness previously found by a U.S. court to lack credibility.[15]

As government lawyers often say, the accused does not have the right to turn an extradition proceeding into a "mini-trial," complete with alibi witnesses and the right to cross-examine his accusers. He is only allowed to "explain" or "clarify" the accusations or evidence.[16] His counsel may not block the introduction of hearsay[17] even though the risks of hearsay are greater in extradition cases, because most foreign witnesses have not been questioned (or had their credibility checked) by American investigators. The U.S. attorneys who attack the accused in the press and at the extradition hearing have no motive to question or produce foreign witnesses for cross-examination. Nor need they fear embarrassment if the affidavits on which they rely are later discredited at trial.[18]

Most defendants in extradition proceedings will not be allowed to challenge foreign documents of doubtful credibility, like the doctored identity card used against Demjanjuk or the "new" affidavits charging Artuković with ordering massacres that never happened.[19] Because extradition proceedings are deemed civil in nature, judges do not imagine that the Fifth or Sixth Amendments allow them to insist that foreign accusations be made under oath and subject to some sort of accountability.[20] Nor do judges believe they should require the requesting state to produce accusers. In *Bingham v. Bradley*, one justice noted that "It is one of the objects [of extradition law] to obviate the necessity of confronting the accused with the witnesses against him."[21]

Similarly, as the Demjanjuk, Artuković, McMullen, and Doherty cases demonstrate, judges feel no obligation to acknowledge that the accused might have a constitutional right to speedy disposition of extradition proceeding.[22] At least two American circuits do not allow the accused in an extradition proceeding to assert his Fifth Amendment privilege against self-incrimination if the feared incrimination would occur under the laws of a foreign regime.[23] Even if the accused defeats extradition, as Artuković did in the 1950s, he cannot claim that the principles of res judicata or double jeopardy protect him from being subjected to the same ordeal again.[24] If at first the government does not succeed, it can try, try again.

It is wrong to claim that extradition is not as much a part of the criminal justice process as any indictment in the United States.[25] Indeed, the Supreme Court has acknowledged that extradition is, in essence, a "case of a criminal nature."[26] Extradition cases initiate criminal trials. Foreign prosecutors initiate extradition. They are represented by American prosecutors who are supervised by the Criminal, not Civil, Division of the Justice Department. The accused is arrested, not summoned, and is normally imprisoned without bail pending completion of the process. In cases involving airline hijackers, the United States has agreed to prosecute those it does not extradite, even when the "crime" was part of a desperate attempt to escape pursuing secret police.[27] To call extradition a civil rather than criminal process, in order to justify a lower level of legal safeguards for the accused, is not just false; it is unconscionable.

One remedy for the low level of rights currently afforded the accused in U.S. extradition proceedings has been suggested by the International Law Association's Committee on Extradition and Human Rights, of which the author was a member.[28] It proposes amending extradition legislation to insure that

1. extradition proceedings, whether labeled as judicial or administrative, are treated as criminal proceedings in which the individual should be entitled to the pertinent safeguards for criminal trials contained in Article 14 of the International Covenant on Civil and Political Rights, Article 6 of the European Convention on Human Rights, Article 8 of the American Human Rights Convention, and Article 7 of the African Charter on Human and Peoples' Rights.
2. the individual is himself entitled to assert these rights in such proceedings.
3. the courts of the requested state should not apply the rule of noninquiry, that is, refuse to inquire into human rights violations in the requesting state.
4. provision be made for a procedure which would allow the fugitive to obtain discovery of pertinent documents in the requesting state to assist him in extradition proceedings. In particular, the requested person should be entitled, upon request, to exculpatory information obtained by the requested state in the course of its investigations on behalf of the requesting state, unless confidential sources or methods would be compromised thereby.
5. evidence obtained in violation of human rights norms shall not be admitted at the trial against the accused person.
6. reports of nongovernmental organizations on the criminal justice system of the requesting state shall be admissible in extradition proceedings in the requested State.

* * *

Another misleading notion is that extradition magistrates do not, in certifying extraditability, exercise the "judicial power of the United States." This claim was broached by Justice Benjamin R. Curtis in 1853, when he argued that the Supreme Court lacked jurisdiction to hear the appeal of a habeas decision that had upheld a finding of extraditability, because extradition magistrates do not, "strictly speaking, . . . exercise any part of the judicial power of the United States."[29]

In December 1996, the U.S. Court of Appeals for the Second Circuit used this theory to strike down a challenge to the extradition statute's constitutionality. The issue had arisen in 1995, when Judge Royce C. Lamberth surprised everyone by ruling that the extradition statute violated the constitutional principle of separation of powers by subjecting the decisions of judges made independent by Article 3 to "revision" by the executive.[30] Lamberth's superiors on the Court of Appeals for the District of Columbia quickly vacated his ruling for lack of jurisdiction,[31] but its novel arguments were promptly reasserted in numerous other extradition cases,[32] including one before the Second Circuit.[33]

In *Lo Duca*, the Court of Appeals for the Second Circuit ruled the extradition statute does not violate the independence of the judiciary, because extradition judges do not exercise Article 3 powers. They do not, the judges reasoned in part, because the treaty (and case law) have recognized in the executive a power to "revise" the magistrate's decision.[34]

Nonsense. The executive has no power to revise a judge's refusal to certify that a person may be extradited. The court's denial has been binding on the executive since 1795.[35] The secretary of state cannot surrender the accused unless and until another judge rules otherwise. Similarly, if the judge certifies that the person is extraditable, his decision does not require surrender, any more than a judge's decision to schedule a case for trial strips the executive of its discretion to drop the case for lack of evidence. A certificate of extraditability simply grants to the executive an option that it would not otherwise have—very much like a warrant that allows but does not compel the executive to search a home or seize a person. Indeed, without a certificate of extraditability, the secretary of state would have no authority to issue a warrant authorizing delivery. The idea that extradition judges do not exercise the judicial power of the United States is an abstruse bit of legal metaphysics, "comprehensible only to a few federal court scholars."[36] No matter what legal theologians say, the work of extradition magistrates is clearly "judicial" in nature.[37] They work for, and under the supervision of, Article 3 judges.[38] Indeed, probable cause decisions in extradition are very much like probable cause findings at the beginning of most domestic criminal cases.[39] As Judge Henry Friendly wryly observed, if extradition were truly administrative, it would be governed by the Administrative Procedure Act, and courts would have to be reclassified as administrative agencies.[40]

To make extradition look administrative, government lawyers often remind us that the Supreme Court has described extradition as a "national" act, performed by the executive branch pursuant to treaties and acts of Congress,[41] ignoring the fact that the president does not have a monopoly on acting for the nation. They also argue, less plausibly, but with some judicial support, that the power to surrender a fugitive for extradition is vested in the president pursuant to the treaty-making and foreign affairs powers granted to him by Article 2.[42] While vaguely true from an international relations perspective, these statements make no sense as a matter of constitutional law, because they mask the fact that the power to deliver a free person for trial is constitutionally subject to judicial check. What political scientists vaguely call the "foreign affairs power" may reside with the president, but the courts and Congress have the authority to limit what the president does with that power. This would be true whether the judges derive their power from Article 3, Amendments Four and Five, or state constitutions (had federal courts not been created).

Nothing in the Constitution supports the idea of extradition as a civil proceeding, or a non–Article 3, non–"case or controversy" subject to executive "revision." Article 3 clearly states that "The judicial Power of the United States, shall be vested in one Supreme Court, and in such inferior Courts as Congress may from time to time ordain and establish." Congress "cannot vest review of the decisions of Article 3 courts in the Executive Branch," or make federal judges advisors to the executive.[43] Article 3 judges have frequently ruled on extradition requests, either in the first instance or in response to habeas corpus petitions, and nothing in the Constitution provides for their constitutional unfrocking in order to carry out this responsibility.

Equally important, the Fourth Amendment's requirement of probable cause, like the Fifth Amendment's guarantee of due process, presupposes that extradition magistrates will be as neutral and detached as any judge deciding whether to issue an arrest warrant or bind a domestic suspect over for trial. Article 3 does not provide that if Congress chooses to shift preliminary hearings in extradition (or domestic criminal cases) from federal (or state) judges to U.S. commissioners or federal magistrate-judges, the hearings somehow cease to be "cases or controversies." The fact that the trial, if any, may occur in a foreign court should not diminish the genuineness of the "case or controversy," any more than a proceeding for a writ of habeas corpus or an arrest warrant should fail to satisfy Article 3's definition of a "case or controversy."

The claim that extradition proceedings are not "cases or controversies" is sometimes associated with the claim that the judicial review required by the Fourth Amendment need not be rendered by a judge at all, much less by one appointed pursuant to Article 3.[44] But this may be a distinction without a difference, because the Fourth Amendment requires that probable cause to arrest a person be assessed by someone independent of the police and the prosecution,[45] not an executive official, or a judge dispensing an "advisory opinion." A decision denying the executive authority to carry out a planned arrest is binding on the executive; it is not subject to "revision" by that executive.[46] As the Second Circuit has ruled, if a magistrate denies extraditability, "the matter is dead."[47] The reason should be obvious: "the Constitution creates no executive prerogative to dispose of the liberty of the individual. Proceedings against him must be authorized by law. There is no executive discretion to surrender him to a foreign government, unless that discretion is granted by law."[48]

Failure by the executive to obey a magistrate's denial of an arrest warrant would not only violate American extradition treaties, the 1848 procedural statute, and the Constitution's Fourth Amendment; it would also exceed the president's authority under Article 2. So too would failure to obey the denial of a certificate of extraditability—at least until a more agreeable magistrate can be found. No incantation of Article 3 theology can do away with this constitutional check on executive power.

An act of Congress transferring probable cause decisions from an independent judiciary ("neutral magistrate") to government investigators, which is what the hated "writs of assistance" did, would also violate the Fourth Amendment, for the obvious reason that executive officials are presumptively not neutral. They are the very people that the probable cause, neutral magistrate requirement was meant to check.[49] So too would a treaty purporting to do the same.[50] Thus, when neither the treaty nor a statute specified who was to ascertain probable cause, the Supreme Court recognized that the power belongs with the judiciary, not the executive.[51]

Practice confirms this reasoning. Never has the executive directly defied a magistrate's ruling that a person was not extraditable.[52] Whether the power to deny a certificate of extraditability comes from a treaty, the procedural statute, Article 3, or the Fourth Amendment, it is a judicial power that the executive must obey.

* * *

Still another dubious proposition is that bail should not be granted to the accused prior to the extradition hearing, except in the most "special circumstances."[53] Government lawyers sometimes claim that courts may not grant bail in extradition cases unless Congress has expressly authorized them to do so,[54] but lower court judges have not accepted this argument. On the contrary, they have assumed an inherent power to grant bail in extradition cases, and then chosen to exercise that power sparingly.[55]

"In general," the State Department has claimed, "it is the practice of the United States courts to allow persons provisionally arrested to remain at large on bond if there is no evidence that the person is about to flee."[56] This misrepresents current judicial practice. In *Parretti v. United States*, the district court denied bail even though the judge expressly found that the accused was not likely to flee.[57] Bail is commonly denied in extradition cases, and its denial is virtually automatic in the First, Second, and Fifth Circuits, where "special circumstances" are almost impossible to prove.[58]

"Special circumstances" that might warrant release on bond are not well developed, but as a general rule, the accused must do more than show that he poses no danger to the community and is unlikely to flee.[59] The hardships of prison,[60] financial difficulties,[61] or bad health[62] are rarely persuasive.[63] The need to consult counsel in civil litigation or to assist in the defense against extradition will rarely move a court to grant bail either.[64]

This is the reverse of domestic law, where in theory "liberty is the norm, and detention prior to trial or without trial is the carefully limited exception."[65] In ordinary criminal cases, the burden is on the government to prove that special circumstances, like the probability of flight or danger to the community,[66] justify *denying* bail. In extradition cases, the burden is on the accused to prove that special circumstances justify *granting* bail. The double standard is sometimes justified on the assumption that all extradition targets are fugitives, which is not true, or more often by the political concern that relations with the requesting state will be harmed if the accused jumps bail.[67] In ordinary criminal cases, vague expressions of "urgency" by prosecutors are not sufficient to block bail; in extradition cases they tend to be decisive, especially when the U.S. government adds its "urgency" to that of the foreign regime.[68]

While bail has been granted in some cases without proof of extra-special circumstances,[69] the bar is impossibly high in most "war on crime" cases. Thus, while Andrija Artuković was released on bail in the 1950s, he was denied release thirty years later.[70] If extradition were genuinely a civil proceeding, OSI could have mailed the eighty-six-year-old invalid a summons, which his attorney could have answered on his behalf. Demjanjuk, a retired motor mechanic, was no more likely to flee (or harm anyone) than Artuković, but he was locked up pending his extradition hearing. Denial of bail was used by OSI to punish both men before trial.

The near total ban on bail in extradition cases should be considered a violation of the Eighth Amendment's prohibition against "excessive bail" and the Fifth Amendment's due process clause. Unfortunately, the U.S. Supreme Court has ruled that neither provision creates a constitutional right to pretrial release.[71] No such right exists, the Court has explained in a deportation case, because the Eighth Amendment does not expressly grant one.[72] Were that reasoning valid, however, all adults could have been denied the right to vote prior to 1868, when the Fifteenth Amendment finally acknowledged that such a right existed. The most cursory review of the Constitution will reveal that the framers expressed numerous liberties in terms of restrictions on the power of government, including the rights guaranteed by the First, Second, Third, Fourth, Thirteenth, and Fourteenth Amendments. There is no reason to read the Eighth Amendment differently.

If the Eighth Amendment is not explicit enough, the Fifth Amendment provides that "No person ... shall be denied ... liberty ... without due process of law." Imprisonment without bail is precisely the kind of arbitrary practice that provoked the American Revolution.[73] Finally, it must be remembered that courts do grant bail in some extradition cases. From where does that authority come, if not from constitutionally appropriate judicial powers?

* * *

The rule against bail is aggravated by treaty provisions authorizing the "provisional arrest" of fugitives in "urgent circumstances," that is, before documents or witnesses establishing probable cause can be supplied.[74] The practice dates from the age of sail, when it took weeks or months for slow-moving mails and slow-traveling witnesses to catch up with telegraphed detention requests, but it remains common practice in the age of fax machines and high-speed air travel. The practice was developed when extradition was entertained only for the most serious of offenses, but it persists now that extradition is allowed for a wide range of relatively minor crimes.

Before a person is subject to a planned arrest, a judge is supposed to subject the allegations and supporting evidence to careful scrutiny. The Fourth Amendment would appear to demand it, or at the very least require the court to make ambiguous treaty language conform to constitutional standards.[75] However, the U.S. Court of Appeals for the Second Circuit has gone so far as to claim that it has the discretion to depart "from usual Fourth Amendment protections" if the foreign policy interest in the executive is sufficiently strong,[76] and no court has ever held a treaty clause allowing for provisional arrests unconstitutional.

The Justice Department has argued that "there is ample probable cause for arrest for extradition if there is reliable information that a specified person is the subject of an arrest warrant in a foreign jurisdiction for an extraditable offense." In other words, the independent judicial review required by the Fourth Amendment need not be exercised by an American jurist; it can be delegated to foreign officials, who do not need to be independent judges.[77] Unfortunately, the Ninth Circuit has accepted this circumlocution, allowing the U.S. government to put a person behind bars, pending an extradition hearing, on the basis of an unsubstantiated foreign warrant.[78] Thus judges have allowed the "urgencies" of international politics to erase a constitutional right.[79]

In 1997, a panel of the U.S. Court of Appeals for the Ninth Circuit finally decided, by a 2–1 vote, that the provisional arrest provision of the extradition statute and its corresponding provision in the U.S.-French extradition treaty were unconstitutional.

In *Parretti v. United States*,[80] the Justice Department had asked the court not to look behind the foreign warrant, much as the Van Buren administration had asked Judge Judson not to question the Spanish documents claiming that the *Amistad* captives were slaves, not freemen. France's accusations, the department claimed, were entitled to "full faith and credit," as if France were the fifty-first state of the American Union. The argument brought back John Stuart Mill's fear of unsubstantiated French charges, expressed in his opposition to extradition without probable cause in the parliamentary debates of 1866.[81] Whether this decision will spread to other circuits, remains to be seen.

* * *

Probable cause hearings in the United States, like trials in foreign lands, are assumed to be just. In truth, as a former Justice Department attorney has written, "the deck is stacked in favor of the government."[82] The most serious loading comes at the investigative stage, where there are no checks on carelessness or misconduct by the requesting regime and where the Department of Justice vouches for an investigation it has not conducted and a regime it may know to be less than just. In domestic criminal cases, American prosecutors feel some obligation to adhere to professional standards, if only because their credibility will be on the line at trial. In extradition, however, there is no such check on carelessness or misconduct, because the trial that might embarrass U.S. attorneys will be held years later in a foreign land.

U.S. attorneys who represent foreign regimes in extradition cases have a conflict of interest, because the same Criminal Division that supervises the litigation of foreign requests also negotiates for the return of fugitives from American law. Recovering such fugitives is a career-enhancing activity; torpedoing a foreign government's request is not. Thus, government attorneys will develop their own rules of noninquiry.

Ethical compromises are even worse when extradition (and deportation) are used to get rid of alleged war criminals. Here the political pressures to cut corners are especially great, because congressional pressures are even more influential than foreign demands. As the Walus, Fedorenko, Artuković, and Demjanjuk cases demonstrate, the Office of Special Investigations has been notorious for prejudicing proceedings with inflammatory charges, mishandling and losing evidence, soliciting extradition requests, and not sharing exculpatory evidence with the defense. As the history of religious wars demonstrated long ago, the worst abuses tend to be committed for the best of causes.

It is no secret, according to a former Justice Department specialist in extradition, that "courts will generally resolve any doubts in favor of finding a person extraditable."[83] Moreover, judges "need not be reminded that these cases are important to the foreign policy interests of the United States."[84] In extradition cases, the thumb of politics weighs heavily on the scales of justice.

That need not be the case. "In dealing with probable cause," the Supreme Court has held, "we deal with probabilities. These are not technical; they are the factual and practical considerations of every-day life on which reasonable and prudent men, not legal technicians, act."[85] Thus, hearsay can be used, provided there is "a substantial basis for crediting the hearsay."[86] Unfortunately, this limit on the use of hearsay is rendered meaningless when both the courts and the executive fail to question the veracity of foreign allegations and do not insist on calling live witnesses whom the defense can cross-examine. If a probable cause determination is to be both factual and practical, it is not enough that foreign prosecutors allege the accused committed a crime. Courts should require that the documents (and witnesses) disclose where the allegations came from and whether they are hearsay. If the documents are inadequate, the magistrate should not hesitate to demand the testimony of eyewitnesses, to make certain that the eyewitnesses were not manipulated, and to insist on documentary corroboration of eyewitnesses whenever possible.[87] This is what courts should mean when they say that submissions "must be tested . . . in a commonsense and realistic fashion."[88]

Unfortunately, the very flexibility that these commonsense judgments invite is forsworn in extradition cases. Courts frequently say that defendants cannot turn an extradition hearing into a mini-trial on the merits. This permits the courts to ignore alibi evidence[89] and any proof that the alleged crimes never happened,[90] that the accusers were tortured,[91] or that previous testimony by them in American courts on the same subject was rejected as not credible.[92]

Nothing in the law prevents extradition courts from allowing the defense far more latitude than they do in "clarifying" the alleged evidence against the defendant. For example, judges could, as the Second and Ninth Circuits have done, assert their "inherent power" to authorize as much prehearing discovery "as law and justice require."[93] Indeed, failure to order adequate discovery in an extradition case might constitute a denial of due process.[94] Since extradition is very much part of the criminal justice process, the governments involved should be required to disclose any information in their possession that "would tend to establish the validity of any defense to extradition."[95] Such a rule, well enforced, could have spared John Demjanjuk and his family their protracted ordeal.

Judges could also admit alibis on occasion and examine public record information to see if the alleged events actually occurred, or occurred as described. When in doubt, they could require additional submissions, sworn statements, presentation of witnesses, and cross-examination.[96] In the case of hijackers-to-freedom and alleged terrorists, they could also hear broader arguments in justification and excuse than are now possible under the political offense exception, much as was done under German law in the Tiede case.[97]

All these modifications of extradition procedure should be as fully within the discretion of an extradition court as any rule restricting bail or refusing to question the willingness or capacity of the requesting regime to do justice. Courts could also allow extradition defendants to conduct pretrial discovery into the evidence against them,[98] and even depose their accusers, if only by telephone. Unfortunately, once the judges begin connecting the numbered dots of misguided precedents, it is enormously difficult for them to back up and embrace a more just and decent procedure.

Probable cause hearings are supposed to involve commonsense judgments, but nothing defies common sense more than the unwillingness of courts to consider what might have motivated the foreign regime to demand surrender of the accused. The so-called "second limb" of the political offense exception, first introduced by the United Kingdom in its 1870 statute, was supposed to protect against trumped-up charges, but in Anglo-American law, questioning the motives of the requesting regime has become a political rather than judicial function.[99] Of course, this does not mean that judges may not quietly take notice of bad motives, as they did when denying dubious requests by communist regimes during the Cold War.[100] Unfortunately, it takes abhorrence of a communist regime to override the powerful presumption that the requesting government is acting legitimately, and even that abhorrence can be overcome by executive allegation that the accused is a heinous war criminal, terrorist, or drug dealer.

When American courts refuse to accept evidence from the defendant that the requesting regime is acting in bad faith, they usually claim that the executive is better equipped to make such sensitive judgments. This is not true. The defense is much better equipped to explain why the request amounts to political persecution. The Departments of Justice and State are in bed with their foreign clients and cannot be trusted to exercise independent judgment.

Extradition, to government lawyers, is not a matter of justice. It is a form of mutual assistance among law-enforcement professionals.[101] It is a corrupt relationship, and should be ended. Only when foreign regimes have to represent themselves in court can we expect the Departments of Justice and State to screen foreign requests with anything approaching a skeptical eye, and then only if the screeners are not compromised by any responsibility for recovering American fugitives from foreign lands.

* * *

When extradition was first allowed, the rule of double criminality was the primary safeguard against unauthorized extraditions. By limiting extradition to a few countries and to a few serious, nonpolitical offenses, and by relying on the doctrine that criminal laws are supposed to be construed strictly, the founders of American extradition law sought to limit the volume, and hence the abuse, of extradition. No longer. Now the United States has allowed both extradition agreements and extraditable offenses to proliferate. Today, the practice of listing crimes has given way, in some treaties, to provisions allowing extradition for all offenses subject to imprisonment for a year or more. Misdemeanors for which the founders would not have allowed extradition have become felonies, which will in time increase the volume, and hence the abuse, of extradition.

Moreover, the Supreme Court has retreated from the principle that criminal laws should be strictly construed, holding instead that extradition treaties should be liberally construed, because that is how commercial treaties are normally read.[102] But extradition should not be treated as just another form of international trade; it involves liberty and justice and should be held to the stricter standards of constitutional and criminal law.

When vague treaties are liberally construed to favor extradition, the accused may later be tried for an offense for which he was not extradited. In its laxity, at least one U.S. court authorized extradition for what the requesting state considered a felony but which in the United States would have been a misdemeanor,[103] thus eroding the principle that extradition will be allowed only for the most serious of offenses. In at least two instances, U.S. courts have upheld extradition even before charges had been filed against the accused in the requesting state's courts.[104]

Yet another outmoded view holds that treaties can grant no rights to individuals, because states are the only parties to them. Thus, while the rule of specialty is included in most U.S. extradition treaties, the accused may not assert it at an American extradition hearing. Nor may he assert it at trial, unless the surrendering state allows him to by filing a diplomatic protest.[105] In practice, this means that the rule of specialty is of no consequence unless the objecting state is so furious at its breach that it cannot be bought off by diplomatic concessions of any kind.

Nothing need prevent treaty makers (or legislators) from granting enforcement rights to individuals as a matter of domestic law,[106] which is what extradition treaties do now when they provide for a judicial hearing on probable cause and charge judges with administering the political offense exception. To say that treaties do not confer rights on individuals is nothing more than a rule of construction that could easily be confined to treaties that do not threaten to deprive individuals of life, liberty, or due process. Where individual rights are at stake, courts should be able to adopt more protective rules, as they did when they (and the executive) decided that extraditability had to be determined by courts (before treaties said so), and that exceptions for political offenses did not just confer duties on the executive but bestowed a judicially enforceable right upon individuals.

Today, U.S. officials find it convenient to insist that individuals have no rights under extradition treaties,[107] but that has not always been the government's position. In 1895, Secretary of State Walter Q. Gresham expressly declared that the idea that treaties conferred rights only on states was "certainly not the law of the United States."[108] Consistent with this view, some U.S. treaties have been found by courts to bestow rights on individuals.[109]

Whatever international law says, treaties are also domestic law,[110] to be interpreted consistently with the higher law of the Constitution. Accordingly, there should be no barrier to a decision overruling the abduction cases, and holding that extradition was meant to be the only lawful way by which the United States may recover people it wishes to prosecute from those foreign countries with which it has extradition treaties.

To say that an accused may not invoke the rule of specialty at his extradition hearing, and may invoke it only at trial and only if the extraditing state objects to additional or different charges, is to make the unwarranted assumption that only the extraditing executive has any interest in, or standing to, invoke the rule. It is to say that because the executive speaks for the United States diplomatically, it can ignore a violation of the rule of specialty, even though that rule is implicit in each judicial certificate authorizing surrender of the accused. This reasoning also overlooks the tripartite structure of American government, and the fact that courts certify extradition only on condition that the accused be tried on those charges for which surrender is authorized.

As certifiers of extraditability, courts have a much greater interest in assuring compliance with the terms of surrender than the executive. Conversely, nothing should prevent a foreign trial court from asking an American extradition court whether the grant of extradition would be violated by trying the accused for a somewhat different, but arguably included, crime.[111] Allowing the courts to communicate directly with each other would provide a useful check against unintentional or deliberate misrepresentations by the diplomats and attorneys of both governments regarding the terms of surrender.[112]

Extradition courts should make the rule of specialty available not only at the extradition hearing either to block or condition surrender, but as a motion to reconsider once the accused discovers that conditions are not being met. Just as Demjanjuk's extradition case was reopened in Ohio after he had been convicted in Israel, so an extradition decision should be subject to reconsideration when it becomes known that the terms of surrender have been violated (or misconstrued). Perhaps all the defendant can expect from the extradition court at this late date is a declaratory judgment clarifying the terms of surrender, but that should be sufficient in most instances.[113]

* * *

Proponents of the political offense exception often overstate its effectiveness in averting foreign injustice. Jefferson's approach was more effective; no extradition with unjust regimes, period. Since then, we have seen an almost promiscuous proliferation of extradition treaties, making the political offense exception even more important.

The exception, however, only protects participants in uprisings. It does not protect people like Jonathan Robbins, the *Amistad* captives, and the East Germans, all of whom hijacked their way to freedom, because not all fugitives from oppression have the time, inclination, or resources to organize an uprising before fleeing. For such people, reformers have proposed applying the *nonrefoulement* principle of asylum law to all extradition cases, because it recognizes that one does not have to be a revolutionary (or deposed official) to be prejudiced at trial or restricted in one's liberty by reason of race, religion, nationality, or political opinions.

Like the so-called "second limb" of the political offense exception, however, the *nonrefoulement* principle means little if it is left solely to the executive, with its conflicts of interest, to enforce. It will also mean little if courts (or the executive) insist that to prove "a well-grounded fear of prosecution," the accused must show something like "clear and convincing proof" that the requesting state has plotted or tolerated plots against him personally.[114] Some people, like kulaks fleeing Stalin or Jews escaping Hitler, cannot prove that the requesting regime has specific plans to send them to Siberia or Treblinka. All they know, and it should be enough, is that people like them are routinely denied justice. Similarly, those who are sent to a Devil's Island cannot prove that the government has specific plans to harm them; they only know that people who are sent to such prisons are routinely brutalized. They may not hijack their way to freedom, like the *Amistad* captives, but they may, like fugitive slaves, commit an extraditable crime in the course of escaping. Such people should not only be eligible for an executive grant of asylum and an executive withholding of deportation; they should be able to ask a court to bar extradition, because the requesting regime is not likely to accord justice to people like them.[115]

How is an extradition judge to know when a foreign regime is unlikely to do justice in similar situations? No easy answer exists, but there are a number of indicators, either of an intent to persecute or a likelihood of discriminatory treatment. These include, but are not limited to, the following.[116]

1. The investigation of the crime was conducted by a different law-enforcement branch than that which normally conducts criminal investigations.
2. The discretion to prosecute deviates from normal prosecutorial discretion in the requesting state, as evidenced, for example, by the resurrection of an unenforced law.
3. A political leader has intervened in the decision to investigate or prosecute.
4. The defendant will be tried in a different court than that used for ordinary criminals.
5. The defendant will be tried by a form of revolutionary tribunal.
6. The requesting state maintains separate penal or interrogation facilities for political prisoners, and the requesting government intends to interrogate the defendant in such facilities.
7. The defendant, or a group with which he or she has been actively associated, is politically controversial or has been the target of systematic discrimination.
8. The defendant has been the target of political surveillance, covert harassment, or official criticism in the requesting state or in the United States.
9. The defendant has actively opposed the policies or the legitimacy of the requesting state's government, either while resident there or elsewhere, in a manner that has provoked reprisals from that government against others similarly situated.
10. The issues involved in the case are so controversial that it is doubtful the accused could receive a fair trial or, if convicted, a fair sentence.
11. The requesting state cannot guarantee the physical safety of the accused if he or she is returned.

If the accused offers proof of factors like these, the requesting state should be allowed to rebut the evidence or offer monitorable assurances. The views of the State Department's human rights office or organizations like Amnesty International could also be solicited.

The standard of proof of possible persecution should be probable cause and nothing higher, because probable cause is the constitutional standard.[117] This is the standard embraced by the British House of Lords when applying the Fugitive Offenders Act, which has also used terms like "reasonable chance," "substantial grounds for thinking," or "a serious possibility."[118] In practice, each of these terms will reflect a variety of subjective factors, and will, like the probable cause standard itself, be subject to some slippage.[119] That said, the accused should not be required to prove the impossible, which unfortunately is becoming the case under Senator Eagleton's misrepresentation of the *nonrefoulement* provision of the supplementary U.S.-U.K. extradition treaty.[120]

For each extradition court to take expert testimony about the state of legal and human rights in the requesting states is inefficient and could turn extradition courts into political forums for irredentist groups. Seeking advisory opinions from international legal bodies would be cumbersome, and would open those groups to political manipulation.[121] A better way to proceed might be to develop systems for "accrediting" legal systems. Nongovernmental groups (like Amnesty International, Human Rights Watch, or the International Commission of Jurists), international bodies (like the U.N.'s Human Rights Committee and the Subcommission on the Prevention of Discrimination and Protection of Minorities), and domestic civil liberties and human rights groups (including local Amnesty chapters) could assess prosecutorial offices, courts, and prisons and produce composite judgments as to whether governments are to be trusted (with or without conditions) to deal justly with the accused.[122] If the requesting state refuses to allow such evaluations or interferes with their conduct, it should be placed on an "unaccredited regimes" list, and all extradition relations should be suspended. Never again should a judge say, as Oliver Wendell Holmes once did, that "We are compelled by the existence of an extradition treaty to assume that the trial will be fair."[123]

Meanwhile, the political offense exception should be modified, as some American courts have tried to do, to permit the surrender of political fugitives credibly charged with wanton and heinous crimes,[124] provided that the requesting regime is able to treat them fairly. It is nonsense to say that the political offense exception is no longer needed because yesterday's freedom fighters have been replaced by today's "terrorists." However, it is equally important to recognize that the exception should not be used to shield a person who indiscriminately kills and maims innocent people, just because the person happened to work for a political organization, governmental or private. People who gas subways, murder Olympic teams, bomb department stores, or try to topple skyscrapers should not be exempt from extradition just because they were hoping to make a political statement. Conversely, people who torture, rape, and maim political opponents on behalf of a murderous regime should not be shielded from extradition, as Commissioner Hocke mistakenly ruled in the first Artuković case. General Pinochet and similar dictators should not be able to escape extradition just because kidnapping, torture, and murder were their way of suppressing uprisings or fighting "terrorists."

The cause of justice is not served by *per se* exemptions from the political offense exception, like the one for all highjackers. Central to the exception is the same moral principle of explanation and excuse applied in the Tiede case.[125] In some respects, the political offense exception approaches a judicially administered grant of asylum, based on an impartial assessment of the nature and quality of the alleged criminal's acts, viewed realistically in context.[126]

Per se exemptions are inexcusably simpleminded and lead to all manner of embar-
rassments and hypocrisies, as the cases of numerous hijackers-to-freedom demonstrate.[127] That some IRA members have been wanton terrorists should not change a
court's evaluation of Joseph Doherty's actions, or lead courts to bias their judgments
in favor of the executive's current political alliances. Courts should not be overly
impressed by governmental or press labels, favoring anti-Castro Cubans who bomb
civilian airliners over IRA soldiers who shoot British soldiers attacking them. Nor
should judges be quick to classify armed settlers and their families who occupy an
indigenous people's lands as "innocent," or assume that modern revolutionaries can
easily avoid civilian casualties and still hope for success.

* * *

Distinguished jurists like Jack Weinstein and distinguished scholars like Alfred P.
Rubin have argued cogently for using the concept of "war crimes" to give content to
the term "political offense." Others, including the American Civil Liberties Union
and this author, have urged a "wanton crimes" exception to the political offense
exception. Both approaches assert moral limits to what may legitimately be done to
advance or suppress an uprising.

The war crimes approach has the virtue of tapping an established, if rarely used,
body of existing law set forth in statutes, treaties, and military regulations. It would
simply extend that law to non-international armed conflicts. The wanton crimes
approach would require ad hoc judicial development, not unlike the way courts have
developed the tort of outrage or, critics might say, the law of obscenity.

If the wanton crimes approach seems too subjective (and hardly something one
might wish to trust to judges who do not get constitutionally outraged over abduction and torture), the war crimes approach might limit the definition of an uprising to something more closely approximating conventional warfare. It might also
discourage judges from granting the political offense exception to people who have
never joined an uprising—like the Polish seamen who hijacked their fishing trawler
to England to avoid standing trial in Poland for their anti-communist opinions.
Limiting the political offense exception to warlike situations may force the accused
to prove membership in a paramilitary uprising group, which may be difficult to
do (because its leaders may not wish to testify), and may be self-incriminating at
some later proceeding. In an age when the surveillance and retaliation powers of
established governments can be substantial, expecting uprising groups to fight like
armies may be unrealistic, particularly when governments do not follow the laws
of war either.

The war crimes approach also risks show trials and verdicts based on guilt by association, because it shifts attention away from the nature and quality of the individual's actions and onto the tactics of his group, some of which may be heinous. The
wanton crimes approach at least focuses attention where it should belong—on the
nature and quality of the defendant's acts. Thus it recognizes that the accused may
belong to a group that has, on occasion, committed heinous acts but, like Joseph

Doherty, did nothing himself that would warrant exempting him from protection as a political offender.

The wanton crimes approach should encourage analyzing what the accused did in the context of what the foreign government was doing in return. For example, it would have made a difference if Joseph Doherty's alleged murder of a British officer had been understood as not just another of the IRA's atrocities, but part of a shoot-out between two squads of plainclothes soldiers, both hoping to kill each other. Similarly, the bombing of civilian marketplaces might seem less heinous once it is understood that, within a few years of capturing Palestinian or Jordanian territory, the Israeli government sought to settle it permanently with armed civilians. An exception for the wanton crimes might encourage a fuller, comparative moral analysis than the laws of war approach.

* * *

Another outmoded view of extradition is that judicial review of a finding of extraditability, done in response to a petition for a writ of habeas corpus, is limited to little more than deciding whether the magistrate had jurisdiction. It is not the function of the habeas court, we are told, "to retry the magistrate's case."[128] The godfather of this view was Justice Holmes, who also insisted, with his usual bias in favor of people in power, that the degree of proof required to certify a person as extraditable need not be great.[129] To Holmes and his colleagues, the function of a habeas review was virtually perfunctory.[130]

But that was in 1925, well before the due process revolution of the 1960s expanded habeas reviews to correct all sorts of constitutional errors.[131] At least one court has chosen to consign Holmes's narrow-mindedness to "the context of its time," which is a polite way of dropping it in the dustbin of history.[132] Habeas courts today not only correct procedural failings "that are of a constitutional dimension," but they consider whether "the substantive conduct of the United States in undertaking its decision to extradite . . . violates constitutional rights."[133]

In addition, the time has come to bury the myth that a judicial finding that a person is extraditable, coupled with an executive intent to surrender, is not sufficiently final[134] to permit a direct appeal. When the defendant has already been convicted abroad, a decision to surrender him is about as final as any court decision gets. Even when he faces a trial, the consequences to his liberty and the risks of injustice are too great not to provide for full appellate review of a finding that the accused may extradited.[135] Recognizing this, the Senate insisted that the supplementary extradition treaty with the United Kingdom provide for direct appeal of adverse decisions under its new *nonrefoulement* clause.[136] That principle should be extended by statute to protect more fully each person's constitutional, statutory, and treaty rights.

* * *

The judicial doctrine is that extradition treaties are "self-executing" is also dubious. Once the Senate has consented and the president has filed a formal ratification, an extradition treaty is as much the law of the land as any statute.[137] This means, in effect, that citizens and aliens alike can be exposed to prosecution in such benighted legal systems as Albania's and Haiti's by action of the president and two-thirds of the Senate, without the consent of the House or the involvement of the House or Senate Judiciary Committees. Were extradition treaties not "self-executing," they would not go into effect until approved, as domestic law, by a majority of both the House and the Senate.

When the framers of the Constitution charged a super-majority in the Senate with the task of approving treaties, they were not thinking of agreements that could put Americans or aliens in U.S. or foreign prisons for years. Extradition then did not exist. The framers envisioned treaties of peace, commerce, and navigation approved by a small, deliberative Senate. Had they anticipated treaties that could severely violate liberty and doom individuals to foreign injustice, they might well have chosen to involve both houses of Congress, and thus both Judiciary Committees, the Senate Committee on Foreign Relations, and the House Committee on International Affairs. Such vetting would substantially reduce the risk that an extradition treaty would threaten individual liberty or due process of law.[138]

Changing the Constitution to correct this problem is not feasible, but nothing should prevent the House and Senate from passing a comprehensive law to govern all extradition treaties. An omnibus law should guarantee that all future treaties receive the same scrutiny as comparable legislation, and make certain procedures and rights common to all agreements. Most extradition treaties would have to be renegotiated, and, with uniform standards, some current arrangements might not survive. Then if each new treaty were deemed self-executing, at least it would conform to, or be measured against, basic principles of justice.

An omnibus extradition statute could set standards for screening all foreign requests, conducting probable cause hearings, protecting political offenders, barring surrender where the foreign legal system is not to be trusted, and conditioning extradition on adherence to basic standards of liberty and justice. The statute also could provide for the suspension of extradition when foreign regimes turn bad, and direct the Secretary of State to transmit to the requesting regime whatever conditions the executive or the extradition court chooses to place on surrender in the interests of justice.

If an omnibus extradition statute cannot be agreed upon, a simple amendment to the current statute could declare that "no extradition treaty is meant to have the force of domestic law unless it is subsequently implemented by legislation." Short of that, the executive could include within (or attach to) each proposed extradition treaty an express declaration that it is not intended to be self-executing but will require full legislative approval via implementing legislation.[139] At bare minimum, the Judiciary Committees of both houses should have authority to review each extradition treaty for its likely impact on liberty and justice.

It is also disturbing that courts have allowed the State Department to perpetuate the myth of a foreign nation's legitimacy as an extradition partner long after it has been taken over by dictators. For example, when fascists came to power in Europe in the 1920s and 1930s, the treaties with Germany and Italy were not formally abrogated or suspended. The 1902 treaty with Serbia remains in force today, long after that country was absorbed into Yugoslavia, after Marshal Tito's Communists slaughtered their way to power, and after the post-Communist Serbs engaged in "ethnic cleansing." More recently, the State Department, the Justice Department, and the U.S. Court of Appeals for the First Circuit allowed the extradition of a Canadian businessman to Hong Kong on the eve of that British Colony's reversion to Communist China, even though he would be tried by courts answering to Beijing.[140] The risks of unfairness had grown radically, but the government pretended that nothing significant had changed. While Secretary of State Albright publicly expressed concern that Hong Kong would be deprived of democratic institutions, her lawyers were claiming that they could declare the old treaty with Great Britain still in force, even after the Communist takeover.[141]

Allowing treaties to survive radical changes in regimes may be convenient for the Department of State, but it mocks the claim that extradition judges need not question the capacity of the requesting regime to do justice, because the president and two-thirds of the Senate (i.e., the Committee on Foreign Relations) made that inquiry for them. The truth is, no systematic study is ever done of the criminal justice system of a foreign government for the purpose of ascertaining whether it is, or remains, an appropriate extradition partner. Nor does any procedure exist for reassessing the administration of justice by current treaty partners, either systematically or when dictators take over.

One function of an omnibus extradition statute should be to establish procedures by which the executive and judiciary would be required, if a foreign legal system loses accreditation, to cease honoring its requests (or subject them to appropriate conditions). Conversely, foreign regimes should apply the same scrutiny to criminal justice systems within the United States.

* * *

One of the most extraordinary myths about extradition today is that the Departments of State and Justice carefully examine requests for extradition for fairness as well as formalities. Such executive screening or review is rarely done when requests come in, and it is almost never done after the departments have persuaded a court to certify that a defendant is extraditable.[142]

Screening foreign requests at the time they are received has not developed, because to do so would alienate the requesting states, make legal representation of them more difficult, and might lead foreign regimes to question the veracity of extradition requests submitted to them by the United States. In the course of defending OSI's reliance on a false affidavit in the Artuković case, one assistant attorney general went so far as to claim that American courts have held that administrative "investigations into the accuracy and veracity of a foreign government's documents and affidavits are not an acceptable practice between treaty parties." Extradition treaties, he declared, are negotiated in order to avoid the possibility that the U.S. government will question the validity of a requesting state's submissions, or that foreign states will question the validity of our documents.[143]

Most U.S. diplomats and their State Department desk officers strive to help foreign regimes fill out extradition forms as if they were tax returns.[144] The department's legal staff and their counterparts in the Office of International Affairs at Justice are not screeners; they are expediters who take pride in the number of alleged criminals they can move across national borders.[145] Attorneys from the Legal Adviser's Office (Law Enforcement and Intelligence Section) help foreign regimes prepare their cases. They work closely with the U.S. attorneys who represent their client regimes in court, and once they have won that battle, they are not suddenly disposed to become impartial and deny surrender (or propose asylum) for reasons of justice. They have become partisans and bureaucrats, and they make no bones about it.[146] Humanitarian appeals should not be routed through the Legal Adviser's Office at all, but should be handled by the Assistant Secretary of State for Democracy, Human Rights, and Labor with full authority to refuse (or condition) extradition out of respect for justice or humanity.

* * *

Another illusion is that the Department of State can be trusted to attach sufficient conditions to surrender to assure that justice will be done. Nothing could be farther from the truth. As a general rule, the State Department avoids conditions because they upset foreign governments, and because its lawyers do not want conditions placed on extradition to the United States.[147] When conditions have been exacted, they have usually been negotiated quietly and used to deflect domestic political criticism, not guarantee justice.

The State Department has never publicly taken a foreign regime to task for conducting an unfair trial, violating the rule of specialty, or consigning an extradited person to a brutal prison. Nor has it conditioned the surrender of nationals on a promise that, if convicted, they must be allowed to serve their sentences in an American (or otherwise approved) prison.[148] The State Department did not object when Yugoslavia failed to allow Artuković to put on a real defense, or when Israel subjected Demjanjuk to a highly prejudicial show trial. Only rarely has the State Department sent observers to foreign trials or made special efforts to assure that the accused was not abused in prison. That is understandable, because consulate personnel are compromised by their need to maintain diplomatic peace. Also, the mistreatment of an alleged criminal is rarely important enough (compared to maintaining good trade relations) to trigger a serious exercise of diplomatic muscle.

On those rare occasions when people question the capacity of the requesting regime to do justice, the focus is usually on whether the trial will be fair. Intense pressure from Arab governments forced the State Department to insist that Abu Eain not be tried by a special military court set up by Israel to deal with terrorists. On the other hand, Irish Americans were unable to pressure the department to deny extradition to the special "Diplock Courts" of Northern Ireland, which enforced emergency legislation against alleged terrorists inside militarized compounds, without granting them the same rights as ordinary criminal defendants.

Worse still has been the willingness of the State Department to surrender people to countries like Turkey and Mexico, which are notorious for their brutal and corrupt prisons. Prisons in some countries are so bad that special treaties now make it possible for Americans convicted in those countries to serve their time in the United States, but that does not protect foreign nationalities (including third-party nationals) whom the United States willingly surrenders to those countries.[149] Internationally, as well as domestically, there is no prison so brutal that American diplomats, prosecutors, and judges have chosen to declare it "off limits" in their administration of what is euphemistically called "justice."[150]

The time has come to abolish the rule of noninquiry, and to limit extradition to those prosecutorial offices, courts, and prisons that have been duly accredited. Legislation (and perhaps treaties) should authorize American courts as well as the executive to deny extradition or to impose appropriate conditions on it in the interests of justice and humanity.[151]

This reform could be expressed in an omnibus statute and in specific treaties. Human rights treaties (e.g., against torture, degrading, or inhumane treatment) could be incorporated by reference into the statute and treaties. Or the standards of fair treatment (at all stages of the criminal justice process) could be made specific (like the first eight amendments to the U.S. Constitution) and open-ended (like the Ninth Amendment) to allow for growth. However the reforms are stated, they should contain four elements:[152]

1. judicial as well as legislative protection at all stages of the criminal justice process, including arrest, investigation, trial, incarceration, or punishment.
2. legal standing in the accused to raise the human rights issues in both the requested and the requesting state, before, during, and after trial.
3. a power in the courts as well as the executive of the requested state to deny extradition or impose appropriate conditions on surrender.
4. provisions to facilitate monitoring of compliance.

The International Law Association's Committee on Extradition and Human Rights has proposed three clauses to effectuate these ends:[153]

1. Extradition shall be refused where, upon return, the requested person would face a real risk of a serious violation of his human rights under any treaty for the protection of human rights to which the requested state is a party or under customary international law.
2. A requested person shall have an effective remedy before an authority of the requested state if he claims that he faces a real risk of a serious violation of his human rights under any treaty for the protection of human rights to which the requested state is a party or under customary international law.
3. If the requested state considers that, in the particular case, the human rights of the requested person under any treaty for the protection of human rights to which the requested state is a party or under customary international law, need special protection, it may make the grant of extradition conditional upon the giving by the

requested state of such assurances as the requested state considers sufficient that the human rights of the requested person will be respected. If such assurances are given to the satisfaction of the requested state, and extradition takes place, the requesting state shall facilitate the monitoring of these conditions by the requested state and shall grant to the extradited person an effective remedy to enforce these conditions.

To these might be added a requirement that the letter by which the United States informs the requesting state that surrender has been authorized shall specify all conditions attendant on the surrender, so that acceptance of the accused constitutes an agreement to abide by the conditions. Failure to abide by the conditions would thus constitute a breach of the treaty, one remedy for which (specified in the letter) might be a contractual obligation to return the accused, subject to an agreed upon procedure for dispute reconciliation.[154]

* * *

The greatest hypocrisy of American extradition practice is the claim that foreign regimes must respect our sovereignty and the legal processes we have set up for recovering fugitives, but our officials need not respect theirs. Domestically, U.S. officials may not conduct planned seizures of persons without a warrant. The Fourth Amendment forbids it. However, if the seizure begins abroad, it may continue within the United States without a warrant.[155] The Fourth Amendment was supposed to prevent government overreaching, but if the overreaching begins in Mexico, the victims (who could be Americans) have no standing to object. They cannot assert a Fourth Amendment right, on behalf of "We the people," to be secure against a government that uses criminal means to enforce the law.

According to the U.S. Supreme Court, our government may hire foreigners to drug, beat, torture, and terrorize persons in other lands so that they may be subdued and dragged onto American soil. "We the people" have no judicially cognizable interest in a government that obeys the laws that bind us. Yet if "we the people" hire police or bounty hunters to kidnap persons from other countries, our Justice Department will properly extradite us for the crime.[156] If the government hires the kidnappers, our courts will receive the persons it steals without objection.

* * *

Extradition was developed to replace the politics of abduction and deportation with the rule of law. Now the United States will do extradition business with some of the least democratic and least just foreign regimes. The political offense exception has been gutted with several important countries, while targeted deportation by executive fiat has become a viable alternative to extradition with its judicial safeguards. Abduction, like deportation and the rule of noninquiry, has become just another way to get the political job done. Meanwhile, wars on crime corrupt the legal process by allowing good ends to justify improper means. The time for reform has come.

Appendix

For rusty readers, extradition is the process by which one state surrenders to a requesting state persons accused (or convicted) of crimes against the laws of the requesting state for prosecution (or punishment).[1] The process cannot begin without a formal request.[2] Thus extradition differs from denials of entry,[3] deportation,[4] and exclusion.[5]

Extradition from the United States usually begins when a foreign government submits a request to the Department of State. If the State Department finds that the request is in order, it will forward it to the Justice Department, which directs the appropriate U.S. attorney to request an arrest warrant from a U.S. magistrate or judge in the district where the accused has been found. Because the accused is alleged to be a fugitive from foreign justice, bail is rarely granted. Instead, the accused is imprisoned until an extradition hearing can be held.

This hearing is similar to a preliminary hearing in a domestic prosecution, in that its purpose is to see if there are sufficient legal and evidentiary grounds to return the accused for trial. The procedure, first enacted in 1848, is set forth in Title 18 of the U.S. Code, section 3184:

> Whenever there is a treaty or convention for extradition between the United States and any foreign government, any justice or judge of the United States, or any magistrate authorized so to do by a court of the United States, or any judge of a court of record of general jurisdiction of any State, may, upon complaint made under oath, charging any person found within his jurisdiction with having committed within the jurisdiction of any such foreign government any of the crimes provided for by such treaty or convention, issue his warrant for the apprehension of the person so charged, that he may be brought before such justice, judge, or magistrate, to the end that the evidence of criminality may be heard and considered. If, on such hearing, he deems the evidence sufficient to sustain the charge under the provisions of the proper treaty or convention, he shall certify the same, together with a copy of all the testimony taken before him, to the Secretary of State, that a warrant may issue upon the requisition of the proper authorities of such foreign government, for the surrender of such person, according to the stipulations of the treaty or convention; and he shall issue his warrant for the commitment of the person so charged to the proper jail, there to remain until such surrender shall be made.

In short, there must be an extradition treaty with the requesting state; the offenses charged must be listed as extraditable under the treaty, and the appropriate statute of limitations—designated by the treaty—must not have run out. The evidence submitted by the requesting state need only establish that a listed crime has been committed and that there is probable cause (or something like it) to believe that the accused committed it. To establish probable cause, the requesting state may submit affidavits rather than live witnesses and rely on hearsay. Accused persons, on their part, may not call witnesses to disprove the evidence offered against them, but they can offer evidence that "clarifies" the nature of that evidence.

If the evidence is sufficient to establish probable cause to believe that the accused has committed an extraditable offense, then the court may certify to the secretary of state that the accused is extraditable. The secretary can then decide whether to order surrender, taking foreign policy, humanitarian values, or changing evidence into account. Once the secretary notifies the requesting government that it may send someone to collect the accused, that government usually has thirty days in which to comply. If it does not, the accused may be released.[6]

Neither the accused nor the requesting state (or the U.S. government on that state's behalf) may appeal a decision certifying, or refusing to certify, that the accused is extraditable.[7] However, the accused may petition the same or a different court for a writ of habeas corpus,[8] but the writ "is available only to inquire whether the magistrate had jurisdiction, whether the offence charged is within the treaty and, by somewhat liberal extension, whether there was any evidence warranting the finding that there was reasonable ground to believe the accused guilty."[9] The reviewing court usually defers to the findings of the magistrate.[10] Although the U.S. government may not appeal a denial of extraditability on behalf of a foreign state,[11] it may file additional extradition requests with other courts until it finds a court willing to grant the request.[12]

Extradition is a national function that in the United States and its mentor, the United Kingdom, has been assigned largely to the judiciary. In both countries the requesting state (usually represented by attorneys of the requested state) must provide sufficient evidence to justify commitment of the accused for trial. If the court rules that the evidence is insufficient, the individual cannot be surrendered.[13] However, a court order does not assure surrender. In both the United States and the United Kingdom, the executive may refuse to surrender a person declared extraditable by the courts.[14]

The normal American rule is that extradition treaties survive changes in administrations, constitutions, and legal systems. Thus, many of the agreements which the United States today has with African military dictatorships and tribal oligarchies were never negotiated with those regimes and then approved by the Senate. Instead, the president and State Department simply decreed that the treaty with the former colonial power (usually the United Kingdom or France) would remain in force, as if the quality of justice developed in Europe had been transferred intact to the colonies and could be sustained there through the turmoils that followed independence. Nothing has ever been done by the State Department or Congress to abrogate extradition treaties with countries that have been taken over by repressive regimes. The Departments of

State and Justice usually decide which countries they will assist or make requests of on a case-by-case basis. In only four instances has the State Department formally announced its unwillingness to make requests of a foreign country. In these instances, involving Cuba, Estonia, Latvia, and Lithuania, the State Department continued to insist that the old treaties, negotiated with noncommunist regimes, remained in force under communism. However, it formally instructed Justice Department attorneys not to request the return of fugitives from them.[15] Department officials hint that requests from certain repressive regimes have been discouraged through diplomatic channels, but no president or Congress has ever formally abrogated an extradition treaty because the country with which it was negotiated has fallen under dictatorial rule.

Extradition law can be made by treaties alone, or by treaties in conjunction with legislation. The substance of American extradition law is to be found in treaties and in court decisions interpreting treaties. Unlike the British Parliament, which enacted a comprehensive Extradition Act in 1870,[16] Congress has seen fit only to legislate the procedure to be followed in applying the substantive provisions of the treaties.

Nations normally enter into extradition treaties in order to:

1. obtain reciprocal return of fugitive offenders.[17]
2. facilitate the punishment of wrongful conduct, and thereby promote justice.[18]
3. avoid harboring within their border those who may commit offenses similar to those which they are accused of committing in another jurisdiction.[19]
4. avoid international tensions caused by one country's refusal to return a particularly wanted person.[20]

Today the United States is a party to more than one hundred extradition treaties,[21] including some with repressive regimes. The treaties with authoritarian regimes often were negotiated in more liberal times[22] or were entered into as expressions of good will toward new regimes.[23]

The United States does not grant every extradition request it receives, even if surrendering the accused would serve one or all of the purposes of extradition. Five doctrines limit the scope of extradition.

First, the United States will not extradite an individual unless it has an extradition treaty with the requesting state. Second, even if a treaty exists, extradition will be granted only for a crime that is enumerated in the treaty. This means that extradition is usually limited to felonies. Third, the allegations against the accused must be sufficient to warrant holding him for trial in the United States had the offense been committed here. Taken together, the requirements of a listed offense and probable cause establish the rule of "double criminality," which means that extradition is only permitted for acts that would be criminal under American law, were they committed in the United States. Fourth, extradition will be granted only for offenses arising out of the acts alleged in the extradition request. This is the so-called rule of specialty, or speciality. Fifth, virtually all American treaties provide that no one will be extradited for "an offense of a political character." In practice, this means protection for people whose alleged crimes were committed to advance (or repress) some sort of political uprising.

Notes

Preface and Acknowledgments

1. Matter of Budlong and Kember (nos. 199/79, Q.B. Div., Nov. 30, 1979); 74 Am. J. Int'l L. 447.
2. "'To Surrender Political Offenders': The Political Offense Exception to Extradition in United States Law," 16 N.Y.U. J. Intl L. & Pol. 169 (1984).

Introduction

1. Cf. John G. Kester, "Some Myths of United States Extradition Law," 76 Georgetown L. J. 1441, 1442–43 (1988).
2. E.g., see Seymour Martin Lipset, The First New Nation (New York: Norton, 1963).
3. See Chapters 20 and 21 on the use of abductions and military capture, and Chapter 16 for the misuse of deportation law.
4. Reform of the Extradition Laws of the United States, Hearings on H.R. 2643 Before the Subcom. on Crime, Com. on the Judiciary, U.S. House of Representatives, 98th Cong., 1st sess. (1983), 36 (statement of Roger Olsen, deputy assistant attorney general, criminal division).
5. Bingham v. Bradley, 241 U.S. 511, 517 (1916).
6. Simmons v. Braun, 627 F. 2d 635, 637 (2d Cir. 1980).
7. First National City Bank v. Aristeguieta, 287 F. 2d 219, 226 (2d Cir. 1960).
8. See Fed. R. Crim. Pro. 54(b)(5).
9. Fed. R. Evid. 1101(d)(3).
10. Quinn v. Robinson, 783 F. 2d 776, 815 (9th Cir.), *cert. denied*, 479 U.S. 882 (1986).
11. Glucksman v. Henkel, 221 U.S. 508, 512 (1911).
12. This case is discussed at length in Chapters 2 and 3.

Chapter One

Epigraph: State Papers and Publick Documents of the United States, 1789–1796 (Boston: T. B. Wait and Sons, 1815), vol. 1, 145, 146.

1. "The Regicide Colonels in New England," Atlantic Monthly, vol. 6 (July 1860), 89, 93.

2. Id., 92.

3. Robert G. Neumann, Extradition and the Political Offender (unpublished Ph.D. dissertation, University of Minnesota, 1946), 82, and Charles Egan, The Law of Extradition (London: W. W. Robinson, 1846), 4–5.

4. Colonial Laws of Massachusetts, 143, 1. The commitment of the Connecticut and New Haven colonies to this policy can be read into the Articles of Confederation they signed with Massachusetts and New Plymouth on May 19, 1643. See Howard W. Preston, ed., Documents Illustrative of American History (4th ed.; New York: Putnam's, 1896), 92–93. Puritan lawmakers also took cognizance of bibical injunctions, including Deuteronomy 23:15 and 16: "Thou shall not deliver unto his master the servant which is escaped from his master unto thee. He shall dwell with thee, even among you, in that place which he shall choose in one of thy gates, where it liketh him best: thou shall not oppress him."

5. See, e.g., Michael Walzer, Revolution of the Saints (New York: Atheneum, 1976).

6. A System of Moral Philosophy (London: Millard T. Longman, 1755), vol. 2, 363.

7. See, e.g., Barton Ingraham, Political Crime in Europe (Berkeley: University of California Press, 1979), 50–57.

8. Paul O'Higgins, "The History of Extradition in British Practice, 1174–1794," 13 Indian Y. B. Int'l Aff. 78, 108 (1964). Between 1718 and 1830, European states concluded ninety-two extradition treaties, mainly focused on the recovery of deserters, robbers, murderers, arsonists, and vagrants. Christine Van den Wijngaert, The Political Offence Exception to Extradition (Netherlands: Kluwer, 1980), 8, citing G. F. de Martens, Recueil des Traités (7 vols.), 1806–26, and G. F. de Martens, Supplements au Recueil des Principaux Traités (20 vols.), 1801–42.

9. O'Higgins, "The History of Extradition," 108–109.

10. Id., 87.

11. William S. Holdsworth, History of English Law (London: Methuen, 1924), vol. 3, 569.

12. 2 Inst. 47. Abjuration was the process by which an alleged felon who had obtained sanctuary in a church could obtain safe passage into foreign exile. Indeed, under abjuration, the felon was required to leave England by the nearest port—a requirement that gave him immunity from a subsequent diplomatic demand for his return. This legal escape route and the immunity from extradition that attended it were effectively destroyed during the fifteenth century when church sanctuary was abolished by the Crown. Holdsworth, History of English Law, vol. 3, 303–307.

13. *"Non trades servum domino suo, qui ad te confugerit."* 3d Inst. 180, quoting Deuteronomy 23:15, 16.

14. 31 Car. ch. 2, sec. 11 (emphasis added).

15. For the debate over the scope of this provision, see O'Higgins, 13 Indian Y. B. Int'l Aff., 110–115.

16. The view that states are bound by natural law to extradite or punish fugitive criminals from foreign states was advanced by Hugo Grotius, De Jure Belli ac Pacis Libri Tres (The Law of War and Peace) (1625; Kelsey trans.; Indianapolis: Bobbs-Merrill, 1925), vol. 2, ch. 21, sec. 5, nos. 1 and 2, and E. de Vattel, Le Droit des Gens, ou Principes de la Loi Naturelle, Appliqués à la Conduite et aux Affaires des Nations et des Souverains (The Law of Nations or the Prin-

ciples of Natural Law, Applied to the Conduct and Affairs of Nations and Sovereigns) (1758; Scott ed.; Washington, D.C.: Carnegie Institution, 1916), vol. 3, bk. 2, ch. 6, sec. 76, 136–137. Sir Edward Coke asserted the contrary view in the Case of Lord Sanchar [1613] 9 Co. Rep. 117a, 121a; 77 E.R. 902 at 908, in his comments on chapter 29 of Magna Carta, 2 Inst. 47, and in his comments on political asylum, 3 Inst. 180. That the duty to extradite was not mandatory but could arise by agreement among nations was also advanced by Samuel Von Pufendorf in his Elementorum Jurisprudentiae Universalis Libri Duo (The Elements of Universal Jurisprudence) (1672; Oldfather trans.; Oxford: Clarendon Press, 1931), bk. 1, def. 12, 206. Georg F. von Martens denied any duty to extradite but thought that host countries should consider punishing fugitives who "attack the safety of [a foreign] state." Précis du Droit des Gens Modernes de L'Europe (The Law of Nations, Founded on the Treaties and Customs of the Modern Nations of Europe) (1788; W. Cobbett trans.; Philadelphia, Pa.: Thomas Bradford, 1795) bk. 3, ch. 3, sec. 23, 108–109.

17. Thomas Hobbes, on the other hand, supported the surrender of political refugees on the theory that individuals surrendered all of their rights, including the right to revolution, to their sovereign. He also recommended a more severe penalty for political than for ordinary crimes, deeming politial offenses to be more serious because of the threat they posed to order in society. Leviathan (1651; Michael Oakeshott ed.; Oxford: Basil Blackwell, 1946), 200, 205. Hugo Grotius shared this view but found reasons why participation in the Netherlands' revolt against Spain was not a crime. De Jure Belli ac Pacis Libre Tres, bk. 2, ch. 21, sec. 5(5).

18. C. B. Beccaria, An Essay on Crimes and Punishment (4th ed.; London, 1775; Farrer trans.; London: J. Almond, 1880), 128–129.

19. I. A. Shearer, Extradition in International Law (Manchester: University Press, 1971), 11. See, e.g., Thomas Jefferson's letter to M. Genêt, infra this chapter, refusing Galbaud's surrender and the writings of Francois Guizot, the French penologist and historian who was a minister in the government of Louis Philippe (1830–1848) when France led the world in liberalism toward political offenders and helped invent the political crimes defense to extradition. Guizot's views are summarized in Ingraham, Political Crime in Europe, 78–83.

20. See, e.g., 1621 treaty between the colonists of New Plimoth and Massasoit, sachem of the Pokanokets (Wampanoags) in William Bradford, Of Plimoth Plantation, 1620–1647 (S. E. Morison ed.; New York: Modern Library, 1952), 80. See also Treaty with the Chickesaws, Upper and Lower Creeks, Chactaws, Cherokees, and Catawba, 1763, art. 3; Treaty with the Deleware, 178, art. 4; Treaty with the Wyandot, Etc., 1785, art. 9; and Treaty with the Choctaw, 1786, art. 5, and Separate Article, in Frederick E. Hosen, ed., Rifle, Blanket and Kettle: Selected Indian Treaties and Laws (Jefferson, N.C.: McFarland, 1985), at 16–17, 21–22, 28, 30, 35, respectively. The federal government has uniformly insisted that Indian tribes may not exercise criminal jurisdiction over non-Indians without the consent of Congress. See Oliphant v. Suquamish Indian Tribe, 435 U.S. 191, 197–198, n. 8 (1978).

21. The Declaration of Independence.

22. See generally Lovejoy, "Rights Imply Equality: The Case Against Admiralty Jurisdiction in America, 1764–1776," 16 Wm. & Mary Q. 459 (1959).

23. Journal, Virginia House of Delegates, 2d sess. (1784), 7.

24. The Statutes at Large; Being a Collection of all the Laws of Virginia (W. W. Hening ed.; Richmond, Va.: George Cochran, 1823), vol. 11, ch. 24, 471–473.

25. Id. at 471.

26. Patrick Henry also supported it, mainly because it might promote more protection for Indians who had been abused by whites, but he left Williamsburg before the vote was taken.

Irving Brandt, James Madison: The Nationalist, 1780–1787 (Indianapolis: Bobbs-Merrill, 1948), 360.

27. B. F. Poore, ed., The Federal and State Constitutions, Colonial Charters, and Other Organic Laws of the United States (2d ed.; Washington, D.C.: U.S. Government Printing Office, 1878), vol. 2, 1908 ff.

28. Letter from James Madison to Thomas Jefferson, Jan. 9, 1785, in Writings of James Madison (Hunt ed.; New York: Putnam's, 1901), vol. 2, 102, 112; Papers of James Madison (R. Rutland ed.; Chicago: Chicago University Press, 1973), vol. 8, 228.

29. Letter from James Madison to Thomas Jefferson, Jan. 9, 1785; Writings of James Madison, vol. 2, 102, 111 (1906); Papers of James Madison, vol. 8, 227–228.

30. Hening's Virginia Statutes at Large, vol. 11, ch. 24, 471.

31. Id.

32. In 1784, Congress concluded that it had no authority to surrender a Frenchman to France for dishonoring his country's consul and referred the question to the President and Supreme Executive Council of Pennsylvania. Doubtful that they could order his surrender, they referred the matter to the Court of Oyer and Terminer, which had already tried and convicted the accused under Pennsylvania law. The court ruled that the executive council did not have the authority "in this case" to deliver the defendant to France but speculated in dicta that the council might have the authority in unspecified cases, when necessary to prevent "atrocious offenders" from evading punishment. Thus, Congress, the Pennsylvania executive, and a Pennsylvania court all agreed that extradition was, by nature, essentially a judicial rather than a legislative or executive matter and chose not to authorize extradition in the absence of a treaty. When France persisted in its demand for the officer's surrender, John Jay, Congress's secretary for foreign affairs, advised Congress not to comply but to let Pennsylvania enforce its verdict against him. If France demanded surrender of the accused after he had served his sentence, Jay added, the issue should be reexamined. France did not, and the issue did not have to be faced until after the new Constitution placed the foreign affairs power in a new executive and created an independent federal judiciary. Respublica v. De Longchamps, 1 Dall. 111 (1784). For Jay's views, see John Bassett Moore, A Treatise on Extradition and Interstate Rendition (Boston: Boston Book Co., 1891), vol. 1, sec. 18, at 25.

33. Hening's Virginia Statutes at Large, vol. 11, ch. 24, at 471; Le Droit des Gens, vol. 3, bk. 2, sec. 176, 136–137.

34. Letter of Thomas Jefferson to George Washington, Nov. 7, 1791, Memoir, Correspondence, and Miscellanies, from the Papers of Thomas Jefferson (Randolph ed.; Charlottesville, Va.: Carr, 1829), vol. 3, 131.

35. Id. at 132. For how secretaries of state chose to interpret this power during the nineteenth century, see J. B. Moore, A Digest of International Law (Washington, D.C.: U.S. Government Printing Office, 1906), vol. 4, 246–257.

36. Letter to Washington, Nov. 7, 1791, at 131.

37. Jefferson, Memoir, Correspondence, and Miscellanies, vol. 3, at 132.

38. Letter from Charles Pinckney to George Washington, Jan. 8, 1792.

39. His proposals were set forth in two documents dated March 22, 1792, which he sent to William Carmichael and William Short, the U.S. negotiators. The first is entitled "Project of a Convention with the Spanish Provinces"; the second, "Heads of Consideration on the establishment of Conventions between the United States and their neighbors, for the mutual delivery of fugitives from justice"; both are reprinted in American State Papers, Foreign Relations (Washington: Gales and Seaton, 1832), vol. 1, 257–258.

40. Id., "Heads of Consideration" at 258.

41. Id., "Project" at 257, and "Heads of Consideration" at 258.

42. Id. at 258.

43. See, e.g., Max J. Kohler, "The Right of Asylum with Particular Reference to Aliens," 51 Am. L. Rev. 381, 405 (1917) (arguing that Jefferson urged Washington to "break with [the] British precedent" of granting blanket asylum, and opting for treaties that would distinguish between common criminals and patriots).

44. Pinckney to Washington, Aug. 18, 1791, cited in Moore, Digest (1906), vol. 4, 247. Pinckney later became a Republican and wrote a pamphlet criticizing the extradition of Jonathan Robbins. (See Chapters 2 and 3, infra.)

45. Letter from Thomas Jefferson to Charles Pinckney, April 1, 1792, in Thomas Jefferson, Memoir, Correspondence, and Miscellanies, vol. 3, 159–160.

46. Id., "Project" at 257.

47. Id.

48. In 1788, Secretary of State John Jay had sought assurances from Spain that the slaves fleeing to Spanish Florida would be returned; the Spanish, concerned with the flight of murderers from Florida to the United States, were inclined to strike an agreement, but none was ever formalized. Moore, Extradition, vol. 1, 84. In 1791, James Seagrove, a U.S. commissioner, signed an agreement with the Spanish governor of Florida regarding the surrender of runaway slaves, but there is no record that it was ever executed. Id. at 85–86. In 1790 and 1796, American slave-owners negotiated with the Creek Confederacy for the return of fugitive slaves from Indian territories, but the Seminoles refused. The Seminoles' acceptance of black fugitives eventually caused them to secede from the Creek Confederacy and helped provoke Andrew Jackson's unauthorized invasion of East Florida in what became known as the First U.S.–Seminole War. Joseph A. Opala, A Brief History of the Seminole Freedmen (Austin: University of Texas African and African-American Studies and Research Center, 1980), 2.

49. Quoted in Moore, Extradition, vol. 1, sec. 77, at 89.

50. Among other things, the treaty won Spanish recognition of the U.S. boundaries established by the treaty with Great Britain in 1783 (the Mississippi to the west and the 31st parallel to the south). The treaty also gave Americans free navigation of the Mississippi. T.S. no. 325, 8 Stat. 138–153 (signed Oct. 27, 1795; entered into force Aug. 2, 1796).

51. See discussion of the Amistad case, infra, Chapter 4.

52. The draft consular convention was submitted to the Continental Congress on July 28, 1781, by Le Chevalier de la Luzerne, the French minister to the United States. It is published in U.S. Continental Congress, Secret Journal of the Acts and Proceedings of Congress (4 vols., Boston: Thomas B. Wait, 1820–1821), vol. 3, 5–19. Luzerne's plan is in Journals of the Continental Congress (Washington, D.C.: U.S. Government Printing Office, 1914), vol. 21, 792. The amended draft, together with the report of the congressional committee that considered it, is in id., vol. 22, 17–28 (Jan. 9, 1782). The convention as finally signed by Franklin is in U.S. Department of State, Diplomatic Correspondence of the United States of America (Washington, D.C.: Blair, 1833), vol. 1, 284–304. See also R. L. Jones, "America's First Consular Convention," Southwestern Social Science Quarterly, vol. 13 (Dec. 1932), 256. Jay's report of July 4, 1786, to Congress on the Convention and his recommendations of August 18, 1786, are in Diplomatic Correspondence of the United States of America, 1783–1789 (Washington: Blair, 1833), vol. 1, 304, 319–320.

53. T.S. no. 84, 8 Stat. 106–15 (signed Nov. 14, 1788; entered into force April 9, 1790).

54. See generally C. L. R. James, The Black Jacobins: Toussaint L'Ouverture and the San Domingo Revolution (1938; 2d ed.; New York: Vintage, 1963); Meade Minnigerode, Jefferson:

Friend of France, 1793; The Career of Edmond Charles Genêt (New York: Putnams', 1928), ch. 5; Alexander DeConde, Entangling Alliance: Politics and Diplomacy Under George Washington (Durham, N.C.: Duke University Press, 1958), chs. 8, 9; and Frances S. Chiles, French Refugee Life in the United States, 1790–1800 (Baltimore, Md.: Johns Hopkins, 1940), ch. 1.

55. Genêt's men obtained warrants for the arrest of Galbaud and his aides from Governor George Clinton of New York (whose daughter Genêt would eventually marry), but could not obtain warrants from the federal courts. See Genêt to Jefferson, Sept. 6, 1793, in State Papers and Publick Documents of the United States, 1789–1796 (Boston: T. B. Wait and Sons, 1815) vol. 1, 144–145.

56. Thomas Jefferson to Citizen Genêt, Sept. 12, 1793, id. at 145, 146.

57. Id.

58. The secretary of state did not identify which French laws needed reformation, but he could have been alluding to a battery of statutes designed to punish loyalists, including one that treated any émigré who did not return to France between November and the end of December 1792 as a conspirator against the new order who could be sentenced to death. See C. D. Hazen, The French Revolution (New York: Holt and Co., 1932), vol. 1, 477; vol. 2, 551, 694–696, 853–854, 984–985.

59. Foreign Relations, vol. 1, 709; Annual Report of the American Historical Association, 1903, "Correspondence of the French Ministers, 1791–1797," vol. 2, 308, 309, 313–316, 345.

60. Charles R. King, ed., Life and Times of Rufus King (New York: Putnam, 1894), vol. 1, 479. Galbaud eventually decided to return to France. He faced a hearing before the National Convention (which by then had disavowed both Genêt and the commissioners in Santo Domingo) and was sent to prison. Maude H. Woodfin, Citizen Genêt and his Mission (unpublished Ph.D. dissertation, University of Chicago, 1928), 423, n. 66, quoting Baltimore Intelligencier, July 8, 1794.

61. E.g., not until 1875 did Congress pass a law denying foreign convicts the right to settle in the United States. 18 Stat. 477. John Bassett Moore noted a similar attitude on the part of the British. Extradition, vol. 1, sec. 8, at 12.

62. The following account is taken from Fauchet's report of the incident, Letter from the Commissioners of the French Republic in the United States to the Commissioners of Marine and Colonies in France, Sept. 1, 1794, in Annual Report of the American Historical Association, 1903: Correspondence of the French Ministers, 1791–1797 (Washington, D.C.: U.S. Government Printing Office, 1904), vol. 2, 397, 401–402. The author is grateful to Prof. Alfred P. Rubin for calling this case to his attention.

63. The Muscadins were young Paris dandies who evaded military service and took pleasure in attacking Jacobins (or anyone wearing the bonnet rouge). They were thus in the vanguard of the Thermidorian (conservative) reaction to the terrorist revolution. C. D. Hazen, The French Revolution, vol. 2, 807.

64. About a year earlier, the French Convention had passed the "Law of Suspects," which ordered the immediate arrest of all persons who, by their conduct, connections, utterances, or writings, have shown themselves to be friends of tyranny and enemies of liberty. Id., vol. 2 at 694.

65. Barré's letter of resignation to Citizen Fauchet was published in the Gazette of the United States, July 28, 1784, and gives Barré's version of the events. Fauchet's version is more complete.

66. United States v. Lawrence, 3 U.S. (3 Dall.) 32, 45 (1795). The Court anglicized Barré's name and mistook the gender of the captain's ship. Judge Laurance had served in Congress

(1789–1793) and was appointed to the bench by President Washington. As judge advocate general on Washington's staff during the Revolution, Laurance had presided at the espionage trial of Major John André.

67. Id. at 45.

68. Id.at 49.

69. Id.

70. Id.

71. Id.

72. Id.

73. 5 U.S. (1 Cranch) 137, 166 (1803).

74. Id. at 53. The justices who participated were Cushing, Wilson, Iredell, and Patterson.

75. Diplomatic Correspondence of the United States, vol. 1, 319–320.

76. Because of the precedential value of the Court's decision, Fauchet also concluded that it was unlikely that American authorities would again allow press gangs from French warships to seize French sailors in American ports in order to fill out a crew. Letter (in French) from the Commissioners of the French Republic in the United States to the Commissioner of Foreign Relations, France, May 6, 1795, in Annual Report of the American Historical Association, 1903: Correspondence of the French Ministers, 1791–1797, vol. 2, 681–683.

Chapter Two

Epigraph: (Philip Freneau), The Aurora, Sept. 3, 1799.

1. T.S. no. 105, 8 Stat. 116–30 (signed Nov. 19, 1794; entered into force Feb. 29, 1796).

2. Article 27 expired in 1807 and was not renewed.

3. The treaty did not become effective in Britain until Parliament enacted it into law. 37 Geo. III, c. 97, sec. XXVI.

4. Jay's draft and the final treaty are set out for comparision in Samuel Flagg Bemis, Jay's Treaty: A Study in Commerce and Diplomacy (New Haven: Yale University Press, 1962), 432, 482.

5. On the other hand, the language did not foreclose future recognition of nonterritorial bases of criminal law jurisdiction.

6. Whether treaties of this sort required subsequent legislation was a matter of some dispute. Attorney General Charles Lee took the position that implementing legislation was required before the extradition article could be enforced by courts. Letter from Charles Lee to Timothy Pickering, Jan. 26, 1797, 1 Op. Att'y Gen. 68, 69–70 (Benjamin Hall ed.; 1852). The French Consular Convention of 1788 had been implemented by legislation.

7. Edward P. Brenton, Naval History of Great Britain (1st ed.; London: C. Rice, 1823), vol. 2, 436. This account also relies heavily on Dudley Pope, The Black Ship (Philadelphia: Lippincott, 1964), 141–142, and Ruth Wedgwood, "The Revolutionary Martyrdom of Jonathan Robbins," 100 Yale L. J. 229, 235–237 (1990), both of which are based on extensive research in the British Admiralty's archives.

8. When the *Hermione* was finally recaptured, she was renamed the *Retribution*.

9. I. A. Shearer, Extradition in International Law (Manchester, Eng.: Oceana, 1971), 9–10.

10. Martin's affidavit is attached to a note from Robert Liston to Timothy Pickering, Feb. 19, 1798, in Notes from the British Legations in the United States to the Department of State, 1791–1906 (National Archives Microfilm Publication M50), roll 3, no pagination.

11. Note from Timothy Pickering to Robert Liston, Feb. 21, 1798, in Domestic Letters of the Department of State, 1784–1861 (National Archives Microfilm M40), roll 10, 358.

12. Article 27 of the Jay Treaty provided for the extradition of alleged murderers; Article 20 pledged that the United States would bring any pirate "to condign punishment."

13. Letter from Charles Lee to Timothy Pickering, Mar. 14, 1798, in 1 Op. Att'y Gen. 83, at 84 (Benjamin Hall ed.; 1852). Whether any of the prisoners were Americans was open to dispute. The *Hermione's* muster book listed Brigstock as a native of Liverpool, England, Evans as a native of Carmarthen, Wales, and Williams (sometimes Williamson) as from Port Royal, Jamaica. Wedgwood, "The Revolutionary Martyrdom of Jonathan Robbins," 276, n. 175. The author gratefully acknowledges his indebtedness to Professor Wedgwood's exhaustive research and analysis of the *Hermione* cases.

14. Wedgwood, "The Revolutionary Martyrdom of Jonathan Robbins," 272 and n. 162.

15. Letter from Charles Lee to Timothy Pickering, Mar. 14, 1798, 1 Op. Att'y Gen. 83, 84 (Benjamin Hall ed.; 1852).

16. Id. at 84.

17. Timothy Pickering to Robert Morris, Mar. 29, 1798, in Domestic Letters of the Department of State, 1784–1861 (National Archives Microfilm Publication M40), roll 10, 378–379.

18. Mrs. Martin's affidavit is attached to the draft of a note from Timothy Pickering to Robert Liston, April 13, 1798, in Domestic Letters of the Department of State, 1784–1861 (National Archives Microfilm Publication M40), roll 10, 386–387.

19. Timothy Pickering to Robert Liston, April 13, 1798 (National Archives Microfilm Publication M40), roll 10, 386–387.

20. Letter from Timothy Pickering to Judge John Sloss Hobart, April 18, 1798, in Domestic Letters of the Department of State, 1784–1861, (National Archives Microfilm Publication M40), roll 10, 389.

21. Letter from Timothy Pickering to U.S. Attorney Lucius Stockton, June 8, 1798, in id., roll 8, at 532.

22. This suspicion is advanced by Wedgwood in "The Revolutionary Martyrdom of Jonathan Robbins," 279.

23. Id. at 279–81.

24. (Philadelphia: Snowden & McCorkle, 1797), ch. 4, 130. Callender would later be convicted under the Sedition Act for calling President Adams, among other things, "a man whose hands are reeking with the blood" of another *Hermione* mutineer, Jonathan Robbins. United States v. Callender, 25 Fed. Cas. 239 (C.C.D.Va. 1800) (No. 14709).

25. Wedgwood, "The Revolutionary Martyrdom of Jonathan Robbins," 283–285.

26. Aurora (Philadelphia), March 21, 1798, at 3, col. 3.

27. These newpaper accounts are summarized by Wedgwood, "The Revolutionary Martyrdom of Jonathan Robbins," 284–286.

28. James Morton Smith, Freedom's Fetters (Ithaca: Cornell University Press, 1956), 56.

29. Thomas Jefferson to James Madison, June 7, 1798, Jefferson's Writings (Ford ed.; New York: Putnam's, 1986), vol. 7, 266–267.

30. 8 Annals of Cong., Fifth Cong., 2d sess, at 1972–73, and appendix, 9 Annals, at 3744–45 (June 18, 1788).

31. Affidavit of William Portlock, reprinted 27 Fed. Cas. at 826.

32. Affidavit of John Forbes, April 18, 1799, reprinted 27 Fed. Cas. at 826.

33. Secretary of State Timothy Pickering to Mr. Robert Liston, June 8, 1796 (regarding request by sheriff of Montreal to the governor of Vermont for an alleged jail breaker), Pick-

ering Papers (F. Allis ed.; Boston: Massachusetts Historical Society microfilm edition, 1966), Roll 36, at 84.

34. Henry Cabot Lodge, "Timothy Pickering," Atlantic Monthly, vol. 41 (June 1878), 739, 745, 752.

35. Letter from Timothy Pickering to John Adams, May 15, 1799, in Adams Papers, Letters Received and Other Loose Papers (Massachusetts Historical Society microfilm edition), roll 394, reproduced chronologically, page marked LI, 219.

36. Letter from John Adams to Timothy Pickering, May 21, 1799, in Adams Papers, Letters Received and Other Loose Papers (Massachusetts Historical Society microfilm edition), roll 219, LI, 219–219a.

37. E.g., see Hayburn's Case, 2 U.S. (2 Dall.) 409 (1792).

38. Letter from Timothy Pickering to Thomas Bee, June 3, 1799, Pickering Papers (F. Allis ed.; Boston: Massachusetts Historical Society microfilm edition, 1966), roll 11, at 209–10. By contrast, the letter sent by Secretary of State Edmund Randolph to Judge John Laurance on Aug. 12, 1794. "requesting your attention" to the French minister's demand for Captain Barré's arrest was highly solicitous of the court's independence. (National Archives Microfilm Publication M40), roll, 7, 156–157.

39. Letter from Thomas Bee to Timothy Pickering, July 1, 1799. The original has disappeared, but it was reprinted in the Aurora (Philadelphia), Feb. 11, 1800, at 2, col. 3, and in the correspondence on the case submitted to the House of Representatives by President Adams on Feb. 7, 1800, 10 Annals of Cong. 516–517 (Feb. 7, 1800).

40. Letter of Abraham Sasportas to Messrs. Freneau and Paine, City Gazette and Daily Advertiser (Charleston, S.C.), Dec. 5, 1799, 3, col. 1, reprinted with United States v. Robins, 27 Fed. Cas. 825, 840–841 (No. 16,175) (1799). The Court mispelled the defendant's alias.

41. United States v. Robins, 27 Fed. Cas. at 827.

42. Id. Forbes departed Charleston before the prisoner had any attorneys who might have questioned him.

43. Letter from Alexander Moultrie, Counsel for Robbins, to Benjamin Moodie, the British Consul, undated, 27 Fed. Cas. at 840.

44. 27 Fed. Cas. at 827.

45. 1 U.S. (1 Cranch) 137 (1803).

46. Bee's credentials with the Federalists were sufficiently strong for him to be mentioned as a possible successor to John Rutledge on the Supreme Court. Documentary History of the Supreme Court of the United States, 1789–1800: Commentaries on Appointments and Proceedings (Maeva Marcus and James Perry eds.; New York: Columbia University Press, 1985), vol. 1, at 720.

47. 27 Fed. Cas. at 830.

48. Id. at 832.

49. Perhaps the judge did not do so because he believed that the prisoner was an Irishman by his accent, but this is not known.

50. William James, the leading historian of the British navy and no admirer of the Hermione's mutineers, admitted that "truth compels us to state that Captain Hugh Pigot ... has been described to us by those who knew him well as one of the most cruel and oppressive captains belonging to the British navy," and volunteered the opinion that "if the Ali Pacha of the ship had been the sole victim of [the mutineers'] rage, the public indignation might have been appeased the instant the daily practices of the tyrant became known." The Naval History of Great Britain (Chaimer, ed.; London: Richard Bentley, 1837), vol. 2, 103.

51. It is possible that the judge was influenced by the publication, about a month before the hearing, of the navy's sixth general order emphasizing the need for strict discipline on all U.S. warships. See Gardner W. Allen, Our Naval War with France (1909; Hamden, Conn.: Archon Books, 1967), 132.

52. Wedgwood, "The Revolutionary Martydom of Jonathan Robbins," 309.

53. United States v. Robins, 27 Fed. Cas. 825, 833 (D.S.C. 1799); Warton St. Trials, 392; 7 Am. Law. J. 18, Bee, 266.

54. Today to try a person for crimes not specified in the extradition order (and therefore in the treaty) would violate the rule of specialty.

55. Reprinted at 27 Fed. Cas. at 842.

56. Id. at 869–70.

57. Proceedings of a Court Martial Held on board His Majesty's Ship Hannibal in Port Royal Harbor Jamaica on Thursday 15 August 1799 for the Trial of Thomas Nash one of the Mutineers of His Majesty's late Ship Hermione (British Public Record Office, Adm. 1/5350), as cited by Wedgwood, "The Revolutionary Martyrdom of Jonathan Robbins," 305.

58. Extract of a letter from Admiral Sir Hyde Parker to Robert Liston, Esq., the British envoy to the United States, Sept. 9, 1799, reprinted in United States v. Robins, 27 Fed. Cas. at 842. Parker's account is confirmed by Dudley Pope, The Black Ship, at 284–285, based on court-martial records on file at the British Public Records Office, and by independent research in the same archives by Wedgwood, "The Revolutionary Martyrdom of Jonathan Robbins," 305–308.

Chapter Three

Epigraph: The Aurora, Sept. 3, 1799.

1. Pinckney's article, which was published in several newspapers and republished as a pamphlet, is reprinted following United States v. Robins, 27 F. Cas. at 835–839. Pinckney had participated in the Constitutional Convention of 1787 and later served as governor of South Carolina. As governor, he had proposed distinguishing between political and other offenses in a treaty with Spain then being negotiated by his Federalist cousin, Thomas. See Ch. 1, *supra*.

2. Id. at 835.

3. Id. at 837.

4. Id. at 838.

5. Id. at 839.

6. Larry D. Cress, "The Jonathan Robbins Incident, Extradition and the Separation of Powers in the Adams Administration," Essex Institute Historical Collections, vol. 111, 99, 108–109, n. 31, and newspapers cited therein.

7. Ruth Wedgwood, "The Revolutionary Martyrdom of Jonathan Robbins," 100 Yale L. J. 229, 332, nts. 387–388.

8. Id. at 339, n. 422.

9. Virginia Federalist (Richmond), Sept. 7, 1799, 3, col. 1, reprinted in The Papers of John Marshall (Charles Cullen and Herbert A. Johnson eds.; Chapel Hill: University of North Carolina Press, 1984), vol. 4, 23–28.

10. Editor's note accompanying 27 F. Cas. 833, 834, col 2, citing 1 Hall. Jour. Jur. 28 as its source.

11. 10 Annals of Congress at 590 (March 5, 1800).

12. Letter from Thomas Jefferson to Charles Pinckney, Oct. 29, 1799; Writings (Ford ed.; 1892–1899), vol. 9, 87.

13. This sympathy waxed and waned. In 1798, at British request, Captain Truxton searched the USS *Constellation* for one of the mutineers, found him, and turned him over to the British navy without provoking a substantial protest. Bradford Perkins, The First Rapproachment (Philadelphia: University of Pennsylvania Press, 1955), 210, n. 28, citing, *inter alia*, Knox, ed., Naval Documents, vol. 1, 365.

14. 10 Annals of Cong., 6th Cong., 1st sess., 511 (Feb. 4, 1800). Unlike most critics of the treaty, Livingston conceded the propriety of surrendering Americans. Id. at 564 (Feb. 27, 1800). He also did not believe that Robbins was an impressed American seaman. Id. at 544 (Feb. 25, 1800).

15. Id. at 533 (Feb. 20, 1800).

16. Id.

17. Id. at 532–533. Livingston's call for censure earned him the president's undying emnity. Writing to Jefferson twelve years later, Adams declared: "Neddy is a naughty lad as well as a saucy one. I have not forgotten his lying Villany in his fictitious case of a Jonathan Robbins who never existed." Letter from John Adams to Thomas Jefferson, May 1, 1812, in The Adams–Jefferson Papers (Lester J. Cappon, ed.; Chapel Hill: University of North Carolina Press, 1959), vol. 2, 346.

18. 10 Annals of Congress at 516–517 (Feb. 7, 1800) and 565 (Feb. 27, 1800).

19. Letter from Thomas Bee to Timothy Pickering, July 1, 1799. Id. at 515 (Feb. 7, 1800) (emphasis added).

20. Albert Gallatin, Observations on Robbins's Case (undated), in Papers of Albert Gallatin, (New York Historical Society microfilm), roll 4 (pages unnumbered).

21. 10 Annals of Congress at 617 (Mar. 7, 1800).

22. Id.

23. Id. at 613.

24. Id.

25. Id. at 615.

26. Quoted in Samuel Spear, The Law of Extradition: International and Inter-State (Littleton, Colo.: F. B. Rothman, 1885), 56.

27. 10 Annals of Congress at 615–616.

28. Some of his rhetoric, however, gave this impression. For example, at one point he declared that "the Judicial power cannot extend to political compacts; as the establishment of a boundary line ... or the case of the delivery of a murderer under the twenty-seventh article of our present Treaty with Britain." Id. at 607.

29. Id. at 614.

30. Thus, all Marshall really argued was that "Till this be done, it seems the duty of the executive department to execute the contract by any means it possesses." Id. In 1848, Congress prescribed a referral procedure, thus rejecting Marshall's concept of an essentially executive practice subject only to judicial review. 9 Stat. 302 (1848). The theory of extradition as a judicial matter was affirmed by the Supreme Court in In re Kaine, 55 U.S.(14 How.) 103 (1852).

31. 10 Annals of Congress at 615.

32. Id. at 614.

33. Charles Lee, Adams's attorney general, agreed with the Republicans that implementing legislation was appropriate. Letter from Charles Lee to Timothy Pickering, Jan. 26, 1797, 1 Op. Att'y Gen. 68, at 69–70 (Benjamin Hall ed.; 1852). For a useful discussion of Pinckney's letter and Marshall's response, see R. C. Hurd, A Treatise on the Right of Personal Liberty and on Habeas Corpus (1876; New York: Da Capo, 1972), 583–587.

34. 10 Annals of Congress at 613.

35. The Papers of John Marshall, vol. 4, 108, n. 4, citing Political Pamphlets, vol. 1, no. 7, Virginia Historical Society. See also Letter from Thomas Jefferson to James Madison, March 10, 1800, in The Writings of Thomas Jefferson (Paul L. Ford ed.; New York: Putnam's, 1896), vol. 7, 432, acknowledging that Marshall distinguished himself.

36. Letter from John Adams to Thomas Jefferson, June 30, 1813, in The Adams–Jefferson Papers, vol. 2, 346–348.

37. See, e.g., Joseph Story, A Discourse Upon the Honorable John Marshall, at the Request of the Suffolk Bar (Boston: J. Munroe & Co., 1835), 44, and Henry Adams, The Life of Gallatin (Philadelphia: Lippincott, 1880), 232.

38. Letter from John Marshall to Reuben George, March 16, 1800, in The Papers of John Marshall, vol. 4, 114–115.

39. In re Kaine, 55 U.S. (14 How.) 103, 113 (1852) (Catron, J.). See also Justice Nelson's opinion in Ex parte Kaine, 14 F. Cas. 78, at 81 (no. 7,597) (C.C.S.D.N.Y. 1853). See also William B. Lawrence, "The Extradition Treaty," 14 Albany L. J. 85, 89 (1876); Edward G. Clarke, Extradition (4th ed.; London: Stevens and Hayes, 1903), 40–41; and John Bassett Moore, Extradition (Washington, D.C.: U.S. Government Printing Office, 1890), vol. 1, 136, 550. On the other hand, Larry D. Cress, "The Jonathan Robbins Incident," vol. 111, 99, 115, believes that the Robbins case was not "a viable campaign issue" in 1800 because commentary about that case in Republican newspapers had declined.

40. 1 Stat. 570. The act was never used and lapsed after the election of 1800.

41. Statutes at large of Virginia (1835; S. Sheperd ed.; reprinted New York: AMS Press, 1970), vol. 2, ch. 7, 302 (Jan. 21, 1801).

42. Ex parte Kaine, 14 F. Cas. 78, 81 (no. 7,597) (C.C.S.D.N.Y. 1853).

43. The caution of subsequent presidents is noted by Ellery C. Stowell, International Law (New York: Holt, 1931), 265, n. 1, and Edward G. Clarke, Extradition (4th ed.; London: Stevens and Hayes, 1903), at 49.

44. In re Kaine, 55 U.S. (14 How.) 103, 112–113 (1852).

45. The Black Ship, 231 (men convicted of offenses not charged against them) and 245 (death sentence given to member of ship's crew who prosecution witnesses swore was blind at the time of the mutiny).

46. Id. at 258–60.

47. Id. at 258.

48. 1924 (Chicago: University of Chicago Press, 1962). Melville finished work on the novella in 1891, but it was not published until 1924.

49. "Struck dead by an angel of God! Yet the angel must hang." Id. at 101.

50. Vere's argument was based mainly on the Articles of War, which made it a capital offense to strike a superior officer. He also invoked the Mutiny Act, which applied only to the British army, but actually disregarded both laws to follow a procedure based entirely on a theory of inherent emergency powers. Budd was manifestly not a mutineer, since mutiny required a combination of persons. Nor was he hanged for murder; Vere conceded that the intent to kill was lacking. Budd was hanged in order to deter future mutinies, and for no other reason. The death sentence was passed even though there was no evidence of any danger of mutiny on board the ship, by a captain who did not know his crew well but who felt a manly need to overcome his feminine intuition and make an example of someone for whom he had affection. Vere reduced the case to one of acts only, ignoring all subjective questions of motive or, for that matter, the sentiments of the crew.

51. For an excellent discussion of these issues in Billy Budd, see John P. Diggins, The Lost Soul of American Politics (New York: Basic Books, 1984).

52. Most of the studies of Billy Budd suggest that Melville took his inspiration from the hanging, without trial, of Philip Spencer on board the American brig-of-war *Somers* in 1842. The main reason for this speculation lies in the fact that one of Melville's relatives was an officer on board the *Somers*. See, e.g., Michael Paul Rogin, Subversive Genealogy: The Politics and Art of Herman Melville (New York: Knopf, 1983), at 294–316. No study of Billy Budd suggests that Melville chose the *Hermione* setting over the *Somers* setting after reading about the Robbins case, but the coincidences are too striking to be ignored. Budd's story takes place in the summer of 1791, after the mutinies at Spithead and Nore. The *Hermione* mutiny occurred in September 1797. In the *Somers* mutiny, no military exigency required execution of the mutineers. The nation was not at war; an American port was close at hand. The *Hermione* mutiny occurred during the Napoleonic wars on a warship, like Vere's, far from England. The earliest descriptions are to be found in E. Brenton, Naval History of Great Britain (1st ed.; London: C. Rice, 1823), vol. 2, 436, and William James, The Naval History of Great Britain (Chaimer ed.; London: Richard Bentley, 1837), vol. 2, 102–104, either of which Melville could have read. The Robbins case remained part of American folklore throughout the nineteenth century and was, as we shall see, recalled frequently during congressional debates, court decisions, and legal treatises in the 1840s when Melville began his artistic career and in the 1880s when he began working on the novella.

Chapter Four

Epigraph: Oral argument in the United States v. The Amistad, 40 U.S. (15 Peters) 518 (1841), reprinted in The Amistad Case: The Most Celebrated Slave Mutiny of the Nineteenth Century (New York: Johnson Reprint Corp., 1968), 26, 29.

1. For an excellent survey of these demands, see Ethan A. Nadelman, Cops Across Borders: The Internationalization of U.S. Criminal Law Enforcement (University Park: Pennsylvania State University Press, 1993), 33–45.

2. The following account draws on Howard Jones, Mutiny on the *Amistad:* The Saga of a Slave Revolt and Its Impact on American Abolition, Law, and Diplomacy (New York: Oxford, 1987); Mary Cable, Black Odyssey (New York: Viking Press, 1971); Christopher Martin, The Amistad Affair (London and New York: Abelard-Schuman, 1970); and Samuel Flagg Bemis, John Quincy Adams and the Union (New York: Knopf, 1965). See also Carl B. Swisher, History of the Supreme Court of the United States: The Taney Period (New York: Macmillan, 1974) vol. 5, 189–96, and Paul Finkleman, ed., The African Slave Trade and American Courts (New York: Garland, 1988).

3. Niles National Register, vol. 57, at 74.

4. Id. at 75.

5. No official versions of the initial court rulings in the Amistad case appear to have survived. Original sources for this account include H.R. Doc. no. 185, 26th Cong., 1st sess. 52–54 (1840), and "Decision of Judge Thomson," Niles National Register, vol. 57, at 75 (Baltimore, 1839). See also pages 73–74 of the Niles National Register for a description of the oral argument. A brief summary of the case also appears in Judge Judson's opinion in Gedney v. L'Amistad, 10 F. Cas. 141–142 (no. 5,294a) (D.Conn. 1840). Secondary accounts begin with John W. Barber, A History of the Amistad Captives (New Haven: Barber, 1840; New York: Arno Press Reprint, 1969).

6. The correspondence is reproduced in The Amistad Case (New York: Johnson Reprint Corp., 1968), reprinting H. Exec. Doc. 185, U.S. House of Representatives, 26th Cong., 1st sess., 1840.

7. T.S. no. 325, 8 Stat. 138–53 (signed Oct. 27, 1795; effective Aug. 2, 1796).

8. Thomas Pinckney's negotiations are discussed in Ch. 1, *supra*.

9. 4 Op. Atty. Gen. 484, at 488–90 (Nov. 1839). Grundy, like Forsyth, had been a longtime defender of slavery.

10. This ignored the obvious fact that piracy, being (at least theoretically) a crime against international law, could have been punished by either the United States or Spain.

11. Id. at 491.

12. 4 Op. Atty. Gen. 484, at 486 (Nov. 1839).

13. United States v. Lawrence, *supra*, Ch. 1.

14. Id.

15. Id. at 492.

16. H. Ex. Doc. no. 185, 26th Cong., 1st sess., at 21.

17. Forsyth to Argaiz (Oct. 24 or Dec. 12, 1839), U.S. Dept. of State, Notes to Foreign Legations in the U.S. from the Department of State, 1834–1906, NA.

18. Quoted in The Memoirs of John Quincy Adams (Charles F. Adams ed.; Philadelphia: J. B. Lippincott, 1876), vol. 10, 398.

19. Bemis, John Quincy Adams and the Union, 390.

20. Jones, Mutiny on the Amistad, 55.

21. Gedney v. L'Amistad, 10 F. Cas. 141 (no. 5,294a) (D.C.D.Conn., 1840).

22. Id. at 148.

23. The cabin boy, with the help of abolitionists, eventually escaped to freedom. Bemis, John Quincy Adams and the Union, 397–398. The judge also denied the claims of Ruiz and Montes and the Spanish government, even as he granted salvage payments on the ship and its non-human cargo to the revenue cutter's crew that had seized them. Barber, A History of the Amistad Captives, 23–24.

24. Order to the United States Marshal to Deliver the Amistad Negroes to the United States Schooner Grampus, Jan. 7, 1840. H.R. Doc. no. 185, 26th Cong., 1st sess. (1840), 69. See also Christopher Martin, The Amistad Affair, 176. The abolitionists were so certain of defeat that they had arranged for a ship of their own to smuggle the blacks to freedom. Id. at 156.

25. Martin, The Amistad Affair, 178. See also Donald B. Cole, Martin Van Buren and the American Political System (Princeton, N. J.: Princeton University Press, 1984), 363–364.

26. James Moore Wayne of Georgia and Philip P. Barbour of Virginia owned slaves; Roger Taney of Maryland had sent his to Liberia.

27. United States v. The Amistad, 40 U.S. (15 Peters) 518, 541–546 (1841).

28. 40 U.S. (15 Peters) at 549–54, 563–566, and 557–558 (1841).

29. Adams's argument was published as a pamphlet entitled "Argument of John Quincy Adams, Before the Supreme Court of the United States, in the Case of the United States, Appellants, vs. Cinque, and Others, Africans, Captured in the Schooner *Amistad*, by Lieut. Gedney, Delivered on the 24th of February and the 1st of March, 1841, With a Review of the Case of the *Antelope*." The pamphlet was circulated as an abolitionist tract and reported in Wheaton's Reports, vols. 10, 11, and 12 (1841). It has been reprinted in The Amistad Case: The Most Celebrated Slave Mutiny of the Nineteenth Century (New York: Johnson Reprint Corp., 1968).

30. The Amistad Case, 38.

31. Id., 26.

32. Id., 29.

33. Id., 71, 75.

34. Id., 80.

35. William Wetmore Story, Life and Letters of Joseph Story (Boston: Charles C. Little and James Brown, 1851), vol. 2, 348–349.

36. United States v. The Amistad, 40 U.S. (15 Peters) 518 (1841). Adams's oral argument was not published with the Court's opinion, apparently because he was offended when the Court's reporter, Richard Peters, asked him to delete, as irrelevant, his attack on the administration. Swisher, History of the Supreme Court of the United States: The Taney Period, vol. 5, 194.

37. 40 U.S. at 593.

38. American missionaries transported most of the blacks back to Sierra Leone. One of the three girls returned to the United States, studied at Oberlin College, and became the principal of a mission school at Bonthe, Sierra Leone. Mary Cable, Black Odyssey, 146.

39. Don E. Fehrenbacher, Slavery, Law and Politics (New York: Oxford, 1981), 19.

40. See generally Howard Jones, "The Peculiar Institution and National Honor: the Case of the Creole Slave Revolt," 21 Civil War History 28 (1975). See also Swisher, History of the Supreme Court, vol. 5, 197–199; dispatch from Secretary of State Daniel Webster to Ambassador Edward Everett, Jan. 29, 1942, Senate Doc. no. 137, 27th Cong., 2d sess.(1841–1842), 2; John Bassett Moore, International Arbitrations (New York: Crane Press, 1914), vol. 4, 4,375; William Jay, The Creole Case and Mr. Webster's Despatch (New York: New York American, 1842); "Case of the Creole," 27 Am. Jur. and Law Mag. 79 (1842); and McCargo v. The New Orleans Insurance Co., 19 La. 111, 10 Rob. 202 (1845).

41. The British minister to Washington, Henry Fox, reminded the secretary that as recently as 1838 federal officials had intervened to prevent the state of New York from surrendering two British subjects accused of murder. Two years later, in Holmes v. Jennison, the U.S. Supreme Court ruled that the American national government could not legally surrender an alleged murderer who had escaped from Canada because of the absence of a treaty. In London, the Crown's law officers informed the ministry of Sir Robert Peel that surrender of the Creole blacks for mutiny and murder would be unlawful because of the absence of any treaty or municipal law authorizing extradition. In Parliament, abolitionists cited the writings of U.S. Supreme Court Justice Joseph Story and the U.S. international law expert and diplomat Henry Wheaton for the same proposition. Howard Jones, To the Webster–Ashburton Treaty: A Study in Anglo-American Relations, 1783–1843 (Chapel Hill: University of North Carolina Press, 1977), 84.

42. Dispatch from Secretary of State Daniel Webster to Ambassador Edward Everett, Jan. 29, 1942, Senate Doc. no. 137, 27th Cong., 2d sess.(1841–1842), at 2. See also Howard Jones, "The Peculiar Institution and National Honor," 43.

43. William Jay, The Creole Case, and Mr. Webster's Despatch, 30.

44. Id., 36. Jay also claimed that his father's treaty exempted "political offences" from extradition. Id., 14.

45. Id., 30.

46. Id., 36–37.

47. See Roman J. Zorn, "Criminal Extradition Menaces the Canadian Haven for Fugitive Slaves, 1841–1861," Canadian Historical Review, vol. 38 (1957) 284–94; Alexander L. Murray, "The Extradition of Fugitive Slaves From Canada: A Reconsideration," Canadian Historical Review, vol. 43 (1992), 298–314; and Roman J. Zorn, "An Arkansas Fugitive Slave Incident and Its International Repercussions," Arkansas Historical Quarterly, vol. 16 (1957), 139–49.

48. However, Ashburton did not offer to change the 1833 statute (the Fugitive Offenders Act, 1833, 3 Will. vol. IV, c. 6.) that empowered Canada's governor to surrender fugitives on his own authority.

49. Id. at 286.

50. Jay, The Creole Case, 53.

51. Howard Jones, "The Peculiar Institution and National Honor," 44–45.

52. Zorn, "Criminal Extradition Menaces the Canadian Haven," 284–94.

53. Alexander L. Murray, "The Extradition of Fugitive Slaves from Canada," at 307.

54. The following analysis draws heavily from the late Robert M. Cover's Justice Accused: Anti-Slavery and the Judicial Process (New London: Yale University Press, 1975).

55. Thomas Sims's Case, 61 Mass. (7 Cush.) 285 (1851). For a report of Shaw's opinion in the case of George Latimer, whom he also returned to slavery, see The Liberator, Nov. 4, 1842. Latimer's case was not reported officially. Latimer's case is also discussed in Stanley W. Campbell, The Slave Catchers: Enforcement of the Fugitive Slave Law, 1850–1860 (Chapel Hill: University of North Carolina Press, 1968), 13.

56. 9 Stat. 462, 463 (sec. 6) (1850).

57. 9 Stat. 465.

58. 1855 (Barre, Mass.: The Imprint Society, 1972).

59. See Amasa Delano, A Narrative of Voyages and Travels (Boston: E. G. House, 1817), ch. 18.

60. Melville's sea-worn black ship is not a Baltimore-built schooner like the Amistad but a former warship like the Hermione. The date of her uprising is also changed to 1799, the year Jonathan Robbins met his fate. The kinship between slaves and seamen, which Melville often noted, was thus acknowledged once again.

61. Herman Melville, Billy Budd, Benito Cereno and the Enchanted Isles (New York: Readers Club, 1942), 182–183. I am indebted to Catherine Allgor for reminding me of the pregnancy of this exchange.

62. Earlier in the same year, however, the Supreme Court struck down state efforts to protect the liberties of free blacks within the United States from fugitive slave hunters. Prigg v. Pennsylvania, 41 U.S. (16 Pet.) 1 (1842). See Ch. 20, infra.

Chapter Five

Epigraph: In re Kaine, 55 U.S. 103, 113 (1852).

1. William Bradford, Of Plimoth Plantation, 1620–1647 (S. E. Morison, ed.; New York: Modern Library, 1952), 80.

2. Articles of Confederation (Massachusetts, New Plymouth, Connecticut, and New Haven), May 19, 1643, Art. 8, in Howard W. Preston, ed., Documents Illustrative of American History (4th ed.; New York: Putnam's, 1896), 92–93.

3. Articles of Agreement made and concluded at Hartford upon Conecticott, September 19th, 1650, betwix the Deligates of the honored Comissioners of the United English Colonies and the Deligates of Peter Styversant, Governor General of New Netherland, Ebenezer Hazard, State Papers (1792; Freeport, N.Y.: Books for Libraries Press, 1969), vol. 2, 170, 172.

4. Articles of Confederation between the Plantations under the Goverment of the Massachusetts, the Plantations under the Goverment of New Plymouth and the Plantations under the Goverment of Conecticott, Etc., Art. 7, id. at 516, 518.

5. State of the State Message, Jan. 2, 1822, N.Y. State Legislature, Assembly Journal, 45th sess., 1822, at 14–15.

6. 1822 N.Y. Laws, ch. 148, at 139 (April 5, 1822).

7. 1829 N.Y. Revised Statutes, ch. 7, tit. 1, sec. 8, at 164: "The governor may, at his discretion, deliver over to justice, any person found within the state, who shall be charged with having

committed without the jurisdiction of the United States, any crime, except treason, which, by the laws of this state, if committed therein, is punishable by death or by imprisonment in the state prison." According to John Bassett Moore, Extradition (Washington, D.C.: U.S. Government Printing Office, 1980), vol. 1, sec. 49, at 59, n. 2, the amendment was enacted in 1827, but no record of any legislative debate could be found in the New York State Library. The author thanks Allan W. Raney of the New York State Library for his research assistance.

8. 1 Op. Att'y Gen. 68 (1797) (Lee), 1 Op. Att'y Gen. 509, 521 (1821) (Wirt), 2 Op. Att'y Gen. 452 (1831) and 2 Op. Att'y Gen. 559 (1833) (Taney), 3 Op. Att'y Gen. 661 (1841) (Legare). Accord: Opinion of the Attorney General and Solicitor General of Great Britain to the Home Office, 30 Sept. 1815, reproduced in International Law Opinions (McNair ed.; Cambridge: Cambridge University Press, 1956), vol. 2, 44.

9. Letter to Gov. Cornelius P. Van Ness of Vermont, March 25, 1825, in Papers of Henry Clay (James P. Hopkins ed.; Louisville: University of Kentucky Press, 1972), vol. 4, 142; Reporter's note to United States v. Davis, 25 F. Cas. 786, 788 (no. 14,932) (C.C.D.Mass. 1837).

10. Letter from Secretary of State Thomas Pickering to Gov. Thomas Chittenden, June 3, 1796, in Pickering Papers (F. Allis ed.; Massachusetts Historical Society, microfilm edition, 1966), roll 36, 85.

11. Ex parte Dos Santos, 7 F. Cas. 949 (no. 4,016) (C.C.D.Va. 1835). Accord: The British case of In re Tivnan et al. [1864] 5 Best & Smith 645 (Compton, J., holding comity was not enough to allow extradition for the allegedly "universal" offense of piracy).

12. One of the defects in Benjamin Franklin's draft of the ship-jumping agreement with France, Barbour recalled, was that it would have required the surrender of passengers on French ships (presumably like Galbaud) whose "acts" would be "rendered criminal by tyrannical laws only." 7 F. Cas. 949 at 955.

13. 7 F. Cas. at 956.

14. Matter of Washburn, 4 Johns ch. 105 (1819) and Commentaries on American Law (New York: O. Halsted, 1826; Da Capo Reprint, 1971), vol. 1, 36: "Every State is bound to deny asylum to criminals, and upon application and due examination of the case to surrender the fugitive to the foreign State where the crime was committed. The guilty party cannot be tried and punished by any other jurisdiction than the one whose laws have been violated." Supreme Court Justice Joseph Story disagreed, aligning himself with Secretary Clay and the four attorneys general. United States v. Davis, 25 F. Cas. 786, 788 (no. 14,932) (C.C.D.Mass. 1837) (in reporter's note). See also Story's Commentaries on the Constitution of the United States, (Boston: Hilliard, Gray & Co., 1833) vol. 3, 677, citing Commonwealth v. Deacon, 10 Sergeant & Rawle R. 125, and 1 Amer. Jurist 297 (a Canadian case, Rex v. Ball).

15. Letter of Timothy Pickering to Gov. Thomas Chittenden, June 3, 1786, in Pickering Papers (F. Allis ed.; Massachusetts Historical Society, microfilm edition, 1966), roll 36, 85.

16. In March 1838, the Canadian Refugee Relief Association was formed in Lockport, New York, in part to conduct paramilitary operations. In June, refugees from Canada and their American sympathizers formed the Sons of Liberty and conducted minor operations in the Detroit area. The most aggressive revolutionary organization, however, was the Hunter's Lodge, which, when it was reorganized in Cleveland in September 1838, claimed a membership of 50,000. It declared independence for Upper Canada and recruited two invasion forces, both of which were defeated and captured on Canadian soil in late 1838. Americans who supported Canadian independence did so for a variety of reasons, including the hope that a free Canada would want to join the United States and that its eventual annexation could counterbalance the potential annexation of Texas as a slave state.

17. Seward had previously refused to ask Canada to surrender a fugitive from New York for the same reason. Message to the New York State Legislature, Niles National Register, vol. 63, at 28 (Sept. 10, 1842).

18. John Bassett Moore, Digest of International Law, vol. 4, sec. 579, at 242.

19. Id., and Albert B. Covey, The Crisis of 1830–1832 in Canadian–American Relations (New Haven: Yale University Press, 1941), 172–173. The 1822 law was finally declared unconstitutional by the New York Court of Appeals in People v. Curtis, 50 N.Y. 321 (1872).

20. In several cases county officials appear to have surrendered fugitives on their own initiative. Moore, Extradition, vol. 1, 67. When Seward became secretary of state under Lincoln, he persisted in the New York view that extradition was an executive power. See the case of Arguelles, infra, ch. 6.

21. Covey, The Crisis of 1830–1842, 172.

22. 39 U.S. (14 Pet.) 540 (1840). The Court mispelled the governor's name.

23. Baldwin thus confused deportation with extradition and imputed the power of deportation, or banishment, to a state. The question of concurrent or exclusive authority would not finally be resolved as a matter of constitutional law until 1886, when the Supreme Court unanimously adopted Taney's view in United States v. Rauscher, 119 U.S. 407 (1886).

24. Ex parte Holmes, 12 Vt. 631 (1840).

25. Id. at 636.

26. Id.

27. Id. at 639.

28. Id. at 636.

29. It was also to be a matter of U.S. law, and not a law inferred from vague assertions about the mutual obligations of "sovereigns" who somehow belong to a "family" of nations. Such familial claims might resonate in postfeudal Europe, where titular royalty still married across national boundaries, but it made no sense to Americans, for whom the people were sovereign and employed government executives as public "servants."

30. For the story of the Caroline raid, see generally H. Ex. Doc. no. 74, 25th Cong., 2d sess., 1838; Covey, The Crisis of 1830–1832, ch. 3; R. Y. Jennings, "The Caroline and McLeod Cases," 32 Am. J. Int'l L. 82 (1938); and Alastair Watt, "The Case of Alexander McLeod," Canadian Historical Review, vol. 12 (1931), 145. See also People v. McLeod, 25 Wend. 483, 484–486 (1841).

31. The attack was authorized by Col. Allan MacNab, commander of the Canadian militia, and was led by Andrew Drew, a captain in the Royal Navy. Covey, 36–37. At his trial, McLeod denied that he had taken part in the raid.

32. Id. at 131.

33. Id. at 137; Watt, "The Case of Alexander McLeod," 153–154.

34. 5 Stat. 355 (March 3, 1839).

35. People v. McLeod, 25 Wend. 483 (N.Y. 1841). The witnesses who could have placed McLeod at the scene of the raid failed to appear, prompting suspicions that the U.S. government had managed, somehow, to prevent their testimony. Watt, "The Case of Alexander McLeod," 158.

36. His name is also spelled McKenzie in some accounts.

37. Opinion of Attorney General Samuel Beardsley to Governor William C. Marcy, Dec. 23, 1837, quoted in Moore, Extradition, vol. 1, 314–315.

38. Id. at 315.

39. Marcy Papers, vol. 3, 32,875, as quoted in Covey, The Crisis of 1830–1832, 171.

40. 1829 N.Y. Revised Statutes, ch. 7, tit. 1, sec. 8, at 164.

41. Despite Mackenzie's popularity in upstate New York, he was convicted in federal court in 1839 of inciting American citizens to attack Canada in violation of U.S. neutrality laws. He served one year of an eighteen-month sentence before being pardoned by President Van Buren. William Kilbourn, The Firebrand: William Lyon Mackenzie and the Rebellion in Upper Canada (Toronto: Clarke Irwin & Co., 1977), 209–10.

42. See, e.g., the first U.S.-France Extradition Treaty, T.S. no. 89, 8 Stat. 580–583 (1843) (art. 5).

43. In re Holmes, 12 Vt. 631, 636 (1840).

44. Letter from Edward Everett, U.S. Minister to Great Britain, to Secretary of State Daniel Webster, Jan. 21, 1842, in Papers of Daniel Webster, Diplomatic Papers, 1841–1843 (Kenneth Shewmaker ed.; Hanover, N.H.: University Press of New England, Dartmouth College, 1983), ser. 3, vol. 1, 491–492.

45. Howard Jones, To the Webster–Ashburton Treaty: A Study in Anglo-American Relations, 1783–1843 (Chapel Hill: University of North Carolina Press, 1977), 146.

46. Daniel Webster, Writings and Speeches of Daniel Webster (Boston: Little Brown, 1903), vol. 1, 124. See also Letter from Joseph Story to Daniel Webster, April 19, 1842, in Papers of Daniel Webster, Diplomatic Papers, 1841–1843 (Kenneth E. Shewmaker ed.; Hanover, N.H.: University of Press of New England, Dartmouth College, 1983), ser. 3, vol. 1, 537.

47. T.S. no. 119, 8 Stat. 572, 576 (1842).

48. Writings and Speeches of Daniel Webster, vol. 11, 302.

49. Id., 302–303.

50. In re Kaine, 55 U.S. (14 How.) 103, 112–113 (1852).

51. Covey, 176–177, citing Public Archives of Canada, Series G, Dispatches from the Colonial Office to the Governors, vol. 114, 108–11.

52. Id., 177.

53. See Ch. 4, *supra.*

54. Id., citing British diplomatic correspondence, Public Archives of Canada, Series G, vol. 114, *passim.*

55. For the British debate regarding the potential applicability of Article 10 to fugitive slaves, see Alexander L. Murray, "The Extradition of Fugitive Slaves from Canada: A Reconsideration," Canadian Historical Review, vol. 43, no. 4 (Dec. 1992), 298–314.

56. Letter from Joseph Story to Daniel Webster, April 19, 1842, in Papers of Daniel Webster, Diplomatic Papers, 1841–1843, ser. 3, vol. 1, 537, 538.

57. Writings and Speeches of Daniel Webster, vol. 1, 124.

58. T. H. Benton, Thirty Year's View: A History of the Workings of the American Government from 1820 to 1850 (New York: Appleton, 1856), vol. 2 (1866), 44.

59. Id.

60. Id., 446–447.

61. Id., 448–449.

62. Id., 449.

63. Id., 448–449.

64. Message of Aug. 11, 1842, 12 Cong. Globe, 27th Cong., 3d sess. (1843), 4.

65. T.S. no. 89, 8 Stat. 580–583 (1843) (art. 5).

66. 94 Consol. T.S. 178–81 (Perry ed., 1969) (signed Feb. 13, 1843). The French, like the Americans, had not included a political offense exception in their 1843 extradition treaty with the United Kingdom. Herslet's Commercial Treaties (1845; New York: Johnson Reprint Corp., 1970), vol. 6, 344–345. But they had included one in their earlier treaty with Belgium, which suggests that the British, more perhaps than the Americans, had initially balked at expressly

exempting political offenders from the extradition provisions of the Webster–Ashburton Treaty.

67. Message of Aug. 11, 1842, 12 Cong. Globe, 27th Cong., 3d sess. (1843), at 4.

68. 13 Cong. Globe, part 2, 28th Cong., 1st sess. (1844), at 248.

69. See generally Patrick Brode, The Odyssey of John Anderson (Toronto: University of Toronto Press, 1989). Other accounts spell Digges's name Diggs. See also Murray, "The Extradition of Fugitive Slaves," 314, and Fred Landon, "The Anderson Fugitive Case," Journal of Negro History, vol. 7 (1922), 233, 242.

70. In the Matter of John Anderson [1860] 20 U.C.Q.B. 124.

71. 20 U.C.Q.B. at 173. The case is described in Roman Zorn, "Criminal Extradition Menaces the Canadian Haven for Fugitive Slaves, 1841–1861," 38 Canadian Historical Review 284–94 (1957), and in Patrick Brode, "In the Matter of John Anderson: Canadian Courts and the Fugitive Slave," 14 Law Society Gazette (of Upper Canada) 92–97 (1980).

72. Brode, The Odyssey of John Anderson, ch. 7.

73. In re John Anderson [1861] 11 U.C.C.P. 1. See also the Toronto Globe's account of Feb. 1, 1861, and Brode, The Odyssey of John Anderson, ch. 8.

74. Id. at 116, citing Morning Chronicle's Parliamentary Debates, 4th sess., 6th Parl., Province of Canada, May 1, 1861.

75. The Founding of New Societies (New York: Harcourt Brace Jovanovich, 1964).

Chapter Six

Epigraph: Letter to Mr. Hulsemann, Sept. 6, 1853, Sen. Doc., 33rd Cong., 1st sess., vol. 1, 34.

1. Article 120 of the Constitution of the First Republic (1793) decreed that the French people would "donner asile aux étrangers bannis de leur patrie pour la cause de la liberté. Il le refuse aux tyrans!"

2. This agreement was renewed by Napoleon in 1803. Lassa F. I. Oppenheim, International Law (H. Lauterpacht, 7th ed.; London: Longmans, Green & Co., 1948), vol. 1, 705.

3. He accused the Senate of Hamburg of violating "the laws of hospitality in such a way that even the wandering tribes of the desert would blush with shame" and broke off diplomatic relations. Quoted in Reale, "Le Droit D'Asile," 63 Recueil des Cours (1938), 547.

4. Id., 546. The British refused.

5. See Barton Ingraham, Political Crime in Europe (Berkeley: University of California Press, 1979), sec. 2.

6. Robert G. Neuman, Extradition and Political Offenders (unpublished Ph.D. dissertation, University of Minnesota, 1946), 98, citing Heinreich Lammasch, Das Recht der Auslieferung wegen Politischer Verbrechen (Vienna: Manz, 1884), 30.

7. Reale, "Le Droit D'Asile," 548.

8. Neumann, Extradition and Political Offenders, 86–87.

9. Oppenheim, International Law (H. Lauterpacht, 8th ed. 1955), vol. 1, 705.

10. L. G. A. Bonald, Legislation Primitive (Paris: Le Clere, 1802), vol. 2, ch. 17, sec. 6, 106–107 ("l'extradition ne doit pas être accordée pro des delits ... politiques, et si le droit d'asile n'est plus attache aux temples, l'Univers entier est un temple pour l'homme infortune").

11. Hollandais Provo Kluit, Dissertio Politico-Juridica Inauguralis de Deditione Profugorum (Politico-Juridical Inaugural Dissertation on the Surrender of Fugitives).

12. Christine Van den Wijngaert, The Political Offence Exception to Extradition (Antwerp: Kluwer, 1980), 12.

13. Id., 549–50.

14. These are summarized in Ingraham, Political Crime in Europe, 123–124.

15. 1 Am. Jurist 297, 301 (1829). Rex v. Ball did not involve extradition because neither Vermont nor the United States had formally requested Fisher's surrender for trial. However, the court upheld the authority of the Canadian executive to expel him, if it wished, over the border into Vermont.

16. Article 6 of the Law of 1833 provided that "no foreigner may be persecuted or punished for any political crimes antecedent to the extradition, or for any act connected with such a crime." Harvard Research in International Law, Extradition, 29 Am. J. Int'l L. at 362 (1935).

17. 22 B.F.S.P. 223, art. 5 (signed Nov. 2, 1833).

18. M. Cherif Bassiouni, International Extradition and World Public Order (Dobbs Ferry, N.Y.: Oceana, 1974), 375.

19. See, e.g., H. Rudman, Italian Nationalism and English Letters (New York: Columbia University Press, 1940).

20. Ingraham, Political Crime in Europe, 219.

21. Quoted in M. Wolfgang, Cesare Lombroso in Pioneers in Criminology (H. Mannheim ed.; London: Stevens, 1960), 189.

22. Criminal Man (G. Lombroso-Ferrero trans.; Monclair, N.J.: Patterson Smith, 1972), App. 294–298. For similar views, see Enrico Ferri, The Positive School of Criminology (Chicago: C. H. Kers & Co., 1906), 78; Raffaele Garofalo, Criminology (R. Millar trans.; Montclair, N.J.: Patterson Smith, 1968), 38; and Havelock Ellis, The Criminal (5th ed.; New York: Scribner's, 1910), App. E, 417.

23. Ingraham, Political Crime in Europe, 124–35, 144–145.

24. Oppenheim, International Law (H. Lauterpacht, 8th ed; 1955), vol. 1, 413.

25. Id.

26. Lora L. Deere, "Political Offenses in the Law and Practice of Extradition," 27 Am. J. Int'l Law at 247, 251 (1933).

27. Reale, "Le Droit D'Asile," 551–552.

28. With the United States. John Bassett Moore, Treatise on Extradition (Boston: Boston Book Co., 1891), vol. 1, 306.

29. Neumann claims that the North German Federation was the first to break ranks but does not acknowledge the treaty between Austria and the United States. Extradition and the Political Offender, 94. Russia's acceptance of the political offense exception is noted in Oppenheim, International Law (H. Lauterpacht, 8th ed., 1955), vol. 1, 706, n. 2.

30. It should not be assumed that the conservative regimes accepted the political crimes exception out of conviction. Four years after Austria accepted the exception in her treaty with the United States, she enacted domestic legislation making it a crime under Austrian law to commit high treason against a foreign government, provided that the foreign government returned the favor by reciprocal legislation. Only Russia reciprocated. Deere, "Political Offenses in the Law and Practice of Extradition," 249, n. 13.

31. See Ch. 5, supra, for accounts of both opinions.

32. With the United States (1842), France (1843), and Denmark (1862). A supplementary treaty with France negotiated in 1852 included an express exemption for political offenders but was never implemented by Parliament because of Liberal opposition to its lax evidentiary standards.

33. Hansard, Parliamentary Debates, 3d ser., vol. 202, col. 301 (1870).

34. Extradition Treaties (London: William Ridgeway, 1868), 34.

35. Report from the Select Committee on Extradition, Parliamentary Papers, 1867–1868.

36. British Digest of International Law (B.D.I.L.) (1965), vol. 6, at 447.

37. A Bill Entitled An Act for the Amendment of the Law Relating to Treaties of Extradition, 29 & 30 Victoria (26 July 1866), Parliamentary Papers, 1866, vol. 3, 39–42. See also Hansard, Parliamentary Debates, 3d ser., vol. 184, cols. 2023–26.

38. Hansard, Parliamentary Debates, 3d ser., vol. 184, col. 2015 (1866).

39. Id., col. 2023.

40. Id., col. 2024.

41. Bernard Potter, The Refugee Question in Mid-Victorian Politics (Cambridge: Cambridge University Press, 1979), esp. ch. 5.

42. Hansard, Parliamentary Debates, 3d ser., vol. 184, col. 2025.

43. Id., col. 2109.

44. Id., cols. 2115–17. As a member of the Select Committee on Extradition, Mill appears to have believed that justice would be best served by requiring the requesting state "to send some witness capable of being cross-examined, who could testify to the main facts of the case." Public and Parliamentary Speeches by John Stuart Mill, July 1869–March 1873 (John M. Robson et al. eds.; Toronto: University of Toronto Press, 1988), 556.

45. Hansard, Parliamentary Debates, 3d ser., vol. 184, cols. 2121–22.

46. Id., cols. 2117, 2115.

47. Id., cols. 2111–12.

48. Id. at col. 2115.

49. Letter from John Stuart Mill to W. D. Christie, Esq., April 20, 1868, in Later Letters of John Stuart Mill, 1849–1873 (Francis E. Mineka and Dwight N. Lindley eds.; Toronto: University of Toronto Press, 1972), letter no. 1221, 1387. See also Mill's question to a witness before the Select Committee on Extradition, in Public and Parliamentary Speeches by John Stuart Mill, July 1869–March 1873 (John M. Robson et al. eds; Toronto: University of Toronto Press, 1988), 555–556. For a description of Louis Napoleon's landing at Boulogne, which was more of a political appearance than a military operation, see F. H. Cheetham, Louis Napoleon and the Genesis of the Second Empire (London: John Lane, 1909).

50. Patrick Quinlivan and Paul Rose, The Fenians in England, 1865–1872 (London: John Calder, 1972), 87–93, 143.

51. J. A. Cole, Prince of Spies: Henre Le Caron (London: Faber & Faber, 1984), 35.

52. Letter from John Stuart Mill to the president of a committee formed for the purpose of securing an amnesty for political prisoners, Feb. 8, 1869, in The Letters of John Stuart Mill (Hugh S. R. Elliot ed.; London: Longmans, Green & Co., 1910), 185.

53. Hansard, Parliamentary Debates, 3d ser., vol. 184, col. 2108.

54. Id., col. 2112.

55. Id., col. 2121.

56. Id., cols. 2120–21.

57. Id., col. 2123.

58. Quoted in 6 B.D.I.L. at 662.

59. Id. Also, Report of the Select Committee on Extradition, Parliamentary Papers, 1867–1868, para. 717–34 (testimony of Sir T. Henry).

60. Correspondence respecting the Extradition of Bennet G. Burley, Parliamentary Papers (41) vol. 82, c. 1528, and Further Return relating to cases of Extradition of Prisoners under the Treaty

between Great Britain and the United States, c. 1621 (1876). See also "In re Bennett Burley," Upper Canada Law Journal, New Series, vol. 1, 34–51.

61. See generally L. N. Benjamin, The St. Albans Raid (Montreal: Lovell, 1865). See also Robin W. Winks, Canada and the United States: The Civil War Years (Baltimore: Johns Hopkins Press, 1960), ch. 14.

62. Benjamin, St. Albans Raid, 470. Accord: In re Tivnan [1864] Best & Smith at 645.

63. Counsel for the defense reminded the court that Great Britain had taken responsibility for the *Caroline* raid, and had argued vociferously that McLeod should not, for that reason, be tried in New York for the shooting of Durfee on American soil. Benjamin, St. Albans Raid, 240. They also noted that an American judge, Talmadge, in reviewing the lower New York court's decision to try McLeod, had found the *Caroline* raid to be "a lawful cause of war," for which the British government and not McLeod should be held responsible. Those engaged in the raid, Talmadge held, were "acting under lawful authority" and, for that reason, "can never be regarded as robbers or plunderers, or liable to be punished criminally." Id. at 270, quoting 26 Wendell's Rep.

64. 6 B.D.I.L. at 664, citing Report of the Select Committee, viii–ix. Citations are to the British Digest of International Law because the Report of the Select Committee is not easily obtained.

65. Id. at ix. The American jurist, David Dudley Fields, made a similar proposal a few years later in his Draft Outline of an International Code (New York: Baker, Voorhis, & Co., 1876), title 5, ch. 18, sec. 1, art. 215(2) at 108. Field's suggestion was embraced by the Association pour la Reforme de la Codification du Droit de Gens at the Hague (1875): "Extradition shall not be granted for an act committed in the course of an internal, political struggle, if that act, had it been committed during a war, could be justified by the law of nations." Heinreich Lammasch, Das Recht der Auslieferung wegen Politischer Verbrechen (Vienna: Manz, 1884), at 81 ff, as quoted in Neumann, Extradition and the Political Offender, 141. The Institute of International Law took a similar position at its meeting in Oxford, England, in 1880: "In order to appraise acts committed in the course of a political rebellion, an insurrection or a civil war, it is necessary to inquire whether or not they were justified by the customs of war." Annuaire de l'Institut de Droit International (Oxford, 1880), vol. 5, art. 14(b), at 118, as quoted by Neumann, 141. This resolution was amended twelve years later: "Acts committed in the course of an insurrection or a civil war by one or the other of the contestants during the struggle and in the interest of his cause, shall not result in extradition, unless they constitute acts of repugnant barbarity and vandalism which are forbidden by the laws of war, and then only after the civil war has come to an end." Annuaire (1892), as quoted by Neumann, 142. Almost a century later, the International Law Association's Committee on Terrorism came to the same conclusion. 26 August 1978, in Terrorism (U.K.: Crane, Russock, 1988), vol. 11.

66. 6 B.D.I.L. 662.

67. 33 & 34 Vict. c. 52 (1870).

68. Autobiography of John Stuart Mill (New York: Columbia University Press, 1924), 210–211. One unforeseen consequence of this Liberal victory was that a century would pass before an Irish rebel would be extradited to the United Kingdom by the United States.

69. It should be noted that this was a proposal; at no time did Fish claim that the administration of the political offense exception did not belong with the courts.

70. Article 2, Extradition Treaty Between the United States of America and Her Britannic Majesty, 26 Stat. 1508, 172 T.S. 169, 12 T.I.A.S. no. 211 (signed July 12, 1889; entered into force April 4, 1890). Sometimes called the Blaine–Pauncefort Treaty.

71. 33 & 34 Vict. c. 52, sec. 3(2). See also sec. 19.

72. United States v. Rauscher, 119 U.S. 407, 418 (1886) (reasoning that extradition treaties are self-executing, and thus become the "supreme law of the land" under Article 6, para. 2, of the Constitution upon ratification by the president.

73. Similarly, the Kentucky Court of Appeals ruled that the 1842 treaty implicitly embraced the rule of specialty. Commonwealth v. Hawes, 76 Ky. (13 Bush) 697 (1878).

74. Article 3, Extradition Treaty Between the United States of America and Her Britannic Majesty, 26 Stat. 1508, 172 T.S. 169, 12 T.I.A.S. no. 211 (signed July 12, 1889; entered into force April 4, 1890).

75. See generally Jacques Semmelman, "The Doctrine of Specialty in the Federal Courts: Making Sense of United States v. Rauscher," 34 Va. J. Int'l L. 71 (1993).

76. In re Castioni [1891] 1 Q.B. 149.

77. Quoted in 6 B.D.I.L. 672.

78. See, e.g., Frederic R. Coudert, Address on Extradition, American Society of International Law, Proceedings (New York: Baker, Voorhis & Co., 1909), vol. 3, 124, 134.

79. In re Castioni [1891] 1 Q.B. 149, 156.

80. 6 B.D.I.L. 672 and Coudert, Address on Extradition, 133. See also Regina v. Governor of Brixton Prison, Ex parte Kolczynski [1954] 1 Q.B. 540, 548 (Cassels, J.) and 550 (Lord Goddard, J.).

81. Sir James F. Stephen, A History of the Criminal Law of England (London: Macmillan, 1883), vol. 2, 71.

82. 33 & 34 Vict. c. 52, sec. 3(1) (1870). The term "second limb" comes from Regina v. Governor of Brixton Prison, Ex parte Kolczynski [1954] 1 Q.B. at 540, 546.

83. Royal Commission on Extradition, Report of the Commissioners (London: HMSO, 1878), at 7–8.

Chapter Seven

Epigraph: No. 78, *The Federalist Papers* (C. Rossiter ed.; New York: Mentor, 1961), 466, quoting Montesquieu.

1. As Secretary of State Elihu Root informed a Honduran minister in 1908, "According to the system of jurisprudence obtaining in the United States, the question as to whether or not an offense is a political one is always decided in the first instance by the judicial officer before whom the fugitive is brought for commitment to surrender. If the judicial authorities refuse to commit the fugitive for surrender on the ground that he is a political offender, the matter is ended. The executive has no authority to review the finding." Letter from Secretary of State Elihu Root to Señor Ugarte, Oct. 1, 1908, quoted in Green H. Hackworth, Digest of International Law (Washington, D.C.: U.S. Government Printing Office, 1942), vol. 4, 46.

2. See generally Carl B. Swisher, History of the Supreme Court of the United States: The Taney Period (New York: Macmillan, 1974), vol. 5, 177–80.

3. James Buchanan to Benjamin F. Butler, Nov. 25, 1846, Works of James Buchanan (Moore ed.; Philadelphia: Lippincott, 1909), vol. 7, 124–125.

4. In re Metzger, 17 F. Cas. 232 (no. 9,511) (S.D.N.Y. 1847).

5. Matter of Metzger, 46 U.S. (5 How.) 176, 181 (1847). For contemporary comment see Note, "Extradition—Case of Metzger, Under the Treaty with France," 5 West. L. J. 141–142 (1847).

6. 8 Stat. 580, 582 (1843).

7. 46 U.S. (5 How.) at 180, 188–189. Metzger's release was eventually ordered by Judge Worth Edmonds of the New York State Circuit Court on the grounds that his commitment had been

illegal. He disappeared before the French government, with the assistance of Secretary of State Buchanan, could initiate extradition proceedings in a federal court. Note, "Extradition—Case of Metzger, Under the Treaty with France," 141–142.

8. Valentine v. United States *ex rel.* Neidecker, 299 U.S. 5, 9 (1936).

9. Ex parte McCardle, 71 U.S. (4 Wall.) 2 (1866). See also the opinion of Judge Betts in In re Kaine, 14 F. Cas. 84, at 87 (no. 7,598) (C.C.S.D.N.Y. 1852) (dictum to the effect that a treaty barring habeas review of an extradition arrest would violate the Constitution).

10. 10 Annals of Congress at 615.

11. 9 Stat. 302, now 18 U.S.C. 3184.

12. The power to refuse to surrender a person certified extraditable by a court was not asserted by the secretary of state until 1871. John Bassett Moore, Treatise on Extradition (Boston: Boston Book Co., 1891), vol. 1, secs. 361–362, 551–555.

13. 17 Cong. Globe 868 (June 23, 1848) (statement of Rep. Charles J. Ingersoll, chairman, Committee on Foreign Affairs).

14. 17 Cong. Globe 1008 (July 28, 1848) (statements of senators King and Badger).

15. The statute was briefly declared unconstitutional in 1995. Lobue v. Christopher, 893 F. Supp. 65 (D.C.D.C. 1995), *reversed* (on jurisdictional grounds), 82 F. 3d 1081 (D.C. Cir. 1996).

16. E.g., Maria P. Imbalgano, "*In re Mackin:* Is Application of the Political Offense Exception an Extradition Issue for the Judicial or the Executive Branch?," 5 Ford. Int'l L. J. 565 (1982).

17. In re Kaine, 14 F. Cas. 84, 86 (no. 7,598) (C.C.S.D.N.Y. 1852).

18. Id. at 90.

19. Id. at 87.

20. In re Kaine, 14 F. Cas. 82 (no. 7,597a) (C.C.S.D.N.Y. 1852).

21. In re Kaine, 55 U.S. (14 How.) 103 (1852).

22. Id. at 108.

23. Id. at 110.

24. Id., 115, at 117.

25. Id. at 136.

26. Id.

27. In re Kaine, 14 F. Cas. 84, 86 (no. 7598) (C.C.S.D.N.Y. 1852).

28. 55 U.S. (14 How.) at 112.

29. 55 U.S. (14 How.) at 138.

30. Ex parte Kaine, 14 F. Cas. 78, 82 (no. 7,597) (C.C.S.D.N.Y. 1853).

31. Id. at 81.

32. Id.

33. In re Mackin, 668 F. 2d 122, 134 (2d Cir. 1981).

34. 14 F. Cas. at 81.

35. Id.

36. Nelson's opinion was shared by British abolitionists at the time, and the Webster–Ashburton Treaty required that all American requests be made by U.S. officials to the British executive before being referred by them to British courts. See Howard Jones, To the Webster–Ashburton Treaty (Chapel Hill: University of North Carolina Press, 1977), 150.

37. 6 Op. Atty. Gen. 91 (1853).

38. Id. at 95.

39. Id. at 96.

40. Edward McPherson, The Political History of the Great Rebellion (Washington, D.C.: Philp & Solomons, 1864), 354. Seward boasted that, merely by ringing a little bell on his desk,

he could bring about the imprisonment of anyone he wished, without giving any reason. William B. Lawrence, "The Extradition Treaty," 14 Albany L. J. 85, 88 (1976).

41. McPherson, The Political History of the Great Rebellion, 355.

42. Id. Legal proceedings against the arresting officer also were abandoned, so the matter did not come under judicial examination. See also Edward G. Clarke, A Treatise on the Law of Extradition (4th ed.; London: Stevens and Hayes, 1903), 73–74, and Wheaton's International Law (8th ed.; Dana ed.; Boston: Little Brown, 1866), 183, n. 73. Spain repaid the favor when it just as peremptorily returned "Boss" Tweed to the United States for prosecution in 1876. Denis Tilden Lynch, "Boss" Tweed (New York: Boni and Liveright, 1927), 398–401.

43. Seward's action was not without historic precedent. In the early 1830s, the British government surrendered to the United States twelve Spanish slavers wanted for attacking and robbing an American vessel on the high seas, even though no extradition treaty then authorized the surrender. United States v. Pedro Gilbert, et al., 2 Summer 19 (1834), and Alfred P. Rubin, The Law of Piracy (Newport, R.I.: U.S. Naval War College Press, 1988), vol. 63 of U.S. Naval War College International Law Studies, 138–139.

44. U.S. Dip. Cor., 1864, part 2, 60–74.

45. 74 U.S. (7 Wall.) 506 (1869). Seward's surrender of Arguelles was, in effect, an executive suspension of the privilege of the writ of habeas corpus, which the Court in McCardle had refused to allow, outside a war zone, even when authorized by legislation.

46. Moore, Extradition, vol. 1, sec. 27, 33–35.

47. Wheaton's International Law (8th ed.; Dana ed.; Boston: Little Brown, 1866), 184, n. 73.

48. 11 Stat. 639, 651–653, 114 C.T.S. 427, 448 (signed Oct. 1, 1855; entered into force Nov. 7, 1866). See also Lawrence, "The Extradition Treaty," 92.

49. See H.R. 5227, 97th Cong., 1st sess. (1981), sec. 3194(e)(2)(B)(v, vi, viii), sponsored by Rep. William Hughes (D.-N.J.) and the Reagan administration.

Chapter Eight

Epigraph: 62 F. 972, 997 (N.D.Cal. 1894).

1. E.g., see Gustavo Tosti, "Anarchistic Crimes," 14 Political Science Quarterly (U.S.) 404, 405–406 (1899): "What has always been understood as a political crime is a deed directed against the persons or things representative of the collective authority, with the purpose of bringing about, directly or indirectly, a violent change in the framework of social institutions, according to a certain plan of reform in opposition to the opinions of the majority which rule the community."

2. See generally James Joll, The Anarchists (2d ed.; Cambridge, Mass.: Harvard University Press, 1980), 111–29.

3. Tosti, "Anarchistic Crimes," 406–408.

4. Joll, The Anarchists, 114. See also Jean Maitron, Histoire du Mouvement Anarchiste en France, 1880–1914 (2d ed.; Paris: Société Universitaire d'Editions et de Librairie, 1955), 215–16, n.1, from which this account is largely taken.

5. In re Meunier [1894] 2 Q.B. 415, 419.

6. The formula adopted by the court in In re Meunier may have been inspired by the Institute of International Law which, in 1892 in Geneva, had resolved that "criminal acts directed against the bases of all social organization, and not only against a certain State or a certain form

of government, are not considered political offences." In Resolutions of the Institute of International Law (J. B. Scott, trans.; New York: Oxford University Press, 1916), 103.

7. Christine Van den Wijngaert, The Political Offence Exception to Extradition (Antwerp: Kluwer, 1980), 14–18.

8. E.g., see In re Ezeta, 62 F. 972 (N.D.Cal. 1894) (granting the political offense exception to a Salvadorian dictator), and Artukovic v. Boyle, 140 F. Supp. 245, 247 (S.D.Cal. 1956) (granting the exception to the second-ranking official in the Nazi puppet regime in Croatia during World War II).

9. Van den Wijngaert, The Political Offence Exception to Extradition, 137.

10. Maitron, Histoire du Mouvement Anarchiste en France, 216, n.1.

11. Lora L. Deere, "Political Offenses in the Law and Practice of Extradition," 27 Am. J. Int'l L. 268–69, n. 107.

12. 32 Stat. 1221 (March 3, 1903).

13. In re Ezeta, 62 F. 972 (N.D.Cal. 1894). See also John Bassett Moore, "The Case of the Salvadoran Refugees," 29 Am. L. Rev. 1 (1895), and reprinted in The Collected Papers of John Bassett Moore (New Haven: Yale University Press, 1944), vol. 1, 347–63.

14. 62 F. at 998.

15. 62 F. at 997.

16. Letter from John Stuart Mill to the president of a committee formed for the purpose of securing an amnesty for political prisoners, Feb. 8, 1869, in The Letters of John Stuart Mill (Hugh S. R. Elliot, ed.; London: Longmans, Green & Co., 1910), at 85.

17. Letter from Mexican Ambassador Juan N. Navarro to Secretary of State John M. Hay, Sept. 3, 1880, and reply from Acting Secretary of State William Hunter to Navarro, Sept. 22, 1880, Papers Relating to the Foreign Relations of the United States (Washington, D.C.: U.S. Government Printing Office, 1880), 787–88.

18. John Bassett Moore, Treatise on Extradition (Boston: Boston Book Co., 1891), vol. 1, sec. 217, 324–25.

19. Also spelled Ignacio.

20. For accounts of this raid, see the diplomatic correspondence excerpted in Moore's Digest of International Law (Washington, D.C.: U.S. Government Printing Office, 1906), vol. 4, 336–51, and articles in the San Antonio Daily Express, Dec. 13–25, 1892. The author thanks Ralph L. Elder of the library of the University of Texas at Austin for supplying copies of these articles.

21. Because Mexico had insisted on a clause barring the extradition of nationals, Benavides enjoyed an immunity that his Mexican followers did not. Moore, Digest, vol. 4, 336.

22. "Outbreak of the Bandits," San Antonio, Texas, Daily Express, Dec. 14, 1892.

23. Id., Dec. 14 and 17, 1892. On December 18, the paper reported that the commander of the northern military zone of Mexico claimed that he had been "informed of the invasion a few weeks before it occurred and [had] warned United States military authorities."

24. "Will Hunt them Down," Daily Express, Dec. 15, 1892, 1.

25. Letter to the Mexican minister, May 13, 1893, quoted in Moore, Digest, vol. 4, at 336. In reaching this judgment, Gresham rejected a contrary opinion reached by the State Department's solicitor. Id. at 337.

26. U.S.-Mexico Extradition Treaty, art. 6 (signed Dec. 11, 1861; entered into force May 20, 1862), 12 Stat. 1199, T.S. 209 (emphasis added).

27. The opinion was not reported.

28. Ornelas v. Ruiz, 161 U.S. 502 (1896).

29. Were the British law of habeas corpus to govern, the justices acknowledged, the reviewing judge would have had wide latitude to reexamine all aspects of the commissioner's finding. But the American law governing such reviews was much narrower. It only permitted reversal if the judge could find that the commissioner had no evidence whatsoever to support his decision. In this case, there was evidence, so the commissioner's decision was reinstated. 161 U.S. 502, 508–509. However, because his decision went unreported, it created no precedent.

30. Two of the three raiders, Inez Ruiz and Juan Duque, were surrendered to Mexico by Gresham's successor, Richard Olney. Ruiz was extradited for common crimes, but the Mexican government, violating the rule of specialty, convicted him for having taken part in the Garza revolt and sentenced him to death. Ruiz managed to escape back to the United States, and when Mexico again asked for his extradition, the State Department refused on the ground that it was now clear that his offense was political. Assistant Secretary of State Wilson to Señor Barra, the Mexican ambassador, Feb. 15, 1910, MS State Dept. File, 2167/14, cited in Robert G. Neumann, Extradition and the Political Offender (unpublished Ph.D. dissertation, University of Minnesota, 1946), at 223. Jesus Guerra was not extradited because, at the time the Supreme Court's decision was handed down, he had escaped from American custody. Moore, Digest, vol. 4, 339.

31. Moore, Digest, vol. 4, at 344.

32. Id. at 340.

33. Quoted in In re Ezeta, 62 F. at 999.

34. Quoted id. at 1000.

35. Moore, Digest, vol. 4, 344.

36. Discussed, *supra*, Ch. 5.

37. Id., and at 346: "In reaching this conclusion, the Department wishes to state that this is a very close case and the decision announced has resolved the doubts in favor of liberty."

38. "Political Offence in Extradition Treaties" (editorial comment), 3 Am. J. Int'l L. 459 (1909).

39. Proceedings of the American Society of International Law, April 23 and 24, 1909 (New York: Baker, Voorhis & Co., 1909), vol. 3, 124, 139–40. Coudert argued Glucksman v. Henkel before the U.S. Supreme Court.

40. Id. at 142.

41. Moore, Digest, vol. 4, at 340.

42. Letter from Eliseo Arrendondo, Confidential Agent of the Constitutionalist Government of Mexico, to Secretary of State Robert Lansing, July 1, 1915, Foreign Relations of the United States, 1915 (Washington, D.C.: U.S. Government Printing Office, 1924), 830–32. Huerta died in El Paso in January 1916, before he could be tried by a U.S. court. Haldeen Braddy, Mexico and the Old Southwest (Port Washington, N.Y.: Kennikat Press, 1971), 223.

43. Letter from Cone Johnson, for Secretary of State Lansing, to Arrendondo, July 10, 1915, id. at 835. This concern for fairness had been made express three days earlier in a letter to the governor of Texas, which counseled that "extradition would be unwise" not only because the crimes were probably of a "political character," but because of "the well-known conditions" and "the lack of orderly machinery of justice by which a fair trial could be expected." Letter to the Governor of Texas from Secretary of State Lansing, July 7, 1915, id. at 834.

44. Hyde, International Law, vol. 1, 573–74 (1922) (facts), and Hackworth, Digest of International Law, vol. 4, 49–50 (1942) (quotation). See more generally Charles Cheney Hyde, "Notes on the Extradition Treaties of the United States," 8 Am. J. Int'l L. 487, 491–95 (1914). Similarly, when a court found Jan Janoff Pouren, another Russian revolutionary, extraditable on charges of "stealing articles of clothing, watches, and other personal property from defenseless peasants and women, the beating of women, and the burning of farmhouses," the State Department

submitted the case to a second magistrate who ruled in Pouren's favor. Foreign Relations of the United States, 1909 (1914), 516 (quotation), 513–23 (correspondence). It did not hurt Pouren's case that one of his attorneys was a sitting member of Congress. See generally The Case of Jan Janoff Pouren, Special Edition by the Pouren Defense Committee, Including Appendix with the Opinion of Commissioner Hitchcock (New York, 1909).

45. Foreign Relations of the United States, 1909, at 518–21.

46. Hackworth, Digest of International Law, vol. 4, 49–50. International practice at this time was split on revolutionary "death decree" cases. In 1907, the Swiss extradited a Polish revolutionary named Kilatschitsky for executing the director of the Vistula Railroad Company in Warsaw, despite the fact that Kilatschitsky was carrying out a "death warrant" issued by his party. Neumann, Extradition and the Political Offender, 161–62. However, Belgium refused to extradite another Polish revolutionary by the name of Chimansky for executing a number of people suspected of being Russian spies. Id. at 182. Art. 4 of the 1930 extradition treaty between the United States and Germany contained one of the strongest anti-terrorism provisions ever negotiated: "a willful crime against human life, except in battle or in open combat, shall in no case be deemed a crime of a political character, or an act connected with a crime or offense of such character." 47 Stat. 1862; T.S. no. 836 (signed July 12, 1930; entered into force April 22, 1931). However, there is no evidence that it was ever used by the United States to extradite anyone comparable to the revolutionary executioners of Russia. The German treaty does not appear to have made any impact on American law or practice.

47. During the so-called "White Terror" of 1905–1906, Russian revolutionaries killed or wounded 114 governors general, governors, high-ranking officials, and gendarme officers, plus 109 officers, 123 lesser functionaries, 452 policemen, and 750 soldiers and Cossacks. Paul Tabori, The Anatomy of Exile (London: Harrap, 1972), 175.

48. For the facts of this case, the author is indebted to James Carney and his book, The Playboy and the Yellow Lady (Swords, Ireland: Poolbeg Press, 1986).

49. (Boston: Luce, 1911).

50. Carney, The Playboy and the Yellow Lady, 184, 183.

51. Id., 190.

52. Hyde, International Law, vol. 1, 573–74; Neumann, 224; and Irish American Victory over Great Britain, issued by the Defense Committee, 1903 (copy in the Harvard Law School Library).

53. Carney, The Playboy and the Yellow Lady, 204–205.

Chapter Nine

Epigraph: 221 U.S. 508, 510 (1910).

1. State v. Mann, 13 N.C. (2 Dev.) 167, 170 (1829).

2. See the discussion of Prigg v. Pennsylvania.

3. Also discussed *supra*, Chapter 4.

4. United States v. Caldwell, 8 Blatchford 131 (Cir. Ct., S.D.N.Y. 1871).

5. Id. at 133.

6. Id.

7. Benedict made a similar ruling in United States v. Lawrence, 13 Blatchford 295 (C.C. S.D.N.Y. 1876), upholding the conviction of an Irishman on several counts of forgery when he had been extradited to the United States by the United Kingdom for trial on only one. In Lawrence, as in Caldwell, Benedict justified his ruling by reference to a case in which the

United States did not protest when the United Kingdom prosecuted a man named Heilbronn for an offense not provided for in the treaty. He also cited Ex Parte Scott, [1829] 9 B. & C. 446, in which the King's Bench refused to deny jurisdiction over a woman who had been abducted by a British officer from Brussels, Belgium.

8. E.g., Judge Ogden Hoffman of the U.S. District Court of California concluded that it was his court's responsibility to honor the rule of specialty, which he found clearly implied by the language of the 1842 treaty with Great Britain, and forbade the trial of the accused for offenses other than the one for which he had been surrendered. United States v. Watts, 14 F. 130 (D.Cal. 1882). In Oregon, federal district court judge Matthew P. Deady ruled that to try Isaac N. Hibbs for any offenses other than the one for which he had been surrendered would not only violate a contract (i.e., treaty) with the United Kingdom, but would violate "the supreme law of this land in a matter directly involving [the defendant's] personal rights." Ex parte Hibbs, 26 F. 421, 431 (D.Ore. 1886).

State courts were divided on the issue. New York seemed to support Judge Benedict's view in Adriance v. Lagrave, 59 N.Y. 109 (Ct. App. 1874); Kentucky, Texas, and Ohio agreed with the federal courts on the west coast that judges had an obligation under the treaties to try extradited persons only on the charges that had brought about their surrender. Like Judge Deady in Oregon, the Supreme Court of Ohio held that the rule of specialty created a personal right in the accused. State v. Vanderpool, 39 Ohio St. 273, 280 (Sup. Ct. Ohio, 1883). Accord: Commonwealth v. Hawes, 13 Bush 697 (C.A.Ky. 1878); Blandford v. State, 10 Tex. Ct. App. 627 (1881); Matter of Cannon, 47 Mich. 481 (1882). Also in accord: Ker v. People, 110 Ill. 627, 642 (1884). Most commentators and treatise writers at the time considered the rule of specialty judicially enforceable on petition from the accused. E.g., see William B. Lawrence, "The Extradition Treaty," 14 Albany L. J. 85 (1876), 15 Albany L. J. 224 (1877), and 16 Albany L. J. 361 (1877); Judge John Lowell, "Winslow's Case," 10 Am. L. Rev. 617 (1875–76); David Dudley Field, Field's International Code, sec. 237, at 122; Samuel Spear, The Law of Extradition: International and Interstate (3d ed.; Littleton, Colo.: F. B. Rothman, 1884), at 94.

9. 119 U.S. 407, 430 (1886).

10. Id. at 422. Accord: Demjanjuk v. Petrovsky, 10 F. 3d 338 (6th Cir. 1993).

11. Id. at 430.

12. Id. Acknowledging this power in trial courts (or in state or federal courts on habeas reviews), Miller noted, would save the federal executive from having to remind state prosecutors that they had overreached themselves.

13. Kelly v. Griffin, 24 U.S. 6, 5 (1916).

14. Id. at 15. Charles Fairman, Miller's biographer, missed this distinction when he claimed that the Justice had "slipped in his language in the Rauscher opinion." "Ker v. Illinois Revisited," 47 Am. J. Int'l L. 678, at 681 (1953).

15. Ker v. Illinois, 119 U.S. 436 (1886). He did have an executive warrant signed by the president.

16. Justice Scott, writing for the Supreme Court of Illinois, acknowledged that the U.S. Navy was involved in the abduction but ruled that the only legal wrong was the invasion of Peru's sovereignty, which he characterized as "an individual wrong" committed by the Pinkerton detective alone. Ker v. The People, 110 Ill. 627, 643 (1884). In any case, Scott added, Ker was not brought into the state of Illinois by any wrongdoing of its officials. Id. at 636. The Illinois court did not consider that, by receiving a stolen person, its trial court would become an accessory after the fact to a kidnapping. However, it did imply that an abducted defendant might have a right to exclude his presence for trial if he could prove that state or federal officials had violated the law in producing him for trial.

17. 119 U.S. at 444. At the time, Peru could not object; most of the country was controlled by the Chilean army. The Chilean commander did not object either. He even loaned the detective an officer to make sure Ker was put aboard the USS *Essex*.

18. "The Path of the Law," 10 Harv. L. Rev. 457, 459 (1897).

19. Morrow's opinion is also well known for giving former dictators as much protection as former revolutionaries, and for refusing to set any standards of acceptable revolutionary or counter-revolutionary conduct.

20. In re Ezeta, 62 F. 972, 979 (N.D.Cal. 1894). Judge Morrow did not mention the Ker decision in his opinion.

21. Id. at 986. Although Judge Morrow cleared Cienfuegos for extradition, the State Department declined to surrender him, on the ground that the offense for which he was committed—attempted murder—was not specified in the Salvadorean government's requisition. John Bassett Moore, "The Case of the Salvadorean Refugeees," The Collected Papers of John Bassett Moore (New Haven: Yale University Press, 1944), vol. 1, 347, 353–54.

22. Id.

23. Lord McNair, ed., International Law Opinions (Cambridge: Cambridge University Press, 1956), vol. 2, 63–64.

24. In re Arton [1896] 1 Q.B. 108. For more background on this scandal, see Jean Bouvier, Les Deux Scandales de Panama (Paris: Collection Archives, Julliard, 1964) and Dictionnaire de Biographie Française (J. Balteau, M. Barroux, and M. Revost, eds.; Paris: Librairie Letouzey et Ane, 1939), vol. 3, 1215–16.

25. In re Arton [1895] 1 Q.B. 108, at 110–11.

26. Id. at 113.

27. See generally Benjamin F. Martin, The Hypocrisy of Justice in the Belle Epoque (Baton Rouge: Louisiana University Press, 1984).

28. Arton's superior, Baron Jacques Reinach, was a member of an Alsatian family that rallied to the defense of Alfred Dreyfus, a Jewish army officer charged falsely with selling defense secrets to Germany. The newspaper's editor was Edouard Drumont, author of a fiercely anti-Semitic diatribe, La France juive (1886).

29. See William D. Irvine, The Boulanger Affair Reconsidered (New York: Oxford, 1989), ch. 6: "From Boulangism to Anti-Semitic Nationalism."

30. In re Arton [1895] 1 Q.B. 108, 110–11.

31. Id. at 115.

32. Royal Commission on Extradition, Report of the Commissioners (London: HMSO, 1878), at 7–8.

33. 33 & 34 Vict., c. 52, sec. 3(1) (1870).

34. Russell, joined by Wills, also concluded that the "second limb" could not be asserted in cases like Arton's where the charged offense (embezzlement) was not, in and of itself, a political one. 1 Q.B. at 114 (Russell) and 115 (Wills). This meant, in effect, that Parliament intended the second limb to be superfluous, which hardly seems likely.

35. In re Arton [1895] 1 Q.B. 108, at 116. Upon his return to France, Arton was acquitted of bribery and corruption but sentenced to prison for eight years on charges associated with the Dynamite Affair. After serving his sentence, he returned to the stock exchange, failed in his new speculations, and rather than face prosecution again, committed suicide on July 17, 1905. Dictionnaire de Biographie Française, vol. 3, at 1215–16.

36. Neely v. Henkel, 180 U.S. 109 (1901).

37. Id. at 122.

38. Id.

39. Id.

40. Id. at 123.

41. 31 Stat. 656–57; today 18 U.S.C. 3185.

42. 180 U.S. 109, 123–24 (1901).

43. In re Neely, 103 F. 626, 628 (C.C.S.D.N.Y. 1900).

44. At no point in the Neely opinion did the Court hold that assuring fairness for the accused was a duty of the executive, and therefore not a duty of the court. Unlike U.S.-U.K. treaties starting in 1890, and the underlying U.K. Extradition Act of 1870, the special extradition statute of 1900 did not contain a two-limb political offense exception, from which such a division of duty might be derived. It simply forbade surrender for "any offense of a political nature." 31 Stat. at 657. In any case, Neely never invoked the political offense exception; his was a clear assertion of the principle that U.S. courts are obliged, by the due process clause of the Fifth Amendment, not to allow themselves to serve as the long arm of a foreign regime's injustice.

45. 221 U.S. 508 (1910).

46. Id. at 512. Accord: Government of Greece v. Governor of Brixton Prison [1971] Appeals Cases [A.C.] 150, at 255. For casual arrogance, Holmes's opinion in Glucksman rivals his ruling in Buck v. Bell, 274 U.S. 200 (1927), upholding the involuntary sterilization of women.

47. Frank v. Magnum, 237 U.S. 309, 345 (1915).

48. Id. at 346–49.

49. In extradition cases, Holmes also took a very narrow view of the proper scope of review by habeas corpus. E.g., see Fernandez v. Phillips, 268 U.S. 311, 312 (1925).

50. Their judgment gained in credibility when another mob later stormed the prison farm where Frank was being held, dragged him to an oak tree, and hanged him. Participating in this final lynching were a clergyman, two former superior court judges, and an ex-sheriff. Liva Baker, The Justice from Beacon Hill: The Life and Times of Oliver Wendell Holmes (New York: Harper Collins, 1991), 481.

51. As Holmes put it to Sir Frederick Pollock, the British legal historian, "I don't pass moral judgments, particularly of all on nations. I see the inevitable everywhere. Also, I do not forget that before we were in the last war a German wrote to me of similar killings on the part of the French. I receive all stories with doubt and, if I believe them, I feel much as I should if the same deaths had occurred by shipwreck or earthquake." Then, as if to underline his own rule of non-inquiry, the Civil War veteran added: "The South still has stories about Sherman's march to the sea that I believe to be fictions." Holmes-Pollock Letters (Cambridge, Mass.: Harvard University Press, 1941), 372.

52. The Transformation of American Law, 1870–1960: The Crisis of Legal Orthodoxy (New York: Oxford University Press, 1992), 130.

53. Merlo J. Pusey, Charles Evans Hughes (New York: Macmillan, 1951), vol. 1, 287.

54. Holmes-Pollock Letters, Feb. 1, 1920, 36. Like many positivists, Holmes rejected the natural rights idea of implied limitations on governmental authority. Germanic notions of the organic state, effectuated through majoritarian rule, appealed to him more.

55. Herman Melville, Billy Budd, Sailor (1924; Harison Hayford and Merton M. Sealts Jr., eds.; Chicago: University of Chicago Press, 1962), 108.

56. 228 F. 70 (E.D.N.Y. 1915), aff'd without opinion, sub nom. Lincoln v. Power, 241 U.S. 651 (1916).

57. 228 F. at 74.

58. Extradition Treaty Between the United States of America and Her Britannic Majesty, 26 Stat. 1508, 172 T.S. 169, 12 T.I.A.S. 211 (signed July 12, 1899; entered into force April 4, 1890), art. 2.

59. During the last half of the nineteenth century, the United States concluded treaties of extradition with such authoritarian regimes as Prussia, 10 Stat. 964 (1852), Bavaria, 10 Stat. 1022 (1853), the Kingdom of the Two Sicilies, 11 Stat. 651 (1855), Austria, 11 Stat. 691 (1856), Mexico, 12 Stat. 1191 (1861), Haiti, 13 Stat. 727 (1865), the Dominican Republic, 15 Stat. 488 (1867), Nicaragua, 17 Stat. 815 (1871), Salvador, 18 Stat. 693 (1874), Peru, 18 Stat. 719 (1874), the Ottoman Empire, 19 Stat. 572 (1875), Spain, 19 Stat. 650 (1877), Japan, 24 Stat. 41 (1886) Colombia, 26 Stat. 1534 (1891), and Russia, 28 Stat. 1071 (1893).

60. For example, in the early twentieth century, the United States concluded extradition treaties with such newly recognized countries as Serbia, 32 Stat. 1890 (1902), Cuba, 33 Stat. 2265 (1905), and Panama, 34 Stat. 2851 (1905), despite the lack of good reasons to trust their legal systems to do justice.

61. On Stepniak (spelled Stepnyak by Moore), see Donald Senese, S. M. Stepniak—Kravichinskii: The London Years (Newtonville, Mass.: Oriental Research Partners, 1987), at 4–5.

62. Both passages are in "The Russian Extradition Treaty," first published in 1893 and reprinted in The Collected Papers of John Bassett Moore (New Haven: Yale University Press, 1944), vol. 1, 256, 262. The article was written two years after Moore left the State Department to join the Columbia Law School faculty.

63. Id. For a contrary view, see " The Proposed Extradition Treaty with Russia," 24 Am. L. Rev. 480–81 (1890), describing the Russian legal system's gross injustices.

64. 162 F. 591, 592 (C.C.D.N.Y. 1908), appeal dismissed, 212 U.S. 589 (1911). Seven years earlier, the Supreme Court had affirmed that hearsay could be used to establish probable cause at an American extradition hearing, just as it was allowed at ordinary domestic arraignments. Rice v. Ames, 180 U.S. 371, 375–76 (1901).

65. E.g., Ex parte La Mantia, 206 F. 330 (S.D.N.Y. 1913), holding that the record of an *in absentia* conviction did not establish probable cause that the accused had been adequately identified as the offender.

66. Re Fedorenko (No. 1) [1910] 20 Man. R. 221, 17 C.C.C. 268.

67. Id. at 225. Although one judge ruled that Fedorenko could not claim protection as a political offender, another judge ordered him released because the Russian government had not made a proper requisition. Re Fedorenko (No. 2) [1910] 20 Man. R. 224.

68. In re Normano, 7 F. Supp. 329 (D.Mass. 1934).

69. Memorandum from Joseph R. Baker of the Legal Adviser's Office, Department of State, April 4, 1933, reprinted in part in G. Hackworth, Digest of International Law (Washington, D.C.: U.S. Government Printing Office, 1942), vol. 4, sec. 339, at 202.

70. 7 F. Supp. at 330.

71. Id. at 330–31.

72. *Supra*, Chapter 5.

73. Id. at 331.

Chapter Ten

1. See generally John Dunn, Western Political Theory in the Face of the Future (Cambridge: Cambridge University Press, 1979), ch. 3.

2. See generally Charles E. Coughlin, A Series of Lectures on Social Justice Published by the Radio League of the Little Flower (Royal Oak, Mich., 1935).

3. The link between Jews from Central Europe and communism was fostered by a 1947 report commissioned by Attorney General Tom Clark. David A. Caute, The Great Fear (New York: Simon & Schuster, 1978), 437–38.

4. See generally Gil Soescher and John A. Scanlan, Calculated Kindness: Refugees and America's Half-Open Door, 1945 to the Present (New York: Free Press, 1986), ch. 1.

5. Caute, The Great Fear, 437–38.

6. Id. at 93.

7. Artuković came to the United States by way of Austria, Switzerland, and Ireland and was admitted under a ninety–day tourist visa made out to Alois Anich. His escape from Yugoslavia was apparently engineered with the assistance of Croatian Catholic clergy. According to one account, he entered the United States disguised as a priest. Larry Keller, "FBI Paper Reveals Vatican Query on Artuković Status," Press-Telegram, March 28, 1986, D4.

8. Allan A. Ryan Jr., Quiet Neighbors: Prosecuting Nazi War Criminals in America (San Diego: Harcourt Brace Jovanovich, 1984), at 155, no source cited. See also Charles Ashman and Robert J. Wagman, The Nazi Hunters (New York: Pharos Books, 1988), 187 (no source cited, either).

9. Fitzroy Maclean, The Heretic (New York: Harper & Brothers, 1957), 124–25.

10. Quoted in Ryan, Quiet Neighbors, 145, from Wilhelm Hoettl, The Secret Front (London: Weidenfeld & Nicolson, 1953), 168.

11. United States v. Artuković, 170 F. Supp. 383, 389 (1959).

12. E.g., see Carlo Falconi, The Silence of Pius XII (1965; Wall trans.; Boston: Little, Brown, 1970) and works cited therein.

13. Ryan, Quiet Neighbors, 146.

14. Id. at 147.

15. Carol Lachnit, "Artuković Questioned on World War II Duties," Orange County Register, April 17, 1986, A2. According to Ryan, who led the U.S. government's effort to extradite Artuković in the 1980s, the directorate ran the concentration camps where between 200,000 and 830,000 Serbs, Gypsies, and Jews were tortured, killed, or starved to death. Quiet Neighbors at 148. As a matter of law and morality, the actual body count is irrelevant, and the scale of the carnage can be established from the postwar openings of mass graves as well as numerous eyewitness accounts. However, given the obligation of Justice Department lawyers to the legal process, it is disturbing that they would rely so heavily for their most damning charges on secondary and even tertiary historical sources. Ryan's figure of 200,000 dead comes from Fred Singleton, Twentieth Century Yugoslavia (New York: Columbia University Press, 1976), 171, who relied solely on Falconi, The Silence of Pius XII, presumably at 298, who gave no source for his estimate that 200,000 died at the Jasenovac camp alone. Falconi's estimates of all Ustashe killings run to 700,000, but (at page 293) he cites only one report, from a Fr. Antun Wurster to the Zagreb foreign ministry, dated 10 May 1943. The figure of 830,000 comes from Nora Levin, The Holocaust (New York: Thomas Y. Crowell, 1968), 514, who relies exclusively on David Alkalay, "The Fate of the Jews of Yugoslavia," Yad Vashem Bulletin, No. 4/5, October 1959, 18.

16. Falconi, The Silence of Pius XII, 271.

17. Carol Lachnit, "Security Tight for Artuković Trial," Orange Country Register, April 13, 1986, A20.

18. Nora Levin, The Holocaust (New York: Schocken Books, 1973), 513–514 (claiming the death of 20,000 Jews in the Jasenovac camp alone).

19. Larry Keller, "Artukovic Denies Knowning of Croatian Concentration Camps," Press-Telegram, April 16, 1986, A1 and back page.

20. Quoted in Carol Lachnit, "Artukovic Questioned on World War II Duties," Orange County Register, April 17, 1986, A20.

21. Falconi, The Silence of Pius XII, 274. Curiously, the Ustašhe appear to have left most Protestants and Moslems alone. Id.

22. Branimir Stanojevic, Ustaski Ministar Smrti [Ustashe Minister of Death] (Belgrad: Nova Knjiga, 1985), 15.

23. See generally John Prcela and Stanko Guldescu, Operation Slaughterhouse: Eyewitness Accounts of Postwar Massacres in Yugoslavia (Philadelphia: Dorrance & Co., 1970).

24. Genocide was not an extraditable offense; murder was, and its prosecution was not barred by a statute of limitations.

25. Ryan, Quiet Neighbors, 155 (no source cited).

26. Id. at 156. Again, no source cited. Federal law at the time expressly forbade the deportation of anyone to a country where he would face persecution. Sec. 243 of the Immigration and Nationality Act of 1952, 66 Stat. 163, 8 U.S.C. sec. 1253(h)(1), repealed by the 1978 Holtzman Amendment, Pub. L. No 95–549, title 1, sec. 104, 92 Stat. 2066 (1978), 8 U.S.C. secs. 1182 (a)(33) and (d)(3), 1251 (a)(19), 1253 (h), and 1254 (e).

27. The reasons for granting bail are set forth in Artukovic v. Boyle, 107 F. Supp. 11 (S.D.Cal. 1952).

28. 32 Stat. 1890, T.S. no. 406 (signed Oct. 25, 1901; entered into force June 12, 1902).

29. 107 F. Supp. 11 (S.D.Cal. 1952).

30. Ivancevic v. Artukovic, 211 F. 2d 565, cert. denied, 348 U.S. 818, reh'g denied, 348 U.S. 889 (1954).

31. Artukovic v. Boyle, 140 F. Supp. 245, 247 (S.D.Cal. 1956).

32. Karadozole v. Artukovic, 247 F. 2d 198, 204, 205 (9th Cir. 1957).

33. Karadzole v. Artukovic, 355 U.S. 393 (1958).

34. United States v. Artukovic, 170 F. Supp. 383, 393 (S.D.Cal. 1959).

35. Curiously, the most liberal members of the Court, William O. Douglas and Hugo Black, dissented from the decision to vacate, also without comment.

36. United States ex rel. Karadzole v. Artukovic, 170 F. Supp. 383 (S.D.Cal. 1959.

37. 170 F. Supp. 383, 388.

38. Charlton v. Kelly, 229 U.S. 447, 456 (1913), In re Wadge, 15 F. 864, 866 (1883), Collins v. Loisel, 259 U.S. 309, 316 (1922).

39. Hocke presented this summary as if it were a quotation. It is not, but it does accurately restate the holding of that case, which was to be misstated repeatedly by the Justice Department in the 1980s.

40. It would have been reasonable for the commissioner to doubt their testimony too. Of the eight major defense witnesses, six were former officials of the Pavelić regime and had every reason to mislead the court.

41. 170 F. Supp. at 390.

42. Id. at 391.

43. Id. at 392.

44. Id. at 392–93.

45. Id. at 392.

46. Eain v. Wilkes, 641 F. 2d 504, 522 (7th Cir.), cert. denied, 454 U.S. 894 (1981). For decisions rejecting its interpretation of the political offense exception, see Abu Eain v. Wilkes, 642

F. 2d at 522, Quinn v. Robinson, 783 F. 2d at 798–801 (9th Cir. 1986); In re Ryan, 360 F. Supp. at 272, n. 4 (E.D.N.Y. 1973); Artukovic v. Rison, 628 F. Supp. at 1376 (C.D.Cal.1985); and Matter of Demjanjuk, 612 F. Supp. at 570 (N.D.Ohio 1985).

47. See, e.g., M. E. Gold, "Non-extradition for Political Offenses: The Communist Perspective," 11 Harv. Int'l L. J. 191 (1970).

48. In re Kolczynski [1955] 1 Q.B. 540.

49. Id. at 551 (Lord Goddard, C.J.).

50. The trial was conducted without the defendant's knowledge, there were numerous "contradictions, variations and changes of position in the testimony of key witnesses," and a suspicious wait of three years before the secret prosecution was begun. Matter of Mylonas, 187 F. Supp. 716, 720–21 (N.D.Ala. 1960).

51. 162 F. 591 (C.C.N.Y. 1908), appeal dismissed, 212 U.S. 589 (1911), discussed in Chapter 5, *supra.*

52. 187 F. Supp. at 721, citing Grin v. Shine, 187 U.S. 181, 185 (1902).

53. Id.

Chapter Eleven

Epigraph: New York Times, Jan. 17, 1991, A14.

1. Compare Thomas S. Kuhn, The Structure of Scientific Revolutions (2d ed.; Chicago: University of Chicago Press, 1962).

2. Michael Abbell and Bruno A. Ristau, International Judicial Assistance, Criminal: Extradition (Washington, D.C.: International Law Institute, 1990), vol. 4, at 12.

3. David Lauter, "There's No Place to Hide," National Law Journal, Nov. 26, 1984, 1, 28. See also 127, Cong. Rec. 9952 (Sept. 18, 1981).

4. S. Doc. no. 34, 97th Cong., 1st sess. (1981); I. I. Kavass and A. S. Sprudzs, eds., Extradition Laws and Treaties of the United States (Buffalo: William S. Hein), 140.1 (signed, Sept. 14, 1979; entered into force March 4, 1982; declared unconstitutional by the Colombian Supreme Court, 1987). Bradley Graham, "Colombia Supreme Court Overturns Extradition Pact with U.S.," Washington Post, June 27, 1987, A16.

5. S. Doc. no. 33, 97th Cong., 1st sess. (1981), 31 U.S.T. 5061, T.I.A.S. 9656 (signed May 4, 1978; entered into force Jan. 25, 1980).

6. S. Doc. no. 33, 97th Cong., 1st sess. (1980), 80 Stat. 271; 1 U.S.C. 113; T.I.A.S. no. 10733 (signed June 24, 1980; entered into force Sept. 15, 1983).

7. Convention on Offenses and Certain Acts Committed on Board Aircraft (the Tokyo Convention), 20 U.S.T. 2941, T.I.A.S. no. 6768, 704 U.N.T.S. 219 (signed Sept. 14, 1963; entered into force Dec. 4, 1969); Convention for the Suppression of Unlawful Seizure of Aircraft (the Hague Convention), 22 U.S.T. 1641, T.I.A.S. no. 7192 (signed Dec. 16, 1970; entered into force Oct. 14, 1971); Convention for the Suppression of Unlawful Acts Against the Safety of Civil Aviation (the Montreal Convention), 24 U.S.T. 565, T.I.A.S. no. 7570, 10 I.L.M. 1151 (signed Sept. 23, 1971; entered into force Jan. 26, 1973).

8. Convention on the Prevention and Punishment of Crimes Against Internationally Protected Persons, Including Diplomatic Agents, 28 U.S.T. 1975, T.I.A.S. no. 8532 (signed Dec. 14, 1973; entered into force Feb. 20, 1977).

9. International Convention Against the Taking of Hostages, Dec. 18, 1979, 34 U.N. GAOR Supp. no. 39) at 23, U.N. Doc. A/34/39 (1979), reprinted in 18 I.L.M. 1456 (1979) (ratified by the United States July 30, 1980).

10. A mirror image of these police wars of cultural self-defense can be found in Jean-Paul Sartre's justification of Algerian atrocities against the French as symbolically necessary to assert the culture of a "Third World" people against the Europeans whose colonial oppression and racism made them moral outlaws, and who could therefore be ousted by any means. See his preface to Franz Fanon, The Wretched of the Earth (New York: Grove Press, 1963), at 20–23.

11. The maxim is usually rendered: "inter arma silent leges." Cicero actually wrote: "silent enim leges inter arma." Cicero, The Speeches (N. H. Watts, trans.; London: William Heinemann, 1931), at 16 and 17 (in Latin and English).

Chapter Twelve

Epigraph: 641 F. 2d 504, 521 (7th Cir. 1981).

1. The "Geneva Conventions" consist of four multinational Red Cross agreements: Convention 1 for the Amelioration of the Condition of the Wounded and Sick of Armed Forces in the Field, Aug. 12, 1949, 6 U.S.T. 3114, T.I.A.S. no. 3362, 75 U.N.T.S. 31; Convention 2 for the Amelioration of the Wounded, Sick and Shipwrecked of Armed Forces at Sea, Aug. 12, 1949, 6 U.S.T. 3217, T.I.A.S. no. 3363, 75 U.N.T.S. 85; Convention 3 Relative to the Treatment of Prisoners of War, Aug. 12, 1949, 6 U.S.T. 3316, T.I.A.S. no. 3364, 75 U.N.T.S. 135; Convention 4 Relative to the Protection of Civilian Persons in Time of War, Aug. 12, 1949, 6 U.S.T. 3516, T.I.A.S. no. 3365, 75 U.N.T.S. 287.

2. U.N. Convention on the Prevention and Punishment of the Crime of Genocide, art. 7, 78 U.N.T.S. 277, 280 (signed Dec. 9, 1948; entered into force for the United States Nov. 4, 1988).

3. "The Genocide Convention—Today and Tomorrow," reprinted in Constitutional Issues Relating to the Proposed Genocide Convention, Hearing before the Subcom. on the Constitution, Com.on the Judiciary, U.S. Senate, 99th Cong., 1st sess. (Feb. 26, 1985), 657, 664–65.

4. Genocide Implementation Act, 102 Stat. 3045–46; 18 U.S.C. sec. 1091–93.

5. Protocol 1 expanded the humanitarian safeguards prescribed by the four Geneva Conventions for international armed conflicts. Protocol Additional to the Geneva Conventions of 12 August 1949 and Relating to the Protection of Victims of International Armed Conflicts (Protocol 1) (signed June 8, 1977; entered into force Dec. 7, 1978, but never ratified by the United States), reprinted in 16 I.L.M. 1442 (1977), and 72 Am. J. Int'l L. 457 (1978). Protocol 2 would bring participants in noninternational armed conflicts under a variant of the humanitarian law prescribed by the Geneva Conventions and Protocol 1 but would not grant any special legal status to persons who participated in "riots, isolated and sporadic acts of violence and other acts of a similar nature." Protocol Additional to the Geneva Conventions of 12 August 1949, and Relating to the Protection of Victims of Non-International Armed Conflicts (Protocol 2), art. 1(2) (signed June 8, 1977, but never ratified by the United States), 16 I.L.M. 1442 (1977), 72 Am. J. Int'l L. 502 (1978).

6. According to Protocol 1, failure to carry arms openly in a military engagement and during deployment prior to engagement would expressly deprive a former combatant of POW (and therefore military) status. As a result, if the accused fled abroad, he would be subject to extradition as a common criminal and denied benefit of the political offense exception. Art. 44(3)(4).

7. President's Message to the Senate Transmitting the Protocol (2), 23 Weekly Com. Pres. Docs. 91, 92 (Jan. 29, 1987). See also Judith Miller, "Reagan Shelving Treaty to Revise Law on Captives," New York Times, Feb. 16, 1987, 1, 5; Clifford D. May, "Terrorist or Insurgent? Diplomacy and the Law," New York Times, May 27, 1988, B5; and Abraham D. Sofaer, "Terrorism and the Law," 64 Fgn. Aff. 901, 916 (1986).

8. Leslie H. Gelb, "War Pact Faces Objection of Joint Chiefs," New York Times, July 22, 1985, A1, A7.

9. U.S. Army training manuals developed from lesson plans at the army's School of the Americas at Fort Benning, Georgia, during the 1980s encouraged murder and torture as legitimate counterinsurgency techniques. "Word for Word/U.S. Army Training Manuals," New York Times, Oct. 6, 1996, E7.

10. However, one federal judge would use the law of armed conflict to distinguish a political offense from a terrorist act. Ahmad v. Wigen, 726 F. Supp. 389 (E.D.N.Y. 1989). Discussed this chapter, *infra.*

11. Anthony Lake, Somoza Falling (Boston: Houghton-Mifflin, 1989), 13.

12. Appeal Decision, In re McMullen, Board of Immigration Appeals, File A23 054 818, at 4 (San Francisco, Cal., May 25, 1984).

13. Petitioner's Brief in McMullen v. INS, no. 84–7468 at 3–4 (9th Cir. Nov. 16, 1984). The Immigration and Naturalization Service rejected McMullen's account of his motivations, but the immigration judge who heard his request for asylum accepted the facts as essentially correct.

14. The foregoing statement of facts also relies on McMullen v. INS, 788 F. 2d 591, 592–93 (9th Cir. 1986).

15. E.g., see "Ex-I.R.A. Member Tells a Judge He'll Be Killed If He Is Deported," New York Times, Sept. 30, 1979, at 24.

16. In re McMullen, Board of Immigration Appeals, File A23 054 818 (San Francisco, Cal., May 25, 1984), at 3.

17. Memorandum Decision, In the Matter of McMullen, Mag. no. 3–78–1099 MG (N.D.Cal., May 11, 1979), at 2–4.

18. Id. at 2, 5.

19. Id. at 3–4.

20. When the U.S. government moved to deport McMullen to the Republic of Ireland, a panel of the Court of Appeals for the Ninth Circuit ignored the revolutionary dimension of the conflict entirely. In the Court's opinion, the IRA's random acts of violence against ordinary citizens of Northern Ireland and elsewhere were "not sufficiently linked to their political objective" and were "so barbarous, atrocious, and disproportionate to the political objective of ridding Northern Ireland of the British that they constitute 'serious non-political crimes.'" McMullen v. INS, 788 F. 2d 591, 598 (9th Cir. 1986). Imputing these nonpolitical offenses to McMullen, the court ordered him deported. Id. at 597. The administration, however, delayed the deportation until December 1986, when the United Kingdom ratified a new supplementary extradition treaty that effectively abolished the political offense exception. McMullen was then seized, while on his way to Ireland, so that his case could provide the factual context for contesting the constitutionality of the new treaty. See Chapter 15, *infra,* for a discussion of McMullen's second extradition case.

21. Id. at 1.

22. For Field's views on this case, see Richard B. Lillich, ed., International Aspects of Criminal Law: Enforcing United States Law in the World Community (Charlottesville, Va.: Michie Co., 1981), 15–33.

23. Letter from Prof. W. T. Mallison, George Washington University Law School, to Rep. William J. Hughes, Chairman, Subcommittee on Crime, Committee on the Judiciary, U.S. House of Representatives, March 1, 1982, at 4.

24. A grand jury refused to believe the allegations, which were made by a twice-convicted convict with a long record of violence and mental disorders. Sullivan, however, believed that

the convict had saved his life and arranged for his release. The convict subsequently committed armed robbery and was convicted. Rob Warden, "PLO Plot to Kill Tom Sullivan?" Chicago Lawyer, Jan. 1982, 3.

25. James Naughtie, "Palestinian, Jailed in Chicago, Fighting Extradition to Israel," Washington Post, July 24, 1981, A5, and American-Arab Anti-Discrimination Committee, "Countdown to Extradition: The Extradition of Ziad Abu Eain," Dec. 15, 1981, 3.

26. Jack Anderson, the syndicated columnist, sent a member of his staff to Ramallah to check these affidavits and found them "persuasive." Washington Post, Aug. 6, 1981, B19.

27. The magistrate's opinion is published as an appendix to Abu Eain v. Adams (Eain 2), 529 F. Supp. 685, 688 (N.D.Ill.E.D. 1980). The quotation is at 691.

28. Id., and Eain v. Wilkes (Eain 3), 641 F. 2d 504, 519 (1981).

29. Eain v. Wilkes (Eain 3), at 520–21.

30. Id.

31. Id. at 521.

32. The Supreme Court denied certiorari, 454 U.S. 894 (1981).

33. The Chicago Reader, June 18, 1981.

34. By contrast, a soldier in an international war who set off a bomb in a civilian marketplace could legally be surrendered under the Geneva Conventions. In fact, however, no soldier has ever been extradited for war crimes or crimes against humanity.

35. On this question, see David K. Shipler, "Boys in West Bank Arrested at Night for Weeks of Questioning by Israelis," New York Times, Feb. 27, 1982, 5; "6 Israeli Army Officers Condemn Troop Behavior in Occupied Areas," New York Times, May 11, 1982, A10; Report of an Amnesty International Mission to the Government of the State of Israel, June 3–7, 1980; and Department of State Human Rights Reports on Israel for 1977, 1978, and 1979.

36. This arrangement was confirmed by an Israeli note dated Dec. 31, 1981, which promised that Abu Eain would be tried before an Israeli "civil court of law" and a U.S. note to the secretary general of the United Nations dated Jan. 4, 1982, reporting this assurance. The notes are reproduced in 2(2) I.L.M. 443–45 (1982). See also undated memorandum of decision by William P. Clark, deputy secretary of state, id. at 445–48.

37. American-Arab Anti-Discrimination Committee, "Countdown to Extradition: The Extradition of Ziad Abu Eain," Dec. 15, 1981, 1, and Testimony of Abdeen M. Jabara, Esq., for the Committee on Foreign Affairs, U.S. House of Representatives, concerning H.R. 6046, July 22, 1982, 14.

38. In November 1983, Abu Eain was one of 4,380 Palestinians whom the Israelis offered to exchange for six of their soldiers. At the last moment, and in violation of the agreement with the International Red Cross, the Israelis pulled him out of that group, threw him on the floor of a jeep, and spirited him out of the airport. In May 1985, he was included in a smaller exchange of 1,150 Palestinians for three Israelis and was actually released, but he was rearrested shortly thereafter for attending a peaceful meeting of a nationalist group. William Clairborne, "Palestinian Terrorist Is Rearrested," Washington Post, Aug. 2, 1985, A24.

39. This procedure was briefly declared unconstitutional in Lobue v. Christopher, 893 F. Supp. 65 (D.C.D.C. 1995), reversed (on procedural grounds) 82 F. 3d 1081 (D.C.Cir. 1996).

40. Quinn v. Robinson, 783 F. 2d 776, 818–819 (9th Cir. 1986).

41. Under similar circumstances, an American policeman would have lacked constitutional authority to search him or detain him further. Sibron v. New York, 392 U.S. 41 (1968).

42. Fingerprints belonging to other members of the unit were found on a letter bomb sent to Sir Max Aiken, chairman of the Daily Express newspaper, which blew off the left hand of a

security guard; on an unexploded bomb left on a loading platform of the Aldershot Railway Station in Hampshire County; and on a bomb left in an attaché case inside the entry to the Kings Arms Pub in Warminster, London.

43. Quinn would later, and properly, make much of the unfairness of this method of identification, but police would also show that the man Blackledge questioned claimed to be William Rogers. "William" was Quinn's first name; "Rogers" was his mother's maiden name. And, of course, there were the fingerprints.

44. See generally Jeanne B. Clarizo, "Report on the Trial of William Joseph Quinn, Central Criminal Court, London, England, February 10–16, 1988," dated May 1, 1988.

45. In re Quinn, No. Cr. 81–146 Misc. (N.D.Cal., Sept. 28, 1982).

46. Eain v. Wilkes, 641 F. 2d 504, 521.

47. Quinn v. Robinson, no. C-82–6688 RPA (N.D.Cal. Oct. 3, 1983).

48. Id. at 37, quoting In re Ezeta, 62 F. 972, 997 (N.D.Cal. 1894).

49. Id. at 38.

50. Id. at 17.

51. Id. at 20.

52. Id. at 21–22.

53. Quinn v. Robinson, 783 F. 2d 776 (9th Cir. 1986), cert. denied, 479 U.S. 882 (1986).

54. Id. at 788, quoting In re Kaine, 55 U.S. (14 How.) 103, 112 (1852).

55. Id. at 789.

56. Id. at 795.

57. Id. at 803, citing In re Doherty, 599 F. 2d at 275.

58. Id. at 804.

59. Id. at 819.

60. Id. at 820.

61. Id. at 813—814; at 814, n. 36, Judges Duniway (at 818) and Fletcher (at 820) both dissented from this "export exception."

62. Id. at 818.

63. Id. at 807.

64. Id. at 808.

65. Id. at 820.

66. Id. at 808.

67. Id. at 807.

68. More disturbing still, the use of the term "indigenous peoples" suggests a racial, tribal, or religious theory of national identity—an odd theory to propose for the American legal system, in which nationhood and citizenship are defined in terms of civic values. On the creedal basis of American citizenship, see generally Samuel F. Huntington, American Politics: The Promise of Disharmony (Cambridge: Belknap, 1981).

69. 783 F. 2d at 820–21. See also Reinhardt's note explaining the holding at 782.

70. Jeanne B. Clarizo, "Criminal Justice in the Old Bailey," 30 N.H.B.J. 79, 85 (1989). Such an instruction by an American court would violate the privilege against self-incrimination. Malloy v. Hogan, 378 U.S. 1, 6 (1964), overturning Adamson v. California, 332 U.S. 46 (1947).

71. Id. at 87. Under British law, Quinn could have been tried by a one-judge, juryless "Diplock Court," specifically set up to try alleged terrorists, even though the offenses occurred in London. The fact that he was not so tried suggests that British authorities were sensitive to the criticism that such a trial would have produced in the United States.

72. According to Article 1 of the U.S.-Israel treaty and 18 U.S.C. sec. 3184, the United States may only extradite, and therefore presumably arrest, persons "found in its territory."

73. In Matter of Atta, 87–0551–M (E.D.N.Y. 1988), at 72. On the abduction question, see Chapters 20 and 21, *infra.*

74. Id. at 52.

75. Id. at 50–51.

76. Id. at 57–58.

77. In re Extradition of Atta, 706 F. Supp. 1032 (E.D.N.Y. 1989).

78. Id. at 1042, quoting In re Doherty, 599 F. Supp. 270, 274 (S.D.N.Y. 1984).

79. Id. at 1047.

80. Ahmad v. Wigen, 726 F. Supp. 389, 408 (E.D.N.Y. 1989).

81. Id. at 409.

82. Id.

83. Id. at 407.

84. Id.

85. Id. at 405.

86. Id. at 410.

87. Id. at 413, citing Gallina v. Fraser, 278 F. 2d 77, 79 (2d Cir.), cert. denied, 364 U.S. 851 (1960).

88. Id. at 416.

89. Id. at 417.

90. Id. at 417.

91. Weinstein published these as an appendix to his decision. Id. at 420–22.

92. Ahmad v. Wigen, 910 F. 2d. 1063 (2d Cir. 1990).

93. Id. at 1066, quoting Jhirad v. Ferrandina, 563 F. 2d 478, 484–85 (2d Cir.), *cert. denied,* 429 U.S. 833, reh'g denied, 429 U.S. 988 (1976).

94. 726 F. Supp. at 410.

95. Id. at 1066, quoting Sindonia v. Grant, 619 F. 2d 167, 174 (2d Cir. 1980).

96. Id. at 1067.

97. Id.

Chapter Thirteen

Epigraph: 599 F. Supp. 270, 275–276 (1984).

1. Liz Curtis, Ireland and the Propaganda War (London: Pluto Press, 1984), chs. 2, 3. The European Court of Human Rights would later rule that the abuse of IRA prisoners did not quite rise to the level of torture but did create "intense physical and mental suffering . . . and acute psychiatric disturbances during interrogation." Ireland v. the United Kingdom (No. 5310/71); judgment of the European Court of Human Rights, 18 Jan. 1978, Council of Europe, Yearbook of the European Convention on Human Rights, 1978, 602, 606.

2. E.g., see Dermont P. J. Walsh, The Use and Abuse of Emergency Legislation in Northern Ireland (London: Cobden Trust, 1983).

3. Shoot to Kill? International Lawyers' Inquiry into the Lethal Use of Firearms by the Security Forces in Northern Ireland (Cork: Mercier Press, 1985).

4. John Stalker, The Stalker Affair (New York: Viking, 1988). Stalker was a highly respected police inspector from Manchester, England, assigned to investigate allegations of a "shoot to

kill" policy after a number of suspicious deaths. He attempted to conduct an independent investigation but was dismissed on bogus charges of conflict of interest.

5. Reprinted in Richard N. Current et al., Words That Made American History (3d ed.; Boston: Little, Brown, 1978), 244–57.

6. One of Mackin's grandfathers was a member of the IRA in County Fermanagh in the 1920s. A grandmother was a member of Cumann na MBan, the women's section of the IRA. Two uncles were jailed in the North during the IRA border war of the 1950s.

7. Interview with Desmond Mackin, June 1985, Dublin, Ireland. See also In Matter of Mackin (Mackin 1), 80 Cr. Misc. 1, 85–90 (S.D.N.Y. 1981).

8. In Matter of Mackin (Mackin 1) at 87.

9. Id. at 88.

10. It would not be unwarranted to suspect that the cab had been abandoned by IRA members after one of their operations.

11. The magistrate's account of the facts is set forth in In Matter of Mackin (Mackin 1) at 92–95.

12. Interview, June 1985, Dublin, Ireland.

13. Id.

14. Interview with a British civil servant responsible for extradition matters, May 1984, London.

15. Id.

16. Id. The same civil servant admitted that it was extremely unlikely Mackin would have been convicted, even by a Diplock Court in Northern Ireland set up specifically to try alleged terrorists. Mackin's companion, Bobby Gamble, was convicted by a Diplock Court, but his conviction was overturned on appeal. At the time Gamble's conviction was overturned, Mackin was in the Metropolitan Correctional Center in Manhattan, awaiting extradition proceedings, but no effort was made to end those proceedings in light of this appellate decision. Jack Holland, The American Connection: U.S. Guns, Money, and Influence in Northern Ireland (New York: Viking, 1987), 160.

17. In Matter of Mackin (Mackin 1) at 7–21, 84–91.

18. Id. at 4–5, quoting from Coleman v. Burnett, 477 F. 2d 1187, 1202 (D.C.Cir. 1973).

19. Id. at 5, quoting Brinegar v. United States, 338 U.S. 16, 174–75 (1949).

20. Id. at 4–21.

21. This is an extraditable offense under art. 3 of the U.S.-U.K. Extradition Treaty, 28 U.S.T. 227, T.I.A.S. no. 8468 (signed June 8, 1972; entered into force Jan. 21, 1977).

22. In Matter of Mackin (Mackin 1) at 37. Accord: Eain v. Wilkes (Eain 3), 641 F. 2d 504, 513 (7th Cir. 1981).

23. In Matter of Mackin (Mackin 1) at 47–98.

24. Id. at 98.

25. In Matter of Mackin (Mackin 2), 668 F. 2d 122, 125 (2d Cir. 1981).

26. Id. at 132, art. 5 (1)(c)(i).

27. 299 U.S. 304 (1936).

28. E.g., see Baker v. Carr, 369 U.S. 186, 211, 212 (1962): "it is error to suppose that every case or controversy which touches foreign relations lies beyond judicial cognizance." Also: "a court can construe a treaty and may find it provides the answer."

29. In Matter of Mackin (Mackin 2) at 134.

30. Id. at 133.

31. Id. at 134.

32. 46 U.S. (5 How.) 176 (1847).

33. 9 Stat. 302, recodified at 62 Stat. 822, and now found at 18 U.S.C. sec. 651.

34. 6 Op. Atty Gen. 91, 96 (1853).

35. United States v. Lawrence, 3 U.S. (3 Dall.) 42 (1795).

36. 668 F. 2d at 131 (1981).

37. His mother's father was a longtime member of the old Official IRA's Belfast Brigade; his mother's father had been an IRA volunteer after the Easter Uprising of 1916; his father's father had been a senior officer in the Belfast battalion of the Irish Citizen Army, which had been formed by James Connolly. The following account is based on court documents, the archives of Belfast newspapers, fact statements issued by the Justice Department and counsel for the defense, and interviews with Joseph Doherty, his family, and attorneys in New York and Northern Ireland. It also draws on Martin Dillon, Killer in Clowntown: Joe Doherty, the IRA and the Special Relationship (London: Hutchinson, 1992), the first full-length book on the Doherty case. A British journalist, Dillon is no admirer of the IRA and was, for a time, a potential witness for the British government in the Doherty case. This stance gave him considerable access to British intelligence files.

38. Interviews with Joseph Doherty and his parents, 1985. In 1974, Doherty's parents and sisters were watching television when a bomb, concealed in a creamery can, was thrown through the front window. The family was not injured by the explosion, but the house was so badly damaged that eventually it had to be demolished. Dillon, Killer in Clowntown, 115.

39. Id. This tactic was also used by the IRA against anyone who might contemplate informing against them.

40. Interviews with Joseph Doherty and his parents, 1985. See also Dillon, Killer in Clowntown, 38–39.

41. Patrick Farrelly, "The Man Behind the Wire," Irish America, June 1987, 20–21. See also Dillon, Killer in Clowntown, 40–44, for a slightly different account.

42. Gene Mustain, "War of Wills: The Story of Joe Doherty," New York Daily News, Dec. 10, 1989, 5, at 60. Parts 2 and 3 of this article were published on Dec. 11 and 12, 1989, respectively.

43. Ireland v. United Kingdom, European Court of Human Rights, 18 Jan. 1978, Council of Europe, Yearbook of the European Convention on Human Rights, 1978, 602, 606.

44. Interviews and Dillon, Killer in Clowntown, 45–48. His sister Anne was later interned without trial, as were more distant relatives.

45. Farrelly, "The Man Behind the Wire," 21.

46. Dillon, Killer in Clowntown, 54, 56, 62.

47. Michael MacDonald, Children of Wrath: Political Violence in Northern Ireland (Cambridge: Polity Press, 1986), 115.

48. Dillon, Killer in Clowntown, 85, 81, 86.

49. Mustain, "War of Wills," Dec. 10, 1989, 5, at 61.

50. Dillon, Killer in Clowntown, 85–86.

51. Id. at 97.

52. Id. at 98.

53. A "Fact Sheet on Proceedings Against Joseph Doherty" circulated by the U.S. Department of Justice in the spring of 1988 erroneously claimed that the escapees used warders as hostages or shields.

54. This account of the escape was provided by Joseph Doherty. See also "Atkins Stresses Gravity of Ulster Gaol Break-Out and Sets Up Top-Level Inquiry," Manchester Guardian, June 12, 1981, at 19; Colin Brown and Paul Keel, "Solicitors Still Held After IRA Escape," Manchester

Guardian, June 12, 1981, at 1; Richard Ford, "Guns Blaze as Eight Burst from Belfast Jail," The Times (London), June 11, 1981, at 1; Paul Keel, "Top IRA Men Shoot Their Way Out of High Security Gaol," Manchester Guardian, June 11, 1981, at 1.

55. Dillon, Killer in Clowntown, 146, 150–51.

56. Id.

57. Quoted in Michael Farrell, Sheltering the Fugitive? The Extradition of Irish Political Offenders (Cork and Dublin: Mercier Press, 1985), 113.

58. In Matter of Doherty (Doherty 1), 599 F. Supp. 270 (1984).

59. Id. at 273.

60. Id. at 276.

61. Id.

62. Mustain, "War of Wills," New York Daily News, Dec. 12, 1989, part 3, 47.

63. In Matter of Doherty (Doherty 1) at 274.

64. Id. at 275. Sprizzo also implied that attacks on civilian representatives of the government and attacks outside the territory where political change was to be effective would also render the political offense exception inapplicable. Id. at 275–76.

65. Id. at 276.

66. Id.

67. E.g., see Tony Gifford, Supergrasses: The Use of Accomplice Evidence in Northern Ireland (London: Cobden Trust, 1984).

68. E.g., see Walsh, The Use and Abuse of Emergency Legislation in Northern Ireland.

69. Shoot to Kill?

70. E.g., see Stalker, The Stalker Affair.

71. Steven Prokesch, "Convictions Overturned for 7 in IRA Blasts," New York Times, June 27, 1991, A7, and William E. Schmidt, "British Court to Review 1974 Bombing Case," New York Times, Sept. 18, 1991, A2.

72. See generally Paddy Hillyard and Janie Percy-Smith, The Coercive State (London: Pinter, 1988).

73. In Matter of Doherty (Doherty 1) at 277.

74. Stuart Taylor, "U.S. Aide Faults Judge's IRA Extradition Ruling," New York Times, Dec. 19, 1984, A23.

75. "Following the Law," National Law Journal, Dec. 31, 1984, 12.

76. Dillon, Killer in Clowntown, 195.

77. The government has been traditionally denied the right to appeal court decisions barring extradition. See generally Collins v. Miller, 252 U.S. 364, 369–70 (1920), and Greci v. Birknes, 527 F. 2d 956, 958 (1st Cir. 1976). The accused, however, may obtain collateral review through habeas corpus. E.g., see Shapiro v. Ferrandina, 478 F. 2d 894, 901 (2d Cir.), cert. denied by agreement of parties, 414 U.S. 884 (1973).

78. 28 U.S.C. sec. 2201 (1988). See also Luckenbach Steamship Co. v. United States, 312 F. 2d 545 (2d Cir. 1963), and E. Edelmann & Co. v. Triple-A Specialty Co., 88 F. 2d 852 (7th Cir.), cert. denied, 300 U.S. 680 (1937).

79. Hurley v. Lindsay, 207 F. 2d 410 (4th Cir. 1953).

80. See generally Susan Kelm Story, "Scope of Review in Extradition Proceedings: The Government Cannot Appeal a Denial of Extradition Request Based on the Declaratory Judgment Act—United States v. Doherty, 786 F. 2d 491 (2d Cir. 1986)," 19 Vand. J. Transnat'l L. 893–910 (1986).

81. In Matter of Doherty (Doherty 2), 615 F. Supp. 755 (S.D.N.Y. 1985).

82. Id. at 760, note 5.
83. United States v. Doherty (Doherty 3), 786 F. 2d 491, 495 (2d Cir. 1986).
84. Id. at 502.
85. Id. at 497.

Chapter Fourteen

Epigraphs: Melville, Mordi and a Voyage Thither (1849; Evanston: Northwestern University Press, 1998), 533; Rogers, Speech to U.N. General Assembly, September 25, 1972.

1. E.g., 1970 Hague Convention for the Suppression of Unlawful Seizure of Aircraft, 22 U.S.T. 1641, T.I.A.S. no. 7192; 860 U.N.T.S. 105 (signed Dec. 16, 1970; entered into force Oct. 14, 1971).

2. Convention on the Prevention of Crimes Against Internationally Protected Persons, Including Diplomats, 28 U.S.T. 1975, T.I.A.S. no. 8532, 1035 U.N.T.S. 167 (signed Dec. 28, 1973; entered into force Feb. 20, 1977).

3. The International Convention Against the Taking of Hostages, art. 12 (opened for signature Dec. 18, 1979), GA Res. 34/146, 34 U.N. GAOR Supp. (no. 39), U.N. Doc. A/C.6/34/l.23 (1979), reprinted in 74 Am. J. Int'l L. 277 (1980), 18 I.L.M. 1456 (1979).

4. U.S.-U.K. Supplementary Treaty Concerning the Extradition Treaty Between the Government of the United States of America and the Government of the United Kingdom of Great Britain and Northern Ireland, S. Exec. Rep. no. 17, 99th Cong., 2d sess. 15–17 (1986); 1 Kavass et al., Extradition Laws and Treaties, 920.20d–h (1979 and 1989 Supp.); 24 I.L.M. 1104 (1985) (signed June 25, 1985; entered into force Dec. 23, 1986).

5. Or if that would impair foreign relations, then a legal technicality might be negotiated, as in the case of Joao Normano, the Jew whom the State Department seemed willing to surrender to Nazi Germany rather than question its treatment of Jews. In re Normano, discussed *supra*, Chapter 8.

6. Regina v. Governor of Brixton Prison [*Ex parte* Kolczynski] [1955] 1 Q.B. 540, 1 All E.R. 31, discussed in Chapter 10, *supra*.

7. In re Kavic, Bjelanovic and Arsenijevic, Switzerland, Federal Tribunal, 19 ILR 371 (case no. 80), 78 Entscheidungen des Bundesgerichts, vol. 1, 39 (April 30, 1980).

8. Id. at 374.

9. 22 Dept. of State Bull. 595 (1950), Whiteman, Digest of International Law (Washington, D.C.: U.S. General Printing Office, 1965), vol. 6, at 810–11. When a Czech engineer was shielded by West Germany after he crashed his train to freedom, the U.S. State Department took the position that he was a nonextraditable political offender. Whiteman, vol. 6, 813. See also "Czech Engineer Flees with Train and 111 Passengers to Germany," New York Times, Sept. 12, 1951. Thirty-one of the passengers chose to stay in the West. "Czechs Are Barred from German Air," New York Times, Sept. 14, 1951, 8.

10. Official morality also changed as the Nixon administration pursued a policy of detente with the Soviet Union. On Nov. 23, 1970, in what the New York Times condemned as "one of the most disgraceful incidents ever to occur on a ship flying the American flag," the U.S. Coast Guard returned an asylum-seeking, ship-jumping Lithuanian to his Soviet ship against his will. "Land of the Free," New York Times, Nov. 30, 1970, 40.

11. In re Holder, reprinted in E. C. McDowell, Digest of United States Practice in International Law, 1975 (Washington, D.C.: U.S. Government Printing Office, 1976), 168–75. For the Reagan administration's reaction, see Abraham D. Sofaer, "The Political Offense Exception and Terrorism," 15 Den. J. Int'l L & Pol'y 125, 128 (1986).

12. Id. at 124–25.

13. "Drama on the Desert: The Week of the Hostages," Time Magazine, Sept. 21, 1970, 18.

14. Id. at 19. See also "4 Jets Hijacked; One, a 747, Is Blown Up," New York Times, Sept. 7, 1970, 1; "Negotiations with Red Cross Official Are Awaited Today," New York Times, Sept. 10, 1970, 1; and John Hess, "Arabs Blow Up 3 Jets in Desert After Taking Off Hostages," New York Times, Sept. 13, 1970, sec. 1, at 1, and sec. 4, at 1.

15. 22 U.S.T. 1641, T.I.A.S. no. 7192, 860 U.N.T.S. 105 (signed Dec. 16, 1970; entered into force Oct. 14, 1971). See also 2 International Civil Aviation Organization, International Conference on Air Law, the Hague, Dec. 1970, ICAO Doc. 8979–LC/165–1 and 2, at 69, 130–80 (1972).

16. "Plan on Hijacking Due Wednesday," New York Times, Dec. 13, 1973, 17.

17. Art. 7 of 22 U.S.T. 1641, T.I.A.S. no. 7192, 860 U.N.T.S.

18. "Two Czechs Flee in Hijacked Plane," New York Times, April 19, 1972, at 2; " Czechs Ask West Germany to Return Two Hijackers," New York Times, April 20, 1972, at 2; "Czech Hijackers Sentenced," New York Times, Aug. 1, 1972, at 9.

19. This account relies heavily on Judge Herbert J. Stern's book, Judgment in Berlin (New York: Universe Books, 1984).

20. Authority to create this court was derived from Law No. 46 promulgated by the U.S. High Commissioner for Germany in 1955. The law is published as an appendix to United States v. Tiede, 86 F.R.D. 227, 261–65 (U.S.Ct. Berlin 1979).

21. Id. at 179.

22. Id. at 162–63.

23. United States v. Tiede at 239, 242. The State Department also argued that the decision of whether the Constitution did or did not apply to occupied territory was a nonjusticiable "political question," and thus beyond the competence of the court to decide. Id. at 239.

24. Id. at 242.

25. See section C of the State Department's brief, reproduced in Stern, Judgment in Berlin, at 97; see also 116–17, and United States v. Tiede at 241.

26. The power would be limited, of course, by the Geneva Conventions of 1949, to the extent they have ever constrained any military force.

27. Stern, Judgment in Berlin, 95–96.

28. Id. at 368.

29. Id. at 115.

30. The State Department's legal adviser was Herbert Hansell. Within his staff, Mark B. Feldman and Lee R. Marks were primarily responsible for the case. Stern, Judgment in Berlin, 196.

31. Stern, Judgment in Berlin, 117.

32. United States v. Tiede at 261.

33. Stern, Judgment in Berlin, 120.

34. Stern, Judgment in Berlin, 212–13.

35. Id. at 344.

36. Id. at 215, 369.

37. Penal Code, Federal Republic of Germany (J. J. Darby, trans.; London: Sweet & Maxwell, 1987).

38. Stern, Judgment in Berlin, chs. 20–22.

39. Id. at 350.

40. Id. at 370.

41. Id.

42. Dostal v. Haig, 652 F. 2d 173, 176 (D.C.Cir. 1981).

43. Id.

44. Andreas Lowenfeld, "Hijacking, Freedom, and the 'American Way,'" 83 Mich. L. Rev. 1000, 1006–1008 (1985).

45. Lewis Caroll, Alice's Adventures in Wonderland (1866, Green ed.; London, Oxford University Press, 1971), at 28.

46. Thomas M. Franck and Scott C. Senecal, "Porfiry's Proposition: Legitimacy and Terrorism," 20 Vand. J. Transnat'l L. 195, at 230 (1987).

47. Id.

48. Id. at 197.

49. Herman Melville, Billy Budd, Sailor (H. Hayford and M. Sealts Jr., eds.; 1924; Chicago: University of Chicago Press, 1962), 111.

50. The inspiration for his candid label comes from Prince Myshkin, the Christ-like figure in Dostoevsky's The Idiot, who has a "single-minded passion for arrow-like truths," "simple principles," and "invariable verities." Franck, "Porfiry's Proposition," 215.

51. Id. at 216.

52. 18 U.S.C. sec. 32.

53. The Articles of War relevant to Budd's case said flatly that "If any person in the Fleet shall strike any of his Superior Officers . . . on any Pretense whatsoever, every such Person being convicted of any such Offense . . . shall suffer Death." 22 George II, c. 33, vol. 2, 22 (1749).

54. For "sophists" law, see art. 34 and 35 of the German Criminal Code, establishing the "justification and excuse" defense, and the U.S. Model Penal Code, sec. 2.09(1) (Proposed Official Draft, 1962).

55. The Germans, as we have seen from their "justification and excuse" rule, are more willing than British and American drafters to acknowledge exculpatory factors up front. Similarly, the French use a more subjective motives test in defining who is a political offender. E.g., see Holder and Kerhow cases in McDowell, Digest of United States Practice in International Law, at 168.

56. The Aurora, Sept. 3, 1799.

57. The obvious analogy, of course, is to the right of revolution. Few requesting states are likely to concede that a fugitive had just cause to revolt, which is why the political offense exception to extradition is administered by the host country. Similarly, those whose lives were endangered by the actions of Tiede and Ruske, the slaves who captured the Creole, or the free blacks who captured the Amistad, should not decide the fate of their hijackers.

58. Bernie Rhodes, D. B. Cooper: The Real McCoy (Salt Lake City: University of Utah Press, 1991.

59. Robert Stetham was a U.S. Navy diver executed by the Palestinian hijackers of an airliner as part of an extortion effort. Leon Klinghoffer was the victim of a gratuitous killing on board the hijacked cruise ship, Achille Lauro.

60. United States v. The Amistad, 40 U.S. (15 Peters) 518, 593 (1841).

61. In 1985, the U.S. government had no compunction about using fighter aircraft to force down an Egyptian airliner carrying the hijackers of the Italian cruise ship Achille Lauro. When the plane landed at a NATO base in Italy, American and Italian ground forces nearly came to blows over which government should take jurisdiction over the suspects. See Chapter 24, infra. This capture, which was far more dangerous to the airliner's crew and people on the ground than anything Tiede had done, was widely excused because the U.S. government had done it. For an argument that the interception was legal, see John Murphy, "The Future of Multilateralism and Efforts

to Combat International Terrorism," 25 Colum. J. Transnat'l L. 35, 80–83 (1986). For an argument that it was illegal, see Oscar Schacter, "In Defense of International Rules on the Use of Force," 53 Chi. U. L. Rev. 113 (1986).

Chapter Fifteen

Epigraph: Martin Dillon, Killer in Clowntown: Joe Doherty, the IRA and the Special Relationship (London: Hutchinson, 1992), at xxv.

1. U.S.–Colombia Extradition Treaty, Sen. Treaty Doc. no. 97-8 Exec. Rep. 97-34 (signed Sept. 14, 1979; entered into force Mar. 4, 1982), art. 4(3),; 1 Kavass and Sprudzs, eds., Extradition Laws and Treaties of the United States (Buffalo: William S. Hein), 140.1; U.S.-Mexico Extradition Treaty, 31 U.S.T. 5061, T.I.A.S. no. 9656 (signed May 4, 1978; entered into force Jan. 25, 1980), art. 5(1); U.S.-Netherlands Extradition Treaty, 80 Stat. 271, 1 U.S.C. 113, T.I.A.S. no. 10733 (signed June 24, 1980; entered into force Sept. 15, 1983), art. 4(4).

2. Extradition Treaty Between the United States of America and the Republic of the Philippines, signed Nov. 27, 1981, reprinted in "Extradition Reform Act of 1981," Hearings Before the Subcom. on Crime, Com. on the Judiciary, U.S. House of Representatives, 97th Cong., 2d sess. (1982), at 327, 329–30 (art. 3).

3. Id. at 346–47.

4. See generally Raymond Bonner, Waltzing with a Dictator: The Marcos and the Making of American Policy (Quezon City, Philippines: Ken, Inc., 1987), and Sterling Seagrave, The Marcos Dynasty (New York: Harper & Row, 1988).

5. Quoted in Fred Poole and Max Vanzi, Revolution in the Philippines (New York: McGraw-Hill, 1984), 63.

6. Amendment 6, Constitution of 1973 (rule by decree whenever the president believes there is a grave threat or emergency) and P.D. no. 1737 (power to order the preventive detention of anyone suspected of "subversion").

7. Poole and Vanzi, Revolution in the Philippines, 347.

8. Jerrold M. Post and Robert S. Robins, When Illness Strikes the Leader (New Haven: Yale University Press, 1993), 127.

9. Id.

10. Seagrave, The Marcos Dynasty, 254.

11. Three members of a pro-Marcos gang were convicted for these crimes, but a forth was killed just before he was to testify that the owner of the murder weapon was an intimate of President and Mrs. Marcos. Id. at 256.

12. Appendix 1 to "Extradition, Political Crimes, and the U.K. Treaty," prepared statement of Prof. Christopher H. Pyle, in United States and United Kingdom Supplementary Extradition Treaty, Hearings Before the Committee on Foreign Relations, U.S. Senate, 99th Cong., 1st sess. (1985), at 98, 119–21. Original sources include members of the Filipino exile community then in the United States.

13. Id.

14. E.g., see remarks of Secretary of State Shultz quoted in Poole and Vanzi, Revolution in the Philippines, 75.

15. "Marcos Foe Slain as He Goes Home From Exile in U.S." New York Times, Aug. 22, 1983, 1.

16. E.g., see H.R. 5227, 98th Cong., 1st sess. (1983), sec. 3194(e)(2)(B) ("A political offense normally does not include . . . an offense that consists of homicide, assault with intent to commit

serious bodily injury, [or] an offense involving the use of a firearm . . . if such use endangers a person other than the offender." When this was revised as H.R. 2643, sec. 3194(e)(3), "normally" was changed to "except in extraordinary circumstances," which were not defined.

17. S. Rep. 97-475, 97th Cong., 2d sess. (1982), at 4.

18. Id. at 4–5.

19. E.T.S. no. 90, art. 1, but see art. 13. The European Convention is in force among Austria, Cyprus, Denmark, Germany, Iceland, Ireland, Liechtenstein, Luxembourg, Norway, Portugal, Spain, Sweden, Switzerland, Turkey, and the United Kingdom, seven of which have entered reservations. Belgium, France, Greece, Italy, the Netherlands, Malta, Israel, Canada, and the United States (which can accede to European Conventions) have not ratified the convention. M. Bowman and D. Harris, Multilateral Treaties, no. 702 at 417 (1984). Ireland signed in 1987. Michael Forde, Extradition Law in Ireland (Dublin: Roundhall Press, 1988), 179.

20. The convention removed from the political offense exception "the use of a bomb, grenade, rocket, automatic firearm or letter or parcel bomb if this use endangers persons." E.T.S. no. 90, art. 1(e).

21. See Michael Forde, Extradition Law in Ireland, 189–99, for these reservations.

22. See also H.R. 2643, 98th Cong., 1st sess. (1983).

23. E.g., see S. Rep. 97-331, at 35–36; S. Rep. 97-475, at 20–21; H. Rep. 97-627, part 1, at 48–49, all in the 97th Cong., 2d. sess. (1982).

24. E.g., see Extradition Act of 1981, Hearing Before the Com. on the Judiciary, U.S. Senate, 97th Cong., 1st sess. (1981): statement of Prof. Christopher H. Pyle, 94, at 102; statement of Wade J. Henderson, Staff Counsel, American Civil Liberties Union, before the Subcom. on Crime, Com. on the Judiciary, U.S. House of Representatives, 97th Cong., 1st sess. (1981), at 5 (photocopy of original).

25. Id. Statement of Morton H. Halperin, Director, Center for National Security Studies, 411, 417.

26. Alfred P. Rubin, "When World Law Should Prevail in Extradition Proceedings," New York Times, Jan. 23, 1982, at 22.

27. 128 Cong. Rec. H6968-70 (Sept. 14, 1982).

28. 1951 U.N. Convention Relating to the Status of Refugees (signed July 28, 1951; entered into force April 22, 1954), art. 33, para. 1, 19 U.S.T. 6257, T.I.A.S. no. 2332, 189 U.N.T.S. 137. See also Protocol Relating to the Status of Refugees (signed Jan. 31, 1957; entered into force Oct. 4, 1967), 19 U.S.T. 6223, T.I.A.S. no. 6577, 606 U.N.T.S. 267. The nonrefoulement principle was also part of U.S. immigration law, sec. 208(a) of the Refugee Act of 1980, 8 U.S.C. sec. 1253(h) ("wellfounded fear of persecution"), and even appeared in the anti-Nazi provision of the Holtzman amendment. 8 U.S.C. sec. 1251(a)(19)(D).

29. For the views of other House members, see 128 Cong. Rec. E4128 (daily ed. Sept. 13, 1982) (Edwards), E4145, E4152 (Stork, Conyers), E4189, E4192, E4201 (daily ed., Sept. 15, 1982) (Moffett, Studds, Fauntroy, Schroeder, Chisholm), id. at E4214, E4222, E4233, E4241, E4245 (daily ed. Sept. 16, 1982) (Wyden, Frank, Brodhead, Bonior, Rosenthal). For senatorial opposition to limiting the exception, see 132 Cong. Rec. S9251–73 (daily ed., July 17, 1986) and 132 Cong. Rec. S9119–71 (daily ed. July 16, 1986). Crockett also proposed amendments to give the accused the right to petition the secretary of state to refuse or condition his extradition, to make the rule of speciality a matter of statutory law, and to require requesting states to hire private legal counsel, thus stripping them of the aura of U.S. government support. 128 Cong. Rec. H6968–70 (Sept. 14,1982).

30. Supplementary Treaty Concerning the Extradition Treaty Between the Government of the United States of America and the Government of the United Kingdom of Great Britain and Northern Ireland, S. Exec. Rep. no. 17, 99th Cong., 2d sess. 15–17 (1986); 1 Kavass et al., Extradition

Laws and Treaties 920.20d–h (1979 and 1989 Supp.); 24 I.L.M. 1104 (1985) (signed June 25, 1985; entered into force Dec. 23, 1986). See also 87 State Dept. Bull., Feb. 1987, at 89.

31. 132 Cong. Rec. S9147 (daily ed. July 16, 1986) (remarks of Senator Lugar, Chair, Com. on Foreign Relations).

32. Quoted by David Lauther, "U.S., Britain Sign New Pact on Fugitives," National Law Journal, July 29, 1985, p. 5.

33. Prepared statement of Abraham D. Sofaer, in United States and United Kingdom Supplementary Extradition Treaty, Hearings Before the Com. on Foreign Relations, U.S. Senate, 99th Cong., 1st sess. (1985), 244, 265.

34. E.g., see Appendix 2 to the prepared statement of Christopher H. Pyle, id. at 121–25.

35. Id. at 258–59.

36. In re Abu Eain, 641 F. 2d 504 (7th Cir. 1981), cert. denied, 454 U.S. 894 (1981); United States v. Doherty, 599 F. Supp. 270 (S.D.N.Y. 1984). The much touted "loophole" did not exist, except in the 9th Circuit, which still followed the amorality of *Ezeta*. But even the 9th Circuit would be able to find a way to extradite Ian Quinn, an alleged IRA bomber. Quinn v. Robinson, 783 F. 2d 776 (1986).

37. "The Target: Thatcher," Time Magazine, Oct. 21, 1984, at 50; R. W. Apple Jr., "IRA Says It Set Bomb That Ripped Thatcher's Hotel," New York Times, Oct. 13, 1984, at 1.

38. William V. Kennedy, "Why Were F-111s 'Misused' in the Raid on Libya?," Chicago Tribune, Aug. 19, 1986, sec. 1, at 15. See also Joseph Lelyveld, "Thatcher Faults U.S. Terror Policy," New York Times, Apr. 28, 1986, at A6 (Thatcher links ratification of the extradition treaty to her decision to allow Americans to bomb Libya from British bases), and Linda Greenhouse, "The War on Terrorism, From Tripoli to Belfast," New York Times, April 30, 1986, B6 (Thatcher tells BBC interviewers that the aid Britain provided for the raid on Libya imposed on the United States a particular obligation to help Britain fight "Irish terrorism". State Department spokesman Charles Redman also urged the Senate to approve the treaty in return for Thatcher's help with the bombing of Libya).

39. 22 Weekly Comp. Pres. Doc. 730–31 (May 31, 1986).

40. Quoted in Greenhouse, "The War on Terrorism," B6.

41. The Anglo-Irish Agreement Support Act, Pub. L. no. 99-415, 100 Stat. 947 (1986).

42. David Shribman, "Senate Debate on Terrorism in Northern Ireland Entangles U.S.-British Treaty on Extradition," Wall Street Journal, May 12, 1986, at 52.

43. 132 Cong. Rec. 16796 (July 17, 1986).

44. Steven V. Roberts, "Pact with Britain on Extraditions Backed by Senate," New York Times, July 18, 1986, A1, A3.

45. Id. at A3.

46. 132 Cong. Rec. at S9161 (remarks of Senator Helms).

47. Id. at S9163.

48. Supplementary Extradition Treaty Between the Government of the United States of America and the Government of the United Kingdom of Great Britain and Northern Ireland (signed June 25, 1985; entered into force Dec. 23, 1986), S. Treaty Doc. 99-8, S. Exec. Rep. 99-17, art. 3(a). The treaty amended the main extradition treaty of Jan. 21, 1977, originally signed at London on June 8, 1972, 28 U.S.T. 227; T.I.A.S. no. 8468.

49. That the exchange was meant to influence subsequent judicial interpretations of the treaty was affirmed during the floor debate by Senator Joseph Biden, 132 Cong. Rec. S9260 (daily ed., July 17, 1986).

50. 132 Cong. Rec. S9260–261 (daily ed., July 17, 1986).

51. Id. at S9253.

52. Id. at S9358. See also S. Rep. 99-17, at 4–5, for assurances from Chairman Lugar that the accused would be able to challenge the fairness of the legal system to which he was to be returned.

53. 132 Cong. Rec. at S9167 (daily ed. July 16, 1986).

54. Id. at S9253.

55. Id. at S9259–61. See also the remarks of Senator Kerry, Id. S9253–57.

56. In Matter of Smyth, 820 F. Supp. 498, 503 (N.D.Cal. 1993); In re Howard, 99 F. 2d 1320, 1330–31 (1st Cir. 1993).

57. With marvelous verbosity, art. 4 provided: "This Supplementary Treaty shall apply to any offense committed before or after this Supplementary Treaty enters into force, provided that this Supplementary Treaty shall not apply to an offense committed before this Supplementary Treaty enters into force which was not an offense under the laws of both Contracting Parties at the time of its commission."

58. Matter of McMullen, 769 F. Supp. 1278, 1285–87 (S.D.N.Y. 1991).

59. Id.

60. McMullen v. United States, 989 F. 2d 603, 604 (2d Cir. 1993 (en banc).

61. 132 Cong. Rec. S9120 (daily ed., July 16, 1986) (text of resolution of consent).

62. Supplementary Extradition Treaty with the Federal Republic of Germany (signed Oct. 21, 1986; entered into force Mar. 11, 1993), S. Exec. Rept. 102–28.

63. Protocol Amending the Extradition Treaty with Canada (signed July 30, 1991; entered into force Nov. 26, 1991), Treaty Doc. 101–17, S. Exec. Rept. 102–12.

64. Protocol Amending the 1974 Extradition Treaty with Australia (signed Sept. 4, 1992; entered into force Dec. 21, 1992), Treaty Doc. 101–23, S. Exec. Rep. 102–30.

65. Signed March 17, 1987, but not entered into force.

66. Thomas M. Frank and Scott C. Senecal, "Porfiry's Proposition: Legitimacy and Terrorism," 20 Vand. J. Transnat'l Law 195, 215 (1987).

67. Id. at 216.

68. Id. at 234.

69. *Supra,* Chapter 1 (opening quotation).

Chapter Sixteen

Epigraph: 149 U.S. 698, 709 (1892).

Epigraph: 60 Minutes, "Joe Doherty and the IRA," CBS-TV broadcast, Oct. 11, 1987.

1. E.g., see statement of Senator Lugar (R.-Ind.) the treaty's chief proponent, 132 Cong. Rec. 16,586 (1986).

2. Doherty v. Meese, 808 F. 2d. 938, 940 (2d Cir. 1986). The Justice Department, in its "Fact Sheet" and arguments before the immigration courts, claimed that no penalties awaited Doherty under Irish law. In fact, the law and politics of Ireland were by then hostile to the IRA. It was the Irish, not the British, government, that had captured and imprisoned most of Doherty's fellow escapees.

3. 8 U.S.C. sec. 1253. As the Court of Appeals for the Second Circuit has explained, "deportation and extradition are two entirely different processes having separate statutory bases. Unlike the subject of an extradition proceeding, a deportee . . . has the right to choose initially the country to which he will be deported." Linnas v. INS, 790 F. 2d 1024 (2d Cir. 1986). See also

Landon v. Plasencia, 459 U.S. 21, 26 (1982), and Maldonado-Sandoval v. INS, 518 F. 2d 278, 280, n. 3 (9th Cir. 1975).

4. Fong Yue Ting, 149 U.S. 698, 725 (1892).

5. Id. at 709.

6. Quoted in Hackworth, Digest of International Law (Washington, D.C.: U.S. Government Printing Office, 1942), vol. 4, 30.

7. 8 U.S.C. sec. 1253(a).

8. The only arguable precedent involved the Amistad captives who could not be extradited to Cuba because there was no extradition treaty with Spain. Had they been ruled slaves, the Van Buren administration would have deported them to Cuba, together with all the relevant documents, so that Cuban authorities could prosecute them for hijacking the ship. Letter from Secretary of State John Forsyth to Secretary of the Navy James K. Paulding, Jan. 7, 1840, doc. no. 185, 26th Cong., 1st sess. (184), 68–69.

9. Id.

10. In re Doherty, A26-185-231, Transcript of Deportation Hearing, Sept. 19, 1986, 57, reprinted in App. to Pet. for Cert. at 158a, filed in INS v. Doherty, 502 U.S. 314 (1992).

11. Unreported decision. See John Riley, "U.S. Refuses to Deport an IRA Member," National Law Journal, Sept. 29, 1986, at 3.

12. Doherty v. Meese, 808 F. 2d 938, 941, n. 3 (2d Cir. 1986).

13. Riley, "U.S. Refuses to Deport an IRA Member," 3.

14. Doherty v. Meese at 944.

15. Id. at 942.

16. Id.

17. See U.S. Dept. of State, Patterns of Global Terrorism: 1988 (1989) (terrorism defined as "premeditated, politically motivated violence perpetrated against noncombatant targets"). Doherty's actions also did not fit the definition of "terrorist activities" set forth in immigration legislation. See 8 U.S.C. sec. 1182(B)(ii).

18. Doherty v. Meese at 943.

19. The reference is to Joseph Heller's novel about a World War II bomber pilot who is crazed by the fact that people are trying to kill him, or get him killed. The Army will release him from duty if he can prove he is crazy. The catch is that anyone who wants to get out of combat duty is, by definition, not crazy. Catch 22 (New York: Dell, 1956), at 46–47.

20. Doherty v. Meese at 944.

21. In re Doherty, A26-185-231 (BIA Mar. 11, 1987), reprinted in App. to Pet. for Cert. at 153a, INS v. Doherty, 502 U.S. 314 (1992).

22. Id., App. at 153a–154a.

23. Id.

24. In re Doherty, A26-185-231 (BIA, May 22, 1987), reprinted in App. to Pet. for Cert. at 140a, filed in INS v. Doherty, 502 U.S. 314 (1992).

25. Id., App. at 140a.

26. Id., App. at 116a.

27. 8 C.F.R. sec. 3.1(h)(1)(iii).

28. In twenty years, the attorney general had certified only eight of thousands of BIA cases for review. All eight involved reviews of law, not findings of fact. Amicus Curiae Brief of Members of the U.S. Congress, Doherty v. INS, 908 F. 2d 1108 (1990).

29. Mem. Att'y Gen. June 9, 1988, reprinted in App. to Pet. for Cert. at 116a, INS v. Doherty, 502 U.S. 314 (1992).

30. Id., App. at 121a.

31. Id., App. at 119a, n. 3.

32. Doherty v. INS, 908 F. 2d 1108 (2d Cir. 1990). Doherty's appeal of Meese's reversal of the BIA's ruling was consolidated with his challenge of Meese's denial of Doherty's designation of Ireland as the country to which he wished to be deported.

33. Id. at 1113.

34. E.g., see Korematsu v. United States, 323 U.S. 214 (1944) (failure to question basis of government allegations that the 110,000 internees might assist the Japanese enemy).

35. E.g., see Dennis v. United States, 341 U.S. 494 (1951) (failure to examine what the defendants had actually done).

36. On Dec. 1, 1987, Ireland's belated ratification of the European Supression of Terrorism Act went into effect, obligating the Irish government to surrender Doherty to the United Kingdom, should he be found on its soil.

37. In re Doherty, A26-185-231 (Affidavit of Mary Boresz Pike, Dec. 2, 1987), reprinted in Joint App. to Pet. for Cert. at 57a, INS v. Doherty, 504 U.S. 314 (1992). See also, Doherty v. INS, 908 F. 2d 1108, 1112 (2d Cir. 1990).

38. In re Doherty, A26-185-231 (BIA, Nov. 14, 1988), reprinted in App. to Pet. for Cert. at 99a, INS v. Doherty, 502 U.S. 314 (1992). Also discussed at 908 F. 2d at 1112.

39. See Articles 32 and 33 of the U.N. Convention Relating to the Status of Refugees (signed July 28, 1951; entered into force April 22, 1954), 19 U.S.T. 6259, and art. 7(1) of the Protocol Relating to the Status of Refugees (signed Jan. 31, 1967; entered into force Nov. 1, 1968), 19 U.S.T. 6224, U.N.T.S. 268. See also Guy Goodwin-Hill, The Refugee in International Law (New York: Oxford Univ. Press, 1983), 69.

40. App. to Pet. for Cert. at 92a, INS v. Doherty, 502 U.S. 314 (1992).

41. Id., App. at 100a.

42. In re Doherty, A26-185-231 (Mem. Att'y Gen. June 30, 1989), reprinted in App. to Pet. for Cert. at 76a, n. 31, INS v. Doherty, 502 U.S. 314 (1992). In March 1990, the Irish Supreme Court refused to extradite two IRA members who had escaped from Long Kesh (Maze) prison in Northern Ireland. Doing so, it held, would violate their Irish constitutional rights by subjecting them to the "probable risk that [they] would be assaulted or injured by the illegal acts of the prison staff." Finucane v. Governor of Portaoise Prison, no. 164-89 slip. op. at 9 (Ir.S.C. 1990). See also Clarke v. Governor of Portaoise Prison, no. 304–89 (Ir.S.C. 1990).

43. Reprinted in App. to Pet. for Cert. at 78a, n. 32, INS v. Doherty, 502 U.S. 314 (1992).

44. Id., App. at 65a–67a. Overlooked in this analysis were the brutal reprisals against prisoners at Long Kesh after a mass escape in 1983. See Finucane v. Governor of Portaoise Prison, no. 164-89, slip op. at 9 (Ir.S.C. 1990).

45. App. to Pet. for Cert. at 66a, INS v. Doherty, 502 U.S. 314 (1992).

46. Compare McMullen v. INS, 788 F. 2d 591, 596 (9th Cir. 1986) ("deportation is a matter solely between the United States government and the individual seeking withholding of deportation. No other sovereign is involved.").

47. Doherty v. INS, 908 F. 2d 1108 (1990), rev'd *sub. nom.* INS v. Doherty, 502 U.S. 314 (1992).

48. 908 F. 2d at 1121.

49. Id. at 1119, citing The Refugee Act of 1980, Pub. L. no. 96-212, 94 Stat. 102, now codified at 8 U.S.C. sec. 1158(a). Prior to 1980, attorneys general regularly evaded the broad humanitarian purposes of asylum, giving ninety-five percent of all grants to fugitives from communist countries. Note, "Political Legitimacy in the Law of Political Asylum," 99 Harv. L. Rev. 450, 458 (1985).

50. 908 F. 2d at 1120 citing 8 U.S.C. sec. 1253(h)(i).

51. Id. at 1119, citing 8 U.S.C. sec. 1253 (h)(i) and INS v. Stevic, 467 U.S. 407 (1984) (attorney general has no discretion once the alien has met these criteria).

52. INS v. Doherty, 502 U.S. 314 (1992).

53. Id. at 322.

54. Id. at 323.

55. Compare, e.g., the opinion of Judge Frank X. Altimari of the Second Circuit, dissenting from a separate decision upholding the length of Doherty's incarceration: "I *do* find it shocking that we would allow the government to indefinitely pursue a litigation strategy, which was essentially designed to circumvent an extradition decision, at the expense of an individual's right to liberty.... A point is reached when all pedagogical distinctions give way to common sense and reason and we say: enough—it is just flat out wrong to confine an individual for eight years when he has not been charged with a crime in this country and has been declared by a court of competent jurisdiction to be guilty of a 'political offense.'" Doherty v. Thornburgh, 943 F. 2d 204, 213–14 (2d Cir. 1991).

56. Under 8 U.S.C. sec. 1253(h) (1988 ed. and Supp. 2) ("The Attorney General shall not deport or return any alien ... to a country if the Attorney General determines that such alien's life or freedom would be threatened in such country on account of race, religion, nationality, membership in a particular social group, or political opinion").

57. INS v. Stevic, 467 U.S. 1407 (1984) (attorney general has no discretion; he must withhold deportation if the alien has shown that his life or freedom would be threatened by persecution).

58. United Nations Convention Relating to the Status of Refugees (signed July 28, 1951; entered into force April 22, 1954), 19 U.S.T. 6259, 189 U.N.T.S. 150, art. 33: "no Contracting States shall expel or return ('refouler') a refugee in any manner whatsoever to the frontiers of territories where his life or freedom would be threatened on account of his race, religion, nationality, membership in a particular social group or political opinion." Protocol Relating to the Status of Refugees (signed Jan. 31, 1967; entered into force for U.S. Nov. 1, 1968), 19 U.S.T. 6223, T.I.A.S. 6577, 606 U.N.T.S. 267. See art. 7(1), forbidding states to escape their obligations under the nonrefoulement principle by entering reservations to the protocol.

59. The U.N.'s Handbook on Procedures and Criteria for Determining Refugee Status Under the 1951 Convention and Protocol Relating to the Status of Refugees (1979), para. 152, at 36, sets forth standards for determining what constitutes a political offense. By any fair application of these criteria, Doherty was a political refugee, entitled to protection under the nonrefoulement principle. Specifically, he acted out of political motives, not seeking personal gain. There was a close causal link between his offense and his political goals, and (as Judge Sprizzo's decision established) the political element of his actions outweighed their common law character. Finally, the killing of Captain Westmacott, who was trying to kill Doherty, was neither atrocious nor disproportionate to Doherty's (and the IRA's) basic political goal, which was to drive the British out of Northern Ireland. Doherty did not pose any danger to the security of the United States or to the community of that country, the two exceptions to the principle of nonrefoulement allowed by the 1951 U.N. treaty, art. 33(2). Nor had he committed a crime against peace or humanity, a war crime, or a serious nonpolitical crime, or otherwise acted in a manner inconsistent with general U.N. principles and policies. Id., art. 1(F)(a)–(c). Nor was he disqualified under the similar provisions of the 1980 Refugee Act, 8 U.S.C. sec. 1101(a) (1980), or 8 C.F.R. sec. 208.8 (1988).

60. On the attorney general's discretion not to reopen the asylum hearing, the Court's vote was 8–0, but on his power to refuse to withhold deportation, it was 5–3. His authority to grant or deny asylum is set forth in 8 U.S.C. sec. 1158(a). For the distinction between the duty to withhold deportation and the discretion to deny asylum, see Davalene Cooper, "Promised Land or Land of Broken Promises? Political Asylum in the United States," 76 Ky. L. J. 931 (1987–88).

61. INS v. Doherty, 502 U.S. at 323, citing INS v. Abudu, 485 U.S. 94 (1988).

62. The majority did not attempt to answer the Court of Appeals' findings regarding Congress's intent, or the attorney general's obligations under the nonrefoulement provision of the U.N. treaty on refugees.

63. James Barron, "I.R.A. Fugitive Sent to Belfast from U.S. Jail," New York Times, Feb. 20, 1992, at A1.

64. See 138 Cong. Rec. H8027–28 (daily ed. Aug. 12, 1992) (remarks of Rep. Engel). "Stiff Term for IRA Man," Washington Post, Aug. 4, 1992, A6.

65. However, in 1996 the U.S. Coast Guard returned six Cubans who, like the Polish seamen, hijacked a tugboat in their bid for freedom. The return was made at sea, pursuant to a 1995 agreement with the Castro regime, and without any specific effort to assure fair treatment on their return. Prior to this agreement, the United States routinely granted refugee status to Cubans who commandeered planes and ships to escape. Since it went into effect, more than 500 Cubans have been returned, despite protests by human rights groups. Larry Rohter, "Cuba Gives Long Prison Terms to Six Who Tried to Flee to U.S.," New York Times (Int'l), Feb. 13, 1997, A10.

66. A fellow defendant in the airline bombing case, Luis Podesta Carriles, escaped from Venezuela and moved to El Salvador, where he helped President Bush's former subordinate at the CIA, Felix Rodriguez, supply arms to the Nicaraguan contras. Alexander Cockburn, "Judge Dreadful," New Statesman and Society, Aug. 10, 1990, 14–15. See also Jeffrey Schmalz, "Furor over Castro Foe's Fate Puts Bush on Spot in Miami," New York Times, Aug. 16, 1989, A1, B8.

67. Larry Rohter, "A Haitian Set for Deportation Is Instead Set Free by the U.S.," New York Times, June 22, 1996, 5 (other alleged human rights violators returned).

68. Garry Pierre-Pierre, "Exile Is Allowed to Stay," New York Times (NE ed.), Aug. 10, 1997, 30.

69. Rohter, "Haitian Set for Deportation . . . Set Free," 5.

70. Id.

71. Id.

Chapter Seventeen

Epigraph: 170 F. Supp. 383, 392–93 (S.D.Cal. 1959).

1. Chapter 9, *supra*.

2. Id.

3. Chapters 12 and 16, *supra*.

4. 78 U.N.T.S. 277, 281 art.7 (opened for ratification Dec. 9, 1948; entered into force for the United States Feb. 23, 1989).

5. On Feb. 19, 1986, the Senate conditioned its consent to the treaty upon the enactment of implementing legislation, which was signed into law on Nov. 4, 1988. Genocide Implementation Act, 102 Stat. 3045–46, 18 U.S.C. sec. 1091–93.

6. E.g., see the opinion of Magistrate Volney V. Brown Jr., reprinted in Artukovic v. Rison, 628 F. Supp. 1370, 1376 (C.D.Cal. 1986), ruling that the accused could only be charged with

382 NOTES TO CHAPTER SEVENTEEN

murder, not genocide, because genocide was not then an offense under American law. But see the extradition of John Demjanjuk, Chapter 18, *infra*.

7. See generally Christopher Simpson, Blowback: America's Recruitment of Nazis and Its Effects on the Cold War (New York: Weidenfeld & Nicolson, 1988). See also Linda Hunt, "U.S. Coverup of Nazi Scientists," Bulletin of Atomic Scientists, April 1985, 16–24.

8. Nicholas R. Roman, "Aftermath of Nuremberg: The Trial of Klaus Barbie," 60 U. Colo. L. Rev. 449, 451 (1989).

9. "Widespread Conspiracy to Obstruct Probes of Alleged Nazi War Criminals Not Supported by Available Evidence—Controversy May Continue," reprinted as Appendix 5 to vol. 1, Alleged Nazi War Criminals, Hearings Before the Subcomm. on Immigration, Citizenship, and International Law, Comm. on the Judiciary, U.S. House of Representatives, 95th Cong., 2d sess. (Aug. 3, 1977), 159–233.

10. For more on the political pressures that led to the creation of OSI, see Charles Ashman and Robert J. Wagman, The Nazi Hunters (New York: Pharos Books, 1988), ch. 7.

11. The Holtzman Amendment establishing OSI's basic authority was enacted as the Immigration and Nationality Act—Nazi Germany, Pub. L. 95-549, 92 Stat. 2065 (1978), codified at 8 U.S.C. secs. 1182(a)(33), 1182(d)(3), 1251(a)(19), 1253(h), and 1254(e). For the legislative history see H.R. Rep. no. 1452 (Comm. on Judiciary), 95th Cong., 2d sess. (1978), reprinted in 1978 U.S. Code Cong. & Ad. News, 4700, 4702, and 124 Cong. Rec. H31640–50 (Sept. 26, 1978).

12. Carroll Lachnit, "Artukovic Case Renews Debate on War-Crimes Investigations," Orange County Register, Feb. 16, 1986, A1 (quoting director Sher). See also Michael Hodges, "U.S. Nazi Hunters Railroaded 'War Criminal,' Experts Say," Washington Times, Sept. 24, 1990, A1, A11.

13. Chapter 10, *supra*.

14. Sec. 243(a) of the Immigration and Nationality Act of 1952, 8 U.S.C. sec. 1253(a).

15. 8 U.S.C. sec. 1253(h), as amended by Act of Oct. 30, 1978, Pub. L. no. 95-549, Title 1, sec. 104, 92 Stat. 2066 (1978). See also 124 Cong. Rec. H31640–50 (Sept. 26, 1978).

16. Id. at H31649. Remarks of Rep. Charles Wiggins (R.-Cal.). Regarding the purpose of the law, see Allan A. Ryan Jr., Quiet Neighbors: Prosecuting Nazi War Criminals in America (San Deigo: Harcourt Brace Jovanovich, 1984), 270. Ryan was the first director of OSI. The constitutional prohibition against bills of attainder and ex post facto laws were held not to apply here because deportation is, technically speaking, not a punishment. Artukovic v. INS, 693 F. 2d 894, 897 (1982).

17. Hearings, at 42. Remarks of Rep. Eilberg (D.-Pa.).

18. H.R. Rep. no. 95-1452, 95th Cong., 2d sess. 3 (1978), 1978 U.S. Code Cong. & Ad. News, 4712. The origin of this standard can be traced to Schneiderman v. United States, 320 U.S. 118, 123 (1943). See also 124 Cong. Rec., Sept. 26, 1978, H.31648. Remarks of Rep. Hamilton Fish Jr. (R.-N. Y.).

19. United States v. Artukovic, 170 F. Supp. 383 (1959).

20. Artukovic v. INS, 693 F.2d 894, 899 (1982).

21. The best known of these show trials was that of the Catholic Archbishop (and later Cardinal) Alojzije Stepinać, who had given qualified support to the Catholic Ustashe against the Communists during the war and who had supported the forced conversion of Orthodox Christians to Catholicism.

22. Declaration of Neal M. Sher, Jan. 29, 1985, 1 and 2 (written in response to charges of perjury on this point).

23. Transcript, In re Artukovic, CV 84-8743-R (B), (U.S.D.C., C.D.Cal., Feb. 13, 1985), at 41. The claim seems improbable both because an OSI historian had gone to Yugoslavia in 1979 in search of evidence for the deportation case and because NBC Television News reported, two

months before the trip took place, that the purpose of the group's trip was to negotiate Artukovic's extradition. Transcript, NBC News, May 12, 1983, at 8.

24. Confidential Cable no. 123179, from Secretary of State, Washington, to American Embassy, Belgrade, May 4, 1983. See also Robert L. Jackson and Ronald J. Ostrow, "Nazi Hunters Investigated in Artukovic Case," Los Angeles Times, Aug. 17, 1990, A3, A26. A second cable confirmed that "The objectives of the USG [U.S. government], as seen by the DOJ [Justice Department] team, [include an] attempt to successfully extradite Artukovic to Yugoslavia." Confidential Cable no. 6747, from American Embassy, Belgrade, to Secretary of State, Washington, Aug. 13, 1983. Neal Sher refused to comment on either cable. Jackson and Ostrow, "Nazi Hunters Investigated in Artukovic Case." See also Confidential Cable no. 013071, from Secretary of State, Washington, to American Embassy, Belgrade, Jan. 16, 1984.

25. "Attorneys Raise Perjury Issue in Artukovic Case," Los Angeles Times, May 29, 1985, 1, 4. The original source is Branimir Stanojević, Ustaski Ministar Smrti (Beograd: Nova Knjiga, 1985), at 12.

26. Benjamin Wittes, "Another Demjanjuk?" Legal Times, Dec. 16, 1996, 4, 16.

27. "Man Held as War Criminal," Washington Post, Nov. 15, 1984, A6 (quoting Neal Sher).

28. See generally Joseph Hecimovic, In Tito's Death Marches and Extermination Camps (New York: Carleton Press, 1962), and John Prcela and Stanko Guldescu, eds., Operation Slaughterhouse: Eyewitness Accounts of Postwar Massacres in Yugoslavia (Philadelphia: Dorrance & Co., 1970).

29. United States ex rel. Karadzole v. Artukovic, 170 F. Supp. 383, 392 (S.D.Cal. 1959).

30. "It's Worth Doing Right," Orange County Register, June 16, 1985, G14.

31. "Soviet Aide Warned U.S. on War Crime Evidence," Los Angeles Times, April 28, 1986, 1, 6, 7.

32. Laipenieks v. INS, 750 F. 2d 1427, 1432, 1435 (9th Cir. 1985).

33. United States v. Kungys, 571 F. Supp. 1104, 1128–29 (D.N.J. 1983). The court found that OSI had used "blatantly leading questions," relied on depositions which Soviet investigators had "orchestrated," id. at 1129, had allowed Soviet procurators to limit questioning of the two most important witnesses, blocking questioning by defense counsel that might have undermined their credibility, and otherwise relied on witnesses who feared that Soviet procurators would return them to prison if they did not give the right answers. Id. at 1131.

34. Dick Chapman, "'Phony' Affidavit Brands Dad Nazi," Sunday Sun (Toronto), Sept. 15, 1985, 25.

35. See generally Arthur D. Morse, While Six Million Died: A Chronicle of American Apathy (New York: Random House, 1967); Henry L. Feingold, The Politics of Rescue: The Roosevelt Administration and the Holocaust, 1938–1945 (New Brunswick, N.J.: Rutgers University Press, 1970); David S. Wyman, The Abandonment of the Jews: America and the Holocaust, 1941–1945 (New York: Pantheon Books, 1984).

36. Wyman, The Abandonment of the Jews, ch. 15.

37. Linda Hunt, "U.S. Coverup of Nazi Scientists," 16—24.

38. Branimir Stanojević, Ustaski Ministar Smrti at 13.

39. Letter from the attorney, Marios Kos, to Radoslav Artukovic, 17 travnja 1986 (copy in author's files).

40. Eric Malnic, "U.S. Seizes Artukovic as Nazi War Criminal," Los Angeles Times, Nov. 15, 1984, 1, 3.

41. "The Case Against Andrija Artukovic: Questions and Answers," Los Angeles Times, Nov. 27, 1984, 1.

42. Id., and Bob Houser, "Artukovic Son Hits 'New' Case," Press-Telegram (Long Beach, Cal.), Dec. 9, 1984, A1, A4.

43. The magistrate's amended opinion, dated Aug. 8, 1985, was adopted by the district court and reprinted in Artukovic v. Rison, 628 F. Supp. 1370, 1372–79 (C.D.Cal. 1986).

44. Id. at 1375.

45. The magistrate erroneously concluded in his opinion that the court-appointed psychiatrist had adjudged the patient sufficiently competent to participate in his own defense. The psychiatrist had not so testified.

46. Seventeen affidavits taken in 1984 were submitted by the Justice Department on behalf of the Yugoslavian government. Of these, fifteen of the affiants had never seen Artuković, and ten of the fifteen did not mention him in their statements.

47. Radoslav Artukovic. Also Robert L. Jackson and Ronald J. Ostrow, "Nazi Hunters Investigated in Artukovic Case," A3, A26. See also Benjamin Wittes, "Another Demjanjuk?," Legal Times, Dec. 16, 1996, 1, 14.

48. Letter from Mark Richards, Deputy Assistant Attorney General (Criminal Division), to Borislav Krajina, Minister of Justice, Yugoslavia, Aug. 1, 1983.

49. Reproduced in Radoslav Artukovic, "The Anatomy of a Fraud: The Affidavit of Barjro Avdic, A Case Study of Fradulent Evidence Used in an OSI Investigation," Feb. 12, 1988.

50. Radoslav Artukovic. When Senator Paul Laxalt (R.-Nev.) later questioned OSI's use of Avdić's statement, Assistant Attorney General John R. Bolton told him that courts had ruled that for the Justice Department to investigate the veracity of foreign government was "not an acceptable practice between treaty parties." However, he assured the Senator that a historian from OSI had determined through research in the Yugoslavian National Archives that "the statement of Barjo Avdic contained no inaccuracy of any import." Letter from John R. Bolton, Assistant Attorney General (Legislative and Intergovernmental Affairs), to Senator Paul Laxalt, March 5, 1987. In Sept. 1990, former OSI historian Dennis Reinhartz told a reporter that he had very serious doubts about the veracity of the Avdić affidavit at the time it was offered for submission to the court. Hodges, "U.S. Nazi Hunters Railroaded 'War Criminal.'" But the affidavit was submitted anyway because, as Bolton explained in his letter, "corroboration is not a requirement in any of our extradition treaties."

51. Larry Keller. Also "An Unhappy Homecoming for Artukovic," Press-Telegram, April 13, 1986, A1, A14.

52. Radoslav Artukovic, "Yugoslavia Sued for 10 Million: New Twist in Artukovic Case," CNC Report (Croatian National Congress), no. 9, Aug. 1985, 7, 8.

53. Radoslav Artukovic.

54. Reprinted in Artukovic v. Rison, 628 F. Supp. 1370, 1373 (C.D.Cal. 1986). The evidence had previously been rejected in Karadozole v. Artukovic, 170 F. Supp. 383 (S.D.Cal. 1959).

55. In a particularly bizarre passage worthy of a Dickens novel, Brown ruled that it would not be enough for the defense to show that the passage of time and the wartime and postwar slaughter in Yugoslavia had made mounting a defense impossible. The defense would also have to show that the delay in bringing the extradition request "was intentional so as to gain a tactical advantage over the accused," as if the government's intent had anything to do with whether it was fair to try a person so long after the events. Odder still, the magistrate ruled that the defense would have to prove that the delay was caused by the United States because, he thought, only an intentional act by the United States could give rise to a due process claim by the defense. Artukovic v. Rison, 628 F. Supp. 1370, at 1375 (C.D.Cal. 1986). In other words,

no violation of due process can occur when a U.S. court knowingly gives legal effect to the deliberate wrongdoing of a foreign government.

56. Similarly, Brown saw no difficulty in extraditing a person for prosecution under an *ex post facto* law. Again, he reasoned, "due process cannot be extended extra territorially," as if the United States is not responsible, under its constitutional obligations to do justice when it delivers a person to certain injustice. Id. at 1377.

57. 628 F. Supp. at 1377.

58. Id. at 1376.

59. 32 Stat. 1890, T.S. 406 (signed Oct. 25, 1901; entered into force June 12, 1902), art. 2.

60. 628 F. Supp. at 1377.

61. For an account of the initial hearings, see William Overend, "Croatian Expert Cut Short in Artukovic Case," Los Angeles Times, Feb. 28, 1985, 1, 10. Also, Reporter's Transcript Proceedings, In re Artukovic, CV 84-8743-R (B), Feb. 27, 1985, 109–114.

62. Reply Brief, In re Matter of Artukovic, Feb. 8, 1985, at 40.

63. Address of Neal M. Sher, Anti-Defamation League National Conference, New York City, May 31, 1984.

64. Aug. 1983 letter quoted in Charley Roberts, "Nazi-Hunting Tactics Being Probed," Los Angeles Daily Journal, March 2, 1990, 1, 9.

65. Benjamin Wittes, "Another Demjanjuk?" 1, 14.

66. Id., 14.

67. Reporter's Transcript of Proceedings, In re Artukovic, CV 84-8743-R (B), at 112.

68. See Chapters 21 and 22, *infra*.

69. Reproduced as Appendix C to Radoslav Artukovic's "The Anatomy of a Fraud," dated Feb. 12, 1988, 159 pp.

70. Radoslav Artukovic could find no one who remembered Avdić from the Ustashe escort service but did locate twelve people who remembered him from Zenica prison in the 1950s. They said he was a snitch, a torturer of other prisoners, and a teller of tall tales. Radoslav Artukovic, "Status of the Extradition Case—What Lies Ahead," Jan. 1986, ll.

71. In re Yamashita, 327 U.S. 1 (1946). For a critique of this decision, see Telford Taylor, The Anatomy of the Nuremberg Trials (New York: Knopf, 1992), 239, and A. Frank Reel, The Case of General Yamashita (Chicago: University of Chicago Press, 1949).

72. Toronto Sun, Jan. 31, 1985.

73. An extensive search by the author of English-language books on the Holocaust and the war in the Balkans has produced no reports of any of the alleged massacres or of Artukovic's alleged importance in the Pavelić government.

74. William Overend, "Attorney for Artukovic Questions U.S. Motives," Los Angeles Times, March 9, 1985, 28.

75. "A U.S. Political Prisoner," Orange County Register, March 25, 1985, A10.

76. Bob Zeller, "Artukovic Likely to Get Bail," Press-Telegram, July 2, 1985, 1, 4.

77. William Overend, "Magistrate Sympathetic to Artukovic's Bail Removed," Los Angeles Times, July 10, 1985.

78. Bob Zeller,"Artukovic Likely to Get Bail," A1.

79. Artukovic v. Rison, 628 F. Supp. 1370 (C.D.Cal. 1986).

80. Artukovic v. Rison, 784 F. 2d 1354, 1355 (9th Cir. 1986).

81. Id. at 1356.

82. Id.

83. Artukovic v. Rison, 784 F. 2d 1354 (9th Cir. 1986).

84. "Artukovic Son Vows Crusade," Santa Monica Outlook, Feb. 13, 1986, A12.

85. Press Telegram, *op. cit.*, Feb. 13, 1986, at A10.

86. "Chronology of Andrija Artukovic," Orange County Register, April 13, 1986, A20.

87. Carrol Lachnit, "Yugoslav Court Refuses Delay of Artukovic Trial," Orange County Register, April 15, 1986, A2 (quoting one of the trial judges at a news conference following the opening hearing).

88. Larry Keller, "Artukovic Shows Up in Court, Falls Asleep," Press-Telegram, April 16, 1986, A3.

89. Larry Keller, "Artukovic Denies Knowing of Croatian Concentration Camps," Press-Telegram, April 16, 1986, and "Son Gets Visa to Artukovic's Trial," Press-Telegram, April 10, 1986, A4. According to the son, the attorneys' phones were tapped and two teams of Yugoslav agents followed him through Germany as he tried to research the allegations. Radoslav Artukovic, "The Andrija Artukovic Case," Press-Telegram, March 27, 1986, B100.

90. Carroll Lachnit, "Security Tight for Artukovic Trial: Officials Fear Croatian Protests," Orange County Register, April 13, 1986, A1.

91. Larry Keller, "Slavs Begin Artukovic Trial," Press-Telegram, April 14, 1986, A1, A5.

92. Carroll Lachnit, "Artukovic Calls Murder Charges 'Complete Lies,'" Orange County Register, April 16, 1986, A1, A2.

93. Carroll Lachnit, "Witness Against Artukovic Falters but Stands by '50s Statements," Orange County Register, April 22, 1986, A1, A2. See also Larry Keller, "Witness Ties Artukovic, Killing," Press-Telegram, April 23, 1986, A1, A6.

94. Jovo Popović, Sudjenje Andriji Artukovicu i Sto Nije Receno [Artukovic's Trial and What Was Not Said] (Zagreb: Stvarnost Jugoart, 1986), 141–50. The author wishes to thank Marija Dokmanovic for her translations of this and other works in Serbo-Croatian.

95. Carroll Lachnit, "Artukovic's Trial Was Symbolic Far Beyond Convicting One Man," Orange County Register, May 18, 1986, A1, A12.

96. War Criminal Sentenced to Die for Killings," San Francisco Examiner, May 14, 1986, A-1. See also Milan Bulajić, Ustaski Zlocini Genocida I Sudenje Andriji Artukovicu 1986. Godine (Beograd: Izdavicka Radna Organizacija, 1986), vol. 1, at 20.

97. Carroll Lachnit, "Artukovic's Trial Was Symbolic."

98. Id.

99. Larry Keller, "Artukovic May Escape Execution," Press-Telegram, May 15, 1986, A1, A12.

100. Id. at A12.

101. Bulajic, Ustaski Zlocini Genocida I Sudenje Ardriji Artukovicu.

102. Ronald L. Jackson and Ronald J. Ostrow, "Nazi Hunters Investigated in Artukovic Case," A3, A26. See also Carroll Lachnit, "Diplomat Calls Artukovic War-Crimes Trial Farce, Says Key Witness Lied," Orange County Register, Aug. 7, 1988, A22, quoting article in NIN, July 17, 1988. See also Milan Nikolić, "Strategija," SVET, Nov. 1, 1989.

103. Hodges, "U.S. Nazi Hunters Railroaded 'War Criminal,'" A11. Srdjan Matić, former executive vice president of the Jewish community in Zagreb, shared the OSI historian's doubts. "I think that there is a lot of room for debate about whether [the crimes for which Artukovic was convicted] happened or not." Quoted by Benjamin Wittes, "Another Demjanjuk?," 1, 14.

104. Hodges, "U.S. Nazi Hunters Railroaded 'War Criminal," A11.

105. Conduct Unbecoming," Legal Times, Aug. 11, 1997, 19–20. See also Benjamin Wittes, "Another Demjanjuk?," 1, 14.

Chapter Eighteen

Epigraph: 397 U.S. 358, 364 (1970).

1. The other two death camps in eastern Poland were Belzec and Sobibor. Others in Poland included Chelmno (Kulmhof), Majdanek (Lublin), and Auschwitz (Oswiecim).

2. The following account draws from Fredric Dannen, "How Terrible Is Ivan?" Vanity Fair, June 1992, 132ff; Tom Teicholz, Ivan the Terrible (New York, St. Martin's Press, 1990); and Allan A. Ryan Jr., Quiet Neighbors: Prosecuting Nazi War Criminals in America (New York: Harcourt Brace Jovanovich, 1984), ch. 4. Dannen's account is sympathetic to the defense, Teicholz's and Ryan's to the prosecution. The author is also indebted to John H. Broadley, Esq., of Jenner and Block, Prof. Sherman Cohn of the Georgetown Law School, and Edward Nishnic of the John Demjanjuk Defense Fund for documents and information pertaining to the case. The author has not relied on Jim McDonald, John Demjanjuk: The Real Story (Brattleboro: Amana Books, 1990), or Alan M. Dershowitz, The Abuse Excuse (Boston: Little Brown, 1994).

3. Quoted from the trial transcript by Teicholz, Ivan the Terrible, 211.

4. Dannen, "How Terrible Is Ivan?" 136.

5. Id.; Teicholz, Ivan the Terrible, 211.

6. Dannen, "How Terrible Is Ivan?" 136; Teicholz, Ivan the Terrible, 212.

7. Had he admitted to living in the Soviet Union between 1937 and 1943, he would have been subject to repatriation under the Yalta agreement and, in all probability, tried and executed for collaborating with the Nazis.

8. Dannen, "How Terrible Is Ivan?," 136.

9. Herbert Romerstein, "The Soviet Role in the Demjanjuk Case," Human Events, April 4, 1992, 12, at 14.

10. (New York: no publisher or date given). According to a note by the author (p. 30), an earlier edition was published in 1973, but no copy of that edition could be located. The 1976 edition did not mention Demjanjuk.

11. Willem A. Wagenaar, Identifying Ivan: A Case Study in Legal Psychology (Cambridge, MA: Harvard University Press, 1988), 96. This account relies heavily on Wagenaar's book, which is the most comprehensive analysis of the use of photos in Demjanjuk's case, as well as the leading treatise on photo displays. Wagenaar testified as an expert witness for the defense at Demjanjuk's trial in Israel, but his book is not a brief for either side. Rather it is a survey of the pitfalls of photo identifications, illustrated primarily with material from the Demjanjuk investigation. For a defense of eyewitness testimony in Nazi expulsion cases, based primarily on the inchoate nature of federal court standards, see Debra H. Nesselson and Steven Lubet, "Eyewitness Identification in War Crimes Trials," 2 Cardozo L. Rev. 71 (1980), and Steven Lubet and Jan Stern Reed, "Extradition of Nazis from the United States to Israel: A Survey of Issues in Transnational Criminal Law," 22 Stan. J. Int'l L. 1, 11–17 (1986).

12. In addition, the INS interviewed twelve Sobibor survivors living in the United States, but none could (or would) identify Demjanjuk. Gitta Sereny, "John Demjanjuk and the Failure of Justice," New York Review of Books, Oct. 8, 1992, at 32.

13. According to a memorandum prepared for the defense in 1981, eighteen survivors could not identify Demjanjuk from the Trawniki card, as opposed to fifteen who claimed they could. Waagenar, at 141. Twenty-one could not identify him from the immigration picture, as opposed to eight who thought they could. Id. at 123. As evidence, however, these failed identifications meant nothing; only the positive identifications counted.

14. United States v. Fedorenko, 455 F. Supp. 893, 900 (S.D.Fla. 1978).

15. Id. at 906.

16. Id.

17. Id. at 907.

18. Id. at 908.

19. Ruth Marcus, " Storm Behind the Nazi Case," National Law Journal, Oct. 27, 1980, 1, 8.

20. Yoram Sheftel, Defending "Ivan the Terrible": The Conspiracy to Convict John Demjanjuk (Haim Watzman, trans.; Washington, D.C.: Regnery Publishing, 1996), at 387–88.

21. United States v. Fedorenko, 597 F. 2d 946 (5th Cir. 1979).

22. 449 U.S. 490 (1981). Fedorenko was deported to the Soviet Union, where he pleaded guilty to treason (for going over to the German side) and to taking part in punitive actions and mass executions of citizens of many countries. He was sentenced to death and executed by a firing squad. Serge Schmemann, "Soviet Dooms War Criminal Who was Deported by U.S.," New York Times, June 20, 1986, A2.

23. United States v. Walus, 453 F. Supp. 699, 704, 710–15 (N.D.Ill. 1978).

24. United States v. Walus, 616 F. 2d 283, 295 (7th Cir. 1980).

25. Id. at 286.

26. Id. at 303–04.

27. Id., at 297.

28. Id. at 299.

29. Id. at 297–99.

30. Id. at 302, 287.

31. Id. at 295, 304. The accusation against Walus apparently came from a disgruntled tenant and was pressed publicly by Simon Wiesenthal. Charles Ashman and Robert J. Wagman, The Nazi Hunters (New York: Pharos Books, 1988), at 193, 196.

32. See Flora Johnson, "The Persecution of Frank Walus," The Student Lawyer, May 1981, 21, 51. For similar abuses in an action to revoke citizenship, see United States v. Kungys, 571 F. Supp. 1104 (1983).

33. Ryan, Quiet Neighbors, 217.

34. 455 F. Supp. at 908 (Epstein). For their testimony against Demjanjuk, see Ryan, Quiet Neighbors, 114–31.

35. Prior to 1978, the Justice Department had a policy of distrusting Soviet evidence and forbade interviews with potential Soviet witnesses. Howard Blum, "New Actions on Alleged Nazi War Criminals Expected," New York Times, June 17, 1978, at 6.

36. The defense attacked the card as a forgery, and it was not until the trial in Israel that it was subjected to forensic analysis.

37. The two camps were about one hundred miles apart.

38. Sereny, "John Demjanjuk and the Failure of Justice," 32.

39. See Gitta Sereny, Into That Darkness: From Mercy Killing to Mass Murder (New York: McGraw-Hill, 1974) (based on extensive interviews with former camp officials and survivors); Alexander Donat, ed., The Death Camp Treblinka (New York: Holocaust Library, 1979) (republishing eyewitness accounts); and Martin Gilbert, Final Journey: The Fate of the Jews in Nazi Europe (New York: Mayflower Books, 1979) (a chapter-length account, with special attention to cruelties). Nor does the appellation "Ivan the Terrible" appear in records of the Dusseldorf trials of 1964 and 1965. See Donat at 295–316, reproducing relevant excerpts from the findings of the German courts that convicted a number of former Nazis for their role at Treblinka. That Ivan was terrible is beyond doubt, but that he was a central figure in the camp—as the label implies—is

not born out by any accounts published before OSI moved against Demjanjuk. It would appear that Ivan was elevated to super war criminal status primarily through the media efforts of OSI.

40. Horn was tried in Dusseldorf in 1964–1965 and acquitted. Donat, The Death Camp Treblinka, 278.

41. United States v. Demjanjuk, 518 F. Supp. 1362, 1370, 1372 (N.D.Ohio, 1981), aff'd 680 F. 2d 32 (6th Cir. 1982), cert. denied, 459 U.S. 1036 (1982).

42. Karl Linnas was also deported to the Soviet Union, where he had already been sentenced to death, *in absentia*, in 1962, for supervising a concentration camp in Estonia. However, he died before he could be executed. Kenneth B. Noble, "U.S. Deports Man Condemned to Die by Soviet Union," New York Times, April 21, 1987, A1. Bill Keller, "Estonian Sent to Face Death in Soviet Dies in a Hospital," New York Times, July 3, 1987, A2.

43. In re Demjanjuk, I.& N. Dec. File A8–237–417 (Cleveland) (B.I.A. Feb. 14, 1985), *aff'd* United States v. Demjanjuk, 767 F. 2d 922 (6th Cir.), cert. denied, 474 U.S. 1034 (1985).

44. Sereny, "John Demjanjuk and the Failure of Justice," 32.

45. Quoted by U.S. Supreme Court Justice Robert Jackson in his Opening Statement for the United States of America at Nurenberg, 2 Trial of the Major War Criminals Before the International Military Tribunal 98, 137–38 (1947). Bohdan Wytwycky, The Other Holocaust (Washington, D.C.: Novak Report on New Ethnicity, 1980), at 70–76, estimates that approximately half of the 5–6 million Soviet POWs perished during captivity.

46. Dannen, "How Terrible Is Ivan?" 179. Accord: United States v. Fedorenko, 455 F. Supp. at 912–14, United States v. Kowalchuk, 773 F. 2d 448, 513 (3d Cir. 1985) (Aldisert, C. J., dissenting). See also Abbe L. Dienstag, "Fedorenko v. United States: War Crimes, the Defense of Duress, and American Nationality Law," 82 Colum. L. Rev. 120 (1982).

47. See cases cited in Dienstag, "Fedoreko v. United States: War Crimes, the Defense of Duress," 137–38, notes 62 and 64.

48. Id. at 139.

49. Section 2.09(1) (Proposed Official Draft 1962). According to Dienstag, "Fedoreko v. United States: War Crimes, the Defense of Duress," eight American states now follow the Model Penal Code's approach.

50. Id. The weight of scholarly opinion favors the Model Penal Code approach. Dienstag, "Fedoreko v. United States: War Crimes, the Defense of Duress," 142, n. 72.

51. 455 F. Supp. at 913.

52. Id.

53. According to Hobbes, "Where a man is captive, or in the power of the enemy, . . . if it be without his own fault, the Obligation of the Law ceaseth; because he must obey the enemy, or dye; and consequently such obedience is no Crime; for no man is obliged (when the protection of the Law faileth), not to protect himself, by the best means he can." Leviathan (1651; W.G.P. Smith, ed.; Oxford: Clarendon Press, 1909), 232.

54. 455 F. Supp. at 913.

55. Fedorenko v. United States, 449 U.S. 490 (1981).

56. Teicholz, Ivan the Terrible, at 72–73.

57. Pal v. Attorney General, 6 Piskei Din 498 (Isr. 1951); Attorney General v. Tarnek, 5 Pesakim Mehoziim 142 (Isr.Dist.Ct. 1952); Attorney General v. Enigster, 5 Pesakim Mehoziim 152 (Isr.Dist.Ct. 1952); and Honigman v. Attorney General, 7 Piskei Din 296 (Isr. 1953).

58. Fedorenko v. United States, 455 F. Supp. at 912–14.

59. On the capacity of "outsiders" to second-guess the moral choices of "insiders" trapped *in extremis*, see Lon Fuller, "The Case of the Speluncean Explorers," 62 Harv. L. Rev. 616 (1949), and

the British case of Regina v. Dudley and Stephens [1884] 14 Q.B.D. 273, described by A. W. Brian Simpson in Cannibalism and the Common Law (Chicago: University of Chicago Press, 1984).

60. Dannen, "How Terrible Is Ivan?" 175. See also Glenn Frankel, "War Crimes Trial Poses Questions for Israelis," Washington Post, Oct. 2, 1986, A31; "Eichmann Prosecutor Asks Israel Trial of Bishop Trifa," Chicago Sun-Times, July 7, 1983, at 36.

61. See, e.g., Fedorenko v. United States, 455 F. Supp. at 899 (threatening demonstrations at Fedorenko hearing).

62. Dannen, "How Terrible Is Ivan?" 175.

63. The Israel warrant for Demjanjuk's arrest was issued on Oct. 18; the extradition request was filed on Oct. 31, 1983.

64. 612 F. Supp. at 548.

65. Matter of Demjanjuk, 612 F. Supp. 544, 563 (N.D.Ohio 1985).

66. Id., citing, inter alia, Bingham v. Bradley, 241 U.S. 511, 516–17 (1916).

67. 603 F. Supp. at 1465, correctly citing Oteiza v. Jacobus, 136 U.S. 330, 336–37 (1890), and 18 U.S.C. secs. 3190–91 (1982). Nothing in the text of sections 3190 or 3191 supports this reading, but see cases cited in Oteiza.

68. 603 F. Supp. at 1465.

69. Matter of Demjanjuk, 612 F. Supp. 544, at 548, 552 (N.D.Ohio 1985).

70. Id. at 550. It should be recalled that this kind of blind acceptance of foreign affidavits had caused John Stuart Mill and fellow Liberals in Parliament to derail Britain's extradition treaty with France in the mid nineteenth century. See Chapter 6, supra.

71. Id. at 553 (N.D.Ohio 1985). Judge Battisti did not acknowledge precedents permitting a more rigorous burden of proof. See, e.g., Argento v. Jacobs, 176 F. Supp. 877 (N.D.Ohio, 1959), in which the extradition court permitted "proof to the contrary" to be raised by the defense to the government's claim that he was the criminal. Battisti applied the probable cause standard from cases where the risks and consequences of misidentification were far less significant— cases in which the judges had contented themselves to judge the plausibility of the government's allegations, as they appeared on paper, unrebutted. 612 F. Supp. 544, at 548, and cases cited therein. See also Lubet and Reed, "Extradition of Nazis from the United States to Israel," 15–16.

72. Dip. Cor., vol. 1, 320.

73. Matter of Demjanjuk, 612 F. Supp.at 552. Compare 455 F. Supp. at 903–04 (Epstein and Czarny).

74. 612 F. Supp. at 553.

75. Id., 554.

76. Id. at 556.

77. Nor were any Jeffersonian arguments heard that Demjanjuk, like the Hermione fugitives, had a federal constitutional right to trial by jury in an American court. That libertarian argument had long since receded into the mists of time. In any case, Congress had not yet passed a law authorizing U.S. courts to try war crimes as they would piracy.

78. 612 F. Supp. at 560–61.

79. Id. at 555, 559–63. The United States had not yet ratified the United Nations Convention on the Prevention and Punishment of the Crime of Genocide, 78 U.N.T.S. 277 (opened for signature Dec. 9, 1948; entered into force for the United States Feb. 23, 1989).

80. 612 F. Supp. at 661–62.

81. Id. at 570.

82. Id., citing Eain v. Wilkes, 641 F. 2d at 521, and Ornelas v. Ruiz, 161 U.S. at 511.

83. 612 F. Supp. at 570, quoting Matter of Doherty, 599 F. Supp. 270, 274 (S.D.N.Y. 1984). Battisti did not acknowledge it, but Judge Sprizzo's opinion in Doherty also declared that the "atrocities at Dachau, Auschwitz and other death camps" should not be considered protected political offenses. 599 F. Supp. at 274.

84. Id.

85. Abu Eain v. Wilkes, 641 F. 2d 504, 522 (7th Cir.), cert. denied, 454 U.S. 894 (1981).

86. Quinn v. Robinson, 783 F. 2d 776, 798–801 (9th Cir. 1984).

87. Although Israel had requested Demjanjuk's extradition in Oct. 1983, the judge allowed him to remain free on bail until April 1985. Then he was arrested, jailed briefly in Cleveland, and eventually transferred, like Artuković, to the federal prison hospital in Missouri, where he would be far from family and attorneys.

88. Demjanjuk v. Petrovsky, 612 F. Supp. 571 (N.D.Ohio 1985).

89. Id. at 574–76, 578.

90. Id. at 576.

91. Id. at 577.

92. United States v. Demjanjuk, 767 F. 2d 922 (6th Cir. 1985) (without opinion).

Chapter Nineteen

Epigraph: Demjanjuk v. Petrovsky, 10 F. 3d 338, 354 (1993).

1. Tom Teicholz, Ivan the Terrible (New York, St. Martin's Press, 1990), at 78.

2. The former auto worker was not indicted until Oct. 18, 1986. His plea was not heard until Nov. 26, and the trial did not begin until Feb. 16, 1987.

3. 4 Laws of the State of Israel, no. 64, at 154 (1950), 57 Sefer Hahukim 281 (1950).

4. For the show-trial aspect of this case, as experienced by Demjanjuk's defense counsel, see Yoram Sheftel, Defending "Ivan the Terrible": The Conspiracy to Convict John Demjanjuk (Haim Watzman, trans.; Washington, D.C.: Regnery Publishing, 1996).

5. United States v. Fedorenko, 455 F. Supp. 893, 908 (S.D.Fla. 1978).

6. Teicholz, Ivan the Terrible, 114–15. Thus, while Judge Battisti had specifically refused to extradite Demjanjuk on charges of malicious manslaughter, the Israeli court allowed evidence of malicious maiming to be used against him.

7. Id. at 121.

8. Id. at 117.

9. Id. at 150–59. At trial, Boraks, then eighty-six years old, could not remember how he had gotten to Florida to testify in the Fedorenko case. First he said he had taken a train from Haifa; later he claimed to have flown there from different cities in Poland, where he thought, mistakenly, he had lived since 1978. Sheftel, Defending "Ivan the Terrible," 60. Czarny's testimony against Fedorenko had also been found not credible by Judge Roettger.

10. Id. at 126, 125.

11. Id. at 128.

12. Id.

13. Id. at 270.

14. Id. In 1978, Rosenberg had failed to identify Demjanjuk as a Treblinka guard. In 1951 he was unsure whether Demjanjuk was at Treblinka, but in 1981, testifying in Cleveland, he was certain. Sheftel, Defending "Ivan the Terrible," 57. At trial, however, he misidentified Ivan's assistant, Nikolai Shalayev. Id., 54.

15. Id., 109.

16. Dannen, "How Terrible Is Ivan?" Vanity Fair, June 1992, 132ff, 176. In May 1987 the Demjanjuk family fired O'Connor and the defense was taken over by John Gill, a Cleveland lawyer. Id., 177.

17. Cambridge: Harvard University Press, 1988.

18. Id., 123.

19. Id., 109–10.

20. See Teicholz, Ivan the Terrible, especially at 44, 46, 83, 198, 199–222, 225, 227–28. See also Michele Leslie and Bill Sloat, "The Devil Knows Where," Cleveland Plain Dealer, Nov. 13, 1994, Special Supplement, 47 pp.

21. Teichholz at 68, 166–68, 182, 190, 240–41, 248, 250, 267–68, 279, 290.

22. Sheftel, 395.

23. The Demjanuk Trial [Israel v/ Demjanjuk, Crim. Cas. (Jerusalem) 373/86] (Tel Aviv: Israel Bar Publishing House, undated).

24. Dannen, "How Terrible Is Ivan?," 177–78.

25. Id., 178.

26. Portions of the confession are reproduced in Sheftel, Defending "Ivan the Terrible," 378–79. Shalayev's name is sometimes rendered Shelaiev in English.

27. Id., 379.

28. Dannen, "How Terrible Is Ivan?" 178.

29. Sheftel, Defending "Ivan the Terrible," quoting the confession, 379.

30. See Dannen, "How Terrible Is Ivan?" 134, for the two photographs.

31. Sheftel, Defending "Ivan the Terrible," 372–73.

32. Demjanjuk had once listed Sobibor as a place he had spent part of the war, later explaining that he had picked the name randomly off a map and meant to write Sambor. Dannen, "How Terrible Is Ivan?" 179. However, Sobibor was so obscure that it was not marked on any prewar maps. Gitta Sereny, "John Demjanjuk and the Failure of Justice," New York Review of Books, Oct. 8, 1992, 33 (quoting the Israeli trial judges).

33. Demjanjuk v. Petrovsky, 10 F. 3rd 338, App. 4A at 366 (6th Cir. 1993).

34. Sereny, "John Demjanjuk and the Failure of Justice," 33.

35. Id.

36. Clyde Haberman, "Prosecutor Answers Doubts on Identity of 'Ivan the Terrible,'" New York Times, June 9, 1992, A6.

37. Id. The rule is set forth in art. 12 of the U.S.-Israeli Extradition Treaty.

38. Order, Demjanjuk v. Petrovsky, no. 85-3435 (6th Cir. June 5, 1992).

39. E.g., Daniel Williams, "KGB Evidence Reopens the Case of 'Ivan the Terrible,'" Los Angeles Times, Dec. 21, 1991, A1; Clyde Haberman, "As the Doubts Grow, 'Ivan' Loses His Fascination," New York Times, Jan. 16, 1992, A7.

40. Interview with John H. Broadley, Esq., June 16, 1992.

41. Nor were they mentioned in Ryan's account of the Demjanjuk case, Quiet Neighbors: Prosecuting Nazi War Criminals in America (San Diego: Harcourt Brace Jovanovich, 1984).

42. Teicholz, The Trial of Ivan the Terrible, 278.

43. Id., 278–79.

44. On April 30, 1986, an article alleging that "The Vampire Lives in Cleveland" appeared in the Communist Party magazine Molod Ukrainy (Youth of the Ukraine). It showed both sides of the Trawniki card and was identical to the copy given to the Justice Department in 1976, with two exceptions. A photograph of someone—not Demjanjuk—appeared on the reverse

side in a formerly blank space. The new photograph was one of six used by Soviet investigators in 1980 in a new effort to find witnesses who could identify Demjanjuk.

In 1981 the Soviet government supplied a summary of this investigation to the U.S. Justice Department. It included photos of six men, along with three photos that the Soviets said were Demjanjuk. According to the summary, the six men, including the one whose photo had been added to the magazine's version of the card, "have no relation to the case." Robert Gillette, "Soviets Offer Different Demjanjuk Accusation," Los Angeles Times, Feb. 15, 1987, 1, 20, 21.

Why someone, presumably within the KGB, would go to the trouble of altering the original card after a copy had already been sent to the Justice Department has never been made clear, but the forgery strengthened arguments that Soviet evidence was not to be trusted.

45. Memorandum to Arthur Sinai, Deputy Director, OSI, from Bernard J. Dougherty Jr., Criminal Investigator, Subj: Horn, Otto—Report of Interview, Ref: OSI #42—Demjanjuk, Iwan, Received Nov. 20, 1979, Office of Special Investigations. Reproduced in Demjanjuk v. Petrovsky, no. 85-3435 (6th Cir. Nov. 17, 1993) (slip opinion), App. 5, at 69.

46. Memorandum to Arthur Sinai, Deputy Director, OSI, from George W. Garand, Historian, Subj: Horn, Otto—Report of Interview, Ref: OSI #42, Demjanjuk, Iwan, Received, Nov. 27, 1979, Office of Special Investigations. Reproduced in Demjanjuk v. Petrovsky, no. 85-3435 (6th Cir. Nov. 17, 1993) (slip opinion), App. 6, at 72.

47. Trial Transcript at 316, 324.

48. The copies were found in the trash in June 1987, while the Freedom of Information Act request was still pending. The originals were recovered by the Demjanjuk family in May 1989 from forty boxes of OSI trash that had been discarded while the document request was pending. The Dougherty and Garand reports were never offered to the defense; nor were they listed in any of the indexes of withheld documents that OSI was required by law to prepare (called "Vaughn indexes"). Interview with John Broadley, June 11, 1992. Ryan, Quiet Neighbors, 113, claims, contrary to the Dougherty and Garand reports, that Horn identified the pictures of Demjanjuk in both sets as Ivan, and that the first set was "taken away" before the second one was shown to him. Dougherty admitted on July 2, 1986, that the affidavit he signed for Israeli prosecutors in May 1986 was false, because by that time he no longer recalled the photo spread with Otto Horn. Sheftel, Defending "Ivan the Terrible," 324.

49. Letter from Michael E. Shaheen Jr., Counsel, Office of Professional Reponsibility, to Rep. James A. Traficant Jr., July 25, 1990. Affirmed by Department of Justice Press Release, June 12, 1992. See also "Barr Defends Nazi Hunters as 'Ivan' Case Deepens," Cleveland Plain Dealer, June 18, 1992, 9.

50. Robert Gillette, "Soviets Offer Different Demjanjuk Accusation," Los Angeles Times, Feb. 15, 1987, 1, 20, at 21.

51. Department of State Telegram, from American Embassy, Moscow, to Secretary of State, Washington, DC, AN: 0780366-0356, Subj: Judicial Assistance, War Crimes Case of Feodor Fedorenko, Aug. 1978 (marked "for Martin Mendelson," an SLU attorney). Leleko's name is sometimes spelled Lyeleko and Lyleko in these documents.

52. From Department of State Telegram to U.S. Embassy, Warsaw, Poland, AN: D8110354-1069, Subj: Judicial Assistance: War Crimes Investigations (OSI: 146-2-47-87), July 1981, Attachment H.

53. Department of Justice Press Release, June 12, 1992 (by Assistant Attorney General Robert S. Mueller 3d) at 3. This admission would seem to contradict Ryan's account (Quiet Neighbors, 106), which implies that OSI did not have any Soviet reports until it received a photocopy of the Trawniki card in Jan. 1980.

54. The summary indicates that by July 1981 the Department was in possession of two state-ments by Vasylyenko, given to the KGB on March 6 and Sept. 19, 1961, respectively, identify-ing Marchenko as Treblinka's Ivan, and three KGB reports on Pavel Leleko dated Nov. 18, 1944, and Feb. 21, 1945, identifying Marchenko as "the motor mechanic of the gas chamber." The atrocities described in these reports were very similar to those described by Jewish sur-vivors of the camps.

55. From Department of State Telegram to U.S. Embassy, Warsaw, Poland, AN: D8110354-1069, Subj: Judicial Assistance: War Crimes Investigations (OSI: 146-2-47-87), July 1981, Attach-ment H. It was later learned that the Polish War Crimes Commission had notified OSI in 1979 that it had identified forty-three of the approximately one hundred Ukrainian guards at Tre-blinka. Ivan Demjanjuk was not among them but Ivan Marchenko was. Letter from Rep. James A. Traficant Jr. to U.S. Attorney General Richard Thornburgh, Feb. 27, 1990, at 1.

56. Statements of Leleko, Shevchenko, Vasylyenko, and Nikolai Kulak. In the course of the FOIA suit, OSI also claimed that it had no reports of its interviews with Richard Glazar, a Treblinka survivor who, according to State Department cables, had been brought to Alexandria, Virginia, from Switzerland by the OSI for questioning. Nor could OSI find any reports on its interviews with Franz Suchonel, an SS officer at the camp, or Kurt Franz, the camp's deputy commandant. Letter from Michael E. Shaheen Jr., Counsel, Office of Professional Responsibility, U.S. Department of Justice, to Rep. James A. Traficant Jr., U.S. House of Representatives, July 25, 1990.

57. Michele Leslie and Bill Sloat, "The Devil Knows Where," Cleveland Plain Dealer, Nov. 13, 1994, Special Supplement, at 38. See also Sheftel, Defending "Ivan the Terrible," 340.

58. In taking this courageous stand, Merritt may have made it impossible for President Clin-ton to nominate him for Justice Blackmun's seat on the Supreme Court. Alan M. Dershowitz, The Abuse Excuse (Boston: Little Brown, 1994), 170.

59. Alan M. Dershowitz has criticized the decision to reopen Demjanjuk's extradition case as high-handed and has argued that the Court of Appeals should have assigned Judge Battisti—the judge who had wrongly cleared Demjanjuk for extradition—to serve as the special master. Dershowitz does not address the evidence of OSI's fraud. Id., 165–70.

60. Haberman, "Prosecutors Answer Doubts on Identity of 'Ivan the Terrible,'" A6.

61. U.S.-Israel Extradition Treaty, art. 13, 14 U.S.T. 1707, 1712–13 (signed Dec. 10, 1962; entered into force Dec. 5, 1963.) (expressly allowing the U.S. government to waive the rule of specialty).

62. Report of the Special Master, Demjanjuk v. Petrovsky, no. 85-3435 (6th Cir. June 30, 1993), at 193. Available through the Library of Congress.

63. Id., 182–95.

64. Id., 195–96.

65. Chris Hedges, "Israeli Court Sets Demjanjuk Free, but He Is Now Without a Country," New York Times, July 30, 1993, A1. See also Sheftel, "Defending "Ivan the Terrible," chs. 13–17.

66. Alex Kozinski, "The Case of Ivan Demjanjuk: Sanhedrin II," The New Republic, Sept. 13, 1993, 16, 18.

67. Chris Hedges, "Israel Recommends That Demjanjuk Be Released," New York Times, Aug. 12, 1993, A15.

68. Id. at 18.

69. Stephen Labaton, "U.S. Vows to Close the Doors to Demjanjuk," New York Times, July 30, 1993, A8. In a brief filed with the Sixth Circuit Court of Appeals a year earlier, OSI contin-ued to insist that Demjanjuk was Ivan, even though it admitted to having not reviewed thou-sands of pages of documents obtained by the Israelis from the former Soviet Union. David John-ston, "U.S. Stands by Actions It Took in Case of 'Ivan,'" New York Times, July 17, 1992, A18.

70. Stephen Labaton, "Justice Dept. Is Pressing U.S. Court to Keep Demjanjuk Out," New York Times, Aug. 19, 1993, A8.

71. Id.

72. Stephen Labaton, "An Appeals Court States Demjanjuk Can Return to the U.S.," New York Times, Aug. 4, 1993, A1, A6.

73. Id., A6 ("irritation"), and Labaton, Aug. 19, 1993, A8 (anger).

74. Stephen Labaton, "U.S., in Reversal, Says Demjanjuk Can Return," New York Times, Sept. 2, 1993, A6.

75. Demjanjuk v. Petrovsky, 10 F. 3d 338, 354 (6th Cir. 1993).

76. Id. at 350.

77. Id. at 355.

78. E.g., see Theodore Lowi's warning that pluralist politics tends to make conflict of interest a principle of government. The End of Liberalism (2d ed.; New York: Norton, 1979), ch. 3.

79. Conversely, those U.S. prosecutors relied to their embarrassment on sloppy eyewitness identifications carried out by the Israeli police.

80. Stephen Labaton, "Return of U.S. Citizenship Sought in Nazi Guard Case," New York Times, Sept. 4, 1993, 6.

Chapter Twenty

Epigraph: "The Democratic Character of Judicial Review," 66 Harv. L. Rev. 193, 207 (1952).

1. Mapp v. Ohio, 367 U.S. 643 (1961). American courts will also refuse to accept jurisdiction over property that has been obtained by fraud or force, Copas v. Provision Co., 73 Mich. 541 (1889); Van Donselaar v. Jones, 195 Iowa 1081 (1923); Abel v. Smith, 151 Va. 568 (1928). See also the opinion of Attorney General Roger Taney denying that U.S. courts should have jurisdiction to condemn jewels stolen from the Princess of Orange, 2 Op. Atty. Gen. 482, 484 (1831). Jurisdiction will also be denied over ships that have been seized in violation of treaties. United States v. Cook, 288 U.S. 102 (1933); Ford v. United States, 273 U.S. 593 (1927).

2. United States v. Alvarez-Machain, 504 U.S. 655 (1992).

3. Nor is it likely that Congress would ever pass a long-arm, strong-arm statute authorizing abductions in foreign countries.

4. United States v. Toscanino, 500 F. 2d 267 (2d Cir.), rehearing denied, 504 F. 2d 1380 (2d Cir. 1974), motion to dismiss denied on remand, 398 F. Supp. 916 (E.D.N.Y. 1975). But see United States *ex. rel.* Lujan v. Gengler, 510 F. 2d 62 (2d Cir. 1975), cert. denied, 421 U.S. 1001 (1976) (no violation of due process because defendant was not subjected to torture, terror, or custodial interrogation).

5. United States v. Lovato, 550 F. 2d 1270, 1271 (9th Cir.) (*per curiam*), cert. denied, 423 U.S. 985 (1975) (the Ker-Frisbie rule of noninquiry is applicable unless defendant "makes a strong showing of grossly cruel and unusual barbarities inflicted ... by paid agents of the United States"); United States v. Lira, 515 F. 2d 68 (2d Cir.), cert. denied, 423 U.S. 847 (1975) (jurisdiction accepted because alleged torture was by Chilean police only, even though defendant alleged that a U.S. agent was present when torture occurred); United States v. Lara, 539 F. 2d 495 (5th Cir. 1976) (jurisdiction accepted because defendant failed to show that U.S. agents played a "direct role" in torture administered by Panamanian authorities); United States v. Reed, 639 F. 2d 896 (2d Cir. 1981) (court not shocked by the holding of a cocked revolver to the head of a securities and mail fraud suspect lured onto a private plane by CIA agents); United States

v. Degollado, 696 F. Supp. 1136 (S.D.Tex. 1988) (jurisdiction accepted where U.S. agents witnessed the injection of hot chili oil and seltzer up the victim's nostrils but left the room when the treatment got "rough"); Matta-Ballesteros v. Henman, 896 F. 2d 255 (7th Cir.), cert. denied, 498 U.S. 878 (1990) (jurisdiction allowed where prison doctor's report confirmed multiple burns from stun gun).

6. Lawrence Preuss, "Kidnaping of Fugitives from Justice on Foreign Territory," 29 Am. J. Int'l L. 502–507 (1935).

7. 119 U.S. 436 (1886).

8. Louis Henkin, "A Decent Respect for the Opinions of Mankind," 25 J. Marsh. L. Rev. 208, 231 (1992).

9. E.g., see the Civil Rights Cases, 109 U.S. 3 (1883) (holding that Congress lacked the power, under the Thirteenth or Fourteenth Amendments, to ban racial discrimination in public accommodations); Chae Chan Ping v. United States, 13 U.S. 581 (1887) (upholding discriminatory immigration policies against the Chinese); and Plessy v. Ferguson, 163 U.S. 537 (1896) (upholding racial segregation on common carriers).

10. The Court's opinion in Ker v. Illinois was written by Justice Miller, who had also produced narrow interpretations of due process in the Slaughterhouse Cases, 83 U.S. (16 Wall.) 36 (1873) and Davidson v. New Orleans, 96 U.S. 97 (1877).

11. See generally Note, "Illegal Abductions by State Police: Sanctions for Evasions of Extradition Statutes," 61 Yale L. J. 445 (1952), and Note, "Interstate Rendition Violations and Section 1983: Locating the Federal Rights of Fugitives," 50 Fordham L. Rev. 1268 (1982).

12. 342 U.S. 519 (1952).

13. E.g., see the decision of the Reagan administration to withdraw U.S. submission to the International Court of Justice when Nicaragua sued it for the covert mining of harbors in support of the rebel *contras*, discussed in Editorial Comment, "*Nicaragua v. United States:* Jurisdiction and Admissibility," 79 Am. J. Int'l L. 373 (1985).

14. E.g., the covert war against Nicaragua in the early 1980s, the invasion of Grenada (1983), the bombing of Libya (1986), and the invasion of Panama (1989).

15. E.g., see Harold Hongju Koh, "'The Haitian Paradigm' in United States Human Rights Policy," 103 Yale L. J. 2391 (1994).

16. The approach, common in the late nineteenth century, was criticized by Roscoe Pound, "Mechanical Jurisprudence," 8 Colum. L. Rev. 605 (1908). It fell into disfavor under the Warren Court but subsequently made a comeback.

17. State v. Brewster, 7 Vt. 48 (col. 117) (1835).

18. Id. at 49 (col. 120).

19. Ex parte Susannah Scott [1829] 9 B&C 446; 109 Eng. Rep. 166.

20. Id., 9 B&C at 448.

21. Id. Compare The Ship Richmond v. United States, 13 U.S. (9 Cranch.) 102, 103 (1815) ("the seizure of an American vessel within the territorial jurisdiction of a foreign power is certainly an offense against that power, which must be adjusted between the two governments. This court can take no cognizance of it."

22. They accepted extradition under the positive law of the United States, not some vague principle of international comity or international moral principle. But the positive law of American extradition treaties was subject to the higher positive law of the U.S. Constitution, which was often interpreted broadly in the Protestant natural rights tradition.

23. Chapter 1, *supra*.

24. Albert Z. Carr, The Coming of War (New York: Doubleday, 1960), 290.

25. See Chapter 5, *supra*.

26. See generally Brief of the Government of Canada as *Amicus Curiae* in Support of Respondent, no. 91-712, United States v. Alvarez-Machain, 504 U.S. 655 (1992). The lapses, one on each side, were R. v. Walton [1905] 11 Ont.L.R. 94, 10 C.C.C. 269, and United States v. Unverzagt, 299 F. 1015 (W.D.Wash. 1924), aff'd *sub nom.* Unverzagt v. Benn, 5 F. 2d 492 (9th Cir.), cert. denied, 269 U.S. 56 (1925). In neither case, apparently, was there a diplomatic protest. Typically, when the United States has protested a Canadian abduction, the Canadians have stayed the criminal proceedings and sent the prisoner back. This occurred as early as 1841, even before extradition provided an alternative to abduction, when the Canadians returned one Grogan who had been abducted from the United States by British soldiers. J. B. Moore, Extradition (1891), vol. 1, sec. 191. ch. 7, p. 281 et. seq. See also secs. 192, 196. In 1876, Canadian authorities subdued a convict in Alaska. Secretary of State Fish protested and Canada released the individual. Reported by Abraham D. Sofaer, Hearing Before the Subcommittee on Civil and Constitutional Rights, Committee on the Judiciary, U.S. House of Representatives, 101st Cong., 1st sess., 1989, at 32. The Canadians also returned a fifteen-year-old boy who had been kidnapped or enticed across the border, even though he had been convicted and sentenced to a reformatory. J. B. Moore, Digest, vol. 4, at 330 (1906).

27. For the Canadian counterparts to Ker, see R. v. Walton [1905] 11 Ont.L.R. 94, 10 C.C.C. 269 and In re Hartnett & the Queen [1973] 1 O.R.(2d) 206.

28. Quoted by Abraham D. Sofaer, Hearings Before the Subcommittee on Civil and Constitutional Rights, Committee on the Judiciary, 101st Cong., 1st sess. (1989), at 32. For example, a U.S. protest obtained the return of Adelard Lafond, who had been kidnapped from the United States to Canada in 1908, and in 1974 a diplomatic protest from Canada was sufficient to cause the United States to give up a U.S. Army deserter who had been chased across the border and captured by American officials. C. Cole, "Extradition Treaties Abound but Unlawful Seizures Continue," Int'l Perspectives 40–42 (Can. Dept. of Ext. Aff. March–April 1975). The Doctrine of "hot pursuit," applicable at sea, does not apply to cross-border chases. Id.

29. In April 1991, the Bush administration took the position that return of a criminal defendant who has been abducted from Canada is not an appropriate remedy. U.S. Embassy Note no. 94, April 8, 1991. Canada disagreed, reaffirming its understanding that the extradition treaty "established the only means under which to obtain the return of fugitive offenders," Dept. of External Affairs Note no. JLAC-0734, April 24, 1991. Canada also informed the U.S. Supreme Court in the *Alvarez* case that the Bush administration had improperly claimed the right to abrogate the extradition treaty on a case-by-case basis. Brief of the Government of Canada as *Amicus Curiae* in Support of Respondent at 12–13, United States v. Alvarez-Machain, 504 U.S. 655 (1992).

30. See generally Andor Klay, Daring Diplomacy: The Case of the First American Ultimatum (Minneapolis: University of Minnesota Press, 1957).

31. Id., 27.

32. Id., 76–97.

33. Marcy to Ambassador Hulsemann, Sept. 26, 1853, Sen. Docs., 33rd Cong., 1st sess., vol. 1, 34.

34. Klay, Daring Diplomacy, 180–81.

35. See generally Norman B. Ferris, The Trent Affair: A Diplomatic Crisis (Knoxville: University of Tennessee Press, 1977).

36. E.g., see the protests that followed the abduction of Walter Linse from the American sector of West Berlin in 1952. New York Times: July 9, 1952, 1; July 16, 1952, 9; Aug. 7, 1952, 6; Aug.

28, 1952, 4;;Sept. 7, 1952, 23, Sept. 10, 1952, 1; Sept. 20, 1952, 1; Nov. 14, 1952, 1; Nov. 16, 1952, 20; Dec. 11, 1952, 8; Jan. 17, 1953, 4; March 13, 1953, 4; April 15, 1954, 6; June 9, 1960, 8.

37. As the State Department put it at the time, "the Government of the United States cannot permit the exercise within the United States of the police power of any foreign government." 19 Dept. of State Bull. 251 (1948) (regarding the refusal of two Russian teachers to return to the Soviet Union).

38. See Chapter 16, *supra.*

39. Chapter 4, *supra.*

40. Those to which the United States is a party include the International Covenant on Civil and Political Rights (ICCPR) (art. 9), G.A. Res. 2200 A (21), Dec. 16, 1966 (guaranteeing an undefined right to liberty and freedom of person for citizens and aliens), and the Inter-American Convention on Human Rights (art. 7), O.A.S. Official Records Serv. 16/1.1 Doc. 65, Corr. 1 (Jan. 7, 1970). In 1991, the U.N. Human Rights Committee ruled that Ecuador had violated art. 9 of the ICCPR by participating in the kidnapping of a person wanted for drug offenses in the United States. Canon Garcia v. Ecuador, Decision of 5/11/91, U.N. Doc. CCPR/C/43/D/319 (1988). Various provisions in the United Nations Charter, including arts. 1(3), 13(1)(b), 55(c), and 62(2) attempt to guarantee universal respect for human rights and fundamental freedoms. The U.N. Declaration of Human Rights attempts to guarantee "the right to life, liberty, and security of persons." G.A. Res. 217A (3), U.N. Doc. A/810 (Dec. 10, 1948). A similar provision is in art. 3 of the U.N. Charter. Art. 5 of the European Convention on Human Rights and art. 6 of the African Charter on Human and People's Rights contain similar protections, which of course are not binding on the United States.

41. E.g., in United States *ex rel.* Lujan v. Gengler, a Second Circuit panel held that the U.N. and O.A.S. charters only protect states and that, in the absence of an objection from a foreign state which is a party to them, no abductee can challenge a U.S. court's jurisdiction to try him. 510 F. 2d 62, 67 (2d Cir.), cert. denied, 421 U.S. 1001 (1975).

42. John S. Bassett, The Life of Andrew Jackson (Garden City: Doubleday, Page, 1911), 234–38.

43. Joseph A. Opala, A Brief History of the Seminole Freedmen (Austin: Univ. of Texas African and African American Studies and Research Center, 1980), 8.

44. Prigg v. Pennsylvania, 41 U.S. (16 Pet.) 539 (1842).

45. Art. 4, sec. 2, cl. 3: "No Person held to Service or Labour in one State, under the Laws thereof, escaping into another, shall, in Consequence of any Law or Regulation therein, be discharged from such Service or labour, but shall be delivered up on Claim of the Party to whom such Service or Labour may be due."

46. Had Margaret Morgan been represented by counsel, she could have advanced a strong claim to not being a "fugitive," having been allowed by her master to marry a free black, live on her master's property as a free person, and move with her free husband to Pennsylvania, where slavery was illegal. See Paul Finkelman, "Sorting out Prigg v. Pennsylvania," 24 Rutgers L. Rev. 605, 610–11 (1993). See also Paul Finkelman, "Story Telling on the Supreme Court: Pennsylvania and Justice Joseph Story's Judicial Nationalism," 1955 Sup. Ct. Rev. 247 (1995).

47. Morgan's husband, a free black, had initially been seized with her.

48. The justices were helped in this venture by the states of Pennsylvania and Maryland. Their attorneys framed the case as an interstate conflict, thereby guaranteeing that abolitionists would not be able to assert the rights of Morgan or her children. The one justice who recognized the danger to free blacks was John McLean. 41 U.S. at 671 (1842).

49. 41 U.S. (16 Pet.) at 625.

50. Id. at 632.

51. See Chapter 4, *supra*.

52. 509 U.S. 155 (1993).

53. U.N. Convention Relating to the Status of Refugees, art.33, (signed July 28, 1951; entered into force for the U.S. Jan. 31, 1967), 19 U.S.T. 6259, 189 U.N.T.S. 150.

54. Sec. 243h of the Immigration and Nationality Act of 1952, codified at 8 U.S.C. sec. 1253(h)(1) (1988) ("The Attorney General shall not deport or return any alien [other than an ex-Nazi] to a country if the Attorney General determines that such alien's life or freedom would be threatened in such country on account of race, religion, nationality, membership in a particular social group, or political opinion.")

55. Ruth Marcus, "In Transition Zone, Clinton's Every Word Scrutinized," Washington Post, Nov. 22, 1992, A1, A9.

56. Victoria Clauson et al., "Litigating as Law Students: An Inside Look at *Haitian Centers Council*," 103 Yale L. J. 2337 (1994).

57. 509 U.S. at 173–83.

58. Id. at 208.

59. As Richard E. Neustadt has pointed out, "The constitutional convention of 1787 is supposed to have created a government of 'separated powers.' It did nothing of the sort. Rather, it created a government of separated institutions *sharing* powers." Presidential Power (1960; New York: Wiley, 1980), 26. See also Louis Fisher, President and Congress (New York: Free Press, 1972), ch. 1.

60. United States v. Toscanino, 500 F. 2d 267, 270 (2d Cir. 1974).

61. Id.

62. Id. at 272.

63. 342 U.S. 165 (1952).

64. 500 F. 2d at 272.

65. Id. at 273, citing Mapp v. Ohio, 367 U.S. 643 (1961).

66. Id. at 274, quoting 277 U.S. at 484–85.

67. Id. at 275. Inclusion of the term "unnecessary" may imply that abductions might be tolerated if there is no other alternative. But there is always the alternative of waiting.

68. Id. at 276.

69. Id. at 277–78.

70. Two years later, in response to the undenied torture in *Toscanino*, Congress passed the "Mansfield Amendment." Responding to intense criticism of U.S. drug agents and police trainers throughout Latin America, the amendment specifically prohibited American drug agents from taking part in the arrest of foreign nationals in other countries. Pub. L. no. 94-329, 90 Stat. 764, 22 U.S.C. sec. 2291(c) (1990). In 1978, U.S. drug agents were prohibited from joining foreign police in the interrogation of Americans unless the Americans consented. Pub. L. no. 95-384, sec. 3, 92 Stat. 730 (1978). See also Andreas F. Lowenfeld, "U.S. Law Enforcement Abroad: The Constitution and International Law, Continued," 81 Am. J. Int'l L. 474, 478–80 (1990). "Internal Security Assistance and Arms Expert Control Act," Report on S2662, S. Rep. no. 605, 94th Cong., 2d sess. (1976), at 55, reprinted in 1976 U.S. Code & Admin. News (1978). During the 1980s, these restrictions were relaxed to allow American agents to assist foreign officers in drug arrests, Pub. L. no. 99-570, sec. 2009, 100 Stat. 3207–64 (Oct. 27, 1986), provided that the local U.S. head of mission consents. The measures seemed more concerned with protecting the image of the United States than with curbing abduction or torture. H. R. Rep. no. 231, 101st Cong., 1st sess. (1989), at 22, reprinted in 1989 U.S. Code & Admin. News 1404, 1425–26. All of this is of limited value, however, because most U.S. arrests can be postponed until the abducting agents

have their captive on U.S. soil, and because the ban on participation in interrogations is limited to drug investigations and does not protect foreign nationals. 22 U.S.C. sec. 2291(c)(5) (1990). Congress has not been much more eager than the courts to require drug agents to wear their constitutional leashes when operating abroad.

71. 398 F. Supp. 916 (E.D.N.Y. 1975).

72. United States *ex rel.* Lujan v. Gengler, 510 F. 2d 62 (2d Cir. 1975), cert. denied, 421 U.S. 1001 (1975).

73. E.g., United States v. Calandra, 414 U.S. 338 (1974) (permitting use of illegally obtained evidence in grand juries); United States v. Janis, 428 U.S. 433 (1976) (evidence illegally seized by a state can be used by federal government in a civil proceeding), Stone v. Powell, 428 U.S. 465 (1976) (deterrant and judicial integrity rationales outweighed by law enforcement considerations); United States v. Havens, 446 U.S. 620 (1980) (illegally obtained evidence admissible to impeach credibility when the defendant allegedly offers false testimony); United States v. Crews, 445 U.S. 463 (1980) (information obtained in course of an illegal arrest not a bar to a subsequent prosecution); United States v. Leon, 468 U.S. 897 (1984) (illegally obtained evidence admitted where officer relied, in "good faith," on a search warrant later declared invalid); Arizona v. Fulminante, 499 U.S. 279 (1991) (dicta that the Fifth Amendment and common law rule against the admission of coerced confessions might be ignored, if the error was thought to be "harmless").

74. In United States v. Toro, 840 F. 2d 1221, 1235 (5th Cir. 1986), the court recognized a defense of outrageous government conduct but held that it could not be invoked by a guilty man.

75. United States v. Cordero, 668 F. 2d 32 (1st Cir. 1982); United States v. Herrera, 504 F. 2d 859, 860 (5th Cir. 1974); United States v. Winter, 509 F. 2d 975, 986–87 (5th Cir.), cert. denied, 423 U.S. 825 (1975); Matta-Ballesteros v. Henman, 896 F. 2d 255 (7th Cir. 1990), cert. denied, 111 S.Ct. 209 (1990); United States v. Darby, 744 F. 2d 1508, 1531 (11th Cir. 1984), cert. denied, 471 U.S. 1100 (1975). Only the Ninth Circuit has endorsed Toscanino's conscience-shocking exception, and then only in theory. United States v. Valot, 625 F. 2d 308 (9th cir. 1980); United States v. Lovato, 520 F. 2d 1270 (9th Cir.), cert. denied, 423 U.S. 985 (1975).

76. 668 F. 2d 32 (1st Cir. 1981).

77. Id. at 37–38.

78. Nor did the executive claim that treaties were to be read narrowly, like contracts, without implied guarantees of just treatment. On the contrary, when critics complained that the Webster-Ashburton Treaty had failed to include an exception for political offenders, President Tyler immediately read one in. See Chapter 5, *supra.* Even where treaties have failed to specify that the decision regarding extraditability belongs to the courts, no court has ever doubted its jurisdiction. Until the 1980s, neither did the executive.

79. 668 F. 2d at 37.

80. On disguised extradition in the first six decades of the twentieth century, see Alona Evans, "Acquisition of Custody Over the International Fugitive Offender—Alternatives to Extradition, A Survey of United States Practice," 40 Brit. Y. B. Int'l L. 77 (1966).

81. The involvement of the Israeli Security Services was admitted by Prime Minister David Ben-Gurion in a letter to Israel Galili, published in the Israeli newspaper Davar on May 27, 1960. See generally Moshe Pearlman, The Capture and Trial of Adolf Eichmann (New York: Simon & Schuster, 1963), ch. 5, and Hannah Arendt, Judgment in Jerusalem (New York: Viking, 1963), 219.

82. 15 U.N. SCOR, Supp. (April-June 1960), 24–28, 30–33, 35, U.N. Docs. S/4334, S/4336 (1960), U.N. Doc. 5/4342 (1960); U.N. Doc. S/4349 (1960); "Israel, Argentina Declare Nazi Case a Closed Incident," New York Times, Aug. 4, 1960, 1, 3.

83. Yosal Rogat, The Eichmann Trial and the Rule of Law (Santa Barbara: Center for the Study of Democratic Institutions, 1961), 24.

84. Attorney General of the Government of Israel v. Eichmann (Dist.Ct. Jerusalem), 36 Int' L. Rep'ts 18, 64–65 (D. Jerusalem 1961), aff'd, 36 Int'l L. Rep'ts 277 (S.Ct. Israel 1962). By the time Eichmann was tried, Argentina's protest had been withdrawn.

85. See The Iran-Contra Affair, Report of the Congressional Investigating Committees (abridged ed.; New York: Times Books, 1988), 344–46.

86. The following account draws heavily on Antonio Cassese, Terrorism, Politics and Law: The *Achille Lauro* Affair (Princeton: Princeton University Press, 1989).

87. Robert D. McFadden, "Judge Says Ship's Bartender Saw Hijackers Kill American," New York Times, Oct. 14, 1985, A12.

88. Bob Woodward, Veil: The CIA's Secret Wars, 1981–1987 (New York: Simon & Schuster, 1987), 414–16; "You Can Run but You Can't Hide," Newsweek, Oct. 21, 1985, 22–32. North's immediate inspiration was probably Israel's successful rescue of hostages held by aircraft hijackers at the Entebbe Airport in Uganda in 1976.

89. John Prados, Presidents' Secret Wars (New York: Morrow, 1987), 390–91.

90. "Piecing Together the Drama," Time, Oct. 28, 1985, at 31.

91. The Italian government could have made a provisional arrest, in the expectation of more information, but chose not to do so, probably in the interest of compromising with the Egyptians and PLO. Abbas also carried a diplomatic passport from Iraq, but that could have been disregarded because it was under an assumed name.

92. Although the four were sentenced to long prison terms, three walked away from custody while on prison-granted leaves. John Tagliabue, "Italy Opens Inquiry into Jail Escape by Achille Lauro Gunman," New York Times, March 5, 1996, A10.

93. E.g., see Samuel G. Freeman, "Across the Country, A Sense of Euphoria and Cries for Blood," New York Times, Oct. 12, 1985, 1, and "Getting Even," Newsweek, Oct. 21, 1985, 20.

94. S1373, 99th Cong., 1st sess. (June 27, 1985). See also Arlen Specter, "How to Make Terrorists Think Twice," New York Times, May 22, 1986, A31; 131 Cong. Rec. S8960–61 (June 27, 1985), 132 Cong. Rec., S1382–1387 (Feb. 19, 1986).

95. John Walcott and Andy Pasztor, "Reagan Ruling to Let CIA Kidnap Terrorists Overseas Disclosed," Wall Street Journal, Feb. 20, 1987, 1, 11.

96. Testimony Before the Subcom. on Security and Terrorism, Com. on the Judiciary, United States Senate, 99th Cong., 1st sess. (1985), 71.

97. Walcott and Pasztor, "Reagan Ruling to Let CIA Kidnap Terrorists," 11.

98. The abduction provision was dropped from the final bill. 132 Cong. Rec., S1382–87 (Feb. 19, 1986).

99. Walcott and Pasztor, "Reagan Ruling to Let CIA Kidnap Terrorists," 11.

100. Under the National Security Act of 1947, the CIA was expressly forbidden to exercise "police, subpoena [or] law enforcement powers." 50 U.S.C. sec. 403(d)(3). However, Executive Order 12333, subpara. 2.6, challenges this flat prohibition by allowing the agency to assist law enforcement.

101. Walcott and Pasztor, "Reagan Ruling to Let CIA Kidnap Terrorists," 11.

102. "Taking On Terrorists," U.S. News & World Report, Sept. 12, 1988, 26; Ihsan A. Hijazi, "Beirut Hijackers Demand Departure of Palestinians," New York Times, June 12, 1985, A10.

103. "Role in '85 Hijacking Denied," New York Times, Dec. 4, 1987, A12; Kenneth B. Noble, "Lebanese Suspect in '85 Hijacking Arrested by the F.B.I. While at Sea," New York Times, Sept. 18, 1987, A1, at A11.

104. "Taking Terrorists," U.S. News & World Report, Sept. 12, 1988, at 26, 28.

105. Sources for this account include "A Sting on the Mediterranean," Newsweek, Sept. 28, 1987, 36 (quotation); Andreas F. Lowenfeld, "U.S. Law Enforcement Abroad: The Constitution and International Law, Continued," 84 Am. J. Int'l L. 444–46 (1990); "Taking On Terrorists," U.S. News & World Report, Sept. 12, 1988, 26–34.

106. United States v. Yunis, 681 F. Supp. 909, 915 (D.D.Cir. 1988).

107. Id. at 921–27.

108. Id. at 918–21.

109. United States v. Yunis, 859 F. 2d 953 (D.C.Cir. 1988). The only issue before the court on appeal was whether the confession was improperly obtained. All other issues, including the legality of the abduction, were excluded by joint stipulation.

110. He was also tried under the Destruction of Aircraft Act, but was acquitted of that charge.

111. 18 U.S.C. sec. 1203 (1988).

112. 681 F. 2d at 918.

113. 18 U.S.C. sec. 1385 ("Whoever, except in cases and under circumstances expressly authorized by the Constitution or Act of Congress, willfully uses any part of the Army or the Air Force as a posse comitatus or otherwise to execute the laws shall be fined not more than $10,000 or imprisoned not more than two years, or both." The extensive use of the navy to carry out the abduction of Fawaz Younis was held not to violate the Posse Comitatus Act in United States v. Yunis, 924 F. 2d 1086, 1093 (D.C.Cir. 1991).

114. Elaine Shannon, Desperados (New York: Viking, 1988), 164.

115. Frederick Kempe, Divorcing the Dictator (New York: Putnam's, 1990), 224.

116. Indictment, United States v. Noriega, no. 88-0079 Cr. (S.D.Fla., filed Sept. 14, 1988).

117. One of the chief opposition leaders, Guillermo Ford, told President Bush that the opposition would never turn the general over to the United States to be tried for drug trafficking; Elaine Sciolino, "Panama Jink: What Should Washington Do About Noriega?," New York Times, Oct. 8, 1989, E1.

118. E.g., see Bernholz, Bernholz, and Herman, "International Extradition in Drug Cases," 10. N. C. J. Int'l L. & Com. Reg. 353, 358–64.

119. 46 Fed. Reg. 59,941, sec. 2.11 (1981) ("No person employed by or acting on behalf of the United States government shall engage in, or conspire to engage in, assassination.")

120. At least that was the official explanation for the president's failure to act more decisively in support of the second failed coup in October 1989.

121. Frederick Kempe, Divorcing the Dictator (New York: Putnam's, 1990), 303–304.

122. Id. at 305.

123. Margaret E. Scranton, The Noriega Years: U.S.-Panama Relations, 1981–1990 (Boulder, Colo.: Lynne Rienner, 1991), 195.

124. The earlier opinion, prepared in response to an FBI proposal to snatch Robert L. Vesco, the fugitive financier, concluded that "U.S. agents have no law enforcement authority in another nation unless it is the product of that nation's consent." 4B Op. Off. Legal Counsel 543, 551 (1980) (prepared after the Bahamian government refused to surrender Vesco or tolerate his abduction). On the Bush administration's opinion, see Michael Wines, "U.S. Cites Right to Seize Fugitives Abroad," New York Times, Oct. 14, 1989, 6. The title of this still secret memorandum is "Authority of the Federal Bureau of Investigation to Override Customary or other International law in the Course of Extraterritorial Law Enforcement Activities."

125. 135 Cong. Rec. S12,679–80 (daily ed. Oct. 5, 1989).

126. Michael Isikoff and Patrick E. Tyler, "U.S. Military Given Foreign Arrest Powers," Washington Post, Dec. 16, 1989, A1. The ruling, by the Justice Department's Office of Legal Coun-

sel, came two months after a U.S. Army Special Forces team was readied to abduct Colombian drug lord Pablo Escobar following intelligence reports that he was visiting Panama. Id., A10.

127. Another secret memorandum advised that the executive order forbidding assassinations need not bar U.S. support for coups d'etat, so long as the death of a leader killed in the process is not the administration's explicit goal. David B. Ottaway and Don Oberdorfer, "Administration Alters Assassination Ban," Washington Post, Nov. 4, 1989, A1, A4.

128. The actual snatch order is published at 25 Weekly Comp. Pres. Doc. 1976 (Dec. 20, 1989).

129. H.R. Doc. no. 127, 101st Cong., 2d sess. (1990) (letter from President Bush notifying Congress of the invasion).

130. Ved P. Nanda, "Agora: U.S. Forces in Panama: Defenders, Aggressors, or Human Rights Activists?," 84 Am. J. Int'l L. 494, 497 (1990).

131. United States v. Noriega, 746 F. Supp. 1506, 1529–32.

132. See generally Louis Henkin, "The Invasion of Panama Under International Law: A Gross Violation," 29 Colum. J. Transnat'l L. 293 (1991).

133. Art. 2, para. 5.

134. 2 U.S.T. 2394, T.I.A.S. no. 2361, art. 17 (opened for signature April 30, 1948; signed by the United States June 15, 1981; entered into force for the United States Dec. 13, 1951).

135. 746 F. Supp. at 2531–34.

136. Id. at 1528.

137. Id. at 1529.

138. Id. at 1539.

139. Even Argentina eventually withdrew its objection to the abduction of Eichmann. Attorney General v. Eichmann, 36 Int'l L. Rep'ts 18, 70–71 (D. Jerusalem, 1961).

140. Huckle v. Money, 2 Wils. K.B. 205, 207 (1763) (upholding a jury's award of punitive damages for false imprisonment for the abduction of the radical Whig journalist John Wilkes pursuant to "a nameless warrant"; Wilkes v. Wood, 19 Howell's State Trials 1153 (1763); Leach v. Three of the King's Messengers, 19 Howell's State Trials 1001 (1765); Entick v. Carrington, 2 Wils. K.B. 275 (1765); James B. Otis Jr., Oral Argument in Petition of Lechmere (The Writs of Assistance Case), Legal Papers of John Adams (L. Kinvin Wroth and Hiller B. Zobel, eds.; Cambridge, Mass.: Belknap, 1965), 139–144. See also United States v. Verdugo-Urquidez, 494 U.S. 259, 288–89 (1990) (Brennan, J., dissenting).

141. In the case of In re Debs, 158 U.S. 564 (1895), the U.S. Supreme Court, erroneously in my judgment, upheld the exercise of inherent judicial power to authorize the president to use the army to break the great Pullman strike without express authorization by Congress under the riot acts.

142. Kear v. Hilton, 699 F. 2d 181 (1983).

Chapter Twenty-One

Epigraph: 939 F. 2d. 1341, 1362 (9th Cir. 1991), reversed, 494 U.S. 259 (1990).

1. Elaine Shannon, Desperados (New York: Viking, 1988); "Man Is Convicted in Drug Agent's Torture Death," New York Times, Dec. 22, 1992, A18.

2. Within forty-eight hours of Camarena's murder, the prime suspect, Rafael Caro-Quintero, bribed his way through a police cordon at a local airstrip and escaped. Affidavit of Special Agent Salvador Leyva (filed Oct. 22, 1987), United States v. Caro-Quintero, 745 F. Supp. 599 (C.D.Cal. 1990) (no. 87-422), aff'd *sub nom.*, United States v. Alvarez-Machain, 946 F. 2d 1466 (9th Cir. 1991), rev'd, 504 U.S. 655 (1992).

3. "Snatching 'Dr. Mengele'," Time, April 23, 1990, 27. Two former high-ranking Mexican law-enforcement officials were subsequently indicted for the killings. Manuel Ibarra Herrera had been the director of the Mexican Federal Judicial Police (MFJP), Mexico's counterpart to the FBI. Miguel Aldana Ibarra had been the director of Interpol, the international police agency, in Mexico. Irving Molotsky, "Physician from Mexico Arrested in '85 Slaying of U.S. Drug Agent," New York Times, April 16, 1990, A2. Another of the defendants, Ruben Zuno Arce, was the brother-in-law of a former president of Mexico, Luis Echeverria.

4. United States v. Caro-Quintero, 745 F. Supp. at 602.

5. United States v. Verdugo-Urquidez, 939 F. 2d 1341, 1343 (9th Cir. 1991), vacated, 505 U.S., 1201 (1992). The Mexican prosecutor in Baja, California, ultimately indicted Verdugo's abductors. United States v. Verdugo-Urquidez, 856 F. 2d 1214, 1216, n. 1 (9th Cir. 1989), rev'd, 494 U.S. 259 (1990). However, the U.S. government, after paying the six abductors $32,000 in bribes, gave them sanctuary in the U.S. Jim Schacter, "Arrest Abroad: Long Arm of Law Bends the Rules," Los Angeles Times, July 17, 1986, sec. 1, 1. The abduction was not approved by the U.S. Department of Justice. Brief for the respondent in United States v. Verdugo-Urquidez, at 6. (Higher officials may have wanted plausible denial if the low-level operation went arwy.)

6. Also known as Juan Ramon Matta del Pozo.

7. Art. 102 ("No Honduran may be expatriated nor handed over to the authorities of the foreign state").

8. The foregoing account draws from Stephen Engelberg, "Suspect in Murder of Drug Agent Is Seized in U.S. Trap in Honduras," New York Times, April 6, 1988, A1, A8; Wilson Ring, "Honduran Wanted by DEA Arrested," Washington Post, April 6, 1988, A1, A34; Bill McAllister, "Trap Set as Honduran Suspect Jogged," Washington Post, April 7, 1998, A8; Philip Shenon, "Meese Links Embassy Riot to Traffickers," New York Times, April 10, 1988, 16.

9. Matta-Ballesteros, ex rel. Stolar, v. Henman, 697 F. Supp. 1040, 1042–43 (S.D.Ill. 1988); Engelberg, "Suspect in Murder of Drug Agent Is Seized in U.S. Trap in Honduras"; Ring, "Honduran Wanted by DEA Arrested"; McAllister, "Trap Set as Honduran Suspect Jogged."

10. Matta-Ballesteros, ex rel. Stolar, v. Henman, 876 F. 2d 255, 256 (7th Cir. 1990).

11. United States v. Caro-Quintero, 745 F. Supp. at 602.

12. Andreas F. Lowenfeld, "Kidnapping by Government Order: A Follow-Up," 84 Am. J. Int'l L. 712, 715 (1990) (based on statement of DEA special agent Berrellez submitted to the district court).

13. United States v. Caro-Quintero, 745 F. Supp. at 602.

14. Id. at 603, 601.

15. Id. at 603. See also Brief for the United States, United States v. Alvarez-Machain, 504 U.S. 655 (1992) at 2–4.

16. United States v. Caro-Quintero, 745 F. Supp. at 603.

17. Alvarez later claimed that he had been shocked on the soles of his feet and injected with a substance that made him feel "dizzy and lightheaded," but the court did not believe him. Id.

18. Id. at 602–604, and "DEA Operative Details His Role in Kidnaping," Los Angeles Times, April 28, 1990, sec. 1, 1. The Agency paid the abductors $20,000 and relocated seven of them to the United States with their families. By November 1992, the United States had paid the witnesses against Alvarez and a codefendant $2.7 million. Id. at 603–604. "U.S. Funds for Camarena Witnesses Are Detailed," New York Times, Nov. 9, 1992, A12.

19. Id. See also Brief for the United Mexican States as Amicus Curiae in Support of Granting Review, United States v. Alvarez-Machain, 504 U.S. 655 (1992).

20. Robert Pear, "Justice Dept. Scrambles to Explain Abduction Plot," New York Times, May 27,1990, 24. DEA did not inform Steven Trott, head of the Justice Department's Criminal Division, of the plan to kidnap Verdugo for fear he would disapprove. Shannon, Desperados, 312.

21. Matta-Ballesteros v. Henman, 697 F. Supp. 1040, 1042 (S.D.Ill. 1988), aff'd, 896 F. 2d 255 (7th Cir. 1990), cert. denied, 498 U.S. 878 (1990).

22. 697 F. Supp. at 1047.

23. Id. at 1047.

24. United States v. Verdugo-Urquidez, CR 87-422Er (C.D.Cal., Nov. 22, 1988), aff'd, 856 F. 2d 1314 (9th Cir. 1988).

25. United States v. Verdugo-Urquidez, 494 U.S. 259 (1990).

26. Id. at 273 (1990).

27. Verdugo-Urquidez v. United States, 856 F. 2d 1241, 1236–37 (9th Cir. 1988). See also Garcia-Mir v. Meese, 788 F. 2d 1446, 1451 (11th Cir. 1986) (limiting the liberty from incarceration without trial guaranteed by the due process clause of the Fifth Amendment to citizens only).

28. 60 U.S. 393 (1856).

29. See also Kenneth L. Karst, Belonging to America (New Haven: Yale University Press, 1989), ch. 4.

30. See generally Testimony of Prof. Christopher H. Pyle, "Foreign Intelligence and Surveillance Act of 1978," Hearings Before the Subcom. on Intelligence and the Rights of Americans, Select Committee on Intelligence, United States Senate, 95th Cong., 2d sess. (1978), 87, 102–104, and sources cited therein.

31. E.g., see Chisholm v. Georgia, 2 U.S. (2 Dall.) 419, 471 (1793) ("The Constitution of the United States is . . . a compact made by the people of the United States to govern themselves").

32. Federalist Papers, nos. 78 and 83 (1788–98; Clinton Rossiter, ed.; New York: Mentor, 1961).

33. The term is Madison's and comes from Federalist no. 51, id. at 322.

34. E.g., see Gordon Wood, The Creation of the American Republic (1969; New York: Norton, 1972), especially ch. 7. The limited government approach eventually became the rationale underlying the exclusionary evidence rule when it was adopted as a constitutional principle in Mapp v. Ohio, 367 U.S. 643 (1961). For an articulation of the structuralist approach to constitutional interpretation, see Charles L. Black Jr., Structure and Relationship in Constitutional Law (Baton Rouge: University of Louisiana Press, 1969).

35. 494 U.S. at 288, citing W. Cuddihy, Search and Seizure in Great Britain and the American Colonies, pt. 2, p. 57, n. 129, 574, n. 134 (1974).

36. 494 U.S. at 289.

37. When the "reasonable expectation of privacy" test was first articulated by Justice Harlan, concurring in Katz v. United States, 389 U.S. 347, 360 (1967), it had both a subjective and objective component. But the Court did not embrace that view. It took the "objective" approach of a "reasonable man," and made a policy-oriented assessment of what the people have a right to expect regarding the investigative behavior of government agents. The majority also declared that "the Fourth Amendment protects people, not places," which could be taken to suggest that the right is a portable personal one, and would protect "the people" against their officials outside the United States. Id. at 351. The exclusionary evidence rule endorsed the expectation that modern government investigators may not, like the customs agents of colonial Boston, overreach themselves.

38. Since the New Deal and the rise of the United States as a world power, the concept of authority, as opposed to power, has declined. The behavioral school of political scientists like Richard E. Neustadt, who came of age following World War II, disparaged constitutionalists like Edward S. Corwin as curmugeonly whigs, more concerned with the Constitution of Limitations than the Constitution of Powers. To the behavioralists, what really mattered was the "power problem" of the president—how could he amass enough political power to bring the nation out of the Depression and fight both hot and cold wars. The inadequacy of this approach became clear during the Watergate affair, when Americans again discovered that they needed not only a Constitution of Powers but a Constitution of Limitations. Unfortunately, the lesson of Watergate was short-lived, and the advocates of executive-centered government became more adept at beating back congressional efforts at limited government and checks and balances during the Iran-Contra scandal.

39. United States v. Toscanino, 500 F. 2d 267, 280.

40. United States v. Caro-Quintero, 745 F. Supp. at 605.

41. Id. at 615, quoting McNabb v. United States, 318 U.S. 332, 345 (1943).

42. Id. at 605.

43. United States–United Mexican States Extradition Treaty, 31 U.S.T. 5059, T.I.A.S. no. 9656 (signed May 4, 1978; entered into force Jan. 25, 1980).

44. United States v. Caro-Quintero, 745 F. Supp. 599, at 608.

45. See generally Jordan J. Paust, "Self-Executing Treaties," 82 Am. J. Int'l L. 760 (1980).

46. See Ex parte Hibbs, 26 Fed. Rep. 421, 431 (D.Ore. 1886) (holding that an extradition treaty is the supreme law of the land, cognizable in all respects by the courts, and not just a political arrangement).

47. See S. S. Lotus (France v. Turkey) 1929 P.C.I.J. (ser. A), nos. 10, 18, 19, and Restatement (Revised) of the Foreign Relations Law of the United States (Tent. Draft no. 6, 1985), sec. 432, comment b: "A state's law enforcement officers may exercise their functions in the territory of another state only with the consent of the other state, given by duly authorized officials of that state."

48. See Chapter 1, *supra*.

49. The affirmance was based on the Court of Appeals' decision in the case of Rene Verdugo, which tracked Rafeedie's reasoning in Alvarez's case. United States v. Verdugo-Urquidez, 939 F. 2d 1341 (9th Cir. 1991), vacated, 505 U.S. 1201 (1992) (in light of Alvarez-Machain).

50. United States v. Alvarez-Machain, 504 U.S. 655 (1992).

51. E.g., see Austin W. Scott Jr., "Criminal Jurisdiction of a State over a Defendant Based upon Presence Secured by Force or Fraud," 37 Minn. L. Rev. 91, 102, 107 (1953); Francis A. Allen, "Due Process and State Criminal Procedure: Another Look," 48 N. W. L. Rev. 16, 27–28 (1953); "Supreme Court 1951 Term," 66 Harv. L. Rev. 89, 126–27 (1953); Manuel R. Garcia-Mora, "Criminal Jurisdiction of a State over Fugitives Brought from a Foreign Country by Force or Fraud: A Comparative Study," 32 Ind. L. J. 427 (1957); Alona Evans, "Acquisition of Custody and the International Fugitive Offender—Alternatives to Extradition: A Survey of United States Practice," 40 B. Y. Int'l L. 77 (1964); Robert M Pitler, "'The Fruit of the Poisonous Tree' Revisited and Shepardized," 56 Calif. L. Rev. 579, 600 (1968); Comment, "United States v. Toscanino: An Assault on the Ker-Frisbie Rule," 12 San Diego L. Rev. 865 (1975); Abraham Abamovsky and Steven J. Eagle, "U.S. Policy in Apprehending Alleged Offenders Abroad: Extradition, Abduction or Irregular Rendition," 57 Or. L. Rev. 51 (1977); "Extradition and Human Rights," Report of the Committee on Extradition and Human Rights to the International Law Association, Buenos Aires, Argentina, August 1994 (John Dugard and Christine Van den Wijngaert,

reporters). Contra: D. Cameron Findlay, "Abducting Terrorists Overseas for Trial in the United States: Issues of International and Domestic Law," 23 Tex. Int'l L. J. 1 (1988).

52. For the current Court's hostility to the exclusionary rule, see Arizona v. Fulminante, 499 U.S. 279 (1991) and cases cited therein.

53. On the similarly between Vere's jurisprudence and Rehnquist's, see Richard Weisberg, "How Judges Speak: Some Lessons on Adjudication in Billy Budd, Sailor, with an Application to Justice Rehnquist," 57 N. Y. U. L. Rev. 1 (1982).

54. Discussed in Chapter 20, *supra*.

55. See generally David L. Shapiro, "Mr. Justice Rehnquist: A Preliminary View," 90 Harv. L. Rev. 293 (1976).

56. 504 U.S. at 682, 687.

57. United States v. Rauscher, 119 U.S. 407 (1886). See Chapter 5, *supra*.

58. Chapter 5, *supra*.

59. Id.

60. 504 U.S. at 676–77.

61. United States v. Rauscher, 119 U.S. 407 (1886).

62. 119 U.S. at 422. Accord: State v. Vanderpool, 39 Ohio 273, 279 (Sup.Ct.Ohio 1883) ("The sole object of the [Webster-Ashburton] treaty was to enable each government to protect its citizens and inhabitants in the right of asylum, except they come within the provisions named").

63. Id.

64. The Apollon, 22 U.S. (9 Wheat.) 362, 371 (1824).

65. "The Path of the Law," 10 Harv. L. Rev. 457, 459 (1897).

66. E.g., see Judge Benedict's opinions in United States v. Caldwell, 8 Blanchford 131 (Cir.Ct.S.D.N.Y. 1871) and United States v. Lawrence, 13 Blanchford 295 (Cir.Ct.S.D.N.Y. 1876).

67. Theodore Roosevelt: An Autobiography (New York: Macmillan, 1913), 388–89.

68. "Excerpts from Interview with Nixon About Domestic Effects of Indochina War," New York Times, May 20, 1977, A16.

69. Federal Data Banks, Computers and the Bill of Rights, Hearings Before the Subcom. on Constitutional Rights, Committee on the Judiciary, U.S. Senate, 92d Cong., 1st sess. (1971), at 598–99.

70. Karl Llewellyn called this the "Formal Style" of jurisprudence, which, he said, was dominant between 1870 and the 1940s. He contrasted it to the "Grand Style," which prevailed from Jefferson's time to Grant's and which began to reappear after the Great Depression. The Common Law Tradition: Deciding Appeals (Boston: Little, Brown, 1960), 5, 6, 36, 38.

71. Youngstown Sheet & Tube Co. v. Sawyer, 343 U.S. 579 (1952).

72. Historically, customary international law was part of the common law of England and the American colonies. Today it is more likely to be characterized as analogous to common law, because it is often difficult to determine when a certain, customary usage has become so widely accepted as to be considered law. This ambiguity, together with ambiguities over who may legitimately abrogate treaties, makes the presidential obligation to obey customary international law tenuous at times, and this tenuousness has been exploited by pro-executive positivists like Chief Justice Rehnquist to allow nearly complete executive discretion, not just at the White House level, but by middle managers in agencies like the DEA. This is not to say that the U.S. government may not sometimes violate customary international law, but only that the power to do so ought to be exercised formally, at the highest level.

73. United States v. Alvarez-Machain, 971 F. 2d 310, 311 (9th Cir. July 27, 1992).

74. 175 U.S. 677, 700 (1900) (admiral could not order seizure of a Cuban fishing boat during the Spanish-American War as a prize, because customary international usage respected the neutrality of local fishing boats).

75. Murray v. The Charming Betsy, 6 U.S. (2 Cranch) 64, 118 (1804).

76. Nor had the government followed the Roman law maxim *nunquam decurritur ad extraordinarium sed ubi deficit ordinarium* (never resort to the extraordinary until the ordinary fails).

77. When the Justice Department secretly rejected the published Carter policy on FBI arrests abroad, President Bush was not even notified. "I'm embarrassed to say I don't know what it is," Bush told a news conference four months later. Ruth Marcus, "FBI Told It Can Seize Fugitives Abroad," Washington Post, Oct. 14, 1989, A1. None of the so-called policy changes allowing CIA, FBI, or military arrests abroad was published by the Reagan or Bush administrations. Their force was minimized by some officials with the claim that they were just legal opinions—an argument they used to justify their failure to disclose the policies to the public or Congress.

78. Garcia-Mir v. Meese, 788 F. 2d 1446 (11th Cir. 1986), cert. denied, *sub nom.* Ferrer Mazorra v. Meese, 479 U.S. 889 (1986).

79. 788 F. 2d at 1455.

80. Id.

81. Nicaragua v. United States, Int'l Ct. of Justice Yearbook, 1985–1986, no. 40 (The Hague: ICJ, 1986), 137–60.

82. Brief for the United States of Mexico as *Amicus Curiae* in Support of Granting Review, United States v. Alvarez-Machain, 504 U.S. 655 (1992); Brief of the Government of Canada as *Amicus Curiae* in Support of Respondent, United States v. Alvarez-Machain.

83. Letter to O. M. Roberts, Governor of Texas, May 3, 1881, Domestic letters of the Department of State, 1784–1906 (National Archives Microfilm Publication, M40, Roll 93).

84. Letter of Secretary of State T. F. Bayard to Thomas Manning, Esq., Feb. 26, 1887, Diplomatic Instructions of the Department of State, 1801–1906, Mexico (National Archives Record Group 59, Microfilm Publication M77, Roll 117), 646–651.

85. Treaty of Cooperation Between the United States of America and the United Mexican States for Mutual Legal Assistance, art. 1(2) (signed Dec. 9, 1987; entered into force for the United States May 3, 1991), Treaty Doc. 100–13, reprinted in 27 I.L.M. 443 (1988). Agreement Between the United States of America and the United Mexican States on Cooperation in Combatting Narcotics Trafficking and Drug Dependency, art. 1(3) (signed Feb. 23, 1989; entered into force July 30, 1990, 26 U.S.T. 1274, reprinted in 29 I.L.M. 58 (1990).

86. Olmstead v. United States, 277 U.S.438, at 485 (1928) (dissenting).

87. Eichmann in Jerusalem (1963; New York: Viking, 1994), 264.

88. Id. Accord: F. A. Mann, Further Studies in International Law (Oxford: Clarendon Press, 1990), 346–47.

89. Moreover, if the enormity of a person's crimes justifies breaking the law to capture him, should it not also justify breaking the law of punishments, on the ground that the enormity of his crime justifies inflicting upon him the most excruciating death imaginable?

90. Dennis v. United States, 341 U.S. 494, 510 (1951).

91. (New York: Vintage, 1962), 37.

92. Id., 52–53.

93. "The Case For and Against Abducting Terrorists," New York Times, Jan. 28, 1986, A24.

94. "Morality and Foreign Policy," 64 Foreign Affairs 205, 214 (1985–1986).

95. Id., 206.

96. Id., 243.

97. Id., 265–67.

98. Arendt did not address the possibility of government assassination. The "heroic" assassins she had in mind were private persons, not agents of the Mossad or CIA, and she believed they should be willing to suffer the legal consequences.

99. "Morality and Foreign Policy," 264–65.

100. See Herbert Wechsler, "Towards Neutral Principles of Constitutional Law," 73 Harv. L. Rev. 1 (1959).

101. In this connection, it is worth recalling that the Nixon administration, like Eisenhower's, made much of historic precedents for covert operations in violation of foreign law. In the tradition of Midwest Oil v. United States, 236 U.S. 459 (1915) and Justice Frankfurter's concurrence in Youngstown Sheet & Tube Co. v. Sawyer, 343 U.S. 579, 611 (1952), they claimed these could place a "gloss" upon presidential powers. One of the proponents of this use of historical precedent was Assistant Attorney General William H. Rehnquist.

102. Loren Jenkins, "Coalition Collapses in Italy," Washington Post, Oct. 17, 1985, A1, A29; "The Price of Success," Time, Oct. 28, 1985, 22.

103. Bernard Gwertzman, "The U.S. May Pay a High Price for Its Triumph," New York Times, Oct. 20, 1985, sec. 4, 1.

104. The presidents of Latin American countries meeting in Madrid passed a resolution urging the U.N. General Assembly to request an advisory opinion from the International Court of Justice condemning the Alvarez decision. "Conclusiones de la Il Cumbre Iberoamerica," El Nacional (Mex.), July 25, 1992, 18.

105. David O. Stewart, "The Price of Vengeance," ABA Journal, Nov. 1992, 50, 52.

106. Tim Golden, "Bush Gives Mexico Limited Pledge on Abductions," New York Times, July 2, 1992, A5.

107. Tim Golden, "Dispute Holds Up U.S. Extradition Treaty with Mexico," New York Times, May 15, 1994, 6.

108. Larry Rohter, "Honduran Anger at U.S. Is Product of Washington Policy, Officials Say," New York Times, April 13, 1988, A10; Wilson Ring, "Honduras Imposes Emergency," Washington Post, April 9, 1988, A1, A18; "Meese Links Embassy Riot to Traffickers," New York Times, April 10, 1988, 16.

109. Larry Rohter, "Anger at Suspect's Expulsion to U.S. Smolders in Honduras," New York Times, April 11, 1988, A11.

110. "Teheran Enables Arrest Abroad of Americans Harming Iran," Washington Post, Nov. 2, 1989, A51. In March 1989, Mrs. Rogers was nearly killed when a bomb went off under the family van while she was driving in San Diego. The bombing followed death threats. "Bombs Across the Ocean?" Time, March 20, 1989, 26.

111. Time, Feb. 27, 1989, at 29, and Time, March 1, 1993, at 13.

112. "Shame," The New Republic, Aug. 12, 1991, 8.

113. London Sunday Times, June 17, 1990, sec. 1, at 30. See also "Sentenced, Mordechai Vanunu," Time, April 11, 1988, 63.

114. In October 1986, two American bounty hunters in the employ of a bonding company abducted Sidney Jaffe from Canada to Florida after he jumped bail rather than face trial for land fraud. Canada protested, and the bounty hunters were returned, via extradition, to stand trial for kidnapping. Kear v. Hilton, 699 F. 2d 181 (4th Cir. 1983) (authorizing extradition).

115. Statement of Abraham D. Sofaer, Legal Adviser, U.S. Department of State, "FBI Authority to Seize Suspects Abroad," Hearing Before the Subcom. on Civil and Constitutional Rights,

Committee on the Judiciary, U.S. House of Representatives, 101st Cong., 1st sess. (1989), 26, 39–41 (on the risks), 41 (quotation).

116. Compare Filartiga v. Pena-Irala, 630 F. 2d 876 (2d Cir. 1980) (civil suit for torture in violation of international law allowed against former Uruguayan police officer).

117. E.g., see Letelier v. Republic of Chile, 748 F. 2d 790 (2d Cir. 1984) (damages awarded against the government of Chile for the death of a bystander in the Letelier assassination).

118. 36 State Dept. Bull. 1027–28 (1957); and New York Times: March 19, 1956, 27; March 21, 1956, 29; March 22, 1956, 71; March 28, 1956, 9; March 30, 1956, 1; April 4, 1956, 10; April 29, 1956, 43; May 14, 1956, 2; May 22, 1956, 16; and May 30, 1956, 1, 6.

119. See generally Taylor Branch and Eugene M. Propper, Labyrinth (New York: Viking, 1982), and John Dinges and Saul Landau, Assassination on Embassy Row (New York: Pantheon, 1980).

120. Fox Butterfield, "Taiwan Arrest in Coast Murder Arouses Concern in Congress," New York Times, Jan. 19, 1985, 8.

121. Richard Lacayo, "Not Again," Time, Aug 14, 1989, 14; Jim Muir, "Lebanese Shiites Dispute Gains to Israel from Kidnapping," Christian Science Monitor, Aug. 2, 1989, 3.

122. Federal Kidnapping (Lindbergh Act), 18 U.S.C. sec. 1201. See also the federal Civil Rights Act, 42 U. S. C. Sec. 1981 and comparable state laws. This also raises the question of whether Alvarez would have been entitled to plead self-defense had he killed one of his captors on the tarmac in El Paso in attempting to escape.

123. "Kidnapping by Government Order: A Follow-Up," 84 Am. J. Int'l L. 712, 715 (1990). Secret (or implicit) executive consent to the violation of criminal laws is no consent at all. The only consent worth any credence is a public consent based on a clear legal mandate, which is best achieved through the normal processes of extradition law.

124. The Complete Writings of Thomas Paine (Philip S. Foner, ed.; New York: Citadel Press, 1945), 588 (and quoted by Stevens, J., dissenting in United States v. Alvarez-Machain, 504 U.S. 655. at 688.

125. Seth Mydans, "Judge Clears Mexican in Agent's Killing," New York Times, Dec. 15, 1992, A20.

126. "Judge Says U.S. Was Told It Held Wrong Doctor in Agent's Killing," New York Times, Dec. 17, 1992, A27.

Chapter Twenty-Two

Epigraph: United States v. Rabinowitz, 339 U.S. 56, 69 (1950) (dissenting).

1. The following analysis builds on the excellent work of John G. Kester, "Some Myths of United States Extradition Law," 76 Georgtown L. J. 1441 (1988), and the Extradition and Human Rights Committee of the International Law Association, led by the incomparable Alfred P. Rubin, Distinguished Professor of International Law, Fletcher School of Law and Diplomacy.

2. Reform of the Extradition Laws of the United States, Hearings on H.R. 2643 Before the Subcom. on Crime, Com. on the Judiciary, U.S. House of Representatives, 98th Cong., 1st sess. 1983, at 36 (statement of Roger Olsen, Deputy Asst. Att'y Gen., Crim. Div., Dep't of Justice).

3. E.g., see Grin v. Shine, 187 U.S. 181, 184 (1902) (extradition defendants are required to "submit themselves to the laws of their country").

4. Neely v. Henkel, 180 U.S. 109, 123 (1901) (U.S. national charged with committing a crime in Cuba may not complain "if required to submit to such modes of trial . . . as the laws [of the requesting country] prescribe for its own people").

5. See David Cressy, Crossing Over (Cambridge: Cambridge Univ. Press, 1987).

6. Jean Baudrillard, America (Chris Turner trans.; New York, Verso, 1988).

7. E.g., see United States v. Galanis, 429 F. Supp. 1215, 1224 (D.Conn. 1977) (refusing to apply criminal law safeguards to extradition because it is not, technically, part of a criminal prosecution under American law). According to the advisory committee's comment on Rule 1101 of the Federal Rules of Evidence, "Extradition and rendition proceedings are . . . essentially administrative in character." Cf. Romeo v. Roche, 820 F. 2d 540, 534–44 (1st Cir. 1987) ("Extradition proceedings . . . are generally not considered *criminal* prosecutions") (emphasis in original). See also Jhirad v. Ferrandina, 401 F. Supp. 1215, 1219 (S.D.N.Y. 1975) ("The extradition procedures afforded by statute seek to preserve an element of judicial surveillance over . . . what is basically an action in international comity"), aff'd, 536 F. 2d 478 (2d Cir.), *cert. denied*, 429 U.S. 833 (1976).

8. Pamela B. Stuart, "Treaty Traps," Criminal Justice, Winter 1992, 24, 25.

9. Id. at 25. In Europe the same doctrine deprives defendants in extradition cases of the right to fair trial provided by art. 6 of the European Convention on Human Rights and art. 14 of the International Covenant on Civil and Political Rights. By labeling extradition as a mere civil proceeding, courts are able to pretend they have no moral or legal responsibility for what happens to the accused upon surrender to a different criminal justice system.

10. County of Riverside v. McLaughlin, 500 U.S. 44, 56 (1991).

11. In the "extradite or punish" case of the East German hijacker, Hans Tiede was held under what was falsely called "protective custody," without charges, bail, or a lawyer for ninety-eight days, again demonstrating why the framers of the Constitution did not trust the liberties of individuals to the executive.

12. "Pretrial confinement may imperil the suspect's job, interrupt his source of income, and impair his family relations." Gerstein v. Pugh, 420 U.S. 103, 114 (1975).

13. As Justice (and former Attorney General) Robert Jackson once noted, denying pretrial release means that "even those wrongly accused are punished by a period of imprisonment while awaiting trial and are handicapped in consulting counsel, searching for evidence and witnesses, and preparing a defense." Stack v. Boyle, 342 U.S. 1, 8 (1951) (Jackson, J., concurring).

14. As Abu Eain claimed.

15. As was the case with accusers in the Demjanjuk and Artuković cases.

16. Eain v. Wilkes, 641 F. 2d 504, 511 (7th Cir. 1981); Hooker v. Klein, 573 F. 2d 1360, 1368 (9th Cir. 1978); Collins v. Loisel, 259 U.S. 309, 317–18 (1923).

17. Jones v. United States, 362 U.S. 257, 269 (1960) (hearsay admissible to establish probable cause if there is "a substantial basis for crediting the hearsay").

18. On the acceptability of hearsay at extradition proceedings generally, despite the higher stakes, e.g., Quinn v. Robinson, 783 F. 2d 776, 815 (9th Cir.) (admitting hearsay), cert. denied, 479 U.S. 882 (1986); O'Brien v. Rozman, 554 F. 2d 780, 783 (6th Cir. 1977) (same); United States *ex rel.* Klein v. Mulligan, 50 F. 2d 687, 688 (2d Cir.), cert. denied, 284 U.S. 665 (1931); cf. Grin v. Shine, 187 U.S. 181, 184 (1902) ("the ordinary technicalities of criminal proceedings are applicable only to a limited extent"). The Federal Rules of Evidence are supposed to apply to habeas corpus proceedings, by which extradition rulings are reviewed, Fed. R. Evid. 1101(b), but see Emami v. U.S. Dist. Court, 834 F. 2d 1444, 1450–51 (9th Cir. 1987) (relying on an affidavit that affirmed unsworn hearsay statements because hearsay was allowed in extradition proceedings by the applicable extradition law and treaty).

19. The Amistad court's decision to question the slave owners' documents was possible because theirs was not an extradition case *per se*, but a civil proceeding for salvage which could

result in surrender. Even so, it took great judicial courage to lift the veil of Spanish legitimacy and reject the documents as false. Chapter 4, *supra*. Compare United States *ex rel.* Sakaguchi v. Kaulukului, 520 F. 2d 726, 728 (9th Cir. 1975) (overlooking inconsistencies among documents submitted by requesting state).

20. E.g., see Zanazanian v. United States, 729 F. 2d 624, 627 (9th Cir.) (admitting unsworn police summaries of witness statements).

21. E.g., Rice v. Ames, 180 U.S. 371, 375 (1901) (confrontation not required when requesting state submits authenticated documents charging the offenses); Bingham v. Bradley, 241 U.S. 511, 517 (1916).

22. See also Jhirad v. Ferrandina, 536 F. 2d 478, 485 n. 9 (2d Cir. 1976) (Sixth Amendment's guarantee of a speedy trial held not applicable in an extradition proceeding); Sabatier v. Dambrowski, 453 F. Supp. 1250, 1255 (D.R.I. 1978) (same), aff'd, 586 F. 2d 866 (1st Cir. 1978).

23. United States v. (Under Seal) (Araneta), 794 F. 2d 920 (4th Cir. 1986); In re Parker, 411 F. 2d 1067 (10th Cir. 1969), vacated as moot *sub nom.*, Parker v. United States, 397 U.S. 96 (1970). Contra: United States v. Gecas, 50 F. 3d 1549 (11th Cir. 1995) (privilege is more than a protection against overreaching by OSI; it is a "matter of individual dignity." The court also found that by trying to coerce self-incriminating evidence out of the accused, OSI was seeking to aid the foreign prosecution).

24. United States v. Doherty, 786 F. 2d 491, 501 (1986) (a second, third, or even tenth request for extradition does not violate principle of res judicata because no trial has taken place); Artukovic v. Rison, 784 F. 2d 1354, 1356 (9th Cir. 1986) (earlier court finding that the offenses charged were political, and therefore exempt from extradition, not binding or relevant because res judicata does not apply in an extradition proceeding); Hooker v. Klein, 573 F. 2d 1360, 1367–68 (9th Cir.) (res judicata not applicable because extradition proceedings are not final judgments on the merits), cert. denied, 439 U.S. 932 (1978). See also Collins v. Loisel, 262 U.S. 426, 429–30 (1923) (allowing a second extradition proceeding based on new affidavits untainted by procedural errors). In re Ryan, 360 F. Supp. 270, 274 (E.D.N.Y.) (refusing to entertain a double jeopardy claim), aff'd, 478 F. 2d 1397 (2d Cir.1973).

25. As stated in Benson v. McMahon [127 U.S. 457, 463 (1888)] "the test as to whether such evidence of criminality has been presented is the same as that 'of those preliminary examinations which taking place every day in this country before an examining or committing magistrate for the purpose of determining whether a case is made out which will justify holding the accused, . . . to ultimately answer to an indictment, or other proceeding, in which he shall finally be tried upon the charge made out against him.'" In re D'Amico, 185 F. Supp. 925, 927–28 ((S.D.N.Y. 1960).

26. Rice v. Ames, 180 U.S. 371, 374 (1901).

27. Chapter 14, *supra*.

28. Report of the Sixty-Eighth Conference of the International Law Association, Taipei, Taiwan, May 24–30, 1998 (London: ILA, 1998), 132–154.

29. In re Kaine, 55 U.S. (14 How.) 103, 120 (1852) (Curtis, J., concurring). Similar assertions have been made by the Justice Department and lower courts from time to time. See, e.g., 10 Op. Atty. Gen. 501, 506 (1863); Austin v. Healy, 5 F. 3d 598, 603 (2d Cir. 1993) ("the function performed by the judicial officer in certifying extraditability has not historically been considered an exercise of the 'judicial power of the United States' at all"), cert. denied, 510 U.S. 1165 (1994); In re Extradition of Howard, 996 F. 2d 1320, 1325 (1st Cir. 1993) ("an officer who presides over such a proceeding is not exercising 'any part of the judicial power of the United States'") (citation omitted); Martin v. Warden, Atlanta Penitentary, 993 F. 2d 824, 828 (11th Cir. 1993) (role of

a judicial officer under the extradition statute does not involve the "essential attributes" of the powers vested in the federal courts by Article 3).

30. Lobue v. Christopher, 893 F. Supp. 65 (D.C. 1995), rev'd on other grounds, *sub nom.* Christopher v. Lobue, 82 F. 3d 1081 (D.C.Cir. 1996).

31. Christopher v. Lobue, 82 F. 3d 1081 (D.C.Cir. 1996).

32. Courts that have upheld the constitutionality of 18 U.S.C. sec. 3186 include In re Lang, 905 F. Supp. 1385 (C.D.Cal. 1995) (denying standing to the accused to challenge the constitutionality of an executive power that could only work to the advantage of the accused); In re Lin, 915 F. Supp. 207 (D. Guam 1995) (noting that the executive's power of "revision" is analogous to prosecutorial discretion); In re Sutton, 905 F. Supp. 631 (E.D.Mo. 1995) (same analogy); Cherry v. Warden, Metro. Correctional Ctr., no. 95 Cr. Misc. 1 p. 7 (LB), 1995 WL 598986 (S.D.N.Y. 1995) (same analogy); Carreno v. Johnson, 899 F. Supp. 625 (S.D.Fla. 1995) (power of secretary to authorize surrender of a person found extraditable is not a "revision" of the court's decision).

33. Lo Duca v. United States, 93 F. 3d 1100 (2d. Cir.), cert. denied, 514 U.S. 1007 (1996).

34. Id. at 1107 (citations omitted).

35. United States v. Lawrence, 3 U.S. (3 Dall.) 32 (1795), discussed, Chapter 1, *supra.* The Court of Appeals admitted as much in Lo Duca, 93 F. 3d at 1104.

36. Andreas Lowenfeld, "Ahmad: Profile of an Extradition Case," 23 N. Y. U. J. Int'l L. & Pol. 723, 732 n. 28 (1990–1991).

37. Benson v. McMahon, 127 U.S. at 463. See also Lo Duca v. United States, 93 F. 3d at 1106 (citing United States v. Ferrandina, 54 U.S. (15 How.) 40, 45 (1852).

38. Ward v. Rutherford, 921 F. 2d at 287 (D.C.Cir. 1990), citing 28 U.S.C. sec. 631.

39. Benson v. McMahon, 127 U.S. at 463.

40. United States v. Doherty, 786 F. 2d 491, 502 (2d Cir. 1986).

41. Citing Valentine v. United States *ex rel.* Neidecker, 299 U.S. 5, 8–9 (1936).

42. Terlinden v. Ames, 184 U.S. 270, 289 (1902). Other vague statements by the Court have encouraged sloppy thinking, such as the observation in Ornelas v. Ruiz that the extradition judge "is to certify his findings on the testimony to the Secretary of State that the case may be reviewed by the executive department." 161 U.S. 502, 508 (1896). The requirement that the judge send the testimony to the secretary along with his finding that the accused is extraditable in no way authorizes the secretary to reverse a court decision that the accused may not lawfully be surrendered. It simply equips him to exercise discretion that he would not have absent the court's finding.

43. Plaut v. Spendthrift Farm, Inc., 115 S.Ct. 1447, 1453 (1995). The earliest ruling against advisory opinions was in Hayburn's Case, 2 U.S. (2 Dall.) 409 (1792). See Chapter 14, *supra,* and the State Department's unsuccessful attempt to turn an Article 3 judge from New Jersey into the equivalent of an Article 2 military judge sitting in "conqueror's court." See also Herbert Stern, Judgment in Berlin (New York: Universe Books, 1984), at 95–98.

44. Shadwick v. City of Tampa, 407 U.S. 345, 348 (1972).

45. Id.

46. The history of the Fourth Amendment's origins in the United States is one of resistance to executive officials deciding for themselves whether they had probable cause to seize persons or property. See James Otis Jr., Oral Argument in Petition of Lechmere (the Writs of Assistance Case), Legal Papers of John Adams (Wroth and Zobel, eds.; Cambridge: Belknap Press of Harvard, 1965), at 139–144.

47. In re Mackin, 668 F. 2d 122, 136 (2d Cir. 1981) (the secretary of state has no authority to surrender a person whom the court has found not extraditable, quoting H. G. Hackworth,

Digest of International Law (Washington, D.C.:U.S. Government Printing Office, 1942), vol. 4, at 46).

48. Valentine v. United States *ex rel.* Neidecker, 299 U.S. 5, 9 (1936).

49. Coolidge v. New Hampshire, 403 U.S. 443, 449–51 (1971) (invalidating warrant issued by state attorney general in his capacity as a justice of the peace because he was also leading the investigation as a law enforcement officer).

50. Reid v. Covert, 351 U.S. 1 (1957).

51. Matter of Metzger, 46 U.S. (5 How.) 176 (1847).

52. When Secretary Seward surrendered the slave trader Arguelles to the Spanish, he did not override a magistrate's decision. He simply acted alone.

53. In 1903 the Supreme Court remarked, rather casually, that "bail should not ordinarily be granted in cases of foreign extradition," but that "special circumstances" could justify release. Wright v. Henkel, 190 U.S. 40, 63 (1903). What those "special circumstances" might be the Court did not say. Nor did it hold that the defendant had failed to met such a test or, indeed, that it intended to create one. Cf. Parretti v. United States, 112 F. 3d 1363, 1386 (9th Cir. 1997) (Reinhardt, J., concurring). Even so, Judge Learned Hand ruled that release on bail should be granted only in the "most pressing of circumstances," In re Mitchell, 171 F. 289 (S.D.N.Y. 1909), and his double standard gradually caught on. In United States *ex rel.* MacNamara v. Henkel, 46 F. 2d 84 (S.D.N.Y. 1912) the Second Circuit Court of Appeals declared that "admission to bail [in extradition] should be in practice an unusual and extraordinary thing." The political reasons behind this rule were acknowledged in In re Klein, 46 F. 2d 85, 85 (S.D.N.Y. 1930): "We have been admonished to exercise the power [to grant bail in extradition cases] very sparingly and only when the justification is pressing as well as plain. . . . [Otherwise, we] would incur a grave risk of frustrating the efforts of the executive branch of the government to fulfill treaty obligations." Like the rule of noninquiry, the rule against bail is a judicial creation. Thus, for example, the pretrial detention provisions of the Bail Reform Act of 1984 literally apply only to persons charged with an offense triable in a federal court. Pub. L. No. 98–473, 98 Stat. 1985, 18 U.S.C. secs. 3140–3150 (Supp. 4 1986).

54. In re Carrier, 57 F. 578, 579 (D.Colo. 1893). See also Fed. R. Crim. P. 54(b)(5) ("These rules [governing pretrial release] are not applicable to extradition").

55. In Henkel, the Supreme Court held that courts have an inherent authority to grant bail, even in the absence of a statute authorizing them to do so. 190 U.S. at 63.

56. John A. Boyd, Digest of United States Practice in International Law, 1977 (Department of State Publication, 1979), 156 (quoting a May 20, 1977, State Department reply to diplomatic notes).

57. 112 F. 3d 1363 (9th Cir. 1997). In another case the Justice Department argued that the mere assertion by government lawyers that denial of bail was required by undisclosed urgent circumstances should render the defendant's eligibility for bail nonjusticiable. Caltagirone v. Grant, 629 F. 2d 739, 744 n. 10 (2d Cir. 1980) (choosing to defer to such claims, rather than rule the issue nonjusticiable).

58. United States v. Williams, 611 F. 2d 914 (1st Cir. 1979) (rejecting as "special circumstances" low risk of flight and willingness of another court, on same facts, to release codefendant brother on bail); United States v. Leitner, 784 F. 2d 159 (2d Cir. 1986) (per curiam) (living openly in the United States will not overcome the presumption of no bail); United States v. Russell, 805 F. 2d 1215, 1216 (5th Cir. 1986) (rejecting as "special circumstances" pending litigation, need to consult with counsel, hardship, and low risk of flight).

59. Leitner, 784 F. 2d at 161 (low risk of flight "would not be dispositive").

60. Williams, 611 F. 2d at 915 (citations omitted).

61. United States v. Russell, 805 F. 2d 1215, 1216 (5th Cir. 1986).

62. Wright v. Henkel, 190 U.S. at 43 (evidence of bronchitis insufficient).

63. United States v. Russell, 805 F. 2d at 1216–17. But see Hu Yau-Leung v. Soscia, 649 F. 2d 914 (2d Cir. 1981) (sixteen-year-old boy allowed to stay at home with parents when no suitable juvenile facility could be found for him).

64. United States v. Russell, 805 F. 2d at 1217. But see In re Mitchell, 171 F. 289 (S.D.N.Y. 1909), in which Learned Hand released the accused on bond because his entire fortune was at stake in civil litigation).

65. United States v. Salerno, 481 U.S. 739, 755 (1987).

66. 18 U.S.C. secs. 3141–3150 (Supp. 4 1986).

67. As the Supreme Court has acknowledged, "The enforcement of the bond, if forfeited, would hardly meet the international demand; and the regaining of the custody of the accused obviously would be surrounded with serious embarrassment." Wright v. Henkel, 190 U.S. 40, 62 (1903). See also Beaulieu v. Hartigan, 430 F. Supp. 915, 917 (D.Mass.) ("The standard of scrutiny and concern exercised by a district court in an extradition case should be greater than in the typical bail situation, given the delicate nature of international relations."), rev'd mem., 533 F. 2d 92 (1st Cir.), vacated, 554 F. 2d 1 (1st Cir. 1977).

68. Leitner, 784 F. 2d 159, 160–61; Russell, 805 F. 2d at 1218.

69. E.g., Matter of Sindona, 450 F. Supp. 672, 674 (S.D.N.Y. 1978); M. Cherif Bassiouni, International Extradition: United States Law and Practice (3d ed.; New York: Oceana, 1996), 539.

70. Chapter 17, supra.

71. United States v. Salerno, 489 U.S. at 751–52.

72. In Carlson v. Landon, 342 U.S. 524, 545–46 (1952) ("the very language of the [8th] Amendment fails to say that all arrests must be bailable").

73. In addition, discriminating against persons because they are accused of violating foreign rather than domestic law would seem to violate the right to equal protection guaranteed by the Fifth Amendment. Bolling v. Sharpe, 347 U.S. 497 (1954).

74. To get a person arrested in the United States, all a foreign regime must provide under 18 U.S.C. sec. 3184 is a sworn complaint from a foreign official declaring that the accused is wanted for an extraditable offense, a statement that an arrest warrant exists, a few facts, a physical description of the accused, and a promise to make a fully documented, formal request later. This is sufficient to put the accused behind bars for between thirty days and three months, depending on the treaty, while the paperwork is being processed. Prehearing incarcerations of seven to eight months are not uncommon.

75. Caltagirone v. Grant, 629 F. 2d 739 (2d Cir. 1980).

76. Id. at 748 (Kaufman, J.).

77. Extradition Act of 1981, Hearings Before the Subcom. on Crime, Com. on the Judiciary, U.S. House of Representatives, 97th Cong., 2d sess. (1982), at 171–172.

78. In re Kraiselburd, 786 F. 2d 1395, 1396, 1397 (9th Cir. 1986) (opinion by Judge, now Supreme Court Justice, Anthony Kennedy).

79. See also In re Russell, 805 F. 2d 1215, 1218 (5th Cir. 1986) ("the question of 'urgency' turns on the perceptions of the requesting and requested countries"); United States v. Leitner, 784 F. 2d at 161 (the urgency usually required by treaties before provisional arrest are allowed "is not merely temporal in nature [but] involves other considerations including importance to the country seeking extradition and foreign policy concerns of the United States"); Kamrin v. United States, 725 F. 2d 1225, 1228 (9th Cir.), cert. denied, 469 U.S. 817 (1984) (persons charged

with violating American law have greater right to bail than comparable suspects wanted for violating foreign law.

80. 112 F. 3d 1363 (9th Cir.) cert. denied, 1998 LEXIS 5702.

81. See Chapter 6, *supra*.

82. Stuart, "Treaty Traps," 24. Or as Justice Holmes once put it, "It is common in extradition cases to attempt to bring to bear all the factitious niceties of a criminal trial at common law. It is a waste of time." Glucksman v. Henkel, 221 U.S. 508, 512 (1911).

83. Stuart, "Treaty Traps," 25.

84. Id.

85. Brinegar v. United States, 338 U.S. 160, 174 n. 13 (1949).

86. Jones v. United States, 362 U.S. 257, 269 (1960).

87. Nathanson v. United States, 290 U.S. 41 (1932); Giordenello v. United States, 357 U.S. 480 (1958); Aguilar v. Texas, 378 U.S. 108 (1964).

88. United States v. Ventresca, 380 U.S. 102, 108 (1965).

89. Thus Abu Eain was not allowed to present a dozen affidavits placing him far away from Ramallah at the time the bomb had to have been planted. Chapter 12, *supra*.

90. In Artuković's case, scholars and Yugoslavian attorneys have established that the crimes for which he was convicted in fact never happened and that some of the weapons with which they were allegedly committed were not then in the possession of Croatian forces. See Chapter 17, *supra*.

91. There was credible evidence in both the Abu Eain case and the Aquino investigation that the accuser was tortured into making his accusations against the accused. See Chapters 12 and 15, *supra*, respectively.

92. This applies to both the Artuković and Demjanjuk cases. Chapters 17–19, *supra*.

93. Quinn v. Robinson, 783 F. 2d 776, 817 n. 41 (9th Cir.), cert. denied, 479 U.S. 882 (1986) quoting Jhirad v. Ferrandina, 536 F. 2d 478, 484 (2d Cir.), cert. denied, 429 U.S. 833 (1976). Other courts have not been so generous. Cf. Sabatier v. Dambrowski, 453 F. Supp. 1250, 1255 (D.R.I. 1978) (denying discovery of legal documents that might shed light on history of the treaty), aff'd, 586 F. 2d 866 (1st Cir. 1978).

94. Quinn v. Robinson, 783 F. 2d at 817.

95. In Demjanjuk, the Justice Department revealed that it calls extradition a civil proceeding in large part so that it need not comply with the requirements of Brady v. Maryland, 373 U.S. 83, 86–88 (1963), which held that the suppression by the government of evidence favorable to a domestic criminal defendant who requested it violates due process if the evidence is material either to guilt or punishment. An end to the government's suppression of exculpatory evidence was proposed as part of H.R. 3347, 98th Cong., 1st sess. (1984). See H.R. Rep. no. 998, 98th Congress, 1st sess. (1984) at 6.

96. E.g., as was done by the magistrate in In Matter of Kraiselburd, 786 F. 2d 1395, 1399 (9th Cir.1986).

97. Chapter 14, *supra*.

98. Had Demjanjuk's counsel been allowed to read the Justice Department's file of Soviet interviews with alleged death-camp guards, they would have discovered hard evidence that the real "Ivan the Terrible" was one Ivan Marchenko.

99. E.g., see Quinn v. Robinson, 783 F. 2d 776, 789 (9th Cir. 1986) (citing In re Lincoln, 228 F. 70 (E.D.N.Y. 1915), aff'd, 241 U.S. 651 (1916), cert. denied, 479 U.S. 882 (1986).

100. E.g., see In re Mylonas, 187 F. Supp. 716 (N.D.Ala. 1960) (request by Greek Communist city council for extradition of anti-Communist opponent convicted *in absentia* of embezzle-

ment denied). See also Ramos v. Diaz, 179 F. Supp. 459, 463 (S.D.Fla. 1959) (requesting state's burden of persuasion increased because of the political nature of the alleged offense, even as the court claimed that "the motive of the Cuban government . . . is not controlling").

101. This point is often overlooked by scholars of international law who, in their diplomatic desire to promote cooperation within the so-called "family of nations," often fail to question official motives or bureaucratic tunnel vision.

102. Factor v. Laubenheimer, 290 U.S. 276 (1933). See also Cucuzzella v. Kelikoa, 638 F. 2d 105, 107 (9th Cir. 1981) (double criminality requirement satisfied if the act is criminal under federal law, state law, or the laws of most states).

103. McElvy v. Civiletti, 523 F. Supp. 42, 48 (S.D.Fla. 1981).

104. Emami v. United States Dist. Court, 834 F. 2d 1444, 1448–49 (9th Cir. 1987) (refusing to second-guess German procedures); In re Assarsson, 635 F. 2d 1237 (7th Cir. 1980) (under the treaty, the term "charged" need only mean accused, not formally charged), cert. denied, 451 U.S. 938 (1981).

105. United States v. Cordero, 668 F. 2d 32, 37 (1st Cir. 1981) (extradition treaties are only made for the benefit of the governments concerned); Berenguer v. Vance, 473 F. Supp. 1195, 1197 (D.D.C. 1979) (rule of specialty is not a right of the accused, but a diplomatic privilege which can be exercised by the extraditing state). Demjanjuk v. Petrovsky, 776 F. 2d 571, 584 (6th Cir. 1985) (accused has no standing at his extradition hearing to invoke the rule of specialty).

106. E.g., see the Head Money Cases, 112 U.S. 580, 598 (1884) ("a treaty may . . . confer certain rights upon the citizens or subjects of one of the nations residing in the territorial limits of the other, which partake of the nature of municipal law, and which are capable of enforcement as between private parties in the courts of the country").

107. E.g., see United States v. Thirion, 813 F. 2d 146, 151 n. 5 (8th Cir. 1987) (rejecting the government's claim that the defendant lacked standing to complain of a treaty violation).

108. John Bassett Moore, Digest of International Law (Washington, D.C.: U.S. Government Printing Office, 1906), vol. 4, sec. 601, at 321.

109. E.g., see Ford v. United States, 273 U.S. 593 (1927) (persons seized on high seas allowed to invoke certain treaty rights); United States v. Ferris, 19 F. 2d 925 (N.D.Cal. 1927) (same); cf. Cook v. United States, 288 U.S. 102, 121 (1933) (owner of a rum-runner seized in violation of treaty allowed to assert treaty rights).

110. Fiocconi v. Attorney General, 462 F. 2d 475, 479–80 (2d Cir.) (Friendly, J.), cert. denied, 409 U.S. 1059 (1972). See also United States ex rel. Neidecker, 299 U.S. 5, 10, 18 (1936) (extradition treaty "equivalent to" a statute).

111. Out of respect for executive prerogatives, such queries could be routed pro forma through diplomatic channels.

112. Legislation could also instruct the secretary of state to transmit to the requesting regime a copy of the judge's certificate, drawing attention to the crimes for which extradition was allowed and specifying how the requesting regime may seek clarification from the judge. Waiver of the rule of specialty by the executive should be considered a violation of the Fifth Amendment's due process guarantee.

113. This ruling could be sent through diplomatic channels, but the duty to send it should be mandatory on the State Department.

114. In Matter of Smyth, 820 F. Supp. 498, 503 (N.D.Cal. 1993).

115. The European Court of Human Rights has acted on this principle, refusing to extradite a murderer to Virginia because that state routinely subjects persons awaiting execution to inhuman and degrading circumstances. The basis for the court's denial was art. 3 of the European

Convention on Human Rights, which does not allow the European Court to extradite persons to legal systems that engage in torture or otherwise subject their prisoners to cruel, inhuman, or degrading treatment or punishment. Soering Case, 161 Eur. Ct. H.R. (ser. A) (1989).

116. The list is taken from Barbara Ann Banoff and Christopher H. Pyle, "'To Surrender Political Offenders': The Political Offense Exception in United States Law," 16 N. Y. U. J. Int'l L. & Pol. 169, 202–203 (1984).

117. Thus the Second Circuit's deportation standard of "a clear probability of persecution to the particular alien" goes too far. Cheng Kai Fu v. Immigration and Naturalization Service, 386 F. 2d 750, 753 (2d Cir. 1967), cert. denied, 390 U.S. 1003 (1968).

118. Regina v. Governor of Pentonville Prison *ex parte* Fernandez [1971] 1 W.L.R. 987, 994. See also The State (Magee) v. O'Rorke, 1971 Ir.R. 205, 213 ("substantial reasons").

119. On the slipperiness of probable cause in other contexts, see Anthony Amsterdam, "Perspectives on the Fourth Amendment," 58 Minn. L. Rev. 349, 374–77 (1974).

120. See Chapter 15, *supra*. See also In Matter of Smyth, 820 F. Supp. 498, 503 (N.D.Cal. 1993) and In re Howard, 99 F. 2d 1320, 1330–31 (1st Cir. 1993).

121. Proposed by the American Bar Association's Model American Convention on the Prevention and Punishment of Serious Forms of Violence, reprinted in 77 Am. J. Int'l L. 664 (1983) (with commentary by R. Lillich) and the International Law Association's Draft Articles on extradition in relation to terrorist offenses (adopted by the Association's 1988 Conference in Warsaw, Poland).

122. If societies can accredit colleges, certify physicians, evaluate airlines, and designate countries as safe for travel, they can assess the competence and fairness of investigators, courts, and prisons.

123. Glucksman v. Henkel, 221 U.S. 508, 512 (1910) (Holmes, J.) (allowing extradition to Tsarist Russia).

124. Eain v Wilkes, 641 F. 2d 504 (7th Cir. 1981); In Matter of Doherty, 599 F. Supp. 270 (2d Cir. 1984).

125. Chapter 14, *supra*.

126. So viewed, it may properly be modified to permit the surrender of persons who commit wanton or heinous killings in the course of an uprising—actions that would be "war crimes" in an international armed conflict.

127. See generally Christine Van den Wijngaert, "The Political Offence Exception to Extradition: How to Plug the 'Terrorists' Loophole' Without Departing from Fundamental Human Rights," 19 Israel Yrbk. Hum. Rts. 297 (1989).

128. Eain v. Wilkes, 641 F. 2d 504, 508 (7th Cir.), cert. denied, 454 U.S. 894 (1981).

129. Fernandez v. Phillips, 268 U.S. 311 (1925). See also Jimenez v. Aritequieta, 311 F. 2d 547, 555 (5th Cir. 1962), and Spatola v. United States, 741 F. Supp. 362, 370–71 (E.D.N.Y. 1990).

130. Id. at 312.

131. E.g., see Caltagirone v. Grant, 629 F. 2d 739, 748 n. 19 (2d Cir. 1980) (violations of Fourth Amendment may be raised in habeas proceeding).

132. In re Burt, 737 F. 2d 1477, 1484 (7th Cir. 1984).

133. Id. See also Plaster v. United States, 720 F. 2d 340, 348 (4th Cir. 1983) (U.S. government, in carrying out its extradition obligations, must conform to the requirements of the Constitution).

134. Under 18 U.S.C. sec. 1291, only "final decisions of the district courts" may be appealed.

135. So long as the U.S. and foreign governments are not bound by res judicata or double jeopardy, there is no reason to grant them a right to appeal. As to them, the decision is not final.

136. Supplementary Extradition Treaty Between the United States and the United Kingdom, Treaty Doc. no. 8, 99th Cong., 1st sess. (1985), art. 3(b). See also In re Extradition of Howard, 996 F. 2d 1320 (1st Cir. 1993).

137. Foster v. Neilson, 27 U.S. (2 Pet.) *253, 314 (1829) ("Our Constitution [art. 6, cl. 2] declares a treaty to be the law of the land. It is, consequently, to be regarded in Courts of Justice as equivalent to an act of the legislature [unless] the terms of the stipulation import a contract [which] the legislature must execute . . . before [the contract] can become a rule for the Court").

138. Under current law, the president and Senate can, without House consent, alter the criminal jurisdiction of the courts. Cook v. United States, 288 U.S. 102 (1933). The Supreme Court has intimated that the president and Senate might be able, in their exercise of the treaty power, to make policies that the two houses and the president may not constitutionally make together. Missouri v. Holland, 252 U.S. 416, 420–21 (1920).

139. Short of that, the Senate Committee on Foreign Relations could invite the Judiciary Committees of both houses to review each proposed extradition treaty, instead of presuming, as they have often done, that such agreements are routine business and not deserving of close scrutiny.

140. United States v. Lui Kin-Hong, 83 F. 3d 523 (1st Cir. 1996).

141. In response to strong criticism, the department finally agreed to impose conditions upon the surrender, and to negotiate a new treaty with China that would govern extradition with Hong Kong and, presumably, bar the transfer of persons surrendered to Hong Kong to any of the Communist provinces.

142. Stuart, "Treaty Traps," 41.

143. Id.

144. Even the director of the Justice Department's extradition staff has admitted to seeing "acute cases of 'clientitis' where the State Department bent over backwards to stroke the foreign country." Howard Kurtz, "Global Role of Justice Dept. Is Irritant to State," Washington Post, Nov. 12, 1986, A1, at A26 (statement of Michael Abbell, Director, Office of Int'l Affairs, Dept. of Justice).

145. "This discretion is almost never exercised, as the United States wants to effectuate the purpose of the treaties. . . . Defenses against extradition that are technical are rejected as inappropriate in dealings with foreign nations." Stuart, "Treaty Traps," 41.

146. In 1973, Judge Friendly could find only two instances in twenty years when the State Department actually refused an extradition request. Shapiro v. Ferrandina, 478 F. 2d 894, 906 n. 11 (2d Cir.), cert. denied, 414 U.S. 884 (1973). The record since then has been no better. Deputy Secretary of State Kenneth Dam signed a warrant authorizing Artuković's surrender without even looking at the humanitarian appeal his family had submitted. The department was equally dismissive, as was Justice, of the humanitarian claims submitted on Joseph Doherty's behalf.

147. The Senate, of course, does not hesitate to demand concessions from foreign regimes as its price for consenting to treaties.

148. For example, Dutch legislation decrees that international cooperation in criminal justice matters must serve "the proper administration of justice," which means, among other things, that a surrendered national, if convicted, must be allowed to serve his sentence in the Netherlands. Bert Swart and Andre Klip, eds., International Criminal Law in the Netherlands (Freiburg: Max Planck Institute, 1997), 17–18.

149. E.g., see United States-Mexico, Treaty on the Execution of Penal Sentences, (signed Nov. 26, 1976; entered into force Nov. 30, 1977), 28 U.S.T. 7399, T.I.A.S. no. 8718. Similar treaties have been signed with Canada, Bolivia, Turkey, Peru, and Panama.

150. It is sometimes argued that to object to brutal prisons would constitute an affront to the requesting state. Perhaps, but that has not prevented the U.S. Army from doing so as a condition to surrendering soldiers under some Status of Forces Agreements (SOFAs).

151. Of course, if the United States begins to place human rights limitations on extradition, foreign regimes are likely to reciprocate. This should be welcome, as the criminal justice processes of the federal and state governments are not always to be trusted. The Justice Department has the authority to accept conditions on extradition to the United States as part of its prosecutorial discretion. Where state prosecutors are constrained in their discretion by state law, compliance can be mandated as a condition of receiving federal assistance in recovering state fugitives from foreign governments.

152. In addition, it might be wise to add that the accused shall have standing to raise the rule of specialty at his extradition hearing, at trial (if the rule is violated), and in the extradition court and with the surrendering executive during and after trial. Similarly, the extraditing court should be able, as the Sixth Circuit Court of Appeals was in the Demjanjuk case, to reopen its proceedings, when necessary, to hear charges that his surrender was obtained through prosecutorial misconduct. That the extraditing court may not enjoin the foreign proceedings should not be considered a bar to reconsideration, as it can always issue a declaratory judgment for transmission to the U.S. and foreign executives, and to the foreign court.

153. Report to the ILA Biennial Meetings, May 24–30, 1998, Taipei, Taiwan.

154. The International Law Association's Committee on Extradition and Human Rights recommends that states consider including a dispute settlement clause in their extradition treaties to the effect that: "Any dispute between two or more of the contracting parties concerning the interpretation or application of this agreement which cannot be settled through negotiation shall, at the request of one of them, be submitted to arbitration. If, within six months from the date of request for arbitration the Parties are unable to agree on the organization of the arbitration, any one of the Parties may refer the dispute to the International Court of Justice by request in conformity with the Statute of the Court." Report to the ILA's Biennial Meeting, May 24–30, 1998, Taipei, Taiwan.

155. United States v. Alvarez-Machain, 504 U.S. 655 (1992).

156. Kear v. Hilton, 699 F. 2d 181 (4th Cir. 1983) (two Florida bounty hunters extradited to Canada for abducting a suspect in a fraud case to Florida); Lobue v. Christopher, 82 F. 3d 1081 (1996) (two Chicago policemen extradited to Canada for abducting a client's wife from her family).

Appendix

1. The Supreme Court has defined extradition as "The surrender by one nation to another of an individual accused or convicted of an offense outside of its own territory, and within the territorial jurisdiction of the other, which, being competent to try and punish him, demands his surrender." Terlinden v. Ames, 184 U.S. 289 (1901). This definition presupposes that the person sought will always be a fugitive. That is the usual situation, but persons who have never set foot in the requesting state also may be extradited for conspiring with others to commit an offense against that state's laws. For example, in In the Matter of Budlong and Kember (nos. 199/79, 200/79, Queen's Bench Division, Nov. 30, 1979), 74 Am. J. Int'l L. 447, the officials of the Church of Scientology sought for prosecution by the United States had never left the United Kingdom but were charged with directing a burglary of a U.S. courthouse from their British

headquarters in Sussex. Similarly, U.S. courts have authorized the extradition of persons alleged to have violated the laws of foreign countries while physically present in the United States. See, e.g., Eatessami v. Marasco, 275 F. Supp. (S.D.N.Y. 1967); Stowe v. Devoy, 588 F. 2d 336 (2d Cir. 1978), cert. denied, 442 U.S. 931 (1979); United States v. Galanis, 429 F. Supp. 1215 (D.Conn. 1977). With the growth of international drug rings and international acts of terrorism, the number of requests for conspirators who have never left the requested country is likely to increase.

2. However, the supporting documentation need not be complete at the time of the initial request. United States ex rel. McNamara v. Henkel, 46 F. 2d 89 (S.D.N.Y. 1912) Indeed, most arrests are "provisional," and the formal requests (complete with copies of foreign warrants, specifications of charges, and affidavits establishing probable cause) may not be received for weeks). Grin v. Shine, 187 U.S. 181, 193–95 (1902).

3. Entry is normally controlled by granting or denying a visa, which is usually done through the screening of visa applications at U.S. consulates and embassies abroad. The standards for deciding who is eligible for a visa—e.g., as an immigrant, tourist, student, refugee, or temporary worker—are set by Congress (at 8 U.S.C. sec. 1181, 1182) but administered (as an instrument of national policy) by the executive.

4. The Supreme Court has defined deportation as "the removal of an alien out of this country, simply because his presence is deemed inconsistent with the public welfare, and without any punishment being imposed or contemplated, either under the laws of the country out of which he is sent, or those of the country he is sent to." Fong Yue Ting v. United States, 149 U.S. 698, 725 (1893). Deportation begins when the host government moves to expel an alien already present in the country, usually because he entered illegally, overstayed his visa, committed a crime, failed to register, or did something else that makes him ineligible to remain. The U.S. government's authority to deport aliens derives from 8 U.S.C. sec. 1251(a). For more on the difference between deportation and extradition see Fong Yue Ting v. United States, 149 U.S. 698, 709 (1893). Deportation only applies to aliens. Extradition from the United States applies to citizens and aliens, unless the treaty specifies otherwise.

5. Exclusion has two meanings in American law. The first refers to the denial of visas to undesirable aliens under the McCarran-Walter Act, 8 U.S.C. sec. 1182. Subsection (a)(27) of that act allows a consular officer or the attorney general to bar from entry aliens who he "has reason to believe seek to enter the United States solely, principally, or incidentally to engage in activities which would be prejudicial to the public interest, or endanger the welfare, safety, or security of the United States." For many years, subsection (a)(28) permitted the barring of "Aliens who advocate or teach or who are members of or affiliated with any organization that advocates or teaches . . . (ii) the duty, necessity, or propriety of the unlawful assaulting or killing of any officer or officers of the government of the United States or any other organized government, because of his or their official character; or (iii) the unlawful damage, injury, or destruction of property; or (iv) sabotage." In 1990, Congress barred the denial of visas to persons for "any past or expected speech, activity, belief, affiliation, or membership which, if held or conducted within the United States by a United States citizen, would be protected by the First Amendment to the Constitution." However, it also provided that visas could be denied to visitors believed to have "engaged in terrorism," which included soliciting funds for an alleged terrorist group. In this way, the attorney general acquired the power to exclude fugitives from foreign revolutions simply by labeling them terrorists.

The second meaning of exclusion is more technical, and refers to the expulsion (ejection) of a person who has been intercepted while entering the United States and has been admitted conditionally. Examples include foreign sailors who land without permits, travelers who land without proper papers, and persons who land while in transit between other countries. The distinction between this form of exclusion and deportation is peculiar to U.S. law. For the law governing these conditionally admitted, expellable persons, see 8 U.S.C. secs. 1101(a)(15), 1182(d)(5). Cf. Petition of Martinez 202 F. Supp. 153 (N.D.Ill. 1962). See also Kleindienst v. Mandel, 408 U.S. 753, 765 (1972), and Leng May Ma v. Barber, 357 U.S. 185 (1958). Excludable persons have very few rights under American law, as thousands of Haitian boat people have learned to their grief. For a discussion of exclusion as an alternative to extradition, see Alona E. Evans, "Acquisition of Custody over the International Fugitive Offender—Alternatives to Extradition: A Survey of United States Practice," 40 Brit. Y. B. Int'l L. 77, 82–87 (1964).

6. Extradition procedures are prescribed by 18 U.S.C. secs. 3181, 3184, 3186, 3188–91, 3195. The hundred or so U.S. extradition treaties currently in force are compiled in Michael Abbell and Bruno A. Ristau, International Judicial Assistance, Criminal: Extradition (Washington, D.C.: International Law Institute, 1990), vol. 5. The procedural details are set forth by Abbell and Ristau in vol. 4.

7. The doctrine of unappealability began with John Marshall's speech to the House of Representatives in the Jonathan Robbins controversy, 10 Annals of Congress 595–617 (Mar. 7, 1800), and was confirmed by the Supreme Court in In re Metzger, 46 U.S. (5 How.) 176 (1847). See also Collins v. Miller, 252 U.S. 364, 369–70 (1920), Greci v. Birknes, 527 F. 2d 956, 958 (1st Cir. 1976).

8. E.g., Shapiro v. Ferrandina, 478 F. 2d 894, 901 (2d Cir.), cert. denied by agreement of the parties, 414 U.S. 884 (1973).

9. Fernandez v. Phillips, 268 U.S. 311, 312 (1925).

10. Extraditability, the Supreme Court has said, "is a question of mixed law and fact, but chiefly of fact, and the judgment of the magistrate rendered in good faith on legal evidence that the accused is guilty of the act charged, and that it constitutes an extraditable crime cannot be reviewed on the weight of the evidence, and is final for the purposes of the preliminary examination unless palpably erroneous in law." Ornelas v. Ruiz, 161 U.S. 502, 509 (1896).

11. Nor may the U.S. government file a backdoor appeal by asking a higher court for a declaratory judgment reinterpreting the relevant law. In Matter of Doherty, 615 F. Supp. 755 (S.D.N.Y.), aff'd sub nom. United States v. Doherty, 786 F. 2d 491, 495 (2d Cir. 1986).

12. E.g., see Hooker v. Klein, 573 F. 2d 1360, 1365–68 (9th Cir.), cert. denied, 439 U.S. 932 (1978).

13. 33 & 34 Vict., c. 52 (1870), 18 U.S.C. 3184.

14. From 1842 until 1871, the U.S. Department of State maintained that the discretion to grant or deny extradition resided wholly with the courts and that the executive function was a purely ministerial one of delivering the accused to officials of the requesting state for transportation out of the country. John Bassett Moore, A Treatise on Extradition and Interstate Rendition, vol. 1 (Boston: Boston Book Co., 1891), 551–55. A brief account of the origins of the revisory power in the United States is contained in Moore, "The Case of the Salvadorian Refugees," Collected Papers of John Bassett Moore, vol. 1, 356–57 (1944). The authority of the British Home Secretary to refuse to surrender a person committed by the magistrate to extradition is affirmed in Atkinson v. United States Government [1969] 3 All E.R. 1317 at 1322.

15. U.S. Department of Justice, Criminal Division, Procedure for Requesting Extradition, A4–A16 (no date).

16. 33 & 34 Vict., c. 52.

17. The failure to fulfill expectations of reciprocity need not be fatal to a treaty. Although the Italian government interpreted extraditable "persons" in its treaty with the United States to

mean non-Italians only, the U.S. Supreme Court still ruled that American citizens could be extradited from the United States to Italy. Charlton v. Kelly, 229 U.S. 447 (1913).

18. Letter from Attorney General Caleb Cushing to Secretary of State William L. Marcy, 7 Op. Attys. Gen. 6, Nov. 2, 1854 (C. C. Andrews ed., 1856).

19. The Report of the British Royal Commission (1878) cited the general deterrence of crime and getting rid of undesirable persons as the two main justifications for extradition. The same commission found that full reciprocity was not essential. Ellery C. Stowell, International Law (New York: Holt, 1931), 265–66, n. 3. See also Evans, "Reflections upon the Political Offense in International Practice," 57 Am. J. Int'l L. 1, 3 (1963).

20. For example, when Chilean courts refused to extradite three former secret police officials accused of ordering the assassination of Orlando Letelier in Washington, D.C., the Carter Administration reduced its embassy staff in Chile, cut off military aid, and curbed international loans. Graham Hovey, "Carter Said to Plan Cutbacks in Chile over Letelier Case," New York Times, Nov. 30, 1979, at A1, col. 3; Department Statement, Nov. 30, 1979, Dep't St. Bull. 65 (Jan. 1980). That same year, the United States' refusal to return the Shah to Iran led to the taking of American hostages in Teheran. In both instances, the refusals were required by law: Chilean law does not permit the extradition of nationals, and the United States had no extradition treaty with Iran.

21. Abbell and Ristau, International Judicial Assistance, vol. 5.

22. E.g., Albania, 1935; Bulgaria, 1924 and 1934; Chile, 1902; Czechoslovakia, 1926 and 1935; Guatemala, 1903 and 1941; Haiti, 1905; Honduras, 1912; Iraq, 1936; Nicaragua, 1905; Paraguay, 1935; Poland 1929 and 1936; Romania, 1925; Seychelles, 1935; South Africa, 1951; and Yugoslavia, 1902.

23. E.g., Panama, 1905; El Salvador, 1911; and Zimbabwe, 1977.

Index

naval discipline, enforcement of, 35, 46
Nazi and Nazi Collaborators Law, Israel, 250
Nazi Germany, international kidnappings by, 263
Neely, Charles F.W., 123–24. *See Neely v. Henkel*
Neely, In re, 358nn 43–44
Neely v. Henkel, 124, 357–58nn 36–40, 410n 4
Nelson, Samuel, 44, 99, 100, 101–102, 104
Netherlands, 197; U.S. treaty with, 144
Netherlands–Hanover treaty, 80
Neustadt, Richard E., 399n 59, 406n 38
neutrality: basis of judicial, 206; need for, 149;
    political character of executive, 206
New Netherlands, treaty with, 64
New York, extradition cases in, 64–65, 68–69
New York Times, 181
Newdegate, Charles N., 88
Newman, Jon O., 167
Nicaragua: contras in, 302; covert war against,
    396nn 13 and 14
Nicaragua v. United States, 408n 81
Nicholas, Philip, 98
Nimmer, David, 222, 231
Ninoy Aquino clause, 203. *See also* "nonrefoul-
    ment principle"
Ninth Circuit Court of Appeals, 158–59, 161–64,
    212, 308–309
Nishnik, Edward, xi, 255
Nixon, Richard, 290
Nixon administration, 371n 10; fear of terrorist
    attacks in, 145
noninquiry, rule of, 6, 20–21, 50, 51, 53, 70, 78, 81,
    118–29, 172, 195, 301; abolition of rule of, 321; in
    Artukovic, 226, 228; in Canada, 76; due process
    exceptions to, 127, 166; and extradition of fugi-
    tive slaves, 57–59, 119, 268; and government
    attorneys, 309; limits of rule of, 140; suspension
    of rule of, 113, 156, 200
"nonrefoulment principle," 201, 212, 213, 268, 269,
    380nn 55 and 58; in asylum law, 313; in supple-
    mentary U.S.–U.K. extradition treaty, 315; in
    U.K., 317
Noriega, Manuel Antonio, 2, 287, 301; abduction
    of, 277–78
Normano, In re, 371n 5, 359n 68
Normano, Joao F., attempted extradition of to
    Nazi Germany, 128–29, 218, 371n 5
North, Oliver, 2, 273, 274, 275, 277
North Carolina Supreme Court, 119
Northern German Federation, 347n 29
Northern Ireland, extradition to in Irish law, 212;
    issue of, 202; powers of police in, 169; Protestant

terrorism in, 170; status of, 162; uprising in, 172,
    173

Obeid, Abdul Karim, 298
Oberdorfer, Louis, 256
Obermaier, Otto, 197
O'Brien v. Rozman, 411n 18
obscenity, law of, 316
O'Connor, Mark, 252
O'Connor, Sandra Day, 288
O'Dempsey, Keara, 171
O'Dwyer, Paul, 153–54, 171
Office of International Affairs (OIA), Justice
    Department, 143
Office of Legal Advisor (OLA), State Department,
    143
Office of Special Investigations (OSI), Justice
    Department. *See* Justice Department, Office of
    Special Investigations
Office on Terrorism and Narcotics, State Depart-
    ment, 155
Olmstead v. United States, 270, 408n 86
Olney, Richard, 354n 30
Operations Sub-Group (OSG), 275
order: preference for in twentieth century foreign
    relations, 142; preservation of, 58–59, 60–61
"ordered liberty," American system of, 148
organic state, 118
organizational base, requirement of, 173
Ornelas, Plutarch, 111. *See Ornelas v. Ruiz*
Ornelas v. Ruiz, 111, 353n 28, 413n 42; 422n 11
Orosco-Orosco, Javier, 282
Oteiza v. Jacobus, 390n 67
outrage, tort of, 316

Paine, Thomas, 299
Palestine Liberation Front (PLF), 273, 276
Palestine Liberation Organization, 157, 164
Palmer, A. Mitchell, 284
Palmerston (Lord), 102
Pal v. Attorney General, 389n 57
Panama, invasion of, 278, 279
Panama Canal fraud, 122
Paquette Habana, The, 292
Paris Commune of 1870, 83, 106
Parker, Barrington, 276
Parker, Hyde, 28
Parker, In re, 412n 23
Parretti v. United States, 307, 309, 414n 53
Pavelic, Ante, 133, 134, 137
Pearson, Drew, 132, 134